REASON'S TRACES

Studies in Indian and Tibetan Buddhism

THIS SERIES WAS CONCEIVED to provide a forum for publishing outstanding new contributions to scholarship on Indian and Tibetan Buddhism and also to make accessible seminal research not widely known outside a narrow specialist audience, including translations of appropriate monographs and collections of articles from other languages. The series strives to shed light on the Indic Buddhist traditions by exposing them to historical-critical inquiry, illuminating through contextualization and analysis these traditions' unique heritage and the significance of their contribution to the world's religious and philosophical achievements.

STUDIES IN INDIAN AND TIBETAN BUDDHISM

REASON'S TRACES

Identity and Interpretation
in Indian & Tibetan Buddhist Thought

Matthew T. Kapstein

WISDOM PUBLICATIONS • BOSTON

Wisdom Publications
199 Elm Street
Somerville, Massachusetts 02144 USA
www.wisdompubs.org

Library of Congress Cataloging-in-Publication Data
Kapstein, Matthew T.
Reason's traces : identity and interpretation in Indian and Tibetan Buddhist thought / Matthew T. Kapstein
p. cm.
Includes bibliographical references and index.
ISBN 0-86171-239-0 (alk. paper)
1. Philosophy, Buddhist. 2. Self (Philosophy)—India—History. 3. Philosophy, Indic. 4. Self (Philosophy)—China—Tibet—History. 5. Philosophy, Tibetan. I. Title.
B162 K37 2002
126—dc21 2001046522

07 06 05 04 03
6 5 4 3 2

Designed by Gopa and Ted2
Cover photo: The site of the excavated Buddhist monastery of Ratnagiri in Orissa, India. 1992. Photo by Matthew Kapstein.

Wisdom Publications' books are printed on acid-free paper and meet the guidelines for permanence and durability set by the Committee on Production Guidelines for Book Longevity of the Council on Library Resources.

Printed in the United States

To the memory of
Alak Gungtang-tshang of Labrang (d. 1999)
and
Dorje Lopön Thuje-pal of Se (d. 2000)
lamps of the teaching in dark places and times

ये च दशदिशि लोकप्रदीपा बोधिविबुद्ध असंगतिप्राप्ताः ।
तानहु सर्वि अध्येषमि नाथांश्चक्रु अनुत्तरु वर्तनतायै ॥

Publisher's Acknowledgment

THE PUBLISHER gratefully acknowledges the generous help of the Hershey Family Foundation in sponsoring the publication of this book.

Contents

List of Illustrations

Unless otherwise noted all illustrations are by the author.

Preface

THE EIGHTH-CENTURY Indian Buddhist philosopher Kamalaśīla, introducing his commentary to his teacher Śāntarakṣita's masterwork, the *Tattvasaṅgraha,* remarked that he could find no dialectical pathway that had not already been well-worn by earlier sages. The established tracks of past generations, however, may become lost with the passage of centuries. Recovering reason's peregrinations in ancient and medieval times by following its traces in the writings that have come down to us is, of necessity, an exploration in the archeology of ideas. Just as the reconstruction of an ancient road network invites our sustained reflection on a now eroded and obscured transportation system's purpose for being, the traffic it bore, and the peoples it brought into communication or conflict with one another, so, too, reason's traces call upon us to imagine, and to imagine ourselves journeying within, unfamiliar worlds of thought, conversation, and practice.

My own travels along the tracks and byways of Indian and Tibetan Buddhist thought have frequently turned on questions of identity and interpretation. Both represent central concerns of Buddhist intellectual traditions, and both demand a self-questioning that at once informs and is informed by the study of traditional textual sources. In the writings of Buddhist philosophers in these areas, moreover, we must attend to a call—at once within and beyond the body of established doctrine—to investigate our own identities and our prospects for understanding. The studies gathered in this book represent a philosophical and buddhological novice's efforts to respond to this call.

The investigations of personal identity presented here were first formulated in connection with my dissertation research at Brown University in the 1980s. It is a pleasure to express in this context my gratitude to the Brown Philosophy Department and to my mentors there: the late Roderick Chisholm, Philip Quinn (now at the University of Notre Dame), Ernest Sosa, and James Van Cleve. I am indebted, also, to the late Arthur L. Basham and to David Pingree, who generously encouraged my work in Indian intellectual traditions at Brown.

I am very much indebted to two scholars who, when we first met, were in the same *āśrama* as I—that is, the transition from graduate school to whatever we call it that follows—and with whom I have shared a broad range of common interests in Buddhist thought and its interpretation. Steven Collins and Paul Griffiths have contributed in a great many ways to the thinking on Buddhism that is represented in this book. I am grateful to them above all for their friendship and for their steadfast refusal to let unchallenged assumptions rest unchallenged.

Frank Reynolds has been at the center of the Buddhist Studies *maṇḍala* at the University of Chicago throughout the period I have taught there. It is a pleasure now to be able to acknowledge, in the year of his retirement, the remarkable generosity of spirit he has extended to all who have had the good fortune to have been his students and colleagues. Above and beyond his many substantive contributions to the study of religion, Frank has shown us something of how the great vehicle can be entered in scholarly practice.

In preparing the present work for publication, I have very much benefitted from the assistance of Daniel Arnold, both in editing the manuscript and compiling the index. Dan's broad background in Indology and philosophy, as well as his finely honed sense of style, made him an ideal reader and critic, improving this book throughout.

Several chapters reproduce, with varying degrees of revision, articles that were published earlier. I thank the editors and publishers mentioned for their kind permission to include here the following:

"Indra's Search for the Self and the Beginnings of Philosophical Perplexity in India," *Religious Studies* 24: 239–56.

"Śāntarakṣita on the Fallacies of Personalistic Vitalism," *Journal of Indian Philosophy* 17 (1989): 43–59. With the permission of Kluwer Academic Publications.

"Mereological Considerations in Vasubandhu's 'Proof of Idealism,'" *Idealistic Studies* 18/1 (1988): 32–54.

"The Trouble with Truth: Heidegger on *Alētheia,* Buddhist Thinkers on *Satya,*" *Journal of the Indian Council of Philosophical Research* 9/2 (1992): 69–85.

"Weaving the World: The Ritual Art of the *Paṭa* in Pāla Buddhism and Its Legacy in Tibet." *History of Religions* 34/3 (1995): 241–62.

"Schopenhauer's Shakti," in Margaret Case, ed., *Heinrich Zimmer: Coming into His Own* (Princeton: Princeton University Press, 1994): 105–18.

"From Dol-po-pa to 'Ba'-mda' Dge-legs: Three Jo-nang-pa Masters on the Interpretation of *Prajñāpāramitā.*" In Helmut Krasser, Michael Torsten Much, Ernst Steinkellner, and Helmut Tauscher, eds., *Tibetan Studies: Proceedings of the Seventh Seminar of the International Association for Tibetan Studies* (Vienna: Austrian Academy of Science, 1997) 1: 457–75.

"Mi-pham's Theory of Interpretation," Donald Lopez, ed., *Buddhist Hermeneutics* (Honolulu: University of Hawai'i Press, 1988), 149–74. With the permission of the Kuroda Institute.

I acknowledge also the San Diego Museum of Art for its generous permission to reproduce here the lovely Rajasthani miniature, "She sees her lover see her," from the Edwin Binney III Collection of Indian painting.

Finally, I wish to thank Tom Tillemanns of the University of Lausanne, and E. Gene Smith and Timothy McNeill at Wisdom Publications, for their welcome efforts to publish this in the series Studies in Indian and Tibetan Buddhism.

M.T.K.
Paris, June 2001

A Note Concerning History and Chronology

THROUGHOUT THIS BOOK I refer to persons, texts, and schools of thought that may be unfamiliar to readers who are not already immersed in the study of Indian philosophical thought. The following remarks are intended to introduce the most important of these within a very general historical and chronological framework.

The earliest literary record of Indian religious thought is the Veda, which consists of several main sections. The most ancient of these is formed by four great collections of hymns, the oldest of which, the Ṛg Veda, perhaps dates to the period 1200–800 B.C.E., though some scholars have held it to be much older. The literature of the Veda also includes a great corpus of prose (and occasionally verse) ancillary works, commenting on all aspects of the Vedic religion. For our present purposes, the most important class of such works is that of the Upaniṣads, which represent the esoteric speculations and teachings of a very large number of sages. Upaniṣads have been composed throughout Indian history, even in recent centuries, but the Upaniṣads that hold special importance for the study of the beginnings of Indian philosophy have been assigned approximately to the period 800–300 B.C.E.

The mid-first millennium B.C.E. represents a pivotal period in the history of Indian thought. Though there were no doubt always tendencies opposing the Vedic religion and the speculative traditions of the Upaniṣads, these had been, from the standpoint of the extant historical record, previously mute. Now, for the first time, we have such tendencies represented in the rise of important new schools, which created their own extensive literatures outside of the Vedic tradition. Among these new schools, two came to be particularly influential: that which gathered around Vardhamāna (c. 599–527 B.C.E.), better known by his epithets Mahāvīra or Jina, whose disciples thus became known as Jainas, and who created a new religious order that, though small, has remained influential in India down to the present day; and that which had as its founder the prince Gautama Siddhārtha (c. 563–483 B.C.E.), known usually as Śākyamuni or Buddha, whose school was eventually to become a world religion, a fountainhead of religious and philosophical developments of continuing importance for much of Asia. During the same period there also flourished many smaller schools, proclaiming a remarkable variety of doctrines: materialism, determinism, skepticism, hedonism, etc. In short, it was an age of intense intellectual and spiritual ferment, in some respects like the closely contemporaneous period during which the Sophists rose to prominence in Greece.

The half millennium or so that follows is of cardinal importance for the history of Indian philosophy, but, lamentably, even the relative chronology of the philosophical and religious literature of this period remains in many respects mysterious. Certainly, the following developments may be assigned to the age in question:

—the redaction of Pāṇini's (c. 450 B.C.E.) grammar and the composition of the first great commentaries upon it (these would henceforth govern formal analysis of language by all schools of philosophy in India);

—the invasion of northwestern India by Alexander (327–324 B.C.E.), resulting in the establishment of regular ties with the Hellenistic world;

—the reign of emperor Aśoka (beginning in 268 B.C.E.), under whose patronage Buddhism first emerged as a world religion;

—the beginnings of the systematic study of inference, argument, and epistemology (all of which emerge as important topics in texts that were composed during the broad period from the last centuries B.C.E. through about 200 C.E.);

—the growth of clearly defined philosophical schools (whose divisions, one from the other, cannot be accounted for strictly in terms of religious sectarianism, but must be sought, in part at least, in substantive differences of ontology, epistemology, theory of agency, etc.).

Among the schools that became clearly defined during the period in question, which adhered nominally at least to the Vedic tradition, the following in particular should be noted: *Sāṃkhya,* aspects of whose doctrines may be seen emerging even in the Upaniṣads, and whose classical version, redacted in the mnemonic verses of Īśvara Kṛṣṇa, dates perhaps to the first two centuries C.E.; *Mīmāṃsā,* whose antecedents go back to the earliest Vedic commentarial literature, and whose main aphorisms are attributed to one Jaimini, who perhaps flourished during the first century C.E.; *Vaiśeṣika,* the atomistic tradition, the dating of which has aroused much controversy, and whose aphorisms, by a certain sage named Kaṇada, have been assigned to sometime during the period 400 B.C.E. through 100 C.E.; and *Nyāya,* the school of logic and argument, the central aphorisms of which were redacted by an Akṣapāda (a.k.a. Gautama), probably toward 150 C.E. (The teaching of the Upaniṣads themselves was greatly amplified, and given philosophical expression, in the Vedānta school, which, despite its ancient sources, became prominent only during the mid-first millennium C.E. and later times.)

The same period was one that brought great changes to Buddhism, too. Though the historical details remain uncertain, we know that the Buddhist order was wracked by a series of schisms, leading to the formation of new and distinctive Buddhist sects, and that in some of these schisms disagreement over doctrinal matters played a major role. In the present work, we will be concerned in part with one of these, the so-called Personalist Controversy, which erupted perhaps as early as the third century B.C.E. The Personalists *(pudgalavādin)* were the adherents of the Vātsīputrīya and Saṃmitīya monastic orders, which held that, above and beyond the stream of psychological and physical events of which experience is constituted, the "person" is in some sense an irreducible reality. Among the schools whose opposition to the Personalists has left some record, particularly important for us are the *Theravāda* school, which has been the dominant school of Buddhism throughout the present millennium in Śrī Laṅkā, Burma, Thailand, and much of Southeast Asia; and the *Sarvāstivāda* school, which, though now extinct (at least as an independent tradition), played a paramount role in the development of Buddhist philosophy in India. The Personalist Controversy, in which these and several other schools took part, represents the beginning of formal debate and argument in Buddhist circles, and so is of particular importance for the history of Indian philosophy.

The Buddhist schools just mentioned are often spoken of (pejoratively) as *Hīnayāna,* the "Lesser Vehicle" of ancient Buddhism, in contradistinction to the *Mahāyāna,* the "Greater Vehicle," which emphasized universal salvation and probably originated toward the beginning of the Common Era. Much of the philosophical creativity of later Indian Buddhism was to come from thinkers affiliated with the Mahāyāna. The first great philosopher who appears to have been so affiliated was Nāgārjuna (fl. c. 150 C.E.), almost certainly a contemporary and opponent of the redactor of the aphorisms of the Nyāya school, and founder of the Buddhist school of philosophy known as Madhyamaka, the "middle" or "central" school, which seeks to remove the dialectical extremes of existence and nothingness (and in this way cleave to a dialectical middle path). Some two centuries following Nāgārjuna, a second major philosophical tradition within the Mahāyāna arose. Frequently referred to as Yogācara ("yoga practice") or Cittamātra ("mind only"), its founders were the brothers Asaṅga and Vasubandhu, to whom a teaching of metaphysical idealism is often attributed.

These remarks permit us to situate historically the main philosophers with whom we shall be concerned here: Vasubandhu, active toward the early fifth century C.E., was, during some part of his career at least, representative of the old schools of Buddhist philosophy, particularly the Sarvāstivāda. His approximate contemporary was Vātsyāyana, the first great commentator of the Nyāya school. Praśastapāda, the most influential thinker of the early Vaiśeṣika school, was probably active not long after Vasubandhu and Vātsyāyana.

The fifth and sixth centuries saw very rapid developments in Buddhist logic and epistemology, primarily owing to the efforts of Vasubandhu's direct disciple Dignāga and the latter's grand-disciple Dharmakīrti. The refinement of Buddhist logic seems to have triggered parallel developments in the Nyāya school, and these are represented above all in the work of Uddyotakara (c. 600), a vociferous opponent of the Buddhist philosophers. An approximate contemporary among the Buddhists was Nāgārjuna's greatest commentator, Candrakīrti, who in many respects opposed the work of his coreligionists, the Buddhist logicians. At the same time, however, we see Buddhist philosophers attempting to synthesize the dialectical approach of Nāgārjuna and his successors with the logical and epistemological research of Dignāga and Dharmakīrti. Two such thinkers will receive considerable attention in these pages, namely, Śāntarakṣita (fl. c. 750) and his direct disciple Kamalaśīla. Among other things, they were responsible for formulating a Buddhist rebuttal to the Nyāya philosopher Uddyotakara.

It should be noted, finally, that recently it has been argued that the date of the Buddha Śākyamuni (and hence also that of his contemporary, Vardhamāna) should be advanced by as much as a century, so that his passing should now be held to have occurred in about 380 B.C.E. This hypothesis has great implications for the *absolute* chronology of Indian religion and culture during the entire period before approximately 350 B.C.E. But, because it neither upsets the *relative* chronology for that period, nor the chronology (whether relative or absolute) for the period that follows, it has few major implications, so far as I can determine, for the present work. Therefore, for simplicity's sake, I have adopted here, without comment in the body of this book, the chronological scheme that Indologists have generally favored until very recently.

REASON'S TRACES

Introduction: What Is "Buddhist Philosophy"?

I

IT IS BY NOW A COMMONPLACE to remark that our attempts to interpret Buddhist thought in Western terms have generally reflected the intellectual perspectives of the interpreters as much as those of the Buddhist thinkers we wish to interpret. Nāgārjuna has seen Hegelian, Heideggerian, and Wittgensteinian readings come and go; Vasubandhu has been incarnated as both transcendental idealist and phenomenologist; the arguments of Dharmakīrti and his successors might have stepped out of the pages of Husserl's *Logische Untersuchungen* or the *Principia Mathematica* of Russell and Whitehead.[1] To take an ungenerous view of our encounter with Buddhism, a great Asian religion turns out to be whatever we happened to have had in our heads to begin with. Like Frank Baum's Dorothy, we visit Oz only to discover that we never had to, and indeed never did, leave Kansas.

Nevertheless, our situation is perhaps inevitable: as Dilthey taught us long ago, understanding must be ever constituted on the basis of prior understanding, and to step altogether out of our skins is an impossibility for us. If we cannot eliminate the conceptual background engendered by our time, place, and personal circumstances, we can, however, with sufficient care, discern some of the ways in which our vision is at once constrained and enabled by it.[2] Our problem is not to discover, *per impossibile,* how to think Buddhism while eliminating all reference to Western ways of thought; it is, rather, to determine an approach, given our field of reflection, whereby our encounter with Buddhist traditions may open a clearing in which those traditions begin in some measure to disclose themselves, not just ourselves. The difficulty presented by our recourse to the resources of the intellectual world that is given to us—a world whose inscriptions permeate our use of the English language—lies not only in our unavoidable employment of the words and concepts we find ready at hand here, but, more subtly and sometimes insidiously, in the manner in which even our grammar defines the modalities of discourse that are authorized for our use: not for nothing did the late Chögyam Trungpa, Rinpoche, sometimes characterize English as a "theistic language." Accordingly, even to speak of "Buddhist philosophy" is already to suggest that the path upon which we now embark lies within the domain of "philosophy," that is to say, that sphere of thought whose horizons and practices have unfolded within those discourses that have been known to the West as "philosophy." If we try to circumvent this conclusion by marking the field of our inquiry not as "philosophy" but as "theology," we gain nothing thereby, but only make explicit our tacit determination to hedge discourse appertaining to religion within the theocentric bounds of Western religious thought.[3]

I do not pretend here that, in an attempt to spring us from the pen of our established ways of thought, I have dug a better tunnel than others have before. On the contrary, I believe that the means available to our efforts to open up the dialectical space I have imagined above are in the first instance those that have been long since deployed: to adduce apparently promising avenues for comparative inquiry, while at the same time not hesitating to criticize those same avenues with rigor, and so to pursue those that seem most durable until they, in their turn, have given way. In posing here the question, "What is 'Buddhist philosophy'?" then, I offer no bold, new synthetic vision, but at most a small gesture; it will be left to time and to others to determine if it suggests a path worth pursuing at length.

When we attempt to speak of "Buddhist philosophy," our expression is strangely hybrid. If its hybridity is no longer unsettling to us, this is only because we have grown accustomed to it by repeated usage; but this is not to say that the strangeness embodied in the phrase has really vanished. For we cannot ask ourselves what Buddhist philosophy might be without at the same time asking what it is that we mean by "philosophy." If we assume that we already certainly know what philosophy is, so that the question is closed even before we have had the occasion to ask it, then evidently we are not thinking philosophically at all—in which case Buddhist philosophy, whatever else it might be, apparently has very little to do with philosophy. Unquestioned, "Buddhist philosophy" is therefore a self-contradictory and self-refuting locution. If we do not welcome this outcome, we have no alternative but to linger somewhat over what we understand philosophy to be, at least when conjoined with the only slightly less problematic term "Buddhist."

Turning to recent scholarship devoted to the chimera called "Buddhist philosophy," it appears that philosophy is often conceived in terms of certain characteristic Buddhist doctrines and ways of reasoning about them. Contemporary work on Buddhist philosophy thus reflects in some respects the "problems and arguments" approach to the study of philosophy that defines much of contemporary philosophical education.[4] In mainstream philosophical circles, precisely this approach has sometimes been deployed in order to exclude from the domain of philosophy those discourses—Buddhist, Hindu, and otherwise—stemming from outside of one's preferred version of the Western Philosophical Canon, and so deemed non-philosophical by the prevailing orthodoxies of our academic philosophy departments. Thus, for instance, the analytic philosopher Antony Flew offers this bit of wisdom to undergraduates:

> Philosophy...is concerned first, last and all the time with argument...[B]ecause most of what is labelled Eastern Philosophy is not so concerned...this book draws no materials from any sources east of Suez.[5]

(In this way, with a late imperial flourish Flew would exclude from Philosophy's sainted halls not only Nāgārjuna and Śaṅkara, but also much of the Aristotelian tradition of medieval Islam!)

The dominant, dismissive prejudgment of the analytic tradition, however, was received by late twentieth-century anglophone students of Buddhist thought with sufficient seriousness that, during the past few decades, many of us who work in this and related areas have in effect devoted our energies to proving Flew wrong—to showing, that is, that classical Indian and Buddhist thinkers *were* concerned with well-formed arguments, and that the problems about which they argued were often closely similar to those that are taken to exemplify philosophy in our textbooks. Thus, recent work has concerned Buddhist examples of the analysis of concepts and categories such as truth, knowledge, perception, and memory; theories of reference and meaning; and ontological questions relating to universals and particulars, substance and attribute, causality and change, the existence of God, and other minds.

It may be fairly proposed, however, that the problems and arguments approach, whatever its heuristic utility, somehow misses the point: it brings to mind the ancient parable about the blind men and the elephant, which—though truly described by them as being at once like a pillar (the elephant's leg), a hose (its trunk), a lance (its tusk), a fan (its ear), and a rope (its tail)—remains nevertheless unknown, so long as all they know of it are these "true descriptions." As good pupils, we have learned, for instance, that the causal theory of perception, the argument from evil against theism, and the conceptualist view of universals are all parts of the elephant that is philosophy; and we can find these and more in certain classical Buddhist works. Ergo, in such works we find Buddhist philosophy. But this is about as good an argument as one that concludes, on the basis of the blind men's report, that a tool-shed is actually an elephant.

There are, of course, alternatives to the problems and arguments approach to our understanding of philosophy. For some, philosophy cannot be dissociated from the historical fact of its Greek origins, so that any inquiry into what we mean by it must proceed by way of the question, "What did philosophy mean for the Greeks?" Philosophy is thus definitionally inalienable from the contingencies of its Greek beginnings, and hence from the project of reason as it unfolded and formed itself within the Greek world and in the entire subsequent intellectual experience of the West. This perspective was most radically articulated by Martin Heidegger, who held the very expression "Western European philosophy" to be tautological; for philosophy is essentially constitutive of Western thought and culture, and of no other.[6] In asserting this, Heidegger was by no means endorsing the Western philosophical triumphalism we have seen articulated by Flew; he does not exclude the possibility that we might find conceptual and dialectical analogues to aspects of our philosophical tradition outside of the West. What he holds, rather, is that the formation of philosophy as a distinct domain of activity is inseparable from its historical constitution in the Greek intellectual and cultural world, and embodies a characteristically Greek preoccupation and astonishment with the categories of being, becoming, and essence.

Heidegger regarded the archaic thinkers, above all Anaximander, Parmenides, and Heraclitus, to be the true exemplars for the Greek world of an at once luminous and occluded presence of being within language and thought. The passage later traced from Socrates through Plato to Aristotle represents, in Heidegger's view, an achievement that is in truth a rupture, whereby thinking became fatefully unhinged from being. As one of Heidegger's interpreters has put it, "The history of *philosophy* becomes a nightmare from which we, Dædalus-like, are trying to awake."[7] In particular, metaphysics and the philosophical project of defining, analyzing, and hence dominating being represent no longer a conquest but a terrible fall.

It is beside the point of our present concerns to pursue Heidegger's path at length here; I have introduced him into my discussion to make just two points. First, our understanding of the obscure self we call "philosophy" is questionable, and our questioning of it must proceed by way of constant reference to Greek thought. Second, Heidegger's critique of "metaphysics," the Western philosophical science of being, should caution us to be particularly wary regarding the deeper implications of the effort to assimilate Buddhist thought, that obscure other, to our category of "philosophy." In considering a bit further the first of these points, I want now to turn from Heidegger to a more recent interpreter of Greek philosophy who I think will help us to shed some light on the second: the implications of things Greek for our reading of things Buddhist.

II

Pierre Hadot, during the past several decades, has elaborated a far-reaching rereading of the classical tradition—one that seeks to restore for us the relationship between thought and being within Greek philosophy, though not along the lines suggested by Heidegger. At the center of Hadot's reflections is the concept of "spiritual exercise," whereby, in his words, "the individual raises himself up to the life of the objective Spirit, that is to say, he replaces himself within the perspective of the Whole."[8] And as Hadot further affirms, "Philosophy then appears in its original aspect: not as a theoretical construct, but as a method for training people to live and to look at the world in a new way. It is an attempt to transform mankind."[9]

An example of Hadot's perspective is his reading of the death of Socrates, its treatment by Plato, and its legacy in the Stoic and other Hellenistic traditions: "For Plato," Hadot writes, "training for death is a spiritual exercise which consists in changing one's point of view. We are to change from a vision of things dominated by individual passions to a representation of the world governed by the universality and objectivity of thought. This constitutes a conversion *(metastrophe)* brought about with the totality of the soul."[10] In Hadot's thought, the implications of this deceptively simple shift of focus ramify throughout our understanding of Greek philosophy; Stoic physics, for example, is now seen to be less concerned with supplying a complete and coherent account of the material world than with the cultivation by the philosopher of a particular attitude to the world, and with the implications thereof for self-understanding. Physics in this system is thus inextricably tied to ethics, and to the formation of oneself as a specific type of agent. It is inseparable from the Stoic "training for death" and as such "is linked to the contemplation of the Whole and the elevation of thought, which rises from individual, passionate subjectivity to the universal perspective."[11]

Now, I think that anyone who has even passing familiarity with Buddhist path texts—works such as Buddhaghosa's *Visuddhimagga (Path of Purity)*, Śāntideva's *Bodhicaryāvatāra (Introduction to Enlightened Conduct)*, or Tsong-kha-pa's *Lam-rim chen-mo (Great Sequence of the Path)*—will appreciate that there is a powerful analogy to be explored here. Take, for example, these verses of Śāntideva:

> By reason of what I cherish and despise, I have done much that is sinful.
> Leaving it all, I will have to go on—as if I didn't know this would be so!
> What I despise will not be, neither will there be what I love.
> I, too, will not be. Everything will come not to be.[12]

Adopting Hadot's way of speaking, Śāntideva directs us here to practice a particular spiritual exercise in which training for death is related both to scrupulous attention to the moral quality of one's actions and to a general meditation on the nature of all conditioned entities as fleeting and impermanent. Acts that flow from our impulse to possess what we find desirable and to avoid what we do not are all grounded in a remarkable illusion, an intellectual error that is at bottom a willful refusal to confront the ephemeral quality of the constituents of our experience, a persistent and tenacious denial of our own mortality. We must, therefore, struggle against this profound disposition to regard ourselves and our properties as secure and enduring realities. The contemplation of universal impermanence reveals to us that we are no more than motes turning within a passing dust-cloud. We must order our values and actions with this humbling vision always in mind.

III

The little I have said so far suggests that Hadot's reading of the Socratic schools, particularly in their Hellenistic iterations, offers a useful model for our thinking on Buddhism in its relation to philosophy. It is a model that depends upon a view of philosophy that emphasizes the "techniques of the self"—systematic spiritual exercises and *ascesis,* and *paideia,* here primarily the formation of the person as a moral agent refined through philosophical education. There is, however, an important challenge to this perspective, in its application both to things Greek and things Buddhist. For, although it is a contribution of inestimable value to delineate with care the manner in which classical philosophy embodied powerful commitments to well-formed regimes of self-cultivation, in which dialectic and argument played central roles, it remains nevertheless true that classical philosophy was also concerned with both speculative and practical knowledge. The Aristotelian project, most notably, with its systematization of scientific research and the acquisition of data, and its strong emphasis on *theoria,* all of which have been regarded as the true ancestors of our modern conceptions of scientific knowledge and discovery, seems to speak for a very different model. Analogously, over and against the Buddhist path texts I have mentioned, we find large numbers of Buddhist writings devoted to logic and epistemology, the categories, and basic ontology. These works are more difficult to interpret according to the conception of philosophy-as-spiritual-exercise that I have been discussing, and it is precisely because they are harder to interpret in this way, and more amenable to the dissection of their "problems and arguments," that we must place them now at the heart of our endeavor.[13]

On reading Hadot's œuvre one is immediately struck by the apparently diminished place of Aristotle, relative to the centrality and weight he is usually accorded. Socrates, Plato, and Plotinus are without doubt the heroes of Hadot's account, together with some, notably Marcus Aurelius, who have been too often neglected in our philosophical syllabi.[14] Nevertheless, Hadot does have a position on Aristotle, and it is one that, perhaps to some degree echoing Heidegger, stresses *our* mistaken tendency to read *theoria* as synonymous with what we now mean by "theory," and accordingly to position *theoria* over and against what we call "practice." For Hadot, *theoria* in Aristotle's sense is itself the most highly valued practice; it is, in fact, that practice through which human beings may come to participate in an activity that is characteristically divine. Where Aristotle departs from Plato is not in valuing theoretical knowledge above practice, but in valuing a specific type of practice, *theoria,* and the way of life that it entails, over the life of political practice that had been so dear to his master.[15]

Now, with this in mind, an approach to Buddhist "theoretical" knowledge may begin to emerge. I would like us to consider, in this regard, a particular text—one to which we shall have frequent occasion to return in the chapters that follow—the *Tattvasaṅgraha,* literally the *Gathering of the Tattvas,* by the great eighth-century Indian master Śāntarakṣita. *Tattva* is an important Sanskrit philosophical term that in both form and meaning resembles the Latin scholastic term *quidditas,* denoting the "essence or true nature of the thing itself." *(Tattva* literally means "that-ness.") Hence, in the extended sense in which Śāntarakṣita uses it in his title, *tattva* refers to "discussions and viewpoints pertaining to the real natures of things."[16] Śāntarakṣita's text, in some 3,600 verses accompanied by the multivolume commentary of his disciple Kamalaśīla, is a veritable encyclopedia of "problems and arguments," treating, together with much else, the existence of god, substance theories of the self, the nature of perception, the ontology of time, and the theory of reference.[17] For those who may harbor doubts, à la Flew, as to whether or not there was philosophical argument "east of Suez," this is the ideal eye-opener. Consider, for instance, the following remarks concerning the logical necessity of positing, besides those cognitive acts that are defined by their reference to an object, a class of self-presenting or purely reflexive acts. Śāntarakṣita here takes up an objection that holds that any and all acts of cognition involve objectification, so that there can be no genuine reflexivity. As Kamalaśīla summarizes the argument:

> The opinion at issue is this: "That [act of consciousness], too, must be known by some knower discrete from itself, [for these reasons:] because it is a phenomenon that comes into being and is annihilated, because it is ponderable, and because it is an object of memory, just like any [other type of] object." [However,] if one act of consciousness must be experienced by a successor, then there may be an infinite regress. For an object cannot be known by an act of awareness that is itself unknown. Thus, to establish a single object, by proceeding through [an infinite] succession of acts of awareness, the entire lifespan of a person must be thereby exhausted! Hence, owing to this danger of an infinite regress, [it must be assumed that] some act of awareness occurs that is essentially self-presenting.[18]

Analogous arguments can be found in the writings of Franz Brentano and Edmund Husserl.[19] If Śāntarakṣita's subject matter and his approach to it are not philosophical, then one might well wonder what is. But, to continue along the path I had set upon earlier, this point is tangential to our concerns.

What we want to know is not whether and in what ways the particular topics discussed by Śāntarakṣita resemble philosophical discussions with which we are familiar, but, rather, what are the larger contours of his project, and how do these relate to the projects we otherwise treat as "philosophy"?

The very dimensions of Śāntarakṣita's work have, I think, caused us to refrain from asking big questions about it. Once more, like the blind men and their elephant, we try to get the feel of only one part at a time; our grasp is just not large enough to embrace the behemoth's whole girth. But the effort is nevertheless worthwhile, and Śāntarakṣita and Kamalaśīla have certainly favored us with some important clues about their intent.[20] Thus, for example, in the six stanzas introducing the *Gathering* (which together form one long sentence), Śāntarakṣita praises his supreme teacher, the Buddha, while providing the general program for his book at the same time. The Buddha is the greatest of all teachers because he has articulated, as no other had done before, the teaching of *pratītyasamutpāda,* the "interdependent origination" or "arising" of all conditioned things, and Śāntarakṣita's verses relate the entire project of the *Gathering* to this cardinal tenet. He writes:

> Movement devoid of prime matter, a divine creator, their conjunction, self and similar constructions;
> Ground for the deed and its fruit, their relationship, ascertainment and such;
> Empty with respect to quality, substance, function, genus, inherence and other superimposed categories,
> But within the scope of words and concepts relating to posited features;
> Ascertained by the two epistemic operations possessing distinct characteristics;
> Unmixed with so much as even a mote of extraneous nature;
> Without temporal extension, without beginning or end, like unto reflections and so on;
> Free from the whole mass of conceptual projections, unrealized by other [teachers]—
> This interdependent arising was propounded by the best of proponents,
> Who was unattached to self-justifying revelations, and moved to benefit the whole world;
> Who throughout no fewer than numberless æons became the very self of compassion;

> Having bowed before him, the Omniscient, I gather here the *tattvas.*[21]

For the sake of the present discussion, it will not be necessary to unpack this in detail (Kamalaśīla devotes some 20 pages to it). Let us consider briefly just the first line, which describes interdependent arising as:

> Movement devoid of prime matter, a divine creator, their conjunction, self and similar constructions...

This sets the agenda for the first eight chapters of the *Gathering,* which provide critical accounts of: the Sāṃkhya theory of prime matter (chapter 1), Śaiva theism (chapter 2), the concept of a creator working as a demiurge upon prime matter (chapter 3), and six different theories of the substantial self, or *ātman* (chapter 7). The word "movement" in the verse alludes to the chapter defending the Buddhist teaching of the ephemerality of conditioned beings over and against these doctrines (chapter 8). "Similar constructions" refers to three chapters refuting, respectively, the notion of spontaneous, causeless creation (chapter 4), the philosopher Bhartṛhari's theory of the "Word-as-absolute" *(śabda-brahman,* chapter 5), and the Vedic conception of the primal man, *puruṣa* (chapter 6). In the remaining lines of the opening verses, Śāntarakṣita similarly introduces, as descriptions of interdependent arising, the other topics he will discuss in the order of their discussion; and in the concluding lines his characterization of the doctrine gives way to a eulogy of the teacher who proclaimed it:

> Who was unattached to self-justifying revelations, and moved to benefit the whole world;
> Who throughout no fewer than numberless æons became the very self of compassion;
> Having bowed before him, the Omniscient...

The last chapters of Śāntarakṣita's treatise will be devoted precisely to refuting the claims of the Vedic revelation (chapters 24–25), and to upholding the omniscience attributed to the Buddha (chapter 26).

There is a further dimension to Śāntarakṣita's introduction to his great work that deserves our attention. His six stanzas strongly echo the first verses of Nāgārjuna's *Treatise on the Middle Way (Madhyamakaśāstra),* where the Buddha is praised in closely similar terms for his declaration of interdependent arising.[22] And elsewhere in his treatise, Nāgārjuna in fact defines the key concept of *śūnyatā,* or emptiness, precisely as this radical contingency of conditioned things.[23] In other words, in its deeper meaning Śāntarakṣita's *Gathering* is perhaps not primarily a work on logic and epistemology, but rather a sustained exploration of a core soteriological theme of Mahāyāna Buddhism in its relation to the full range of the preoccupations of late first-millennium Indian thought. The *Gathering,* then, is not gathered together in the manner of a miscellany; it is a dialectical gathering-in, a passage through Indian systematic thought whose spiraling flight finds its center in the Buddha's message and in the person of the Buddha himself. The dialectical path of the work is defined by its continual oscillation between moments of affirmation and of negation. On the one hand, this means that Śāntarakṣita is occupied throughout in presenting the affirmations of his intellectual rivals, Śāntarakṣita's refutation of which points the way to successively stronger positions. But Śāntarakṣita does not proceed via negative argument alone; there is a positive content to his thought as well, which finds its culmination, once again, in the teaching of interdependent origination and in the affirmation of the Buddha's surpassing omniscience and omnibenevolence.

The Madhyamaka philosophy of Nāgārjuna and his successors (including Śāntarakṣita) is one of the areas in Buddhist thought in which we are prone to find an exemplification of philosophy-as-theoretical-activity, according to something like what we mean by "theory."[24] We sometimes speak, for example, of "establishing emptiness," as if the point here were to demonstrate apodictically the soundness of the particular thesis that "all things are empty of essential being."[25] As the Madhyamaka teaching of emptiness, however, is sometimes said to dispense with all expressed tenets, even this one, more nuanced readings favor finding here a type of scepticism, specifically a sceptical view of the referential capacity of language and conceptual activity.[26] None of this seems to me to be wrong, but it raises the question: what connection could this possibly have with the program of spiritual exercise I introduced earlier? Indeed, we must entertain this question, for within the Mahāyāna the Madhyamaka teaching is always valued soteriologically, and from our standpoint it is perhaps difficult to see precisely how salvation flows from assenting to a sceptical view of language. But consider how Nāgārjuna's great commentator Candrakīrti, for instance, introduces the suitable aspirant's response to the teaching of emptiness:

Even as a mundane person, on hearing of emptiness,
He is inwardly moved to rejoice,
To rejoice until tears wet his eyes
And the hairs of his body stand on end.
In that one there is the seed of the Buddha's intention.
That one is the vessel fit for this intimate teaching.
It is to him that you should teach this ultimate truth,
For in him the virtues that flow from it will emerge.[27]

Whatever else we may say of this, it should be evident that Candrakīrti is not speaking here of "theory" as something set over and against "practice." The teaching of emptiness gives joy to the receptive individual who possesses the seed of the Buddha's intention, in whom the soteriological orientation of the teaching is well-planted. For such an individual, "emptiness" cannot be understood primarily in propositional, or "theoretical" terms; rather it fundamentally determines one's orientation to the Buddha's salvific project. This is also clearly expressed by Śāntarakṣita's disciple Kamalaśīla in commenting upon his master's verse ("This interdependent arising was propounded by the best of proponents"):

> By teaching interdependent arising the Lord [Buddha] engenders the attainment of worldly excellence and supreme beatitude, in this way: by the inerrant teaching of interdependent arising and the ascertainment of its meaning, the basis for an excellent destiny *(sugatihetu),* namely, the inerrant comprehension of deeds and their results, their connections, and so on, is born; and the basis for supreme beatitude, the realization of selflessness, both personal and in principle, develops progressively through audition, reflection and contemplation. For when that has developed, the unknowing that is the basis of the worldly round is undone; and with its undoing all that is rooted in it—the affective and cognitive obstructions—is undone. It is from dispelling all these obstructions that beatitude is won.[28]

The dialectical path of Śāntarakṣita's text, therefore, is not to be followed solely through study and critical reflection culminating in intellectual certainty; it must be pursued further in contemplation, *bhāvanā*—a word often translated as "cultivation," and literally meaning "bringing into being." This philosophy, in the end, is not primarily about objects of thought *(jñeya),* but is rather a way of coming-to-be *(bhāvanā)*—one that we are enjoined to bring to fruition within ourselves.[29]

Some further specifications are called for. As we have seen above, much of Śāntarakṣita's text is devoted to the critical scrutiny of doctrines propounded by rival schools, for instance, the Hindu Sāṃkhya theory of prime matter. Now, how does the study of this and its refutation properly belong to the program of self-culture through spiritual exercise that we have been discussing? For on the surface, at least, it appears that Śāntarakṣita's purpose is primarily to dismiss the teachings of Buddhism's opponents and to defend the faith; philosophical argument, so it seems, is deployed here primarily in the service of doctrinal apologetics.

It is undeniable that this is an entirely legitimate way of reading Śāntarakṣita's text, and that it succeeds very well in capturing one of the dimensions to which it is directed. Nevertheless, even here I believe that Śāntarakṣita's dialectical course suggests an alternative reading. As Kamalaśīla insists, the doctrines Śāntarakṣita is concerned to refute all involve "mistaken views of the self" *(vitathātmadṛṣṭi).*[30] As such, the importance of critical reflection upon them lies precisely in the fact that they are not just *others'* views of *them*selves, but that, potentially at least, they are views that any of us may harbor, whether explicitly or not, with respect to *our*selves. Śāntarakṣita's critical journey through the byways of Indian philosophy is therefore no mere exercise in doxography; rather, it is a therapy whereby one must challenge one's own self-understandings so as to disclose and finally uproot the misunderstandings that are concealed therein. This process involves equally the positive construction of a conceptual model of the Buddha's teaching and of the Buddha himself, a conceptual model that is to be progressively assimilated until, in the end, concept and being have merged.[31] This is a self-transcending project, oriented toward that omniscient being who, as the very self of compassion, is oriented to benefit all beings.

IV

The perspective I am adopting here depends in part upon an accentuation of the Madhyamaka architecture of what, after all, is classified as a treatise on logic and epistemology. Within later Tibetan Buddhist circles, however, it was in fact sometimes disputed whether the epistemological doctrines of the philosophers Dignāga and Dharmakīrti—who, as we have seen, were among Śāntarakṣita's major sources of inspiration—had any clear soteriological role, or instead offered merely an *organon.*[32] Nevertheless, the assimilation of even these thinkers to the project of spiritual exercise, contested though it may have been, offers what I believe is a particularly forceful confirmation of the general validity of the approach I am adopting. For whatever may be concluded regarding Dignāga's and Dharmakīrti's exact intentions, it is certain that many thinkers trained within their tradition understood their thought, too, in its connection with a clear program of spiritual exercise.

This is very well illustrated in the writings of the great eighteenth-century master, Lcang-skya Rol-pa'i rdo-rje (1717–86), a figure of commanding importance in the Manchu empire's religious affairs. Identified at the age of four as the incarnation of a famous lama, Lcang-skya was sent to Beijing to be educated at the court. There he became the playmate of the fourth-ranking Manchu prince, who, despite his rank order, was selected by his father, the Yongzheng emperor, to succeed to the throne. Known by his reign title Qianlong (reigned 1736–99), the prince became the greatest of the Qing monarchs. Lcang-skya rose with his boyhood friend to become the empire's preeminent Buddhist clergyman.[33]

The text I present here is drawn from one of Lcang-skya's most esteemed and puzzling works: it records a dream-vision in which the relationship between the systematic study of Dharmakīrti's epistemology and progress on the Buddhist path is set out in general terms. Kept secret during the final year of Lcang-skya's life, it was published posthumously in the superb biography authored by his disciple, Thu'u-bkwan Blo-bzang-chos-kyi-nyi-ma (1737–1802). The text does not propose to examine particular arguments in detail, but rather presents a strategy for relating the study of Dharmakīrti's magnum opus, the *Pramāṇavārttika (Exposition of [Dignaga's system of] Logic and Epistemology),* to the soteriological concerns of Buddhism. The visionary aspect of the text tends to undermine the assumption that there was any great divide between the worlds of the Buddhist logician and the Buddhist mystic. Lcang-skya, by placing this sketch of Buddhist rationalism in the context of a dream-vision, effectively annuls the gulf separating religious experience from reason. He writes:

> I, Rol-pa'i rdo-rje, traveled to Mount Wutai, the supreme abode of the emanation of Mañjuśrīghoṣa,[34] during the wood serpent year of the thirteenth cycle (1785). Sealing myself in meditational retreat for some months, I prayed to the three supreme jewels

[Buddha, doctrine, and community], when, during the night of the seventeenth day of the sixth Mongolian month,[35] there was a great torrential rainfall, and, because it brought great danger of flood, my opportunity to sleep was stolen. Spontaneously, the verbal significance of the *Hymn of the Glorious One Excellent with the Virtues of Knowledge* occurred to me clearly, as if explained by another, and I wrote it down the next day.[36]

During that retreat I experienced many altered states, in which mystical experience and dream intermingled. Mostly they seemed to be experiences mixed up with portents of obstacles, so that it was difficult to distinguish the good from the bad. Nonetheless, there were some that caused me to frequently wonder whether they might be [due to] the blessing of the deity and guru.

When I left the retreat and was returning [to Beijing], after the sun had set during the first day of the ninth Mongolian month, when I was in the vicinity of the great Chinese fort called "Baoding Palace" [in Hebei Province, en route between Mt. Wutai and Beijing], I recited about five chapters of the text of the *Guhyasamājatantra* together with my attendant Ja-sag Bla-ma Dge-legs-nam-mkha', and in my mind I had various pleasurable experiences. Afterward, having turned in, I fell asleep reciting a Mañjuśrī prayer as I drifted off. Then, at some point, while experiencing myself to be seemingly awake, someone arrived suddenly and I asked who it was. "I'm 'Jam-dbyangs," he said.[37] I thought it must be my monk called "'Jam-dbyangs" who was sleeping outside my door, and I looked to see. Because my eyes were unclear I saw neither the form nor the garments of a human being; but just then there was a small, young reverend, wearing a new blouse of yellow silk, to whom I said, "Look at the wall-clock to see what time it is!" He acted as if to look at it, and said that it had reached the halfway point of the hour of the pig. After I said, "Then it's still early. Go back to sleep!" he straightened himself up right there, but did not go off. At that time, a recollection suddenly popped into my mind of [the title and opening verses of Dharmakīrti's *Exposition of Logic and Epistemology*].

Right then, that small reverend just sat there and, though it was not clear that he was speaking, there was a voice in my ear:

"This *Exposition of Logic and Epistemology* is a superlative treatise! In those who strive for liberation and omniscience a faith in our teacher and teaching that reaches the depths must be born from the heart. About that, even though certainty brought forth by pure reason is not born in the fideists, a faith involving conviction may well be born in them; still, it is hard [for them] to get beyond a conditional [sort of faith]. If certainty is born on the basis of genuine reason, it won't be turned back by conditions; a firm disposition is established.

"In the second chapter of the *Exposition,* it explains at length...the manner in which our Teacher [the Buddha] is Epistemic Authority for those seeking liberation.[38] Owing to this, fully comprehending that the plentiful talk among the Outsiders [i.e., non-Buddhists] of liberation and the path to reach it is like childish babble, there will come to be the uncontrived production of deep faith in our Teacher and Teaching, brought about on the path of reason.

"Further, when one well investigates by reason the Transcendent Lord's declarations of the four truths, along with the injunctions, prohibitions, and methods [that follow from them, one finds that] there is not even the slightest fault, contradiction, lack of proof, or uncertainty. Not only that, but when investigating all the reasons that are articulated [in the Buddha's teaching] through study and reflection, they are [found to] really penetrate the heart of the matter. You must reflect on that [intellectual penetration], intermingling it with your present experience: these varied pleasures and pains that occur to you now in the course of things are ephemeral occurrences. Regarding them, these pleasures and pains—whatever the degree of their intensity—are experientially proven to occur on the basis of causes and conditions. Having taken the measure of this, [one comes to know that] the acquisitive *skandhas*[39] certainly depend on causes, and that, regarding those causes, they do not arise from permanent or heterogenous causes. Thus you arrive at the thought that [the teachings of impermanence, suffering, and causality] that have been proclaimed by the Teacher are certainly established..."[40]

Thus, for Lcang-skya—the urbane servant of an eighteenth-century empire, whose awareness of contemporary Russia, Germany, and France led him to scoff at traditional Tibetan Buddhist knowledge of the world from an early modern perspective[41]—the cultivation of reason was nevertheless tied to the exercises of the path in much the same manner that it had been for Śāntarakṣita and Kamalaśīla a millennium before. The reasoned investigation of the teaching is to be intermingled with one's experiences; it must flow from, and in turn inform, one's engagement in the culture of the self.

V

In view of all that I have said above, it seems fair to affirm that what we may term "Buddhist philosophy" has unfolded within those realms of discourse that might be more precisely called, in the proper sense of the term, "Buddhology," that is, the hermeneutics of buddhahood and of the message propounded by the Buddha.[42] Because this suggests that we remain nevertheless within the domain circumscribed by the authority of a revealed religious tradition, one may well object that this "Buddhist philosophy" is not really philosophy at all; it is, to appropriate an expression well-known to historians of philosophy in the West, merely the "handmaid" of the Buddhist analogue to theology. That such thinkers as Nāgārjuna and Candrakīrti remain firmly within the ambit of the Buddhological project, despite the impressively sceptical dimensions of their path, may be taken by some as proof positive that Buddhist philosophy has never claimed for itself the perfect autonomy of reason that is often supposed to be a hallmark of the Western traditions of rational inquiry derived ultimately from the Greeks. Buddhist scepticisms, like those of Western "sceptical fideists,"[43] in the end remain relatively tame; the trenchant impulse to overthrow all prior assumptions that we find perhaps in a Jayarāśi Bhaṭṭa in India or in a Solomon Maimon in the West seems altogether alien to the Buddhist tradition.[44] Even the most radical deconstructions of the world and the self in Buddhist contemplative experience, where the disposition to hanker after the merest grain of reality in body or mind is undone, must be seen to be indexed to specific soteriological projects and the axiological assumptions that accompany them.[45]

I do not raise these objections in order to quibble about the relative degrees to which the freedom of reason has (or has not) been realized and expressed in various historical settings in the West and in the Buddhist world. My point is not to underwrite a stance that values an assumed Western freedom of thought as a unique achievement, now best emulated by all those others who, despite their best efforts, have never quite hit the mark. For, as emphasized earlier, the impossibility of our just stepping out of our skins should counsel caution regarding our presumptions of perfect intellectual freedom. And far from proposing a negative assessment of the achievements of past Buddhist thinkers, I hope that I have made clear above that I regard theirs to be an intellectual tradition of supreme and enduring value. What I wish to emphasize, nevertheless, is that, whatever we may rightly assert of the powerful analogies between certain important trends in Buddhist thought and equally important aspects of the enterprise we call philosophy, the relationship between Buddhism and philosophy must continue in some respects to perplex us, even after we have grown to accept the locution "Buddhist philosophy." In the work presented here, therefore, I wish to consider "Buddhist philosophy" not as an achievement, but as a still unrealized potentiality.

The elaboration of doctrine and argument in traditional Buddhist settings necessarily responded to the intellectual cultures of the times and places concerned. We cannot rightly expect to find there ready-made answers to the problems that confront our contemporary philosophical culture. And one of the hallmarks of philosophy is that it must forever renew itself in response to the specificities of place and time, that there is a strong sense in which there can be no perennial philosophical doctrine. From this perspective, the very notion of a "perennial philosophy" risks finishing as an annulment of the philosophical spirit. However, in suggesting that perhaps the richest analogue between traditional Buddhist thought and Western philosophies is to be found not in the comparison of particular arguments so much as in the overriding project of philosophy as a vehicle for the formation of the person through spiritual exercise, as has been emphasized by Hadot, a new perspective may also be disclosed, not only for comparative reflection on arguments and practices elaborated in the past, but in considering also our unactualized prospects. If Buddhism is to emerge as a viable current in Western thought over the long duration, its point of departure will have to be sustained and critical reflection upon its ideals of the good in relation to our contemporary predicaments. Thus, Buddhist philosophy, despite its great and ancient history, remains for us a project as yet unborn.

The essays that follow in the body of this book relate to the perspective I have traced out here in a number of different ways. In the first part, "Situating the Self," the connection between critical reflection on the self and the "techniques of the self" is implicit throughout and is underscored especially in chapters 2 and 5. It will also be clear, I believe, that the questions at issue in part 2, "Reality and Reason," represent, in important respects, the extension of particular inquiries whose initial points of departure were among the problems of the self: Vasubandhu's "proof of idealism," discussed in chapter 7, turns on an analysis of part-whole relationships that is directly related to the analysis of persons in terms of their parts, considered in chapters 2 and 3; while the Madhyamaka teaching of two truths, taken up in chapter 8, flows from distinctions that were first adumbrated, so far as we now know, in the context of the debates on the self that are surveyed in chapters 3 and 4, concerning the complementary themes of the absence of the self and its synthesis.

The inclusion, in part 3, of three essays on tantrism may strike some as unusual in a book of philosophy, and perhaps requires some explanation. Not long ago, given the widespread presupposition in philosophical circles of an near-absolute dichotomy between "mysticism and reason," it was almost unimaginable that some of the greatest reasoners in the Indian and Tibetan Buddhist traditions could have also been involved in "tantric mysticism."[46] The evidence now available to us, however, demonstrates that in both India and Tibet there were many important figures whose mature work involved both the tantric and dialectical dimensions of Buddhist thought and practice. This is exemplified, as we have seen above, in the life and work of Lcang-skya Rol-pa'i rdo-rje, and in the body of the book by such figures as Bhāvaviveka and Abhayākaragupta in India, or Dol-po-pa and Mi-pham in Tibet. It is therefore a prima facie problem for the interpretation of the tradition to understand just how these two spheres are related to one another. (The importance of this question in relation to the hermeneutics of Indian religious culture generally was suggested as early as the 1920s, in the writings of Heinrich Zimmer, considered in chapter 11.) Of course, tantrism engages philosophical reflection to the extent that thinkers within Buddhist traditions were influenced by tantrism in their philosophizing—this is illustrated in chapter 9, as well as in the two chapters of part 4 on "Doctrinal Interpretation in Tibet." Perhaps more significant, however, was the role of tantric ritual and meditational practice in the formation of the religious agent; for, in this respect, tantrism complemented and cooperated with the educational formation that, as I have argued here, was essential to the project of Buddhist philosophy overall. In chapter 10, "Weaving the World," I seek to illustrate the manner in which Buddhist tantric ritual embodied a dynamic process of world-construction in which adepts and artisans might participate in divine agency. Such a process has the formation of a Buddha-realm as its ideal culmination, and, as I have suggested above, it is the realization of the Buddha's wisdom and love that is the proper *telos* of reason as well.

Notes

1 Scharfstein 1998 provides useful surveys of contemporary interpretation of some of the major Asian philosophical thinkers, including (in chaps. 8, 12, and 13) the three mentioned here. Tuck 1990 studies the history of Nāgārjuna's reception in the West. For the Western encounter with Indian thought more generally, see esp. Halbfass 1988; and with Buddhism, Lopez 1995.

2 Or, as Thompson 1981: 38, puts it: "What historians seek to understand is what they themselves have produced." Makreel 1992: 54–55 explains that, for Dilthey, "inner experience is limited in scope by personal dispositions and presuppositions. Such individual perspectives need not be denied, but through reflection their horizons of meaning can be shifted so as to be made more and more encompassing.... The solution is to make the perspective explicit, thereby rendering it less restrictive and more amenable to refinement."

3 Jackson and Makransky 2000 examines and engages the category of "theology" in its relation to Buddhism.

4 My remarks here apply not only to the study of Buddhist philosophy, but to that of Asian philosophies more generally. See, for example, Deutsch and Bontekoe 1997, where the chapters on Buddhism (24–31) take up "ideas of the good," "social and political ideals," "causality," "humankind and nature," "reality and divinity," "concept of self," "rationality," and "ontological truth." Consider also Scharfstein 1998.

5 Flew 1971: 36.

6 Heidegger 1958: 31. On Heidegger's relationship with Asian thought, refer to Parkes 1987 and now, esp., May 1996. See, further, chap. 8 below.

7 David Farrell Krell, in Heidegger 1975: 7. The italics are in the original.

8 Hadot 1995b: 82.

9 Hadot 1995b: 107.

10 Hadot 1995b: 96.

11 Hadot 1995b: 97.

12 *Bodhicaryāvatāra,* chap. 2, vv. 35–36.

13 For surveys of the Buddhist *pramāṇa* schools, to which I refer here, Stcherbatsky 1962 offers the classic study, now very much out of date. Dreyfus 1997 provides an excellent survey of Dharmakīrti's epistemological tradition from a Tibetan scholastic perspective that serves as the best overview of this material at present. In contemporary scholarship, there has sometimes been a strong presupposition

that the concerns of the *pramāṇa* schools were entirely removed from the properly religious interests of Buddhism. This is reflected by Conze, who writes (1967: 265): "Buddhist logic, studied only by one section of the Yogācārins, failed to win approval elsewhere, and aroused the misgivings of many who condemned it as an utterly profane science.* At variance with the spirit of Buddhism, it can indeed be tolerated only as a manifestation of 'skill in means'." Conze's asterisked note here reads: "These misgivings must have been further increased when, observing the behaviour of people like Dharmakīrti (BL [*Buddhist Logic*] I 36, Gnoli, p. xxxvi) one could not fail to notice that this branch of studies produces people who are boastful and inclined to push themselves forward." It is difficult to see just how the passages cited support such a strong conclusion; perhaps Conze had privileged knowledge of Dharmakīrti's behavior!

14 Hadot 1992, 1995a, 1995b.

15 Hadot 1995a: 123–44, esp. 143–44: "Aristote, comme Platon, fonde sur les hommes politiques son espoir de transformer la cité et les hommes. Mais Platon considérait que les philosophes doivent être eux-mêmes les hommes politiques qui réaliseront cette œuvre...Pour Aristote, au contraire,...[l]e philosophe, pour sa part, choisira une vie consacrée à la recherche désintéressée, à l'étude et la contemplation, et, il faut bien le reconnaître, indépendante des tracas de la vie politique. La philosophie est donc, pour Aristote, comme pour Platon, à la fois un mode de vie et un mode de discours." A further, useful correction to any inclination there may be to emphasize one-sidedly the "techniques of the self" in the context of Hellenistic philosophy is found in Nussbaum's (1994) insistence on what she felicitously terms the "dignity of reason." Her observations about this apply equally, I believe, to the Indian traditions studied here. For a valuable consideration of the place of "theory" in classical Indian thought, see Pollock 1985.

16 *Tattvasaṅgrahapañjikā,* p. 20, stipulates that *tattva,* as used in the *Tattvasaṅgraha*'s title, refers particularly to the topics treated in that text insomuch as they are characterizations of interdependent origination *(yathoktāny eva pratītyasamutpādaviśeṣaṇāni tattvāni).* Cf. *Nyāyakośa,* pp. 309–11, which surveys the range of definitions of *tattva(m)* in Sanskrit philosophical texts.

17 The twenty-six chapters of the *Tattvasaṅgraha* examine: 1. the Sāṃkhya doctrine of 'nature,' that is, prime matter; 2. the lord (God); 3. nature and the lord as 'cocreators' of the world; 4. the notion that the world is a chance occurrence; 5. *śabdabrahma,* that is, the absolute as Word; 6. the Cosmic Man (the anthropomorphic cosmology of the Veda); 7. the self; 8. the existence of persisting entities; 9. the relationship between act and result; 10. substance; 11. quality; 12. act; 13. universal; 14. particular; 15. the inherence of quality in substance; 16. word and meaning; 17. perception; 18. inference; 19. whether there are other means of knowledge; 20. the logic of 'may be'; 21. past, present, and future time; 22. materialism; 23. the existence of the external world; 24. scriptural authority; 25. the self-validation of religious claims; 26. the seer's extrasensory perception.

18 *Tattvasaṅgrahapañjikā,* p. 107.

19 Brentano 1973: 124: "[W]hen I remember having heard something, in addition to the presentation of hearing I have a presentation of the present remembering of hearing, which is not identical with it. This last presentation, however, must also be conscious, and how would this be conceivable without the assumption of a third presentation which has the same relation to it as it has to the remembering? This third presentation, however, would likewise demand a fourth, and so on, *ad infinitum.*" Cf. Husserl 1962, vol. 2, part 2, p. 155.

20 One of the first obstacles we face in appraising these texts, however, is traditional classification. In the Jaina manuscript collections in which Śāntarakṣita's text was preserved in Sanskrit, and equally in the Tibetan Buddhist commentarial canons, which give us its eleventh-century Tibetan translation, the *Gathering of the Tattvas* was classified among works of *pramāṇavidyā,* that is to say, the science of logic and epistemology. There is nothing particularly wrong about this classification, for many of the topics Śāntarakṣita discusses—for instance, perception and inference, reference, and particulars and universals—were generally allocated here, and many of Śāntarakṣita's particular arguments ultimately derive from the writings of Dignāga and Dharmakīrti, the founding masters of the Buddhist epistemological school. Nevertheless, Śāntarakṣita indexes his work to other currents in Buddhist thought as well, and the overall architecture of his text, as he himself sets it out, suggests that while logic and epistemology indeed constitute his *organon,* his overriding concern is by no means their exposition alone. For the Jaina reception of the *Tattvasaṅgraha,* see the comments of Guṇaratna Sūri in *Ṣaḍdarśanasamuccaya,* p. 75, line 7.

21 *Tattvasaṅgraha,* vv. 1–6.

22 *Mūlamadhyamakakārikā,* vv. 1–2 *(maṅgalaśloka):* "I praise the best of proponents, the perfect Buddha who declared interdependent origination—without cessation, without origination, neither discontinuous, nor persisting, neither unicity, nor multiplicity, neither arriving, nor departing—to be free from elaboration and at peace."

23 There are several proof texts, but the clearest statement is *Mūlamadhyamakakārikā,* chap. 24, v. 18ab: "That which is interdependent origination is what we call emptiness."

24 For Śāntarakṣita's major Mādhyamika work, the *Madhyamakālaṃkāra,* refer to Ichigō 1989.

25 This has been no doubt fostered by the study of Tibetan scholastic approaches, as represented, for example, in Hopkins 1983.

26 Siderits 1989 offers a clear point of departure here. For a nuanced consideration of the similarities between Madhaymaka and classical scepticism, see Garfield 1990. Garfield 1995 provides an insightful and thorough reading of Nāgārjuna's *Mūlamadhyamakakārikā.*

27 *Madhyamakāvatāra,* chap. 6, vv. 4–5: *so so skye bo'i dus na'ang stong pa nyid thos nas// nang du rab tu dga' ba yang dang yang du 'byung// rab tu dga' ba las byung mchi mas mig brlan zhing// lus kyi ba spu ldang bar gyur pa gang yin pa//* 4 *//de la rdzogs pa'i sangs rgyas blo yi sa bon yod// de nyid nye bar bstan pa'i snod ni de yin*

tel/ de la dam pa'i don gyi bden pa bstan par bya// de la de yi rjes su 'gro ba'i yon tan 'byung// 5 //

28 *Tattvasaṅgrahapañjikā,* p. 13.

29 The progressive development of wisdom through study *(śrutamayīprajñā),* critical reflection *(cintāmayīprajñā),* and contemplative cultivation *(bhāvanāmayīprajñā)* is a widely invoked template for Buddhist education and reflects the similar progression described in the Upaniṣadic literature, e.g., *Bṛhadāraṇyakopaniṣad,* 2.4.5: *śrotavyo mantavyo nididhyāsitavyaḥ,* "it should be heard, thought about, and contemplated."

30 *Tattvasaṅgrahapañjikā,* p. 18.

31 This is clearly expressed in the definition, given in *Tarkabhāṣā,* p. 24, of contemplative cultivation *(bhāvanā)* as a "repeated formulation within the mind" *(bhāvanā punaḥ punaś cetasi samāropaḥ).*

32 On this, see Kapstein 2000a: 96–97, and the sources referred to therein.

33 Smith 1969 provides a useful survey of Lcang-skya's life. On his relations with the Qing court, see now Rawski 1998: 257–58.

34 Wutaishan, Mañjuśrī's sacred abode in Shanxi Province, is a popular place of pilgrimage for both Chinese and Tibetan Buddhists. Lcang-skya himself wrote an excellent Tibetan guidebook to the sites of Wutaishan.

35 This would have fallen in July or August. The custom of counting the months beginning from the Chinese New Year was introduced into Tibet during the Yuan period of Mongol rule, owing to which the months so counted are called "Mongolian months" *(hor-zla).*

36 *Dpal ye shes yon tan bzang po'i bstod pa,* a popular hymn to Mañjuśrī, learned by heart by every Tibetan schoolchild. Lcang-skya's commentary, entitled *Dpal ye shes yon tan bzang po'i bstod pa rnam par bshad pa mkhas pa dga' bskyed tam bu ra'i sgra dbyangs,* is preserved in the fourth volume of his *Collected Works.*

37 "'Jam-dbyangs" is both a common Tibetan proper name and the Tibetan rendering for the Sanskrit "Mañjuśrī," the bodhisattva of wisdom.

38 The *Pramāṇasamuccaya (Compilation of Epistemic Authority)* by Dignāga forms the basis for Dharmakīrti's *Exposition,* and its opening verse is the topic under discussion here. See, especially, Hattori 1968. Hattori (p. 23) translates the verse under discussion as follows: "Saluting Him, who is the personification of the means of cognition, who seeks the benefit of [all] living beings, who is the teacher, the *sugata,* the protector, I shall, for the purpose of establishing the means of valid cognition, compose the [*Pramāṇa-*]*samuccaya,* uniting here under one head my theories scattered [in many treatises]." The relevant portions of Dharmakīrti's work, as understood within the Dge-lugs-pa tradition in which Lcang-skya was educated, are studied in Jackson 1993. For the background in the available Indian sources, see Vetter 1984, Van Bijlert 1989, and Franco 1997.

39 The five "bundles" *(skandha,* Tib. *phung-po)* constituting the individual—form, sensation, perception, volitions (and other "factors"), and consciousness—are "acquisitive" *(upādāna)* in that they form the causal basis for the future states of the continuum that they constitute.

40 *Tshad-ma lam-rim,* pp. 634–37.
41 Smith 1969.
42 See esp. Griffiths 1994.
43 Popkin 1979.
44 On Jayarāśi, see Franco 1987; and on Maimon, Hadas 1967.
45 I do not wish to minimize, however, the intensity and depth with which skeptical tendencies were sometimes expressed in traditional Buddhist circles. Consider the case of Karma Pakshi (1206–83), on which see Kapstein 2000a: 97–106.
46 This, of course, has a precise analogy in the tendency (now mostly discredited) to regard the cult of relics and related developments in early Buddhism as belonging to the domain of popular lay practice, and not pertaining to the clergy. This has been trenchantly criticized in the work of Gregory Schopen; see, in particular, Schopen 1997, chap. 6.

I SITUATING THE SELF

1. Personal Identity in a Comparative Perspective

In his introduction to *A History of Philosophy* (1982), the Swedish philosopher Anders Wedberg makes the following remarkable statement:

> There is...much that will be passed over in silence; above all, the Indian and Chinese philosophy which is independent of this Western tradition.... My silence in these matters is mainly due to my ignorance of the subject.[1]

What is unusual here is the affirmation by a contemporary Western historian of philosophy of the possible existence of philosophy outside of the West; and in affirming this possibility the author acknowledges the limits of his own project, withholding judgment about that which falls beyond its scope. Wedberg's brief remarks thus stand in sharp relief against some (usually inexplicit) dogmas of philosophical history, namely, that the kind of rational discourse that is exemplified above all in philosophical activity originated in Greece and nowhere else, that this has remained the unique heritage of the West, and that whatever is known by the name of "non-Western philosophy" is invariably of little real philosophical value.[2] Given the intensive interest in social and historical questions among English-speaking philosophers in the past two decades, however, such prejudgments regarding non-Western philosophies seem less assured than they once were. At the very least, we have begun to appreciate that they have often had their source not in their supposed objects, but in our constructions of the other *as* object. Without taking account of the data provided by the study of other philosophical cultures, we risk misinterpreting the historical data we derive from our own.[3]

The traditional Western philosopher's ignorance of non-Western thought has not, to be sure, been uniquely characteristic of philosophy among the human sciences. Historians, religionists, art historians, and literary scholars alike have often shared a deep and abiding Eurocentrism. The perspective in question has been so deeply ingrained in our intellectual life that, for instance, during the late 1970s a bibliographical guide to the history of ideas not only omitted the non-Western world altogether, but apparently regarded that omission as standing in no need of explanation.[4] And this was mirrored soon after in a bibliographical survey of philosophy as well.[5] Given the assumption that "the East" never enjoyed the life of the mind in its philosophical or scientific manifestations, there was apparently no reason for the scholar to explain his or her complete neglect of non-Western sources.

The historical background of academic Eurocentrism was thoroughly intertwined, as we now know, with the phenomenon known as Orientalism, the historical deconstruction of which was begun some years ago by Edward Said.[6] Said was concerned primarily with the formation of modern Western conceptions of the Arab world, and only peripherally with the Indian and Chinese spheres of civilization; and he was concerned preeminently with Orientalism as a distinct cultural/intellectual manifestation, and not so much with such related phenomena as the general ignorance of Asia among the non-Orientalist disciplines. Returning now to philosophy in particular, its marked aversion to the study of non-Western developments was itself certainly a manifestation of the same historical background, and in its own right no doubt merits an exercise in thorough historical deconstruction; but that is not the task to which I address myself here. My brief remarks about this topic are only intended to clarify my own relation to what seems to be an unfortunate and mistaken imbalance in the cultural perspective of much that is called the "history of philosophy."

It is possible to identify more or less precisely the point at which the history of philosophy, as a distinctive sub-discipline, acquired in "canonical" form the view of the great Asian traditions to which it has adhered ever since: this was 1833, the year in which Hegel's (1770–1831) *Lectures on the History of Philosophy* first appeared in print.[7] Hegel, reacting in part to the idealization of ancient India and China that had marked romantic scholarship[8] and mistakenly assuming that the small body of material that had become available to European thinkers by the beginning of the nineteenth century was a sufficient sample to permit generalization about the nature of Oriental thought, not surprisingly concluded that a true philosophical consciousness had never arisen in traditional Asia, that the closest one came was religious speculation of a quasi-philosophical character. In the early part of the nineteenth century such a view of the matter provided a tenable alternative to the approach taken by the romantics,[9] but now there can be no excuse for it. I think it is safe to say that the mainstream among twentieth-century historians of philosophy, with respect to Indian and Chinese thought, seldom progressed significantly beyond, or in some cases even equalled, Hegel.[10]

Because this chapter limits itself to aspects of the problem of personal identity as it was discussed in India, it will not attempt to review the large body of relevant material that, taken together, thoroughly demolishes the Hegelian view of Asian philosophies. Instead, it will concern one specific area of philosophical research in which are exemplified both impressive philosophical achievement outside of the West and historical misunderstanding on the part of some contemporary philosophers. Moreover, because our scope is limited to classical Indian philosophy, it does not take account of philosophical developments in other parts of Asia.[11] Even with this restriction, many examples could have been chosen from among the problems of philosophical logic,[12] universals,[13] theory of reference,[14] epistemology,[15] philosophical theology,[16] and philosophy of mind,[17] to name but a few of the many areas in which Indian contributions have begun to receive the sustained philosophical consideration they merit. But here the problem is just that of personal identity through time.

The Enigmatic "I"

There are some very strong assumptions that we sometimes make about the historical contingencies that contributed to the emergence of the problem of personal identity in eighteenth-century Europe. Amélie Rorty, for example, argues that "from a large world-historical perspective this version of the problem of personal identity is one that could only appear under very special social and intellectual conditions," conditions that include, for example, "the movement from the Reformation to radical individualism" and "Romanticism and the novel of first person sensibility."[18] Indeed, personal identity may be said to belong to a nexus of problems regarding the self and persons that is so closely bound to specific historical and cultural conditions that the very possibility of significant communication among divergent cultures in this area might at best seem very remote.[19] As Charles Taylor expresses it:

> If someone summons you to decide between the Buddhist view of the self and Western conceptions of personality, you are going to be in trouble. I am not saying that even this kind of issue is ultimately unarbitrable; but clearly we start off without the remotest idea of how even to go about arbitrating it.[20]

At the same time, and in contrast to the opinions just noted, several contemporary philosophers have thought that they have discerned interesting resemblances between modern Western and classical Indian theories of the self and personal identity. For Derek Parfit, the apparent convergence between Buddhist views and his own suggests not a problem of arbitration, but rather the conclusion that his claims "apply to all people, at all times."[21] And Robert Nozick has referred to "a contention massively and inconclusively debated between Vedantists and Buddhists" in his discussion of a theory of the self-synthesizing activity of the self.[22] Have these philosophers profoundly misunderstood the alien traditions to which they refer, and about which they can claim no specialized knowledge, or have they in fact located some philosophically interesting similarities among differing traditions? Such similarities would be *philosophically* interesting, and not merely curiosity pieces, in part because they challenge our assumptions about the historical contingencies underlying our modern Western problem of personal identity.

Before any of this can be of more than purely speculative interest, however, it must be established that the problems with which we are concerned were actually topics of learned discussion outside of the modern West. It will not suffice merely to point to some Brahmanical or Buddhist text that, given sufficient strain to the imagination, might be taken as vaguely suggestive of possibly rational awareness of the problem. But what kind of evidence is required in order to establish what we wish to establish here? Some clarification may be gained by considering Jonathan Barnes' arguments in regard to notions of personal identity within the Pythagorean tradition. Barnes, of course, is challenging received opinion by contending that the problem of personal identity is not strictly a modern problem, but that it was also known to certain pre-Socratic philosophers:

> It may be thought fanciful to connect the obscure superstitions of Pythagoras with modern studies on personal identity: 'In Pythagoras' time,' it will be said, 'no one knew or cared about the problems of personal identity; and Pythagoras himself was

> promulgating an eschatological dogma, not propounding a philosophical thesis.' A piece of Epicharmus will refute that skeptical suggestion…[23]

I shall return to the actual content of the selection from Epicharmus, a Sicilian dramatist of the early fifth century B.C.E., in the following chapter. Here, however, I am concerned with what appears to be Barnes' evidential principle, namely, that one relevant fragment in an appropriate context is all that we need.

Clearly, in the study of the pre-Socratics, where fragments are all that we have, one either accepts some principle of this sort or else abandons the project altogether. But, generally speaking, it is not a very good principle; for it is always possible that a talented writer like Epicharmus has had a flash of insight, but lacks any enduring awareness of, or, for that matter, interest in, the implications of his or her own discovery. And if such insightful episodes may thus not guarantee significant awareness of the problem at hand on the part of the subject of the episode in question, how much less can single fragments be taken as evidence of such awareness within extended intellectual traditions?

What is required, rather, is evidence of sustained interest in the problem, whether on the part of a single thinker or of several historically connected thinkers. But something more than this must be sought as well: the range of conceptual perspectives and philosophical arguments elaborated in connection with the problem should bear upon it in a manner that we can appreciate as being intelligible and coherent.[24] Without this, we are not entitled to assume that the problem we find discussed in the texts upon which we focus *is* the problem we thought we had found there.

To say this, of course, is to risk being rebuked by many as begging all sorts of questions pertaining to the issues of cultural relativism, indeterminacy of translation, objectivity of understanding, etc. Why, one might object, should one permit modern Western notions of intelligibility and coherence to play any role whatsoever in the study of non-Western or premodern thought and culture?

I think that the correct response to this objection is roughly as follows: assuming, *per impossibile,* that we were in fact capable of completely bracketing out of our investigations the concepts of intelligibility and coherence (which we have acquired through the education and acculturation we have undergone in our own place and time), would we then be capable of forming any judgments at all, such as would permit us to undertake any systematic research of human culture whatsoever? I am certain that we would not; we would merely have succeeded in creating for ourselves a "buzzing, booming confusion" such as William James supposed infants to be up against. So let us assume instead that we retain our notions of intelligibility and coherence, at least to some limited degree, and that we discover that the manner in which, say, the members of community T discuss the problem P makes no sense to us whatsoever. Of course, this may reflect simply the poverty of our own understanding, but the crucial point here is this: should we find ourselves in such a predicament, we are then in no position to assume that the problem under discussion by the members of T is in fact what we call "the problem P." In short, the apparent failure to meet the criteria of intelligibility and coherence should lead us simply to withhold judgment about the precise nature of the question being discussed by the members of T. But if, on the contrary, we appear to understand what others say, and if what they say appears to us to be coherent, then we have the best evidence we shall ever have that they are discussing what we think they are. To look for anything less fallible would be just silly. As in any other scientific investigation, should we discover at some later stage in our researches that our earlier conclusions cannot be sustained in the light of more recently acquired evidence, or of new interpretive insights, then we do not curse the lack of apodictic certainty but get on with the business of generating new, or revised, hypotheses. It is not clear to me that such an approach need involve any prior commitment to one side or the other in the debates between relativists and objectivists.

I will not pause to consider these difficult issues at greater length in this context: if understanding is not merely mysterious, but frankly impossible, then the interpretive project of this book is not the only one that will suffer. And I can see no good reason to assume that the problems of cultural relativism preclude understanding of Indian or Chinese philosophers, but that this is not the case when the object of our study is, say, an ancient Greek or a medieval Spaniard. If classical, medieval, and renaissance philology, given adequate allowance for characteristic sources of error within those disciplines, permit us to undertake the study of, for instance, the Pythagoreans, or ibn Gabirol, or Ficino as philosophers, then what would convince us that Sinology and Indology do not also pave the way for similarly studying Zhuxi and Wang Yangming, or Jetāri and Vijñānabhikṣu? As with understanding in general, so too with understanding between diverse cultural traditions: it is a mysterious phenomenon, but it *is* a phenomenon nevertheless.

Given just this, we can begin the philosophical investigation of traditions outside our own, and with respect to our present subject matter we may reasonably ask: is evidence to be found in classical Indian sources, as understood through the contemporary disciplines of textual-historical research, of sustained and systematic interest in problems closely resembling the modern Western philosophical problem of personal identity through time? Are the doctrines and arguments elaborated in such contexts apparently intelligible and coherent?

The short answer is that certainly there is an abundance of evidence of the required sort. (The next section of this chapter will suffice to suggest that this is so. The remaining chapters in part I will then fill in some of the details.) Before surveying the relevant history, however, it may prove useful to have before us a clear statement of the problem of personal identity in a mature formulation of its Indian version. To illustrate the seriousness with which Indian thinkers were to confront the problem of personal identity, a passage from Kamalaśīla (late eighth century) provides an unequalled beginning:

> [The opponents of the Buddhist view that there are continuants but no persisting substances ask:] If everything is affirmed to be instantaneous, then how do you go about establishing causal connection, etc., which are well known to the world and to science? The "etc." here refers to the whole mass of objections raised by our opponents concerning: inductive knowledge of cause and effect, recognition of what had been previously experienced, desire for something on the basis of prior experience of another [similar] thing, bondage and liberation, memory, resolution of doubt, recovery of what had been entrusted to another, absence of astonishment when it is the case that the [astonishing] thing had been seen before.[25]

Consider for a moment the range of phenomena that, according to Kamalaśīla, had thus been considered by some as counterexamples to the Buddhist scholastic view that the continuity of persons through time does not involve strict and perfect identity. The first was induction. We presume to know, for example, that we can be injured by fire. We assume that this knowledge represents the cumulative result of a series of experiences with fire, rather than our being endowed with an innate idea thereof; and we take as evidence for this assumption, for instance, the fact that small children are careless with fire. But if we are really just continuants, and not persisting entities at all, then how is it that we can ever undergo a series of experiences and acquire knowledge based on their cumulative effect upon us? Similarly, it seems odd to say that I recognize something seen previously if at the same time I assume that I exist only now, without temporal extension; or that I can resolve my doubts, given that the subject of doubt and the subject of its resolution are not supposed to be one and the same. So too, I should not be motivated to recover the copy of the *Bhagavadgītā* that Devī borrowed, if I believe that I am not the same person who gave it to Devī on loan. And why is it that I am no longer surprised to see a new bridge spanning the river, when every day a new "I" sees all this for the first time? It appears to be only the reference to bondage and liberation here—that is, the unenlightened individual's bondage in the painful round of saṃsāra, and the liberation from it that comes with enlightenment—that reminds us that the context in which Indian thinkers first framed the problem of personal identity was entirely unlike that in which Locke and Reid, Butler and Hume, formulated the version about which Western philosophers have argued for close to three centuries. But can it be said that Kamalaśīla is here concerned with a wholly disparate problem?

The Development of the Debate on the Self: Some Central Themes

The passage just quoted from Kamalaśīla, like Barnes' citation from Epicharmus, lends a certain plausibility to the view that something much like the post-Cartesian problem of personal identity was also known to other philosophically reflective civilizations. However, I argued above that there is a limit to what the historian of philosophy can reasonably hold on the basis of such isolated fragments. It is also essential, I maintained, to demonstrate that the problem in question was the object of *sustained* philosophical interest. The present section and the chapters that follow will serve to fulfill that requirement.

I have no intention, however, to attempt to offer here a comprehensive survey of the development of Indian concepts relating to the questions at issue, or to survey the now extensive secondary literature on the subject. Accordingly, my approach throughout will involve isolating a few important and paradigmatic texts for consideration as representative of some of the main phases of the historical development of the debate before and during the scholastic period, which reached its apogee from about 400 through 1000 C.E.[26]

The study of classical Indian philosophy has by and large been the study of rival schools of thought, often considered in complete isolation from one another. This approach is not peculiar to contemporary research in this area: it partially characterizes, too, the indigenous Indian doxographical traditions, represented above all by Sāyaṇa Mādhava's (fl. c. 1350) compendium, the famous *Collection of All Viewpoints (Sarvadarśanasaṅgraha).*[27] Progress made during recent decades in the historical interpretation of the philosophical heritage of India has, however, made it abundantly clear that the schools did not develop in pure isolation from one another; they were not only actively engaged in philosophical controversy with one another, they were also nourished by that controversy. The refined positions of such thinkers as Uddyotakara (c. 600), Kumārila Bhaṭṭa (c. 700), and Śāntarakṣita (fl. mid-eighth century) reflect an intention to vindicate their respective traditions, certainly, but underscore at the same time the great extent of their indebtedness to those whom they attack.

The problems of identity and individuation first confronted the philosophical and religious imagination of India during the remote age in which the Vedic literature took form. Under the guise of the search for the individual self, *ātman,* and its macrocosmic correlate, *brahman,* there emerged the central concepts around which speculative thought blossomed, the matrix from which a distinctively Indian vision of reality grew. The search itself was fueled in part by an extreme sense of anxiety aroused by a sharpening appreciation of the fundamental instability of the world of experience, increasingly thought of as saṃsāra, a realm of action and law-like retribution for action, and of death and regeneration without beginning or end. The knowledge of ātman and of brahman and of their ultimate identity—these alone were saving, revealing to the knower an eternal and stable ground that was free from the bondage of deeds, free from death and redeath. With the rise of Buddhism during the last centuries B.C.E., the problems of identity and individuation gained renewed significance for Indian thinkers owing to the challenge presented by the rejection, attributed to the Buddha, of the notion that liberation was to be gained through the discovery of an immutable substratum, the ātman.

Some centuries earlier than this Indian thinkers had already begun to delineate a considerable range of views regarding the "self" *(ātman).* In a famous passage from the *Chāndogya Upaniṣad* (c. 600–400 B.C.E.), which will be discussed in detail in the following chapter, the self is identified in turn with the body, with dream consciousness, with the blissful unconsciousness of deep sleep, and finally with brahman, the unifying ground of being beyond all of these. This last-mentioned identification represents perhaps the most well-known and characteristic of Upaniṣadic doctrines: that of the all-embracing ātman-brahman, a concept that is elaborated in the later Vedāntic teaching of Śaṅkara (eighth century) into a singularly imposing brand of monistic pantheism. It is this doctrine that many Western thinkers frequently and mistakenly take to be emblematic of the whole range of classical Indian philosophy and religion, and which a tenth-century Buddhist doxographer summarizes in these words:

> The proponents of the Upaniṣads hold that there is a single pervader, which penetrates the continua of all life forms, and is eternal knowledge. All of this world, including earth, water, air, and fire, appear through the transformation of its form. Its essential nature indeed is the self. The well-known objects of cognition belonging to the external world, i.e., wholes and atoms and so forth, do not exist at all.[28]

This, however, does not exhaust the range of early Indian theories of the self: some held the self to be breath; others said it was a very fine substance "the size of a thumb" within the heart of man; and others still identified it with "the controller within."[29] The preoccupation of ancient Indian thought with the proper identification of the self, as the means whereby freedom from saṃsāric entanglement might be secured, provided the contextual background from which the famous dictum of the Buddha—"all things are non-selves" *(sarvadharmā anātmanaḥ)*—drew its power. It is possible, in fact, to construe the rich and complex debates about the self, together with the wide range of related epistemological and metaphysical discussions that those debates aroused—and that would unfold in India from the third century B.C.E. down to the early second millennium C.E.—as a continuing exploration of the philosophical challenge that this posed. To construe the course of Indian philosophy in this manner would be something like construing the development of Western metaphysics as an ongoing response to the Eleatic *elenchus;* for the Buddha's teaching of *anattā,* "non-self" *(anātman),* was especially prominent among the challenges that encouraged Indian thought to rise from the inspired, but generally unsystematic, speculations of the ancient brahmanical and ascetic sages, in whose teachings can be found anticipations of many of the theories later systematically developed in the long history of Indian philosophical psychology.

Among the philosophers who attempted to meet the challenge posed by the Buddhist refutations of the reality of ātman were the adherents of the several schools of realists and pluralists, who rejected alike the monistic and pantheistic tendencies often associated with the Upaniṣads, and the reductionism of early Buddhist scholastic doctrine. Four of these schools became especially prominent philosophically, their representatives occupying central roles in the conflict between Buddhism and the Brahmanical tradition. These four were: (i) *Sāṃkhya,* which conceived of the self as an immaculate spiritual substance standing in absolute opposition to the dynamic realm of nature, the latter thought of as the transformations of a single prime matter;[30] (ii) *Mīmāṃsā,* whose main focus was the elaboration of a metatheory of the Vedic cult, in which the self's role as agent was of special importance;[31] (iii) *Vaiśeṣika,* which sought to establish a fundamental categorial scheme through which to analyze reality in all its aspects;[32] and (iv) *Nyāya,* whose focus was the study of knowledge, including both the means whereby it is acquired, and the means whereby it is transmitted to others through reasoned argument.[33] For simplicity's sake, I will limit my remarks here to the confrontation of Buddhism with the closely related Nyāya and Vaiśeṣika schools, whose respective logical-epistemological and ontological concerns were in most respects complementary, and so led to the formation of a syncretic Nyāya-Vaiśeṣika tradition.

The Buddhist philosopher Śāntarakṣita tells us that the Nyāya-Vaiśeṣika philosophers ascribe to the self these properties: it is the support for desire and the like, not conscious in and of itself, permanent and ubiquitous, the doer of good and evil deeds, and the enjoyer of their fruit.[34] His disciple Kamalaśīla, commenting on this, explains that the self is a substance that is discrete from body, sense-faculty, and intellect; that, following the common tradition of the *Nyāyasūtra* and the *Vaiśeṣikasūtra,* it is the support for desire and aversion, willful effort, pleasure and pain, knowledge, and the conditions of moral rightness and wrongness; and that "support" means here "ground for inherence" (that is, of the properties mentioned above). He goes on to suggest, moreover, that a strong motivation underlying the positing of such a substantial self was the thought that the doctrine of *karman* would be incoherent otherwise. The problem that this raises is one of personal identity:

> If there were no self, then who, having passed away, would enjoy the fruit of action? For one does not enjoy the fruit of what another has done, besides which, it would be an error to affirm that one reaps what one has not sown; for the fruit would enter

> into relation with him who has not performed the deed, and what had been done would thereby be lost, because the doer would have no relationship with the fruit.[35]

So, the motivations that led Nyāya-Vaiśeṣika philosophers to elaborate their version of the substance theory of the self may be in some respects similar to the considerations that inform modern Western philosophical work on the philosophical problem of personal identity in relation to the religious problems of judgment and resurrection.[36] The difference is, of course, that here we are operating within the parameters of a karmic cosmology, whereas the works of modern Western philosophers of religion usually presuppose a Jewish or Christian theistic cosmology. This difference, however, should not obscure the fundamental similarity that obtains between the two sets of problems: the question puzzling the Nyāya-Vaiśeṣika philosopher is essentially how it could be that anyone other than myself might reap the karmic rewards or retributions for my deeds, while his Western counterpart wants to know how it could be that anyone other than myself might be rewarded or punished by the Lord for my deeds.[37] It seems plausible to suppose, then, that the disanalogies we find here concern not the question of personal identity in and of itself—that is, the question about just who it is who realizes the result of the action that I perform—but concern rather the cosmological theory held to account for there being results corresponding to the moral qualities of actions that are realized at all.[38] The analogies obtaining in the microcosmic sphere of human affairs within this one lifetime are those of crime and punishment, achievement and reward—in brief, all of our institutions of praise and blame. We are not comforted by the thought that the person sent to the gallows might not have been the one who committed the act for which capital punishment was prescribed.

The odd thing, at first glance, about the Nyāya-Vaiśeṣika view of the self, is the notion that the self is not essentially conscious, but yet an agent and an enjoyer. This theory immediately contrasts with, for instance, that of the rival Sāṃkhya school, which maintained that "awareness is the essential nature of the person."[39] Śāntarakṣita explains that the Nyāya-Vaiśeṣika thinkers hold the self, though not essentially conscious, to be nonetheless capable of entering into conjunction with consciousness. We might wish to paraphrase this by saying that, on this account, the self is *possibly* conscious, and *actually* so whenever appropriate conditions obtain. Thus, although the notion of "conjunction with consciousness" may seem a mysterious one, it is not, prima facie at least, an absurd one.

There would appear, then, to be some ground for comparing the self as conceived by the Nyāya-Vaiśeṣika school with the Cartesian Pure Ego as conceived by John Locke; it is to all intents and purposes a "bare particular," virtually devoid of intrinsic properties but serving as the elusive something in which psychological and other properties associated with personhood inhere.[40] The notion of the self's permanence raises some immediate puzzles, which Kamalaśīla sums up in these words:

> If it is eternal, then how can it be agent and enjoyer? How does it come to be born, to die, to be alive? For none of this can apply to something that is eternal and uniform...[41]

These are, I think, among the fundamental problems facing the substance theorist, in the West as well as in India—considering which, as Locke again clearly perceived, we come to confront a problem of personal identity even if we assume a substance theory of the self.[42] The problem for the Nyāya-Vaiśeṣika thinker is this: what can an eternal (and, *ex hypothesi,* unchanging), ubiquitous (or non-spatial) something possibly have to do with this world of continuous phenomenal change? If, in response to this, one assumes that the self is something that undergoes change and is in some sense itself phenomenal, then it is difficult to see where to draw the line between the resulting view of the self and a type of continuant theory, as is associated with "non-Cartesian" (or "Humean") dualism.[43] But if one insists on the self's absolute freedom from change, it becomes difficult to explain how it is to be related to the manifold states of the person whose self it is supposed to be.

The problems that arise here had clearly become urgent in India by the age in which the *Bhagavadgītā* was redacted;[44] for there the notion that one's self is a simple immutable substance, utterly distinct from the changing physical realm it inhabits, reaches its logical conclusion: to slay a body is not to slay a person.[45] We have already seen that the Nyāya thinkers assumed it to be possible for the self to enter into relationships that permitted of its being conscious. In this case, the approach to the difficulty was similar to what we have just seen: when knowledge, will, and the effort to act inhere in the self, it may be spoken of as an agent; and when presentations of pleasure or pain inhere in it, it may be spoken of as an enjoyer. Similarly, through *commercium* with bodies it may be said to undergo birth, death, etc. Thus, we can bring harm to a person, but only indirectly, by interfering with the body to which that person's self is related.

Buddhist opposition to the Brahmanical proponents of the concept of the individual and substantial self, such as the Nyāya-Vaiśeṣika, reached its first culminating philosophical formulation in the *Treatise on the Negation of the Person (Pudgala-pratiṣedha-prakaraṇa)* of scholastic philosopher Vasubandhu (c. 400).[46] There, he argues that there is no substantial self, because no reliable epistemic operation verifies the existence of such an entity. Vasubandhu's primary argument against the view that the self is a discrete substance rested on the claims that the self posited by his opponents is the object neither of immediate acquaintance nor of sound inference, and hence that it is altogether unknown. It appears that this argument should be understood not as an attempt to provide an apodictic refutation of the substance theory, but rather as a challenge to the substance theorist to demonstrate that we are sometimes subject to veridical acts of acquaintance or to sound inferences of the required sort. In the absence of an adequate response to this challenge, Vasubandhu holds, as the mainstream of Buddhist thought has maintained, that it is most plausible to regard persons as continuants *(santāna),* conceptually constructed on the basis of aggregated primitive and momentary elements. There is no *tertium quid* that is neither primitive substance nor conceptual construct that the posited self might be.[47] Vasubandhu recognizes that the conception of persons as continuants is not unproblematic; among the many objections to the Buddhist theory that Vasubandhu considers, this example will not seem too foreign to contemporary philosophers:

> If, then, there is no self whatsoever, how is it that among instantaneous mental events there occurs memory or recognition of objects experienced long before?
>
> It is because there is a distinctive mental event...which has a resemblance to and connection with the experience of that [remembered object]...For even if it resembles that [object], a distinctive mental event not causally connected to it is not a memory; and even if it is causally connected to [that object], a [mental event] which resembles another [object] is not a memory.
>
> Then, how is it that what has been seen by one mind is not remembered by another?
>
> That does not occur, because there is no appropriate causal connection.[48]

Continuants of the type "person," therefore, like other kinds of continuants, are individuated primarily by their causal relationships.[49] While Vasubandhu's causal analysis of memory recalls Hume to some,[50] its elaboration is suggestive, too, of more recent philosophy, for instance, the work of Martin and Deutscher.[51]

As mentioned above, contrary to popular belief (which regards Hindu thought to have always been predominantly idealistic and monistic), the leading philosophical critics of Buddhism were mostly realists and pluralists, who held that each one of us has a unique and persisting soul. Uddyotakara, a noted logician, undertook to refute Vasubandhu by attacking the epistemological argument directly:[52] a substantial self, Uddyotakara holds, is known to exist; for there are indeed sound inferences affirming its existence, and we are directly acquainted with it. Among the inferential arguments he advances, Uddyotakara emphasizes in particular the phenomena of the unity of consciousness and first-person reference. (Because I consider some of Uddyotakara's arguments in more detail in chapters 3 through 5, for illustrative purposes I will concern myself here only with aspects of his treatment of first-person reference.)

Uddyotakara holds that "the word 'self' is the designator of something distinct from the aggregate of intellect, sense, and so on."[53] We are directly acquainted with the self, he maintains, because the cognition "I" *(ahaṃ-pratyaya)* is present in every self-presenting *(svātmasaṃvedya)* act of awareness.[54] As Arindam Chakrabarti has pointed out,[55] Uddyotakara's argument here is dependent upon his treatment of singular terms in general, for it is one of his cardinal assumptions that all statements can be reduced to statements whose only terms genuinely refer. Thus, statements in which non-referring terms are found (for instance, "sky-flowers don't exist," or "there are no rabbit-horns") are to be reduced in translation to statements involving only genuinely referring terms, e.g., "no flower grows in the sky," or "no rabbit has a horn." Irreducible terms must then be admitted into Uddyotakara's ideal language as being genuinely referential. The words "I" and "self," he maintains, are ultimately irreducible.

Uddyotakara was answered from the Buddhist side by Śāntarakṣita, whose disciple Kamalaśīla presents Śāntarakṣita's main arguments on the present point as follows:

> We do not think that just because it is a unique term, [the word "self"] is a designator of a distinct something; for the synonyms for "mind," "sense," "sensation," and "body" are all similarly unique terms...Hence, your argument is uncertain because the absence of a counterexample has not been established.

> Nonetheless, one might object: "It is distinct from [other] established conventions"...But this qualification of the argument is itself not established. Why so? It is because mind [in this context, "the continuum of mental events"] is indeed the foundation of first person reference, that it is called "self."[56]

Thus, Śāntarakṣita holds that the term "I" just picks out a particular mental continuum, whenever it is thought or uttered. Against Uddyotakara, he wishes to argue that it is not a genuine referring term, as his opponent had insisted.

Śāntarakṣita's project was not limited to elaborating refutations of arguments for the substance theory; he also overhauled the causal theory of persons in an attempt to put aside the many objections that we have seen reported above by Kamalaśīla. And, of course, the substance theorists were not content to let the debate end there: with arguments suitably rebuttressed, they renewed their attacks on the causalists,[57] and so it goes. The particulars of the story, and all the many arguments it involves, are interesting enough in their own right, but it is difficult to avoid here a profound sense of déjà vu. Are we condemned to an unresolvable struggle between Reductionists and non-Reductionists, that will end only when at last we tire of battle?

It is, perhaps, instructive to note that this last reflection was also not foreign to Indian philosophers. The Buddhist Candrakīrti (c. 600), for instance, basing himself on the earlier work of Nāgārjuna (c. 150 C.E.), came to hold that the confrontation of philosophical views on personal identity was indicative of something profoundly incoherent about the very concept of "self," and that this could be demonstrated in the formulation of a strict antinomy between the substance and continuant theories of persons.[58] Candrakīrti's antinomies, however, were not elaborated in support of a Kantian conclusion: in the work of Candrakīrti there is little suggestion of Transcendental Idealism; persons, I believe he would hold, are constructed at the level of language and social convention.[59] (We shall return to consider some of the questions that may be raised in this connection in fuller detail in chapters 3 and 4 below.)

From Language to Conversation

Drawing on classical Indian discussions of the self and personal identity, I have described philosophical developments often held to be uniquely characteristic of the modern West unfolding in a radically distinct cultural milieu. I would hold that, even if the discussion were to treat *in extenso* the differences of cultural and historical background, nonetheless, upon turning from the early speculations of the Upaniṣads, the Buddhist canon, and other very ancient materials, to the scholastic writings of thinkers such as Vasubandhu, Uddyotakara, and Śāntarakṣita, we would still be struck by powerful resemblances with the researches into personal identity and related topics that have been undertaken in the modern West. Though we would also remark on many differences, I think that we would still have to admit that the problem of personal identity through time, and such allied problems as those of first-person reference, unity of consciousness, memory and causation, were no less vexing to Indian philosophers of the mid- and late-first millennium C.E., than they have been to Western thinkers since Locke.

To all of this, however, one objection, which some would regard as being extremely powerful, might yet be brought to bear. Any time we find, as we do with respect to personal identity, strong resemblance between Indian and Western philosophical problems and arguments, there will be a temptation to suspect that, if the problems in question are not grounded in historical and cultural contingency, they may yet be grounded in linguistic contingency; for Sanskrit and Pali, the main languages of Indian philosophy, are, like Greek, Latin, and the other main languages of Western philosophy, Indo-European. Is it not possible, then, that the philosophical problems shared by India and the West reflect certain peculiarities of Indo-European languages, for instance, their highly inflected morphologies?[60] I do not think that there can be a really decisive demonstration that this is not the case, but there are certainly grounds for doubting it to be so. In the absence of any precise identification of the features of language that are supposed to account for the phenomena in question, we would have strong reason to suppose that there are indeed some such features to be identified if it could be established, for example, that non-Indo-European speakers find the philosophical problems with which we are concerned here to be unintelligible, or at least particularly difficult to make sense of. But this is probably not the case in the present instance: the problem of personal identity in its Buddhist guise was disseminated throughout East, Central, and Southeast Asia, where the languages are not Indo-European, but Sinitic, Tibeto-Burman, Thai, Altaic, Turkic, etc. Not only did thinkers in these linguistic communities find the problem of personal identity to be intelligible, but it is also known that sustained discussions of the problem were conducted in some of the non–Indo-European languages in question.[61] These considerations, I must emphasize, prove nothing definitively; but they show that, lacking the support of really solid evidence, linguisticism as yet does not overturn what some would take to be an undesirable conclusion, namely, that we do not yet deeply understand the general historical, cultural, or linguistic conditions that have given rise to a consciousness of the problem of personal identity and all that it entails. That the peculiarities of given languages or language families may play a role in the formation of philosophical perspectives is, to be sure, something that I do not doubt. (In fact, in chapters 6 and 8 we shall consider instances that may exemplify in part just this sort of linguistic determination.) But unless supported by reasonably specific evidence—to the effect that some particular feature *a* of language L is clearly related to a certain feature *b* of philosophical discourse among speakers of language L—linguisticism remains little more than an ad hoc assumption, and merits treatment only as such.

The final section of Richard Rorty's *Philosophy and the Mirror of Nature* is entitled "Philosophy in the Conversation of Mankind."[62] The fragility of the splendid vision that that phrase conjures up is revealed, perhaps unintentionally, in the very last sentence of the book: "The only point on which I would insist," Rorty writes, "is that philosophers' moral concern should be with continuing the conversation of the *West*..." (emphasis added). What I have argued here, is not that the concern for history upon which Rorty and other philosophers have insisted is misplaced, but rather that their project has sometimes been too narrowly conceived. It is possible to broaden the scope of that concern, and so to seek our conversation partners without parochialism. In so doing, I suggest, we will discover that many of our problems are not uniquely our own—they are not culture-, race-, or language-specific. Whatever the historical contingencies involved, a strange possibility begins to emerge: philosophical problems are sometimes human problems, and in recognizing their humanity we may recover our own.

Notes

1 Wedberg 1982: 2.

2 These dogmas were made explicit, for instance, in the popular introductory textbook of Western philosophy by Antony Flew, referred to in the introduction, n. 5.

3 The "new historicism" found its manifesto in Rorty 1980. Some other works, appearing shortly thereafter, that encouraged the historical investigation of philosophical questions were: Putnam 1981; and Rorty, Schneewind, and Skinner 1985. For philosophers schooled in nineteenth- and twentieth-century Continental philosophies, it perhaps seemed that these "Anglo-Saxon philosophers" were Johnny-come-latelies: Rorty traced his own historicism back to Heidegger, and Putnam traced his to Foucault. Nevertheless, Continental philosophers have been almost as reticent as their Anglophone counterparts to devote attention to non-Western ways of thought. Particularly telling in this regard are the remarks of Hadot 1995a: 418–19: "J'ai été longtemps hostile à la philosophie comparée, parce que je pensais qu'elle pouvait créer des confusions et des rapprochements arbitraires. Mais il me semble maintenant...qu'il y a réellement de troublantes analogies entre les attitudes philosophiques de l'Antiquité et de l'Orient, analogies qui d'ailleurs ne peuvent s'expliquer par des influences historiques, mais qui, en tout cas, permettent peut-être de mieux comprendre tout ce qui peut-être impliqué dans les attitudes philosophiques qui s'éclairent ainsi les unes par les autres."

4 Tobey 1975–77. Note that Tobey saw fit to include here Joseph Needham's *A History of Embryology,* but omitted entirely Needham's greatest contribution to the history of ideas, *Science and Civilization in China.*

5 Tice and Slavens 1983, a standard volume on philosophical reference materials, devoted but one paragraph (p. 310) to the topic of Eastern/Western Philosophy, which I reproduce here in its entirety. "Very little comparative analysis of Eastern and Western sources has been done that is not only critical but also displays a truly knowledgeable understanding of both. A volume by Ben-Ami Scharfstein and his Israeli associates, *Philosophy East/Philosophy West,* 1978...bears these qualities. The usual effort is to interpret Eastern thought to Western readers, as in the periodicals *Philosophy East and West, Journal of Chinese Philosophy,* and *Journal of Indian Philosophy.* This is largely true of three volumes edited by Charles A. Moore (1967), fruits of the four East-West philosophers' conferences held at the University of Hawai'i from 1939 to 1964. This area of inquiry is still in its infancy, held back by the relative inaccessibility of Eastern sources and by the widely held assumption that theories authentic to Eastern cultures consist primarily of mythology and of moral and religious doctrines irrelevant to modern philosophical interests." Though this is fair enough, so far as it goes, I believe that the references given in the notes throughout this book will make it clear that there was, by 1980, much relevant literature, which Tice and Slavens might have uncovered had they only looked a bit harder. For a recent, comparative treatment of Asian philosophies with extensive bibliographical reference to work in this field, see Scharfstein 1998.

6 Said 1979. The relationship between Orientalism, the body of disciplines especially entitled to interpret Asia to the West, and academic Eurocentrism becomes especially clear on pp. 43–46: "Orientalism was ultimately a political vision of reality whose structure promoted the difference between the familiar (Europe,

the West, 'us') and the strange (the Orient, the East, 'them')...I mean to ask whether there is any way of avoiding the hostility expressed by the division, say, of men into 'us' (Westerners) and 'they' (Orientals). For such divisions are generalities whose use historically and actually has been to press the importance of the distinction between some men and some other men, usually towards not especially admirable ends. When one uses categories like Oriental and Western as both the starting and the end points of analysis, research, public policy...the result is usually to polarize the distinction—the Orient becomes more Oriental, the Westerner more Western—and limit the human encounter between different cultures, traditions, and societies." Cf. Inden 1990 and Lopez 1995.

7 Hegel 1928. The section to which I refer here is "Orientalische Philosophie," pp. 151–84. I do not think that, in my reading of Hegel here, I am merely reflecting the prejudice of one who has a particular interest in non-Western philosophies. Cf. the remarks of a historian of modern European thought, Löwith 1967: 29ff.

8 On this, in relation to India, see Winternitz 1972, vol. 1: 18–25 and Halbfass 1988, esp. chaps. 5–8.

9 Of course, the formation of nineteenth-century views of Asian thought had much to do with the growth of European imperialism, which had accelerated rapidly during the preceding century. This historical development required a corresponding ideological shift, whereby Asians (here, particularly, the Chinese and Indians) were not to be regarded as civilized heathens, but rather as childlike, not yet fully rational, peoples who required for their own good the benevolent care of paternal Europeans. Hegelian historiography thus nicely fulfilled an ideological demand.

10 A major historian who sought to achieve some redress here was Émile Brehier, who commissioned a distinguished authority on Asian thought, Paul Masson-Oursel, to write a supplementary fascicle to Brehier's *Histoire de la Philosophie: La Philosophie en Orient* (1938). Unfortunately, Masson-Oursel thought himself obliged to attempt a comprehensive survey of ancient Near and Middle Eastern cosmology, mythology and religion as part of the bargain, so that the volume in question has very little to say about philosophy proper, thus, incidentally, reinforcing the very misconceptions it was intended to counteract. (Masson-Oursel's supplement was not included in the English translation of Brehier's *Histoire de la Philosophie* (1963).) For a good example of a recent history that attempts to do some justice to India and China while remaining in its basic conception still within the Hegelian framework, see Störig 1962. Störig's accounts of Asian philosophies owe a great deal to Paul Deussen's *Allgemeine Geschichte der Philosophie,* a work that treated selected aspects of Indian and Chinese philosophy in extenso. A recent Continental thinker who attempts to consider non-Western philosophers and religious thinkers alongside those of the West is Karl Jaspers, *The Great Philosophers.* While this is one recent work that breaks almost completely from the Hegelian historiographical background, its highly personal style and uneven scholarship (not to mention the fact that it was

never completed), greatly reduce its value for methodical research. A noteworthy effort on the part of a philosopher with no specialized background in non-Western materials to encourage the systematic investigation of a major field for comparative research is Bocheński 1970, part 6, "The Indian Variety of Logic." Frederick Copleston, among the most distinguished twentieth-century English-speaking historians of philosophy, did not consider non-Western philosophies in the great work for which he is justly famous. However, in his later writings he did draw attention to some of the problems of comparative philosophy. See, for instance, Copleston 1980, 1982. I am not sure that any of this, however, has had any pronounced effect on most English-speaking philosophers' views of Asian thought. The historical perspective that I have been characterizing here as "Hegelian" pervades the general study of the history of civilization no less than it does that of philosophy in particular. It arrives at its quintessential vulgarisation in Will and Ariel Durants' *The Story of Civilization,* in which "Our Oriental Heritage"—volume 1—represents, in Hegelian fashion, the beginning of the long teleological march culminating in the twentieth-century West; India, China, Japan, etc. thereby being consigned symbolically to the same slot as Sumeria and dynastic Egypt!

11 In general I believe that Indian philosophy is rather more akin to Western philosophy than is the third great, original philosophical tradition, that of China. This has been totally obscured by those who insist on speaking of "Oriental Philosophy" without recognizing that, except in some areas of Buddhist thought (which China imported from India), there seems to be relatively little that the two Asian traditions actually have in common. In any case, the structure of Chinese thought seems to be much more poorly understood, from a philosophical standpoint, than are the main characteristics of classical Indian thought. For the philosopher who wishes to know something of philosophy in China, an exceptional brief introduction is the remarkable essay by A.C. Graham, "The Place of Reason in the Chinese Philosophical Tradition" (1964). Graham 1989 works out many of the ideas adumbrated there in detail. Symptomatic of the general state of awareness of Chinese (and Asian) thought in analytic philosophy, however, was Flew 1979, and the response of Daor and Scharfstein 1979. See also chap. 5, n. 2 below.

12 For instance, Matilal 1968, 1971, 1998; McDermott 1970; Mohanty 1992; and Ganeri 2001. On Nāgārjuna, in particular, in relation to philosophical logic, see now Bugault 1994. This and the notes immediately following are not intended to provide a thorough bibliographical guide, but only some useful orientations.

13 E.g., Dravid 1972, Siderits 1982, Chakrabarti 1985, and Halbfass 1992.

14 E.g., Sharma 1969 and Siderits 1985, 1986. On philosophy of language in India generally, Matilal 1990 affords an exceptional introduction.

15 See esp. Jayatilleke 1963, Hattori 1968, and Matilal, 1986.

16 Chemparathy 1972. If we can speak of buddhology (in the strict sense) as a form of philosophical theology, then Griffiths 1994 should certainly be noted here as well.

17 Hulin 1978.

18 Rorty 1976: 11.

19 Carrithers, Collins, and Lukes 1985 very well illustrates the complexity of the cultural/historical problems involved in this particular area. On the more general questions of relativism that are involved here, see especially Hollis and Lukes 1982, as well as Rorty, Schneewind, and Skinner 1985 on historical relativism in connection with the study of philosophy.

20 Taylor 1985: 30.

21 Parfit 1984: 273. Though Parfit identifies his position with that of Buddhism, it should be pointed out that all major Buddhist schools of thought have upheld the doctrine of transmigration, which is not consistent with Parfit's particular brand of Reductionism. Parfit's views are examined in relation to Buddhist thought in Kapstein 1986, Duerlinger 1993, Collins 1994, and Siderits 1997.

22 Nozick 1981: 94. Of course, the main line of the Buddhist debate with the orthodox schools of Hinduism involved not the Vedāntists, as Nozick believes, but rather the adherents of Sāṃkhya, Nyāya-Vaiśeṣika, and Mīmāṃsā. In fact, Buddhist philosophical assessments of the Vedānta tended to be more generous than contentious; see below, chap. 4, n. 1 and chap. 9, n. 40.

23 Barnes 1979: 106.

24 In fact, Barnes would probably argue that his fragment from Epicharmus, when considered not in isolation but in connection with the whole mass of evidence bearing upon the Pythagorean doctrine of the soul, does provide evidence of just the kind that we require. On p. 107 of the work cited, he says, "I suppose that his play is evidence of a lively debate on matters of personal identity in early Pythagorean circles." My point here is not to argue that Barnes is wrong about the Pythagoreans—I claim no particular expertise in the field of pre-Socratic philosophy. My concern is, rather, purely methodological.

25 *Tattvasaṅgrahapañjikā*, pp. 207–8.

26 For relevant social-historical and philosophical background, see Silburn 1955, Hulin 1978, Organ 1964, and Collins 1982a.

27 The influence of the *Sarvadarśanasaṅgraha* on modern texts on the "history" of Indian philosophy has been so pervasive that to attempt to enumerate the works so influenced would be virtually no different from compiling a general bibliography on the topic in question. Cf. the comments of Raju 1985: xx–xxi. However, I do not agree with Raju that Sāyaṇa Mādhava originated the particular pattern of doxographic exposition that he adheres to: the same pattern is followed, e.g., in the eighth- or ninth-century *Sarvasiddhāntasaṅgraha* (attributed to Śaṅkara). For detailed discussion of all this, see Halbfass 1988, chaps. 15, 16, and 19.

28 *Bodhicaryāvatārapañjikā*, p. 215.

29 See Organ 1964 for a general survey of these and other early theories.

30 For a general account of this school, see Larson 1979.

31 On the doctrine of the self in classical Mīmāṃsā, see Biardeau 1968 and Taber 1990.

32 For surveys of this tradition, refer to Potter 1977, Matilal 1977, and esp. Halbfass 1992.

33 Consult the works given in the preceding note for background on this school, and for current work, refer to Ganeri 2001.

34 *Tattvasaṅgraha,* vv. 171–76.

35 *Tattvasaṅgrahapañjikā,* p. 102.

36 Cf. Quinn 1978: 343–59.

37 Compare here the views of Jonathan Edwards, on which see Quinn 1978 and Chisholm 1979: 138–40.

38 Of course, in India there were skeptical thinkers who doubted that the theory of karman and retribution was true, just as the cosmologies of Western theism have been the object of much skepticism. Refer to Chattopadhyay and Gangopadhyay 1990. Especially notable, in this regard, is the work of Jayarāśi Bhaṭṭa, studied in Franco 1987. But, again, just as most philosophical reflection in the pre-modern and early modern Christian West has involved the tacit acceptance, at least, of the dominant cosmology, so too in India. The philosophical discussion of the karman-and-saṃsāra cosmology in its own right is a fascinating topic that has yet to receive thorough consideration. That, however, lies beyond the bounds of the present book. For work in this area in general, see O'Flaherty 1983. More recently, there has been growing interest in Indian Buddhist efforts to demonstrate the plausibility of the teaching of rebirth; in particular, refer to Franco 1997.

39 *Tattvasaṅgrahapañjikā,* p. 102: *yathā varṇayanti kāpilāḥ—"caitanyaṃ puruṣasya svaṃ rūpam."*

40 Locke 1974: II.xxvii.14.

41 *Tattvasaṅgrahapañjikā,* p. 102.

42 Locke 1974: II.xxvii.12–14: "...those who place thinking in an immaterial substance only...must show why personal identity cannot be preserved in the change of immaterial substances."

43 On non-Cartesian dualism, see Shoemaker 1984: 139–58, "Immortality and Dualism."

44 The precise dating of the *Bhagavadgītā* is uncertain, but the text must have been established roughly during the broad period 200 B.C.E.–400 C.E.

45 See, especially, *Bhagavadgītā,* II.11–37.

46 Also known as the *Ascertainment of the Person (Pudgalaviniścaya).* A translation will be found in chap. 14 below. For recent interpretation of this and related works, see Oetke 1988 and Duerlinger 1989, 1993, 1997–2000.

47 Compare the mutually exclusive opposition of Reductionism and non-Reductionism, as set out in Parfit 1984, part 3. See also n. 21 above.

48 *Abhidharmakośa,* vol. 4, p. 1215.

49 Cf. Sydney Shoemaker's contributions to Shoemaker and Swinburne 1984.

50 The parallels between Hume and Buddhism have been often remarked upon. A relatively detailed study of the resemblance is Hoffman 1982. See, too, Giles 1993.

51 Martin and Deutscher 1966. See chap. 4 below for further elaboration.
52 *Nyāyavārttika,* sections 1.1.10 and 3.1.1.
53 Following the discussion in *Tattvasaṅgraha,* v. 182 and its commentary.
54 A modern philosopher who argues in a similar vein is Chisholm 1976, 1981.
55 Chakrabarti 1982.
56 *Tattvasaṅgrahapañjikā,* p. 112.
57 Śāntarakṣita was directly attacked, for instance, by Vācaspatimiśra, in the latter's *Nyāyatātparyaṭīkā,* on *Nyāyasūtra,* 1.1.10.
58 *Madhyamakāvatāra,* chap. 6, vv. 120–65. See chaps. 3 and 4 below for further discussion. I do not agree with Duerlinger's (1993) characterization of Candrakīrti as a non-Reductionist in quite the senses that Parfit intends. Candrakīrti's argument, rather, is that the apparently Reductionist Ābhidharmikas are nonetheless tacitly non-Reductionist themselves, owing to their supposition of a genuinely individuating continuum. For Candrakīrti, I believe, the entire Reductionist–non-Reductionist problematic is one further instance of conceptual elaboration *(prapañca)* that must be abandoned in the attainment of discernment *(prajñā.)*
59 For one influential comparison of Candrakīrti and Kant, see Murti 1960: 293–303.
60 For more on this, see chap. 5, n. 2, and chap. 8 below.
61 Especially in Chinese and Tibetan. Some aspects of the impact made by Buddhist theories of the self on Chinese thinkers are discussed in Pachow 1980: 117–62. The Tibetan debates on topics relating to personal identity have just begun to be studied: the bone of contention was Tsong-kha-pa's (1357–1419) controversial interpretation of the work of Candrakīrti, particularly with reference to the continuity of karman. See Cabezón 1992, esp. pp. 314–16. A second topic of relevance here was the treatment of reflexivity, on which refer to Williams 1998a and Kapstein 2000b.
62 Rorty 1980: 389–94.

2. Indra's Search for the Self and the Beginnings of Philosophical Perplexity in India

OUR CONCERN HERE will be with some of the earliest Indian reflections on the puzzles of personal identity. These are derived from the Upaniṣads, which exemplify a type of discourse that some philosophers may regard as wisdom literature but not as philosophy. What I will be proposing here is that we attempt to regard such ancient sources of Indian thought more philosophically, more in the manner that some recent writers have begun to re-examine the pre-Socratics.[1] I wish to show that although philosophical method had not yet developed in the early literature under consideration (as equally it had not in Anaxagoras or Heraclitus), several important arguments were nonetheless already emerging there *in limine*. In surveying these proto-arguments, we will also have occasion to remark on their historical and/or conceptual affinities with the developed philosophies of later ages.

The self, as an object of philosophico-religious speculation, is conspicuous in the most ancient literature of India only by its absence. The early hymns of the Ṛg Veda, whose composition may date to about 1200–800 B.C.E., do not yet hint at what was to become the central problem of Indian philosophy.[2] The self makes its appearance in the middle period of Vedic thought, in the magical *Atharva Veda* and in the extensive ritual texts called *Brāhmaṇa*. Franklin Edgerton has described the evolution of some of the foremost ideas involved here as follows:

> In the Puruṣa hymn of the Rig Veda we find a crude evolution of various parts of the physical universe from parts of the physical body of the cosmic 'Man'. But in the later Vedic texts, the feeling grows that man's nature is not accounted for by dissecting his physical body—and, correspondingly, that there must be

> something more in the universe than the sum total of its physical elements. What is that 'something more' in man? Is it the 'life-breath' or 'life-breaths' *(prāṇa),* which seem to be in and through various parts of the human body and to be the principle of man's life (since they leave the body at death)? So many Vedic thinkers believed. What, then, is the corresponding 'life-breath' of the universe? Obviously the wind, say some. But even this seems presently too physical, too material. On the human side, too, it begins to be evident that the 'life-breath', like its cosmic counterpart the wind, is in reality physical. Surely the essential man must be something else. What then? Fittingly, here and there, it is suggested that it may be man's 'desire' or 'will' *(kāma),* or his 'mind' *(manas),* or something else of a more or less 'psychological' nature. But already in the Atharva Veda, and with increasing frequency later, we find as an expression for the real, essential part of Man the word *ātman* used. *Ātman* means simply 'self'; it is used familiarly as a reflexive pronoun, like the German *sich.* One could hardly get a more abstract term for that which is left when everything unessential is deducted from man, and which is at the same time to be considered the principle of his life, the living soul that pervades his being.[3]

I have quoted this passage at length because, with the brevity and insight that often characterize his reflections on ancient Indian religion and philosophy, Edgerton has encapsulated many of the essential themes that run throughout the vast literature that is actually preserved. In discussing here some prominent aspects of archaic Indian concepts of the self in particular, I will only introduce certain pertinent features of their development in the earlier Upaniṣads (attributed roughly to the period 800–300 B.C.E.),[4] the last section of the Vedic literature to have evolved.

The thought of the Vedic sages turned on what was perceived to be a system of analogies obtaining between microcosm and macrocosm, between man and world. This pervading interest in analogy had its origins in the Vedic cult, which depended on the efficacy of ritual or magical action, especially in the context of sacrificial performance. The hierophant, in order to manipulate events in the larger cosmos, enacted appropriately analogous events in the purified space consecrated for the sacrifice; and to do this he required knowledge of the appropriate analogies, particularly those obtaining between himself as ritual or magical actor, and the world he was to influence through his action. The principle[5] of analogy concerns us here, because, as later Indian thought evolved, subtle and philosophically interesting analogies among diverse classes of things were discovered and discussed from an increasingly critical standpoint. The beginnings of this process can be seen already in the earliest Upaniṣad, the *Bṛhadāraṇyaka:*

> Indeed, [all] this is three[-fold]: name, form, and action. Of them, what is called "speech" is the source of all names, for hence arise all names. This is common to them all, for it is the same with respect to all names. This is their *brahman,* for this supports all names.
>
> Now, what is called "eye" is the source of all forms [i.e., visual objects], for hence arise all forms. This is common to them all, for it is the same with respect to all forms. This is their *brahman,* for this supports all forms.
>
> Now, what is called "self"[6] is the origin of all actions, for hence arise all actions. This is common to them all, for it is the same with respect to all actions. This is their *brahman,* for this supports all actions. That which is these three, is this one self; and the self, being one, is these three. That is this which is deathless, hidden by what manifestly is; indeed, breath is what is deathless, and name and form are what manifestly is. This breath is hidden by those two.[7]

As word to speech, so form to eye, and action to the embodied self. Words, forms, and actions, as objects, are respectively united by the organs whose objects they are; and these thus become the *brahman,* the ultimate ground or fundamental principle, underlying each. But the ultimate ground of each class also points the way to the ultimate ground of all: as each member of the trio is unified in its ground, so the trio itself is united in the deathless and simple *ātman.* It is here that the principle of analogy converges with a principle of identification, which will be elaborated further below. We should note, too, that the passage here cited represents an early formulation of the basic intuition underlying what later emerges as an important philosophical argument for the reality of the self: as the organs of sense and of action stand in a one–many relationship to their objects, so there must be a *one* related to the entire manifold of the individual's experience.

The principle of analogy, however, not only points out hidden unity, but at the same time underscores multiplicity. From the *Taittirīya Upaniṣad* comes an interesting example of the use of numerical categories in analogical thought, an example that equally represents a very ancient instance of the principle of analysis by reduction to parts, to which we will have several occasions to return:

> Earth, atmosphere, heaven,
> the [main] quarters and the intermediate quarters;
> Fire, wind, sun, moon and stars;
> Water, plants, trees, space and body[8]—
> So it is with regard to the domain of the elements.
> Now with regard to what is within:
> *Prāṇa, vyāna, apāna, udāna, samāna* [the five vital energies];
> Eye, ear, mind, speech, touch;
> Skin, flesh, muscle, bone, marrow.
> The sage, having reflected on this, said:
> Quintuple, indeed, is this all.
> With the quintuple, indeed, does one acquire the quintuple.[9]

Both world and man, then, can be analyzed into triplets of fivefold categories. These reflections of an ancient sage are evocative not only because they apparently anticipate the threefold and fivefold classificatory schemes which will abound in early Buddhist scholasticism, but also because, again anticipating Buddhism, the self does not occur in the list of "what is within" (though the word *ātman,* translated above as "body," *is* found in the list of what is *without* in the domain of the elements). One further example, again from the *Bṛhadāraṇyaka,* parallels the preceding text in its reduction of the whole to its parts, but takes the process of analogical reflection one step further, by inquiring into the causal order of things. Analogy here gives way to pure metaphor:

> As is a great forest tree so, in truth, is a person; his hairs are leaves and his skin is its outer bark...
> His flesh is its inner bark, his nerves are tough like inner fibers.
> His bones are the wood within and the marrow is made resembling the pith.
> A tree when it is felled springs up from its root in a newer form;
> *from what root does man spring forth when he is cut off by death?*
> Do not say "from the semen," for that is produced from what is alive...[10]

The analogical reasoning of the Upaniṣadic tradition thus concludes with the recognition of significant disanalogy; man's life is thought to spring from some source beyond the natural order of physical generation, unlike the life of a tree, though the two are alike in having a protective skin, inner organs, etc. The thought of the Upaniṣadic sage here contrasts with that of Plato's Socrates, as expressed in the *Phaedo:*

> If you would grasp my point more readily don't think only of mankind, but of the whole animal and vegetable world, in short of everything that comes into being: and let us put the general question: isn't it always a case of opposite coming to be from opposite whenever the relation in question exists?[11]

Here Socrates seeks a universal principle of generation, common to plant, animal, and man, and further imagines that that principle must be one of generation from opposites. To the author of the Upaniṣad, however, the possibility of there being two radically distinct orders of causation has already dawned; indeed, the dualism implied here was also apparent in the earlier quotation, which sought to analyze, in parallel columns as it were, analogous but otherwise utterly distinct outer and inner worlds. Again, later Buddhist scholasticism, with its notions of outer and inner causation formally expressed in contrastive paradigms of the principle of dependent origination, seems to inherit something here from the more ancient Brahmanical background.[12]

If analogical reason found its culmination in the beginnings of a clear appreciation of difference, other elements were still required to pave the way for the more sophisticated (and no longer preeminently analogical) ratiocination that was just dawning when the Upaniṣads were composed. One such element was a principle of identification, which clearly was closely tied to analogical thought, insofar as the latter demanded the proper identifications of the terms of any ritually efficacious analogy. Edgerton says of this principle, as it is found expressed in the Upaniṣads:

> If I now know that the *brahman,* which is the *ātman* of the universe, is my own *ātman,* then not only do I control the fundamental principle of the universe, because knowledge is magic power; but even more than that, I *am* the fundamental principle of the universe, by mystic identification.[13]

Though identification in the Upaniṣads is often, indeed, the so-called "mystic identification" in which individual and universal soul are realized as one, this is not always the case. We shall see below that identification also takes the form of a determination of defining marks, and that mystic identification sometimes is that to which one takes recourse where the apprehension of a definition will no longer suffice. So perhaps it is more correct to speak of several notably different *principles* of identification. These will remain with us throughout this chapter owing to the centrality of the question, "What is this self?" *(ko'yam ātmā?),* the resolution of which is held to be the secret to liberation.

We have already seen some examples of the principles in question: in the identification of the eye as the *brahman* of sight, speech as the *brahman* of words, etc.; in the fivefold analysis of the outer and inner, which seemed to identify each with the aggregation of its parts; and in the parable of the tree, which calls us to question the identity of the source of human becoming. In the analytic dismemberment of the person that was to occupy a central role in the development of Buddhist systematic meditation, one is, in effect, directed to try and fail to identify the self among the parts of which one is constituted.[14] A particularly interesting text, which perhaps bridges the gulf between the Upaniṣadic love of analogy and such systematic analytical meditation as will be fully realized in early Buddhism, is found in the *Aitareya Upaniṣad:*

> If speaking is through speech, if breathing is through breath, if seeing is through the eyes, if hearing is through the ears, if touching is through the skin, if meditation is through the mind, if exhaling is through the outbreath, if emission is through the generative organ, then who am I?[15]

Let us note the contrast between this and the parable of the tree, on the one hand, and the fivefold analysis on the other: the latter, after analyzing the inner domain into three groups of five parts each, elaborates no special category for the self; but the metaphor of the tree and our present text both leave us with questions asked in such a way as to suggest that there may be some mysterious element in the constitution of a person, above and beyond the enumerated parts. It is important that we emphasize here that even in the earliest Upaniṣadic speculations, it became apparent that identifying the *self* (whether with the universal *brahman,* or in any other context) was somehow to be distinguished from identifying the *objects* given to the senses, or to the intellect. This emerges from a particularly striking passage, again from the *Bṛhadāraṇyaka:*

> Uṣasta Cākrāyaṇa said: "This has been explained by you just as one might say 'This is a cow, this is a horse.' Now explain to me the *brahman* that is immediately present and directly perceived, that is the self within all." "This is your self that is within all." "Which is within all, Yājñavalkya?" "You cannot see the seer of sight, you cannot hear the hearer of what's heard, you cannot think the thinker of the thought, you cannot know the knower of knowledge. He is your self which is within all. Everything else is wretched."[16]

Given the abstractness, noted by Edgerton, of the reflexive pronoun *ātman,* it should not surprise us to see here a distant anticipation of the problem of pronominal reference, which was later to occasion much philosophical puzzlement in India. What still requires some clarification is *why* it was that the abstractness of the reflexive pronoun should have troubled classical Indian thinkers, as it does us. Certainly, the absence of an ostensible referent corresponding to "self," to which our text is so finely attuned, is one major factor here. But an answer must be sought also in the attention given to the analysis of language in ancient India, the early development there of linguistic science having been the direct outcome of the need to preserve the text of the sacred Veda intact after the Vedic language itself was no longer spoken.[17] It is therefore of considerable interest that even here, in a passage that belongs to the germinal age in the history of Indian linguistics, Uṣasta adopts a linguistic model to indicate what he considers to be an unsatisfactory explanation of *brahman.* He does not say, "You have explained this as you explain cows," but rather, "...*as one might say* 'This is a cow, this is a horse'" *(yathā vibrūyād asau gaur asāv aśva ity evam).* In this way, he suggests that a particular form of utterance, an act of designation in which a demonstrative is placed in apposition to a noun, is in this case inadequate to the task at hand. The question thus is not merely one of seeking the *what* with which to identify the self, but equally the *how,* whereby the very identification may become a possibility. How, that is, can language refer at all to what has no determinate defining marks? Yājñavalkya's solution, we have seen, was to adopt a course that would henceforth remain supremely influential in Indian philosophy and religion, namely, to attempt to refer indirectly, by means of the *via negativa.*

One last theme that pervades Upaniṣadic thought deserves mention here. The ritualist, we have seen, could control the universe by virtue of his special knowledge of the correspondences between microcosm and macrocosm. The principles of analogy and identification, and their significance for the ritual hierophant, then imply a further concept that becomes increasingly important throughout the later Vedic period; namely, the notion that the individual who does not possess the special knowledge of the self and its identity is without any ability to determine his own destiny. Thus, in the words of the *Īśa Upaniṣad:*

> Unholy, indeed, are those worlds, smothered in darkness,
> To which those people who slay the self depart after death.[18]

The intuitive knowledge of the self to which the Upaniṣadic sage aspires is thus not to be regarded as a sort of theoretical insight devoid of practical significance; rather, it is the knowledge that confers liberation from the evils of saṃsāra, and whoever lacks such knowledge is hopelessly bound to a round of perpetual misery. This cosmological setting thus insures that the supreme categorical imperative of the Upaniṣadic world is: "Know then thy self!"

We may now turn to a text of great importance, one in which the various themes we have so far examined are woven together into a philosophically richly evocative fabric. It is from the eighth book of the *Chāndogya Upaniṣad* where we find for the first time a clear expression of the problem of the self posed in terms of *identity through time.* Significantly, this is also one of the earliest passages in which we can clearly discern the outlines of a philosophical *argument* (rather than just philosophically pregnant insights of the sort we've examined thus far)—informally stated, to be sure, but already suggesting possibilities for relatively formal expression.[19]

Like so much of the philosophical gold that is to be mined from Upaniṣadic ore, the argument is found in the midst of a remarkable tale: Indra, lord of the gods, and Virocana, lord of the antigods (who resemble the Greek Titans), both hear Prajāpati, the divine preceptor, say that "The self...has vanquished evil, and is unaging, deathless, free from grief...He who has discovered and knows that self, he obtains all worlds and all desires." Eager to acquire these boons, they approach Prajāpati to learn of this wonderful self:

> Prajāpati said to them, "The person seen in the eye is the self," and said further, "This one, immortal and fearless, is *brahman*..." And he instructed them to study their own physical reflections to learn of it.
>
> "But Lord, who is this one who is seen reflected in the waters, and in a mirror?" To this he said, "This one, indeed, is seen reflected in all of these...Look at your self in a pan of water, and whatever you do not understand of the self, tell me..."
>
> Then the two said, "We both see the self thus altogether, Sir, a picture even to the very hairs and nails...Just as we are, Sir, well adorned, with our best clothes and tidy, thus we see both these, Sir, well adorned, with our best clothes and tidy." "That is the self," said he. "That is the immortal, the fearless, that is *brahman*." They both went away with tranquil hearts.
>
> Then Prajāpati looked at them and said, "Not having found the self, not having discovered it, they depart!"

Let us begin by considering the preliminary identification of the self with the "person that is seen in the eye...who is seen reflected in the water, and in a mirror." Contemporary philosophical readers may recall here Wittgenstein's saying that "the human body is the best picture of the human soul."[20] It is possible that Prajāpati's intention, too, was, in a certain sense at least, not so very different from Wittgenstein's, that is, if both be taken as saying, in effect, that it is the actual bodily presence of a person that permits us to gain our truest understanding of that person. This is not, however, how Indra and Virocana understand Prajāpati's cryptic statement: they take him instead to be saying that the one reflected *is* the self, *not* an image or picture thereof. The tale continues:

> But Indra, even before reaching the gods, saw this danger: Even as this self [here: the body] is well adorned when this body is well adorned, well dressed when the body is well dressed, tidy when the body is tidy, that self will similarly be blind when the body is blind, lame when the body is lame, crippled when the body is crippled. It perishes just when the body perishes. I see nothing enjoyable in this.

It is precisely in this passage that a central philosophical argument emerges (albeit, in embryonic form): if the body *is* the self, then the body's infirmities will belong to the self, as well.[21] But Prajāpati had previously declared that "the self is free from old age…," etc. That is, it is liberated from all infirmities. So, Indra has located a logical inconsistency—one that betokens a departure from what is true, from being, from what is enjoyable or valuable. That ontology and axiology are not clearly distinguished is characteristic of early Indian (as of Greek) thought,[22] and we shall see that it is this feature that is most pertinent to an understanding of the significance of the argument within its Indian context.

Having introduced, in a general manner, some of the questions arising in connection with what I take to be the first relatively clear expression in India of the problem of personal identity through time, let us return briefly to the version of that problem that Jonathan Barnes argues is the earliest in the West, which we mentioned briefly in the preceding chapter. It comes from the work of the ancient Sicilian dramatist Epicharmus, and so may reflect Pythagorean inspiration:

> *Debtor.* If you like to add a pebble to an odd number—or to an even one if you like—or if you take one away that is there; do you think it is still the same number?
> *Creditor.* Of course not.
> *D.* And if you like to add some length to a yard-measure, or to cut something off from what's already there, will that measure still remain?
> *C.* No.
> *D.* Well, consider men in this way too—for one is growing, one declining, and all are changing all the time. And what changes by nature, and never remains in the same state, will be something different from what changed; and by the same argument you and I are different yesterday, and different now, and will be different again—and we are never the same.[23]

Thus, the debtor maintains, he's just not the same man who took out the loan, and so shouldn't be held accountable. Epicharmus's argument shares with Indra's reflections an acute perception of the incompatibility of identity and change; but unlike the Upaniṣadic author, the ancient Sicilian does not presuppose here an unchanging something over and against the domain of change and transformation. If, with Barnes, we agree that Epicharmus's argument is evidence that the issue of personal identity was actively discussed in Pythagorean circles, we will no doubt want to hold with him also that the Pythagoreans supposed the *psychē* to be a stable entity relative to the other constituent elements of a person, the elements which "are changing all the time."[24] Note, though, that the courtroom scene as presented above is, rather, a mocking rejection of the supposed Pythagorean assumption.

Barnes considers it to be of great significance that the setting for Epicharmus's argument is a forensic one, and he quotes Locke's observation that "person is a forensic term." This explains in part why bodily identity is all that the argument concerns, for in the forensic context in which third-person identity is most prominent, apparent bodily identity *is* the actual criterion upon which we base the majority of our judgments of identity. Where the *Chāndogya Upaniṣad* and Epicharmus agree, then, is in a common assertion (which they share no less with Joseph Butler) that *bodily identity is not really identity at all.* But Locke, we should recall, uses the term "forensic" in a peculiarly broad sense, comprising not just the proceedings of courts of law, but also the entire nexus of nomic relationships holding among intelligent agents, their actions, and the reward or punishment, divine or human, which they receive therefore: "forensic," for Locke, describes the forum of God's law no less than man's.[25] And it is this assumption, that personal identity is somehow fundamental to the realization of human ends, conceived now in cosmological terms, that serves to expose the deeper analogy between the Western problematic and its Indian counterpart. This analogy will be strengthened when, below, we turn to some Kantian reflections. Before taking up these issues, however, some remarks on the form of the Upaniṣadic argument itself are required.

In the modern West, there is a family of arguments for dualism that are associated primarily with the Cartesian tradition, versions of which have been powerfully defended in recent philosophy by Saul Kripke.[26] These arguments generally turn on the so-called Leibniz-Russell definition of identity:[27]

> For any *x* and any *y* whatsoever, if *x* and *y* are identical, then *x* has all and only the properties of *y*.

This permits us to say what must be true for any two things to be established as being not identical:

> For any *x* and any *y* whatsoever, if it is not the case that *x* has all and only the properties of *y*, then *x* and *y* are *different. (Principia Mathematica,* *13.14.)

An argument often attributed (probably erroneously) to Descartes that apparently makes use of this principle is as follows:[28]

(1) The existence of my body is dubitable, but my existence is not.
(2) Therefore, my body has a property (dubitability with respect to its existence) that I do not.
(3) Therefore, (by (2) and *PM,* *13.14) my body and I are *different things.*

This version of the Cartesian argument has been generally discredited on the grounds that Leibniz's Law does not apply to *intentional* properties.[29]

Clearly, Indra's misgivings regarding the identity of body and self can be cast in the same mold as the foregoing "Cartesian" argument without too much difficulty:

(1) The body is subject to infirmity, but not so the self.
(2) Therefore, the body has a property (subjection to infirmity) that the self does not.
(3) Therefore, (by (2) and *PM,* *13.14) body and self are different.

Significantly, *this* version of the argument involves an entirely straightforward application of Leibniz's Law: no messy intentional properties or modalities here.[30] Rather, the properties that distinguish the body from the self are those that it possesses in virtue of being something that *changes in time,* which the self, *ex hypothesi,* does not. But the argument will carry no weight unless we are willing to affirm, with the first premise, that there *is* such a thing as "the self" and that it is not the sort of thing that grows old, gets sick and dies, i.e., that it is an *incorruptible* self. In the Cartesian argument for dualism, the existence of the conscious subject would be assumed to have been already proven on the basis of the *cogito*-argument. But why, according to the *Chāndogya Upaniṣad,* should one affirm such a thing as the independent reality of the self? The text suggests to us two arguments in the passage we are considering, one explicit and the other only implied: we may call them the *argument from authority* and the *axiological argument,* respectively.

The argument from authority would have us maintain, in effect, that the controversial part of premise (1)—namely, the part concerning the self's reality and freedom from corruption—must be affirmed just because Prajāpati was heard to say that the self was of thus-and-such a nature. For one who had actually *heard* Prajāpati (in a Western religious context read, perhaps, "the voice of the Lord") this may be a very good (that is, convincing) argument, as also it may be for the members of a community that consciously and deliberately adhere to what are agreed to be Prajāpati's dicta. The reasons for its being a good argument in that context, but probably not so good in other contexts, are substantially similar to the reasons James adduced in *The Varieties of Religious Experience* for holding that mystical experience provides good reasons for belief only to the subject of mystical experience, but not so to others.[31] Thus, the argument from authority cannot be expected to carry much weight among those who are neither subject to the experiences in question nor members of a community affirming the dicta of one who is. This was recognized by Indian philosophers of the scholastic period, who would have recourse to arguments from authority only in debates *within* schools adhering, by mutual consent, to the same authorities.[32] But a Brahmanical philosopher, for example, would not expect to convince a Buddhist by an argument from authority leading back to the Upaniṣadic Prajāpati. And, as Indian philosophy developed, it became widely recognized that the argument from authority, even within a single school, could seldom be affirmed without additional support in the form of evidence derived from sources other than the scriptural authority in question. Thus, for example, Vātsyāyana (c. 400 C.E.), introducing his discussion of arguments for the substantial reality of the self, says:

> [Among the substances] the self is not grasped through direct acquaintance [of an ordinary sort, excluding here mystical intuition]. But then is it established only through received scripture? No; for it is to be established through inference.[33]

In short, the limitations of arguments from authority came to be felt no less keenly in Indian philosophical circles than they have been in the West (though, at the same time, orthopraxy—the authority of tradition with respect to practice—has been always an extremely powerful force in all aspects of Indian religious and social life).

The second argument, which I think is of greater importance here, is still not very clearly developed in the text that we are investigating. This is an axiological argument, indicated in Indra's lament that he sees "nothing *enjoyable*" in the self's being identified with a mortal body.[34] In order to comprehend better the axiological argument, it will be helpful to review briefly some of the terrain covered by Indra as he further pursues his search for the secure realization of *brahman.* After Indra abandons the notion that the self is to be identified with the body, Prajāpati instructs him in two other doctrines, each of which Indra goes on to abandon after reflecting upon them with care. The first of the new doctrines states that: "He who moves about happy in a dream, he is the self; he is the immortal, the fearless. He is *brahman.*" Delighted, Indra departs, but:

> Even before reaching the gods he saw this danger: even though this self...is not slain [when the body] is slain, is not one-eyed [when the body] is one-eyed, yet it is as if they kill him, as if they unclothe him. He comes to experience as it were what is unpleasant, he even weeps as it were. I see nothing enjoyable in this.

Returning, then, for further instruction, Prajāpati tells him that "When a man is asleep, composed, serene, and knows no dream, that is the self, that is the immortal, the fearless. That is *brahman.*" And following the same pattern as before:

> Even before reaching the gods he saw this danger: in truth this one does not know himself that "I am he," nor indeed the things here. He has become one who has gone to annihilation. I see nothing enjoyable in this.

Thus, one ought not to identify oneself with that which is not, in the final analysis, worthy of enjoyment: the body with all of its infirmities, or the dream-world with its uncertainties and evils, or the unconscious repose of deep sleep. What *is* worthy of final enjoyment can only be that which is free from all the many defects of this painful round; that is, it can only be the deathless, the pure, the true self of all. Thus, Prajāpati finally declares to Indra:

> Mortal, indeed, is this body. It is in death's grasp. But it is the support of that deathless, bodiless self...pleasure and pain do not touch one who is bodiless...Now he who knows, "Let me think this," he is the self, the mind is his divine eye...He obtains all worlds and all desires who discovers and knows the self.

So one ought to identify oneself with that alone which is one's own essentially conscious self, and is the self of all worlds.

It is simple enough to construct a hypothetical ethical syllogism on the basis of this informally constructed argument. Let us call it the "Liberation Argument":

> (1) If one ought to value above all freedom from saṃsāra's defects, then it must be the case that one's true identity is that supreme self that instantiates such freedom.
> (2) Indeed, one ought to value above all such freedom.
> Therefore, (3) one's true identity is that supreme self that instantiates such freedom.

As C.D. Broad indicated early in the last century,[35] arguments of this type may certainly be valid, but in most cases their premises are suspect: the argument given above is certainly one such case. Among arguments familiar to contemporary philosophers, one with which this may profitably be compared is the one characterized by Broad as "the Argument that the World would be very evil unless Men are immortal."[36] Broad summarizes it as follows:

> If we and all men die with our bodies the world is very evil. The world is not so evil as this. Therefore some men, at any rate, are immortal.

The analogy between the two arguments may be seen by converting the foregoing to *modus ponens:*

> (1) If the world is not extremely evil, then not all of us die when our bodies do.
> (2) The world is not all that bad.
> Therefore, (3) some of us, at least, survive bodily death.

Where the arguments concur, of course, is in the movement from an assumed value—freedom from saṃsāra in the one case and the (at least partial) goodness of the world in the other—to an actual state of affairs that the value in question entails—be it identity with what transcends saṃsāra or immortality. We should note, too, that immortality was valued in classical Indian thought only insomuch as it was understood to involve freedom: merely to persist beyond this lifetime as a being bound within the round of saṃsāra was conceived not as positively valued immortality, but rather as a sort of hyper-mortality, an infernal passage through death after death. Hence, the emphasis on freedom rather than on survival per se.

In the argument on evil and immortality, as Broad has shown, both premises are at least very doubtful. One is inclined to wonder just how evil the world has to be in order to be "very evil"—unless some clear sense be given to this, it is hard to see how either premise can be properly assessed. If "not very evil" is taken to be equivalent to "good," then the second premise is of doubtful truth-value at least. And this is to say nothing of the difficulties involved in the assumption that the world's not being very evil implies that at least someone is immortal! In short, the argument seems to be not very promising.

What of the Liberation Argument, which we derived from Indra's search for the self? It seems clear to me that the second premise—one ought to value freedom from saṃsāra above all—is its strong suit, being (from this writer's standpoint, at least) intuitively far more plausible than either of the premises of the argument taken up by Broad: taking freedom from saṃsāra in its most basic sense to be freedom from death and sorrow, this does seem to be worthy of the highest valuation; and in practice this is affirmed by virtually the whole of human science, philosophy, religion, and politics, each of which, in its own sphere, has sought to free us from misery, and at least from some of the anxieties and torments of death. So, in as much as freedom from saṃsāra is simply freedom from the harsh trials and tribulations of our world, the imperative to value such freedom above all is one to which much of humankind yields.[37]

But the Upaniṣadic teaching, I am arguing, involves a passage from the value of freedom to the fact of a secure ground, an ultimate reality, in which that freedom is perfectly actualized. This is represented in the first premise of the argument, and it is particularly this premise, I think, that merits our careful attention; for it is this premise that represents what is most central to the debate that would emerge later between the Brahmanical and Buddhist traditions.

Let us re-pose the question: does the value of freedom have as its necessary condition the actuality of a perpetually free self? Or is it just necessary that there be a *bound* self that is possibly such as to instantiate that freedom? Or is that freedom actualized when self is relinquished and we yield to an entirely impersonal reality? Or is the actuality of freedom something of which we can have no positive theoretical knowledge, but must nonetheless affirm, as Kant would have it, as a "postulate of pure practical reason?" Or is freedom no more than whatever it happens to be that humans can actually accomplish at any given period in their history in the way of making their lives go well? We might continue in this manner, no doubt, at great length; but this much will suffice to make the essential point here: premise (1), whose consequent is "it must be the case that one's true identity is that supreme self that instantiates freedom from saṃsāra," will remain in doubt so long as there are a plurality of possible alternative, but mutually exclusive, consequents amenable to substitution here.

Now, it seems quite certain that most of the major philosophico-religious traditions of India would have accepted some form of the Liberation Argument.[38] Kamalaśīla, for instance, writing in the eighth century C.E., declares that the value of freedom from saṃsāra is something that all educated persons affirm.[39] And we have seen that there is a very broad sense, at least, in which many contemporary Westerners might concur, though usually without wishing to go along with the cosmological particulars of the classical Indian worldview. But in the present context, where that worldview is a fundamental presupposition, what was debated by Indian philosophers was this: whether the necessary condition for the freedom to which we aspire is (i) the presence in each and every one of us of a possibly free, substantial self (the view of the Brahmanical realist schools and of the Jains); or (ii) the actuality of an all-pervading, ultimately real ground, in which individual identity is ultimately lost (the view of Upaniṣadic monism); or (iii) the entirely nomic structure of saṃsāra itself, whereby if certain causal conditions cease to operate, the process of saṃsāra itself comes to a halt, which cessation is freedom (the view of the mainstream of scholastic Buddhism). The diversity of opinion here (and the three options given represent only a schematic view of the full range of speculation about this), suggests a possible reformulation of the Liberation Argument that would have appealed to a very broad consensus of learned opinion in ancient India, and whose major premise might be:

> (1a) If, given the accepted cosmology, one ought to value freedom from saṃsāra, then, given that same cosmology, it must be possible to realize that freedom.

Such an argument, of course, would tell us nothing at all of the actual conditions in virtue of which freedom is a possibility; it merely affirms that it is.

I have already suggested one other line of objection to the Liberation Argument that will perhaps trouble some contemporary readers: premise (2) and the antecedent of premise (1) were both defended on the basis of a very free interpretation of the notion of "freedom from saṃsāra," one that deliberately stressed the convergence between modern Western and classical Indian concepts of "freedom from." (I deliberately exclude the notion of "freedom to" from the present discussion, as this would involve us in a great many additional complications.) But what of the implications for the argument if we emphasize, instead, the specific character of the various freedoms with which we might be concerned? Of course, it will not be possible to discuss all the many paradigmatic examples of freedom that might be adduced here: freedom from disease, from political oppression, from poverty, from damnation by an all-powerful God, from death and rebirth in saṃsāra, etc. Clearly, the precise conditions for the realization of these various freedoms will not all be the same. But in the present context, where freedom from saṃsāra is conceived as the highest good, I think we can show that the direction of Upaniṣadic speculation is not completely without its modern Western parallels.

The Liberation Argument, formulated in an Upaniṣadic version, would have us posit an axiological scale, which requires, for its own completion, that we also posit the real existence of the eternal *ātman-brahman,* together with the realization of it which is *mokṣa,* liberation from the lower values of saṃsāra. What this may recall is the argument in Kant's Second Critique concerning "the immortality of the soul as a postulate of pure practical reason." Kant writes:

> The realization of the *summum bonum* in the world is the necessary object of a will determinable by the moral law. But in this will the *perfect accordance* of the mind with the moral law is the supreme condition of the *summum bonum.* This then must be possible, as well as its object, since it is contained in the command to promote the latter. Now, the perfect accordance of the will with the moral law is *holiness,* a perfection of which no rational being of the sensible world is capable at any moment of his existence. Since, nevertheless, it is required as practically necessary, it can only be found in a *progress in infinitum* towards that perfect accordance, and on the principles of pure practical reason it is necessary to assume such a practical progress as the real object of our will.
>
> Now, this endless progress is only possible on the supposition of an *endless* duration of the *existence* and personality of the same rational being (which is called the immortality of the soul).[40]

The objections to this argument are notorious, and so will not be rehearsed here; they will apply, moreover, to any closely similar argument.[41] But here I am interested only in pointing out an analogy. In the Upaniṣadic context, Kant's moral imperative requiring that a man be holy would be replaced by the imperative to realize the *summum bonum* as perfect freedom of the self from the limitations of death, grief, etc. But the condition for this realization is the perfect accordance of the individual self *(ātman)* with that which is in its essence free from those very limitations, namely, *brahman*, the ultimate ground of all being. This perfect accordance with *brahman* cannot be realized by the body, or dream consciousness, or the unconsciousness of deep sleep; in fact, it can only be realized on the condition that the individual self, *ātman*, is essentially similar to *brahman*, that is to say, that *it is* in its own essence free from death, etc. So the postulate of the Upaniṣadic *summum bonum* may be seen to require the practical postulate of the immortality and perfect freedom of the individual self. Kant's supposition, too, of the "endless duration of the existence and personality of the same rational being" finds a curious analogue in the Upaniṣad: Indra's discipleship under Prajāpati, during which he progresses from the crude identification of self and body to the profoundest realization of *ātman*, is described as a process that continues over centuries; Upaniṣadic perfection is actualized in cosmic time.

I do not think that the axiological argument was ever developed in quite this form in ancient India—comparison with Kant provides not an exact description of the Indian argument, but rather a prescription for its possible reformulation. Nonetheless, something very much like it is clearly involved in much classical Indian philosophico-religious speculation. The Buddhists would certainly have accepted some of its premises—those which establish the basic scale of values—though they decisively rejected the conclusion that its completion demanded the posit of an eternal and immutable being of any kind; what they accepted was the posit of *mokṣa*, or *nirvāṇa*, as liberation, but they generally thought it incapable of characterization in positive assertions of being.[42] And even when Indian philosophy had reached the scholastic phase of its development, we find the same basic axiological scheme informing arguments that had first appeared in the Upaniṣads and in the early scriptures of Buddhism. The logician Vācaspatimiśra, for instance, argues that:

> This one who is experiencer, rememberer, inferer, and desirer, is the self; for the body is not worthy *(arhati)* so to be; because that

> becomes other, according to the distinctions of infancy, childhood, youth, and adulthood.[43]

The logical point, of course, is the one concealed in Indra's original line of argument, namely, that the body's properties are not those of the self; but those properties inform us of more than mere difference, for they speak equally of an order of worthiness.

It may be objected, more generally, that the attempt to find a parallel to the ancient speculations of Brahmanical sages in Kant is just too arbitrary and contrived to be taken seriously. I do not deny that the cultural-historical differences between them are very great indeed, perhaps even great enough to vitiate any such comparison. Nonetheless, it remains a curious fact in the history of ideas that two of the scholar-philosophers who contributed most to the philosophical study of the Upaniṣads in the West, namely, F. Max Müller and Paul Deussen, were both neo-Kantians,[44] and that Kant has been held in the highest esteem by the Indian philosophers of the neo-Vedantic movement.[45] I think it not unlikely that when such sympathy between philosophers from diverse backgrounds occurs, there is some basis for it in the conceptual convergences of the philosophies in question; and one of the topics concerning which such convergence seems greatest in the case we are considering here is certainly that of the value and prospects of freedom,[46] that is, the logical passage from its "oughtness" to the real possibility thereof.

Notes

1 I refer, for example, to Barnes 1979.

2 Refer esp. to Deussen 1965, Keith 1925, Willman-Grabowska 1929–30, Silburn 1955, Abegg 1956, Horsch 1956–58, Organ 1964, and Hulin 1978. The early development of Indian reflection on questions pertaining to personal identity, particularly within ancient Buddhism, has been considered in depth in Collins 1982a.

3 Edgerton 1965: 25–26.

4 For the Sanskrit text of the Upaniṣads, I have referred to: *Daśopaniṣad, Śrīśaṅkaragranthāvalī,* and Radhakrishnan 1953. References are given according to the title, and numbering of the passage, of the particular Upaniṣad cited. The translations given here sometimes follow those of Radhakrishnan (who I

think leans too heavily on Śaṅkara) or Zaehner 1966 (who perhaps does not take the indigenous commentaries seriously enough), with minor emendation when it appears to me to be required. Olivelle 1996 provides now excellent translations of the major early Upaniṣads.

5 The use of the word "principle" in the present chapter is not intended to suggest that Upaniṣadic thought involved the application of formal *laws* of reason. "Principle" is used to underscore only that there are recurrent motifs that do characterize the type of thinking we find here. Still, while systematization belongs rather to a much later stage in Indian history, the motifs that I here term "principles" nevertheless have regular analogues in the formal systems of developed Indian philosophy.

6 The traditional commentators interpret this occurrence of the word *ātman* as meaning "body" rather than "self," which, in this context, is lexically possible. It is important to recall that this remained an important usage of the word even in later classical literature, e.g., in Kālīdāsa, *Raghuvaṃśa,* chap. 1, v.21a.

7 *Bṛhadāraṇyakopaniṣad,* I.vi.1–3.

8 "Body" here is *ātman* again. The interpretation of its meaning follows Śaṅkara. It must be understood here as referring to the living, breathing body, and not to the body as a mere physical thing.

9 *Taittirīyopaniṣad,* I.7.

10 *Bṛhadāraṇyakopaniṣad,* III.ix.28.

11 Hackforth 1955, par. 70d–e.

12 Cf. my comments in "Mi-pham's Theory of Interpretation," chap. 13 below.

13 Edgerton 1965: 27.

14 See, e.g., Conze 1969: 95–107.

15 *Aitareyopaniṣad,* IV.3.

16 *Bṛhadāraṇyakopaniṣad,* III.iv.2.

17 On the early evolution of Indian linguistics, see Scharfe 1977.

18 *Īśopaniṣad,* v. 3.

29 All remaining Upaniṣadic citations in this chapter will be from *Chāndogyopaniṣad,* VIII.7–12.

20 *Philosophical Investigations,* II.iv: "Der menschliche Körper ist das beste Bild der menschlichen Seele." I am also reminded here of a popular saying from Eastern Tibet: "To know someone's past deeds, look at his present body. To know someone's future embodiments, look at his present deeds." (*snga ma'i las shes 'dod na, da lta'i lus la ltos. phyi ma'i lus shes 'dod na, da lta'i las la ltos.)* There are, of course, many other ways to interpret Prajāpati's laconic remarks. "The person seen in the eye" is taken by traditional commentators to refer suggestively to the seer *(draṣṭṛ)* himself, who is here mistakenly grasped as a reflected form. See, e.g., *Śrīśaṅkaragranthāvalī,* pp. 316–17.

21 This point, of course, is one that mind-body identity theorists have always and everywhere accepted as an entailment of their position. Gassendi, a proponent of mind-brain identity, writes, for instance: "For you yourself are perturbed when it is perturbed, and oppressed when it is oppressed, and if something

destroys the forms of things in it, you yourself do not retain any trace." Quoted in Wilson 1982: 178.

22 Some of this tension is what is involved in the disputes, inspired by Martin Heidegger, over the proper sense of the Greek *alētheia.* See "The Trouble with Truth," chap. 8 below.

23 Barnes 1979: 106–7.

24 Barnes 1979: chap. 6, *passim.*

25 Locke 1974: II.xxvii.26: "*Person,* as I take it, is the name for this self. Wherever a man finds what he calls himself, there, I think, another may say is the same person. It is a forensic term, appropriating actions and their merit, and so belongs only to intelligent agents, capable of a law, and happiness, and misery...whatever past actions it cannot reconcile or appropriate to the present self by consciousness, it can no more be concerned in than if they had never been done; and to receive pleasure or pain, i.e. reward or punishment, on the account of any such action, is all one as to be made happy or miserable in its first being, without any demerit at all. For, supposing a man punished now for what he had done in another life, whereof he could be made to have no consciousness at all, what difference could there be between that punishment and being created miserable? And therefore, conformable to this, the apostle tells us that, at the great day, when everyone shall *receive according to his doings, the secrets of all hearts shall be laid open.*" Curiously, it is characteristic of the ancient Buddhist Jātaka tales, stories of events in past lives, that the hero's undergoing retribution for a past misdeed is often accompanied by a recollection of the original misdeed.

26 Kripke 1981, esp. 144ff.

27 See, e.g., Brody 1980: 6–10 and Whitehead and Russell 1962.

28 On this attribution see Wilson 1982: 190.

29 Wilson 1982 and Rorty 1980: 55–56. Given, however, a Chisholmian view of intentional attribution, it is not clear that Wilson and Rorty are entirely correct on this point.

30 Of course, one might wish to argue that "subjection to infirmity" cannot be made intelligible without reference to some modal property or other, e.g., "being such that it possibly dies." However, I do not think that such monadic modal properties vitiate the application of Leibniz's Law.

31 James 1925: 422ff. James maintains, in essence, that while mystical states are "absolutely authoritative over the individuals to whom they come... No authority emanates from them which should make it a duty for those who stand outside of them to accept their revelations uncritically."

32 Useful introductions to the treatment of authority in classical Indian philosophies are given in Saksena 1951 and Potter 1963, chap. 5. Among recent works, see Halbfass 1991, Mohanty 1992, and Matilal and Chakrabarti 1994.

33 *Nyāyabhāṣya* on *Nyāyasūtra,* 1.1.10.

34 The term that I here render as "enjoyable" *(bhogyam),* i.e., worthy of enjoyment, is glossed by the great Vedāntic philosopher Śaṅkara with the term *phalam,* "fruit, reward, end, goal." Radhakrishnan translates it as "good," but while I

concur that the term is valuational, I do not think that it is so decisive in its axiological implications as English *"the* good," or Greek *agathón,* or, for that matter, the Sanskrit *śreyas.* It certainly refers, however, to "goods" in a broad sense. See also Krishna 1991: 52–56.

35 Broad 1925: 487–91.

36 Broad 1925: 500–504.

37 Philip Quinn has called my attention to an objection here, namely, that there are many persons who value religious, political, or other ideals above freedom from death and suffering. Otherwise, he asks, why would there be martyrs? In response, I should stress that it's not exclusively one's own freedom from death and suffering that seems to be so highly valued, though that is often enough the case in ordinary life. Rather, what is valuable is freedom from death and suffering, whether it be one's own, or that of some particular group one particularly cares for (i.e., family, friends, allies, compatriots, correligionists, etc.), or that of all human beings, or that of all sentient beings. It seems to me at least plausible to hold that even a great many martyrs are motivated by some such values, else why the emphasis, in the diction of spiritual, political, and medical martyrs alike, on "liberation," "salvation," and "freedom"?

38 The skeptical, materialist, and determinist traditions, e.g., the Cārvāka, Lokāyata, and Ājīvaka, would have been among the dissenters here; but these were never so influential as the Brahmanical, Buddhist, and Jaina schools, all of which concur on this point. And in the case of the Cārvāka and Lokāyata, given their association with a type of hedonism, one might argue that the refined pursuit of pleasure *was* regarded as flowing from the value of freedom, although they held complete freedom from the flaws of saṃsāra to be an impossibility.

There have been many discussions of the notion and value of "freedom" in classical Indian thought. Particularly relevant here are Potter 1963, chaps. 1–4, who examines the relationship among freedom, self-knowledge, and philosophical speculation in India, and Bugault 1994, chap. 2, on suffering. Krishna 1991, chap. 3, argues that the emphasis on *mokṣa* in writing on Indian philosophy has been largely misplaced, and that its function in the classical literature is largely rhetorical. I am inclined to agree with him, at least to the extent of concurring that some correction is required. However, I believe that this must take the form, in large part, of an effort to examine the positive constitution of freedom through the culture of the self, somewhat along the lines I suggest in the introduction and in chapter 5. Cf. also Collins 1994, where selflessness is considered as part of a "process of self-cultivation" (78).

39 *Tattvasaṅgrahapañjikā,* pp. 6–7.

40 Kant 1927: 218–19.

41 For a thorough discussion, see Beck 1960: 265–71.

42 The most striking exception in the early literature has sometimes been taken to be this passage, from *Udāna,* p. 80 (Pali Text Society ed.): "There is, O monks, that which is unborn, unbecome, unmade, uncompounded. For, O monks, if there had not been what is unborn, unbecome, unmade, uncompounded, then

the passing beyond what is born, become, made, compounded, would not be known here. Wherefore, O monks, because there is what is unborn, unbecome, unmade, uncompounded, therefore is the passing beyond what is born, become, made and compounded known." It is not at all, clear, however, that the Pali text intends the verb *atthi* ("there is") to be read as an existential affirmation of a substratum.

43 *Nyāyatātparyaṭīkā,* p. 185.

44 See Halbfass 1988: 128–35, and *passim.* Nineteenth-century interest in the Upaniṣads owed much, as well, to the reflections of Arthur Schopenhauer, on whom see chap. 11 below.

45 Halbfass 1988, esp. 295–98, on K.C. Bhattacharya. Cf. also Murti 1960.

46 Cf. Deussen 1965: 45–50: "[The] three essential conditions of man's salvation—God, immortality, and freedom—are conceivable only if the universe is mere appearance and not reality (mere *māyā* and not the *ātman*), and they break down irretrievably should this empirical reality, wherein we live, be found to constitute the true essence of things."

3. Missing Persons: The Inapprehensible "I"

In this and the following chapter I wish to examine two complementary themes in Indian Buddhist philosophical thought: the absence of direct apprehension of a self *(ātmānupalabdhi),* and the synthetic cohesiveness of psychic life *(pratisaṃdhāna).* It is not my intention to attempt a thorough historical account of these notions and the arguments surrounding them. I have chosen instead to focus upon a small number of pertinent texts, in order to emphasize just what appears to have been at stake here philosophically. Among the opponents of Buddhist views on these matters, some attention will be given to the arguments of the Naiyāyikas, particularly Uddyotakara, in whose polemics certain philosophical objections to mainstream Buddhist scholastic assumptions are very sharply delineated.

The Beginnings of an Argument

It is clear that, even if we disregard the difficult questions surrounding the precise nature of early Buddhist doctrine, some of the most ancient among the scriptures attributed to the Buddha unmistakably call into question the notion that each one of us possesses a unique and persisting self.[1]

From these, from the conflicting interpretations of them that arose among the Buddha's followers in the generations following the founder's passing, and later from their disputes with the non-Buddhist schools of Indian thought, there evolved in scholastic circles a rich array of increasingly rigorous arguments all to support one conclusion: the "self" *(ātman)* or "person" *(pudgala),* conceived as an enduring entity that somehow individuates an otherwise fragmented continuum of mental and physical events, simply does not exist. Among the many arguments bearing upon this one point, it seems that Buddhist scholastic thought was forever dominated by two master arguments—twins, in fact, that shared a common origin and that achieved some measure of independence from one another only when Indian philosophical thought had begun to distinguish more or less systematically topics that Western philosophers would assign to the departments of "ontology" and "epistemology," respectively.[2]

An important statement of the problem we are considering is found in the *Saṃyuttanikāya* section of the Pali canon, where it is related that the nun Vajirā was once approached by Māra, evil personified, who intended to frighten her from the path to nirvāṇa. Māra sought to sow doubt and confusion in her mind with this puzzle:

> Who has fabricated this being?
> Where is the being's maker?
> Whence has the being arisen?
> Whither does the being cease to be?[3]

"Being" *(satta)* is here taken as referring to a stable, persisting entity that underlies the constant change of an individual's life. The term is used conventionally in Buddhist discourse to refer to any animate and conscious creature, human or animal, divine or demonic. In this instance, however, Māra speaks of a being in a "metaphysical," rather than in the conventional, sense. The good sister Vajirā, recognizing this, and recognizing too the emptiness of speculation about hypostatized "beings" above and beyond the ever-changing flow of things, rebukes him as follows:

> Do you think, O Māra, that there is a "being"?
> You're under the spell of views!
> This is purely a heap of conditions;
> No being is found here.
>
> Just as when there's an assemblage of parts,
> The word "chariot" comes to mind,
> In the same way, depending on the bundles *(khandha, skandha),*
> One speaks of a "being" conventionally.

These verses attributed to the nun Vajirā are among the canonical passages most frequently cited in the whole of later Buddhist philosophy; for we find condensed here as nowhere else the fundamental themes that are interwoven throughout the Buddhist inquiry into the reality of the self and the nature of persons.[4] Throughout these developments Vajirā's verses remained the epitome of the founder's teaching on the matter of the reality of the self. As will be seen in the appendix to this chapter, they remained a fundamental topic of reflection in later Tibetan scholastic traditions, fully two millennia after they were composed.

Here, I will be concerned initially with the claim made in the last line of the first verse of Vajirā's rejoinder, i.e., "No being is found here." This claim came to represent, in one form or another, a fundamental assumption made by Buddhist thinkers seeking to establish epistemological grounds for the denial of the existence of a substantial self; and hence it was also regarded as the fundamental Buddhist claim to be refuted by Brahmanical philosophers who desired to prove that there *is* such a self, and that, as the Upaniṣadic tradition affirmed, its being is known.

In Pali the line we are considering reads, *"nayidha sattūpalabbhati."* The crucial portion is the phrase *na... upalabbhati*, "is not found." In later Buddhist epistemology this was to become a technical expression, which, when it occurs, I will render, "is not (objectively) apprehended." There is no reason to suppose, however, that the phrase had yet acquired a technical sense during the early period in the formation of Buddhist doctrine represented by the *Saṃyuttanikāya*, and so the non-technical translation is to be preferred in the present context. Indeed, verbs meaning "to be found" are frequently used in Indic languages as synonyms for "to exist."[5] In Vajirā's usage, then, there is nothing whatever that precludes "is found" from being intended in an existential rather than epistemic sense, except for the general tendency for derivatives of *upa-labh* to be used with at least some epistemic connotation. Other occurrences of the same verb in other early passages in the Pali canon reinforce this conclusion.[6]

We must recall, though, that a closely similar phrase does occur at least once in a text usually thought to be pre-Buddhist, and there, strikingly, in much the same context. The passage in question occurs in the final chapter of the *Chāndogya Upaniṣad*, which we have examined in chapter 2. There, as we have seen, Indra and Virocana approach Prajāpati, the creator of all, to learn of the self *(ātman)*, knowledge of which will fulfill all desires. Prajāpati, testing their worthiness, explains that the self is none other than "the person seen in the eye," and, on being questioned further, goes on to assert that this very self is beheld when one looks into a mirror or a reflection in water. Delighted with this simple teaching, the two depart for their respective abodes. Indra, of course, was later to grow dissatisfied with

Prajāpati's initial, superficial teaching, and to return for a prolonged course of discipleship culminating in his receipt of the esoteric doctrine originally withheld. What is of interest in our present context, however, is Prajāpati's exclamation following the departure of his two foolish pupils: "Not having found the self, not having come to know it, they depart!" *(anupalabhyātmānam ananuvidya vrajataḥ).* The Sanskrit for "not having found the self" here parallels the Pali for "no being is found" in every respect: the same verb is used, in this case in an unambiguously epistemic sense; and the Sanskrit of the Upaniṣad speaks of a "self," whereas Vajirā's Pali uses "being." The difference in the manner in which the two phrases function in their respective contexts, however, could hardly be greater: Prajāpati's is a tragic exclamation, despairing for those who have missed the true path, while Vajirā's represents a confident refusal to blunder, tragically, onto the path of unwarranted speculation. It is here that the remarkable dichotomy between the speculative psychology of the Brahmanical tradition and its Buddhist rejection seems incontrovertible; and it is this dichotomy that stands at the heart of all later debate. Already in the Upaniṣadic literature the notion that the self was to be known in some special way, if it was to be known at all, was well established.[7] This is clearly stated in the *Kaṭha Upaniṣad,* which, though perhaps post-dating the beginnings of Buddhism, offers us another interesting example of the use of the verb *upa-labh* in connection with the self:

> It may not be obtained by speech, or mind, or eye.
> How is it found, except in the assertion "it is"?
>
> It is to be found both that "it is," and is of the nature of reality;
> When it is thus found that "it is," reality's nature shines clear.[8]

Curiously, however, even many Brahmanical philosophers were hesitant to affirm that this "finding" of the self spoken of in the Upaniṣads could be taken to consist in immediate acquaintance with the self, in anything like the sense in which "immediate acquaintance" *(pratyakṣa)* is conceived in other contexts; rather, they interpreted this "finding" as a sort of privileged occurrence, about which we ordinary folk know only through the authority of scripture.[9] This standpoint, however, was particularly resisted by the early Nyāya and Vaiśeṣika schools. Vātsyāyana (fourth or fifth century C.E.), for instance, begins his discussion of our knowledge of the existence of the self by saying:

> [Among the substances] the self is not grasped through direct acquaintance. But then is it established only through received scripture? No; for it is to be established through inference.[10]

Later commentators, though, were hard-pressed to reinterpret this to accord with their own assertions that we are all immediately acquainted with the self, in a sense that involves no equivocation between ordinary and extraordinary uses of "immediate acquaintance."[11] We shall return to this point in our discussion of Uddyotakara below.

The "Personalist" Controversy

From its first promulgation, the Buddhist teaching of selflessness was not just troubling to ignorant laymen alone. Even during the Buddha's lifetime, the suttas tell us, the more deluded among the master's disciples failed to grasp this subtle point, which occasioned much confusion among them. It comes as little surprise, then, that even within the Buddhist fold the non-self teaching became a ground for dissension, and that the earliest detailed Buddhist scholastic debates of which we now have record are concerned in large measure with rebuking a rebellious Buddhist school that affirmed the reality of a persisting basis for individuation, which they called the "person" (Pali, *puggala*, Skt., *pudgala*). It will not be our concern here to attempt a reconstruction of the doctrines of these Buddhist philosophical renegades, called the Personalists (Pali, *puggalavādin*, Skt. *pudgalavādin*).[12] Rather, we will focus instead on a single issue that appears to have some importance for later Buddhist reflections on the self overall, namely, the role played by the idea of "finding the person" in the extant records. In this section, I will limit my analysis to certain features of the debate on the "person" as it appears in the *Kathāvatthu*, which records the controversy from the perspective of the Theravāda school of Buddhism.[13]

My discussion will raise some questions regarding the logical form of the *Kathāvatthu*'s arguments. Properly speaking, these might better belong in a work on the early history of Indian logic, but because I believe that the discussion of the *Kathāvatthu*'s logic, as it has been conducted so far,[14] has obscured rather than clarified questions of philosophical content even while illuminating the text's formal features, I will attempt to provide an improved analysis of certain dimensions of the arguments in question here.

The *Kathāvatthu* opens as follows, with an adherent of the Theravāda *(Th.)* posing the initial question and the Personalist *(P.)* responding:

Th. "Is the person found truly and ultimately?"
(1a) *P.* "Yes, it is."
Th. "Is the person found truly and ultimately, just as what is true and ultimate?"
(1b) *P.* "That may not be said."
Th. "Acknowledge the refutation:
(2) "If the person is found truly and ultimately, then indeed it must be said that the person is found truly and ultimately, just as what is true and ultimate.
(3) "What you have said, namely that it must be said that the person is found truly and ultimately, but not that the person is found truly and ultimately, just as what is true and ultimate, is false.
(4) "If one must not say that the person is found truly and ultimately, just as what is true and ultimate, then one must not say that the person is found truly and ultimately.
(5) "What you have said, namely that it must be said that the person is found truly and ultimately, but not that the person is found truly and ultimately, just as what is true and ultimate, is false."[15]

Buddhaghosa (fl. c. 400–450 C.E.), the greatest scholastic commentator of the Theravāda tradition, tells us that "is found" is here to be taken to mean "is apprehended having been approached by discernment; is known."[16] And "truly and ultimately" tells us that the object thus found is genuine, unlike a mirage or illusion, and not merely affirmed through hearsay. However, I wonder whether Buddhaghosa, in defining "is found" in this way, was not reflecting the pronouncedly epistemological interests of his own era; for the text does not seem to require that "is found" be used in anything other than the more or less neutral sense (with respect to its epistemic and existential connotations) that it had in Vajirā's verses.

Concerning the form of the argument itself, much recent scholarship has interpreted the *Kathāvatthu* as representing a sort of propositional calculus.[17] Certainly some features of the *Kathāvatthu's* argumentation may be elucidated in this way. Thus, substituting p for "the person is found truly and ultimately" (the proposition affirmed in 1a above) and q for "the person is found truly and ultimately, just as what is true and ultimate" (the proposition denied in 1b), we can symbolize the foregoing argument as follows. (To save words and to clarify the issue, I will say "the person is found ultimately" instead of "the person is found truly and ultimately," and "it is found to be ultimately real" in place of "the person is found truly and ultimately, just as what is true and ultimate.")

(1) The person is found ultimately, *but* it is *not* found to be ultimately real.

$p \cdot {\sim}q$ ASSUMPTION (CONJUNCTION OF 1A AND 1B ABOVE)

(2) *If* the person is found ultimately, *then* it is found to be ultimately real.

$p \supset q$ ASSUMPTION

(3) *Therefore, it is false that:* the person is found ultimately, *but* it is *not* found to be ultimately real.

$\therefore {\sim}(p \cdot {\sim}q)$ FROM (2) BY DE MORGAN'S LAW

(4) *If* the person is *not* found to be ultimately real, *then* it is *not* found ultimately.

${\sim}q \supset {\sim}p$ FROM (2) BY CONTRAPOSITION

(5) *Therefore, it is false that:* the person is found ultimately, *but* it is *not* found to be ultimately real.

$\therefore {\sim}(p \cdot {\sim}q)$ FROM (4) BY DE MORGAN'S LAW

What we have here, then, is apparently a valid test for logical consistency: the conjunction of the opponent's assumptions (here premise (1)) is shown to be inconsistent with step (3), derived from the second assumption (2). To verify this conclusion, it is derived once again (5) from the contrapositive form of the same assumption (4).[18] Because premise (2) is taken (by the Theravāda proponent, at least) to be incontrovertible, the argument shows, by *reductio ad absurdum,* that premise (1) must be abandoned. The propositional calculus nicely serves the purpose of demonstrating that the test is indeed a valid one in this case. There is, however, a problem: on this reading both the present argument, which the commentator says is good, and the following argument, which he will declare to be bad, are shown to be equally valid tests for consistency, and we have no way of distinguishing between them on formal grounds alone; but there must be *some* way of distinguishing between them since, unless Buddhaghosa was a very bad logician with shamelessly partisan intentions, there should be some difference between the good argument and the bad. To clarify the problem, then, let us turn now to examine the "bad" argument that the Personalists put forward in their attempt to overturn the "good" argument just presented:

P. "Is the person not found truly and ultimately?"

(1a) *Th.* "No, it is not."

P. "Is the person not found truly and ultimately, just as what is true and ultimate?"

(1b) *Th.* "That may not be said."

P. "Acknowledge the refutation:

(2) "If the person is not found truly and ultimately, then indeed it must be said that the person is not found truly and ultimately, just as what is true and ultimate.

(3) "What you have said, namely that it must be said that the person is not found truly and ultimately, but not that the person is not found truly and ultimately, just as what is true and ultimate, is false.

(4) "If one must not say that the person is not found truly and ultimately, just as what is true and ultimate, then one must not say that the person is not found truly and ultimately.

(5) "What you have said, namely that it must be said that the person is not found truly and ultimately, but not that the person is not found truly and ultimately, just as what is true and ultimate, is false."[19]

Those who have interpreted the *Kathāvatthu* logic to be a propositional calculus have read this argument as follows:

(1) The person is *not* found ultimately, *but it is not the case that* it is *not* found to be ultimately real.

$\sim p \cdot \sim\sim q$ ASSUMPTION (CONJUNCTION OF IA AND IB ABOVE)

(2) *If* the person is *not* found ultimately, *then* it is *not* found to be ultimately real.

$\sim p \supset \sim q$ ASSUMPTION

(3) *Therefore, it is false that:* the person is not found ultimately, *but it is not the case that* it is *not* found to be ultimately real.

$\therefore \sim(\sim p \cdot \sim\sim q)$ FROM (2) BY DE MORGAN'S LAW

(4) *If it is not the case that* the person is *not* found to be ultimately real, *then it is not the case that* it is *not* found ultimately.

$\sim\sim q \supset \sim\sim p$ FROM (2) BY CONTRAPOSITION

(5) *Therefore, it is false that:* the person is *not* found ultimately, *but it is not the case that* it is *not* found to be ultimately real.

$\therefore \sim(\sim p \cdot \sim\sim q)$ FROM (4) BY DE MORGAN'S LAW

The "bad" argument, then, is no less valid when taken as a test for consistency than is the "good" one. How, according to this account, are we to differentiate satisfactorily between the two?[20] To find a solution, I think that we must break into the propositions themselves and search for our answer among their parts. I limit myself here to a consideration of the first two exchanges in the *Kathāvatthu*'s critique of the Personalists, which are the ones we have just surveyed above. I believe that once we have found an adequate solution to the problems raised here, it will be possible to develop analogous solutions to the problems raised by the various exchanges that occur in subsequent passages in the *Kathāvatthu* (which I will not, however, take up at this juncture).

The question we are trying to answer is this: in virtue of what is it affirmed as true that "if the person is found truly and ultimately, then the person is found truly and ultimately, just as what is true and ultimate" ($p \supset q$), but denied as sophistical and false that "if the person is not found truly and ultimately, then the person is not found truly and ultimately, just as what is true and ultimate" ($\sim p \supset \sim q$)?

Let us begin by noting that one element in these complex propositions is repeated twice in each one, affirmatively in the first, and negatively in the second, namely, "the person is found truly and ultimately." To simplify it somewhat, we represent this with the symbolic expression "*Fa*," where "*F*" = "is found truly and ultimately" and "*a*" = "the person." Then, the negative proposition—"the person is not found truly and ultimately"—may be represented by the expression "$\sim Fa$."

To resolve the phrase "just as what is true and ultimate" I suggest, on the basis of the commentarial tradition, that we take this to be elliptical for "just as whatever belongs to the fifty-seven categories is found truly and ultimately."[21] The "fifty-seven categories" represent the complete list of real entities affirmed by the authors of the *Kathāvatthu.* The details of that list, which involve many redundancies, need not concern us here, except to note that, in accord with the lists formulated by the mainstream abhidharma schools, such things as "person," "soul," "self," and "being" are never included therein.[22] The important point to note here is that whatever belongs to the list of categories is something that is assumed *to exist.* Symbolizing the phrase "belongs to the fifty-seven categories" with the letter *"B,"* we can proceed to represent the proposition "the person is found truly and ultimately, just as what is true and ultimate," in short as "$Fa \supset Ba$"; that is to say, "if the person is found ultimately, then it belongs to the fifty-seven categories." This formulation, however, does not yet make explicit the existential assumption that is involved here. That assumption can be clarified by interpreting "the person is found truly and ultimately, just as what is true and ultimate" as an instance of the general principle, to which the Theravāda adheres, that *whatever is found ultimately belongs to the fifty-seven categories and thus really exists.* This may be expressed symbolically in this way: $x(Fx \supset \exists x(Bx))$. That is to say, "for all *x,* if *x* is found ultimately, then *there exists* some *x* that belongs to the fifty-seven categories."

I am assuming, therefore, that there must be a strict relationship between the expression *"Fa"* and any other expression predicated by *"F,"* such that any equivocation in the meaning of *"F"* is precluded. The upshot of this is that to say that "the person is found, etc." implies its membership in the categories—an implication that all schools of early Buddhist scholasticism regarded as anathematic, insomuch as it amounts to asserting that the person *really exists,* either as an ephemeral constituent of the *skandhas,* or perhaps as an unconditioned entity beyond the psycho-physical constituents. (This latter alternative recalls the substantial self of the Brahmanical pluralist schools.) Because the Personalists, as Buddhists, joined the Theravāda in seeking to avoid affirming either of these alternatives, the first argument from the *Kathāvatthu* does succeed in revealing an inconsistency in their position; for it shows that one cannot hold both that the person "is found," and at the same time that it is not something really existing.

But what of the second "bad" argument? Does the Personalist there succeed in his effort to demonstrate an inconsistency in the Theravāda position? To see what is at stake here, consider again the representation of "the person is found truly and ultimately, just as what is true and ultimate," as an instance of the principle expressed by the formula $x(Fx \supset \exists x(Bx))$. In other words, $Fa \supset \exists a(Ba)$, "if the person is found ultimately, then *there exists* a person that belongs to the fifty-seven categories."

Now, what would be the analogue in the case of the relevant sentence from the second argument, "the person not found truly and ultimately, just as what is true and ultimate"? Given what has already been said, it would be most natural to take it as saying, $\sim Fa \supset \sim\exists a(Ba)$; that is, "if the person is *not* found ultimately, then *there does not exist* a person that belongs to the fifty-seven categories." This would seem to be, from the Theravāda perspective, quite unobjectionable.

As we have seen above, however, the existential commitment required clarification in the course of our formalization of the argument. This suggests that there may be an important ambiguity in the Pali text; specifically, an ambiguity in the precise force of the particle of negation. For there is nothing in Pali grammar that necessitates our placing the negative sign in the consequent—$\sim\exists a(Ba)$ "*there does not exist* a person that belongs..."—just as we have. It may also be read in this way: $\exists a(\sim Ba)$, that is, "*there does exist* a person, but it does not belong..." What the Personalist wishes the Theravāda to affirm, and what the latter refuses to affirm, then, is this: $\sim Fa \supset \exists a(\sim Ba)$; that is, "if the person is *not* found ultimately, then *there does exist* a person, but one that does not belong to the fifty-seven categories." I think that it will be plain enough that this has some very undesirable implications indeed; for given the affirmation of the antecedent, with which all parties to the debate concur, the existence of the person must then follow. *Not* finding the person would in this way *entail* its existence.[23]

The argument of the *Kathāvatthu* thus remains essentially a test for consistency within the Buddhist tradition, but a test which involves not only the application of the rules of a rudimentary propositional calculus, but additionally the application of principles derived from the common acceptance of a specific categorical scheme. What's "bad" about the Personalist's argument is not the "sophistical" manipulation of the rules of the calculus, but rather that it violates the fundamental principle that holds that "finding" (in the relevant sense) implies *real being*. The realist schools of brahmanical Hinduism, which simply did not accept the early Buddhist categorical system, were therefore not directly challenged by arguments like these; for the self which they posited was *ex hypothesi* a real being outside the Buddhist categories. When the debate broadened beyond Buddhist circles, a broadening which appears to have occurred during the early centuries

C.E., Buddhist philosophers were therefore required to refashion their arguments in order to refute thinkers who refused to accept the fundamental categorical framework within which Buddhist philosophy had so far developed.

Milinda's Chariot

An early example of a Buddhist text that attempts to rework the arguments of the *Kathāvatthu,* without explicitly presupposing all and only its categories, is the *Milindapañha (Questions of King Milinda),* redacted in about the first century C.E.[24] Interestingly, the *Milindapañha* does not attempt a refutation of any of the particular brahmanical soul-theories, but addresses itself instead to the unanalyzed belief in a persisting self harbored by an ordinary individual, a non-philosopher. The individual in question is here the historical Graeco-Bactrian king Menander (reigned c. 150 B.C.E.),[25] but though it is certain that this figure was indeed a patron of Buddhism, it is now impossible to determine what, if any, historical value the *Milindapañha* might have. The text is in any case constructed as a series of dialogues between the king and the learned and saintly Buddhist monk Nāgasena. Their first discussion begins with the king's courteous inquiry: "How, reverend, are you addressed? What is your name?"[26] Nāgasena's response might well have led his royal questioner to affirm Russell's quip, that in philosophizing we start with common sense but end with what is frankly unbelievable:

> "I am addressed, my lord, as 'Nāgasena,' and 'Nāgasena,' my lord, is what my correligionists ordinarily call me. What's more, though parents assign such names as 'Nāgasena,' or 'Sūrasena,' or 'Vīrasena,' or 'Sīhasena,' indeed, my lord, this 'Nāgasena' is a designation, an appellation, a conceptual construct, a convention, a mere name. For here no person is apprehended."

This last sentence is by now familiar to us. We should note only that "person" is perhaps intended more generally here than it was in the *Kathāvatthu,* where it referred to a particular entity posited by the Personalist school; in the present text, it may refer to any stand-in for the concept of a persisting self. Milinda is, understandably, surprised by Nāgasena's assertion, and proceeds with his interrogation:

> "If, good monk Nāgasena, no person is apprehended, then who is it who gives you [the donations which you receive as a Buddhist monk]? Who uses those things? Who practices disciplined conduct? Who enters into contemplation? Who discloses nirvāṇa, which is the fruit of the path?... If, good monk Nāgasena, one were to slay you, his would not be the crime of murder. And you, good monk Nāgasena, have no master, no preceptor, and hence no ordination."

Milinda is attempting to show, in other words, that various absurdities follow from taking Nāgasena at his word; the denial of there being persons cannot be made to cohere with our notions of agency, or of persons as objects of action. But Milinda does not stop at this; significantly, he proceeds to elaborate a genuine *reductio* argument, an argument which he fashions using some elements from the scholastic categorical schema, but mixed here with details from an anatomical inventory that, while occurring in early Buddhist meditation manuals, is not normally spelled out in the scholastic lists of the categories.[27] Thus, Milinda asks Nāgasena whether Nāgasena is to be identified with the hair, or with the nails, etc., and, after running out of anatomical parts, lists cursorily the five *skandhas* of physical form, sensation, conceptualization, motivation, and consciousness. Being told that Nāgasena is none of these things, he asks if Nāgasena is to be identified with their totality, or with something altogether different, and again receives negative responses. Similarly, he is rebuked when he attempts to identify Nāgasena with the word "Nāgasena." From all of this he then concludes: "Who then is this Nāgasena?...There is no Nāgasena" *(ko pan' ettha Nāgaseno?...natthi Nāgaseno).* And it is here, of course, that we find ourselves confronting a formal contradiction; for, now, Nāgasena *both* is *and* is not.

Nāgasena's response to his royal assailant develops one of the most poetic of ancient philosophical metaphors, which was known in one version or another to both the Greek and the Indian traditions, and which we have encountered already in Vajirā's verses. It is the metaphor which compares man and chariot, found early on in Parmenides and in the *Kaṭhopaniṣad,* and later beautifully expressed in Plato's *Phaedrus.*[28] In these and many other Indian and Hellenic works, the chariot always carries a passenger, but in Vajirā's version and the one we have here there's a difference: we are concerned only with the chariot and its parts; horses and driver are not considered.

In chapter 7, I provide a more detailed analysis of the mereological assumptions that may be derived from Nāgasena's version of the chariot metaphor. Here I confine my remarks to those aspects of the metaphor that bear upon Nāgasena's conception of the self. Questioning Milinda, Nāgasena establishes that: (i) the chariot is not any one of its parts, (ii) the chariot is not simply the aggregation of all the parts (i.e., it is not a "mere sum"), and (iii) the chariot is not something above and beyond the parts. What is it then? When Milinda finally gets Nāgasena's point, he expresses it thus:

> "It is depending on the axle, the wheels, the chassis, and the pole, that there is this designation, appellation, conceptual construct, convention, mere name, i.e., 'chariot.'"

What is intended here, as we have seen, is a doctrine similar to the one that some contemporary philosophers have called "logical constructivism"; that is, the view that some apparent entities are in fact reducible to complexes of more primitive entities, and so need not be granted any position whatsoever in a fundamental ontology. Such an ontology would ideally provide an inventory of only irreducible primitives, an ontology rather like the early Buddhist categorical system we have referred to above. The author of the *Milindapañha,* while endeavoring to generalize some aspects of the arguments of the earlier tradition so as to illustrate their application to questions defined more broadly than they had been in the context of Buddhist intrasystemic scholastic debate, nonetheless is still philosophizing within the confines of that tradition. Nāgasena summarizes the argument as follows:

> "Very good, my lord! You understand the chariot. Just so, it is depending on hair [and other physical parts], and [the five skandhas of] physical form, sensation, conceptualization, motivation, and consciousness, that the designation, appellation, conceptual construct, convention, mere name 'Nāgasena' applies to me. In an absolute sense *(paramaṭṭhato),* no person is apprehended."

And he completes his summation by quoting the nun Vajirā's verse about the chariot.

How does this "proto-logical constructivism" bear upon the contradiction—Nāgasena must be and yet is not—that seemed to flow from Milinda's *reductio* argument? For this is precisely the sort of passage that has often given rise to the impression among Western philosophers that Buddhism ignores the basic laws of thought, especially the laws of contradiction and of the excluded middle. Nāgasena's use of the phrase "in an absolute sense" suggests that he has in mind the metalinguistic solution to this problem that plays a prominent role in later Buddhist thought.[29]

Certainly, one does not want to say, "Nāgasena does not exist," *simpliciter*. But we can say that "Nāgasena, whatever else he may be, is not a primitive in our fundamental ontology; he is a logical construct." In other words, the logical constructivist may be taken as urging that the verb "exists," as it occurs in ordinary speech, can be interpreted in at least two importantly different ways: "exists as a primitive" ("exists^{p}"), which is predicated only of the *irreducible* primitives of the fundamental ontology; and "exists as a construct" ("exists^{c}"), which is predicated of all those things that are *reducible* to the primitives of the fundamental ontology, but are not themselves to be admitted among those primitives. We may say that, in Buddhist scholastic terms, "exists^{p}" is predicated of whatever exists in an absolute sense, while "exists^{c}" is predicated of whatever exists at the level of conventional reality. Returning to Milinda's *reductio* argument, we see now that Milinda's questions, couched in everyday speech, equivocates between these two predicates. His argument is defective in the sense that it obscures a crucial distinction that must be made in the very concept of being. Milinda's error, then, is that, as Nāgasena sees it, he wishes to make a logical passage from "exists^{c}" to "exists^{p}," a passage that is wholly unwarranted. The *Milindapañha*, therefore, though simplifying the *Kathāvatthu*'s more formal argumentation, appears at the same time to suggest a significant refinement of it.

The Epistemological Argument of Vasubandhu

Based on what we have seen so far, the main Buddhist argument in favor of the *anātma* doctrine is one that has its roots in the early antiquity of the Buddhist teaching. Its central point is that the self is never apprehended; indeed, this is one of the main features of Buddhist thought that has led not just a few modern interpreters to suggest that there is some similarity here with the philosophy of David Hume.[30] This notion of not apprehending the self had its origins in part in the practice of systematic contemplative introspection, in which the meditator was to undertake a methodical search for the self by conducting an inventory of the physical, sensorial, and psychological elements of which he or she is constituted. Repeated failure to find something corresponding to a concrete self eventually catalyzes the insight that there is no such thing. Such meditational practices, interpreted by the scholastic philosophers of the abhidharma schools, reinforced the tendency to formulate comprehensive lists of *dharmas,* irreducible principles that constitute the impersonal building-blocks of reality.[31]

None of the arguments we have examined so far requires that we carefully disambiguate the use of the verb *upa-labh,* "to find, apprehend"—as we have seen, it may be taken in both epistemic and existential senses. Nonetheless, the arguments from the *Kathāvatthu* which we examined above betrayed a distinct tendency to make a logical passage from the act of *apprehension* to the apprehension of *being:* to find some *x* entails its membership among the categories of irreducible, primitive dharmas. At the same time, the argument of the *Milindapañha* underscored a distinction between two orders of existence, the "absolute" existence of the irreducible principles and the "conventional," or "relative" existence of whatever is conceptually constructed on the basis of their aggregation.

In this and the following section I wish to illustrate the manner in which the original argument about finding the self, with its attendant ambiguities, gave way to two separate arguments, one epistemological and the other ontological, concerning the reality of the self. These developments took place during a period (c. 150–400 C.E.) of very rapid advancement of philosophical method in India, a development whose historical background remains in some respects obscure.[32] Some have argued that, just before the beginning of this period, Indian thought made a quantum leap that cannot be explained without positing some transmission of philosophical knowledge from beyond India, namely, from the Hellenistic world.[33] Nevertheless, I do not think that this was at all the case with respect to the arguments we are here considering, whose refinement is perhaps better explained by the influence of developments in Indian linguistics.[34] Even if it could be reasonably established that some philosophical exchange took place between greater Greece and India (and certainly we cannot rule out this possibility), such exchange seems not to have been an essential element in the development of Indian philosophy overall.

The epistemological version of the argument against the reality of the substantial self is known primarily from the work of Vasubandhu, who writes:

> How is it known that this designation "self" applies to the bundle-continuum alone, and not to some other designatum?
>
> Because there is neither acquaintance with nor inference of [the posited self]: Thus, whatever things there are are apprehended by acquaintance whenever there is no obstruction. So, for example, the six objects and the intellect. On the other hand, [they may be apprehended] inferentially, as are the five sense faculties. In that case this is the inference: There being [some] cause, the absence of an effect is noted in the absence of some other cause, and in the presence [of that additional cause] the presence [of the effect in question is noted]. So it is, for instance, in the case of a shoot. Now, [in the case of the inference that establishes the sense faculties], there is a manifest object and a cause [that contributes to the perception of that object, namely] the attention [of the subject directed upon it]. But the apprehension of the object may be absent or, again, present. For instance, [it is absent] among the blind, deaf, etc., and [it is present] among those who are not blind, not deaf, etc. Hence, in that case, the absence or presence of another cause is ascertained. And that which is that other cause is the sense faculty. That is the inference [in the case of the sense faculties]. But because there are no such [perceptions or inferences] of the self, [it follows that] there is no self.[35]

To begin to interpret this, Vasubandhu's argument may first be restated as an obviously valid syllogism:

> (1) If there were a self, then it would be known either by immediate acquaintance or by inference (there being, in Vasubandhu's view, no other valid sources of knowledge).
> (2) But, it is not known either by immediate acquaintance or inference.
> (3) Therefore, there is no self.[36]

There seem to be two main approaches one might adopt in seeking to challenge this. First, one might declare that there is a self, but that it is not such that it can be known. But where would that leave the substance theorist? How can an unknowable self be invoked to explain any of the known facts of our existence, such as apparent identity through time? As Terence Penelhum says, referring to Locke's doctrine of unknowable spiritual substance, "The difficulty with this is that it leaves the doctrine of substance without any connection to those entities whose unity it was supposed to explain."[37]

The second approach involves attempting to demonstrate that Vasubandhu errs in his second premise, and that the self *is* known through either immediate acquaintance or inference. Concerning, then, the first conjunct, "the self is not known through immediate acquaintance": Vasubandhu's condition that the objects of immediate acquaintance be "unobstructed" *(asaty antarāye)* seems to amount to his maintaining that they are directly evident to the perceiver. The "six objects" are the objects of the five physical senses and those of mental states; and "intellect" refers to the perceiving subject (here taken to be an instantaneous event, not an enduring self). Vasubandhu's account is neutral with respect to the questions separating direct realists, representational realists, and phenomenalists: "objects" *(viṣaya),* here, may be taken equally to refer to the things themselves, representations of those things, or sense-data, depending on one's epistemological stance.

Now, it does seem to me that Vasubandhu is unquestionably correct to assert that the self is not one of the six objects: it most certainly is not a sensory object, and, when I think of the self, the fact that my intentional object is the self does not entail the real *being of self,* but only that of a *concept of self.* More controversial would be Vasubandhu's claim that the direct acquaintance of a state of consciousness with itself as subject is not direct acquaintance with the self. This claim has been challenged at length by such thinkers within the Indian tradition as Uddyotakara and Udayana, and in the West by, among others, Leibniz, Reid, Brentano, and, recently, Chisholm.[38] I rather doubt that Vasubandhu had developed all the epistemological and psychological tools needed to answer satisfactorily the challenges put forth by such philosophers, and I will consider below one of the most influential of the objections articulated in India, that of Uddyotakara. For the moment, however, let us recall that Vasubandhu's primary claim here—that the self is not an object of immediate acquaintance—would not have been affirmed by Buddhists alone, but was equally maintained by the early thinkers of the Nyāya-Vaiśeṣika tradition. In any case, Vasubandhu would certainly have held that, while every state of consciousness may well contain a reference to self, this phenomenon is merely a manifestation of the reflexivity of consciousness, and, thus, each such "self" referred to is discrete from every other.[39] For the moment, I will leave this issue to one side with the remark that it seems to me that Vasubandhu is not obviously wrong on this point: my *sense of self* is far from sufficient to confirm me in the belief that there is *a persisting, substantial self.*

The second conjunct of Vasubandhu's second premise is the assertion that the self is not known by means of an inference. The example given by Vasubandhu is of an inductive inference of a causal relationship. In fact, there is noteworthy agreement between Vasubandhu's form of induction and Mill's "method of difference":

> If an instance in which the phenomenon under investigation occurs, and an instance in which it does not occur, have every circumstance in common save one, that one occurring in the former; the circumstance in which alone the two instances differ, is the effect, or the cause, or an indispensible part of the cause, of the phenomenon.[40]

However, while this may appropriately characterize Vasubandhu's exemplum, the seed-and-shoot argument (where the prior presence or absence of a seed is ostensively correlated with the subsequent presence or absence of the shoot), it is less certain that it can be taken as a description of the argument from the functioning of the senses to the faculties thereof. (In this case, the "faculties," of course, are not to be taken as the externally visible sensory organs—a blind man, after all, may have what appear to be perfectly ordinary eyes—but rather the invisible, sensitive powers of the organs in question.) Nor does it apply to the argument which his opponents, one guesses, might advance in support of the substance theory of the self. For in these two cases, the inferred cause is not to be found among the observed phenomena under investigation at all. It seems to me, then, that Vasubandhu wished to assert something more. To see what that may have been, let us consider Brentano's statement concerning conditions that must be fulfilled by a causal argument for unconscious mental states:

> In order to be able to draw any conclusion concerning an unconscious mental phenomenon as a cause, from a fact which is supposed to be its effect, it is necessary, first of all, that the fact itself be sufficiently established. This is the first condition...
>
> There is a further condition, namely, that, on the hypothesis of a mental phenomenon of which we are not conscious, the fact of experience can really be explained as an effect brought about by a corresponding cause...

> Finally, a third condition for the validity of the conclusion concerning unconscious mental phenomena as the cause of certain empirical facts would consist in the proof that the phenomena under discussion cannot be understood, at least without the greatest improbability, on the basis of other hypotheses.[41]

In the later passages of his treatise, Vasubandhu takes up some of the phenomena—memory, rebirth, reference to seemingly persistent subjects, and so on—that had been variously claimed as explicable only on the supposition that there exists a substantial self. In each case, he seeks to show either that the phenomenon concerned is not as it is purported to be, or that the supposed self cannot explain it in any case, or that there are alternative explanatory hypotheses that are adequate to the task. Thus, Vasubandhu's argument here appears to be that the weakest acceptable inferential argument in favor of the existence of the self would be an inductive inference to the effect that there must be some cause *x* for a particular empirical effect, and that the only reasonable candidate for cause *x*, even if merely hypothetical, is a substantial self. Such an argument, we must note, could hardly be construed as constituting certain proof that there exists a substantial self, but only as providing reasonable grounds for belief in the existence of the self. In the absence of such, or of any stronger inferential argument, we simply cannot assert there to be even reasonable ground for belief in the self. This, I think, is the real thrust of Vasubandhu's argument.

Uddyotakara on Direct Acquaintance with the Self

Vasubandhu's was not the only argument advanced by Buddhist philosophers seeking to refute the substance theory of the self. Nonetheless, his *Treatise on the Negation of the Person* was among the most influential discussions of this topic. The epistemological argument of Vasubandhu, we have seen, cannot be construed as an apodictic proof of the falsehood of the substance theory; at best, it provides us with grounds for reasonably doubting the veracity of that theory. Of course, such doubt may in some individuals become strong enough to give rise to *non-apodictic* certainty,[42] that is, the sort of certainty experienced by one who, for instance, having searched every nook and cranny to find a missing pair of eyeglasses, concludes in exasperation that "they're certainly gone." Psychologically, at least, such certainty is often just as good as the kind experienced by one who's just solved and double-checked an elementary algebraic equation. Vasubandhu's argument, then, may produce in some a very high degree of conviction. (An analogous conclusion, as will be shown below, applies to Candrakīrti's "ontological" argument.) Nevertheless, some philosophers might assert that in Vasubandhu's case the argument never really gets off the ground, because his assumption that the reality of the self is neither known inferentially nor through direct acquaintance is simply false. In this section we will focus upon the objections of one such philosopher, the acute polemicist of the old Nyāya school, Uddyotakara (c. 600 C.E.). Though Uddyotakara objects both to the assumption that the self is not known inferentially and to the assumption that it is not known through direct acquaintance, our comments in this chapter will be restricted by and large to an examination of his views on direct acquaintance with the self, which, as we shall see, are in certain respects closely tied to his views on first-person reference.[43]

It was one of Uddyotakara's tenets that to deny the reality of the self entails a self-contradiction. This follows from his doctrine of genuine referring terms, which was summarized in the first chapter. Uddyotakara's notion of the self, like Anselm's of God, is one that analytically includes the concept of being. The argument about the self, he holds, is not about whether there is or is not such a thing, but about its nature: is it the body or a part thereof? a mental event? or a substance of the sort Nyāya-Vaiśeṣika philosophers had traditionally affirmed it to be? Even a materialist, who holds that the body is the self, cannot deny the self's reality; for that would be equivalent to a denial of the body's reality, and hence to the materialist's denial of his own thesis.[44]

In effect, then, Uddyotakara is maintaining that the proposition "the self exists" is tautologically true, in that the concept of "self" includes the concept of being in its analysis. But it should be clear that this affirmation of the reality of the self is ad hoc: Candrakīrti's argument (with which, I am quite certain, Uddyotakara was not familiar) will underscore that unless we are prepared to hold that the self is to be uniquely identified with this or that specific thing, or is to be related to our experience in this or that specific way, it becomes uncertain just what is to be gained by positing its real existence. Hence, Uddyotakara's argument on this point might be taken by his critic not as a demonstration of the substantial reality of the self, but rather as an indication that something has gone seriously awry with his theory of reference!

Nevertheless, when Uddyotakara introduces his notion of direct acquaintance with the self, he does not actually presuppose the foregoing argument, which holds the reality of the self to be entailed by its very concept. He writes:

> The consciousness of "I," which conforms to the distinctions of the nature of the object, and which does not depend upon memory of marks, the possessor of the marks, and their relationship, is direct acquaintance just as is the cognition of physical form. Concerning what you yourself, with perfect confidence, establish to be direct acquaintance, in virtue of what is it that it is [said to be] direct acquaintance? You must establish it as being consciousness alone, which does not depend upon the relationships among marks, etc., and which is self-presenting. So then you think there to be an I-cognition, but that its object is not the self? Well, then show us its object![45]

Uddyotakara's main point is thus that the knowledge of one's own being, as given in every conscious act of the form "I am F," is non-inferential, and that such acts are self-presenting acts, in which the self that is presented *is* the persisting and substantial self. Conscious awareness of the self, according to Uddyotakara, is given in every self-referring mental event—it is not inferred on the basis of marks or signs, warranting the knowledge of the self in the manner that smoke may be taken as a mark that warrants the conclusion that fire is present. Uddyotakara's argument, therefore, bears a noteworthy resemblance to Descartes's celebrated *cogito*-argument.

In our discussion of Vasubandhu's epistemological argument above, we have seen that, in so far as a subject is given in acts of awareness, some Buddhist philosophers were in fact in agreement with Uddyotakara's key assumption concerning the givenness of self-reference. But, from the Buddhist perspective, the subject so given is none other than the momentary act of awareness itself, and not a persisting, substantial subject as conceived by the Brahmanical philosophers. As Śāntarakṣita remarks, if *that* were directly evident to us then none of this debate would have arisen.[46] The view of the subject with which he opposes the Nyāya philosophers will be among our concerns in the chapters that follow.

Candrakīrti's Sevenfold Revolution of the Chariot

In the first section above ("The Beginnings of an Argument"), I referred to two broad types of argument—epistemological and ontological—that were elaborated on the basis of Sister Vajirā's verses (or similar early formulations) on the impossibility of finding the self. The argument that I am calling *epistemological* was, as we have seen, given clear formulation in the writings of Vasubandhu. The *ontological* argument, however, came to characterize the Mādhyamika tradition stemming from Nāgārjuna (c. second century).

Nāgārjuna's is perhaps the most celebrated name in Indian Buddhist philosophy, and the Mādhyamika teaching associated with him is often regarded as a radical break with earlier Buddhist thought.[47] Nevertheless, much of Nāgārjuna's work can be seen as continuous with the Buddhist scholastic tradition that preceded him—there is no "quantum leap" we need posit in order to explain the appearance in India during the second century C.E. of this master of dialectic. This is not to say that Nāgārjuna's ingenuity was less than we might have thought otherwise, but only that Nāgārjuna, like brilliant thinkers everywhere and at all times, did not just appear in a vacuum; he, like others, consolidated, developed, and transformed a pre-existing tradition. However, it must be granted that Nāgārjuna was responsible for initiating an important paradigm shift within Buddhist philosophical circles—one that would henceforth influence Buddhist thought in a great many areas. In connection with our present subject matter, this shift involved a reinterpretation of the self/non-self controversy so that this was to be regarded henceforth as an instance of a more general problem about concepts of substantial existence, or, to put it somewhat differently, a puzzle raised in connection with an all-encompassing question of being. Nāgārjuna's impact becomes clearest when we consider his remarkable legacy down to the present day: besides developments in medieval Asia as varied as the Chinese master Zhiyi's theory of three truths, or Kūkai's reflections on esoteric ritual in Japan,[48] contemporary interpretations as distinctive as the Wittgensteinian reflections of Gudmunsen or Thurman,[49] or the Heideggerianism of the philosophers of the Kyoto school,[50] would be quite unimaginable if all Buddhist thought had to offer was abhidharma scholasticism; but after Nāgārjuna everything seems possible.

This being said, let us note that Nāgārjuna's treatment of the question of the substantial reality of the self was nevertheless strikingly conservative. In fact, it was one more variation on precisely the same argument we have already seen in the *Kathāvatthu* and in Nāgasena's dialogue with the Greek king Menander. Nāgārjuna condenses the entire argument into a single verse:

If the self is the *skandhas,*
Then it must come into being and be annihilated;
If it is other than the *skandhas,*
Then it must be without the *skandhas'* defining marks.[51]

As we have already seen in the preceding sections, although this argument was adequate within the context of Buddhist intrasystemic debate, it could not have been expected to carry much weight among the adherents of non-Buddhist schools, who in any case would not have accepted the Buddhist categorial schemes presupposed here.

Nonetheless, this was by no means all that Nāgārjuna had to say about the self. Indeed, his *Root Verses on the Madhyamaka (Mūlamadhyamaka-kārikā)* contain so many arguments that might apply to the self, that it is easy to see why, upon reaching the eighteenth chapter of that work, in which the self is the ostensible subject matter, he decided simply to provide the most generally accepted argument from the Buddhist perspective in the first verse, cited above. The remainder of the chapter is then devoted to the elucidation of particular topics, beginning with the groundlessness of the notion of "mine," that are entailed by the denial of the self's real being.[52]

Despite this, one might be curious to know just how the many arguments that I have said *might* apply to the self actually *do* apply to the self, and this is something that Nāgārjuna does not make very clear. For clarification we can turn, however, to the most influential of the classical commentators on Nāgārjuna's work, Candrakīrti (c. 600 C.E.). In his remarks on Nāgārjuna's brief verse about the self and its relationship with the bundles, Candrakīrti is quite cognizant of its shortcomings: "One may urge," he says, "that the non-Buddhists hold that the self is distinct from the bundles, and has separate characteristics from them. Therefore, this formulation is no way to refute them."[53] Candrakīrti, however, reserved the task of working out the argument in accord with the suggestions scattered throughout Nāgārjuna's work, and developing a version of the argument that no longer depends exclusively on the older Buddhist scholastic categories, for his own magnum opus, the *Introduction to the Middle Way (Madhyamakāvatāra).*[54] The resulting argument came to be known in later Tibetan scholastic circles by the colorful name "the sevenfold revolution of the chariot" *(shing-rta rnam-bdun 'khor-lo).*[55] This argument, an obvious successor to Nāgasena's deconstruction of King Menander's carriage, is the one with which we will here be concerned.

Earlier, I suggested that a single argument against the substantial reality of the self evolved into two distinct arguments, one *epistemological* and the other *ontological,* and that the original argument was one that concerned "finding" the self. The point of the epistemological version of the argument, as developed by Vasubandhu, was that the self is not apprehended by any valid epistemic operation, and so its existence is to be strongly doubted. By contrast, what I am calling the ontological version of the argument, as developed by Candrakīrti on the basis of Nāgārjuna's work, moves from the presumed being of a persisting substantial self, to the absolute impossibility of such an entity's entering into any sort of coherent relationship with the world of our actual experience.

Candrakīrti attempts to make his case by assuming and negating in turn seven possible relationships between the posited self and the ephemeral constituents of our being, and these he considers via the ancient metaphor of the chariot and its parts. The first five possible relationships that he mentions are derived from Nāgārjuna's enumeration of them in the latter's version of the ancient argument concerning the incoherence of the relationship between fire and fuel:[56] identity, diversity, possession, support, and dependency. Candrakīrti asks us to imagine, in other words, that the chariot (self) may be thought to be: (a) identical *(eka)* to its parts, such as the wheel, axle and so forth (equivalent, in the case of the self, to the skandhas comprising the ephemeral psychic and physical elements of our being); or it may be (b) diverse *(anya)* from them; or it may be (c) their possessor *(-vān);* or (d) their support *(ādhāra);* or it may be (e) dependent *(ādheya)* upon them.[57] Because Candrakīrti's remarks on identity and diversity do not add to what we have seen earlier in connection with the *Milindapañha,* I will not comment further on those relationships here. And alternatives (c), (d) and (e) are all rejected by Candrakīrti because, as he sees it, these relationships can only hold if the chariot is a substantial entity—something that must be identical to or diverse from its parts. For instance, when we consider a landlord and his house (possession), or a container and its contents (support and dependent), we are considering relationships that presuppose the *diversity* of the things in question. But in these instances we are concerned with discrete physical entities; their being diverse and yet related as possessor-to-possession, or container-to-contents is in such cases perfectly intelligible. But in what sense does a chariot "own" its parts, "support" them, or "depend" upon them? Candrakīrti is arguing, in effect, that these relationships, derived from our conceptions of physical objects, extend only metaphorically to the relationships between primitive elements (the chariot's parts) and the constructs ("chariot") supervening upon them. By mistaking mere metaphors for actual states of affairs, we lead ourselves philosophically astray.

The sixth and seventh alternatives, which Candrakīrti has added to Nāgārjuna's original five, are: (f) that the chariot is the sum of its parts (and not merely the parts themselves), and (g) that it is the form into which the parts are organized. He rejects (f) because in that case the chariot might just as well be a mere heap, or a scattered object, so long as the requisite parts are all included in the sum called "chariot." But (g) must also be rejected, in essence because the *form* of a thing presupposes the thing and not merely the collection of its parts. That is, the form of a chariot cannot be individuated apart from concrete chariots, and so cannot explain the relationship of the chariot to its parts; to say that "these parts instantiate the form of a chariot" is to say only that "these parts form a chariot," and thus the original puzzle is merely reintroduced. Clearly Candrakīrti does not wish to countenance anything even approximating an Aristotelian (much less a Platonic!) view of substance.[58]

These remarks are intended only to supply a brief introduction to Candrakīrti's approach to the problem of the self, and will be continued in the final section of the following chapter. I will not attempt a thorough analysis or critique of his arguments here. It seems to me that they are flawed in some respects, especially in a very general account such as I have just described. Thus, for instance, *pace* Candrakīrti, possession *is* a relationship that various kinds of abstract or logically constructed entities—nations and corporations are examples—do indeed have to concrete physical things. Even with this objection, however, it remains very mysterious just how this might enable us to understand the possession of our properties by an unchanging, substantial self. Candrakīrti's argument therefore does lead us to call into question the puzzling nature of the relationship between the self (conceived as an autonomous and persisting substance) and our experienced being. So far as it is concerned to call this enigma to our attention, Candrakīrti's revolution of the chariot certainly achieves some success. Nevertheless, for Candrakīrti, recognition of the conceptual incoherence of the posit of a substantial self does not require us to abolish our common notions of personal identity from conventional discourse, any more than the example he uses requires us to stop speaking of "chariots." The discovery that our conventions are not *ultimately* grounded may be disconcerting for some, but for Candrakīrti this is precisely what being *conventional* means.[59]

In concluding this discussion of the inapprehensibility of the self, I wish to emphasize that, in both Vasubandhu's and Candrakīrti's formulations, the Buddhist arguments contra the substance theory of the self preserved powerful evidence of their origin in the context of systematic training in meditation—and its analogue (and reinforcement) in abhidharma modes of analysis—where the exercise of *trying and failing* to find the self was key. As suggested above, the point here was not so much the achievement of logical certitude as it was to arrive at what I have called "non-apodictic certainty." Against the suppositions of Uddyotakara, and those who like him have claimed to find the self concealed in the phenomena of self-reference, the Buddhist thinkers we have examined were concerned not so much to demonstrate that the concept of the self thus found was incoherent in itself (whatever that might mean), so much as they were to show that the self so conceived—as an unchanging foundation for our ephemeral acts of self-consciousness—could have no interaction with the ever changing flow of experience it was supposed to explain. Despite this, as we shall see in the chapter that follows, there was one important question about which the reflections of the Nyāya philosopher Uddyotakara and the Mādhyamika Candrakīrti did nevertheless converge.

Appendix: A Tibetan Comment on Sister Vajirā's Chariot

The following remarks on the Tibetan scholastic interpretation of Vajirā's verses are drawn from the work of a celebrated Dge-lugs-pa thinker, Gung-thang Dkon-mchog-bstan-pa'i sgron-me (1762–1823), *Grub mtha' bzhi'i 'dod tshul sogs dris lan sna tshogs kyi skor zhal lung bdud rtsi'i thigs 'phreng* (Lhasa Zhol xylographic edition). They illustrate the perspective of Dge-lugs-pa Mādhyamika interpretation, which holds Candrakīrti to represent the culmination of Indian Buddhist philosophy. Gung-thang's exposition follows the established progression of the four Buddhist philosophical schools *(siddhānta):* Vaibhāṣika, Sautrāntika, Cittamātra, and Madhyamaka. The first two are here treated indifferently as "realists" *(don-smra),* whereas the Madhyamaka, in accordance with Tibetan interpretations, is divided into Svātantrika and Prāsaṅgika subschools.

Translation

Because the self must be made the ground of all bondage and liberation, the outsiders and insiders [i.e., non-Buddhists and Buddhists] all disagree about it. In particular, the insiders think that if the parameters within which it is posited have extreme affirmative implications, then that would contradict the axiom that all principles are non-selves; whereas if there are extreme negative implications, then the foundation of deed and consequence will be overthrown, which would obstruct even the entrance to the higher destinies [by leading one to become skeptical about *karman*]. Hence, with great caution they each, in accordance with their own attitudes, formulate the parameters within which it is posited. They all concur that the fundamental text on the positing of the person is this, from a sūtra:

> Just as one speaks of a carriage,
> On the basis of an assemblage of parts,
> So based upon the bundles,
> One speaks conventionally of a "sentient being."

Nonetheless, they have dissimilar ways of drawing out the force of these words.

Most of the realists [i.e., the adherents of the abhidharma schools] say that "bundles" *(phung-po, skandha)* must refer to the five bundles in sum. Because the assemblage must be posited on the basis of them in sum, the meaning of the scripture is that the assemblage of such bundles must by itself alone be posited to be the person. This, [they believe], is clearly indicated by these lines:

> So based upon the bundles,
> One speaks conventionally of a "sentient being."

The idealists say that there must exist an object of the imputation of the person, which [object] is to be gotten at. Because it cannot exist apart from the bundles, it must be sought and gotten at among the bundles. That is the meaning of "based upon the bundles." When it is sought from among them [i.e., among the bundles], because nothing other can rightly be the ground for the designation of the person, it must be posited to be the universal ground *(ālaya(vijñāna))* alone. Thus reason demonstrates the meaning of the scripture.

The Svātantrikas, [who, among the schools of Mādhyamika philosophy, maintain that the role of philosophical argument need not be restricted to the negative dialectic,] say that because it is stated that the person is posited on the basis of the bundles, it is implicit that there must be some other positing agent. If it be asked why that is, then because imagination alone cannot posit it, it must be posited by force of being apparent to an incorrigible mind that is unerring with respect to the individuating characteristic of its object. However, just being apparent will not suffice: it must be established among the features of the ground of imputation. If not referring to its being established or not established among the features of that, there would arise the flawed implication that the human bundles, etc., may be the ground of imputation of other species. Hence, here "based upon the bundles" may be understood in two ways. For, negatively, absence of reference to another positing agent is not established; and, affirmatively, [the person] must be established, too, among the features of the ground of imputation itself.

The Prāsaṅgikas, [proponents of that school of Mādhyamika thought that adheres strictly to the negative dialectic], refute everyone by means of that very sūtra citation. So, to the realists: Your positing that the mere assemblage of the bundles itself is the person[60] has invalid implications; for the person must be posited *on the basis* of that mere assemblage of the bundles. The inclusion holds; for what has risen on the basis of Devadatta must be other than Devadatta, there being no way that something can arise on the basis of itself. And [your position] is invalid even if you say that, although the person is posited on the basis of the bundles, the sūtra has not stated that the person is posited on the basis of the *mere assemblage* of the bundles; for the sūtra has explicitly stated that the carriage is posited on the basis of the mere assemblage of its parts, and both example and object must cohere. Moreover, it is implied that the mere assemblage of the parts of the carriage *is* the carriage, because the mere assemblage of the bundles *is* the person. If you hold that, then you explicitly contradict the sūtra by identifying act and agent.

To the idealists: Your positing that consciousness alone, divided out from among the bundles, is the ground of the designation of the person has unreasonable implications; for that contradicts the sūtra, which, when indicating the ground of its designation, without dividing out, speaks in common of "the bundles." If, when you search among them by means of reason, you light inappropriately upon the universal ground, then you contradict the sūtra even if you say that the universal ground is indicated by application of the general term [i.e., "bundles"] primarily to a particular; for the sūtra states that the person is posited on the basis of that, but not that that itself is the person. Thus, the refutation.

To the Svātantrikas: Your holding that the person is established *among the features of* the bundles that are the ground of its imputation has invalid implications; for the sūtra states that it is posited *on the basis of* the bundles that are the ground of imputation. The inclusion holds; for what is posited among the features of the ground of imputation does not fall under the category of imputed principle. For example, although "nearer peak" has reference to "further peak," it is in no way established to be among the features of the further peak; and although the long has reference to the short, it is in no way established to be among the features of the short.

Notes

1 Collins 1982a, esp. chaps. 3 and 6.

2 Note, however, that although Indian thinkers did carefully distinguish such characteristically philosophical problems as those of perception, the existence of external objects, the nature of universals, and many others, they never defined the "departments" of philosophical research in quite the same way that the West has.

3 *Saṃyuttanikāya*, i.135.

4 Among Theravāda scholastic works these verses are quoted in: *Kathāvatthu*, I.1.240; *Milindapañha*, II.i.1 (= p. 45 of the Rhys Davids translation); and *Visuddhimagga*, p. 508. Among non-Theravāda abhidharma works, they are found in *Satyasiddhiśāstra*, sections 38 and 141; and Vasubandhu, *Treatise on the Negation of the Person* (see chap. 14 below). Citations by Mādhyamika authors include: Bhāvaviveka, *Tarkajvāla* on *Madhyamakahṛdaya*, chap. 3, v. 97; and Candrakīrti, *Madhyamakāvatāra*, chap. 6, pp. 246 and 258. It is the last verse, in particular, that is most frequently cited in these sources.

5 These comments seem also to apply to Indo-European languages in general; for instance, in English, "No ostriches are found in Greenland." That the verb in question here could be used in either an epistemic or existential sense was well known to traditional Indian lexicographers. See, for instance, the entries under *upa-labh* in *Śabdakalpadruma*. That it was treated as more or less interchangeable with the root *vid* in its passive sense, "be found," is demonstrated by the occurrence of this instead of *upa-labh* in some versions of Vajirā's verses.

6 Cf. *Saṃyuttanikāya*, iv.384, where the referent is the Tathāgata. Warder 1970:

125 n., comments: "... *upa-labh* may, especially later, mean 'be perceived', but still in the sense that 'not perceived' implies definitely not there at all."

7 Cf. Bhattacharya 1973: 9, n. 4: "L'ātman n'est pas un objet à 'saisir'...mais, transcendant au moi empirique, il est notre essence veritable..."

8 *Kaṭhopaniṣad,* II.iii.12–13.

9 Though in the case of the early Sāṃkhya school, perhaps only inference was recognized as an alternative to privileged discovery. See Larson 1979: 169.

10 *Nyāyabhāṣya,* introducing *Nyāyasūtra,* 1.1.10.

11 Thus, Vācaspatimiśra, *Nyāyatātparyaṭīkā,* p. 184, offers the following comment on the passage just quoted: "The cognition 'I', manifesting with reference to the body, as having pale or other features [e.g., 'I am pale'], cannot immediately demonstrate the self in the manner of the cognition of a pot [i.e., in the way that 'here's a pot' immediately demonstrates to the cognizer, under normal circumstances, that there is a pot here]—this is [Vātsyāyana's] intention. Or else his intention has reference to selves associated with other bodies."

12 Among texts belonging to the earlier (the so-called Hīnayāna) schools of Buddhism that treat of the Personalist controversy, the most ancient that are now extant appear to be the Pali *Kathāvatthu* (*Matters under Discussion,* or, following Aung and Rhys-Davids, *Points of Controversy*), and the *Vijñānakāya (Body of Consciousness),* composed originally in Sanskrit, but now surviving only in a Chinese translation. Both of these texts purport to represent *verbatim* accounts of debates traditionally believed to have taken place during the great convocation of Buddhist clergy said to have been held at Pāṭaliputra during the mid-third century B.C.E. (Contemporary scholarship considers this account apocryphal.) There is a consensus among scholars that their redaction antedates the beginning of the Christian Era, and the striking agreements between the two texts, particularly in the formal features of the debates they record, suggests that they draw on a common tradition that may well go back to something like the debates in question, even if no formal "council" was ever held. In addition, there are a small number of texts that actually represent the view of the Personalists themselves, especially the *Saṃmitīyanikāyaśāstra (The Treatise of the Saṃmitīya Sect),* which like the *Vijñānakāya* exists today only in the Chinese. Later documents in which the arguments are summarized include Vasubandhu's *Treatise on the Negation of the Person* (see chap. 14 below), Harivarman's *Satyasiddhiśāstra* (or *Tattvasiddhiśāstra),* and Śāntarakṣita's *Tattvasaṅgraha* (on which see here Schayer 1931–32). For the earliest documents, the texts and translations referred to here are: *Kathāvatthu,* La Vallée Poussin 1925 (for the *Vijñānakāya*), Venkataramanan 1953 (for the *Saṃmitīyanikāyaśāstra*). On the Personalist controversy generally, see also Conze 1967: 122–34; and Watanabe 1983, chap. 11; and, for an interpretation of Vasubandhu's position, Duerlinger 1997–2000.

13 The complete record of the controversy as it appears in the *Kathāvatthu* is very extensive, comprising the first 243 paragraphs of book I.

14 Works on this topic include: Shwe Zan Aung, in Aung and Rhys Davids 1915: xlvii–li; Schayer 1932–33; Jayatilleke 1963: 412–15; Warder 1963; Bocheński 1970;

Daye 1978: 128 (where Daye argues that the *Kathāvatthu* does not involve "the recognition of any metaconcepts about logic"); Ichimura 1980; Watanabe 1983, chap. 11; and, most recently, Matilal 1998: 33–37.

15 *Kathāvatthu,* I.1.1. I have numbered the particular propositions contained within this passage and those that follow.

16 *Kathāvatthu Aṭṭhakathā* on *Kathāvatthu,* I.1.1, trans. Law 1969.

17 Refer to n. 14 above.

18 The test of the argument by deriving an identical conclusion from the contraposition of a premise is a typical device in classical Indian argumentation, and though obviously redundant in the symbolic version of a fairly simple argument such as the one given above, is nonetheless a valuable device for checking more complex arguments expressed, as is the case here, in quasi-formal ordinary language. See Staal 1962.

19 *Kathāvatthu,* I.1.2.

20 Watanabe, who views the logic of the *Kathāvatthu* as a propositional calculus, suggests this answer (1983: 160): "It seems that by showing the form $\sim p \supset \sim q$ which is equivalent to the form $q \supset p$, in the above the Pudgala school tries to demonstrate sophistically p and $\sim q$, which are both the standpoint of the Pudgala school."

Assuming that what Watanabe means here by "p and $\sim q$" is only that, given the assumption $q \supset p$, these two propositions are not incompatible (for $q \supset p$ is, of course, equivalent to the *disjunction* of p and $\sim q$, and *not* to their conjunction), then this solution to the puzzle would be an elegant and ingenious one; but, unfortunately, it cannot be correct. To see that this is so, consider these points: (i) we are given no grounds whatsoever on this account for assuming that the premise $p \supset q$ (premise (2) of the Theravāda argument) is to be regarded as true, but $\sim p \supset \sim q$ (premise (2) of the Personalist's rebuttal) as false, so that prima facie at least, the Personalist's argument *is* just as good as that of his opponent; and (ii) we must assume that the principle of material implication is the one actually intended by the various Pali grammatical particles and expressions used in these dialogues, and that the authors of these dialogues thus had a sure concept of the truth-conditions for material implication.

It is not clear, however, that material implication was at any time the form of implication accepted among Indian logicians, who would certainly have considered the seemingly paradoxical instances of material implication to be senseless and ill-formed, e.g., the proposition "if flowers bloom in space, then 2 + 2 = 4." The occurrence of such a proposition within the framework of the *Kathāvatthu* logic is, I believe, quite unthinkable. (Cf. Douglas Daye's remarks on material implication in relation to implication in Indian logic inter alia in Daye 1985.)

21 *Kathāvatthu Aṭṭhakathā* on *Kathāvatthu,* I.1.1.

22 The entire list is given in *Kathāvatthu,* I.1.17–73. All of these categories can be reduced to the five bundles (physical form, sensation, conceptualization, motivational and other conditions, and consciousness), with the addition of the

unconditioned elements (i.e., space and cessations, which are not counted among the bundles). There are many differences among the details of the categorizations adopted by the several abhidharma schools. See now Cox 1995, esp. chap. 9.

23 The distinction I am drawing here is indeed given formal expression in Indian grammatical and later philosophical literature through the notions of two types of negation: *paryudāsapratiṣedha* ("implicative (or 'predicate') negation") and *prasajyapratiṣedha* ("non-implicative (or 'existential') negation"). Refer to Kajiyama 1973.

24 The approximate date given here follows Warder 1970: 330. It seems likely, however, that some of the material contained in this work is much older, c. first century B.C.E. See also Lamotte 1976: 465–69.

25 There is still no exact consensus about the dates of his reign. See Narain 1957: 75–77; Lamotte 1976: 414–17 and 461–69; and Warder 1970: 330.

26 *Milindapañha,* II.1.1.

27 For the complete list, see Conze 1969: 95–100. Indeed, the anatomical elements should properly be reduced to the more primitive constituents of the skandha of form, i.e., atoms and things compounded of the elements.

28 Parmenides, fragment 1 (Kirk and Raven 1971, no. 342); Rawson 1934: 122–27 and 216–23; Hackforth 1952: 69–77; Pérez-Remón 1980: 57–63; and Collins 1982a: 230–33.

29 But note that the *Kathāvatthu* makes considerable use of just the same phrase, which, when it occurred in the passages given above, was rendered "ultimately." So I do not wish to suggest that the author of the *Milindapañha* is particularly innovative in this respect. What is novel, however, is his manner of introducing the distinction after the conflict has first arisen in ordinary, relatively nontechnical language. On the pervasive role of the absolute/conventional distinction in later Indian philosophy, see Sprung 1973 and chap. 8 below.

30 Refer to Conze 1963. Conze, however, rejects the equation between Hume's denial of self and the Buddhist *anātma* doctrine primarily on contextualist grounds. Cf. the remarks on this same topic in Jacobson 1974, chap. 8, "The Buddha and Hume"; and Hoffman 1982.

31 For a recent attempt to relate all this to philosophical abstraction, see Griffiths 1990.

32 The beginning of the period in question is marked by the works of Nāgārjuna and Gautama (author of the *Nyāyasūtra*), the end by those of Vasubandhu, Vātsyāyana, and possibly Praśastapāda.

33 This was famously the supposition of Vidyabhusana 1971 (first published in 1921): 497–513, "Influence of Aristotle on the Development of the Syllogism in Indian Logic." Though Vidyabhusana's arguments have been generally rejected, it is now known that Aristotelian philosophy was indeed taught in Greek colonies as far east as present-day Afghanistan. See L. Robert in Bernard 1973, chap. 12.

34 See esp. Stall 1965.

35 See below, chap. 14, par. 2.

36 A modal version of this syllogism—"(1) If...it would *possibly* be known... (2) It is *not possibly* known..."—would certainly be stronger; but I do not think that that is what Vasubandhu has in mind here. As it stands, the present syllogism can yield no more than reasonable grounds for the denial of self, unless all possible perceptions and inferences have been tested. Thus, complete certainty is only possible for an omniscient mind, i.e., for the Buddha alone.

37 Penelhum 1967: 98.

38 Udayana's classic work on the subject is his *Discrimination of the Reality of the Self (Ātmatattvaviveka),* a useful summary of which may be found in Potter 1977: 526–57. The Western discussion of the problem is detailed in Chisholm 1979, especially chap. 1.

39 As presented here, it does appear that the abhidharma philosophy got rid of persistent selves only to substitute streams of momentary selves. This is precisely the point of many of the attacks on the old abhidharma schools by the philosophers of the later Mahāyāna, and especially Candrakīrti; on this, see the following chapter. Concerning reflexivity in Buddhist philosophy, refer now to Williams 1998a.

40 Quoted in Mackie 1967.

41 Brentano 1973: 106–9.

42 Generally, it seems to me that contemporary discussions of certainty *(niścaya)* in Indian and Buddhist thought too often presuppose that it must be *apodictic certainty* that is at stake, without entertaining the possibility that Indian thinkers may have other sorts of certainty in mind. To the best of my knowledge, the distinction between what I am calling apodictic and non-apodictic certainty is nowhere clearly thematized within the traditions I am considering.

43 Note that Uddyotakara was likely familiar with Vasubandhu's *Treatise on the Negation of the Person (Pudgalapratiṣedhaprakaraṇa),* and was no doubt criticizing that work directly in the relevant passages of his *Exposition of the Aphorisms of Reason (Nyāyavārttika),* for selections from which see chap. 14 below.

44 *Nyāyavārttika,* pp. 700–701.

45 *Nyāyavārttika,* p. 704.

46 *Tattvasaṅgraha,* v. 215.

47 Some, however, have argued that his thought is better understood in relation to early Buddhism; note, in particular, Warder 1973.

48 See chap. 8, nn. 48–49.

49 Gudmunsen 1977 and Thurman 1984.

50 Refer to chap. 8, n. 6, below.

51 *Mūlamadhyamakakārikā,* chap. 18, v. 1.

52 *Mūlamadhyamakakārikā,* chap. 18, vv. 2–6. The remaining verses of the chapter (vv. 7–11) emphasize the awakening that follows from relinquishing all grasping of both self and selflessness.

53 *Prasannapadā,* p. 146.

54 *Madhyamakāvatāra,* vi.151–61, pp. 271–81 and Huntington 1989: 176–77.

55 See, especially, Engle 1983 and Hopkins 1983: 175–96.

56 *Mūlamadhyamakakārikā,* chap. 10. An interesting comparative discussion of this chapter may be found in McEvilley 1982.

57 *Madhyamakāvatāra,* pp. 265 ff.; *Prasannapadā,* p. 91.

58 *Madhyamakāvatāra,* pp. 272–77.

59 Refer to chap. 1, n. 58, above, on James Duerlinger's interpretation of Candrakīrti as a Nonreductionist.

60 The text erroneously reads *phung-po.*

4. Synthetic Selves

EARLIER, we considered the Upaniṣadic search for freedom from saṃsāra, a freedom that was to be won, above all, through the achievement of self-knowledge. But just what was the nature of this self, knowing which one might be free? About this there was much disagreement, until, with the teaching of the Buddha, a fundamental assumption of the religious milieu that produced the Upaniṣads was cast into doubt: possibly there was no concrete thing corresponding to "self"; possibly "self-knowledge" was to consist not in the discovery of a firm ground underlying the constant flux of becoming, but rather in the discovery that we are in a profound state of error about ourselves, and that "selves" are no things at all.

The challenge posed by the Buddha's difficult teaching soon gave rise to an interpretive conflict among his own followers, who mostly came to hold that, in the pursuit of a viable theory of persons, the competing views could be reduced to two: either each of us is individuated by a unique and persisting substantial self; or we are continuants, individuated by contingent relationships holding among our many temporal parts. Interestingly, monism (of the Upaniṣadic variety) was not taken seriously during the course of these early debates, as indeed it would not be until the rise of the non-dualist school of Upaniṣadic philosophy (that is, Advaita Vedānta) toward the mid-first millennium C.E., when Buddhist philosophers would reject it as yet another Brahmanical hypostasis of self (though one thought not to be so vicious as that of the pluralists; for Advaita at least concurred with Buddhism in doing away with individual selves).[1] Another option that was generally neglected was physicalism, which holds that personal identity supervenes upon some relevant type of physical continuity. Given the absence of any really well-developed school of philosophical materialism in classical India, this position, which has attracted many contemporary

Western thinkers, seems not to have been seriously countenanced at all.[2] Neither was what Derek Parfit calls the "Further Fact View" particularly prominent in the classical Indian discussions.[3]

I suggested above, however, that the confrontation in ancient India between divergent views of the self was similar to the opposition of Reductionism and non-Reductionism about which Parfit has written. The foregoing remarks suggest a further specification of that observation: the confrontation was one between two forms of dualism, roughly similar to Cartesian and non-Cartesian (or "Humean") dualism, respectively.[4] On the Brahmanical side, leading philosophers argued that the psychological features of our existence inhere in some substance, which they termed the "self," while the Buddhists for their part insisted that psychological continuity does not presuppose any such bearer. And as we have seen, the Buddhist attack on the Brahmanical theory at the very least succeeded in casting doubt upon the notion that the posited self could be known immediately, through an act of direct acquaintance. Equally, it raised serious questions concerning the nature of the self's relationship with all that it was supposed to bear. Nevertheless, Buddhist thinkers generally retained the conviction that the continuous stream of mental events was incapable of physical reduction—idealism, in fact, became the preferred alternative to dualism.[5]

The strength of the view that persons are continuants is, it seems to me, that such a view does ample justice to our sense that we are changing things, things that come into being and grow, learn and forget, sin and achieve absolution, and finally die. The most powerful objection to this view is perhaps that it does *too much* justice to the dynamic aspect of human existence; it emphasizes *becoming* at the expense of *being*. That is, the notion that persons are continuants appears to neglect our unity and purposefulness, and, above all, the unity that I experience whenever I turn my gaze inward, to reflect on what I have been, and on what I expect to be. This objection turns on a group of assumptions that philosophers in the West have often discussed under the headings of *personal identity* and the *unity of consciousness*.[6]

These two expressions are sometimes taken as more or less synonymous. More often, however, philosophers prefer to distinguish what are obviously two related but nonetheless distinct problems, and it is this usage that I shall follow here. Accordingly, the *problem of personal identity* will be taken to be the problem of what it is that individuates persons through time; in other words, to address this problem will be to ask, in virtue of what is it that Jones yesterday and Jones today are held to be *the same person?* The *problem of the unity of consciousness,* on the other hand, will be taken to be the problem of the unity of the subject at any given time; that is, why is it that I always experience *myself* as the same one who sees, hears, thinks, etc., simultaneously? Why is it, in other words, that my consciousness appears to have just one center?

Many particular problems raised in this connection were known to the Indian philosophers with whom we are here concerned. In the remainder of this chapter, we shall consider some of their observations on the problem of personal identity, while in the chapter that follows we shall also turn to questions raised in connection with the unity of consciousness. In discussing both problems, Indian philosophers frequently speak of *pratisaṃdhāna,* "connectedness," a term referring to the synthetic cohesiveness of psychic life. The term is often translated as "memory," a rendering that is not incorrect, but much too narrow for our present context. Nonetheless, as we shall see below, the analysis of memory figures prominently in these discussions.

Early Buddhist Reflections on the Problems of Personal Identity

A crucial point of contention for Buddhist thinkers engaged in the Personalist controversy, as for Indian thought more generally, involved the relationship holding between the doer of an action and the one who reaps the consequences of the action done. As it said in the *Sammitīya-nikāya-śāstra:*

> If the self were totally unreal... [t]here would be neither the doer nor the deed, nor any result thereof. There being no deed, the results also would not be. There being no deed and no results, there would not be either birth or death. But beings turn in the wheel of birth and death on account of their deeds and their results...[7]

Nonetheless, the dominant streams of early Buddhist scholastic thought were constrained by their denial of the Brahmanical soul-theories on the one hand, and of Personalism on the other, to elaborate an account of personal identity through time that would ground the intuitions underlying the notion of karman, while avoiding any compromise with the anathematic doctrines just mentioned. The result was the elaboration of the hypothesis that personal identity through time is to be interpreted in terms of the concept of a bundle-continuum *(skandha-santāna);* that is, a causally continuous aggregation of psychological and physical "substances" thought to be atomic, simple, and instantaneous. The theory, however, did not emerge as a *fait accompli:* the earliest records of the Personalist controversy make it clear that the redescription of persons as continuants was puzzling even to its proponents from the very outset. An excellent summary of these early struggles with the doctrine in question is to be found, once more, in the *Milindapañha:*

> The king said: "He who is born, Nāgasena, does he remain the same or become another?"
>
> "Neither the same nor another."
>
> "Give me an illustration."
>
> "Now what do you think, O king? You were once a baby, a tender thing, and small in size, lying flat on your back. Was that the same as you who are now grown up?"
>
> "No. That child was one, I am another."
>
> "If you are not that child, it will follow that you have had neither mother nor father, no! nor teacher. You cannot have been taught either learning, or behaviour, or wisdom. What, great king! is the mother of the embryo in the first stage different from the mother of the embryo in the second stage, or the third, or the fourth? Is the mother of the baby a different person from the mother of the grown-up man? Is the person who goes to school one, and the same when he has finished his schooling another? Is it one who commits a crime, another who is punished by having his hands or feet cut off?"
>
> "Certainly not. But what would you, Sir, say to that?"
>
> The Elder replied: "I should say that I am the same person, now I am grown up, as I was when I was a tender tiny baby, flat on my back. For all these states are included in one by means of this body."
>
> "Give me an illustration."
>
> "Suppose a man, O king, were to light a lamp, would it burn the night through?"
>
> "Yes, it might do so."
>
> "Now, is it the same fire that burns in the first watch of the night, Sir, and in the second?"

"No."

"Or the same that burns in the second watch and in the third?"

"No."

"Then is there one lamp in the first watch, and another in the second, and another in the third?"

"No. The light comes from the same lamp all the night through."

"Just so, O king, is the continuity of a person or thing maintained. One comes into being, another passes away; and the rebirth is, as it were, simultaneous. Thus neither as the same nor as another does a man go on to the last phase of his self-consciousness."

"Give me a further example."

"It is like milk, which when once taken from the cow, turns after a lapse of time, first to curds, and then from curds to butter, and then from butter to ghee. Now would it be right to say that the milk was the same thing as the curds, or the butter, or the ghee?"

"Certainly not; but they are produced out of it."

"Just so, O king, is the continuity of a person or thing maintained. One comes into being, another passes away; and the rebirth is, as it were, simultaneous. Thus neither as the same nor as another does a man go on to the last phase of his consciousness."

"Well put, Nāgasena!"[8]

Early Buddhist scholastic thought appears to have had particular difficulties with the logic of relationships, especially the relationships of identity and difference. These difficulties confront us again at the very beginning of the passage just given, where Nāgasena responds to the king's query ("does he [who is born] remain the same or become another?") with the words, "neither the same nor another." What could he possibly mean here, where the question is one of human maturation and growth?

The dialogue proceeds to clarify Nāgasena's apparently paradoxical words by inquiring first into one's relationship with the infant from whom one has grown. There is a clear sense in which one is not the same as that infant, and so king Milinda states that, "That child was one, I am another." But as Nāgasena points out, an absurdity follows from this: that infant had parents; but one is not identical to that infant; therefore, one has no parents. The argument as it stands, of course, is enthymematic, and thus requires the clarification of its suppressed premises: one has parents now only if one was once an infant who was born to parents; and one's parents could only have been the parents of that very infant. But since our ordinary concept of parentage seems to involve some such notions, I think it is not unreasonable to allow Nāgasena this much. Similar considerations may apply to the other absurdities enumerated by Nāgasena as flowing from the assumption of difference. But if that is so, then how could it have seemed plausible for King Milinda to state that he and his infant predecessor were different?

Clearly, the discussion must be taken as turning on a certain ambiguity deriving from the failure to specify *in what respect* they are same or different. Once this is pointed out, then, despite the apparently paradoxical diction, there is nothing at all mysterious about the assertion that one is somehow the same as and yet different from the child from whom one grew. But it is not the case that one is at once the same and different with respect to just the same thing in just the same mode. Now, Nāgasena makes it clear enough where he sees difference between one's present and childhood selves: for instance, in learning, behavior, and wisdom. What is most striking in this ancient dialogue, however, is his conception of what it is in virtue of which there is also an identity relationship: "For all these states are included in one by means of this body." Does Nāgasena thus hold that personal identity is to be reduced to physical continuity?

The examples that he adduces strengthen the impression that this is so: he speaks of the continuity of a single flame, and of that of milk that is curdled, churned, and finally refined into ghee. In both of these cases we have "identity" only so long as we have physical continuity along a single spatio-temporal path. Some modern philosophers have suggested too that such an account can be adapted to serve as an appropriate model for the explanation of personal identity. Nevertheless, it is very difficult to see how a Buddhist philosopher could seriously maintain a physicalistic view of personal identity. This becomes apparent when we consider the paragraph which Nāgasena repeats twice in the foregoing dialogue:

> "Just so, O king, is the continuity of a person or thing maintained. One comes into being, another passes away; and the rebirth is, as it were, simultaneous. Thus neither as the same nor as another does a man go on to the last phase of his consciousness."

If I understand Nāgasena correctly, he is maintaining in effect that when bodily continuity is broken by the process of rebirth, some other relevant sort of continuity is operative under the circumstances, and temporal continuity is at least part of what's involved. Clearly, however, temporal continuity alone cannot account for the continuity of a person from one lifetime to the next; for if Nero dies at 11:53:16 P.M., and a swarm of fireflies and a half dozen fiddler-crabs are all born at precisely 11:53:17 P.M., then, on the assumption that temporal continuity is all that matters for personal identity across lifetimes, it would follow that Nero is reborn as a swarm of fireflies and a half dozen fiddler-crabs; and that seems unlikely.[9] So the problem for Nāgasena is to specify just what must be added to temporal continuity to get the relevant continuity across lifetimes.

Nāgasena hints at an approach to the resolution of the difficulty in the very last sentence of the paragraph just cited: "Thus neither as the same nor as another does a man go on to the last phase of his consciousness." In other words, some sort of psychological continuity must also be involved here. The problem of specifying precisely what sort of psychological continuity is required became itself the source of considerable dispute within early Buddhist philosophical circles. The details of these arguments, and of the theories that developed in connection with them, need not be surveyed here. However, it would appear that the theories that became most influential were all markedly dualistic in that they posit consciousness—not, to be sure, as an enduring thing, but as a series of causally related, if very short-lived phenomena—to be capable of continuity, for a limited time at least, even if utterly disembodied. With the adoption of such theories, temporal continuity between bodies in a rebirth sequence gradually waned in importance: there could be gaps during which one continued to exist only as a disembodied mind-stream.[10] How this could be I find very puzzling, as did the abhidharma scholars themselves, to judge from the profusion of speculation this problem generated. Let us note, however, that even a philosopher so opposed to Hume's conception of a serial self as Franz Brentano acknowledges the logical possibility of immortality in a Humean world: the series of psychological events would in that case just go on forever.[11] The puzzlement here, I think, stems not from a difficulty about *logical* possibility, but rather one about *empirical* possibility. Just what, in fact, is the case if we inhabit a Buddhist world?

Vasubandhu on Memory and Personal Identity through Time

We turn now to Vasubandhu's treatment of some of the puzzles that thus seem to flow from the doctrine that persons are selfless bundle-continua. Vasubandhu, roughly a contemporary of the Nyāya philosopher Vātsyāyana, was concerned to answer opponents who, like Vātsyāyana, did not see how a theory such as the Buddhist one could provide an account of the unity and continuity we experience in our lives, as illustrated by the phenomena of volition and memory.[12]

I will focus here primarily on Vasubandhu's treatment of memory, for memory paradigmatically illustrates the sort of psychological continuity that Vātsyāyana sees as grounded in the real existence of a persisting self. Once we have comprehended Vasubandhu's strategy in treating of memory, then, we will be in a position to understand his approach to the problems of personal identity through time more generally. Moreover, because memory has also figured prominently in modern discussions of personal identity, ever since Locke made his famous attempt to explicate personal identity in terms of it,[13] Vasubandhu's discussion will be of particular interest in this context. But one should note that Vasubandhu at no point advances a memory-theory of personal identity. I suspect, in fact, that he would have agreed with those who, like Joseph Butler, hold that memory theories tend to presuppose the concept of personal identity, rather than to explain it.[14] Still, some may wonder, given the concept of a person as a continuum of somehow-linked, discrete events, does not the notion of memory itself become altogether paradoxical? That is, does not our very concept of memory presuppose, or in some way require, the concept of a persisting self? This was Vātsyāyana's point, namely, that if I now truly remember my former pleasurable experience of thus-and-such a type, then indeed it was *I* who had the very experience in question.[15]

Refusing any such conclusion, Vasubandhu outlines his theory as follows:

> If, then, there is no self whatsoever, then how is it that among instantaneous mental events there occurs memory or recognition of objects experienced long before?
>
> It is owing to a distinctive mental event, following from an act of concept-formation directed upon the object of memory.
>
> What sort of distinctive mental event is it, from which memory immediately follows?
>
> From one endowed with an act of concept-formation, etc.,[16]

which has a resemblance to and connection with the enjoyment of that [object], and whose force is not destroyed by peculiarities of the support, grief, distraction, etc. For even though it may resemble that [object], a distinctive mental event not caused by it has not the capacity to produce memory, and even if it follows from it, that [mental event] which resembles another [object] has not the capacity to produce memory; for the capacity is not found elsewhere.[17]

Now, Vasubandhu's intention is here anything but crystal clear. Certainly, he wishes to hold that our concept of memory does not commit us to maintaining there to be substantial selves. In any case, I take Vasubandhu's discussion to suggest roughly the following attempt at analysis:

A psychological act *m* is a memory of *x* if and only if: (i) at some time prior to the occurrence of *m* there was an act of concept-formation *a* which had as its object *x;* (ii) that *a* occurred was a condition for the occurrence of *m;* (iii) *m* has an appropriate resemblance to *a.*

In examining this analysis, the first question to be raised is: what sort of thing is *x?* Clearly, it should stand in for whatever may be an object of memory: the big cookout last summer, Hamlet's soliloquy, Marilyn Monroe's hair color, the feeling of depression, how to ride a bike, etc. Indeed, I think that one of our initial difficulties in dealing philosophically with memory stems from the many kinds of mental acts we call memory, in accordance with the many kinds of objects remembered: facts, states of affairs, sentences, phenomena, our own psychological states, physical objects, skills. A good analysis of memory should be rich enough to encompass the several specific types of memory that we may have.[18]

It follows from this that special care must be taken in interpreting the third clause of the analysans: *m* has an appropriate resemblance to *a.* What counts as the appropriate resemblance of a given memory to an earlier psychological event will vary according to the exact type of psychological event in question, and to the type of object to which it was directed. In some cases, moreover, the object, its concept, and the content of the act of memory may even converge. Thus, one remembers the Pythagorean theorem just in the event that one remembers that the square of the hypotenuse of a right triangle is equal to the sum of the squares of the two remaining sides; that is to say, the appropriate concept of the Pythagorean theorem *is* the Pythagorean theorem (or, perhaps, some sort of "conceptual-token" thereof), and so, too, the memory of it. But what of the cookout last summer? In a case such as this, we permit a very wide range of concepts of the event in question to count as the possible contents of memories of that very same event.

These considerations suggest that any very brief account of memory, such as the one under discussion here, will have to be to some extent vague, at least so long as one does not elaborate as part of that account a relatively detailed typology of the objects of memory and the memory-appropriate concepts corresponding to each type of object.[19] But the lack of greater clarity on this score would not seem to have much bearing in the present context, for the question is not one of seeking the self among the *objects* of memory, but rather of determining whether the concept of memory itself requires our positing a persisting self as *subject*. Therefore, acknowledging that a fully satisfactory account would require that more complete consideration be given to the objects of memory, we will proceed, leaving this problem to one side.

A philosopher like Vātsyāyana would probably raise an objection to the proposed analysis along these lines: Granted that memory is a very complex affair, and that we do not expect here to do full justice to the complexities involved in the analysis of memory according to its objects, it appears nonetheless certain that something of crucial importance has been left out of the proposed analysis. For is it not possible that the act of concept-formation spoken of in the first clause is the act of one person, but that the *apparent memory* is then the act of another, in which case the analysis would appear to be defective?[20] The question we are facing, then, boils down to this: would not the analysis be counterexemplified by a case in which an act of concept-formation occurring to one person is a condition for an apparent memory occurring to someone else?

It is clear that, in attempting to come to grips with this objection, we will have to proceed with much caution; for we have reached a thicket in which the perils of *petitio principii* lurk all about. To the foregoing objection, for instance, the non-self theorist may wish to respond: in the case you imagine, in which A's act of concept-formation is a condition for the occurrence of B's apparent memory, why is it that you assume A and B to be other than what we would term "discrete stages of what is conventionally thought of as 'the same person?'"

It seems to me exceedingly difficult to resolve this dispute in the absence of some set of neutral assumptions, about which the Reductionist and non-Reductionist can concur without equivocation. The non-Reductionist, for instance, might maintain that the inadequacy of the analysis becomes apparent as soon as we contemplate a possible universe in which, say, the formation of concepts by a certain inhabitant of an ashram in Hardwar is regularly followed by a well-known Hollywood actress's having apparent memories of an appropriate sort. The (logical) possibility of such a universe, it will be argued, shows that the Reductionist's approach to memory cannot be correct.

To this the Reductionist will respond, however, that in a universe such as the one described—assuming, for the sake of the argument, that we were unable to distinguish *apparent* memories of the sort in question from what we think of as *real* memories—our notions of persons would be considerably different from what they are in this world. And from our Reductionist point of view, she would continue, that poses no problem; for it is precisely our contention that personal identity is not in fact a matter of necessary and sufficient conditions holding in *all* possible worlds, but is, rather, a matter simply of the *actual* conditions that obtain contingently in our world as we happen to have it. And in *our* world, as a matter of fact, there are no regular, non-trivial relationships (none which we know about, anyway) holding between the thoughts of Hardwar ashramites and apparent memories in Beverly Hills.

There is, however, a clearer, and perhaps less easily contested, counterexample to the Reductionist view: Consider, if you will, Pythagoras (or whoever it was that discovered the famous theorem that bears his name). His formation of a concept of his theorem certainly was a condition for countless later acts of memory on the part of numberless generations of math students.

That it was a condition in these many cases is beyond dispute, but what is not so clear is just what kind of condition it was. In any case, the objection makes it clear that clause (ii)—that *a* occurred is a condition for occurrence of *m*—is inadequate as it stands. This raises two questions, one of which I shall pursue briefly, while deferring the other: what kind of condition did Vasubandhu have in mind? and just what kind of condition is *in fact* required here? I shall not investigate the second here because I do not think that I have anything to add here to what Martin and Deutscher have already said about what they term "operative conditions."[21]

In regard to the first question, it appears that Vasubandhu wished to rule out the possibility of interpreting "condition" as meaning "sufficient condition" *simpliciter.* This much is indicated by his qualifying clause, "whose force is not destroyed by peculiarities of the support [i.e., the body], grief, distraction, etc." But he may still be taken to mean something like "sufficient, given the absence of obstructions." This, however, seems to be ruled out by his phrase "capacity to produce memory"; that is, the earlier act of concept-formation is sufficient, given the absence of obstructions, to produce a *capacity* for memory, but not memory itself. Given that capacity, memory will actually occur whenever co-operating conditions obtain, but just what these are will vary greatly, depending on the type of memory involved, its object, the freshness of the memory, etc. Nonetheless, it seems clear from Vasubandhu's remarks elsewhere, and those of his commentators and critics,[22] that the "capacity to produce memory" was to be taken as a necessary condition for the occurrence of actual memory.

With all this in mind the original analysis may be emended as follows:

> A psychological act *m* is a memory of *x* if and only if: (i) at some time prior to the occurrence of *m* there was an act of concept-formation *a* which had as its object *x;* (ii') that *a* occurred was a sufficient condition, given the absence of obstruction, for there to have been a capacity for *m* to occur; (ii") that capacity was a necessary condition for *m*'s occurrence; (iii) *m* has an appropriate resemblance to *a.*

Let us return now to the counterexample about Pythagoras and the later generations of schoolchildren who "remember" his theorem. It seems clear that Pythagoras's formation of the concept of his theorem could not have been a *sufficient* condition, in our world as we have it, for anyone but Pythagoras to have had the capacity to remember the theorem later. And, as suggested, there appears to be no reason for Vasubandhu to respond to a counterexample derived from the concept of a world other than our world as we have it; for in a world in which Pythagoras' theorem-thoughts might be sufficient for countless later generations to have the capacity to remember his theorem, our notions of persons and personal identity would not be quite what they are. But one may still object that when a given schoolchild in our world remembers the Pythagorean theorem, one cannot be sure that at some prior point in the history of the continuum of which that schoolchild is the present stage, there was an act of concept-formation directed upon the theorem; that is, it remains a possibility, on Vasubandhu's account, that the original act occurred in some other continuum.

What Vasubandhu must concede to the non-Reductionist, then, is that memory presupposes, without itself constituting, what we call personal identity. What is therefore needed to flesh out his analysis is the qualification that the memory and the act of concept-formation which is its condition must both occur in the same continuum—and this is precisely parallel to Vātsyāyana's demand that they be states of the very same subject.

Regardless of the philosophical or exegetical deficiencies that may be found even in the reformulated analysis, I do think that Vasubandhu was correct to insist that our concept of memory must involve both resemblance and causal connection. Thus, psychic trauma is not usually thought of as memory precisely because, while bearing a causal connection to past conscious events, it does not appropriately resemble them. On the other hand, neither are one's fantasies about life in ancient Egypt memories; for even if they might sometimes resemble the conscious acts of certain ancient Egyptians, they have no relevant connection with them.

Before leaving this topic, let us recall the main elements of the Martin and Deutscher analysis of memory, where the criteria that must be fulfilled if someone can be said to remember something are:

1. Within certain limits of accuracy he represents that past thing.
2. If the thing was "public," then he observed what he now represents. If the thing was "private," then it was his.
3. His past experience of the thing was operative in producing a state or successive states in him finally operative in producing his representation.[23]

Martin and Deutscher's first criterion seems to be similar to Vasubandhu's insistence on resemblance, while their third criterion clearly parallels Vasubandhu's assertion that some sort of causal connection is at work here. The most remarkable difference seems to be that where Vasubandhu's analysis requires an impersonal formulation of clause (i)—at some time prior to the occurrence of *m* there was an act of concept-formation *a* which had as its object *x*—Martin and Deutscher specify that it must be the very subject of the memory who first observed what he now represents, or (as they put it), that it was *his*. This of course reinforces the conclusion arrived at above: namely, Vasubandhu's analysis *presupposes* the concept of personal identity; it does not explain it.

But Vasubandhu can still hold that the concept of memory in no way commits us to substance theories of the self, since what's missing from the proposed analysis might, on his account, just as well be supplied by the posit of the continuum. It is in this connection that he raises a remarkably contemporary-sounding puzzle case:

> Now, how is it that what has been seen by one mind is remembered by another? For thus, [according to your account, in which different person-stages seem equivalent to other minds,] what was seen by Devadatta's mind might be remembered by Yajñadatta.
>
> Not so, owing to lack of connection. For those two [Devadatta's act of seeing and Yajñadatta's apparent memory] have no connection as do two [mental events] belonging to the same continuum, because they are not related as cause and effect. Moreover, we do not say, "what was seen by one mind is remembered by another," but rather that the other mind which remembers comes into being from the mind which sees, as has been said, through the transformation of the continuum. What fault is there here? Moreover, recognition occurs only owing to memory.[24]

It is here that Vasubandhu answers the charge, which was articulated in fact by Vātsyāyana,[25] that the Buddhist theory levels the distinction between diachronic unity of persons and synchronic difference. Again, we must note: memory is *not* here called upon to *explain* personal identity—to say that *m* is a memory connected with some earlier mental act *a* is to say that they occur in the very same personality-continuum, but not to say that it is the continuity of memory itself that is constitutive of the person.

Still, on this account, the person is nothing more than a continuum, which may still seem puzzling. Vasubandhu introduces another question:

> And how does Devadatta go?
>
> The instantaneous conditions in an unbroken continuum—which is regarded by childish persons, who grasp it as a unified lump of existence, as the so-called "Devadatta"—are the cause of its own coming-into-being elsewhere, which is spoken of as "Devadatta goes." For "going" is that very coming-into-being-elsewhere. E.g., "goes" designates the passage of the continua of flames and words. Similarly, too, there being causes of consciousness, they are spoken of as "Devadatta cognizes."[26]

If I am not mistaken, this brings us to the heart of the matter: the unity of the bundle-continuum consists in a type of causal continuity. This is, of course, just the theory that Hume suggests, but never fully develops.[27]

Interpreting Vasubandhu on this point is no straightforward matter, and I am not sure that I can do justice to his viewpoint here. Let me say at the outset that I think that Vasubandhu, like the author of the *Milindapañha*, damages his own case from the very outset by relying rather heavily on examples of characteristically *spatio*-temporal continua—for instance, a moving fire, a lamp-light, and a growing plant. What is never made completely clear is just what it is that these examples are supposed to reveal about the unity of a continuum that is only partially physical, and which at times may be completely non-physical. We might try to think in terms of the continuity of a rope, that includes, say, fibers of both hemp and jute, but sometimes is only hemp; but though that illustrates that there are continuous things formed of various different substances, it does not help us when we ask, inevitably: how do you explain continuity of a person when the physical element drops out of the picture altogether?

Vasubandhu makes it clear that he believes psychological succession to be an entirely lawlike, but remarkably complex, sort of of process. An example he gives here strikingly presages associationist psychology:

> Also, there is fixed order among mental states, because what is to arise from such-and-such only arises from that. For when some similarity of features occurs, then there is a potency, owing to the specifics of the class. E.g., if, following the thought of a woman, the thought of rejecting her body, or the thought of her father, son, etc., should arise, then again when, later on, owing to the transformation of the continuum, the thought of a woman arises, then, because of its being of that class, it is capable of giving rise to the thought of rejecting her body, or the thought of her father, son, etc., but is not otherwise capable.[28] Moreover, if from the thought of a woman a great many thoughts have gradually arisen, then those which are most frequent [or clearest] or most proximate arise because they have been most forcefully cultivated, except when there are simultaneous special conditions external to the body.[29]

In essence, Vasubandhu is telling us here that the causally individuated continuum of a mind exhibits a peculiar causal density, characterized by the indefinitely complex associations among mental events occurring within the same causal stream.

It is, however, one thing to acknowledge the complexity of a scientific project and another to work it out in full detail. The attempt of the Ābhidharmikas to elaborate the nomic principles of psychological succession probably fared no worse than the similar efforts of the early modern associationists and their successors. In the final analysis, however, even the Ābhidharmikas admitted defeat on this score; a complete account, they said, could only be known by the omniscient mind of the Buddha:

> The totality of the causal features of a single peacock feather's eye
> Is not knowable except by an omniscient one;
> For the knowledge of that is the power of omniscience.
> How much more is this true of the distinctions of immaterial minds![30]

Of course, there is a sense in which this is quite correct: only an omniscient mind can know everything about everything—that much is analytically true. So let us assume, for the sake of argument, that psychological succession can, in principle, be fully described in terms of some set of causal-cum-associative laws, even though we might never be able to specify all the laws involved. And let us say that whatever series of psychological events occurs in conformity with such laws exhibits a special kind of continuity, call it ψ-continuity. Then, what Vasubandhu is claiming, in essence, seems to be that ψ-continuity is really just as good as spatio-temporal continuity; that is, a ψ-continuum is just as well-unified as a physical continuum is—it is "one thing" in much the same sense that a continuous flame or a living fruit tree remains "one thing" throughout the duration of its existence. Persons, then, are ψ-continua that are capable of interacting with certain kinds of physical continua (for instance, animal bodies), and, indeed, very often do so. As Vasubandhu expresses it:

> That which, preceded by deeds, is an ongoing coming-to-be of mental events, is a continuum. Its arising otherwise is transformation. And, moreover, that potency, which immediately produces the fruit, being distinct from [that involved in] other transformations, is the distinctive feature of the transformation. E.g., a mind at the point of death which grasps for rebirth. And though various sorts of deeds precede, that deed which is

> weightier, or proximate, or reinforced by practice, is one which has generated a potency that shines forth, but not so another.[31]

The view that persons are ψ-continua will be attractive, I think, primarily to those who, like the early Buddhists, become convinced that the notion of a persisting, substantial soul is for some reason false (or at least very unlikely to be true), but who nonetheless insist upon some form of psycho-physical dualism. As we shall soon see, however, the concept of the ψ-continuum is one about which many objections can be raised.

Where Uddyotakara and Candrakīrti Agree

We have already seen that there is considerable difficulty involved in specifying just what the laws are that must be assumed to govern the ψ-continuum. We turn now to consider briefly two further objections to the abhidharma version of the theory, one of which came from the Nyāya philosophers, and the other of which came to be articulated by Buddhists themselves. In particular, I wish to point out a curious convergence between the thought of the Nyāya philosopher Uddyotakara and the Buddhist Candrakīrti, who was his approximate contemporary. Both rejected the hypothesis that persons are continuants, and did so for similar reasons; but Uddyotakara upheld the Nyāya theory of the reality of a substantial self, while Candrakīrti, we have seen, was a proponent of the Buddha's non-self teaching.

Uddyotakara's fundamental objection to the notion of the continuum is given in this assertion:

> Affirming unification to be due to there being [the relationship of] cause and effect does not preclude diversity.[32]

We are causally related with all sorts of things—about that there is no question. And most of those things, we would concur, are not in any sense ourselves. But if we are unified as persons only in virtue of the causal relationships obtaining among discrete person-stages, and if we do not have a very good theory about just which causal relationships individuate persons and which ones do not, then it would seem that Devī yesterday and today are no more stages of the same person than Devī yesterday and Līlā today are usually held to be, so long as Devī and Līlā are related causally in *some* way or another.

Strikingly, this is precisely Candrakīrti's objection, too:

> The principles which depend on Maitreya and Upagupta,
> Being different, do not belong [to the same continuum] at any instant;
> And whatever is essentially different
> Cannot belong to a single continuum at all.[33]

Candrakīrti, I think, saw the hypothesis of the continuum as another effort, in reaction to the Buddha's rejection of the persisting self, to reintroduce such a thing through the back door, as it were. As he perceived it, the Ābhidharmikas went wrong in seeking to find something "out there" with which the concept of the person has a one-to-one correspondence, namely, the continuum. But the radical causalism of Buddhism, on Candrakīrti's view, in effect turns the entire world into a single, interdependent continuum, in which no really self-individuating continua are to be found.

In sum, Candrakīrti argues that on the assumption that the person is something strictly identical through time, the inquiry into its relationships with the changing series of psychological and physical elements with which it must be somehow connected leads to various absurdities. But if a person is simply the changing series, then we are left without any clear reason to suppose that, say, Devī today is not someone other than Devī yesterday. In other words, Devī yesterday might just as well have been Līlā. The notion of a persisting self doesn't "correspond" to anything at all; it's simply an illusion, and this is what the Buddha pointed out in declaring all things to be non-selves.[34]

I will not attempt a more detailed account of Uddyotakara's and Candrakīrti's arguments about this here. This short summary, however, should underscore for us that the convergences among differing Indian philosophical schools (here, Nyāya and Madhyamaka), as well as the divergences within single traditions (Buddhism in the present case), were sometimes more intricate and subtle than they are often supposed to be. At the same time, we must recall that Uddyotakara and Candrakīrti advanced their arguments in support of quite different ends, and these, for the most part, were determined by the schools to which they belonged.

Notes

1 See here *Tattvasaṅgraha,* v. 330, and its commentary; and chap. 9, n. 42, below.

2 Nonetheless, materialism was a well-known position, even to the authors of the Upaniṣads. *Bṛhadāraṇyaka,* II.iv.12, for instance, says: "The mass of consciousness, having arisen, verily, from these elements, dissolves back into them; having died, there is no awareness."

3 Parfit 1984: 210: "[The Further Fact View] denies that we are separately existing entities, distinct from our brains and bodies, and our experiences. But this view claims that, though we are not separately existing entities, personal identity is a further fact, which does not just consist in physical and/or psychological continuity." What Parfit terms the Further Fact View may, in fact, be similar to the view of the Buddhist Personalists, who affirm an "ineffable" person. And Candrakīrti's critique of the more mainstream abhidharma view of persons as continuants suggests that he regarded the abhidharma perspective as tacitly non-Reductionist, in which case it, too, would be a variety of Further Fact View. Duerlinger 1993, however, argues that Candrakīrti, given his assault on abhidharma Reductionism, was himself espousing a sort of non-Reductionism, but here I am inclined to disagree. I believe that he would have regarded *both* Reductionism and non-Reductionism as aporetic, and, hence, *ultimately* untenable. Duerlinger, however, may be broadly in accord with Candrakīrti's *conventional* position.

4 Cf. Shoemaker 1984: 139–58: "Immortality and Dualism."

5 On the general Buddhist problematic of psychological continuity, see in particular Griffiths 1986.

6 I have in mind here particularly the discussions of Kant 1965: A 98–130, A 345–49, B 131–38; Broad 1925, chap. 13, "The Unity of the Mind"; Brentano 1973, chap. 4, "On the Unity of Consciousness"; Chisholm 1979, chaps. 1 and 3; and 1981, chap. 7, "Certainty and the Unity of Consciousness."

7 Venkataramanan 1953: 177–78.

8 Rhys Davids 1890: II.2.1.

9 Note, however, that the Reductionist may allow for the possibility of some sort of continuity between one "person" and several simultaneous successors. Consider some of the more bizarre puzzle-cases in Parfit 1984: 298–306. Most Buddhist traditions insist upon a one-to-one correspondence between the deceased and his or her successor. Tibetan Buddhism, however, does admit multiple incarnations of a single master, or reabsorptions of these into a single successor. Nevertheless, this tends to be explained on the basis of buddhological theories of emanation, and not according to the conception of regular rebirth in the world. The issues raised here have not been much considered in current investigations of Buddhist thought, but see Piatigorsky 1984.

10 Cf. Collins 1982a: 238–61, on the so-called "*bhavaṅga*-mind" posited in Theravāda Buddhism. Cf. also Griffiths 1986.

11 Brentano 1973: 16–17.

12 Vātsyāyana's arguments are detailed below in chap. 5, in the section entitled "The Dancing Girl's Brow."

13 John Locke 1974: II.xxvii, "Of Identity and Diversity." For critical discussions of Locke's theory, see Perry 1975: 33–155.

14 Joseph Butler, "Of Identity," in Perry 1975: 100: "And one should really think it self-evident, that consciousness of personal identity presupposes, and therefore cannot constitute, personal identity, any more than knowledge, in any other case, can constitute truth, which it presupposes."

15 See below, chap. 14, part II, passage A.

16 According to Yaśomitra, one of Vasubandhu's most influential commentators, "etc." here refers to, e.g., deliberate practice, repetition, and other such acts which tend to promote retention by memory. *Abhidharmakośa,* vol. 4, p. 1216.

17 See below, chap. 14, part I, par. 7.1.

18 Refer to Martin and Deutscher 1966 and, for "memory" in traditional Buddhist thought, Gyatso 1992.

19 Martin and Deutscher 1966: 161–67.

20 In the present discussion, *apparent memory* refers to a mental act that appears to its subject to be a memory, whether or not it really is one. Experiences of *déjà vu* frequently seem to exemplify experiences of apparent memory whose credentials as real memory we doubt, or at least find puzzling.

21 Martin and Deutscher 1966, sections VI, "Necessary and Operative Conditions," and VII, "A Distinction between Operative in the Circumstances, and Operative for the Circumstances."

22 Cf. the remarks of Uddyotakara in the selections given in chap. 14, part II, passage B, below.

23 Martin and Deutscher 1966, section II.

24 Chap. 14, part I, par. 7.1, below.

25 Refer to Vātsyāyana's comments in chap. 14, part II, passage A.

26 Chap. 14, part I, par. 7.2, below.

27 Cf. "The Problem of Personal Identity," in Perry 1975: 26–30.

28 It is to be regretted that the example Vasubandhu gives here so blatantly reflects the pervasive misogyny of classical Indian ascetic culture. One note of clarification is called for: "the thought of rejecting a woman's body" is the attitude appropriate for a celibate monk, while "the thought of her father or son" is appropriate for the layman. In both cases, the associations in question are deliberately cultivated in order to encourage one's adherence to the vows of celibacy on the one hand, and the avoidance of adultery on the other.

29 Chap. 14, part I, par. 7.3, below.

30 Chap. 14, part I, par. 7.3, below.

31 Chap. 14, part I, par. 7.7, below.

32 *Nyāyavārttika* on *Nyāyasūtra,* 1.1.10, translated in chap. 14, part II, passage B, below.

33 *Madhyamakāvatāra,* vi.61.

34 My interpretation of Candrakīrti on this point is supported by his own remarks on *Madhyamakāvatāra,* vi.129ab (pp. 249–50 in the Tibetan text). I quote here

the translation of Engle 1983: 159–60: "...it might be said that, 'Although these moments occurring at an earlier and later period are different, still, as they make up a single continuum, we are not guilty of the alleged fallacy.' To this it is replied:

> If the error is denied because of a really existent continuum,
> In an earlier analysis the error of the continuum was explained.

"This occurs where it was said: 'Things based on Maitri and Upagupta...' (*Madhyamakāvatāra,* chap. 6, v. 61). It is also stated that:

> If a human were different from a god
> Then there would be impermanence.
> If a human were different from a god
> There could not be a continuum. (*Madhyamakakārikā* XXVII, 16)

"Thus, since it cannot be the case that things which have defining properties *(lakṣaṇa)* different from one another should make up part of a single continuum, the unwanted consequence is not averted."

5. The Sensualist, the Sage, and the Dancing Girl's Brow: Personal Identity and Self-Cultivation

The true mystery of the world is the visible, not the invisible.
—Oscar Wilde

It is clear now that philosophical disputes in ancient and medieval India surrounding problems of the self and personal identity sometimes anticipated modern Western discussions. Locke and Hume had their counterparts among Buddhist thinkers who sought to explain apparent personal identity through time by treating persons as continuous streams of short-lived events, while the opposing non-Reductionist theories of the self were anticipated in the writings of the Buddhists' Brahmanical opponents. Parallels such as these between the Indian and Western philosophical traditions rightly invite comparative inquiry, but this in turn seems generally to invite a question of great breadth that we have not yet succeeded in addressing with much clarity: if Indian and Western philosophy are in some respects so similar, why are they at the same time so very different? If the apparent similarities obtaining between the two traditions incline us to a strong version of anti-relativism, asserting that human thought is always and everywhere similar in its essential features, then we perhaps have reason to re-examine with some skepticism our own presuppositions and methods: just what, after all, ought to count as an "*essential* feature" of human thought? If we drop this qualification, we are left with a platitude ("human thought is always and everywhere similar"), and one that is—at least on some readings—likely false to boot.[1]

The case of Indian philosophy is in some respects unlike that confronted by students of classical Chinese thought. It is sometimes argued that China offers us an intellectual universe largely diverse from that of the West, and that apparent resemblances between them should be considered with circumspection. China invites ruminations on radical incommensurability, on the problems of interpreting and explaining an altogether alien realm, on the possibility that something like the Whorf-Sapir hypothesis might be correct.[2] India, on the other hand, beguiles us with an appearance of familiarity set in an alien landscape; and this, of course, leads us to wonder whether the similarities we thought we had perceived were merely imagined, or were in some sense basic and "real." Assuming that this is not just an illusion, does the perceived conformity orient us to genuine universals of thought, or does it only reflect something peculiar about the Indo-European languages? (It has sometimes been suggested, for instance, that the Indo-European copula might be a factor here.[3])

It will be urged that India developed sophisticated and critical approaches to epistemology and metaphysics, often resembling our own; but then why, given the close attention to conceptual analysis in those spheres, the conspicuous absence of sustained philosophical discussion in such areas as ethics and politics?[4] Or that India elaborated advanced systems of logic and the philosophy of language; but in that case why are the modalities of necessity, possibility, and actuality seemingly neglected?[5] India, to mention one specific example, produced arguments very much like the standard Western arguments for the existence of god (excepting of course their modal versions); but why is it that the philosophers drop these so quickly, to elaborate instead a series of arguments that turn on the revealed status of Vedic lore?[6] Regarded from this perspective, Indian philosophy begins to look like a misshapen version of Western philosophy, like Western philosophy seen through a distorting lens.

Part of the problem we confront here stems from the relative lack of attention contemporary students of Indian philosophy have paid to the context of the development of Indian philosophy. I do not propose now to enter upon a lengthy digression on contextualization.[7] Some, of course, will hold that when we are discussing philosophical arguments, consideration of context is to all intents and purposes irrelevant: we should focus just on the precise content of the argument, on the crispest possible formulation of questions bearing upon its soundness and validity, abstracting the philosophical meat from its contextual shell as perfectly as is possible. Issues of context just muddy the waters.[8] I am willing to accept, for the sake of the discussion, that this sometimes may in fact be a legitimate position to adopt; I don't think, for example, that reflection on the logical entailments of Leibniz's Law requires us to worry overly much about the man Leibniz, or about his historical situation. But clearly this is not always the case: if I wish to inquire more broadly into the concept of identity in Leibniz's thought, I am inevitably going to delve into *The Monadology* and *The Theodicy*, and any non-superficial consideration of these will in turn force me to study seventeenth-century thought more generally.[9] The topic for our present discussion, personal identity, is certainly an instance in which some measure of contextualization must be countenanced. It matters very much to our reading of Locke, for example, that we understand what he means when he insists upon what he terms the *forensic* character of the concept of the person.[10] We cannot fully comprehend Hume's real disquiet over his own conclusions about personal identity, if we do not grasp the manner in which that question is framed within Hume's concerns regarding persons as moral and historical agents.[11] Derek Parfit's intriguing puzzles of identity seem mere brain-teasers, unless we take seriously their relevance to his ethical reflections.[12] The point I am trying to make here has, of course, been very prominent in recent philosophical writing on personal identity, above all in Charles Taylor's magisterial *Sources of the Self*.[13]

As a student of Indian philosophy, this leads me to ask how we ought to frame the problem of personal identity in its Indian setting. What are the considerations in virtue of which we might understand how the problem was *felt* by Indian thinkers? In attempting to make some progress here, I offer in what follows not a sustained analysis of a single aspect of the Indian discussion, but rather three vignettes, which I hope will cooperate to suggest some of the broad contours of the larger picture, and so perhaps indicate something of the richness of the problem and of the sources that must be considered in relation to it. The three topics that I shall consider here are: the identity of persons as narrated in literature, in this case in a poem of the Buddhist author Aśvaghoṣa (first or second century C.E.); aspects of the debate between adherents of the Hindu Nyāya school and the Buddhists concerning the unity of consciousness, as exemplified in a peculiar trope, the "dancing girl's brow," which is discussed by the philosophers Uddyotakara (c. 600) and Śāntarakṣita (c. 750); and the implications of the Indian Buddhist interest in poetics for our conception of the formation of the educated person. What I hope to suggest is that, while there is indeed a correspondence between certain of the formal features of classical Indian and modern Western debates on personal identity, these common concerns are framed in interestingly disparate ways.

Beautiful Nanda

The figure of Nanda is well situated for us by the poet Aśvaghoṣa.[14] The handsome son of a royal family of great antiquity, glory, and piety, he is Siddhārtha's younger half-brother, and it is Siddhārtha's return—long after renouncing the palace to become the Awakened One, the Buddha who has realized the peace of nirvāṇa—that marks the beginning of a turn in Nanda's own life. For Nanda has been up to now content to situate himself in the realm of the senses, and even as his brother preaches his message of spiritual liberation to their common clansmen, Nanda, in Aśvaghoṣa's words, "remained in the palace with his darling, with nothing to do but make love" (*SN,* 4.1).

Aśvaghoṣa marks the complementarity and the opposition of the siblings early in his poem, soon after describing their birth. He metaphorically describes king Śuddhodana's nurturing of them as resembling wealth *(artha)* that is used to uphold moral and religious obligations *(dharma)* on the one hand while nourishing the sensual pleasures *(kāma)* on the other (*SN,* 2.60). There is perhaps no statement in the literature that indicates more concisely the core of classical Hindu value theory.[15] We must by no means read Aśvaghoṣa's words at this point as involving any tacit condemnation of sensual pleasure, for, in the particular context of the ancient Indian ideal of kingship, Epicurean refinement was always held to be a virtue, one to be harmonized with the proper fulfillment of mundane and religious obligations in the life of the cultivated individual.[16] It is only with Śākyamuni's later rejection of his princely estate in order to achieve the freedom of buddhahood that we find a distinctive and destabilizing virtue introduced into that potential harmony of the values—specifically freedom *(mokṣa)* itself. For in Indian thought freedom was counterpoised to religious duty, as well as to both material prosperity and the cultivation of the senses, and thus was placed in an asymmetrical relationship with those goods as they were often traditionally affirmed.[17] By leaving the palace, Śākyamuni had in effect issued a declaration of spiritual autonomy, a refusal to remain entangled within the radically heteronomous condition of ordinary worldly life.[18] That condition, requiring an unending expenditure of energy in an inevitably futile effort to maintain or improve one's station, was thought in the final analysis to be no more than a painful round of self-defeating desire and fear. All of the classical Indian systems of salvation agreed about this.[19] Beautiful Nanda, however, is still happy to remain in the round, gleefully relishing imaginative love-play with his wonderfully beautiful wife. Aśvaghoṣa

figure 1. The complementarity of values: donor figures and buddhas. Cave 3, Kanheri, Maharashtra. Second century.

intended no doubt that in Nanda we should see ourselves, both in his affinity with the Buddha, and in his actual inability to comprehend the deeper significance of that affinity.

One of the games Nanda enjoys with his love, Sundarī, involves the mirror that he holds for her as she makes herself up (*SN*, 4.13–22). Her reflected beauty, both present and removed from its source, seems to be within his grasp but forever slipping away from it. The motif of the mirror, in Aśvaghoṣa's narration, is suggestive of the diaphanous and ephemeral quality of worldly enjoyment, as also of its capacity to entice us to unending distraction. The world glitters and sparkles, but it is not substantially real.[20] So immersed in their mirror-game are Nanda and Sundarī, however, that they are caught entirely unawares when one day Śākyamuni arrives at their household in the course of his begging rounds (*SN*, 4.24–25). The servants, too preoccupied with preparing unguents and garlands and all that is required for the delight of their master and his lady, take no notice of the sage as he reaches the threshhold, and he, perceiving at once that he is unnoticed, quietly departs and proceeds on his way. As he walks off, one of the servant-girls recognizes what has happened and runs to tell Nanda, who is dismayed that such a breach of hospitality toward his own brother, the spiritual mentor of his clan, should have taken place. Nanda, after all, for all his immersion in his own enjoyments, is nonetheless a Śākya prince, and his devotion to eros has by no means annulled his devotion to his family, and to the brother who is now well honored for his attainments on a path opposite to Nanda's own. He dresses in haste and takes his leave from Sundarī, who agrees to let him depart "so long as you return before my make-up has dried" (*SN*, 4.34). Thinking of her words and at the same time of his need to make amends for the rude reception accorded the Buddha, he sets off, and suddenly finds himself torn by his own feelings, "seized by his lust, even as he was drawn on by a yearning for the Dharma" (*SN*, 4.44). It is precisely here that Aśvaghoṣa establishes the dramatic center of his poem: it is the story of a man who discovers to his dismay that, far from being the carefree playboy he thought himself to be, he is profoundly divided against himself.

Nanda catches up with the sage and, with considerable embarrassment, proffers his apology and prepares to return home before Sundarī's make-up sets (*SN*, 4. 40–5.14). But the Buddha, knowing Nanda's mind, gives him his begging-bowl, that symbol of renunciation that is filled by the faithful to sustain the ascetic (*SN*, 5. 11). The empty begging-bowl, a sign of one's refusal to grasp, represents in Aśvaghoṣa's poem the mendicant's attainment of the only really substantial nutrition that is to be found, that of the enlightened spirit, and it stands here in implicit contrast with the mirror, which, though deliberately grasped, can hold only fickle reflections.

When the Buddha at last addresses Nanda, his gentle self-assurance establishes a counterpoint to the latter's confused state of mind. "The world," he tells him, "is no more satisfied with the senses than is a fire, stirred by the breeze, with oblations" (*SN*, 5.23). Beautiful Nanda is quite shaken by the impact his brother's calm presence makes upon him, and, thinking to change his ways, renounces the worldly life to become a monk in the order.

Conversions, though they may be decisive events, are seldom straightforward and untroubled. Having entered into mendicant life, Nanda continues to mull over what he has lost and grows despondent, finding himself immersed in memory and in longing. He craves to return to his beloved, and though outwardly a member of the order, in his heart he is "neither monk nor householder" (*SN*, 7.49). This is not to say that he is just caught between opposing roles; for Nanda's dilemma, though certainly brought to a head by the conflict between monastic and lay roles, is much less about the part he should play than it is about the condition of his self-understanding. Nanda's conflict is fundamentally a crisis not over role, but over his very identity.[21]

Desiring nothing more than to reestablish his own equilibrium, he reflects on the sages and heroes of legend who sacrificed possessions, status, sanity, and sometimes even life itself for the women they loved (*SN*, 7.24–52). He concludes that his own course must be similar, that it is a sham for him to remain a monk. His state of mind becomes known to a fellow member of the order, who tries to convince Nanda to reconsider by lecturing him on the evil nature of women (*SN*, canto 8). Regardless of Aśvaghoṣa's real intentions here, it is to his credit as a poet that this harangue *does not* have the desired effect.[22]

The Buddha eventually comes to learn of his brother's imminent departure from the order and decides that he himself must intervene (*SN*, 10.1–2). He takes Nanda on a visionary journey during the course of which, among other things, Nanda comes to behold the beauty of the celestial nymphs. This vision inspires him to adhere to a chaste and virtuous life in order to acquire the positive *karman* needed to ensure his rebirth in a heaven populated by such beauties (*SN*, 10.3–64). He becomes zealous in his religious practice, inspired by the expectation of future bliss. After some time, however, his hypocrisy is exposed, and it finally dawns on him that in both his former relationship with his wife and his aspiration for the pleasures of heaven, he was impelled by a passion for objects, a passion that inevitably brings loss, frustration, and pain (*SN*, canto 11). The Buddha, by granting him a vision of paradise, had not intended that Nanda should merely alter the objects

figure 2. The persistence of images: the mirror-game in a miniature. Bundi, Rajasthan. c. 1765.

of his thirst, but that he should become aware of his own proclivity to indulge in self-defeating objectifications. It is the turn in Nanda's inner trajectory, attending this discovery, that sets him upon the course that will culminate in his attainment of genuine enlightenment. Nanda attains that realization in the poem's seventeenth canto, and it is here that the normative doctrine of the selflessness of all conditioned things is at last underscored.

The construction of Nanda represents in crucial respects a fluid and open conception of persons. As the motif of his beloved's mirror image suggests, the person is disclosed in its aspects, and these are tenuous and unsure. Likewise, Nanda, his wife, and his brother are all poetic constructions; tropes and figures convey their personæ in the mirror of Aśvaghoṣa's words. In this reflected image of his spiritual and visionary path, Nanda changes and grows, and the person who had at first been restlessly immersed in sensual delight, in the end becomes a sage at peace with the truth of selflessness.

In Aśvaghoṣa's telling of it, then, Nanda's story may be read so as to accentuate the fragility and mutability of the self. A person may be rent by profound conflict, and may change in unanticipated ways. In such circumstances, to know a person means not to know some fixed and determinate thing, but to be familiar with some part of a *narrative,* to have followed crucial developments through time. Let us note, however, that this is still a very far cry from the negation of the person, or the denial of the self, which is frequently (and for good reason, as we know) regarded as the most characteristic of Buddhist philosophical doctrines. If Nanda's tale is plausible to us at all, it is only because we understand there to be some person, Nanda, who is torn against himself and is the subject of the great changes he endures. Aśvaghoṣa's poem makes sense, paradoxically, only on the condition that there are persons who are capable of realizing the truth of their selflessness.

The poet in fact deliberately emphasizes this apparent contradiction. For after Nanda describes his experience of enlightenment to his brother, the latter affirms Nanda's realization, saying:

> Today you are a genuine renunciate, O conqueror of the *self,*
> Who has mastered his own *self;*
> For the fine renunciation possessed by the conquered *self,*
> Is not found where the *self* is fickle, the senses uncontrolled
> (*SN,* 18.23).

The fact that the word "self" *(ātman)* is repeated four times in this verse is surely intended to fix our attention upon it, to highlight both the puzzlement that attends this term, and the Buddha's resolution of that puzzlement in a philosophical teaching of selflessness, which corresponds to a practical achievement of self-mastery. Passages similar to the one just quoted have been frequently seized upon by those who are of the opinion that the Buddha's teaching involved some sort of "hidden doctrine" of the self,[23] but Aśvaghoṣa surely is more subtle than that. For numerous passages here and in his other great poem, the *Buddhacarita,* establish that, in perfect accord with the early Buddhist philosophical mainstream, Aśvaghoṣa will in fact countenance no objectification of the self whatsoever; and if the assertion that "there is a self but its nature is hidden" is not an objectification of the self, I am not certain what is.[24] Relinquishing objectification entails not an esoteric doctrine, but genuine silence. It is in a spirit of gently ironic playfulness that one who has realized that peace and silence may now be spoken of as one who has "conquered the self."

The tale of Nanda thus may seem to have been contrived so as to propagate a peculiarly Buddhist message. Its emphasis on the primacy of Śākyamuni's teaching and the enlightenment to be realized through it undoubtably impress upon the reader Aśvaghoṣa's own religious commitment. Moreover, Aśvaghoṣa's stated views on the self appear to be perfectly consistent with normative early Buddhist doctrine. Nevertheless, it is not at all certain that any fundamental difference divides Buddhist from Hindu narrations of persons. A consideration of David Shulman's wonderfully perceptive reading of the tale of Nala, an episode from the Mahābhārata, makes this at once clear. It is a tale "about a man who lost his 'self'—along with everything else that was his,"[25] in the course of episodes in which he finds himself quadruplicated by the gods, only to be later transformed into a dwarf, and at one point seized by the very spirit of Kali, the dark age in the history of the world, who is also the demon of defeat in the game of dice. In the space available here, it will not be possible to summarize Shulman's arguments in detail; some words extracted from his conclusions will have to suffice:

> Nala stumbles, is possessed, goes mad, careens wildly and foolishly from one terrible mistake to the next...It is an internal process, characterized by conscious alienation, the perceived presence of alien being within.
>
> The self, as Nala knows it, is a point of conflagration. Man, at his best, most knowledgable, is a self-consuming, hence self-transcending being. In this system, the words "not I" are the strongest possible affirmation.

> For Nala, or for the poets who sang his story, the self itself is other; possession by Kali is not a moment to be reclaimed or integrated but an awakening, through intoxication and madness, to this fragmented alienness within us and to the process of self-consummation, in a double sense, that is felt to be constitutive of human experience.[26]

Any attempt, therefore, to find a simple correlation between Hindu and Buddhist philosophical doctrines of the self and their narrations of persons is probably doomed to failure. In Aśvaghoṣa's poems, as in other Buddhist narratives, we discover that we must attribute some sort of personhood to the characters whose lives are narrated just in order to make coherent sense of the tale; and this despite the explicit affirmation of the philosophical doctrine of no-self. In the Nala episode, on the other hand, we find the entire notion of the self problematized to a frighteningly radical degree. The stories of Nanda and Nala are stories of liquid selves, selves that can shatter and break, if not in a Parfitian sense, then nonetheless to a degree that calls the receptive reader's own assurances of selfhood into question. To be sure, neither Hindu nor Buddhist poets were primarily concerned to generate metaphysical puzzles of personal identity. Both wished us to hold that the persons we meet at either end of a particular tale are in some sense the same—rake Nanda and sage Nanda, young prince Nala and old chief Nala. In either case, the integrity of the narrative is predicated upon the assumption that personal identity, though fluid, fragile and endlessly puzzling, is nevertheless part of the way in which we make sense of the stories we are told, and of those that we live.

Some may wish to argue that Aśvaghoṣa, as a Brahman seeking to present Buddhism in terms acceptable to the tradition in which he was raised, would naturally have assimilated the Buddhist story to Brahmanical models. This is no doubt in some respect true, but it remains nevertheless the case that Indian Buddhist and Hindu Sanskrit narratives belong to a single continuum, and that no decisive mark of separation, besides sectarian self-identification, can be found to set them apart. Indian tales, both Buddhist and Brahmanical, often seem to emphasize the surprising and frequently disquieting transformations to which persons may be subject—transformations requiring them to become somehow other, to become alien unto themselves—while at the same time challenging us to puzzle over just what it is that has endured such great change. It was left to the philosophers, not to the poets, to seek more perfect clarity and definition, to attempt to resolve the puzzles of our protean selves.

The Dancing Girl's Brow

Indian philosophers were interested in the problem of personal identity in part because, as we have seen, the identity of persons was sometimes thought to be a problem in Indian culture more generally. This is not so glib an observation as it may initially seem, for many of the problems philosophers tackle, in India as in the West, appear to be problems for philosophers alone. It is possible to imagine, I suppose, a community in which roles are so well defined and life so harmonious that, except perhaps for a small number of specialized thinkers who are interested in the logic of identity, no one ever gives much thought to the question of personal identity. (The specialists, for example, may have discovered Leibniz's Law in quite another context and then asked, "now, how does this apply to persons?") In modern Western thought, however, as Charles Taylor has argued eloquently and at length, the puzzles formulated by Locke and by Hume have sustained our interest because they are profoundly intertwined with a rich network of questions about our identity, which ramify throughout our political and moral lives, and which are reflected throughout our literature, too. I would like to suggest that something similar was likely the case in India; in other words, that differing philosophical approaches to the problem of personal identity not only marked off, from a dogmatic perspective, the boundaries between diverse schools of thought, but also reflected deeply troubling concerns. These included questions of social status in relation to caste and lifestyle, of ritual purity, and of temporal and spiritual freedom or the lack thereof.

Literary and historical narratives may permit a way of ingress into the lived worlds of (spatially or temporally) distant communities. For the historian of philosophy they are valuable precisely because they permit us to assess, to some extent at least, the relationship between the topics addressed by the philosopher, and the issues confronting the world in which the philosopher lived and thought. Some familiarity with fifth- and fourth-century B.C.E. Athenian political life, and with the role of the sophists in the education of its elite, for instance, are crucial to our reading of Plato. From another perspective, however, it is the task of the philosopher to reduce a problem to its most simple and abstract terms; in this respect, it may seem unimportant to distinguish very sharply between, say, arguments concerning the logic of predication, and those focusing upon the rights of possible persons. The levelling that seems to occur here ("all p-s and q-s are created equal") is, of course, a sort of philosophical illusion: all problems may be equal to the extent that they share certain formal features, though we know that in real life they are not so. Abstraction of the sort I am referring to must, I think, be borne in mind in connection with our present subject matter; for when we turn from the problem of personal identity in the context of classical Indian narrative to some aspects of its philosophical treatment, we notice a distinct change of emphasis. In brief, we may characterize this by saying that, whereas the poets seemed to accept and indeed to accentuate the very problematic character of the issue, the philosophers wished to find a clear and, so they hoped, unproblematic resolution to it.

Let us recall now that Nanda, when we first met him, was subject to powerful and sometimes conflicting desires. Does it shed any light on the metaphysical problems we are considering to remark that whatever else we may be, we are subjects possessing desires? Among the Brahmanical philosophical traditions of India, as we have seen elsewhere, the Nyāya school of epistemologists certainly thought this point to be crucial. This emerges clearly among the arguments that are developed in the work of Vātsyāyana (c. 400 C.E.) concerning the proof of the self's existence. His remarks take the form of a comment on *Nyāyasūtra (Aphorisms of Reason)*, 1.1.10, the locus classicus of the Nyāya attempts to prove the reality of the self. The aphorism in question reads:

> Desire and hatred, willful effort, pleasure and pain, and knowledge are the marks of the self. *(icchā-dveṣa-prayatna-sukha-duḥkha-jñānāny ātmano liṅgam.)*

Vātsyāyana's comment begins:

> The self, having [previously] acquired pleasure through contact with an object of a certain type, desires to possess an object of that very type whenever it sees it. It is the mark of the self that this desire-to-possess occurs, because a single seer synthesizes *(pratisaṃdhā-)* the seeing. For even with respect to a determinate object, that [synthesis] cannot be based solely upon discrete mental events *(buddhibheda)*, e.g., [the discrete mental events associated with] different bodies.[27]

The argument is then developed by substituting for desire various other sensations, volitions, and psychological states, in order to drive home the contention that the relationships holding among these states "would not be the case if there were not one seer of the many [mental and perceptual acts] that synthesizes the seeing." Vātsyāyana's intuitions accord with those we have brought to bear in our reading of the *Saundarananda*—we found there that we had to imagine some one, namely Nanda, who both desired Sundarī and renounced her. Nanda, as Aśvaghoṣa's narrative center, was in this sense equivalent to Vātsyāyana's philosophical center, the single seer.

For the philosophers of the early Nyāya tradition the existence of a unique, substantial self was thus established by the phenomenology of the individual subject's synthetic experience of such states as desires and so on. Synthetic cohesion *(pratisandhāna),* that is, demonstrates not, as the Buddhists would have it, that there are some regular principles in virtue of which discrete events hang together to form what we conventionally label a "person," but rather confirms that there must be some one thing, the self, causing the synthesized events to cohere. But just how is it, we may ask, that these states of the ego cause us to know of a substantial self with which we are not otherwise directly acquainted? Vātsyāyana's commentator, Uddyotakara, thought that in fact we are each directly acquainted with our own unique self; hence, in responding to this question, he was attempting to establish that reason also confirms the existence of the self, independent of introspection. In adopting this tack, he was rebutting the objections of his Buddhist opponents, by whom an appeal to putative non-inferential self-knowledge would have been rebuked as an instance of *petitio principii.*

The attempt to adduce reasons that demonstrate the substantial existence of the self was, as we have seen, addressed by Vātsyāyana in arguing that singularity of agency is established because desire and other such states share a common orientation to the same objects as memory, and that this can only be explained by assuming them to be states of the same knowing subject. This synthetic cohesion would not occur were there a diversity of agents, corresponding to the diversity of objects and diversity of stimuli involved. It is here that, though taking as his point of departure Vātsyāyana's argument, which concerns primarily the identity of consciousness through time, that is, the problem of personal identity, Uddyotakara subtly shifts the argument, asking us instead to consider the unity of consciousness at one time:

> [If there were no singularity of agency] there would be no synthesis of diverse agents, diverse objects, and diverse stimuli. For the cognitions of form, taste, odor, and texture would in that case not be synthesized; for it would not be true [under that

> description] that "what form I have seen, that is this texture, and what texture I have felt, that is the form I see."[28]

That is to say, assuming no identity of agency, there can be no synthesis of the diverse cognitions of form, odor, etc., into an organic whole—in what sense, then, could we understand ourselves to be both seeing and smelling the same rose? We would not be able to say that the very object I see is the very same object I feel, unless we can affirm that it is one "I" that does both the seeing and the feeling. To drive this point home, Uddyotakara sets out what must be one of the most colorful examples in the history of philosophy:

> Devadatta's cognitions of visible form, flavor, odor, and texture bear the mark of one and many; for they are synthesized by the cognition "I." Similarly, the cognitions of many persons, who have previously entered into an agreement, [are linked together] during the single instant when the dancing-girl raises her brow.[29]

Śāntarakṣita's successor Kamalaśīla, commenting upon Uddyotakara's argument as a prelude to his master's criticism of it, explains it as follows:

> [Uddyotakara's] meaning is this: just as many might enter into an agreement, saying, "As soon as the dancing-girl raises her brow let us all throw fine fabric [onto the stage as a gesture of our common approval]," so that the many agents and their many cognitions—"I have seen [her raise her brow], I have seen it"—are synthetically united because of the singularity of the sign, the raising of the brow; so, too, in the present case, cognitions with many different objects should be synthesized owing to the singularity of a sign, and that singular sign is the self. The synthesis, moreover, is of many cognitions, such as "I have seen, I have heard," which are linked together by the characteristic of possession by a single knower. But in the case of the dancing-girl raising her brow, the cognitions [of the many spectators] are connected because they have a common object. In all these cases, a "synthesis" is spoken of whenever there is a relationship among cognitions, some single feature being considered the reason.[30]

Uddyotakara's fundamental intuition here clearly develops Vātsyāyana's assertion that, whenever we have reason to think of many things as being somehow unified, then those many things must all have some *one* thing in common. This intuition is a very ancient one in Indian thought, and informs many passages in even the earliest Upaniṣads.[31] In the present instance, Uddyotakara seeks to stress in particular our repeating property of egoity—our punctuated consciousness of an "I"—which, he holds, may be interpreted as a *sign,* one signifying an enduring, substantial self. Besides the philosophical content of the argument, however, what is of interest here is also an implicit gesture made through the example of the dancer: in Uddyotakara's philosophical ruminations, the play of sign and signification unfolds in the world of the theater. Philosophical reflection, like dramaturgy and poetics, finds its foundations in semiotics and its expression in the arts of performance. Through the dancing girl's brow, Uddyotakara, the philosophical dramatist, appears to be winking at us.

Śāntarakṣita and Kamalaśīla, in their response, in fact do accept much of Uddyotakara's argument. They affirm, as perhaps Hume did not, that at any one time there is indeed a single center of consciousness, and one that is conscious, all at once, of the various objects of the senses and of the intellect.[32] In this Śāntarakṣita fully agrees with Uddyotakara: what the latter set out to prove, he says, is therefore accepted as proven.[33]

Śāntarakṣita, however, in accord with much of Buddhist scholastic tradition, wishes us to imagine that at any time *t,* a given person-continuum may be subject to an instantaneous act of consciousness (the so-called "condition of immediate continuity") by which the contents of immediately precedent sensory and mental acts are synthesized. When such an act occurs, its phenomenological character is one of unity and egocentricity, and thus, despite the ephemeral character of such consciousness-events, we are generally subject to an illusion of unified and enduring selfhood. As Kamalaśīla tells us:

> Moreover, if what is proven is only that, generally speaking, there is a causal precedent, then what [Uddyotakara] has set out to prove is in any case accepted… Thus, from a single succeeding act of consciousness, which is the condition of immediate continuity, the [preceding] occurrence of the six consciousnesses of the eye, etc., are clearly known. So it is that what sees the dancing-girl's figure also hears the sounds of the drum and other instruments, smells aromas like that of the blue lotus, tastes camphor and so forth, feels the breeze from the fan, etc., and thinks of presenting a gift of cloth. It is not correct to assert that this is

due to extreme rapidity of movement, as when one sees a circle formed by a whirling torch.[34]

Thus, this is not a question of our somehow running together a stream of discrete events, as we do the frames of a film, for that would suggest there to be an enduring observer standing outside of the stream, who perceives objects blurred into apparent identity. For Śāntarakṣita and Kamalaśīla, by contrast, *phenomenal* identity is *phenomenologically* as good as *real* identity, and hence not blurred or fuzzy. Because self-consciousness, the subject's apparent awareness of the "I," is a unique property of all acts of intellectual consciousness, Śāntarakṣita holds that there will be a phenomenal unity of consciousness whenever an act of intellectual consciousness occurs, but there will never be a *real* unity of consciousness in time. Though there is indeed a conscious subject, there is no persisting self, and so no real personal identity through time. Kant provided a somewhat simpler model with his example of a row of billiard balls, each communicating its force to the one that follows.[35] Uddyotakara's charming example of the dancing-girl's gesture, too, can be redeployed to illustrate Śāntarakṣita's case, for here it is a question of an atomic, ephemeral event, standing in a one–many relationship with the perceptions and responses that it arouses. There is neither real unity, nor real identity through time, to be exemplified in this way.

Śāntarakṣita and Uddyotakara remain, nevertheless, participants in a common theater of discourse. Its dramatic conventions provoke varied interpretations of the reality they are presumed to disclose. But one cannot hold—as so often one imagines one can on reading philosophy as also criticism of the theater—that they were not even present at the same performance.

Authoring the Self: Literary Composition and Hyper-refinement

In the study of ancient and medieval India, whose are the names we know? Whose *identities* are in some sense recalled? It is not difficult to list the main types who have escaped the obliteration imposed by time: there are the sages and kings, the poets, philosophers, and grammarians. Enduring identity was won in India through imposing deeds of worldly or spiritual conquest, or through surpassing mastery of language—the Sanskrit language above all. Aśvaghoṣa, in singing to us of the Buddha, his family, and his disciples, recalls for us the identity of a sage, and those glorified by association with him, but we recall Aśvaghoṣa himself thanks to his poetic virtuosity alone. Similarly, Śāntarakṣita and Uddyotakara are enduring presences in the domain of Indian philosophy, thanks to the skill with which they articulated their thought upon the shared stage of the Sanskrit language. These observations suggest, then, one further dimension to the problem of personal identity in the Indian Buddhist context, which we shall explore briefly here. In addition to the construction of the person in narrative, and the deconstruction of the person in philosophical analysis, we may speak of the refinement of the person through the *hyper-refinement* of language, the field within which both narrative and philosophy unfold.

The word "Sanskrit" *(saṃskṛta)* literally means that which is "refined." It is opposed to what exists in its natural or unrefined state *(prākṛta)*, for which reason common, vernacular speech is called "Prakrit." The mastery of Sanskrit is an achievement through which the individual himself is refined and comes to participate in an ennobling and even divine sphere of being, for Sanskrit is also the tongue of the gods. I speak of this mastery as a "hyper-refinement" in order to suggest a domain of activity in which an excellence is cultivated far beyond the demands of ordinary social convention, and certainly beyond any obvious utilitarian requirements. All societies probably value hyper-refinements of one kind or another: they are exemplified by virtuosity in the arts, in sports and games, in learning, ritual, social etiquette, and cuisine, among many other things. The hyper-refinements valued by a particular culture tell us much (though certainly not everything) about the goods it cherishes overall. Persons who are thought to exemplify a given culture's hyper-refinements to the highest degree similarly disclose to us important aspects of the construction of personal identity within the communities in question. Such persons frequently become exemplars who are admired to the point of awe, and they are often emulated.

Hyper-refinements generally involve a peculiar feature that, superficially at least, appears to be paradoxical. The exemplification of a hyper-refinement is felt to be the achievement of an *objective* excellence, and so in an important sense hyper-refinements are impersonal. But at the same time their exemplification confers upon the person exemplifying them a unique personal identity, to which special honor is accorded. Michael Jordan's antigravitational jump-shots represent an attainment whose excellence is thought to be judged according to an objective and impersonal standard, but Jordan is unique in our eyes for possessing such excellence. This is no doubt the case in part because we delight in the manner in which hyper-refinements are always made personal by their possessors: no two great basketball players make their moves in quite the same way. Improvisational skills and art forms, including many sports, accentuate this personal appropriation of impersonal excellence, but the case is similar even where performance is stipulated to an exceptionally high degree: we might consider the performances of a single violin concerto by, say, Gil Shaham and Itzhak Perlman, or the practice of the tea ceremony by different masters. It is as if the distinctive character of the person were brought into sharpest relief as she or he draws closest to an ideal that is thought to stand apart from any particular individual.

In our present context, it is not difficult to find evidence in Sanskrit literature for the assumption of a fundamental relationship between education emphasizing the refinement of language and the formation of the morally refined individual. Accordingly, there was a remarkably high valorization of cultivated speech in the cultural world that produced this literature. The famous collection of fables, *Hitopadeśa,* which identifies itself as a pedagogical text, tells us at the outset that its study offers "skill in the Sanskrit language and brilliance of speech," in addition to the knowledge of polity, which is nominally its proper subject matter.[36] To mention a text that was popular among Buddhists, we may note Daṇḍin's stipulations regarding poetic excellence in his *Kāvyādarśa (Mirror of Poetics),* above all his assertion that the arts of composition, of the "brilliantly varied pathways of speech," were intended for the formation of cultivated persons.[37]

Because we have often understood the Buddhist conception of *anātman,* "non-self," to be a teaching of abnegation, the Buddhist participation in, and indeed commitment to, the Indian culture of personal aesthetic refinement has sometimes seemed counterintuitive. But there can be no doubt that Indian Buddhist thinkers were thoroughly engaged in this culture of the self. An illustration may be found in Jñānaśrīmitra's *tour de force,* the *Vṛttamālāstūti (Metrical Garland Hymn),* a praise-poem eulogizing the bodhisattva Mañjuśrī in 154 verses exemplifying 150 distinct metrical forms, the name of each being embedded in the verse which exemplifies it. As an example, consider verse 80, in the meter Vasudhā, whose name refers to the earth as the "store of riches":

> If one contemplates you even in part, mind unwavering,
> Respectful in every way, with powers well-bound,
> Before long this person will certainly by himself bind
> This Store of Riches, adorned with her belt of seas.[38]

Jñānaśrīmitra here stresses an isomorphism holding among the mind well-bound in contemplation—cultivated by the devotee, but epitomized in the figure of Mañjuśrī—the king who binds the earth under his rule, and, implicitly, the poet, by whom language is bound in well-formed verse. Bodhisattva and aspirant, prince and poet, here partake of, and indeed instantiate, a common order of moral discipline, of refined self-control. The culture of selflessness is here fully harmonized with the cultivation of the self. As two rivers that mingle in the sea surrounding the well-bound earth, *ascesis* has here merged with *poesis.*

Philosophy and Self-Cultivation: The Whole in the Center

The juxtaposition here of three approaches to the question of personal identity—in relation to narrative, philosophical discourse, and the educational formation of the refined individual—leads us to ask further how these three are connected with one another. There should now be no question but that there are deep connections among them; our task, rather, is to accentuate those that seem most pertinent in the present context. It is clear, to begin, that educational systems are very strongly linked with ideal narrative constructions: we imagine (or, at least, in earlier generations we imagined) the individual who succeeds brilliantly in the challenges of classroom and playing-field, and goes forth, well-rounded and affirming of life, to succeed with equal brilliance in the challenges of family and career. The picture is so simple that it can be evoked in just a few words, even if projected into cultural and historical frames far removed from our own: a fine example is Herman Hesse's characterization of his youthful hero in the opening paragraph of the novel *Siddhartha:*

> Shadows passed across his black eyes in the mango grove during play, while his mother sang, at the holy sacrifices, while learning from his learned father, when conversing with the sages.[39]

Similarly, consider the impression one derives from the opening of the Hāthigumphā inscription of the Orissan king Khārevala, composed over two millennia ago:

> [Khārevala,] who has a handsome brown complexion, played childhood games for fifteen years. Thereafter, being proficient

> in writing, coinage, arithmetic, law and procedure, and skilled in all arts, (he) ruled as the Crown Prince for nine years.[40]

The relationship between the narration of a life and an ideal pattern of development grows more interesting, of course, when we take account both of the idiosyncratic ways in which the ideal may be in some sense actualized, and the numberless deflections whereby its actualization may be frustrated or defeated: divine or human opposition from without, personal failings from within, willful determination not to accord with the ideal, bad luck, the inevitability of decline and death, and endless twists on these and other themes. Hesse's Siddhartha becomes intriguing to us when this perfectly virtuous heir to the brahmans moves in with his courtesan, likewise Aśvaghoṣa's Nanda when he finds himself rent between the opposing values of erotic pleasure and spiritual freedom. In both of these stories the hero's detour becomes part of the path whereby he realizes an ideal end; such tales are attractive no doubt in part because so many of us, if we are to realize our highest aims at all, must likewise do so via circuitous and often tortured paths.

For much of classical Indian thought, internal conflict betokened the heteronomy of the will and the dispersion of one's energies in a deceptive and ephemeral world. The cultivation of the person was intended to counter the entropic tendencies this involved, by harmonizing one's energies, leading to conscious mastery of them, and by arousing a continuous vigilance to the dangers of succumbing to illusion. Such cultivation, of course, found its most extreme articulation in yoga and soteriological practice, but similar themes surround the formation of scholars and kings. Not for nothing was the grammatical science of India thought to have represented the grace of Śiva, or the great poet Kālidāsa to have been a bumpkin blessed by the goddess, or the king the deity's living presence. For that which was well-ordered was divine, and the individual who had attained self-mastery, or had mastered the rule-bound grammar of the Sanskrit language, or the laws of poetic meter and ornament, or the principles required for the governance of a pacific and prosperous kingdom were all isomorphic in this regard. Buddhism, despite its doctrinal differences with the Brahmanical schools, and its ambivalent ties with aspects of Indian social structure, was nevertheless a paradigmatically Indian tradition in these respects. Neither Aśvaghoṣa's narration of Nanda, nor the pedagogical ideals embodied in his and other Buddhist Sanskrit poetry incline us to any other conclusion.

We are left then to question the role of philosophical conflict here, particularly that of the conflict about the metaphysics of our identity. I should like to suggest that the foregoing observations provide at least part of the answer. For conflicted thought, like emotional conflict, represents the failure to achieve a perfect harmony and self-integration. The philosophical impetus thus parallels the soteriological; as later Hindu thinkers would have it, thought itself becomes a kind of yoga.[41] The resolution of intellectual conflict, however, cannot for long be a matter of purely internal contemplative practice, for thought has its home in shared language, and so must itself be shared. The conflicts that inevitably arise are engendered by and thus belong to an entire community of discourse. The notion of a perfectly harmonious philosophical doctrine remains an unactualized ideal of reason so long as persons are themselves subject to conflicting impulses of whatever kind. So it was that, even after Vedānta had successfully established its hegemony in the domain of later Hindu philosophical thought, it found itself eventually shattered into a plurality of contentious subschools. And not very surprisingly, in the light of what has been said, the problems of the self would loom large in their disputes.[42]

It is sometimes thought that the ancient Buddhist teaching of selflessness undermined concern and care for the self, except perhaps insomuch as it supported a negatively construed ideal of freedom. I have tried to suggest here that things in fact were not nearly so simple, for the Indian Buddhist discourse of the self was multivalent, informed by a variety of complementary goods. The doctrine of selflessness, by refusing to countenance any objectification of the self, by accentuating our fluidity and our capacity for change, and by encouraging us therefore to attend to the task of self-formation, played a central role in that discourse. Clearly, therefore, we would err, were we to reduce all this to the negative proposition alone.

The teaching of selflessness according to the readings suggested above begins perhaps to appear as a vortex theory of the self: metaphysically speaking, there is *nothing* there. There is a vacuum, an absence around which the person is configured. In this regard we remain close to the observations articulated with reference to the tale of Nala by Shulman. For the person who inhabits the world that we have sought to explore here in its general contours, one's supreme task is to be stationed at once in the emptiness of self and in the fullness of being. The fortunate individual may achieve this by pursuing a clear and well-defined path leading to an optimal level of harmony and self-integration. Such individuals, however, are few. The rest of us, alas, are condemned to fight terrible battles, self against self, before we can enter that sure sphere of peace.

Notes

1 On the question of relativism generally, see Hollis and Lukes 1982; and in connection with comparative philosophy in particular, Larson and Deutsch 1988, and Biderman and Scharfstein 1989.

2 For a judicious survey of this question in relation to both its philosophical and philological aspects, see Graham 1989: 389–428 (app. 2, "The Relation of Chinese Thought to the Chinese Language"). The so-called Whorf-Sapir hypothesis to which Graham refers was summarized by Whorf (1956: 213) in these words: "We dissect nature along lines laid down by our native languages. The categories and types that we isolate from the world of phenomena we do not find there because they stare every observer in the face; on the contrary, the world is presented in a kaleidoscopic flux of impressions which has to be organized by our minds—and this means largely by the linguistic system in our minds."

3 Refer to comments on words for "being" and "truth" in chap. 8 below.

4 Of course, ethics and politics are indeed very much discussed in the literature of ancient and medieval India. What we do not seem to find, however, is the philosophical investigation of ethical and political concepts along lines similar to those that are evident in the Indian treatment of matters pertaining to logic, epistemology, philosophy of language, and metaphysics. It is striking, for instance, that in an encyclopedic work of markedly philosophical character like Śāntarakṣita's *Tattvasaṅgraha* (for the contents of which see the introduction, n. 17), no specifically ethical topics are treated (though, as I have argued earlier, there is a discernible *ethical orientation* governing the work as a whole).

Dasgupta 1961, still one of the fullest explorations of Indian ethics, takes as her point of departure that, in Indian thought at least, "morality implies a system of practical rules of conduct of a man in the light of his religion" (p. 4). And many writers (e.g., Potter 1963, Matilal 1982, and Ganeri 2001) emphasize the ethical dimensions of soteriology in the Indian framework. For recent treatments of specific ethical issues in Hindu and Buddhist thought, see now Coward et al. 1989, Perrett 1998, and Harvey 2000. See, too, Raju 1985, chap. 2, on Mīmāṃsā thought in relation to Indian ethics.

5 On the treatment of necessity in Indian logics, see especially Matilal 1982, chap. 7, and Mohanty 1992: 118–22. Of course, necessity is often *expressed* in Indian arguments, for instance, through the use of the gerundive, but what is in question here is whether it was *theorized* as a feature of logical operations. Similarly, we do find, on occasion, informal remarks on possibility and probability, e.g., *Pramāṇavārttika,* Svārthānumana chapter, 8ff., on results born of causal aggregations, and *Tattvasaṅgrahapañjikā,* p. 4. As Matilal (1982: 150) remarks, however, "Possibility as a modal notion had a very limited use in the whole of Indian philosophy."

6 See, in particular, Chemparathy 1972, on Udayana's *Nyāyakusumāñjali;* and on Mīmāṃsā approaches, D'Sa 1980.

7 Scharfstein 1989 offers a thoughtful and perceptive study of this issue.

8 See, for instance, Griffiths 1990.

9 Or as Rorty, Schneewind, and Skinner (1985: 10) put it: "No matter how philistine the historian of philosophy may want to be, he will need translations of what Spinoza wrote which will let him get a handle on the truth-value of Spinoza's sentences. This will require him to examine present translations critically to see whether they are infected with the philosophies of some intervening epoch, and eventually to work out his own translations. He will become an historical scholar...whether he wants to or not."

10 See above, chap. 2, n. 25.

11 Hume 1888, book I, sec. VI, "Of Personal Identity," and, famously, Hume's reconsiderations, which he elaborates on pp. 633–36.

12 Parfit 1984. On the relationship of Parfit's work to Buddhist thought, see Kapstein 1986, Duerlinger 1993, Collins 1994, and Siderits 1997.

13 Taylor 1989: 34: "To ask what a person is, in abstraction from his or her self-interpretations, is to ask a fundamentally misguided question, one to which there couldn't in principle be an answer."

14 Throughout the present section I refer to Aśvaghoṣa's *Saundarananda* by the abbreviation *SN,* followed by the number of the canto and verse as given in Johnston's edition.

15 Zimmer 1969, parts I and II, provides an attractive, albeit romanticized, introduction. But see Krishna 1991, chap. 11, for critical remarks.

16 As the photograph of Cave 3 at Kanheri, reproduced here, demonstrates, this conception of the complementarity of values was iconized at Buddhist monastic settlements.

17 Krishna 1991, chaps. 2 and 3, usefully calls into question the role of *mokṣa* in classical Indian thought. In *SN,* however, it is certainly more than a rhetorical gesture.

18 See Dumont 1970 and 1980 for a thoroughgoing analysis of the contrast between renouncer and householder in traditional India.

19 As Matilal 1982 puts it, the achievement of freedom from worldly pain is "the most common theme of all Indian religions" (p. xi).

20 As suggested by the miniature painting illustrating this chapter, the mirror offered an enduring trope in Indian art. In relation to Buddhist meditation, too, it is a frequently employed metaphor for the mind, as is underscored in Mahāyāna gnoseology by the concept of the buddhas' "mirror-like gnosis" *(ādarśajñāna).* The contemplative and erotic resonances of the mirror motif are beautifully combined by the great Tibetan Rdzogs-chen master Klong-chen Rab-'byams-pa (1308–63) in his *Sems nyid rang grol,* pp. 5–6: "Like a small child seeing a mirror, an infantile person refutes or proves outer objects. Like his mother who sees [the child playing with the mirror] and then wipes it clean, the causal vehicle seeks to transform the external. But when the coquette gazes [in that mirror] she uses it to make up her face; so, too, one who knows just what is, looks to the mind alone."

21 Compare, for instance, the conflict of roles and individuation in Greek thought, above all in Sophocles' *Antigone,* on which consider especially the insightful comments of Nussbaum 1986, chap. 3.

22 The topic of misogyny in *Saundarananda* is a complex and interesting one that merits full and separate treatment. Aśvaghoṣa's treatment of the character of Nanda's wife Sundarī is probably more important in this regard than is the sermonizing text of canto 8.

23 Among recent authorities, one who seems to argue that early Buddhism held some sort of theory of a real individual self, is Pérez-Remón 1980. But on this book see Collins 1982b. Collins sees Pérez-Remón as arguing that "the real but hidden teaching of the Buddha was equivalent to that of the Sāṃkhya school of Hinduism, such that the denial of self only refers to a 'lower,' psycho-physical or phenomenal self, and not to the 'higher' real self, which is taken to be an individual, monadic soul or 'person' *(puruṣa).*" However, I do not think that Pérez-Remón's thesis is so clear-cut as Collins here makes it out to be. On p. 7, for instance, Pérez-Remón says: "The 'soul' is supposed to be wholly involved in all bodily and mental processes, vivifying the body and constituting the substrate of all intellectual and emotional phenomena. It is obvious that this kind of *attā* or 'soul' is emphatically rejected in many a passage of the Nikāyas." Does he mean that the "real self," then, is involved only in some bodily and mental process, or in none whatsoever? I suspect that he holds the latter view, in which case one wonders whether Pérez-Remón really thinks it to be the "individual, monadic soul" which Collins attributes to him, or something more like the Upaniṣadic *ātman-brahman.*

24 On objectification, compare chap. 13, par. 1.4.4. below.

25 Shulman 1994: 1.

26 Shulman 1994, from pp. 25, 26, 27, respectively.

27 *Nyāyabhāṣya,* in *Nyāyadarśana,* pp. 185–87; see also chap. 14 below.

28 *Nyāyavārttika,* in *Nyāyadarśana,* p. 186; see also chap. 14 below.

29 *Nyāyavārttika,* in *Nyāyadarśana,* p. 192; see also chap. 14 below.

30 *Tattvasaṅgrahapañjikā,* pp. 104–5.

31 Refer to chap. 2 above.

32 Hume 1888: 634, is rather ambiguous: "I never can perceive this *self* without some one or more perceptions..."

33 *Tattvasaṅgraha,* v. 198.

34 *Tattvasaṅgrahapañjikā,* pp. 110–11.

35 Kant, *Critique of Pure Reason,* third paralogism of pure reason, "Of Personality" (1965, p. 342 n.): "An elastic ball which impinges on another similar ball in a straight line communicates to the latter its whole motion, and therefore its whole state...(similarly) we can conceive a whole series of substances of which the first transmits its state together with its consciousness to the second, the second its own state with that of the preceding substance to the third...The last substance would then be conscious of all the states of the previously changed substances, as being its own states...and yet it would not have been one and the same person in all these states."

36 *Hitopadeśaḥ,* Prastāvikā, v. 2.

37 *Kāvyādarśa,* chap. 1, v. 9. For the role of Sanskrit poetics in Tibetan Buddhist thought, see further Kapstein 2002.

38 Hahn 1971: 153.

39 Hesse 1950: 1: "Schatten floß in seine schwarzen Augen im Mangohain, bei den Knabenspielen, beim Gesang der Mutter, bei den heiligen Opfern, bei den Lehren seines Vaters, des Gelehrten, beim Gespräch der Weisen."

40 Sahu 1984: 332–33.

41 The notion of *jñānayoga* seems in large measure derived from *Bhagavadgītā,* chap. 4, where the acquisition of soteriologically valued knowledge is explicitly tied to the resolution of indecisiveness and doubt.

42 Hulin 1978 well illustrates the variety of theories of the ego that arose within the Advaita traditions alone.

6. Śāntarakṣita on the Fallacies of Personalistic Vitalism

Introductory Remarks

THE STUDY OF INDIAN BUDDHIST PHILOSOPHY has, for the most part, been connected closely to the study of the Buddhist religion. This, of course, is just as it should be, and to say that this is the case is in one sense only to state the obvious. What I wish to point out here, however, is how this may bias in certain respects our perceptions of Buddhist thought: we are drawn to focus on those issues which lend themselves to discussion in the contexts of contemporary Religious Studies or Philosophy of Religion, perhaps neglecting topics which have no immediate bearing on the concerns of these disciplines. The problem arises in part because Indian Buddhists did not categorize their intellectual pursuits in quite the same way we do—a difficulty that besets not only the study of non-Western civilizations, for similar considerations apply to the study of the pre-modern West. The topic for the present chapter is a case in point: the conflict between mechanism and the various types of vitalism is currently thought to belong to the domain of natural science and the philosophy thereof, but in Greek and medieval philosophy it crops up frequently in discussions of what we now call "philosophical psychology" or "philosophy of mind." What I will propose here is that significant features of this debate are to be found in the conflict between Buddhist thinkers and their opponents over the existence of a substantial self *(ātman)*. Given the many issues this conflict raises, as well as the prolonged and intense philosophical research it generated in India, it is not surprising that quasi-scientific problems would have arisen in this context; for the debate about *ātman* was, in the end, a debate about the nature and ends of living beings.[1]

Under the general heading of "vitalism,"[2] historians of philosophy and science unite a great many biological and pseudo-biological doctrines. Their unifying feature is the notion that an animate organism lives in virtue of something other than its inanimate parts and their interaction alone, that is to say, that the organism is in possession of some special element upon whose presence its animate condition depends. This element is often called simply "life." Generally conceived in this manner, vitalism has appeared throughout the history of human thought in many different cultural settings. Its primitive versions, as known from the literatures of early antiquity and from the evidence of anthropological research, have always been very widespread. Indeed, colloquial speech preserves many expressions that embody vitalistic notions, for instance, in modern English, "the pressures of her career left her lifeless," or, "since his vacation in Fez he's been full of vitality." The particular form of vitalism with which I shall here be concerned has been exemplified among both the beliefs of so-called primitive cultures and the sophisticated metaphysical doctrines of philosophers, and, though personalistic vitalism has had few adherents in very recent philosophy, it continues to exercise an influence among spiritualists and theosophical thinkers.

The central tenet of what I am calling "personalistic vitalism" is this: there is a particular substance that is at once the self-conscious subject and the ground for personal identity through time, and which, when appropriately associated with a functional animal body, causes that body to be alive. This substance is often called "self" or "soul" in English. Astral body theories may also exemplify personalistic vitalism. The personalistic vitalist, therefore, holds that the substantial self, besides individuating the person, also acts as a sort of "psychic battery," imparting life to a body that is physically capable of living and which it "inhabits" or otherwise enters into intercourse with. When the self withdraws the body in question dies, whether or not it is still physically capable of living, just as a battery-operated toy ceases to operate when the batteries are removed, regardless of the mechanical condition of the toy they had powered. Personalistic vitalism, as I understand it here, thus falls within the range of, but is more narrowly defined than, what C. D. Broad has termed "substantial vitalism."[3]

Let us review, briefly, the history of personalistic vitalism in the West: It is the doctrine of Plato's Socrates in the *Phaedo,*[4] and something like it may have been held by some of the Pythagoreans as well.[5] It is debatable, at least, whether or not Aristotle sought to espouse any form of personalistic vitalism through his teaching of the tripartite soul, which treats the vitalizing aspect of the soul as distinct from the soul's rational part, and not in and of itself separable from the body which it informs.[6] Nonetheless, thinkers in the later Aristotelian tradition have sometimes interpreted Aristotle's teaching as a species of personalistic vitalism.[7] The philosophy of Descartes clearly involves a rejection of vitalism in all of its forms, through the hypothesis that living bodies are automata,[8] but it is equally clear that interactionist versions of Cartesianism can be elaborated in which the presence of the Pure Ego is regarded as a necessary condition for the life of the body with which it interacts: from this is derived a Cartesian form of personalistic vitalism.[9] This last version of the doctrine is historically very important, since it is this doctrine that Kant criticizes in connection with the fourth paralogism of pure reason. Kant's discussion of it represents perhaps the first attempt in modern Western philosophy to arrive at a clear analysis of the conceptual basis for personalistic vitalism. He characterizes the doctrine he is criticizing in these words:

> [T]he relation [of the substantial self] to objects in space gives *commercium* with bodies, and so leads us to represent the thinking substance as the principle of life in matter, that is, as soul *(anima),* and as the ground of *animality.* This last, in turn, as limited by spirituality, gives the concept of *immortality.*[10]

Kant, however, was inclined to sort out the problems which he believed were involved here in terms of his peculiar doctrines of the representation of space and of transcendental idealism, the discussion of which would take us far from the subject matter of this essay.[11] Thus, he never undertook to analyze in its own right the conflation of the concepts of life and selfhood (upon which conflation personalistic vitalism is founded), except insofar as the remarks just quoted suggest such an analysis.

The preceding summary provides background for our consideration of the arguments of classical Indian thinkers in respect to notions of personalistic vitalism. Vitalism, in one form or another, was present in Indian thought from the period of the Ṛg Veda onward, and by the age of the earliest Upaniṣads (c. 800–500 B.C.E.), a wide range of vitalistic theories had already been elaborated.[12] While the early history and evolution of the Indian versions of the doctrine will not be detailed here, it should be noted that personalistic vitalism may have been attractive in the Indian context for at least one fundamental reason that was relevant, too, among the Greeks and speakers of Latin, and whose seductive influence must not be overlooked in the present context. I am referring to some of the lexical peculiarities of the languages in question, whereby soul-words and life-words were from the earliest times only imperfectly differentiated. Concerning the state of affairs which obtains in Greek and Latin, Antony Flew provides this summary:

> The word ψυχή, always translated *soul,* is etymologically related to several other words: such as ἔμψυχος, meaning *alive* (literally "ensouled"), and λιποψυχιά, meaning *swooning* or *death* (literally, "abandonment by the soul"). There is the same sort of relationship in Latin, the language in which Aquinas thought; between *anima,* taken as the equivalent of ψυχή; and *animatus* and *inanimatus,* the words from which animate and inanimate are derived. These features smooth the way for a use of *soul* in which *to have a soul* is merely synonymous with *to be alive.*[13]

Sanskrit, like Greek, Latin, and English, is an Indo-European language, and its lexicon similarly includes not just a few soul/life ambiguities. Thus, from √*jīv,* a verbal root meaning "to live," is derived *jīva,* "life-force, soul";[14] and *ātman,* the most common word for "self," is to be derived either from a verb meaning "to breathe," or from one meaning "to move."[15] Hence, "vital breath," usually referred to as *prāṇa* in the classical literature, regularly comes to be regarded as a power of the self, or as strictly identical to self. One final example is in order here: *sattva,* literally "being," may refer, among many other things, to an empirical living creature, a substantial self, or vital energy.

Obviously, there is a sense in which, in the languages we have just been considering, "to be alive" *does* mean "to be ensouled," and so to affirm their synonymity is simply to give expression to a tautology. It is important that we bear in mind, however, that the "soul" whose existence is thus tautologically affirmed is *not* the soul of the personalistic vitalist. It is, in fact, no *thing* at all: we must resist becoming confused by the use of a substantive to denote a state of affairs, in this case the condition of being alive. Nevertheless, that the soul/life conflation is avoided by the speakers of languages in which it is semantically embedded only with difficulty is indicated, I think, by the historical sketch given above: in the West we have only recently succeeded, despite the persistence of vitalistic idioms in ordinary speech, in disambiguating the terminology involved here.[16] Nonetheless, we should recall too that the influence of language was never so great as to preclude the development of conceptions opposing personalistic vitalism: purely mechanistic theories appeared in both India and Greece at an early date, and were occasionally quite influential,[17] and so, too, various kinds of non-personalistic vitalism.[18]

In the remainder of this chapter I will examine the manner in which three prominent representatives of the Vaiśeṣika, Nyāya, and Svātantrika-Mādhyamika schools respectively treated the question of personalistic vitalism. It will emerge from this that the Vaiśeṣika school was committed to some form of the doctrine, that it was virtually irrelevant to the purposes of the Nyāya philosophers (who nonetheless lent it their weak support), and that the Svātantrika-Mādhyamika, as a Buddhist school, was thoroughly determined to expose personalistic vitalism as fallacious. The three paradigmatic thinkers with whom we will be concerned are Praśastapāda (c. 500), Uddyotakara (c. 600), and Śāntarakṣita (mid-eighth century). We should note at the outset why it was that the disagreements about the doctrine in question immediately placed it in the context of the Buddhist-Brahmanical debate over the ontological status of the self: from the standpoint of the proponents of personalistic vitalism, this represented one possible way of challenging the Buddhist non-self theory *(anātmavāda);* whereas for the Buddhists the decisive rejection of this brand of vitalism provided one further ground for rejecting the Brahmanical (and Jaina) hypostasis of selfhood. The essential point here is that, given the assumption that some relationship with a substantial self is a necessary condition for a body's being alive, one can then demonstrate that there is in fact some such self just by affirming that there are living bodies. In what follows I will attempt to survey from a historical perspective the philosophical development of arguments bearing on the fundamental assumption that is made here.

Personalistic Vitalism in Classical Nyāya-Vaiśeṣika Thought

The basis for the Vaiśeṣika commitment to personalistic vitalism and the corresponding Nyāya ambivalence about it are explained by reference to the aphorisms which constitute their respective scriptural authorities. These were probably compiled during the early centuries of the Common Era, but in many respects also reflect more ancient traditions.[19] The complementary character of the two schools already emerges from the two collections of aphorisms, for there is much duplication of material between them. The aphorisms that are of particular interest in the present context are those that concern the proof of the self's existence, which are closely similar in the versions preserved in the two texts. In the *Nyāyasūtra,* 1.1.10, it reads:

> Desire and hatred, willful effort, pleasure and pain, and knowledge are the marks of the self. *(icchā-dveṣa-prayatna-sukha-duḥkha-jñānāny ātmano liṅgam.)*

But in the *Vaiśeṣikasūtra,* 3.2.4,[20] it takes the following form:

> Inhalation and exhalation, opening and shutting of the eyes, life, imagination, and sensory changes, pleasure and pain, desire and hatred, and willful effort are the marks of the self. *(prāṇāpāna-nimeṣônmeṣa-jīvana-manogatîndriyavikārāḥ sukha-duḥkhêcchā-dveṣa-prayatnāś cātmano liṅgāni.)*[21]

Whether the Nyāya version is to be regarded as attributing a vitalizing function to the self depends largely on one's interpretation of the role to be played by desire and hatred, and, above all, willful effort *(prayatna).* It is probable that early Nyāya intended that this last mentioned activity of the self should somehow link the self to the body's vital forces, so that the self becomes at least indirectly the agent of vitality. The Vaiśeṣikas, on the other hand, attributed the vital forces directly to the self. Thus, the Vaiśeṣika school, in contrast to the Nyāya, appears to have adhered to a form of personalistic vitalism as a fundamental tenet involved in its essential concept of the self. Praśastapāda, certainly the most influential of early medieval Vaiśeṣika scholastic writers, has two arguments that are of interest to us here. The first is his argument against identifying consciousness with the body, viz.:

> Consciousness does not belong to the body; for, like a pot, it [i.e., the body] is a product of the elements, and when it dies it is without [consciousness].[22]

The second is an independent argument, apparently derived from *Vaiśeṣikasūtra,* 3.2.4, quoted above:[23]

> [The existence of the self is inferred] "by inhalation, etc.," so it is said. How so? Because, when the vital wind *(vāyu)* is conjoined with the body, changing activity is seen, as when a bellows is pumped...[24]

According to Praśastapāda, then, life and death are respectively indicative of the presence and absence of a substantial self, which is also the basis for the presence or absence of consciousness.

The argument that we will be primarily concerned with in what follows is one that appears to be very closely related to those of Praśastapāda. It is summarized by Śāntarakṣita, who attributes it, however, to the Naiyāyika Uddyotakara. Śāntarakṣita's verse summary is followed here with the comment of Kamalaśīla, Śāntarakṣita's disciple, who restates the argument in conformity with the formal conventions of Buddhist logic:

> Assuming there to be no self at all,
> This living body must be disjoined
> From vital force, just like a pot.
> Therefore, selfless it is not. (*Tattvasaṅgraha*, v. 184.)

> That very one [Uddyotakara] has utilized this contrapositive reason to establish the self: "This living body is not selfless, because that would imply it to be devoid of vital force, etc., like pots and such like." (*Tattvasaṅgrahapañjikā*, p. 105.)

Reformulated in the fashion to which Western philosophers are accustomed, the argument may be expressed:

(1) If the living body were selfless, then it would be without vital force.
(2) But, the living body is not without vital force.
(3) Therefore, the living body is not selfless.

The argument is called "contrapositive" *(vyatirekin)* owing to the form of the major premise. It is clear, moreover, that the argument is a formally valid one.

Though its elements recall the argument we have seen from Praśastapāda, so that it seems certainly to represent the position of at least some adherents of the Vaiśeṣika school, this argument, as already noted, is supposed by Kamalaśīla to be derived from the work of Uddyotakara, whose arguments on the self form the subject matter of the immediately preceding verses. Kamalaśīla's commentary is altogether clear about this attribution. The problem is, however, that Uddyotakara nowhere seems to advance the argument in just this form, and this is rather odd; after all, Kamalaśīla usually goes to pains to provide verbatim citations of the philosophers whom Śāntarakṣita subjects to criticism, and Uddyotakara's *Nyāyavārttika* is frequently quoted by him with perfect accuracy.

What, then, was Uddyotakara's argument? In Jhā's translation the first two lines, which here are all-important, read as follows:

> Others again, having stated the Proposition in the form—'the living body is not with Soul'—put forward, in support of it, such premises as 'because it exists' and the like. This also is not right; because none of the alternatives possible under this is admissible. (*Nyāyavārttika,* book 3, intro.)

It is not clearly stated who the "others" referred to here might be. In the arguments preceding this one, Uddyotakara had addressed himself precisely to well-known Buddhist arguments against the substance theory of the self, and probably he addresses the Buddhist logicians in the present instance, too. It would be easier to resolve this point if we had some definitive interpretation of the reason given here for denying the living body's possession of soul, namely, the premise "because it exists." I am inclined to agree with A. Chakrabarti that this is an oblique reference to the equation, in the philosophy of Dignāga and his followers, of existence with impermanence and causal efficacy.[25] Thus, the causally efficacious body's existence would be held to entail its utter difference from the permanent and, so, inefficacious self.

Let us assume that this interpretation is correct. Then, the next puzzle is to determine just what the "this" is that Uddyotakara thinks "also is not right." Is it the denial that the living body has a soul, or the denial that the soul exists? This is the crux of the matter; for if it is the former, then we can see how Śāntarakṣita came to attribute the argument of personalistic vitalism to Uddyotakara, while if the point is only to refute the denial of the soul's existence, then there would appear to be no basis at all for attributing that argument to him. In fact, Uddyotakara's text turns out to be curiously equivocal about this: he *does* object to the opinion that the living body is soulless, but he then turns about and makes it clear that he is not wedded to that line of objection, since even if we deny any relationship between self and body we will still have to affirm the reality of the self! Evidently, Śāntarakṣita took Uddyotakara's disowning of personalistic vitalism to be more a rhetorical ploy than a statement of serious intent, and so saw himself obliged to refute that doctrine in addition to those which Uddyotakara weighs more heavily.

Śāntarakṣita's Refutation of the Doctrine

Before turning to the text of Śāntarakṣita's arguments against the positions just surveyed, we should first review briefly the background for the Buddhist point of view. The Buddhist critique of personalistic vitalism began during the early stages of the evolution of Buddhist thought: *jīva,* with its ambiguous evocation of the concepts of both life and soul, is, with *ātman,* regularly treated by Buddhists as a pseudo-entity, whose existence is flatly denied. In a famous passage, the Buddha refuses to answer Vatsagotra's question as to whether the *jīva* is the same as or different from the body, a refusal which, in the later commentarial literature, is said to follow from the very non-existence of the thing in question.[26] In fact, it sometimes appears that early Buddhism was opposed to vitalism in all of its aspects, though Buddhism was never to exorcise entirely the vitalist ghost from its world-view. An example of the tendency toward a mechanistic concept of living organisms is found, for instance, in the *Milindapañha:*

> "Reverend sir, whatever is the inner mobile principle, the life-principle that enters and issues forth, I think that is 'Nāgasena.'"
>
> "But if this breath has issued forth and does not enter (again) or has entered but does not issue forth (again), could that man live?"
>
> "O no, reverend sir."
>
> "But when those who are conch-blowers blow on a conch, does their breath enter (again)?"
>
> "No, reverend sir."
>
> "Or when those who are blowers on bamboo pipes blow on a bamboo pipe, does their breath enter (again)?"
>
> "O no, reverend sir."
>
> "Or when those who are horn-blowers blow on a horn, does their breath enter (again)?"
>
> "No, reverend sir."
>
> "Then why do they not die?"
>
> "I am not competent to converse on this assertion with you. It were good, reverend sir, if you uttered the meaning."
>
> "This is not the life-principle; in-breathing and out-breathing are bodily activities."[27]

At the same time, it is clear that the Ābhidharmikas refused to endorse mechanism *simpliciter.* What they posited was the existence of a special faculty possessed by living organisms, which was termed *jīvitendriya,* "life-force."[28] The result of their efforts to mediate between the apparently conflicting demands of mechanistic and vitalistic lines of thought within their own tradition led to the formation of a curiously hybrid doctrine, an interesting and, in the present context, highly relevant, instance of which may be found in the *Mahāprajñāpāramitāśāstra,* attributed by Chinese tradition to Nāgārjuna.[29] There *Vaiśeṣikasūtra,* 3.2.4., is put forward by a disputant who argues against the *anātma* doctrine, and who is then rebuked as follows:

> But all these features are features of consciousness! It is because there is consciousness that there is breath, direct and peripheral vision, etc. And when consciousness leaves the body, all of this disappears. According to your conception of an eternal and ubiquitous *ātman,* even a corpse would still have to possess direct and peripheral vision, breath, life, etc.
>
> What's more, breath, etc., are material dharmas, moving in the wind of mind: these are features of consciousness and not features of the *ātman.* As for life, which is a formation disassociated from the mind, it is also a feature of consciousness.[30]

Consciousness thus comes to assume here precisely the functions of the Vaiśeṣika *ātman,* the differences between them being with respect to the properties of permanence and pervasiveness, which are attributed to the *ātman* but not to consciousness.

The viewpoints just outlined belong to the ancestry of the position which Śāntarakṣita seeks to defend. But Śāntarakṣita is the product of an age of greater philosophical sophistication, and this is reflected in his attention to matters of logical form and conceptual analysis, which is without parallel in the literature of early Buddhism. His argument against personalistic vitalism thus provides us with a fine example of philosophical progress in classical Indian thought; for though the problem addressed was in his day an already ancient one, his analysis of it would have been possible only after the age of Dignāga and Dharmakīrti.

Because, as we have seen, the argument attributed to Uddyotakara is a formally valid one, any criticism of it must revolve around an inquiry into the truth of the premises themselves. Śāntarakṣita proceeds accordingly, giving his main objections in two cryptic verses (*Tattvasaṅgraha,* vv. 207–8), which are amplified by Kamalaśīla in his commentary:

> If vital force, etc., were proven to have some connection with the self, whether through an internal or a causal relationship, then the implication that absence of vital force in the body would follow from the absence of its self would be reasonable. For, otherwise, in the event that they are unrelated, but such that it is implied that the absence of the one entails the absence of the other, [despite their being] unrelated, absurd consequences follow. For it is not the case that in the absence of a barren woman's son there is the absence of the vital force, etc., that are not related to that [non-existent barren woman's son]. Therefore, as the argument is an uncertain one, with ruinous implications, as illustrated by "there being no barren woman's son, the absence of unrelated vital force, etc., follows, as in the case of a pot," just so your [argument], in which absence of self implies absence of vital force, etc., is uncertain, because the [relevant] relationship has not been proven. (*Tattvasaṅgrahapañjikā,* pp. 113–14.)

Let us set out this argument with some care. It turns, of course, on the theory that relationships can be reduced to two categories: internal relationships *(tādātmyalakṣaṇasambandha);* and causal relationships *(tadutpattilakṣaṇasambandha).* Things that are not related in one or the other of these two ways are simply "unrelated" *(asambaddha).* A detailed investigation of this theory will not be attempted here, but some of its salient features must be surveyed nonetheless, in order to avoid possible misunderstanding. My account here will, for simplicity's sake, be a contemporary restatement, rather than a straightforward exposition.

Following Dharmakīrti's *Investigation of Relations (Sambandhaparīkṣā),* the later Buddhist scholastic traditions explicitly opposed the realist account of relations. Thus, for these Buddhists, the relationship is not an additional thing existing above and beyond the relata; rather, relationships are conceptual or linguistic constructs. However, we should not conclude that every kind of relationship that is thus constructed is just as good as every other: some putative relations are either formally defective or utterly vacuous, while others, though they are similarly constructs, are nonetheless contentful. Contentful relations can be reduced to the two categories of *internal* and *causal* relationships. Objects not related by any such contentful relationship are "unrelated," though there is a sense in which it is always possible to stipulate some relationship holding between them, however vacuous it might be. Thus, the "non-being of a barren woman's son" is vacuously related to everything, or, in the terms of the present discussion, *significantly* related to nothing. What Śāntarakṣita and Kamalaśīla seem to be arguing under the rubric of "unrelatedness," then, is that their opponents have failed to point out any *non-vacuous* relationship holding between the posited substantial self and "vitality."

The precise interpretation of the two relational categories is not by any means unproblematic. Among Western philosophical concepts, the relationship that I have referred to as "internal" has often been interpreted as identity, but, strictly speaking, that cannot be correct: a material thing, e.g., a pot, has this relationship not only to the stuff of which it is made, but also to the properties of being an artifact, being impermanent, being causally efficacious, etc. But despite the apparent appropriateness of the concept of internal relations here, the so-called "causal relationship" cannot be identified with external relations in general, but only with a sub-class thereof. This, however, is not very problematic: recalling the reduction of contentful relations to the two categories in question, it seems clear that, from the perspective of the Buddhist logicians, contentful external relations *are* all and only causal relations.

These considerations will help to clarify Śāntarakṣita's elaboration of his examination of the relationships in question. Again, because Śāntarakṣita summarizes his own views in just two short verses (*Tattvasaṅgraha,* vv. 209–10), it will be clearer to follow his commentator, Kamalaśīla:

> In what sense is their relationship not proven?...There is no internal relationship connecting the self and vital force; for their essential difference has been affirmed, as follows: the vital forces are impermanent, non-pervading [that is, spatially determinate], and corporeal, while self is just the opposite. Neither is there a causal relationship, because given the totality of the vital forces' causes, [their] occurrence-all-at-once *(yaugapadya)* is implied. And there is no relationship besides these. Therefore, why is it that the vital forces abandon that body, that is, a body qualified by life? (*Tattvasaṅgrahapañjikā,* pp. 114–15.)

In other words, an *internal* relation between the self and vital energy is necessarily precluded because the essential definitions of the terms in question are mutually exclusive; and a causal relationship cannot be supposed because if, *per impossibile,* an eternal and ubiquitous entity were causally efficacious, its effects would come into being not sequentially, but everywhere in an instant.[31]

In closing his discussion of the Nyāya-Vaiśeṣika soul theory, Śāntarakṣita reaffirms that the processes of life are to be explicated only in terms of the universal principle of causation; plants and persons are just alike in this respect. Though his view of consciousness, which is elaborated elsewhere, does not permit us to conclude that he was a thoroughgoing mechanist, his diction at this juncture is strongly suggestive of such a view: "The similarity with pots, etc.," he says, "whereby our opponents seek to refute [the doctrine of] non-self with respect to living bodies, becomes in this instance our proof."[32]

Conclusions

What was the fate of personalistic vitalism in later Indian thought? That question is too large to be considered here in full detail, but it is certain that the doctrine did reemerge and was to remain influential. Nonetheless, there is some reason to believe that Śāntarakṣita's critique of personalistic vitalism did have an immediate impact on philosophers within the Nyāya tradition: Vācaspatimiśra, Uddyotakara's sub-commentator, whom we know to have been familiar with Śāntarakṣita's *Tattvasaṅgraha,* simply passes over Uddyotakara's already equivocal argument without making any effort to defend it.[33] Surely, he had concluded that Uddyotakara's weak assertion of personalistic vitalism was either not important, or else a lost cause. Is it too much to suppose that he might have let himself be convinced, in this case, by a Buddhist?

The ancient debate between *ātmavādin* and *anātmavādin* was at the heart of a conflict between opposing systems of salvation. To construe this, however, in accordance with our contemporary categorical schemes involves a fundamental error; for "systems of salvation" in ancient India were concerned with human nature and the human world, in a rich and full sense. What I have tried to indicate here is that one strand of the debate in question can be isolated and shown to involve progressive developments in the conceptual analysis of a basic biological doctrine. Other strands that might similarly be analyzed bear upon the theories of agency and causation, and rational and empirical psychology. To study these and many other topics in classical Indian thought from the perspective here advocated does not require our losing sight of the essentially religious interests that motivated and informed the Indian discussions with which we are concerned; what it does require is an involvement in the history of ideas quite broadly conceived. In this context we should recall that it is now possible to treat much of classical Indian thought from a truly historical, and not merely doxographical, vantage-point. By focusing less upon belief and doctrine within single systems, and more upon the dynamic tension that arose where competing systems came into conflict, we discover that there was indeed historical progress, and that it is characterized in part by the application of methodological refinements in the areas of logic and epistemology to problems that had been first defined in antiquity. This sounds very much like the history of philosophy in other settings; what must be done is to fill in the details with respect to the splendid array of questions which Indian thinkers posed and the answers about which they argued.

Notes

1 A contribution on an altogether different topic, which also illustrates the need to approach the study of Indian religions from the standpoint of the history of ideas more broadly conceived, is Staal 1982.

2 For a general introduction to the philosophical use of this term, see Beckner 1967.

3 Broad 1925: 56ff. Broad writes: "The doctrine which I will call 'Substantial Vitalism'...assumes that a necessary factor in explaining the characteristic behaviour of living bodies is the presence in them of a peculiar component, often called an 'Entelechy', which does not occur in inorganic matter or in bodies which were formerly alive but have now died." Broad contrasts this with what he calls "Emergent Vitalism," which maintains that living bodies are to be differentiated from inorganic matter not because the former includes some special substantial component, but rather because of structural differences which nonetheless cannot be described in purely mechanistic terms. What I am calling here "personalistic vitalism" differs from Broad's "Substantial Vitalism" just in its assertion that the "necessary factor" is none other than the self or soul which also individuates the person, and explains his or her personal identity through time.

4 Plato's *Phaedo,* in Gallop 1975: 59:

"Answer then, and tell me what it is, by whose presence in a body, that body will be living."

"Soul."

"And is this always so?"

"Of course."

"Then soul, whatever it occupies, always comes to that thing bringing life?"

"It comes indeed."

5 This is suggested by such interpreters as Chaignet 1873: 175ff. and 1887: 53. More recent writers, however, have not generally implied that Pythagoras and his school held the doctrine I have been calling "personalistic vitalism." See, especially, Barnes 1979, vol. 1, chap. 6, "Pythagoras and the Soul." In the extant relevant fragments the only one which seems to me to be indicative of the doctrine we are considering, however weakly, is no. 271 in Kirk and Raven 1971: 223. It comes from Porphyrius, *Vita Pythagorae:* "...he maintains that the soul is immortal; next that it changes into other kinds of living things..."

6 Aristotle, *On the Soul,* 413b25–30 (trans. J.A. Smith): "mind...seems to be a widely different kind of soul, differing as what is eternal from what is perishable; it alone is capable of existence in isolation from all other psychic powers. All the other parts of the soul, it is evident from what we have said, are, in spite of certain statements to the contrary, incapable of separate existence though, of course, distinguishable by definition." See, also, Brentano 1977, esp. 28–41.

7 The teaching of Saint Thomas Aquinas' *Treatise on Man* (= *Summa Theologica,* Questions 75–89), is sometimes understood to involve this. Consider his remarks in Question 75, Article 1: "To seek the nature of the soul, we must premise that the soul is defined as the first principle of life in those things in our world which live; for we call living things animate, and those things which have no life, inanimate. Now life is shown principally by two activities, knowledge and movement." (From Pegis 1945, vol. 1: 683.) Cf., also, Copleston 1955: 160: "in virtue of his one rational soul the human being can exercise not only the vital activities of plants and of animals but also a still higher range of vital activities, namely, those which are linked with the possession of mind."

8 See, e.g., Dampier 1971: 186 and 357–58.

9 A good example of this line of thought is represented by the biological speculations of Georg Ernst Stahl (1660–1734), on whose vitalist notions see Dampier 1971: 186; and Vartanian 1967.

10 Kant 1965: A 345, B 403.

11 On this, see, for instance, Strawson 1966: 170–74, "The Complications of Transcendental Idealism."

12 I do not know of any attempts to study systematically the history of vitalism in India. Nevertheless, most works on early Indian thought will be found to contain a great many references to vitalistic notions *inter alia.* Besides those already mentioned in chap. 2, n. 2, above, see, in this context esp. Heimann 1964, chap. 3, "India's Biology."

13 Flew 1964: 15.

14 The use of this term is, of course, particularly prominent among the Jains, who, however, may have partially emptied it of its vitalist connotations at an early date. See Mehta 1954, chap. 2, "Nature of Soul."

15 Cf. Monier-Williams 1899: 135.

16 The retention of vitalist idiom in colloquial language may be compared with our continued use of such terms as "sunrise" and "sunset," though we have long known that the phenomenon involved is really one of "earthspin." Examples of

terms which have been more or less purified of soul/life ambiguities in recent times include "animate" and its derivatives. Consider, also, "ghost," which is still associated with vitality in a few quaint expressions, e.g., "he gave up the ghost."

17 Cf. *Bṛhadāraṇyakopaniṣad,* II.iv.12, quoted in chap. 4, n. 2, above.

18 See, for example, my remarks on *jīvitendriya,* below.

19 Concerning the historical questions involved here, see Matilal 1977.

20 This sūtra occupies the same position even in the various divergent redactions of the *Vaiśeṣikasūtra.*

21 The notion of the self and its "marks" embodied in these sūtras can already be found in numerous Upaniṣadic passages. An interesting example comes from *Taittirīya Upaniṣad,* I.7, which was quoted in chap. 2, n. 9.

22 *Praśastapādabhāṣya,* p. 171: *na śarīrasya caitanyam, ghaṭādivad bhūtakāryatvāt, mṛte cāsambhavāt.*

23 This is fairly clear from Praśastapāda's own text, which, following the argument of the sūtra, takes up the implications of the opening and shutting of the eyes immediately after sketching out the argument from inhalation and exhalation. Śrīdhara, in his *Nyāyakandalīvyākhyā,* also states that Praśastapāda intends the phrase "by inhalation, etc." to stand as an abbreviation for the entire sūtra.

24 *Praśastapādabhāṣya,* pp. 199–200: *prāṇādibhiś cêti. katham? śarīraparigṛhīte vāyau vikṛtakarmadarśanād. bhastrādhmāpayitêva....*

25 Chakrabarti 1982.

26 See chap. 14, part I, par. 6.5.

27 Horner 1963, vol. 1: 41. Cf. also 76ff.

28 According to some accounts, this seems to have been conceived in substantial terms, in which case the doctrine in question is a form of substantial vitalism. But according to some later Ābhidharmikas and the Mahāyāna philosophers, this "life-force" is itself a conceptual construct, in which case we approach mechanism more closely (though it is still possible that the doctrine is to be interpreted as a type of what Broad terms "emergent vitalism"). Cf. Collins 1982: 228–30. Cox 1995, chap. 8, provides a valuable discussion of "vitality" as treated in the Sarvāstivāda traditions. She demonstrates that its existential status, as imputed or real, was deeply contested and concludes (p. 130) that: "the factor of vitality had become increasingly significant doctrinally as the quality that distinguishes life from death, a function not traditionally listed among its activities."

29 On this important text in general, see Robinson 1976: 34–39. Lamotte's five-volume translation and summary (1949–76) provides a magisterial doctrinal survey.

30 Lamotte 1970: 1449–50: "Mais tous ces caractères sont des caractères de la connaissance *(vijñānalakṣaṇa)!* C'est parce qu'il y a connaissance, qu'il y a respiration, regard droit ou oblique, vie, etc. Et quand la connaissance quite le corps tout cela disparaît. Selon votre conception d'un Ātman éternel *(nitya)* [Lamotte gives *anitya.*—M.K.] et omniprésent *(vyāpin),* le cadavre *(kuṇapa)* lui-même devrait posséder encore regard droit ou oblique, respiration, vie, etc.

"En outre la respiration *(ānāpāna),* etc., sont les dharma matériels *(rūpidharma)* se mouvant au vent de la pensée: ce sont des caractères de la connaissance *(vijñāna)* et non pas des caractères de l'Ātman. Quant à la vie *(āyus)* qui est une formation dissociée de la pensée *(cittaviprayuktasaṃskāra),* c'est aussi un caractère de la connaissance."

Lamotte, however, did not notice the precise correlation with *Vaiśeṣikasūtra,* 3.2.4, which was first pointed out by Robinson 1976: 69.

31 This assumption recurs throughout Buddhist discussions of both the self and of God. Cf. Hayes 1988. For analogous concerns in Western philosophical theology, see Kretzmann 1966.

32 *Tattvasaṅgraha,* v. 220. But cf., here, Buddhaghosa, *Visuddhimagga,* xviii.32, quoted in Collins 1982: 133:

> The mental and the material are really here,
> But here there is no human being to be found.
> For it is void and merely fashioned like a doll,
> Just suffering piled up like grass and sticks.

But while such mechanistic imagery is found throughout Buddhist doctrinal literature, the question about whether it really is indicative of opposition to substantial vitalism can only be resolved with reference to the doctrine of *jīvitendriya,* referred to above. Śāntarakṣita, certainly, would have held this "life-force" to be a conceptual construct, and not a substantial constituent of a human being. I am not yet clear as to what Buddhaghosa's views about this may have been.

33 Introduction to *Tātparyaṭīka,* book 3, in *Nyāyadarśana,* vol. 2.

II REALITY AND REASON

7. Mereological Considerations in Vasubandhu's "Proof of Idealism"

And the venerable Nâgasena said to Milinda the king: "You, Sire, have been brought up in great luxury, as beseems your noble birth. If you were to walk in this dry weather on the hot and sandy ground, trampling under foot the gritty, gravelly grains of the hard sand, your feet would hurt you. And as your body would be in pain, your mind would be disturbed, and you would experience a sense of bodily suffering. How then did you come, on foot, or in a chariot?"

"I did not come, Sir, on foot. I came in a carriage."

"Then if you came, Sire, in a carriage, explain to me what that is. Is it the pole that is the chariot?"

"I did not say that."

"Is it the axle that is the chariot?"

"Certainly not."

"Is it the wheels, or the framework, or the ropes, or the yoke, or the spokes of the wheels, or the goad that are the chariot?"

And to all these he still answered no.

"Then is it all these parts of it that are the chariot?"

"No, Sir."

"But is there anything outside them that is the chariot?"

And still he answered no.

"Then thus, ask as I may, I can discover no chariot. Chariot is a mere empty sound. What then is the chariot you say you came in? It is a falsehood that your majesty has spoken, an untruth! There is no such thing as a chariot! You are king over all India, a mighty monarch. Of whom then are you afraid that you speak untruth?" And he called upon the Yonakas [Greeks]

> and the brethren to witness, saying: "Milinda the king here has said that he came by carriage. But when asked in that case to explain what the carriage was, he is unable to establish what he averred. Is it, forsooth, possible to approve him in that?"
>
> When he had thus spoken the five hundred Yonakas shouted their applause, and said to the king: "Now let your Majesty get out of that if you can?"
>
> And Milinda the king replied to Nâgasena, and said: "I have spoken no untruth, reverend Sir. It is on account of its having all these things—the pole, and the axle, the wheels, and the framework, the ropes, the yoke, the spokes, and the goad—that it comes under the generally understood term, the designation in common use of 'chariot.'"[1]

Some two millennia ago, in northwestern India, the Buddhist sage Nāgasena and the Greek king Menander came together to discuss problems of philosophy and religion. In the passage reproduced above their dialogue enters a territory that has continually given rise to philosophical puzzlement, within both the Indian and Hellenic traditions and their offshoots: how are we to understand the mereological structure of matter? What is the relation of the whole to its parts? The answer that Menander finally produces in response to Nāgasena's Socratic questioning is recognizably an early version of a theory that has not been without its modern proponents: wholes are not entities that exist in addition to their parts; they are merely logical constructions.

I will not be concerned here with this ancient logical constructivism *per se,* though I will seek to indicate something of the manner in which it formed the conceptual background for the development of Vasubandhu's "proof of idealism," which belongs to a more developed phase of Buddhist mereological thought. Before, however, turning to the arguments themselves some introductory remarks of a general nature are called for.

Vasubandhu, a founder of Buddhist philosophical idealism, has been the object of considerable philological research since the latter part of the nineteenth century. Historical data alone justify the efforts that have been made, for, with the translation of his works into Chinese, Tibetan, and not a few other languages, Vasubandhu's thought became, from about the sixth century onward, a dominant force in central and east Asian intellectual life. Moreover, his substantial contributions to logic, epistemology, and metaphysics are more than sufficient to justify his prominent position in the history of Indian philosophy, even if his impact abroad be totally disregarded. Still, for the philosopher, the relative lack of attention paid by philologists to Vasubandhu's actual philosophy remains an obstacle to study. What Jonathan Barnes has said of the pre-Socratics may be restated, *mutatis mutandis,* in the present instance:

> If the linguistic expression and the historical context of the pre-Socratics have been exhaustively discussed, the rational content of their thought has been less thoroughly scrutinized. By and large, scholars have asked what the Presocratics said, and what external circumstances may have prompted their sayings; they have not asked whether the Presocratics spoke truly, or whether their sayings rested on sound arguments.[2]

Two particular difficulties stand in the way of our attempt to formulate a philosophical reconstruction of Vasubandhu's teaching, even after philology makes clear (at least in principle) what, exactly, he said.[3] First, he was, like many another classical Indian writer, an elliptical stylist to an extreme degree: Vasubandhu assumed himself to be writing for the beneficiaries of a thorough Buddhist scholastic education in Sanskrit, and so presupposed an audience for whom much could be left unstated. Today, we must fill in the gaps to the best of our ability by relying upon the entire corpus of his surviving work, the writings of others in his tradition, and the demands of reason. In the second place, Vasubandhu, perhaps in part because he was engaged in the difficult task of forging new philosophical tools, did not always achieve the perspicuity for which he certainly aimed, and which marks the work of several of his philosophical successors.[4] Often, for instance, he will voice an intuition only in terms of a concrete example, leaving it for the reader to penetrate to the abstract reasoning beneath the surface. With this in mind, then, I offer here an exposition and interpretation of the rational content of Vasubandhu's "proof of idealism."[5]

Let us begin by returning to the conversation between Nāgasena and Menander. The following mereological principles are certainly implied there:

> (P1) For all x and all y, if x is a composite material whole and y is a proper part of x, then it is not the case that $x = y$. [Is it the pole that is the chariot?]

> (P2) For all *x* and all $y^1, y^2, \ldots$, if *x* is a composite material whole and $y^1, y^2, \ldots$ are the proper parts of *x*, then it is not the case that $x =$ the mere sum of $y^1, y^2, \ldots$. [Then is it all these parts of it that are the chariot?]

> (P3) For all *x* and all $y^1, y^2, \ldots$, if *x* is a composite material whole and $y^1, y^2, \ldots$ are the proper parts of *x*, then it is not the case that there exists some *z* such that (i) $x = z$ and (ii) *z* is discrete from $y^1, y^2, \ldots$ [But is there anything outside them that is the chariot?]

One possible objection to this scheme may immediately be raised when we consider (P2) alone. True enough, one might say, the whole is no *mere sum* of its proper parts. But is it not, rather, a unified, ordered collection of those parts? One who advances this objection might wish to affirm the following to supplement (P2):

> (P4) For all *x* and all $y^1, y^2, \ldots$, if *x* is a composite material whole and $y^1, y^2, \ldots$ are the proper parts of *x*, then $x =$ the unified, ordered collection constituted by all and only $y^1, y^2 \ldots$ [It is on account of its having all these things...that it comes under the generally understood term..."chariot."]

Now, if a *mere sum* and a *unified collection* are collections of just the same parts *a, b,* and *c,* then what is it that distinguishes them? One way to answer this question is to assume there to be some relation of, say, *strong conjunction,* which is to be differentiated from the weaker notion of logical conjunction. With reference to the latter it is true that for all *x* and all *y,* where *x* and *y* are discrete, concrete, individual things, there is a *mere sum* which is the *logical conjunction* of *x* and *y.* Assuming instead the (undefined) relation of *strong conjunction,* we can say that *a, b,* and *c,* in the example above, form a *mere sum* if and only if *strong conjunction* does not obtain among them; and that they form a *unified collection* if and only if it does so obtain.

How are we to respond, though, to one who points out that in what has been said so far there is nothing to preclude each of the parts of some whole from being itself a unified collection of parts, each of which is itself a unified collection, and so on, *ad infinitum?* In that case, any material whole must actually have infinitely many material parts, which seems absurd. One hypothesis which avoids this difficulty by denying that any unified collection actually has infinitely many material parts is atomism; namely, the theory which holds that any unified collection actually has only a finite number of material parts. These parts must be thought to be spatially extended (being material), simple (for they do not themselves have parts), and empirically indivisible (for, if empirically divisible, then they must have parts). Let us call such atoms *minimal parts.* And let us further stipulate that for all x, where x is a composite material whole, there is some set S of minimal parts such that (i) S has a finite number of members and (ii) each member of S is discrete from every other. Then we may restate our four mereological principles as *principles of minimal part atomism* (Pa), thus:

> (Pa1) For all x and all S, if x is a composite material whole and S is the set of the minimal parts of x, then it is not the case that x = any member of S.
>
> (Pa2) For all x and all S, if x is a composite material whole and S is the set of the minimal parts of x, then it is not the case that x = the *mere sum* of all members of S.
>
> (Pa3) For all x and all S, if x is a composite material whole and S is the set of the minimal parts of x, then it is not the case that there exists some z such that (i) $x = z$ and (ii) z is discrete from all members of S.
>
> (Pa4) For all x and all S, if x is a composite material whole and S is the set of the minimal parts of x, then x = the unified, ordered collection constituted by all and only the members of S.

These four principles have been implied, if I am not mistaken, by most of the ancient schools of atomism. They admirably preserve many of our ordinary intuitions about the material world, and burden our ontology with only one putative entity, the minimal part, and one putative relationship, the relation of strong conjunction. Minimal part atomism is thus attractive to some because it retains the metaphysical simplicity of logical constructivism, while refusing to countenance the absurd notion that corporeal substances might actually be composed of an infinite number of extended parts. Still, not a few ancient philosophers found atomism to be a flawed doctrine. Zeno, Aristotle, and Vasubandhu agree in rejecting various theories which explicitly or implicitly embrace minimal part atomism, but their alternatives are, respectively, monism, the theory of extended continua, and idealism.

It is instructive to ponder the considerations that led Aristotle to shun idealism in favor of his continuity theory, and that led Vasubandhu to make just the opposite move. For Aristotle, the notion that a body might be "nothing but an appearance" is patently absurd and is tantamount to maintaining that "its constituents are nothings,...it might both come-to-be out of nothings and exist as a composite of nothings."[6] If we agree that this cannot be correct, and reject atomism at the same time, then we have no choice but to seek, with Aristotle, an alternative theory of matter.

Vasubandhu, on the other hand, aims to demonstrate that the atomic theory is *both* false *and* necessary: "...atomic distinctions must be supposed; and there can be no simple atom." Wherefore, matter is naught but ideal. Vasubandhu, if he is to make his case, must demonstrate the truth of the premises of a simple *modus tollens* argument:

> (1) If material things exist independently of the perceptions in which they are given, then they must be atomic in composition.
> (2) But they cannot be atomic in composition.
> Therefore, (3) material things do not exist independently of the perceptions in which they are given.[7]

This becomes a "proof of idealism" if supplemented by the following definition:

> *x* is ideal = Df *x* does not exist independently of the perception(s) in which it is given.

The main body of Vasubandhu's argument (sections ii and iii in the translation below) is devoted to the demonstration of premises (1) and (2). This is preceded, however, by a summary statement of the alternatives to idealism, and their defects (section i). The alternatives enumerated are:

> (i) the whole is a simple "part-possessing form" *(avayavirūpa);*
> (ii) it is a *mere sum* of atomic parts; and
> (iii) it is a *unified collection* of atomic parts.

It is important to consider how it is that Vasubandhu intends these to be understood, and how they are to be related to the main body of the argument that follows.

(i) The "part-possessing form"

Against the early Buddhist logical constructivism represented in such texts as the *Questions of King Milinda,* the Hindu philosophers of the Nyāya-Vaiśeṣika school posited that the whole is something in addition to the unified collection of its parts.[8] There are two lines along which their doctrine might be interpreted: both the unified collection of parts and the whole actually exist; or only the whole actually exists. The latter line of interpretation suggests an analogue to the Aristotelian continuity theory and is taken up by Vasubandhu in section iii, where he challenges the doctrine of simple, extended wholes. In section i, however, his target is the notion that the whole exists above and beyond the actually existing parts. Vasubandhu maintains that such a whole is "not apprehended," that is to say, its concept is in some sense counterintuitive. How so? Certainly, when we see, for example, a carriage, we do not see those parts of the carriage which are visible to us and the carriage besides. But I suspect that Vasubandhu intends something more than that, and what it might be I shall try to make clear in what follows.

Assume a given whole to be the conjunction of a unified collection of parts and something *x* existing above and beyond that collection. This may commit us, of course, to abandoning (P3) and its atomist analogue (Pa3). If *x* is an *abstractum,* then it is difficult to see in what sense it actually *exists* in addition to the unified collection of parts. Indeed, the doctrine of the part-possessing form would, in that case, be nothing but a fancy sort of logical constructivism. If, on the other hand, *x* is a *concretum,* is it simple or complex? If simple and existing in addition to the unified collection, then we are indeed committed to abandoning (P3)/(Pa3). Now, empirical considerations aside, *x* obviously can, under these conditions, be thought of as a simple entity which is logically independent of the unified collection. As such, it merits no special discussion apart from the doctrine of simple, extended wholes in section iii. However, if it be deemed *complex* and existent over and above the unified collection, then the entire mereological puzzle is merely reintroduced with reference to *x,* and nothing whatever has been gained by its supposition. Finally, should it be assumed that there is a part-possessing form, but that it does not exist in addition to the unified collection, then Vasubandhu is quite correct in asserting that it is nothing discrete from the minimal parts of the unified collection. In short, Vasubandhu seems to maintain that if the hypothesis of the part-possessing form has any substance to it at all, it can only be according to the continuity theorist's reading of it, and that will be taken up below.[9]

(ii) The whole as mere sum

Vasubandhu's rejoinder to the proponents of this second view—"single atoms are not apprehended"—suggests that he considered this alternative, too, to be counterintuitive. The thoughts which led to our distinguishing mere sums from unified collections and positing the relation of strong conjunction do lend support to Vasubandhu's intuition. Still, the assertion that this doctrine—which holds that wholes are mere collections of minimal parts—entails our being able to perceive minimal parts *directly* may seem to be excessive. But consider: if wholes *are* mere sums and not even unified collections, then in fact there *is* no difference between what we ordinarily take to be mere sums and wholes. Nonetheless, there *appears* to be some difference between them. So, wholes are only apparent things, that is, they do not exist independently of the perceptions in which they are given. Thus, even if we do posit noumenal atoms of some sort, as long as they do not form unified collections, we must accept some form of idealism, at least with respect to apparent wholes—which is just what Vasubandhu set out to prove in the first place.

(iii) Wholes as unified collections of atoms

This thesis is to be given thorough consideration in section ii. Note that at this point in the argument, we are left with two viable theories of matter: atomism and the continuity theory. The refutation of these will give Vasubandhu the premises he requires.

Section ii. Contra atomism

The refutation of atomism is in two parts: ii.a, in which Vasubandhu argues that the supposition of the *conjunction* of partless minimal parts entails various absurdities; and ii.b, where he seeks to demonstrate that *spatial extension* and *simplicity* are, in any case, mutually exclusive properties. It appears that both arguments are intended to support one and the same conclusion, namely, that the atomist's concept of simple minimal parts is defective and so cannot be made to account for complex wholes.

Section ii.a requires, I think, that we suppose Vasubandhu to have intended some such argument as:

(1) If there exists an atom which is a simple substance, it must be able to enter into conjunction with other atoms.
(2) But it is not possible for it to do so.
Therefore, (3) there does not exist an atom which is a simple substance.[10]

The first premise—which requires the atomic theory to posit atoms that do form unified collections, and not only mere collections—has already been established. Only the second premise need now be proven. To do so, Vasubandhu presents the atomist with two dilemmas: one arising from the notion of minimal parts conjoining directly with one another, the second arising from an alternative "molecular" theory of conjunction.

ii.a1. The first dilemma of conjunction

Consider one partless atom entering into conjunction with six others. Either all occupy discrete spaces, thus:

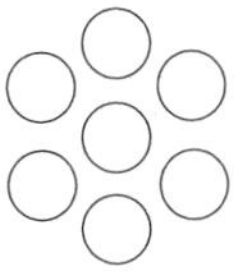

or else they all occupy the very same space:

"To occupy" a space means here *to fill* that space, and not simply *to fall within* it.

If we grasp the first horn of the dilemma then surely we are committed to the view that our atoms have parts; for they have discrete parts that are in contact with discrete atoms. Should we opt for the second alternative, by contrast, we must admit that all the atoms in the group must collapse into the same atom-sized space.

The above, or something close to it, is what I take Vasubandhu to have in mind here. I confess that while the problem posed by the first horn of the dilemma seems to me clearly to be a real difficulty, I am by no means confident in the interpretation of the second. Let us examine it somewhat more carefully.

Is it possible that Vasubandhu had in mind here not extended minimal parts, but unextended points? In that case, the dilemma elaborated in ii.a1. would have us choose between, on the one hand, extended atoms which must have parts in order to conjoin; and, on the other, unextended material points, an infinite number of which might "conjoin" without any space being thereby filled. However, I doubt very much that Vasubandhu is here entertaining the idea of there being unextended material points, an omission that, though partially remedied below, might prove to be devastating for his "proof of idealism."[11] At the same time, should we adhere to the first interpretation proposed, which in any case better accords with Vasubandhu's own words, it may be well to ask whether or not the notion of several atoms occupying the very same space is, in fact, problematic. Do the "molecules" formed of the compresent atoms conjoin or not? What is to prevent all the atoms in the universe from occupying the same space? Is it possible for any two, or more, material things to occupy one and the same space? The second horn of the dilemma calls upon us to consider these questions.

Vasubandhu's own answer to the last question would certainly have been "no."[12] It is one of the properties of matter, as we ordinarily understand it, that no two bits of it can occupy simultaneously the very same space. Any theory that denies this fundamental intuition must be prepared to explain just why it is that *all* the matter in the universe does not simply collapse into the same space. Moreover, should such a theory in some way limit the quantity or number of extended substances that may be compresent, it will be faced with the first question posed above: for, if the "molecules" do not conjoin with one another, we confront again the problem of mere collections; and if they do conjoin, we are left with the puzzle of conjunction itself, but this time with reference to atom-sized clusters rather than atoms. As Vasubandhu's second dilemma presents that puzzle all over again, in fact with reference to "molecules" and not atoms, it seems not unlikely that he well realized that the second horn of the first dilemma might be taken to be the lesser of the two evils offered, the point of departure for a molecular theory requiring clusters of atoms to serve as the finest actual parts of coarse matter—though, as seen above, he would not have countenanced the idea that the atoms making up those clusters might be literally compresent.

ii.a2. The second dilemma of conjunction

It was the Vaibhāṣika school of Buddhist realism that, with remarkable genius, developed a molecular theory not clearly susceptible to objections such as those raised in the first dilemma of conjunction; and it is this theory that Vasubandhu attacks in section ii.a2.[13] The Vaibhāṣika theory in its developed form seems to have required unextended points of resistance, indivisible even in thought, falling within, but not filling, given spaces, and at the same time capable of existing only in clusters. These clusters conjoin to form gross matter. This, according to Vasubandhu, merely introduces a new dilemma for the atomist: the cluster must be either the same as, or different from, the atoms which compose it. If it be different, then of what is it a cluster? On the other hand, if it is the same, then for what reason should we suppose it to be capable of conjunction at all, when its atomic parts are not? Surely Vasubandhu is right to object to the notion that the atomic clusters might be discrete from the atoms of which they are composed. Aggregations that are not aggregations of anything are, like dollars worth no cents, meaningless fictions. Assuming, then, that the aggregations are mere collections of unconjoined atoms, can we assume unified collections ever to be generated from them? Vasubandhu found such an assumption wholly untenable. Some contemporary philosophers would, I think, not be so ill disposed to it.[14] Their views, however, must be examined in the light of modern physical theory, an undertaking for which the present writer is not qualified, and which, in any case, is far removed from the subject matter at hand.

It should be noted, though, that a cogent point-particle theory would mitigate severely the force of Vasubandhu's argument: so long as such a theory cannot be decisively rejected, Vasubandhu's "proof of idealism" is, in fact, no proof at all. Nonetheless, it should not be forgotten that Vasubandhu aimed to challenge pre-modern minimal part atomism, not twentieth-century particle physics. His conclusion to section ii.a.—that his pair of dilemmas has shown the atom to be incapable of conjunction and that, hence, the existence of the minimal part cannot be established—is not at all unwarranted, given the ancient theories against which he directed his assault.

Section ii.b. Extension and simplicity

The second argument against atomism must be understood to be entirely independent of the first. It is also the argument one most frequently encounters in Western criticisms of atomism: spatial extension and simplicity cannot be properties of one and the same substance.[15] As Vasubandhu plainly puts it, the atom, if spatially extended, "has a front part that is different from its bottom part."[16] It may be recalled that, in formulating the concept of the minimal part, all that was required in addition to extension and simplicity was *empirical* indivisibility. Vasubandhu and most other opponents of minimal part atomism object that so long as the *logical* possibility of division remains—that is to say, so long as we can conceive of the atom as having parts—the minimal part cannot be simple. This claim will have to be reexamined below, in connection with the question of extended, simple wholes; for the notion that having possible parts entails having actual parts is just what the continuity theorist will deny. Still, the objection does succeed in pointing out a certain arbitrariness in the atomist's bringing the process of division to a halt with his hypothetical atoms. We are driven, in effect, to choose between the apparent absurdity of infinite division and the continuity theory.

At this point in the text, Vasubandhu adds a peculiar argument concerning shade and shadow. His intuition may be represented with the aid of a diagram:

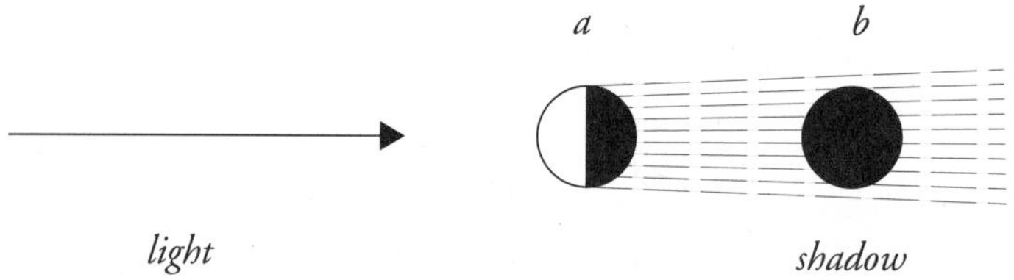

Consider two particles, *a* and *b*, such that *a* is struck by light and *b* is in the shadow of *a*. If we think of *a* as an extended thing, then we must think of it as having a part that is illumined and a part that is shaded. But if we assume it to be partless this cannot be: the light must either stop short of *a*, or else it must penetrate *a* through and through. If the former, we must explain the light's strange behavior; if the latter, then there is no reason to suppose that the light does not reach *b* as well.

It is obvious that this example is intended only to illustrate the intuition that extended things have parts and, as such, it remains susceptible to the continuity theorist's objections. Moreover, the point-particle theorist can maintain without absurdity that *a* might be an unextended point of resistance at which the light simply terminates, and so does not need to be troubled by Vasubandhu's example. That Vasubandhu did not seriously consider the implications of the point-particle hypothesis is almost certainly indicated by his equation, in this passage, of resistance with extension: "If no atom whatever has discrete parts, such as might obstruct passage from one place to another, then, in the absence of such obstruction, owing to the co-spatiality of all, an entire cluster must be a mere atom." If atoms are extended, they must have parts; if unextended, the universe is swallowed in a mere point.[17]

Section ii.b. closes with a response to the philosopher who supposes the phenomena of shade and shadow to depend upon atomic clusters rather than upon single atoms. That supposition requires the clusters to be discrete from the atoms that compose them, for otherwise there is no reason to suppose these phenomena not to depend on the atoms themselves.

Section iii. Against continuity

The abandonment of the atomic theory leaves us still with the data supplied by our physical senses intact: "So long as the defining characteristics of material wholes are present, does it matter whether their concepts correspond to atomic collections, or not?" Having denied the atomic theory (that is, the postulate that wholes are complex substances composed of minimal parts), Vasubandhu is still faced with another possibility: namely, that wholes are simple, extended continua, possibly divisible, but not composed of *actual* parts. This is, of course, the notion at the heart of both Aristotelian and Nyāya-Vaiśeṣika mereological speculation, a way to avoid the terrible conclusion that a body might be "nothing but an appearance." Vasubandhu calls on four alleged counterexamples in his attack on the continuity theory. They may be presented as follows:

> (1) Consider a continuous, extended whole *w*, which is traversed by a moving object *x*. If *w* is simple, then *x* can at no time have traversed only part of *w;* hence, *x* must traverse *w* not gradually, but in an instant, which is absurd.
>
> (2) Consider a whole *w* and an observer *o*, who can not see all of *w*. *O* sees one part of *w*, but not another; hence, *w* has parts. To say that *o* sees *w*, but does not see *w*, at one and the same time, is a contradiction.

> (3) Consider a continuous field *f*, with various elephants *e*, horses *h*, and cattle *c*, grazing upon it. If *f* is simple, then *e*, *c*, and *h* are all in the same place, which again is an absurdity.
> (4) Consider a little fish f^1 and a big fish f^2, which are similar in all respects but size. An observer stationed at an appropriate distance from f^1 and f^2 will be able to discern f^2, but not f^1. But how is this possible if they have just the same characteristics and the same number of parts?

Are these counterexamples really damaging to the continuity theory? If any one of them is, that will be quite enough for Vasubandhu's purposes. Each requires more careful consideration. In particular, it will be necessary to weigh them against Aristotelian suggestions put forth by R. M. Chisholm, to the effect that our "part of" locutions may be replaced by clauses in which "partly" is used as a predicate modifier.[18]

(1) There can be no doubt that a sentence such as, "*x* has traversed part of *w*," can be rendered, for instance, "*w* has been *partly* traversed by *x*." But what of, "By now *x* has traversed a larger part of *w* than it had a minute ago"? We might try something like:

> (i) By now *w* has been partly traversed by *x*; (ii) a minute ago *w* had been partly traversed by *x*; (iii) *w* is possibly such that it is divided into *either* F and G, *or* H and I, but not into *both* F and G *and* H and I; (iv) F is (tenselessly) smaller than H; (v) if *w* had been divided into F and G a minute ago, *x* would have traversed F; and (vi) were *w* divided into H and I now, *x* would have just traversed H.

The atomist, who can simply say, "By now *x* has traversed numerically more minimal parts of *w* than it had a minute ago," does have the advantage of relative simplicity of expression in this instance. Nor is our example, by any means, a terrifically complex one: the mind boggles to think how an Aristotelian might describe the progress of a number of objects, traversing the same object along various paths and at different speeds. This is not to say that the Aristotelian theory must be false, but was it not advanced in the name of simplicity?

(2) The Aristotelian response to Vasubandhu's second counterexample might be: "*W* is partly seen by *o*, and partly not." Complexity again becomes a problem, though, if we turn our attention to possible translations of fairly

straightforward part-expressions, such as: "*O* sees part of the red part of *w*, and that part which he sees is partly soiled."

(3) The challenge here is to banish reference to parts from such sentences as: "*E* stands on one part of *f*, *h* on another part, *c* on another, and there are parts of *f* intervening between, and surrounding, the parts on which *e*, *h* and *c* are standing; and on those parts there is nothing at all."

Intricate juggling of the "possibly such that it is divided" locution may enable the Aristotelian to accomplish the appropriate translations in (2) and (3)—I leave it to the reader to experiment—without loss in meaning. Certainly, a great harvest of convoluted expression may be reaped in this fashion.

(4) Vasubandhu's final counterexample is quite strange, and I am not at all certain that I have grasped his meaning.[19] The point seems to be that difference in size between otherwise similar objects is explicable in realist terms only by assuming either that the objects have different quantities of minimal parts, or that the relations among their respective parts somehow differ. But if things have no parts, there can be no such differences. If this be so, then distinctions of size become unintelligible. Now, if there is any truth to this, it will be somewhat more troublesome for the Aristotelian than counterexamples (1)–(3); for, as we have already seen, any spatially extended whole, of whatever size, has precisely an *infinite* number of *potential* parts. Thus, the doctrine of *possible* division cannot meaningfully be invoked here. That is, if the number of, or relations among, minimal parts are fundamental to difference of size, then only *actual* parts will do. The intuition is, I think, clarified if we consider a possible universe, along lines once suggested by Max Black, containing only two spheres similar in every respect except size: both have infinite possible parts, and the relations among these parts are in every aspect similar. Of course, one might posit absolute space, and go on to ground size-difference in the relations that hold between possible parts and points in absolute space. But this would necessitate *actual* relations among *possible* parts, and would require the supposition of real atomic points as well. So it is not clear that we have thus gained any ground.

But, one might ask, is not "bigger than" a primitive relationship? Is it not simply the case that the one sphere is bigger than the other?

If "*seeming* bigger than" is what is meant here, then of course it is a primitive relationship holding between phenomenal objects—even the idealist can agree to that! But phenomenal relationships, in the absence of other considerations, imply nothing ontologically; they merely tell us something about how things appear to perceivers. On the other hand, it is not nearly so clear that "*being* bigger than" *is,* in fact, a *primitive* relationship. Imagine that the aforementioned two spheres are in far distant corners of the universe. In the region possessing the smaller sphere, matter is more dense, gravitational conditions are different, and so the people are "smaller" than in the region that has the larger sphere. Scientists from the two regions make radio contact and discuss their respective spheres. Incredibly they conclude that both spheres are two yards in diameter and weigh 1500 pounds.

An obvious objection to this line of argument is that the scientists' inability to *know* there to be a size difference hardly goes to show that there *isn't* one.

True enough, but minimal part atomism permits knowledge, too, in this instance. If atoms are similar throughout the universe, then eventually the scientists will discover differences between the spheres and realize that they had been mistaken up until that time. And is not a science that corresponds to *being* preferable to one that does not?

At this writing, I am not at all certain that Vasubandhu's four counterexamples can be made to do the work demanded of them—i.e., demonstrate that, if matter is real, atomism necessarily follows. They do, however, underscore several of the difficulties which must be resolved by the continuity theory if it is to be made capable of fully expressing our commonplace intuitions with respect to parts and wholes.

Vasubandhu, like Kant, sought to prove idealism by demonstrating first that our concept of composite material wholes necessarily entails there being simple, atomic substances, and, secondly, that atomism is incoherent and so must be false. In so doing, he, no less than Kant, underestimated the potential strengths of the continuity theory, and of the point-particle theory. It may be asked: Would even a fully successful argument of this type be sufficient to demonstrate the truth of idealism? It is of interest to remark that, among Vasubandhu's successors in the Buddhist tradition, few seem to have thought so: Dharmakīrti, for example, though probably leaning in favor of some form of idealism, saw in Vasubandhu's mereological argument at best a supplement to profounder epistemological arguments for idealism.[20] And Śāntarakṣita, who refined Vasubandhu's argument to a greater degree than did any other classical Indian thinker, saw here not a "proof of idealism," but a step on the way to a near total rejection of speculative metaphysics.[21] Still, Vasubandhu must be credited with making significant progress in the development of Indian mereological thought, and with constructing not a few puzzles for which decisive answers are wanting even today.

I have endeavored here to provide a clear and critical account of Vasubandhu's chief argument in support of an idealist ontology, an argument that represents but one aspect of a richly elaborated philosophical system, which merits more thorough *philosophical* interpretation overall than it has received to date. It is my own conviction that the value of such an inquiry as this derives not from the discovery that, for instance, the ancient Indian philosopher in question was in his musings particularly right or wrong. What is of interest is that he mused on these matters at all. When we begin to appreciate Vasubandhu's insights from the vantage point of our own philosophical understanding, what is most human about us leaps through centuries, rushes across continents, and greets what is most human in what had formerly been alien. We meet Vasubandhu face-to-face, incline towards one another, and commune in our perennial capacity to puzzle over what is real.

Appendix: Viṃśatikā, 11–15, The Proof of Idealism[22]

i. Rejection of possible alternatives to idealism (v. 11)

How, moreover, can it be known that the Transcendent Lord spoke of the existence of the domain of form with this intention *(abhiprāya)*,[23] and that no object of any particular perception of form, etc.,[24] does, in fact, exist?

v. 11 *The object is not simple,*
Nor is it atomically complex,
Neither is it an aggregation;
For the atom cannot be proven.

What does this assert? Whatever, in the domain of form, etc., may be an object of a particular perception of form, etc., is possibly either (i) a part-possessing form, as conceived by the Vaiśeṣikas; or (ii) atomically complex; or (iii) an aggregation of the atoms together. But (i) the object is not simple, because there is no apprehension whatever of a part-possessing form discrete from the parts; (ii) neither is it complex, because single atoms are not apprehended; and (iii) their aggregation is not the object, for the atom *qua* simple substance cannot be proven.[25]

ii. Refutation of atomism (vv. 12–14)

ii.a. Refutation of the atomist supposition of the conjunction of partless minimal parts (vv. 12–13)

ii.a1. A dilemma for one who affirms the conjunction of such minimal parts (v. 12)

Why can it not be proven? Because:
v. 12ab *Owing to the simultaneous conjunction of six,*
The atom must be six-parted.

If there be simultaneous conjunction with six atoms from six directions, then the atom must be six-parted; for in the place of one there cannot be another.[26]

v. 12cd *If the six occupy the same place,*
Then the cluster must be a mere atom.

Now, let the place of one atom be that of six. In that case, because all occupy the same place, the entire cluster must be a mere atom; for they do not exclude one another. Thus, no cluster whatever is found.

ii.a2. A dilemma for those who posit the conjunction of aggregations (v. 13)

The Kāśmīri Vaibhāṣikas, to avoid the fault implicit in partlessness, namely, that the atoms cannot conjoin, maintain that it is the aggregations that conjoin with one another. Let us demand of them whether or not the aggregations of atoms be objects discrete from those [atoms].

v. 13ab *If not a conjunction of atoms,*
Their aggregation is that of what?

"That" here stands for "a conjunction."

v. 13cd *And it is not merely owing to partlessness*
That their conjunction cannot be proven!

Now, should it be that the aggregations, too, do not conjoin with one another, then let it not be said that partlessness is the reason that the conjunction of atoms cannot be proven; for the conjunction of aggregations which have parts cannot be affirmed, either.

ii.a3. Conclusion of ii.a

Therefore, it cannot be proven that the atom is a simple substance.

ii.b. The incompatibility of spatial extension and simplicity (v. 14)

Whether the conjunction of atoms be affirmed or denied:

> v. 14ab *That which is spatially extended*
> *Cannot be simple.*

If the atom be spatially extended—that is, e.g., if it has a front part that is different from its bottom part—how can the simplicity of such an atom make sense?

> v. 14c *How can there be shade and shadow?*

If not a single atom is spatially extended, then, when the sun is shining, how is it that in one place there is shade, while there is sunlight in another? [Under such circumstances, the atom] does not, after all, have other parts that are *not* struck by the sunlight. And how can one atom be in the shadow of another, if spatial extension be denied? Moreover, if no atom whatever has discrete parts, such as might obstruct passage from one place to another, then, in the absence of such obstruction, owing to the co-spatiality of all, an entire cluster must be a mere atom, as has already been asserted.

But do you deny that shade and shadow are [properties] of the cluster, rather than of the atom?

Are you, then, maintaining them to be [properties] of a cluster which is discrete from the atoms? That cannot be, for:

> v. 14d *If the cluster be not discrete,*
> *They are not [properties] of it.*

If the cluster is not held to be discrete from the atoms, then it is established that they [i.e., shade and shadow] are not [properties] of it [i.e., the cluster].

iii. Refutation of the doctrine of simple, extended wholes (v. 15)

So long as the defining characteristic of form, etc.,[27] is not negated, does it matter whether or not the constructed idea[28] [of a particular form corresponds to] atom or aggregation?

What, then is their defining characteristic?

"Being an object of the eye, etc." and "being blue, etc."[29]

This must be examined: is that blue, yellow, or other, which is held to be the object of the eye, etc., a simple substance, or is it complex?

What are you driving at?

The fault of complexity has already been stated, and:

> v. 15 *If it were simple, there could not be gradual motion;*
> *Neither would simultaneous apprehension and non-apprehension be possible;*
> *Neither could there be separate, varied presence;*
> *Nor could there be unseen minuteness.*

If one imagines that, so long as the visual object [blue, yellow, etc.] is unbroken, it is not many but is one substance, then gradual traversal of the earth becomes impossible, "traversal of" meaning "motion across"; for a single step would have to traverse the whole.

Neither could there be apprehension of the near-part [of some object] simultaneous with non-apprehension of the far-part. For apprehension and non-apprehension at once of the very same thing is impossible.[30]

Neither could there be the presence in a single place[31] of separate and varied elephants, horses, and so forth; for, if one be in the location of another, how can they be held to be separate? How is it that [the places] they occupy and do not occupy are one, when empty space is apprehended between them?

Moreover, minute aquatic creatures having the same features as large ones would not be imperceptible if discreteness of substance were known only through characteristic difference, and not otherwise.[32]

iv. Conclusion

Therefore, atomic distinctions must be supposed; and that [atom] is not proven to be simple. It being unproven, it is not proven that forms, etc., are the objects of the eye, etc. Thus, it is proven that they are mere perceptions.

Notes

1 Rhys Davids 1890: 43–44. The Graeco-Bactrian king Menander (Pali: Milinda) reigned during the latter part of the second century B.C. (See chap. 3, n. 25, above.) His dialogues with Nāgasena were not set down until a somewhat later date and have little historical value. In particular, they offer no dependable evidence of possible philosophical exchange between Greece and India. Arguments based on the dissection of a thing into its constituent parts were well known in India from at least the first half of the first millennium B.C.E. Cf. chap. 2 above, and Collins 1982: 78–84 and *passim.* Several centuries prior to the age of Menander the elements of the person had already been metaphorically compared to the parts of a chariot, including horses and driver, in *Kaṭhopaniṣad,* III.3ff., and in many of the early Buddhist *suttas.* See, further, chap. 3, n. 24.

2 Barnes 1979, vol. 1, p. ix.

3 This is not to say that philology has in fact already completed its work in this case. On the contrary, we still face the vexing problem of whether the name "Vasubandhu" was that of one philosopher or of several. Nonetheless, the text studied in this essay is unquestionably well enough established for present purposes. On the entire problem, see, most recently, Skilling 2000.

4 I am thinking chiefly of the brilliant line of logicians beginning with his disciple Dignāga.

5 Quotations from Vasubandhu given below are based on my own translation, which is appended to this chapter. I have, however, allowed myself some liberties in the body of the paper, so as to avoid the more stilted style of the appendix, reference to which is given by means of the lowercase Roman numerals used in the section headings.

6 Aristotle, *On Generation and Corruption,* book 1, chap. 2, 316a. 25–30. Cf., also, Miller 1982.

7 Vasubandhu, unlike many of his successors, seldom gives clear syllogistic expression to his arguments. Hence, reconstructions like this one can only be given with some reservations. The conclusion (section iv.) of Vasubandhu's discussion, however, comes very close to setting out the present syllogism in unambiguous terms.

8 A useful discussion of Nyāya-Vaiśeṣika mereology will be found in Potter 1977: 74–86, and *passim.*

9 One question not raised here is: even if the whole is not a substance in addition to the unified collection of parts, is it not still true that the whole is something more than the sum of its parts? I see no objection, from Vasubandhu's standpoint, to the notion that a unified collection might have properties which neither its individual parts, nor any mere collection of those parts, might have. Strong conjunction is, in fact, just one such property.

10 The considerations mentioned in n. 7 apply here as well.

11 I think it at least questionable whether Vasubandhu ever did, in fact, seriously entertain the notion of unextended material points. It is referred to explicitly

in none of his works, so far as I know. His commentators who do mention it, e.g., Saṃghabhadra and Yaśomitra, may have posited such points in an attempt to formulate a realist response to Vasubandhu's idealism. See below, n. 13; as well as section ii.b., v. 14c.

12 Karunadasa 1967: 12–14, esp. p. 13: "Where there is one *sapratigha* (resistant) object there cannot be (at the same time) another..." Karunadasa here bases his statement on works of Vasubandhu and his commentators.

13 In my discussion, I interpret Vasubandhu *as if* he were addressing himself to a fully developed form of the theory in which atoms are supposed to be unextended. As has already been noted, however, *that* form of the theory may well have post-dated Vasubandhu. Here, his concern was probably an earlier version which postulated conjunction, not among atoms, but among clusters of unconjoined, simple, but extended, atoms.

14 Cf. Broad 1978: 224: "I do not see the slightest objection to the view that every body occupies the region which it *does* occupy only discontinuously." Similarly, Strawson 1966: 184: "...there would be no contradiction or absurdity in a physical theory according to which a composite material body was made up of a finite number of simple and unextended point-particles each of which was the sole occupant of a part of the space occupied by the material body as a whole..." Strawson's theory, however, allows for the formation of unified collections; for each particle might "...exert some causal power throughout the region of space of which it was the unique occupant."

15 Cf., e.g., Barnes 1979, vol. 1, chap. 12; Aristotle, *Physics,* 231b.15; and the antithesis of Kant's second antinomy.

16 Compare Pierre Bayle: "every extension, no matter how small it may be, has a right and a left side." Quoted in Van Cleve 1981: 483.

17 Herman 1983: 336–40, offers an analysis of Vasubandhu's attack on atomism which, I believe, is flawed. Rather than undertake a point-by-point critique of Herman's discussion, it will be sufficient to consider his proposed counterargument addressed to Vasubandhu's argument from shadow and shade, for it seems to me that most of Herman's difficulties are revealed in this one short passage. He writes:

> The realist defender of atoms, whoever he may be, is in a good position to attack the apparently devastating dilemma of atomism with a plausible and sensible counter-dilemma of his own. Let's call it "the counter-dilemma of atomism":
>
> 1. If the atom (or an aggregate) has spatial divisions then there would be shadows, etc.
> 2. If the atom (or an aggregate) has no spatial divisions then it can be a unity.
> 3. But the atom (or an aggregate) either has spatial divisions or it has no spatial divisions.

4. Therefore, either there are shadows, etc., or there is a unity, either of which is perfectly sensible.
5. Therefore, the atomist's position is perfectly sensible and not absurd.

As things stand, who is to say which dilemma or counter-dilemma, Vasubandhu's or the atomist's, is the most defensible? Thus the atomist's possible reply to Vasubandhu.

It should be clear that Herman has got himself into a muddle here by, among other things, completely failing to understand Vasubandhu's first dilemma of conjunction (ii.a1. above); for Herman's third premise asserts precisely what Vasubandhu there refuted. Neither has he, in speaking of "a unity," drawn any distinction whatsoever between the unity of a continuous whole, that of an extended minimal part, and that of a point-particle, which distinction, as I indicated above, does in fact reveal the weakness in the argument from shadow. This being so, it is altogether unclear just how his fourth step provides us with sensible alternatives. I ignore here several purely formal flaws in the argument, which require only relatively simple reformulation.

18 On this, see Van Cleve 1981: 490.

19 A somewhat different interpretation may be found in Hamilton 1938: 57, n. 103: "On the hypothesis of unity, each occupying subject must fill the whole of the place occupied. Hence in a single body of water each animalcule would have to be equal to the whole. Consequently small and large would be of the same measure—an absurdity."

20 *Pramāṇavārttika,* Pratyakṣapariccheda, v. 360. Refer to chap. 15, p. 413 below.

21 Śāntarakṣita develops the argument at great length in his "Examination of External Objects" *(Bahirarthaparīkṣā),* in his *Tattvasaṅgraha,* vol. 2, chap. 23. He applies it to the general critique of substantialist theories in his *Ornament of the Middle Way (Mādhyamakālaṃkāra),* which, with its commentaries, survives now only in Tibetan translation. Refer to Ichigō 1989.

22 In translating this passage from the Sanskrit, with reference to the eighth-century Tibetan translation, I have utilized the texts listed under *Viṃśatikā* in the bibliography, with reference also to Hamilton 1938, and Gangopadhyaya 1981. Translations may also be found in Anacker 1984, and Kochumuttom 1982.

23 The Buddhist idealist must argue that the references to material objects made by the Buddha in his discourses are intended not as metaphysical declarations concerning the real order of things, but merely as popular expressions, conforming to philosophically uninformed convention.

24 "Form, etc." = "visual objects and the objects of the remaining four physical senses."

25 "Cannot be proven" *(na sidhyati)* = "cannot be shown to exist," or "is an inadmissable hypothesis."

26 *ekasya yo deśaḥ tatrânyasyâsaṃbhavāt,* cf. n. 12 above.

27 See above, n. 24.

28 *Sanniveśaparikalpa eṣaḥ,* the Sanskrit phrase with which this passage opens (rendered here as "the constructed idea") is somewhat obscure, as is its Tibetan translation at this point. See Hamilton's note on it (1938: 53, n. 93), and Sastrin's remarks based on the gloss of Vinītadeva *(Viṃśatikā,* pp. 47–48, n. 50).

29 This is, of course, an abbreviated, enumerative definition: physical things are considered by Buddhist realism to be possibly such that they are objects of the five senses, or possibly such that they instantiate the properties that are perceived by those senses. See, e.g., Karunadasa 1967, chap. 1.

30 *na hi tasyâiva tadānīṃ grahaṇañ câgrahaṇañ ca yuktam.*

31 The Sanskrit text reads *anekatra* "here and there," but this is to be emended to *ekatra* "in a single place"; cf. the Tibetan *gcig-na,* "in one place."

32 Compare Hamilton's translation of Xuanzang's Chinese version: "Moreover there should also be no such scarcely perceptible tiny things as water animalcules, because being in the same single space with the coarse things they should be of equal measure." (Hamilton, 1938: 57).

8. The Trouble with Truth: Heidegger on *Alētheia,* Buddhist Thinkers on *Satya*

> What is questionable can sometimes be worthy of thought, and what is unthinkable can sometimes be glimpsed as that which thinking is about. Both Heidegger and Vedānta thought amply illustrate this. No other justification can be offered for the following very questionable enterprise of bringing together two disparate ways of thinking, so wide apart in time and in their entire context.[1]

IN THESE WORDS, the late J. L. Mehta set the appropriate cautionary tone for the dialogue which we are here attempting, thereby echoing Heidegger's own tentative explorations of the possibility for such a dialogue. In the 1946 "Letter on Humanism" Heidegger had written:

> But even the Western world is not thought of regionally as the Occident in contrast to the Orient, nor merely as Europe, but in the frame of world history from the closeness to its origin. We have hardly begun to think of the mysterious relations to the East, which find expression in Hölderlin's poetry.[2]

During the next decade Heidegger would begin to disclose some of these "mysterious relations" himself, most famously in the 1953 "A Dialogue on Language," and in several allusions to Laozi.[3] Nonetheless, his reflections both on the historicity of human thought and on the uniquely intimate relationship between language and Being seem to have counselled cautious restraint here: "comparative philosophy" would play no explicit role in Heidegger's enterprise, and, indeed, as Mehta clearly suggests in the perceptive essay cited above, Heidegger's way of thinking would appear to raise severe questions regarding the very possibility of "comparative philosophy." In *What is Philosophy?* he writes:

> The word *philosophia* tells us that philosophy is something which, first of all, determines the existence of the Greek world. Not only that—*philosophia* also determines the innermost basic feature of our Western-European history. The often heard expression "Western-European philosophy" is, in truth, a tautology.[4]

"Philosophy," Heidegger tells us, "is speaking Greek." As Evan Thompson rightly notes, Heidegger is not here arguing jingoistically for the superiority of Western thought. Rather, "Heidegger's conception is...a philosophical one: it is a conception of the form or *eidos* of a culture and the essential relation of philosophy to that form."[5]

The task of engaging together in dialogue the thought of Martin Heidegger and Buddhism is, therefore, something of a quixotic enterprise. This is so for many reasons, of which, at the outset at least, the most formidable will be the sheer difficulty for us of both ways of thought. And this difficulty stems not just from terminological and conceptual complexity and subtlety of reason in each instance, but is intensified also by the problematic nature of our own historical and cultural relationships with the parties we wish to engage in dialogue here.

Heidegger, to begin, assumed something of mythic proportion even during his own life; and he shows little sign yet of shrinking to a more manageable dimension. To put the point somewhat whimsically: Martin Heidegger was the Darth Vader of late twentieth-century intellectual life. Regarded by some as the supreme exponent of the force of authentic thinking-and-Being, he appeared also to have been turned, terrifyingly, to the dark side of that force. Whether our inquiry be in the domain of philosophy, religion, history, or criticism, he looms thus above our path as one with whom we must struggle, if only to avoid; and in struggling with him we will likely face some disconcerting revelations of our own intellectual paternity.

Our second difficult conversation partner is "Buddhist thought." Of course, there is no way for us to enter into dialogue with Buddhist thought *überhaupt.* We must choose either to engage the thought of a single individual, or perhaps that of a well-defined group of some sort, and our decision about our symposium's guest list will, to a very great extent, skew the course of the entire dialogue: in searching for aspects of Buddhism to introduce in dialogue with Martin Heidegger we will almost inevitably set our sights on those which seem, initially at least, to have the greatest affinity with his thought. Because we engage in the conversation in this manner, we have determined even before the onset of the dialogue that it should be relatively harmonious in nature, that it should underscore fraternity and not incompatibility. It is difficult to imagine that, under the rubric of "Heidegger and Buddhist Thought," one might attempt to contemplate the abhidharma, Tibetan debate logic, or Nichiren, for instance.

These considerations by no means discredit the present effort, but they should make us very humble about what we are willing to claim for it: the rubric of "Heidegger and Buddhist Thought" (and a fortiori "Heidegger and *Asian* Thought"!) is a denomination of convenience, referring to what will necessarily be a severely restricted undertaking. In point of fact, the dialogue between Heideggerian and Buddhist thought, as it has evolved to date, has involved almost exclusive representation, on the Buddhist side, of the dialectical aspects of Mahāyāna thought—as exemplified above all by the Mādhyamika tradition, or by traditions in which Mādhyamika thought plays a particularly prominent role: consider Sprung or Sinari on Nāgārjuna, Guenther on Mahāmudrā, or the thinkers of the Kyoto school on Zen.[6] In surveying the contributions emerging from these quarters, it is impossible to avoid the suspicion that, rather than genuine philosophical dialogue, what we have here in fact represents the growth of a peculiar brand of contemporary apologetics. And it is apparent, too, that in this effort representatives of East Asian, and particularly Japanese Buddhist, traditions have been preeminent.

One of the initial difficulties we face in attempting to reflect on Buddhist thought in relation to Heidegger is thus partially obviated once we recognize the severe and inevitable cultural/historical/doctrinal limitations of the project. The apparent simplification of our problem in this sense, however, does not by any means yield a corresponding simplification of philosophical content: for Madhyamaka and the traditions closely allied to it embody highly complex currents in the history of ideas, extended through some two millennia, intermingling with the major cultural traditions of South, Central, and East Asia, and articulated in some half a dozen or so languages. In attempting to understand this movement in human thought, we are faced—the Kyoto school philosophers are perhaps among the partial exceptions here—with what Luis O. Gómez has felicitously termed the "double distance"—historical and cultural—between ourselves and the tradition into which we inquire.[7]

With this in mind, the present essay must be placed in the forum of the discussion as only a very tentative experiment. We may ask: for one engaged in the study of Indian Buddhism from a critical historical and philosophical perspective, does the encounter with Heidegger offer a possibly fruitful path through the wilderness of interpretation? And does that encounter further advance our understanding of Heidegger? Because no simple and straightforward answers can be offered in response to such questions, it will be preferable to choose one precise and well-defined area in Heidegger's thought that seems to correspond or contrast in an interesting fashion with some equally well-defined aspect of Indian Buddhist thought. In this manner, a dialectical pathway may begin to open before us; but like the *Holzwege* of which Heidegger speaks, it is a path whose destination we cannot determine in advance, and which very possibly has no fixed destination at all. For the purposes of this experiment, then, the topic to which we shall address our inquiries will be the concept of truth.

Heidegger's radical, and much criticized, interpretation of the Greek concept of *alḗtheia,* which he developed in considerable detail in his seminal essay *Plato's Doctrine of Truth,*[8] presents us with a central theme in Heidegger's historical critique of Western philosophy: Greek thought bears witness to a great upheaval in the history of Being, characterized by the growing alienation of thought from an authentic engagement in Being and by the corresponding rise of metaphysics; and this alienation is epitomized in a shift in the very meaning of truth. On this reading, Plato's parable of the Cave (*Republic,* book 7, 514 seq.) is significant to us not only owing to what Plato seeks to convey through its explicit symbolism, but even more so because of its unspoken revelation of precisely this shift in meaning.

Heidegger, treating the Greek *alḗtheia* as a term composed with the *alpha*-privative particle and thus literally meaning "*un*hiddenness" or "*un*concealment," identifies four stages in the career of the prisoner of the Cave.[9] At first, the prisoner is chained, seeing only shadows, hearing only echoes. These are the things which seem to him to be "unhidden" *(alēthés,* 515c, 1–2). Then, he is freed from his bonds and permitted to turn toward the fire and the objects whose reflected shadows he had previously beheld. These things, painfully regarded through blinded eyes, are now "unhidden," in a certain respect, but it is the shadows dancing on the wall, seen with ease rather than pain, that appear to be "more unhidden" *(alēthéstera,* 515d, 6). In the third stage the prisoner is dragged out into the open, where his eyes, gradually growing strong, come to see that which is "most unhidden"[10] of all: the solar orb that is the "Idea of the Good." Witnessing it in its radiant splendor, the former prisoner now recognizes the true order of things and the fact that all that he had seen in the Cave, though false, was nonetheless dependent on this for its shadowy existence. The fourth and final stage occurs when the prisoner returns to the Cave to free his former companions. No longer able to see "correctly" in the Cave's dark recesses, he courts death by proclaiming a truth to which the still chained prisoners react as to the ravings of a madman.

The transformation of the soul which has progressed through these stages consists in a reorientation through which one comes to behold the "unhidden," the truth that was previously concealed, precisely because one's gaze was turned in the wrong direction. With the soul's reorientation, then, the truth is laid bare, or, in Heidegger's words, it is "wrested from a base and stubborn concealment."[11] Moreover:

> Where there is pure education the soul itself is seized and transformed as a whole, while at the same time man is transplanted to the region of his essence and oriented to it.[12]

Thus, the revelation of the "unhidden" has two aspects: it involves the radiant presence of the "unhidden" itself; and it requires a proper human orientation, one which faces the "unhidden" directly. Heidegger contends, in effect, that the historical shift in the concept of truth (Plato's "unspoken" doctrine of truth) is to be found in a shift in emphasis to the second of these aspects, to the "correctness" of the human glance; and that through this shift sight has been lost of what was, in the first place, to be beheld in its mysterious self-disclosure.[13] The result of this transition, as George Steiner expresses it, is the emergence of "the Aristotelian-Thomistic view of truth as that of an agreement or adequation between subject and object... [which] places man at the commanding fulcrum of being. It must lead," he continues, "to that pragmatic and technological imperialism over knowledge which proceeds via Cartesian rationality to the Nietzschean exaltation of will and modern nihilism."[14]

Whatever we may conclude with regard to the full details of Heidegger's account, we must concede to him at the outset that the Greek notion of *alētheia,* "truth," cannot be thought of reductively as signifying only *adæquatio intellectus et rei.* Even in the writings of Aristotle, who sought to disambiguate the term as far as possible, *alētheia* remains a problematic concept. This was almost certainly brought to Heidegger's attention when he was still quite young, through his reading, in 1907, of Brentano's *On the Several Senses of Being in Aristotle,* the third chapter of which is entitled

"Being in the Sense of Being True" *(on hos alēthés, ens tanquam verum).*[15] Further reflections of Brentano on truth became available posthumously, in 1930, with the publication of *The True and the Evident (Wahrheit und Evidenz).*[16] In 1889 Brentano had presented the Vienna Philosophical Society with a lecture on "The Concept of Truth"—this was among the pieces later published in *The True and the Evident*—in which he elaborated in popular terms some of the ambiguity with which, he maintained, Aristotle had been struggling:

> We call many *thoughts,* ideas, or presentations *(Vorstellungen)* true, and we call others false (hallucinations, for example, we call false); we call concepts true or false, we call *judgements* true or false; we call conjectures, hopes, and anxieties true or false; we call a heart, a mind, true or false *(un esprit faux);* we call external things true or false; we call sayings true or false; we call conduct true or false; we call expressions, letters of the alphabet, and many other signs, true or false; we call a friend, we call gold, true or false. We speak of true happiness and of false happiness.... Similarly, we say on occasion: a false woman..., but in another sense a false woman would be a man posing as a woman...; and still in another sense a false woman would be a man who has no thought of pretending to be a woman but nonetheless is taken for one, a thing that actually happened to me at dawn one morning in the entrance to the Würzburg fortress. At that time I was wearing a cassock....[17]

As Brentano argues, Aristotle sought to resolve some of the difficulties flowing from the ambiguity of the concept of truth by reference to his doctrine of analogy. What is true in the primary sense is the judgment that accords with its object. Other sorts of truth are so-called only insomuch as they "all stand in close relation to" such judgment. This is similar to the manner in which a concept such as "healthy" is to be explained: in that case, one thinks primarily of the healthy animal body, but the parts of that body, as well as foods, medicines, exercise routines, and attitudes, may all be called "healthy" too, owing to their close relations to the health of the body.

By the time Brentano delivered his talk on truth in Vienna, several of his senior contemporaries had already challenged the Aristotelian doctrine of truth, above all the historian of philosophy Windelband and the father of contemporary philosophical hermeneutics, Wilhelm Dilthey.[18] While

Brentano ultimately defends a version of the Aristotelian doctrine against these thinkers in the 1889 lecture, it is already clear that he regards that doctrine as a troubled one. By 1915 he would abandon the correspondence theory altogether, saying:

> We cannot possibly know that there is an agreement between things unless we know each of the things between which the agreement holds. Hence if all knowledge were thought of as knowledge of agreement, we would be required to complete an impossible *regressus ad infinitum.* The real guarantee of the truth of a judgement lies in the judgement's being evident.... Truth pertains to the judgement of the person who judges correctly—to the judgement of the person who judges about a thing in the way in which anyone whose judgements were *evident* would judge about the thing; hence it pertains to the judgement of one who asserts what the person whose judgements are evident would also assert.[19]

But though Brentano has now abandoned the doctrine of adequation, he retains, as had Windelband and Dilthey, Aristotle's view that truth primarily pertains to the true judgment. It is here that the genuine radicalism of Heidegger's thesis concerning *alētheia* becomes apparent, even without regard to its historical ramifications; for Heidegger's thesis deracinates truth from its tenacious implantation in the ground of human judgment and reason. Nonetheless, we must note in Brentano's invocation of the "evident" a striking anticipation of Heidegger's notion, first introduced in *Sein und Zeit,* of Being-true as disclosedness.[20]

With this in mind, let us turn now to the consideration of the concept of truth in some of its classical Indian manifestations.

The Sanskrit term most frequently rendered in English as "truth" and in German as "Wahrheit" is *satya.* Any comparative inquiry into the conceptual nexus associated with this term must begin by asking: what does the word *satya* literally mean, and how was its basic meaning understood in India? Only when we know this, will we be able to investigate particular instances of the "philosophical" use of the term in question without that investigation being unacceptably tendentious from the outset.

There can be no question of *satya's* ever having *literally* meant anything like "unhidden."[21] As is well known, it is derived in a straightforward manner from a participial form of the verb "to be," and can be traced right back to the Indo-European copula, which is preserved in Sanskrit *as,* Greek *eimí,* Latin *esse,* English *is,* and German *Sein.* This is not merely a discovery of modern comparative philology: Sanskrit grammarians, though not engaged in Indo-European historical linguistics, were always acutely sensitive to the derivational principles of their own language, and they explained the term *satya* thus: *sate hitaṃ yat.*[22] This terse formula means: [the secondary derivational suffix] *ya* has been applied to [the present participle] *sat.* The suffix *ya* has several functions; typically, it expresses derivation, affinity, relatedness. It may express this rather strongly, as for instance in the formation of patronymics—e.g., "son of so-and-so," "descendent of so-and-so"—or so weakly that the derived term is virtually synonymous with its etymon. *Satya,* therefore, given a strong interpretation of the semantic influence of the derivational suffix, is "what stands in relation to, has affinity with, being." Read more weakly it is simply "what has being."

From the Vedic period onward, Indian thinkers regarded speech as one of the things that, in some instances at least, could be characterized as *satya,* "related to being."[23] The epithet *satyavādī*—truth-speaker, one who "tells it like it is"[24]—comes into use during the same early period, and suggests that true speech was regarded as that speech which discloses being through some sort of correspondence thereto, a conception that was later given systematic expression in Hindu philosophical literature.[25] That very early Indian thinkers *did* regard language as capable of standing in a relationship of correspondence or adequation to being is confirmed beyond reasonable doubt by even so ancient a text as the *Bṛhadāraṇyaka Upaniṣad,* where the apparent *impossibility* of designating some objects—*brahman* or *ātman*—in this manner had already become a topic of lively discussion.[26] It was here that the seed was planted for the eventual emergence of the theory of "two truths" *(satyadvaya)* that became prominent in much later Buddhist and Vedāntic scholasticism, and to which we shall return below.

Throughout the history of Indian Buddhism the paradigmatic notion of "truth" (Skt. *satya,* Pali, *sacca)* was revealed in the teaching of the four noble truths. Even so late a Mahāyāna epistemologist as Mokṣākaragupta (twelfth century), separated from the age of the Buddha by no less a span of time than was Luther from Jesus, in his exposition of the peculiar mode of perception or knowledge possessed uniquely by the insightful sage, refers to the four noble truths as the "genuine objective," contemplation of which is productive of the knowledge in question.[27] When we inquire into what "truth" meant to Indian Buddhists, therefore, we would do well to begin by asking, what sort of "truth" is meant when one speaks of the "four noble truths"?

The sūtra in which the Buddha first reveals his teaching of the four truths is reported universally to have been his first sermon. Though the various available redactions in the surviving canons of the early Buddhist schools reveal some discrepancies in the precise wording of the text, one is struck above all by its stability in its several transmissions.[28] The best known version is the *Dhammacakka-ppavattanasutta (The Discourse Setting into Motion the Wheel of the Dharma)* of the Pali canon, where the crucial passage with which we are here concerned reads as follows:

> Now this, O monks, is suffering, a noble truth: birth is suffering; aging is suffering; illness is suffering; death is suffering; coming in contact with what is unpleasant is suffering; separation from what is pleasant is suffering; not getting what one desires is suffering; in short, the five acquisitive *skandhas (khandha)* are suffering. Now this, O monks, is the origination of suffering, a noble truth: it is this thirst, causing further birth, accompanied by delight and desire, taking pleasure here and there, namely, erotic thirst, thirst for being, thirst for annihilation. Now this, O monks, is the cessation of suffering, a noble truth: it is that thirst's cessation due to complete dispassion, [its] abandonment, releasement, liberation, deracination. Now this, O monks, is the path conducing to the cessation of suffering, a noble truth: it is this eight-limbed path, namely, correct view, correct intention, correct speech, correct limits on action, correct livelihood, correct effort, correct presence of mind, correct meditation.[29]

It is by no means certain that the term "truth" is used univocally in these passages. The manner in which the first truth, that of suffering, is expressed, suggests above all a roughly propositional conception of truth articulated in statements of the form: *it is true* that *x* is suffering, *it is true* that *y* is suffering, etc. But in the case of the second truth, that of the origination of suffering, it is a particular property, "thirst," that is identified with the truth in question; and in the third the cessation of that property. Finally, the fourth truth embodies a recommended course of action. "Truth," therefore, would appear to be what is really the case, or a fact about the world, or an appropriate course of human action, or else it is a proposition or assertion corresponding to such a reality, or fact, or action. "Noble truths" are those truths, contemplation of which culminates in the attainment of the status of a "noble" (Pali *āriya,* Skt. *ārya*) in the classical Buddhist sense; that is, one whose final liberation is secure.

As we have seen earlier (in chap. 3), a distinction is sometimes made in the scholastic literature of early Buddhism between those terms or statements which are of "ultimate significance" *(paramattha)* and those which are matters only of conventional usage *(sammuti)*. Thus, for instance, *The Questions of King Milinda (Milindapañha),* paraphrasing here the much earlier *Kathāvatthu:* "In an ultimate sense, no person is apprehended...'there is a being' is conventional usage."[30] It is this distinction that, refined and further developed, becomes a distinction between "two truths." Nāgārjuna introduces it thus:

> Relying on two truths is the Dharma instruction of the buddhas:
> The truth of the world's conventional usage, and the truth in an ultimate sense.[31]

Though I do not accept the general thesis of those who seek to disassociate Nāgārjuna from the Mahāyāna, I can see no reason not to take the technical terms in this verse as meaning just what they do in the tradition represented by *The Questions of King Milinda.* It is true that instead of the Pali *sammuti* we find here the Sanskrit *saṃvṛti,* but, as will become apparent below, that should not in itself convince us that any semantic shift has yet taken place.

The context of Nāgārjuna's verse is also worth noting: it occurs in the middle of his discussion of the four noble truths, and is clearly introduced here, as it had been in *Milinda,* to provide a metalinguistic device through which to interpret differing, apparently incompatible, assertions of doctrine, in this case the teaching of emptiness and that of the four truths. The two truths can plausibly be regarded as originally hermeneutical categories, and not as a metaphysical doctrine at all, much less a theory about the general concept of "truth." Nonetheless, it would appear that during the first centuries of the common era, Buddhist scholiasts came increasingly to regard the two truths as a scheme parallelling, or supplementing, that of the four noble truths. Vasubandhu writes:

> Four truths were uttered by the Lord, and also two truths: the truth of conventional usage and the truth of ultimate significance. What are the defining characteristics of these two?
>
> With reference to some thing, upon there being a breaking up or mental reduction to other [constituent elements],
> If no perception of that [thing remains], as in the case of a pot or of water,

> Then it is truth of conventional usage; otherwise, the truth
> of ultimate significance.[32]

In the ensuing autocommentary, Vasubandhu makes clear that truth is conceived according to a linguistic paradigm: *satyam evāhur na mṛṣā,* "they speak truth, indeed, not lies." And Yaśomitra, in his subcommentary (which incidentally quotes in full the verse of Nāgārjuna that we have already cited above), glosses *saṃvṛti* with the expression *saṃvyavahāreṇa,* "according to common usage."[33]

If Nāgārjuna's *explicit* doctrine of the two truths can thus be plausibly understood as simply a variant on earlier Buddhist scholastic usage, is it not yet possible that his teaching as a whole nonetheless necessitated a transformation in the understanding of that doctrine? As Heidegger tells us:

> The "doctrine" of a thinker is that which is left unsaid in what he says, to which man is exposed in order to expend himself upon it.[34]

Indeed, the later history of Mahāyāna thought, above all within the Mādhyamika tradition, reveals a deepening and ever-widening preoccupation with the problem of the two truths, as that tradition expends itself upon what remains unsaid in Nāgārjuna's doctrine. The history is long and complex, but thanks to the recent intensification of research in the sphere of the history of Indian Mādhyamika philosophy, many significant details have now come into view.[35] For present purposes it is not necessary to survey this material in full detail, so to suggest something of the great changes that were to take place, we shall leap ahead to the final phase in the history of Indian Madhyamaka, and consider briefly some of the remarks on the two truths found in Prajñākaramati's (tenth- or eleventh-century) commentary on Śāntideva's (seventh-century) *Introduction to Enlightened Conduct (Bodhicaryāvatāra).* Śāntideva's evocative verses, Prajñākaramati's comments on which will concern us here, are these:

> Convention and ultimate significance—this is thought to be the
> pair of truths.
> Reality is not the field of intellect; intellect is said to be conventional usage. 9.2.
> So it is that the world is twofold, [there being the worlds of]
> adepts and commoners.

> Thus, the common world is overcome by the adept's world. 9.3.
> Overcome, too, according to distinction of thought, are the adepts in ascending succession. 9.4ab.[36]

A superficial resemblance with the parable of the Cave will be noticed immediately: just as the condition of the prisoners is separated from that of the realizer of the "Idea of the Good" by an intervening realm in which one has turned painfully away from the shadows flickering on the wall, so too, here the commoner who knows only convention is separated from the realizer of the truth of ultimate significance by a hierarchically ordered realm of adepts, who, though free from the constraints of the commoner, have not yet realized that reality which is the truth of ultimate significance. Thus, the apparent bivalence of the two truths notwithstanding, the scheme, as presented here, can be made out to comport rather well with Heidegger's reading of the Platonic progression from that which merely appears to be "unhidden"—Plato's *alēthés,* Śāntideva's *saṃvṛtisatya*—through that which is "more unhidden"—*alēthéstera, yogisaṃvṛti*[37]—to that which is "most unhidden"—*tò alēthéstaton, paramārthasatya.* Let us turn now to Prajñākaramati's discussions of the essential concept of the two truths.[38]

Prajñākaramati opens his comments on verse 9.2 by explaining the term *saṃvṛti,* so far translated as "conventional usage." He writes:

> *Saṃvṛti* is so called because by it the comprehension of what is as it is is concealed, occluded, by reason of the occlusion of essential being, and because of disclosing [what is itself] occluded. Ignorance, stupefaction, and error are synonyms. For ignorance, being the imputation of the forms of non-existent things, and of the nature of occlusion of the vision of inherent being, is *saṃvṛti.*[39]

Concealment has now displaced convention as the primary signification of *saṃvṛti.* It is not without interest to note that here, as in Heidegger's novel interpretation of *alḗtheia,* the rhetorical medium for the reassessment of the word's meaning is etymological explanation—by explaining, or seeming to explain, a word from its root, we seek to probe its archaic resonances, to uncover in its depths a message lost to the commerce of ordinary chatter. The later Mādhyamika interpretation of *saṃvṛti,* it should be emphasized, is etymologically correct: the root-form from which it is derived, *saṃ-vṛ,* means essentially "to cover over, to close." Hence, "closing of the throat, articulation,"[40] but also "concealment." That Mādhyamika thinkers came in time to emphasize the latter signification was a historical decision, linguistically correct to be sure, but not given unto them by the language even prior to their reflection upon it.

Prajñākaramati's discussion of *paramārtha* reveals a subtle intermingling of two themes that had been associated with this term from antiquity. On the one hand, following a tradition established in the analytical aspects of abhidharma thought, as represented above primarily in the selection from Vasubandhu, it is that which is ultimately real, that which is not destroyed through a reductive analytical procedure. For Vasubandhu this meant that it was paradigmatically two sorts of things: physical atoms and phenomenal atoms, or *dharmas.* For Prajñākaramati, as a Mādhyamika thinker, analysis can find no such points of termination; it must proceed until it reveals the radical contingency of all conditioned phenomena, their ultimate emptiness:

> The ultimate, highest, significance, is...the uncontrived form of things, owing to the comprehension of which there is the abandonment of affliction that is bound up with all dispositions [involving] obscuration. It is the absence of inherent being of all dharmas, [their] emptiness, just-so-ness, genuine limit, the sphere of dharma—these are among its synonyms.[41]

As this passage makes clear, however, analytical ultimacy is closely associated with soteriological ultimacy—at the limit of analysis there is an "abandonment of affliction." While the Buddhist tradition seems always to have associated the two, the later Mādhyamika tradition accentuates this in a manner that is in certain respects to be distinguished from the earlier tradition. For *paramārtha* can mean not just "ultimate significance" in an analytic sense, but equally it can stand for *paramapuruṣārtha,* that is, the highest end of man, *mokṣa,* liberation. In the tradition represented by Prajñākaramati, there is an apparently perfect convergence between these notions. One result is that the two truths scheme is no longer essentially a hermeneutical device used to interpret four truths discourse, nor is it merely an alternative classificatory scheme; rather, the two truths embrace and include the four noble truths themselves:

> It has been explained in the abhidharma by the Lord that there are four noble truths, whose defining characteristics are suffering, origination, cessation and the path. How, therefore, can

> there be just two truths?... It is because of their being included in the two, in this manner: the truths of suffering, origination, and the path, being essentially concealment, are included in the truth of concealment, and the truth of cessation in the truth of ultimate significance. Thus there is no contradiction [between the two schemes].[42]

The doctrine of two truths, having assumed an all-embracing character, begins to look increasingly like a general doctrine of truth. But we have not yet said just how it is that truth, *satya,* is here to be understood. In particular, if *saṃvṛti* is concealment, occlusion, then in what sense is it *satya,* truth, at all?

> *Saṃvṛti* is one truth, inerrant, and *paramārtha* is the other truth. "And" conjoins them as being equivalent insomuch as they are just truth. In this connection, the truth of concealment is the non-inadequate form of [i.e., adhered to by] the common world. The truth of ultimate significance is the incorrigible reality of [i.e., realized by] the nobles.[43]

The world of common experience, including linguistic and cognitive experiences, is true just insofar as it is not actually falsified. Its "truth" is not a question of adequation, but rather of non-inadequation: whether my concept of a vase involves a relationship of adequation to that vase, in the Aristotelian-Scholastic sense, can never be established,[44] but the Mādhyamika's notion of non-inadequation (*avitatha,* lit. "non-not-thus") is no mere double negation of the Western scholastic concept. So long as my concept of the vase is not defeated in experience, it is not inadequate. In quotidian life that is generally all the truth we need. Prajñākaramati adds:

> It may be [objected], how is it that *saṃvṛti,* being of the nature of what is revealed in ignorance, and which is devastated by hundreds of investigations, because it is of the nature of imputation of what is not, is truth? This too is truth. However, it is spoken of as the truth of concealment in that it is a determination of the common world. For it is the world that is here the truth of concealment. In conformity with it, the Lord too has just so spoken [in terms of] the truth of concealment, without reference to those seeking reality. Hence, the qualification "and the truth of the

world's conventional usage" has been also asserted by the venerable teacher [Nāgārjuna] in [his] treatise [or, perhaps, "in a śāstric context"]. In reality, ultimate significance is the only truth.[45]

It is precisely here that we may return to Heidegger's reflections on *alētheia;* for it is the concealment that is the world, which is known as truth insofar as there is no deprivation of adequation, that is the ground realized also as the truth of ultimate significance. In the two truths doctrine, dualism is overcome, much as it is in Heidegger's thinking on the unhidden, according to which the unhidden is vouchsafed to the thinker in virtue of its very concealment. Concealment *is* the abode of emptiness, that which is of ultimate significance; and because its abode is concealment, "in reality, ultimate significance is the only truth."

In the soteriological dimension of the two truths doctrine as well, some will be inclined to find some harmony with the later Heidegger's reflections on "releasement." Indeed, the possible points of harmonious contact now seem to be many, and the path that seems to find its beginning in these reflections urges us forward. However, in accord with the spirit of the wanderer on the *Holzwege* of thought, I must end by abruptly changing my course.

Heidegger's reinterpretation of the Greek notion of *alētheia* was offered in part as a *historical* thesis. Moreover, it is not the case here of a philosopher's historical accuracy or inaccuracy being to all intents and purposes irrelevant to his intentions; for Heidegger's interpretations of the history of philosophy are absolutely central to his thought, and his thinking on the historicity of the concept of truth contains the distilled essence of his historical vision. On Heidegger's view, the archaic conception of the unhiddenness of Being was, at some place and time in the history of Being (namely Greece in the last half of the first millennium B.C.E.), transformed into and supplanted by the notion of truth as a correspondence between idea and object; and it was this transformation that betokened the entire later development of Western "rationality," under the banner of "metaphysics." This is pretty strong stuff, and we need to ask what bearing, if any, our Indian Buddhist researches might have here.

It seems fairly certain that the doctrine of two truths, in the developed form in which we have described it above, does not represent the archaic thought of India, which regarded truth loosely as "that which has affinity to being," and more precisely as the real state of affairs obtaining in the world, or as speech or thought according with that reality. This is not, of course, to say that there was an archaic doctrine of truth, and that that doctrine corresponded more or less to the correspondence theory. Rather, the archaic conceptual nexus associated with the notion of truth was somewhat indefinite, pregnant with possibilities for reflective and theoretical disclosure. Our conclusions about this thus conform quite closely to those of Charles Kahn regarding the relationship between the concepts of truth and being in Greece,[46] so that, insofar as Sanskrit and Greek are closely related cognate tongues, we have some reason to be skeptical of Heidegger's arguments concerning the *historical* primordiality of truth-as-unhiddenness.

Because archaic Indo-European notions of truth were indefinite, and thus offered many avenues for possible development, it should not be too astonishing that reflective civilizations, such as those of India and Greece, generated diverse theories or doctrines of truth. Plato's interest in the theory of knowledge may perhaps be traced in part to the polysemy of "truth" in his time. Consider too that in India, epistemologists and logicians of the Nyāya and allied schools, among Hindus, Buddhists, and Jains, advanced markedly positivistic theories of truth, which traditions of thought like the Madhyamaka and Vedānta were, in part, determined to overcome. Again, the evidence may be read so as to undercut Heidegger's account.

But does it? Granting that "unhiddenness" can be accorded no historical priority, at least among Greeks and Indians, we must not thereby assume that it is without priority in the unfolding of that thinking in which the Being of beings announces itself. Despite the evident fact that the radical dichotomy of subject and object, with its attendant repercussions for thinking on truth, was no less prominent in Indian thought than in Greek, we cannot conclude that Heidegger has failed to identify a crucial feature of Western-Hellenic-Christian thought—crucial precisely because that tradition itself fatefully chose that it should be preeminent—much as the Mādhyamika tradition fatefully chose to destroy classical Indian "metaphysical" thought by means of the antidote offered by its doctrine of two truths.

Appendix: The Legacy of the Two Truths beyond India

The spread of the Buddha's teaching throughout much of Asia in late antiquity and the early medieval period engendered a great proliferation of new approaches to Buddhist thought, reflecting in part the efforts of thinkers to assimilate the doctrine to the requirements of diverse communities and cultures. The richness of these developments as they bear upon the conception of the two truths cannot be adequately reflected here, but to exemplify them in part we shall briefly consider some salient innovations articulated by philosophers of the Mahāyāna in China, Japan, and Tibet. The teaching of the two truths, as befitted its origins, always remained a problematic doctrine, destabilizing, and thereby opening, thought in varied and creative ways.

Despite the many pronounced differences between the East Asian Buddhist traditions (including those of China and Japan), which relied upon the Buddhist scriptures and philosophical treatises as they had been translated into classical Chinese, and the Tibetan Buddhist schools, which followed distinctive scriptural canons in literary Tibetan, both were united in their puzzlement concerning the relationship between the two truths. We have seen already that Indian sources provided no simple solution to this problem, and so it is not surprising that it would generate considerable interest when the difficulties to which it gave rise were compounded by issues of translation and transmission across linguistic and cultural boundaries.

One of the most daring solutions to the problem was proposed by the Chinese monk and scholar Zhiyi (538–97), whose teachings formed the basis for the Tiantai (in Japanese, Tendai) school of Buddhism. What Zhiyi proposed was to resolve the dialectical tension between the two truths by positing a third truth. In its essential structure, then, Zhiyi's theory very roughly reminds us of the Hegelian conception of the *synthesis* that arises from the dialectical opposition of *thesis* and *antithesis.* It is a theory with its own distinctive twist, however, as is made clear in the interpretation of Neal Donner:

> The third truth is generated from the other two by regarding them as extremes, dialectically reconciled in the middle truth. That things *are* is the first truth (provisional); that they are *not* is the second (ultimate); and that they *both* are and are not, as well as *neither* are nor are not, is the third truth, considered necessary by Chih-i [Zhiyi] in order to avoid the extreme of negation into which he perceived many of those falling who clung to the doctrine of emptiness as an ultimate.... The third or middle truth, expressible as above in two equivalent ways ("both" and "neither") is not truly a compromise, a "middle way" between extremes as we might think, but instead emphasizes the paradoxical nature of reality: that the truth cannot be reduced to a single formulation.[47]

Zhiyi's three truth theory, however, did not meet a favorable reception in all quarters. It invited, among others, the objections that by identifying the ultimate with the "not," Zhiyi had misunderstood the second truth, and that by propounding a third truth he had failed to grasp the significance of complete freedom from conceptual alternatives. Thus, for instance, Kūkai (Kōbō Daishi, 774–835), the founder of the Shingon school of esoteric Buddhism in Japan, clearly suggested that Zhiyi, though deriving his teaching partly from that of Nāgārjuna, had not really comprehended the depths of the latter's insights.[48] Kūkai's own view of the two truths was, by contrast, elaborated primarily on the basis of the esoteric teachings he championed. In esoteric Buddhist practice, in contradistinction to other approaches to Buddhist meditation, there is a powerful emphasis on ritual performance and positive symbolism (including visual imagery, incantation, and gesture). In this approach, emptiness suffuses the brilliance of divine and sacred forms, and these, in turn, are identified with the manifest nature of living beings. Expressing this in relation to the doctrine of two truths, Kūkai elaborates the very passage from Nāgārjuna we considered above:

> In Buddhism there are two standards of truth, that is, the conventional truth and the ultimate truth. For the conventional truth it is explained that there are sentient beings. For the ultimate truth it is explained that there are no sentient beings at all. But here again there are two standards. For those who do not know the characteristics of expression and esoteric symbols, it is explained that from the point of view of the ultimate truth there are no sentient beings; and for those who know the characteristics of expression and esoteric symbols, it is explained that from the point of view of the ultimate truth there are sentient beings.[49]

Kūkai's conception here is similar to that of some of the esoteric traditions of Tibetan Buddhism, which speak in this context of a "coalescence of appearance and emptiness" *(snang-stong zung-'jug)*. A recent doctrinal manual of the Rnying-ma-pa tradition, for example, states:

> The body of reality according to the vehicle of dialectics has fallen into the extreme of emptiness, whereas the body of reality according to the mantras [that is to say, esoteric Buddhism] does not fall into extremes of eternalism and nihilism since there is no dichotomy between appearance and emptiness.[50]

Passages such as these, however, are deliberately framed to reflect the polemic of certain proponents of the esoteric traditions against dialectical philosophers (in Kūkai's words "those who do not know the characteristics of expression and esoteric symbols"), and so to some extent stereotype the viewpoint of the latter. At the same time, however, the dialectical traditions of Tibetan Buddhism, basing themselves upon the close study of the writings of the Indian philosophical masters, arrived at a whole range of differing interpretations of the two truths, while seeking to avoid those perspectives characterized as "extreme." Among these interpretations the most controversial, certainly, was propounded by Dol-po-pa Shes-rab-rgyal-mtshan (1292–1361), who was famous for his peculiar doctrine of the "extrinsic emptiness" *(gzhan-stong)* of the absolute, that is to say, its emptiness with respect to all relative or conventional phenomena, that are thus extrinsic to its proper nature.[51] Entailed by this doctrine is a radical division between the two truths: the nature of the absolute is such that relative reality is in some sense wholly other with respect to it. The following remarks are drawn from Dol-po-pa's remarkable essay entitled "The Sun Illuminating the Two Truths":

> The defining characteristic of relative truth is that it is an object of consciousness that in its fundamental nature is itself essentially empty of veridical being, while the defining characteristic of absolute truth is that it is an object of authentic, sublime gnosis that in its fundamental nature is itself essentially not empty of veridical being....
>
> Because the relative does not exist in fact, it is intrinsically empty, and appears to consciousness but not to gnosis. Because the absolute exists in fact, it is not intrinsically empty, but is extrinsically empty, and appears to gnosis but never at all to consciousness....
>
> Thus, to those who are childish, according to their own dispositions, only inauthentic characteristics appear, but not the authentic suchness, and in the same way, to the bodhisattvas, according to their own dispositions, only the authentic appears, but not what is inauthentic.[52]

Dol-po-pa's views were hotly contested by those who thought they amounted to a form of radical dualism; his most vociferous opponents even charged that he was a covert adherent of the Hindu Sāṃkhya philosophy!

Among those who articulated opposing interpretations of the teaching of two truths, the renowned Tsong-kha-pa Blo-bzang-grags-pa (1357–1419), founder of the Dge-lugs-pa school that would later dominate Tibetan Buddhism, sought to re-emphasize an essentially dialectical conception of their relationship.[53] A successor to his teaching, the Mongolian cleric Ngag-dbang-dpal-ldan (b. 1779), summarizes the reasons for regarding the radical separation of the two truths as unacceptable:

> If the two truths were different entities, then (1) the mind realizing the emptiness of true existence would not overcome the conception of true existence; (2) the emptiness of true existence of a form would not be the mode of abiding of that form; (3) the non-affirming negative that is the mere excluder...of the true existence of a form would not be the real nature of that form; and (4) Buddha[s]...would see forms as truly existent and would see emptiness as truly existent separately.[54]

The supposition here is that the extreme bifurcation proposed by Dol-po-pa effectively underwrites the metaphysical equivalence, while undermining the identity, of the two truths. Thus, for instance, to conceive that something exists veridically and to realize its emptiness ((1) above) are no longer dialectically opposed as contradictories, one negating the other, but are now independent intentions directed upon disparate objects (the veridical existence of *x* and the emptiness of the veridical existence of *x*). Such a theory of the two truths, far from revealing to us a soteriologically valuable dialectic, leaves us with the unedifying vision of two mutually exclusive, but somehow compresent, orders of being, in which our discovery of a higher truth does nothing to overcome our previous unknowing. The central ontological and epistemological dimensions of the two truths theory, as understood in Tsong-kha-pa's tradition, have been well-summarized by Jeffrey Hopkins:

> The division of the two truths is not an ontological division. Both exist only conventionally...with *saṃvṛti* here referring to a valid dualistic cognizer; both truths exist for valid dualistic cognizers and not in ultimate analysis. The division of the two truths emphasizes two types of objects of consciousness, truths and falsities. Both, however, are falsely existent or falsely established because neither is independent; each depends on its imputing consciousness and on the other....

> The division into two truths on epistemological grounds is a call to eradicate ignorance and to attain the highest wisdom. It is a call to recognition that a conventional cognizer, even if valid with respect to the existence or non-existence of objects, is not valid with respect to their suchness. It is a call to a new mode of perception, to a cognition of a reality that has been ever-present.[55]

As Hopkins's reference to "a cognition of a reality" makes clear, however, there are some strong ontological commitments at work here, despite the refusal to countenance an ultimate ontological basis for the distinction between the two truths themselves. Perhaps we may say that, on this account, the dialectic of the two truths discloses ontological truth, or reality, which involves nothing to be posited over and against the dual aspect of its disclosure.

Realists, as the late B. K. Matilal remarked in a critique of Mādhyamika thought, tend to be "rather suspicious of such bifurcation of truths into two levels." He continued to argue, however, that "such criticism misses the mark if we do not take into account the soteriological significance of the doctrine."[56] The theory of the two truths provided a means for Buddhist thinkers to interpret the apparent contradictions that obtain between the Buddha's conventional and practical teachings, on the one hand, and the insights that are only to be realized by the most accomplished and perceptive of disciples, on the other. By accepting that convention had the status of a sort of truth and was not to be regarded as sheer falsehood, a bridge was effectively established over which those receptive to the teaching might be guided until they themselves arrived at the highest realization.

Still, the puzzling aspect of the two truths theory is again underscored when we return to contemplate the contrast between propositional and ontological conceptions of truth. For the two truths theory is at once a theory of ontological truth,[57] that is, a theory about how things are, and at the same time a theory of the system of convention in which propositional truths may be expressed. In order to think on the two truths theory at all, we must entertain it propositionally. In such a framework, the theory *must* result in paradox, because propositional truth operates wholly within the sphere of the conventional. The discourse of an ultimate truth, undermining convention, must in the end undo the very framework upon which such discourse depends. Nonetheless, we may wish to hold that, *per impossibile,* were we perfect cognizers, our thought would never become involved in this destabilizing dialectic at all, and so would never involve the two truths. From the perspective of a perfect cognizer, it will be urged, the truth of things must be one. As we have seen above, some Buddhist thinkers—Prajñākaramati and Tsong-kha-pa were examples—arrived at just this conclusion. And it is a conclusion that, within the domain of conventional truth, appears to be eminently reasonable.

Notes

1 Mehta 1978.

2 Heidegger 1971b: 208. Also translated in Heidegger 1998: 257.

3 The "Dialogue on Language between a Japanese and an Inquirer" appears in Heidegger 1971c. For valuable information on Heidegger's knowledge of and interest in East Asian thought, see Otto Pöggeler, "West-East Dialogue: Heidegger and Lao-tzu"; Joan Stambaugh, "Heidegger, Taoism, and the Question of Metaphysics"; and Paul Shih-yi Hsiao, "Heidegger and Our Translation of the *Tao Te Ching,*" all in Parkes 1987. See now also May 1996.

4 Heidegger 1958: 29–31.

5 Thompson 1986: 235.

6 For example: Sprung 1979: 1–27; Sinari 1984, chap. 6; Guenther 1963; Takeuchi Yoshinori, "The Philosophy of Nishida," in Francke 1982: 179–202; and Abe 1989, chap. 5. References to Heidegger, whether explicit or tacit, are ubiquitous in the writings of the Kyoto school philosophers.

7 Gómez's remarks on this were made to the conference on Buddhist hermeneutics held at the Kuroda Institute in Los Angeles during the spring of 1984.

8 Heidegger 1971a. Also translated in Heidegger 1998: 155–82. The essay was composed in 1940 on the basis of a lecture Heidegger had first delivered in 1931–32.

9 Heidegger 1971a: 180–83; 1998: 171–74.

10 *tò alēthéstaton.* Unlike the two preceding, this term is not actually used in the parable of the Cave. As source for it Heidegger cites *Republic,* book 6, 484c, 5 seq., where the context does seem to support Heidegger's use of it here.

11 Heidegger 1971a: 182; 1998: 172.

12 Heidegger 1971a: 178; 1998: 167.

13 Heidegger 1971a: 187–89; 1998: 176–79.

14 Steiner 1978: 114–15.

15 Brentano 1975.

16 Brentano 1966. I do not yet know whether Heidegger had any familiarity with

this work, which in any case first appeared in print after Heidegger's own *Sein und Zeit*, in which Heidegger's interpretation of *alētheia* was first articulated.

17 Brentano 1966: 5.

18 Brentano 1966: 9–15.

19 Brentano 1966: 120–22.

20 Heidegger 1962: 261ff. (=*Sein und Zeit*, pp. 219ff.)

21 Note, however, the close association of *satya*, in some Upaniṣads, with the occlusion and disclosure of Brahman. E.g., *Muṇḍakopaniṣad*, 3.1.6–8.

22 Apte 1958, part III, p. 1614.

23 "Being" is here intended only in its participial sense, and by no means as a substantive. Nevertheless, truth was clearly valued as an almost divine property. A good example of an early text concerning true and false speech is *Śatapatha Brāhmaṇa*, II.2.2, where truth-speaking is compared to an oblation of butter poured on the sacred fire, and falsehood to extinguishing it with water.

24 Cf. Kahn 1978 on this colloquial English phrase, and its relationship to Greek notions of truth and being.

25 Thus, for example, *Nyāyakośa*, p. 945, lists *yathārthajñānam*, "knowledge that accords with its object," among the technical definitions of *satya*.

26 See chap. 2, above.

27 *Tarkabhāṣā*, p. 24: *bhūtārthabhāvanāprakarṣaparyantajaṃ yogijñānaṃ... bhūtārthaś caturāryasatyaṃ.*

28 For a convenient edition of the Pali text, based on the Pali Text Society edition, see Anderson 1968: 66–67. The versions given in the *Mahāvastu* and *Lalitavistara* are most easily available in Edgerton 1953b: 17–23.

29 *Idaṃ kho pana bhikkhave dukkhaṃ ariyasaccaṃ: jāti pi dukkhā, jarā pi dukkhā, vyādhi pi dukkhā, maraṇaṃ pi dukkhaṃ. appiyehi sampayogo dukkho. piyehi vippayogo dukkho, yam p'icchaṃ na labhati tam pi dukkhaṃ, saṃkhittena pañc' upādānakkhandhā pi dukkhā. Idaṃ kho pana bhikkhave dukkhasamudayaṃ ariyasaccaṃ: yāyaṃ taṇhā ponobbhavikā nandirāgasahagatā tatratatrābhinandinī, seyyath'īdaṃ: kāmataṇhā bhavataṇhā vibhavataṇhā. Idaṃ kho pana bhikkhave dukkhanirodhaṃ ariyasaccaṃ: yo tassā yeva taṇhāya asesavirāganirodho cāgo paṭinissaggo mutti anālayo. Idaṃ kho pana bhikkhave dukkhanirodhagāminī paṭipadā ariyasaccaṃ, ayam eva ariyo aṭṭhaṅgiko maggo, seyyath'īdaṃ: sammādiṭṭhi sammāsaṃkappo sammāvācā sammākammanto sammāājivo sammāvāyāmo sammāsati sammāsamādhi.*

30 *Milindapañha*, p. 21: *paramatthato panettha puggalo nūpalabbhati...hoti satto ti sammuti.*

31 *Mūlamadhyamakakārikā*, chap. 24, v. 8: *dve satye samupāśritya buddhānāṃ dharmadeśanā/ lokasaṃvṛtisatyaṃ ca satyaṃ ca paramārthataḥ//*

32 *Abhidharmakośa*, vol. 3, p. 889: *catvāry api satyāny uktāni bhagavatā, dve api satye saṃvṛtisatyaṃ paramārthasatyaṃ ca. tayoḥ kiṃ lakṣaṇam? yatra bhinne na tadbuddhir anyāpohe dhiyā ca tat/ ghaṭāmbuvat saṃvṛtisat paramārthasad anyathā//*

33 *Abhidharmakośa*, vol. 3, p. 890.

34 Heidegger 1971a: 173; 1998: 155.

35 See esp. Ruegg 1981, Lindtner 1981, Eckel 1987, Williams 1989 (esp. chap. 3), Huntington 1989, and Garfield 1995.

36 *Bodhicaryāvatāra,* pp. 170, 177–78: *saṃvṛtiḥ paramārthaś ca satyadvayam idaṃ matam/ buddher agocaras tattvaṃ buddhiḥ saṃvṛtir ucyate//* 9.2. // *tatra loko dvidhā dṛṣṭo yogī prākṛtakas tathā/ tatra prākṛtako loko yogilokena bādhyate//* 9.3. // *bādhyante dhīviśeṣeṇa yogino 'py uttarottaraiḥ/* 9.4ab.

37 This term is actually introduced by Śāntideva in *Bodhicaryāvatāra,* 9.8a.

38 In the interest of simplicity and brevity, the topic of *yogisaṃvṛti* is omitted from the present discussion.

39 *Bodhicaryāvatāra,* p. 170: *saṃvriyate āvriyate yathābhūtaparijñānaṃ svabhāvāvaraṇād āvṛtaprakāśanāc ca anayeti saṃvṛtiḥ. avidyā moho viparyāsa iti paryāyāḥ. avidyā hi asatpadārtharūpāropikā svabhāvadarśanāvaraṇātmikā ca satī saṃvṛtir upapadyate.*

40 For the main derivatives used in the technical vocabulary of Indian linguistic science, see Abhyankar 1961: 379, entries for *saṃvaraṇa, saṃvāra,* and *saṃvṛta.*

41 *Bodhicaryāvatāra,* p. 171: *paramaḥ uttamaḥ arthaḥ paramārthaḥ, akṛtrimaṃ vasturūpam, yadadhigamāt sarvāvṛtivāsanānusaṃdhikleśaprahāṇaṃ bhavati/ sarvadharmāṇāṃ niḥsvabhāvatā, śūnyatā, tathatā, bhūtakoṭiḥ, dharmadhātur ityādiparyāyāḥ/*

42 *Bodhicaryāvatāra,* p. 175:...*catvāri āryasatyāni duḥkhasamudayanirodhamārgalakṣaṇāni abhidharme kathitāni bhagavatā, tat kathaṃ dve eva satye iti?...amīṣāṃ dvayor evāntarbhāvāt/ tathā hi—duḥkhasamudayamārgasatyāni saṃvṛtisvabhāvatayā saṃvṛtisatye 'ntarbhavanti, nirodhasatyaṃ tu paramārthasatye, iti na kaścid virodhaḥ//*

43 *Bodhicaryāvatāra,* p. 174: *saṃvṛtir ekaṃ satyam aviparītam, paramārthaś ca aparaṃ satyam iti/ cakāraḥ satyatāmātreṇa tulyabalatāṃ samuccinoti/ tatra saṃvṛtisatyam avitathaṃ rūpaṃ lokasya, paramārthasatyaṃ ca satyam avisaṃvādakaṃ tattvam āryāṇām.*

44 Cf. the argument of Brentano, cited above, n. 19.

45 *Bodhicaryāvatāra,* p. 175: *syād etat—saṃvṛtir avidyopadarśitātmatayā abhūtasamāropasvarūpatvād vicārāt śataśo viśīryamāṇāpi kathaṃ satyam iti/ etad api satyam/ kiṃ tu lokādhyavasāyataḥ saṃvṛtisatyam ity ucyate/ loka eva hi saṃvṛtisatyam iha pratipannaḥ/ tadanuvṛttyā bhagavadbhir api tathaiva anapekṣitatattvārthibhiḥ saṃvṛtisatyam ucyate/ ata eva lokasaṃvṛtisatyaṃ ceti śāstre 'pi viśeṣa ukta ācāryapādaiḥ/ vastutas paramārtha eva ekaṃ satyam.* Cf. the discussion of Abhayākaragupta, chap. 15 below.

46 Kahn 1973 and 1978.

47 Donner 1987: 205.

48 Kūkai, "The Precious Key to the Secret Treasury," in Hakeda 1972: 210. On Kūkai's thought overall, see Abe 1999.

49 Kūkai, "The Meanings of the Word Hūṃ," in Hakeda 1972: 260.

50 Dudjom Rinpoche 1991, vol. 1, p. 144.

51 Useful background, albeit from the standpoint of a sharp critic, will be found in Ruegg 1963. See also chap. 12 below.

52 *Bden gnyis gsal ba'i nyi ma* ("The Sun Illuminating the Two Truths"), in *Dol-po-pa,* vol. 5 (series vol. vii), pp. 812–15.

53 For a thorough account of Tsong-kha-pa's interpretation of the two truths theory, see especially Tauscher 1995.

54 Quoted in Newland 1992: 65.

55 Hopkins 1983: 418–19.

56 Matilal 1973: 57.

57 Nagao 1991, chap. 12, "Ontology in Mahāyāna Buddhism," rightly expresses caution regarding the application of the concept of "ontology" to Mādhyamika thought, but concludes (p. 187): "If an ontology of a Buddhist kind is to be considered seriously, then it would have to be based, not on an ontology of 'being'—that is, not in an ontic sense, but on transcending both existence and non-existence—that is, in the movement towards *śūnyatā.* In other words, ontology in a Buddhism (sic!) context is not an ontology of 'being,' but that of *śūnyatā.*"

III THE STUDY OF TANTRISM

9. Scholastic Buddhism and the Mantrayāna

The categories that have dominated much of contemporary reflection on religious phenomena—categories like magic and religion—have no precise equivalents in the languages of the traditions of India and those derived from them. This is not only because the categories in question are themselves imprecise and problematic.[1] More importantly, it is because the conceptual landscape of India was early on divided according to principles that, though often resembling those operating in what we have come to refer to as the West, nevertheless often differed from them in important and interesting ways.

It may therefore seem plausible to argue that our concepts of magic and religion, however we understand them, have little or no utility in the study of India. On this view, to invoke them would be to do violence to a domain in which our distinctions have no clear equivalents whatsoever. This is not, however, what I shall argue here. Rather, it seems to me that the traditions of India often *do* introduce distinctions that may strike us initially as being substantially similar to those that some Greeks and Romans, as well as Frazerians and other moderns, have invoked in distinguishing between magic and religion,[2] however distinctively these may have been thematized in the Indian context. Such cases raise interesting questions for our researches: are the distinctions we find drawn in India really similar to our own, or are we, for want of appropriately refined conceptual tools, just allocating them to the categories that seem to us to be ready to hand?

The problem will become clearer with the aid of an example: It has been customary, when treating of the early traditions of the Veda, to describe the Fourth Veda, that is, the Atharva Veda, as "magical."[3] This is because it contains many formulæ for rituals intended to effect tangible worldly results: the alleviation of illness, maintenance of sexual potency, increase of wealth, destruction of enemies, and so on; and the Atharvans, the priests who were the guardians of this corpus, were specialists in the rituals intended for ends of this sort. The initial impression that the Atharva Veda is particularly related to what we think of as magic finds additional support in the rather marginal status it had within the early Brahmanical traditions themselves: for a very long time, indeed, in some quarters well into the medieval period, it was held that there were only *three* Vedas, and the status of the Atharva was treated with no small measure of doubt.[4] So then, in the case of the early Vedic traditions it may seem that we would be entitled to regard the cults promoted by the first three Vedas—which focus upon solemn and domestic rites—to represent something analogous to what we call "religion," and the Atharva to represent "magic." Indeed, this seems to be precisely what many Indologists in the nineteenth and early twentieth centuries tacitly assumed in their references to the Atharva Veda as "magic."[5]

Fortunately—at least for those of us who relish the messiness of most things human (this is, after all, what keeps many of us in business)—matters turn out to be not nearly so simple. For the ritual cults of the Brahmanical mainstream early on converted the Vedic gods into forces whose agency was determined by the priestly ritual itself. Thus, according to one way of understanding "magic," the Vedic tradition was concerned with magic through and through.[6] As Louis Renou put it, "La discrimination est malaisée entre sacrifice et acte magique."[7] But in that case there is no interesting difference to be made in our terms between the first three Vedas and the Atharva. This conclusion, however, cannot be correct; for, as we have already seen, the tradition itself hesitated to accord a common status to all four.

Because my concern in what follows will be with certain aspects of Buddhist esotericism, I do not intend to belabor any further the semantical question regarding the application of the term "magic" to the study of the Veda. My point in introducing this problem has been a purely heuristic one: to underscore that, by employing the categories of our own world of discourse—which certainly is something we must do—to describe Indian religious phenomena, we risk creating the illusion that these categories will be employed in familiar ways in the new landscape in which we find ourselves now situated. This illusion is one, surely, that in the past has brought many a comparative project to ruin.

Early Buddhism in India has frequently been characterized as a highly rational, ethical, and philosophical movement that, by and large, was profoundly opposed to magical beliefs and practices of all kinds. The promotion of such a view among some Buddhists of Sri Lanka and southeast Asia, and above all among Western students of Buddhism, during the nineteenth century has been aptly described by Richard Gombrich as "protestant Buddhism."[8] The Buddha's tradition never seems to have been so denatured as some of its modernizing apologists asserted that it was. Nevertheless, it is probably correct to hold that the mainstream of early Indian monastic Buddhism maintained a stance of disinterest regarding most forms of purposeful ritual. A few minor spells were countenanced (for instance to counteract snakebite), and some protective rituals were also permitted.[9] Beliefs and practices that we might characterize as "magical" are also evident in, for instance, the cult of relics that began after the Buddha's death.[10] Nevertheless, while Indian Buddhists believed that greatly advanced persons, especially the Buddha, were capable of working wonders of many kinds, they also believed that such powers were likely to be dangerous for those whose minds were dominated by stupidity, hatred, and lust.[11]

Some of the schools of early Buddhism appear to have emphasized the Buddha's own transcendent character, and may have adopted a near docetic view of him. We find sometimes references to magical apparitions and conjuring such as would proliferate in the sūtras of the Mahāyāna.[12] And it is with the emergence of the Mahāyāna as a distinctive tendency within monastic Buddhism during the first centuries C.E. that we find clear evidence for a growing domain of ritual action, paving the way for the appearance of what we have come to call "esoteric" or Tantric Buddhism.

Until very recently, the study of esoteric Buddhism represented a conspicuous gap within the study of Buddhism generally.[13] Its neglect can be traced to a variety of reasons: the superficial impression that tantrism was no more than a manifestation of late Indian Buddhist "decadence," or that it was morally repugnant, or simply unimportant; the extreme esotericism of the relevant documents, which frustrates our efforts to understand them; the complex and widely scattered nature of both textual and material evidence; etc. Recent researches, however, have begun to alter this state of affairs: we have begun to investigate the Buddhist tantric movement with the recognition that it must be regarded as the last great creative movement within Indian Buddhism, whose dynamic vision of the Buddhist enlightenment profoundly influenced not only later Indian religions—for instance, in the Vīraśaiva, Sahajīya, and Nāth traditions—but even more so the religious, artistic, and political life of peoples throughout East, Central, and Southeast Asia. The great rise of Buddhist esotericism occurred during the mid- and late first millennium C.E., and involved the growing acceptance, within segments of the monastic communities, of rites and practices that earlier Buddhism had regarded as anathematic and dangerous, or, at best, marginal to the real concerns of the Buddha's teaching.

To what extent did the emergence of Buddhist esotericism represent a sort of paradigm shift within the Indian Buddhist traditions? Opinion differs concerning whether its development involved a clear break with or a gradual evolution from the earlier tradition. David Snellgrove, for instance, writes that, "Although...many of the roots of the Vajrayāna were already present in the Mahāyāna...the differences between the Vajrayāna and the earlier forms of Buddhism are extreme. The main difference derives from the Vajrāyana use of incantation and ritual as means towards the ultimate goal, whereas in the earlier phases of Buddhism their use was largely peripheral."[14] That "incantation and ritual" had long been used in Buddhism as a means to achieve at least some non-ultimate ends is something we need not doubt, and indeed, the origins of what would eventually be classed as the lower orders among the tantras may well be sought in early Mahāyāna and perhaps, in some cases, even before.[15]

Here, I wish to inquire a bit more into some aspects of the background of tantric Buddhism in earlier Mahāyāna theory and practice. In particular, I believe that we may find evidence of a phenomenon which in fact smoothed the way for and presaged the development of the full-blown Vajrayāna Buddhism that appears from about the seventh century onwards. This phenomenon I call "scholastic *mantrayāna,*" that is, the scholastic mantra vehicle. As the term is unfamiliar and not unambiguous, let me begin to clarify it somewhat by saying that I am not referring here to "*Vajrayāna* scholasticism," by which I mean the philosophical and exegetical literature on the subject of Vajrayāna, or aspects thereof, the developed tantrism that becomes prominent only during the last few centuries of Indian Buddhist history, and is later much elaborated in Tibet. Examples of what I am calling "Vajrayāna scholasticism" include the commentaries on major tantras such as the *Guhyasamāja, Hevajra,* and *Kālacakra,* as well as independent treatises like the *Guhyasiddhi* and *Jñānasiddhi.*[16] To be sure, the development of Vajrayāna scholasticism definitely presupposed scholastic mantrayāna. This latter phrase, however, I intend to refer to the practice of the *mantranaya,* that is, "the way of mantras," as it was conducted in the monastic universities of India during the mid-first millennium.[17] My hypothesis is that some forms of "incantation and ritual" belonging to the mantranaya were indeed sometimes devoted to Buddhism's ultimate ends, and that these had become accepted practice among monastics adhering to the Mahayāna roughly during the third through sixth centuries. The important features to bear in mind here are that the goals of such practice were not limited to mundane protection and power, and that the practitioners cannot be dismissed as devotees of "popular forms of Buddhism" that were shunned by the intelligentsia. Indeed, I would hold that much of the effort devoted to driving wedges between popular and learned forms of Buddhism has been misplaced, and when this effort is relaxed it becomes plausible to hold, for instance, that the *dhāraṇī* found alongside Vinaya texts and Mahāyāna sūtras at Gilgit and elsewhere may be seen to represent the very phenomenon in question.[18]

One important objection that may come to mind here is this: why is there no evidence of this so-called "scholastic mantrayāna" in the abundant scholastic literature of the exoteric Mahāyāna? In response, one might appeal to the strictures of secrecy among adherents of esoteric practice. But that, in fact, will not be necessary; for there is indeed evidence of the required type—not a great deal of it, to be sure, but what there is merits our careful attention.[19]

One of the earliest normative scholastic texts that sheds some light here is found in an extremely influential treatise redacted probably during the late fourth or early fifth century. This is the excursus on dhāraṇī found in the *Bodhipakṣyapaṭala,* the seventeenth chapter of the first section of the *Bodhisattvabhūmi.* Dhāraṇī are here presented in four categories: doctrinal dhāraṇī *(dharma-dhāraṇī),* semantic dhāraṇī *(artha-dhāraṇī),* mantra-dhāraṇī, and those dhāraṇī which give rise to the receptivity of a bodhisattva *(bodhisattva-kṣānti-lābhāya dhāraṇī).*[20] The first two categories are explicitly related to the bodhisattva's faculty of retention, i.e., memory, which is the literal significance of the term "dhāraṇī."[21] The bodhisattva, the text tells us, is able to retain for unlimited time both the doctrine—that is, scripture—and its meaning. These two categories may thus be related to the mnemonic use of the formulaic dhāraṇī well known in Mahāyāna sūtras.

The author of the *Bodhisattvabhūmi* then describes the third category as comprising those mantra-expressions *(mantra-padāni)* that promote the appeasement of sentient beings, in particular the appeasement of their ills. This probably alludes to the use of mantras in protective rites, to which reference has been made above—a practice whose antecedents can be traced even to the *paritta-suttas* of the *Dīghanikāya,* and which we should therefore refrain from interpreting as an allusion to particularly tantric phenomena.[22] The tantras, however, would certainly incorporate various mundane rites of protection as an important dimension of the practice which they espoused, and elaborate such rites enormously.[23]

It is in the discussion of the fourth category of dhāraṇī that we may detect, I think, the inception of a novel and striking view of mantra- practice. Here, we are told that the bodhisattva, whose conduct is properly moderated, undertakes to investigate those mantra expressions "which have been proclaimed by the Tathāgata" *(tathāgatabhāṣitāni)* as giving rise to the receptivity of the bodhisattva—receptivity, that is, to the ultimate nature of reality.[24] One such formula is: *tadyathā iṭi miṭi kiṭibhiḥ kṣāntipadāni svāhā.* The bodhisattva discovers that such expressions are without meaning, indeed, that their meaning is only their meaninglessness *(ayam eva caiṣām artho yaduta nirarthatā).* Extending by analogy his inquiry to all phenomena, he comes to realize that their essential significance is, similarly, their essential ineffability *(yā punar eṣāṃ nirabhilāpyasvabhāvatā ayam evaiṣāṃ svabhāvārthaḥ).* Attaining thus the receptivity of a bodhisattva, he soon realizes the purity of an enlightened aspiration *(adhyāśayaviśuddhi).*

The passage just summarized is a difficult one, and not all aspects of its interpretation are secure. That mantra expressions are represented here as the dicta of the Buddha is noteworthy. However, given the many dhāraṇī (both mnemonic and protective), found in even relatively early Mahāyāna sūtras, we should refrain from reading too much into this feature of the discussion. What strikes me as most remarkable is, rather, the association of mantra with the attainment of *kṣānti,* the bodhisattva's receptivity with respect to the realization of the essential nature of things. Recall now Snellgrove's assertion that "the main difference derives from the Vajrayāna use of incantation...as means towards the ultimate goal." Is Snellgrove wrong about this, or does the *Bodhisattvabhūmi* reflect here what we might term "proto-Vajrayāna"?

I do not think that it is yet possible to provide a decisive answer to this question. If we are inclined, as indeed I am, to perceive here some connection with the later emergence of tantric Buddhism, we must be prepared to accept that the connection is but a tenuous one. Nonetheless, the notion that mantras may be used for a purpose that is neither simply mnemonic nor simply protective, but that is additionally clearly associated with progress on the bodhisattva's path, was at the very least an element that would have encouraged the extension, during subsequent centuries, of the employment in Mahāyāna circles of mantras and the rituals associated with them. In short, the *Bodhisattvabhūmi* provides us with some of the earliest available evidence for the elaboration of a doctrinal warrant for the expansion of practices allied with those of esoteric Buddhism. Let us recall, too, that later developed tantric Buddhism would always maintain its twin ends to be the attainment of benefit to others through proficiency in mundane rites and the attainment of one's own realization through insight born of yogic practice.[25] This bivalence seems curiously presaged in the last two dhāraṇī categories of the *Bodhisattvabhūmi.*

Some indications concerning the increased employment of mantras by monks belonging to Mahāyāna scholastic circles may be gleaned from Śāntideva's (c. eighth century) magnificent *Śikṣāsamuccaya (The Compendium of Lessons),* a florilegium, with brief commentarial glosses, of scriptural passages pertaining to the practice of the bodhisattva's path.[26] Here, in closing the chapter on "self-preservation" *(ātmabhāvarakṣā),* a selection of useful mantras is given. "Self-preservation" is itself emphasized as part of this path of selflessness, because, while the bodhisattva must strive to protect all beings, he obviously cannot succeed if he is not even able to take care of himself. In order ultimately to serve others, he must learn to nourish himself properly even while adhering to a life of ascesis, and to treat what illnesses may befall him with appropriate medications.[27] He must strive, however, not to feed his attachments in the name of corporeal maintenance.[28] In order to achieve the proper balance between necessary self-preservation and detachment, he learns to protect his own mind by performing his ablutions, conducting his begging rounds, and partaking of his meals in the midst of the circle *(maṇḍala)* of buddhas. And to enter that circle, he recites the *vidyā,* the "gnostic mantra" of the Buddha as *King of the Triple Vow (Trisamayarāja).*[29]

To enter into the living presence of the Buddha in this way is, in Śāntideva's view, "the supreme protection, overcoming the Māras and all other foes."[30] However, he goes on to provide other formulæ as well: the mantra of all "wielders of the vajra sceptre," to pacify all demonic forces; a mantra that, used with sanctified water, purifies foodstuffs and other substances; the inevitable mantra to be used in case of snakebite or poisoning; etc.[31] The mantras themselves combine apparently "meaningless" words with occasional clear phrases: the mantra to protect one from the dangers of the wilderness, for instance, which is one of the most intelligible, includes the words: "protect me on the path, protect me on detours, protect me from crowds, protect me from thieves, protect me from princes, protect me from lions, protect me from tigers, protect me from elephants, protect me from snakes, protect me from everything!"[32]

As Śāntideva's work makes clear, the use of mantras made great inroads in Mahāyāna Buddhist circles during the mid-first millennium. And although the passage from the *Bodhisattvabhūmi* that we considered above suggested some approaches to the doctrinal legitimation of such developments, we should not be surprised to learn that the question was not thus put to rest. One very important passage, dating to the mid-sixth century, provides us with an intriguing glimpse of the monastic disputes about esoteric practices. It is found in the writings of the philosopher Bhāvaviveka, who raises a curious question in the great autocommentary to his *Madhyamakahṛdaya (The Heart of the Middle Way),* the *Tarkajvāla (The Blaze of Reason),* which survives now only in its eleventh-century Tibetan translation.[33] Surprisingly, perhaps, but significantly, the question arises in his chapter on the philosophy of the śrāvakas, that is, the adherents of the early traditions of Buddhism that Mahāyānists disparagingly term "Hīnayāna." The question is given as an objection posed by the śrāvaka to an opponent adhering to the Mahāyāna:

> In the Mahāyāna there are taught dhāraṇī, mantra, and vidyā,[34] which are inappropriate in both word and meaning, but for which many benefits are claimed, so as to deceive the childish, and which resemble the Vedas of the others [i.e., non-Buddhists]. Without meditative cultivation even minor faults cannot be exhausted, so how can those [mantras, etc.] exhaust evil so long as conflicting emotions are gross and their roots still present? Moreover, the dhāraṇī do not pacify evil, for they counteract its basis no more than do injurious actions, etc. So, too, mantras do not exhaust evil, for they are uttered in foreign languages, for instance, in the languages of Mlecchas, etc.

Bhāvaviveka, as is well known to students of the history of Indian philosophy, was much interested in the formal features of argumentation. Accordingly, in criticizing the foregoing objection, he seeks to demonstrate formally that it is unsound. The argument to be refuted may be restated, according to the conventions of medieval Indian logic, as follows:

(1) Mantras, etc., are of no value. *(pratijñā)*
(2) Because they are not among the antidotes to the *kleśa,* or conflicting emotions. *(hetu)*
(3) Thus, they are like the useless practices of non-Buddhists, and unlike, for instance, the Buddha's teaching of loving-kindness. *(dṛṣṭānta)*

In elaborating his refutation, Bhāvaviveka will argue that (3) the statement of exemplification, or *dṛṣṭānta,* is false, wherefore (2) the warranting reason, or *hetu,* must also be false. Hence, the objection must be abandoned. To demonstrate the falsehood of the *dṛṣṭānta* and *hetu,* Bhāvaviveka will insist that: (i) dhāraṇī and the like are indeed aspects of meditative practice which effect progress on the path, just like other widely accepted types of Buddhist meditative practice; (ii) their occurrence in unusual languages is indicative of their transcendental nature; and (iii) their role in meditative progress distinguishes them altogether from the worldly practices with which they might otherwise be confused. Let us take up these points in turn.

(i) In defense of the assertion that dhāraṇī, etc., do have a role in meditative discipline, Bhāvaviveka introduces a selection of scriptural passages concerning these formulæ as well as examples of the formulæ themselves. Two items, in particular, merit our attention. The first is a citation from the *Anantamukhanirhāradhāraṇī*—a text probably of some antiquity even in Bhāvaviveka's day, for there is an early Chinese translation of it attributed to Zhiqian (active c. 223–53 C.E.) and a second by Buddhabhadra (408–29).[35] The citation reads:

> The bodhisattva who ponders this dhāraṇī ponders neither conditioned nor unconditioned principles, nor does he grasp them, posit them, hanker after them, or denominate them. He meditatively cultivates only the recollection of the Buddha.[36]

Up to this point, Bhāvaviveka's argument very much resembles the perspective we have already seen articulated in the *Bodhisattvabhūmi,* and so by itself would therefore be unremarkable, were it not for what follows in his text:

> Most vidyā, too, only teach the six perfections, and the extinguishing of kleśa by word and meaning indicative of the noble truths and the principles allied with enlightenment, for instance: *śamaya śamaya dānte śānte dharmarāja bhāṣite mate mahāvidye sarvārthasādhane*... Similarly, "emerging from the supreme principle is *tāre,* from the original principle *tuttāre,* and from the ineffable principle *ture,*" which, clarifying emergent realization, remove one's own ignorance, and are capable of generating knowledge in others. This being so, relying upon them, why should not evils, along with their basis, be thus pacified? Because [these mantras] have such potency, they are just like [such practices as] loving-kindness, etc.

This is perhaps the earliest decisive Indian Buddhist reference to the cult of Tārā, whose ten-syllable mantra is *Oṃ tāre tuttāre ture svāhā*.[37] And the cult of the goddess Tārā can be taken, I think, as strongly suggestive of the rise of Buddhist tantrism; so that what we have here is perhaps the first sure evidence of the acceptance of tantrism (or at least aspects thereof) within Buddhist scholastic circles. It therefore seems plausible to hold that the theoretical understanding of dhāraṇī, as enunciated in the *Bodhisattvabhūmi* (which was consistent with Bhāvaviveka's point of departure), has provided the ingress through which a steadily expanding repertoire of "incantations and ritual" was introduced into Mahāyāna circles to aid in the practice of the path, and not merely for mundane ends.

(ii) The scriptures of the Mahāyāna had from an early date countenanced the possibility of *buddhavacana* being pronounced in any language whatsoever. Thus, for instance, the *Bhadracaripraṇidhānarāja* section of the *Gaṇḍavyūhasūtra* (46.18) says:

> In the tongues of gods and nāgas,
> In the tongues of trolls, fairies, and men,
> In all the tongues of beings,
> I'll teach the doctrine in all of them![38]

Bhāvaviveka, inspired by this, or any one of many similar passages, takes a route different from that followed by the author of the *Bodhisattvabhūmi* in addressing himself to the apparent meaninglessness of some mantras: if we do not comprehend them, he says, it is due to their transcendent character and to the fact that they were taught in the languages of, for instance, nāgas and yakṣas. It is tempting, too, to read Bhāvaviveka on this point in the light of oft-repeated Mahāyāna and Vajrayāna historical legends, to the effect that the scriptures of these traditions that had been taught by the Buddha were preserved by non-human beings until the human world was ready for them. It may, however, be anachronistic to read the versions of these legends known from later Buddhist tantric sources into the present context.[39]

(iii) Bhāvaviveka's third point concerns the distinction between Buddhist and non-Buddhist practices involving dhāraṇī and other such formulæ. He declares:

> [Because they reveal the nature of ultimate reality,] they indeed belong to the scope of those who know *samaya* and have acquired

> dhāraṇī [here: retention of the doctrine].... So, how can there be any similarity between the [ritual] knowledge of, for instance, Cāmuṇḍā, which is replete with coarse and unbearable affliction, teaching a mundane purpose, and that of, for instance, Tārā, which is knowledge of absolute significance?

I hesitate to say what, exactly, Bhāvaviveka intends by his use of *samaya* here. In later Buddhist tantric literature it comes to mean something like "spiritual commitment," where it is a technical term for the special vows of esoteric Buddhism.[40] Here, however, it may well be used in a cognitive sense, to describe the special knowledge in virtue of which the practice in which one is engaged may be performed efficaciously. Of supreme interest, in any event, is the deliberate juxtaposition of the goddess Cāmuṇḍā—one of the eight "mother goddesses" *(aṣṭamātṛkā)* particularly popular among adherents of tantric Hinduism in northern India and Nepal[41]—with the Buddhist goddess Tārā. We must note especially that Bhāvaviveka was by no means a rigid opponent of whatever was not clearly Buddhist; just a few pages after the passage under discussion he says:

> Whatever is well-taught in Vedānta,
> All of that is proclaimed by the Buddha.[42]

Clearly, then, Bhāvaviveka is unlikely to have found the Cāmuṇḍā cult to be objectionable simply for being non-Buddhist. He characterizes its unacceptability, however, only by saying that it "is replete with coarse and unbearable affliction, teaching a mundane purpose." What this in fact means can only be a matter of speculation. It is most likely that, because the Hindu Cāmuṇḍā cult certainly involved live sacrifice, that alone was sufficient to condemn it in the eyes of a Buddhist monk.[43]

However, esoteric Buddhism also took over many other Hindu deities whose cults similarly may have been objectionable to Buddhist sensibilities for one reason or another, altering them to suit Buddhist strictures.[44] Though there is no evidence that the Cāmuṇḍā cult was ever incorporated into Buddhism in exactly this fashion, this goddess was nevertheless permitted a place in the retinue of some of the great gods of late Indian Buddhist tantrism, such as Cakrasaṃvara, and figures also in some traditions as the consort of the wrathful Yamāntaka.[45] It is possible, then, that Bhāvaviveka's objection is not primarily directed to the Hindu cult of the mother goddess Cāmuṇḍā, but to tendencies within Buddhist esotericism of the sort that eventually were consolidated as the Anuttarayoga Tantras.[46] One passage in the writings of Bhāvaviveka's junior contemporary, the logician Dharmakīrti, indeed suggests that tantric texts emphasizing a wide range of goddesses were beginning to circulate among Buddhists, and that, unlike Tārā, they were not finding ready acceptance among the monastic elite.[47]

figure 3. Cāmuṇḍā, the wrathful mother-goddess whose cult Bhāvaviveka considered repugnant. Paraśurāmeśvara Temple, Bhubaneswar, Orissa. Eighth century.

Given the materials here surveyed, it seems plausible to hold that the practice of "incantation and ritual," directed to both ultimate and mundane ends, had become normal Mahāyāna practice, and not merely popular cult shunned by the learned clergy, prior to the sixth century, and probably as early as the third. Over the course of the centuries the volume of ritual lore incorporated into the Mahāyāna in this fashion increased without any but general doctrinal restriction: the fact, for instance, that some of the developing ritual texts included spell-like formulæ in strange and often incomprehensible languages was not theologically problematic. It was only after this corpus had grown sufficiently massive to take on a life of its own however, that conditions came to favor the emergence of the mantranaya and later Vajrayāna as distinct ways of Buddhist practice, apart from the pāramitānaya, the ethico-philosophical tradition of the Mahāyāna. I believe that this development occurred within a century or two following Bhāvaviveka's day, and perhaps had begun already during his lifetime. Once it took place, it became possible to attempt an *ex post facto* classification of the whole mass of mantric lore that had accumulated during the preceding centuries. Thus, the so-called "outer tantras" had been part and parcel of Mahāyāna practice long before anyone ever conceived of them as a class apart.[48]

Indian monastic Mahāyāna thus had to justify its engagement in the entire class of practices involving "spells," but succeeded in establishing doctrinal bounds that were remarkably inclusive in this regard. The rationalizations that were employed, moreover, could be redeployed to admit an ever broadening circle of esoteric disciplines and texts. In later times even sorcery could be countenanced, so long as its powers were won "incidentally, through the practice of the doctrine," as a thirteenth-century Tibetan author says.[49] I shall leave it to my readers to judge what relationship the materials surveyed above may have to the categories of religion and magic as we conceive of them in connection with contemporary scholarship in religion. For myself, I would prefer to speak of the dynamics of what may be termed the "transgressive employment of uncommon power" and the rationalization of such power. What counts as transgressive will depend on where the boundaries are drawn, and in the history of any community these change with time. One generation's dangerous magic becomes the domesticated practice of another.

Appendix: Bhāvaviveka on Dhāraṇī

Translation

"In the Mahāyāna there are taught dhāraṇī, mantra, and vidyā, which are inappropriate in both word and meaning, but for which many benefits are claimed, so as to deceive the childish, and which resemble the Vedas of the others [i.e., non-Buddhists]. Without meditative cultivation even minor faults cannot be exhausted, so how can those [mantras, etc.] exhaust evil so long as conflicting emotions are gross and their roots still present? Moreover, the dhāraṇī do not pacify evil, for they counteract its basis no more than do injurious actions, etc. So, too, we can assert that mantras do not exhaust evil, for they are uttered in foreign languages, for instance, in the languages of Mlecchas, etc."

If that is the objection, then this should be said to those who hold that the dhāraṇī, etc., of the Mahāyāna are mere syllabic compositions:

Sometimes the dhāraṇī are indeed aspects of meditational cultivation *(bhāvanā)*; for, as it says in the *Anantamukhanirhāradhāraṇī:*

> The bodhisattva who ponders this dhāraṇī ponders neither conditioned nor unconditioned principles, nor does he grasp them, posit them, hanker after them, or denominate them. He meditatively cultivates only the recollection of the Buddha.

Similarly,[50] in the *Sāgaranāgarājaparipṛcchāsūtra:*

> O nāga-king! All that has been taught is inexhaustible. This, indeed, is the dhāraṇī called the "inexhaustible container." The bodhisattva who enters in the way of this dhāraṇī of the inexhaustible container knows all of this: the inexhaustible emergence of penetrating insight *(pratisaṃvit)*, gnosis *(jñāna)*, discernment *(prajñā)*, and brilliance *(pratibhāna)*—these four; similarly, that which is exceedingly difficult to realize, and the limitless blaze of vigor without complacency, and the invisible, and freedom from support, and blamelessness, and the four fearlessnesses *(catvāri vaiśaradyāni)*, and the emergence of the four treasures of essence, ascertainment, disclosure, and power; and, similarly, he penetrates the way of the phonetic units *(akṣara)*, names, conventions, and conventions of dharma. So it is: *all principles (dharma) are primordially pure!*

figure 4. The emerging goddesses of tantric Buddhism: Tārā and Bhṛkuṭī with Avalokiteśvara. Cave 90, Kanheri, Maharashtra. Sixth or seventh century.

Similarly:

> The bodhisattva who abides in this dhāraṇī-mantra seeks and penetrates awakening *(bodhi)* on the basis of the phonetic units alone. The phonetic units are vital power. Their arrangement is

> the body. The elevated vision[51] that enters the gate of the Dharma is the forehead. Discernment is the eye...

The root of the contemplative cultivation of this and more is discernment. For, where there is discernment, ignorance vanishes. If they lack roots, then neither desire nor hatred will emerge, because [discernment] is in opposition to their root [i.e., ignorance]. Therefore, [in the objection quoted above], to say that [the dhāraṇī] are not in opposition with the root remains unproven.

Moreover, there is a rebuttal that overturns what was to be proven [by the proponent of the objection above]: the *dhāraṇī-mantra* indeed do pacify misdeeds; for they have the features of contemplative cultivation and so indeed counteract the roots [of misdeeds], just as does the contemplative cultivation of ugliness [which counteracts passion], etc. Similarly, with reference to the secret mantras *(guhyamantra):* when, within the continuum,[52] the penetration of contemplative cultivation is established owing to the nature of the composition of esoteric phonetic units that reveal the secret of the Tathāgata's gnosis, one then has the power to achieve rightly whatever one wishes. Because they have the nature of great occult power, they are like the wish-granting tree. Most *vidyā,* too, only teach the six perfections, and the extinguishing of *kleśa* by word and meaning indicative of the noble truths and the principles allied with enlightenment, for instance: *śamaya śamaya dānte śānte dharmarāja bhāṣite mate mahāvidye sarvārthasādhane...* Similarly, "emerging from the supreme principle is *tāre,* from the original principle *tuttāre,* and from the ineffable principle *ture,*" which, clarifying emergent realization, remove one's own ignorance, and are capable of generating knowledge in others. This being so, relying upon them, why should not evils, along with their basis, be thus pacified? Because [these mantras] have such potency, they are just like [such practices as that of] loving-kindness, etc.

[Moreover, their being expressed in unknown languages is no objection,] because the gnostic expressions whose meanings are not understood are taught in transcendent language, and because they are taught in the languages of gods, nāgas, yakṣas, etc.

Neither is it the case that they do not teach reality *(dharmatā),* for they indeed belong to the scope of those who know *samaya* and have acquired dhāraṇī. As it says in the *Sūtra of Secret Intelligence:*[53]

> What are here called "suffering," "origination," "cessation," and

> the "path," are the *ene,* and *mene,* and *dam po,* and *da dam po*[54] of the divinities of the class of the four great kings *(caturmahārājika)...*

This being said, how can there be any similarity between the [ritual] knowledge of, for instance, Cāmuṇḍā, which is replete with coarse and unbearable affliction, teaching a mundane purpose, and that of, for instance, Tārā, which is knowledge of absolute significance?

One may also say this: by reciting, reflecting upon, and contemplatively cultivating the dhāraṇī, mantra, and vidyā in accord with the Tathāgata's instruction, evil, together with its basis, is pacified. Because they thus accord with the path, they are like the sūtras and other scriptural transmissions.

The Tibetan Text

The text as given here is a transcription based upon the Derge *(D.)* and Peking *(P.)* editions of the *Tanjur.* In some cases, where the differences between these two editions are noteworthy, I have included variants in brackets, but have otherwise provided only a diplomatic edition. The passage begins at *D.* 183a and *P.* 82.1.2.

theg pa chen po las yi ge dang don shes par mi rung ba'i gzungs sngags dang/ gsang sngags dang/ rig sngags la sogs pa phan yon mang po can byis pa'i skye bo slu bar byed pa bstan pa de rnams ni gzhan gyi rigs byed dang 'dra'o// bsgom pa med pa ni skyon phra rab tsam yang zad par byed nus pa ma yin te/ nyon mongs pa bsags pa dang de'i rtsa ba yod na sdig pa zad pa ga la 'byung bar 'gyur/ gzungs sngags kyis kyang sdig pa zhi bar byed pa ma yin (*D.* 183b) te/ de'i rgyud dang mi 'gal ba nyid kyi phyir 'tshe ba la sogs pa bzhin no// de bzhin du gsang sngags kyis kyang sdig pa zad par byed pa ma yin te/ skad gzhan gyis brjod pa'i phyir kla klo la sogs pa'i skad bzhin no zhes kyang smra bar nus so zhe na/ gang yang theg pa chen po'i gzungs sngags la sogs pa yi ge sbyar ba tsam du 'dod pa 'di la brjod par bya'o// re zhig gzungs sngags ni bsgom pa'i rnam pa nyid yin te/ ji skad du *sgo mtha' yas pa sgrub pa'i gzungs* las/

> gzungs 'di sgom par byed pa'i byang chub sems dpa' ni 'dus byas dang 'dus ma byas kyi chos rtogs par yang mi byed/ len par yang mi byed/ gnas par mi byed/ mngon par zhen par mi byed/ tha

> snyad 'dogs par yang mi byed/ sangs rgyas rjes su dran pa 'ba' zhig sgom par byed do/

zhes bya ba la sogs pa gsungs pa dang// //dbu ma'i snying po'i 'grel pa rtog ge 'bar ba// bam po bcu drug pa/ de bzhin du *klu'i rgyal po rgya mtshos zhus pa'i mdo* las kyang/

> klu'i rgyal po (*P.* 82.2) gang yang bstan pa thams cad ni mi zad pa ste/ 'di ni mi zad pa'i za ma tog ces bya ba'i gzungs yin no// so sor yang dag par rigs pa dang/ ye shes dang/ shes rab dang/ spobs pa bzhi yang mi zad par rjes su 'byung ba dang/ de bzhin du shin tu rtog par dka' ba dang/ ngoms pa med pa'i brtson 'grus 'bar ba dang mthar thug pa med pa dang/ mthong ba med pa dang/ rton pa med pa dang/ dmod pa med pa dang/ 'jigs pa med pa bzhi po rnams dang/ snying po dang/ nges par 'byed pa dang/ snang ba dang/ stobs kyi gter bzhi 'byung ba dang/ de bzhin du gang yi ge'i lugs dang/ ming dang/ brda dang/ chos kyi brda'i rjes su 'jug pa de dag thams cad kyang mi zad pa'i za ma tog gi gzungs 'di'i rjes su zhugs pa'i byang chub sems dpas shes te 'di lta ste/ chos thams cad ni gdod ma nas dag pa'o/

zhes bya ba la sogs pa dang/ de bzhin du

> gzungs sngags 'di la gnas pa'i byang chub sems dpa' ni yi ge kho (*D.* 184a) na las byang chub 'tshol bar byed/ rjes su 'jug par byed de/ yi ge ni stobs so// dgod pa ni lus so// chos kyi sgo la 'dzud pa'i mgo bo blta ba ni dpral pa'o// shes rab ni mig go

zhes bya ba la sogs sgom pa'i rtsa ba ni shes rab yin la/ shes rab yod pa'i phyir gti mug med par 'gyur ro// rtsa ba med na 'dod chags dang zhe sdang 'byung bar mi 'gyur te/ rtsa ba dang 'gal ba yod pa'i phyir ro// des na rtsa ba dang 'gal ba med pa'i phyir zhes bya ba 'di don ma grub pa yin no// phyir rgol ba'i rtog ges kyang sgrub par bya ba la gnod pa nyid te/ gzungs sngags kyis ni sdig pa zhi bar 'gyur ba nyid yin te/ bsgom pa'i rnam pa yod pa nyid kyi phyir de'i rtsa ba dang 'gal bar gyur pa nyid kyi mi sdug pa la sogs pa (*P.* 82.3) bsgom pa bzhin no// de bzhin du gsang sngags kyang de bzhin gshegs pa'i ye shes kyi gsang ba ston par byed pa'i sbas pa'i yi ge sbyar ba ngo bos bsgom pa la rab tu 'jug pa rgyud la gnas pas ji ltar 'dod pa'i bsam pa yang dag par bsgrub par nus pa yin te/ mthu chen po'i bdag nyid yin pa'i phyir dpag bsam gyi shing bzhin no// rigs sngags kyang phal cher pha rol tu phyin pa drug dang/ 'phags pa'i bden pa dang/ byang chub kyi phyogs kyi chos ston par byed pa'i yi ge dang don gyis nyon mongs pa zad par byed pa ston par byed pa nyid yin te/ ji ltar

> sha ma ya sha ma ya// dha na te shan te dar ma rā dza// bha ṣi te ma te ma dha bid tye// sa rba rtha swad ni na/ [*D.* reads: sha ma ya sha ma ya/ dante shānte dharma rā dza/ bha shi te ma te ma hā bī dya/ sarbārtha sā dha na ni]

zhes bya ba lta bu dang/ de bzhin du

> chos kyi mchog las byung ba ni tā re/ dang po'i chos las byung ba ni tud tā re/ brjod du med pa'i chos las byung ba ni tu re

zhes bya ba lta bu ni mngon par rtogs pa gsal bar byed pa ste/ bdag ma rig pa dang bral bar gyur pas gzhan dag gi rig pa yang bskyed par nus pa yin na de sten par gyur na ci'i phyir sdig pa gzhi dang bcas pa zhi bar mi 'gyur te/ de'i nus pa dang ldan pa'i phyir byams pa la sogs pa bzhin no//

rig pa'i tshig gang dag gi don rtogs par ma gyur pa ni de dag 'jig rten las 'das pa'i skad kyis bstan pa'i phyir dang/ lha dang/ klu dang/ gnod sbyin la sogs pa'i skad kyi (*D.* 184b) bstan pa'i phyir ro// chos nyid ston par mi byed pa yang ma yin pas dam tshig rig pa dang/ gzungs thob par gyur pa rnams kyi spyod yul yang yin te/ ji skad du *gsang ba blo gros kyi mdo* las/ gang 'di na sdug bsngal dang/ kun 'byung ba dang/ 'gog pa dang/ lam zhes bya ba rnams la rgyal chen bzhi'i ris kyi lha rnams kyi ni e ne dang/ me ne dang/ dam po dang/ (*P.* 82.4) da dam po zhes bya ba la sogs par brjod do zhes 'byung bas 'jig rten ba'i don ston par byed pa bzod par dka' ba'i nyon mongs pa bdo bas 'khrigs pa tsa munda la sogs pa'i rig pa dag dang/ sgrol ma la sogs pa'i don dam pa'i rig pa rnams 'dra ba lta ga la yin/ des na dpe ma grub pa yin te/ bsgrub par bya ba'i chos dang mi ldan pa'i phyir ro// 'di skad brjod par yang nus te/ gzungs sngags dang/ gsang sngags dang/ rig sngags rnams de bzhin gshegs pa'i man ngag bzhin du dag tu brjod pa dang/ bsams pa dang/ bsgoms pas sdig pa rgyu dang bcas pa zhi bar byed pa yin te/ lam dang rjes su mthun pa yin pa'i phyir mdo sde la sogs pa'i gsung rab bzhin no//

Notes

This chapter has seen a long and slow evolution, beginning its life as a presentation to the Association for Asian Studies meeting in 1988 and approximating its present form as a paper read at Prof. Peter Schäfer's seminar on "Magic in the World's Religions" at the Institute for Advanced Study, Princeton, in 1994. I am grateful for the comments received from many colleagues at these and other points along the way. After the present essay was largely completed I received Braarvig 1997, which discusses some of the same texts I analyze here, above all the important passage from Bhāvaviveka's *Tarkajvāla.*

1 The papers collected in Schäfer and Kippenberg 1997 reflect much of the range of current reflection on the relation between these two categories in the study of Western traditions. As the editors remark in their introduction (p. xi): "Magic essentially belongs to religion (and, indeed, language), and any attempt to separate one from the other turns religion into bloodless spirituality and magic into an uncontrollable and destructive force (and language into lifeless convention)." For a judicious review of the question, see Versnel 1991.

2 On the criminalization of magic in the classical world (which, of course, presupposed the ability to clearly distinguish it), see esp. Hans G. Kippenberg, "Magic in Roman Civil Discourse," in Schäfer and Kippenberg 1997: 137–63. Frazer's effort (1922), following Tylor (1871), to maintain a clear conceptual distinction (and evolutionary order) among magic, religion, and science was, of course, the *bête noire* for much of early twentieth-century anthropology and history of religions.

3 Renou and Filliozat 1985: 270, and on the "magical" character of the Atharva Veda in particular, pp. 284–88; and Gonda 1979: 22–23.

4 Renou and Filliozat 1985: 271: "[O]n discerne qu'à haute époque les teneurs atharvaniques étaient sans grandes garanties, et flottaient pour ainsi dire en marge du canon. Nous savons d'ailleurs que l'*Atharva* n'a été accrédité que tardivement et progressivement comme <<quatrième Veda>>, que certaines écoles ne l'ont jamais reconnu, qu'il avait à tous égards une dignité inférieure à celles des autres Veda."

5 See, for example, Basham 1959: 232–33, whose remarks seem to embody many of Frazer's evolutionary conceptions.

6 Consider, for instance, the survey of magic in the Vedas in Gonda 1979: 135–42.

7 Renou and Filliozat 1985: 346. See also pp. 368–72.

8 Gombrich 1988, chap. 7.

9 The *Āṭānāṭiya Sutta* of the *Dīghanikāya,* now conveniently available in the translation of Walshe 1995: 471–79, is perhaps the best-known protective scripture in the Pali canon. On the use of spells to cure snakebite, see Zysk 1991: 101.

10 On the early growth and elaboration of the Buddhist relic cult in India, see especially Schopen 1997, chaps. 6–8.

11 Thus, for example, the Buddha's condemnation of the miracles associated with the "Gandhāra Charm" by which a "monk becomes many." Walshe 1995: 176.

12 That early Buddhism was sometimes very reserved with respect to miracles is clearly demonstrated by the *Kevaddha Sutta* and the *Pāṭika Sutta,* both in the *Dīghanikāya,* translated in Walshe 1995: 175–80 and 371–83. But other *suttas* in the same corpus refer to wondrous events of various kinds, for instance, the *Mahāsamaya* (Walshe 1995: 315–20) in which the gods visit the Buddha en masse. Compare here, for example, the *Mahāvastu,* especially on the "Attributes of the Buddha" and "Apparitions" (Jones 1949: 124–51).

13 Snellgrove 1987 may perhaps be taken as marking the coming-of-age of Buddhist Tantric Studies, with reference particularly to South Asia and Tibet. On the state of the field with regard to East Asian Buddhist Tantrism, see in particular Strickmann 1996.

14 Snellgrove 1987: 130; cf. also pp. 121–24.

15 See, esp., Skilling 1992 on the question of protective rituals in early Buddhism.

16 For the Sanskrit and Tibetan texts of the last two mentioned, refer to *Guhyādi-aṣṭasiddhisaṅgraha.*

17 On the distinction between *pāramitānaya* and *mantranaya,* see *Vimalaprabhāṭīkā,* vol. 1, p. 41, and vol. 3, p. 100. Cf. also *Acintyādvayakramopadeśa,* v. 90, in *Guhyādi-aṣṭasiddhisaṅgraha,* p. 204: *eko 'bhiprāyaḥ sarveṣām advayajñānam uttamam/ mantravādam aśeṣaṃ ca tathā pāramitānayaḥ//*

18 E.g., in Dutt 1942, vols. 1 and 4.

19 One text I shall not consider in this regard is the *Mahāyānasūtrālaṃkāra.* There has been a long debate concerning the interpretation of chap. 9, v. 46, which describes the "reversal" *(parāvṛtti)* of sexual intercourse. Some—including most recently Snellgrove 1987: 127–28—insist that this must refer to "sexual yoga." Opposing this view are those (including the present author) who believe that neither the historical nor the textual context support this, and that, in accord with mainstream Yogācāra teaching, the "reversal of sexual intercourse" is essentially the sublimation of sexual desire in enlightenment.

20 *Bodhisattvabhūmi,* pp. 185–86. For an interesting paraphrase of this passage, from the perspective of the Tibetan scholastic tradition in the thirteenth century, see *Sa-skya mkhas-'jug,* p. 103.

21 Relevant discussions of *dhāraṇī* include: Lamotte 1944, chap. 10; Braarvig 1985; Janet Gyatso, "Letter Magic," in Gyatso 1992: 173–213; and Strickmann 1996, chap. 1.

22 See Skilling 1992. For the *paritta*-rites in Sri Lanka, refer to de Silva 1981, and, concerning their possible relations with Tantrism, Jackson 1994.

23 Skilling 1992 demonstrates this very well. As he emphasizes (p. 167), "by definition the *rakṣā* literature is devoted to worldly ends."

24 Suzuki 1930: 126–27 and 396 offers valuable comments on the meaning *kṣānti* in similar contexts. Cf. the remarks of Edgerton 1953a, vol. 2, p. 199.

25 This is ritually embedded in Buddhist tantric practice, where the cultivation

of *bodhicitta,* the will to attain enlightenment oneself on behalf of all beings, is regularly followed by rites to "destroy all obstacles" *(sarvavighnavināśārtham),* as is the case in *Sādhanamālā,* vol. 1, p. 3.

26 For discussion and analysis of this work, see Hedinger 1984 and Griffiths 1999: 133–39.

27 *Śikṣāsamuccaya,* pp. 67–79, especially pp. 71–76, on v. 6.13ab: *eṣā rakṣātmabhāvasya bhaiṣajyavasanādibhiḥ.*

28 *Śikṣāsamuccaya,* pp. 76–79, on v. 6.13cd: *ātmatṛṣṇopabhogāt tu kliṣṭāpattiḥ prajāyate.*

29 *Śikṣāsamuccaya,* p. 77, lines 9–20.

30 *Śikṣāsamuccaya,* p. 77, line 19: *ayam eva paramāṃ rakṣāṃ mārādibhyaḥ sarvaduṣṭebhyaḥ karoti.*

31 *Śikṣāsamuccaya,* p. 78, lines 4–27.

32 *Śikṣāsamuccaya,* p. 78, lines 29–31: *pathe me rakṣa/ utpathe me rakṣa/ janato me rakṣa/ caurato me rakṣa/ rājato me rakṣa/ siṃhato me rakṣa/ vyāghrato me rakṣa/ nāgato me rakṣa/ sarpato me rakṣa/ sarvato me rakṣa/*

33 Among studies of this work that have appeared to date, see, in particular, Iida 1980, Qvarnström 1989, and Eckel 1992.

34 The tripartite distinction of dhāraṇī, mantra, and vidyā is explained in an early ninth-century Tibetan lexicon, *Sgra sbyor bam gnyis,* pp. 97–98, as follows: "*Mantra* is explained by *mantre guptibhāṣaṇe* ["'mantra' in the sense of 'secret utterance'"]. Secret mantra is so-called because it captures and secretly invokes the deity of the mantra, etc. *Vidyā* is explained by *vid[a] jñān<a>[e]* ["'vid[yā]' in the sense of 'knowledge'"]. The vidyā-mantra is so-called because it is the term for the antidote to ignorance, embodied as a goddess. *Dhāraṇī* is explained by *arthagranthan dhārayatīti dhāraṇī* ["*dhāraṇī* maintains meaning and text"]. The dhāraṇī-mantra is so-called because it is the term for retaining without forgetfulness, and acquisition of the special sequences."

35 The text was in fact translated into Chinese no fewer than nine times: Taishō nos. 1009, 1011–18, in Demiéville, Durt, and Seidel 1978: 91–92, and, for brief biographical notes on the translators mentioned here, pp. 275–76 (Shi Ken, i.e., Zhiqian) and p. 238 (Butsudabatsudara, i.e., Buddhabhadra).

36 In the scripture from which it is drawn, this passage follows immediately after, and therefore is taken as directly pertaining to, the teaching of the dhāraṇī itself. Refer to Inagaki 1999: 69.

37 Braarvig 1997: 36, n. 12, also mentions this point. He questions, however, "whether Tārā...was already in existence at the time of Bhavya," rightly noting that the earliest epigraphical evidence is much later. It is significant, however, that Bhāvaviveka/Bhavya is roughly contemporaneous with the earliest *sculptural* representations of goddesses resembling Tārā, notably cave 90 at Kanheri in Maharashtra, photographically reproduced here. At Ellora caves 8, 9, and 10, the identification of Tārā seems certain. Malandra 1993 dates these Ellora caves to the seventh century.

38 *Āryabhadracaripraṇidhānarāja,* v. 18.

39 Consider, in this regard, the remarks of Tāranātha, in Chimpa and Chattopadhyaya 1980: 343–46.

40 *Samaya* (Tib. *dam-tshig*) in this sense reflects the well-established use of the word to mean "oath," or "pledge."

41 On the cult of the mothers and the yoginīs, of which the development and spread embraced the period of Bhāvaviveka's career, see Dehejia 1986. On Cāmuṇḍā in Nepal, refer to Slusser 1982, vol. 1, pp. 329–34.

42 Refer to Gokhale 1958, 1963; and to Qvarnström 1989.

43 Bhāvaviveka's condemnation remains somewhat obscure, as the crucial phrase "replete with coarse and unbearable affliction" *(bzod par dka' ba'i nyon mongs pa bdo bas 'khrigs pa)* is not explained in detail.

44 Kubera, Gaṇeśa, and Mahākāla are among the several examples that come to mind. Possibly, too, the deified yoginīs in general (Dehejia 1986).

45 See, for instance, de Mallmann 1986: 135, on Cāmuṇḍā's inclusion in the Vāgīśvara and Kālacakra maṇḍalas.

46 The chronological development of the Buddhist tantras remains an area of much uncertainty. For a recent study of the art historical evidence, see Linrothe 1999. The presuppositions that have informed much of the historiography in this area are critically scrutinized in Wedemeyer 2001.

47 *Pramāṇavārttika-svavṛtti,* p. 163, lines 3–5: *dharmaviruddhānām api krauryasteyamaithunahīnakarmādi-bahulānāṃ vratānāṃ ḍākinībhaginītantrādiṣu darśanāt.* Thus, Bhāvaviveka and Dharmakīrti illustrate a degree of resistance to the "ritual eclecticism" of medieval India that has recently been discussed in Granoff 2000.

48 In Tibetan tantric nomenclature the "outer tantras" *(phyi-yi rgyud)* are the three classes of *kriyā-, caryā-,* and *yoga-tantra,* excluding the "highest yoga tantra" *(anuttarayogatantra).* The "outer tantras" of the Tibetan traditions overlap in large measure with the Buddhist esoteric texts that were introduced into East Asia, and remain current in the Shingon and Tendai sects in Japan.

49 Dudjom 1991, vol. 1, p. 765.

50 In the text "similarly" *(de bzhin du)* is preceded by the notation (marked in the transcription of the Tibetan text by an underline): "*Madhyamakahṛdayavṛtti-tarkajvāla,* sixteenth fascicle."

51 *mgo-bo blta-ba.* The exact significance of this expression is unfamiliar to me. I assume—and this appears to make good sense in context—that *mgo-bo* is used here for Skt. *śiras,* "head," which is used euphemistically in compound with verbs to refer not only to actions that pertain to the head, but also those that tend upward, or are preeminent, or otherwise elevated.

52 *rgyud,* here, is best understood as meaning *santāna,* the personality-continuum (in this case, of the adept), and not *tantra.*

53 The *gsang ba blo gros kyi mdo (*Guhyamatisūtra)* appears to be unknown, besides this reference to it.

54 As Braarvig 1997: 34 indicates, this seems to be a version of the mantra *īne mīne dapphe daḍapphe* studied in Bernhard 1967.

10. Weaving the World: The Ritual Art of the *Paṭa* in Pāla Buddhism and Its Legacy in Tibet

I

PERHAPS YOU'LL RECALL a scene from Federico Fellini's *Satyricon,* a gaudy vision of life on the wild side in old Rome. The setting resembles a loft space, and the characters are upper class, well-togaed connoisseurs, enjoying tasty snacks and punchy drinks, and admiring already-ancient fragments of sculpture and painting at a chic gallery opening. If you don't know the film, just try imagining a toga party in Soho.

Fellini's studied anachronism was itself an exercise in Roman excess, but, its silliness notwithstanding (or perhaps in virtue of it), the scene is one that often comes to mind when I visit gallery or museum exhibitions, particularly grand exhibitions that seek to survey vast expanses of the very old or the very alien. So it was that Fellini's pompous Romans had their lips to my ears when I attended the sumptuous 1990 exhibition of "The Art of Pāla India and Its International Legacy," asking me to reflect for a few moments on the set that had been constructed in order to situate these rags and stones from medieval India, Nepal, and Tibet.

The grand exhibition, a form of theater within our own cultural world, projects and undergirds values refined for us in academic art departments, museums, auction houses, galleries and collections, by expert scholars, curators, dealers, and collectors: these are the places and agents that in our world govern the construction of the value attributed to these old and mostly damaged goods. Now, one question this raises is: what value might these things have for us, if they didn't have *this* value? Specifically, what were some of the values that were refined through the construction of these objects in Pāla India, and among those who partook of the Pālas' "international legacy"? That these questions, bearing upon the manner in which the artistic traditions concerned were embedded in and integrated with the world that created them, have not been much pressed is itself a remarkable and characteristic feature of much of the contemporary study of the arts of esoteric Buddhism and related traditions.

Possibly we are gazing at idols. With this notion, at least, we confront our vision with some idols of our own. A deeply problematic category in the thought of the West, idolatry may be conceived as having outer or inner significance—the former associated, for instance, with the worship of Mammon, the latter the object of Bacon's fury when he writes of the "four classes of Idols which beset men's minds."[1] A presupposition that seems to have informed much of the early modern European encounter with its many Others was the usually unexpressed conviction that the ontogeny of the critique of idolatry had always to recapitulate its Western phylogeny: the benighted heathens of Asia, Africa, and the Americas could not be expected to attack the Baals lurking within their souls until they had first cast them from their altars. Thus, it comes as no surprise to find an early eighteenth-century Jesuit traveller in India reporting that "...you wou'd scarce believe me, shou'd I name the vile and infamous creatures to which they pay divine honours. 'Tis my opinion, that no idolatry among the antients was ever more gross, or more horrid, than that of these Indians."[2] And, despite the relatively tolerant interest in Hinduism and Buddhism shown by at least some European missionaries and scholars in Asia in the late eighteenth and nineteenth centuries, it was not at all uncharacteristic for L. Austine Waddell, in a magnificent compendium of copious learning and equally rich Orientalist nonsense, to have written of later Indian Buddhism's "introduction of innumerable demons and deities as objects of worship, with their attendant idolatry and sacerdotalism..."[3]

The presuppositions involved here may seem quaintly antiquated to us today. Nevertheless, we may still find attractive the thought that, in the case of medieval Indian Buddhism, we find ourselves confronted with the apparent paradox of the idol that's no idol at all, whose mere materiality accentuates the uncanniness of its sanctity. Nāgārjuna, for instance, writes (*Suhṛllekha,* v. 2):

> An image of the Sugata, though made of wood,
> Is nonetheless worshipped by the wise...

And a Tibetan commentator does not hesitate to gloss the word "wood" as it occurs here with the phrase "base material" *(rgyu dman pa)*.[4] Remarks such as these will no doubt suggest to some that the cognoscenti had always recognized the "true" character of their idols, thus tacitly maintaining the arrogation of the criterion of *the true* to the self-consciously anti-idolatrous perspective of our own tradition.[5]

Nevertheless, if the thought of idolatry has led us tentatively to consider these artifacts more or less as base matter, that is not, I think, a bad place for us to begin. In consideration of what is yet unformed, and thus in a crucial sense empty, the construction of value emphatically appears as a matter of intentional practice by human agents within human communities. The art of esoteric Buddhism is appropriate subject matter for our reflections on this; for esoteric Buddhism in its several particular cultural forms—Indian, Newari, Tibetan, Javanese, Japanese, and so on—seems always to accentuate the *constructedness* of human values, with particular attentiveness to the unformed character of the stuff from which those values are constructed, and to the requirement that they be reconstituted continuously in a world of ongoing change.

In the present context, "construction" must be thought of as carrying its full, literal weight: we refer here not solely to the construction of values in systems of symbols conceived in purely abstract terms, but equally to the concrete, physical construction of temples, paintings, statues, maṇḍalas, offering-cakes, and other material objects, ephemeral and enduring. Our topic is in a crucial sense, then, not fine art narrowly conceived, but world-building, in its physical, symbolic, and conceptual dimensions. Indian and Tibetan Buddhists may have seen things similarly, and so spoke of *śilpaśāstra*, the arts and crafts, as being divisible into the arts of body, speech, and mind. Painting, sculpture, and architecture were thought of as the primary arts of body; poetics and drama the primary arts of speech; and philosophy and meditation the primary arts of mind, all being here regarded as aspects of a complete world-constructing project.[6]

These general considerations should serve to problematize an assumption often encountered in the study of Indo-Tibetan Buddhist art: namely, that there was in principle a very great gulf separating the artist from the virtuoso practitioner of the religion, with the former manufacturing objects of cultic utility on behalf of the latter. This account requires that artisans and adepts occupy two parallel, occasionally interactive, but nonetheless essentially separate domains. Indeed, this has sometimes been advanced as a corrective to an alternative caricature, according to which the artist is depicted as a yogin or meditator, whose work, as a projection of his personal meditation, is related to the cultural system in which he acts above all through its unalterable adherence to a stipulated iconography. Both of these conceptions are evident in the words of art historian Peter H. Pott:

> The art of Tibet is indeed an art with a purpose. The artist created a work for ritual use. Beauty was of subordinate importance, in so far as it was conditioned by the power of expression with which the artist succeeded in embodying in his work the tradition handed down to him and the formal language of symbols. The artist is therefore not motivated by an impulse to produce a work of art but *merely executes a commission* to produce an object for meditative practices or for the extensive rites of Lamaism. In a certain respect the production of the work can in itself be an exercise in meditation; in this case the artist must make himself so familiar with the object he is producing that he brings it forth entirely from his own self, and yet must do this in such a way that not only does a universally valid specimen emerge but each detail can be ritually justified; otherwise the result cannot serve the desired end. [Emphasis added.][7]

I believe this picture to be a distorted one, obscuring an on-going project of world-construction in which artist and dharma-master (and possibly also king, patron, and poet) were collaboratively engaged. The creation of Buddhist icons in the esoteric traditions of Pāla Buddhism, as well as in their Tibetan offshoots, was itself preeminently understood as an integral aspect of a collective virtuoso religious practice, contributing to a holistic world-constructing enterprise. This view of things is supported by extant textual evidence, and, although the norms described in the texts were not rigidly maintained throughout the course of the transmission of esoteric Buddhism from India to Nepal and Tibet, they can nevertheless be seen to inform Tibetan practice even today. In support of such a perspective, we shall analyze the compositional paradigms informing a ritual of artistic creation. To make sense of the relationship between Indian and Tibetan artistic practice and religious practice, we must inquire not into the manner in which art served ritual, nor postulate that artistic practice was itself soteriological practice, but look instead into the way in which ritual embraced and included artistic production as part of a regular, rule-governed enterprise.[8]

II

Our most substantial textual source for the study of Buddhist artistic practice in Pāla domains is the massive *Mañjuśrīmūlakalpa* (*The Root Ceremonial of Mañjuśrī, MMK* hereinafter), redacted in the forms in which we now have it somewhere in northeastern India probably during the eighth century.[9] Its substantial discussions of paintings on cloth *(paṭa)* and the creation of temporary maṇḍalas for initiatory purposes have been well-studied by Marcelle Lalou and Ariane Spanien-Macdonald, and so are readily accessible to anyone engaged in research in this field.[10] We must note here also that Lalou has, in a separate article, made short work of the possible objection that the *MMK* represents but a single, perhaps idiosyncratic, tradition and so offers no reliable data that might inform the study of Pāla-period Buddhist artistic practice more generally: parallel passages in contemporaneous texts, as documented by Lalou, demonstrate that the *MMK* represents some very influential tendencies indeed.[11]

Of particular interest for our present investigations are the *MMK's* several detailed discussions of *paṭa.*[12] *Paṭa* are the Indian antecedents of the *paubha* of Newari Buddhist art and of the *thang-ka* of Tibet; also, possibly, of similar East Asian Buddhist paintings on cloth, such as the Korean *tangwa.* The *MMK* (p. 40) provides instructions for the creation of these painted fabrics in three sizes: large *(jyeṣṭha),* measuring 8 x 4 cubits (Skt. *hasta,* units of about 18 inches); medium *(madhyama),* measuring 5 x 2; and small *(kanyasa),* measuring 1 x ½. The three sizes are further distinguished according to their appropriate ritual functions: generally speaking, the highest attainments *(siddhi),* especially that of enlightenment, are to be won through the great *paṭa;* major mundane accomplishments, such as kingship, through the medium one; and ritual efficacy through the small *paṭa.* (*MMK,* pp. 40–41, vv. 14–18.)

Before the painting can be produced, however, one must have the fabric on which it is to be painted: the term *paṭa* in fact denotes the fabric; compare our use in English of "canvas." The manufacture of the fabric is itself specified as a part of the manufacture of the painted *paṭa,* and so it is with this that the text begins its actual practical prescriptions.

The adept must start *(MMK,* p. 39) by gathering cotton wool at a site that is "pure" or "clean" *(śuci).*[13] The cotton is initially to be cleansed by persons who are adherents of the special vows and commitments of esoteric Buddhism *(samayapraviṣṭaiḥ sattvaiḥ),*[14] after which it is ritually purified through the recitation over it, by the master of the maṇḍala, of a purificatory mantra that is to be repeated 108 times:

> *namaḥ sarvabuddhabodhisattvānām apratihatamatigatipraticāriṇām/*[15] *namaḥ saṃśodhanaduḥkhapraśamanarājendrarājāya tathāgatāyārhate samyaksaṃbuddhāya/ tadyathā—Oṃ śodhaya śodhaya sarvavighnaghātaka mahākāruṇika kumārarūpadhāriṇe vikurva vikurva/ samayam anusmara/ tiṣṭha tiṣṭha/ hum hum phaṭ phaṭ svāhā//*[16]

The adept must then find a virgin girl belonging to the higher castes *(brāhmaṇa, kṣatriya,* or *vaiśya),* who does not conform to the vulgarities of village life *(avitathagrāmyadharma),* who is beautiful and physically mature, compassionate and religious, and who, permitted by her parents, has assumed the vows of the penitential fast *(upoṣadha).* On an astrologically auspicious day, causing her to dress in pure and fresh garments, he takes her to a pure location where the sky is cloudless and there is no wind, and has her bathe there. After she has dressed he sanctifies her with protective mantras. Purifying the cotton-wool once more, he calls upon the buddhas and bodhisattvas to consecrate *(adhi-sthā)* the thread that will be spun from it.

At the completion of these initial rites of protection and consecration, the adept observes closely the signs that become manifest in the surrounding environment: the appearance of birds associated with water, sky, or whatever is pure and bright, such as peacocks, herons, geese and brahmani ducks; or the sounds of drums, cymbals, and other musical instruments; of persons singing auspicious songs or shouting gay exclamations; of bells and benedictions—all of these signify success:

> This rite of mine will be fruitful! I am blessed by the buddhas, who are transcendent lords, and by the great bodhisattvas! The thread of the *paṭa* is vitalized here in my life! My accomplishment of mantra will not be barren! (*MMK,* p. 39, lines 3–4.)

On the other hand, he may hear people shouting inauspicious or harsh phrases—"catch it!" "eat it!" "smash it!" "break it!" and the like—or he may see or hear animals such as the monkey, buffalo, ass, cat, and so on, which are here regarded as base and inauspicious, as in some sense messy. The practitioner then knows, "I will have no successful accomplishment." So what does he do then? He picks up and starts all over, that's what.

The entire process must then be repeated and the omens rechecked. Of course, one can well imagine certain locations in northeastern India where the chances of performing this rite without even so much as a monkey turning up are well nigh nonexistent. The hapless practitioner may attempt as many as seven times to get his cotton and the virgin properly protected and consecrated, even if bad omens occur each time. But not to worry: the *MMK* now tells us that after seven repetitions even one who has performed the five inexpiable sins *(pañcānantaryakārin)* will be assured of success.

The virgin is now to be protected once more and should be made to sit on a mat woven of pure *kuśa* grass, facing east or north. Preparing a ritual meal fit for a god, the adept serves her. He will have instructed the virgin earlier on in the art of spinning the cotton so that the thread is soft and fine; she now practices her spinning, remaining on the same *kuśa* seat, the measure of cotton thread to be spun being specified in the text of the *MMK* by weight in accord with the intended size of the *paṭa.*

It will not be too difficult to pick out an essential pattern in the material we have surveyed so far: at each stage of the process culminating in the spinning of the thread, we find higher levels of order brought out of precedent disorder, with an attendant effort to exclude possible sources of new disorder from the entire process. Thus, for instance, the cotton wool, a relatively disordered substance, must be gathered from a "pure," that is, relatively ordered, location by relatively ordered persons, the vow-adherents. When it is at last spun into thread, the final goal of this phase of ordering, there must be neither surplus nor lack, since either of these conditions betokens disorder. Because, in several important dimensions at least, esoteric Buddhist practice is a way of ordering the entire world, it is clear that the gathering of cotton and the spinning of thread are not to be understood solely as utilitarian acts in the service of a ritual practice with which they enjoy no inherent relationship; there is no distance here between craft and ritual—we are engaged at all times in the weaving of a world.

Once this is recognized, it becomes clear that the practice of world-weaving can tolerate certain characteristic minor, or even sometimes major, disorders, and that these may be compensated for in the larger process of ordering: thus, for instance, the repeated occurrence of inauspicious omens in connection with the purification of the cotton wool fails to scuttle the entire project. It is crucial that we reflect on this point carefully, for it provides a key to our understanding how it was that so many of the precise ritual prescriptions we encounter in texts such as the *MMK* came to be seen in the later history of the esoteric Buddhist traditions as options, yet without the larger outlook that these prescriptions reflect being abandoned. The Tibetans, for example, never concerned themselves, so far as I know, with the manufacture of cotton thread and fabric—these they had to import—yet the spinning of the ordered thread of the Buddha's dharma out of the rough wool of worldly life was for that no less a fundamental theme governing the practice of their ritual arts.

To return, then, to the *MMK.* The thread that has been produced as described above is itself so powerful that reflection upon it has the power to annihilate traces of evil *karman.* Such a powerful object must be handled with extreme care, so that accordingly the thread is to be placed in a purified container, and perfumed with saffron and sandal, and with fragrant flower-blossoms, making certain that no insect particles come into contact with it. The receptacle containing the thread is removed to a pure site, where it is further protected and consecrated by the mantra-adept. Finding a weaver, the practitioner offers him the wage he desires in order to produce the fabric. The weaver should be neither crippled nor emaciated, neither diseased nor aged, free from respiratory ailment, not a eunuch, not yet greying, and should also be devoted to virtue, well regarded, handsome, and an upholder of appropriate worldly conventions. The quality of the weaver—superior, middling, or inferior—will be correlated too with the ritual efficacy of the final product. The text further remarks that no time is to be lost in bargaining: when the artisan names his price the practitioner is to exclaim "great deal!" (lit. "heroic price," *vīrakraya*) and so seal the agreement. The superior *paṭa,* we are reminded, is beyond all price.

It is worth noting here the transition that has taken place between the spinning of the thread and the weaving of the cloth: the virgin spinner was to be as uncontaminated by the world as possible, but yet not a child—that is, she was to be one who had the unactualized potential to be engaged in worldly life; the weaver, on the other hand, is a householder-tradesman, whose involvement with the world is actualized but not corrupted. One's dealings with him are to be straightforward and unproblematic. The ritual project thus reaches out at this point to embrace the world—ultimately in a sense to coerce it—without being sullied by it.

The actual weaving of the fabric must take place on an astrologically propitious day, preferably during the spring, when mangos and other fruits are ripening, when flowers are fully blossomed. The practitioner bestows on the weaver the precepts of the purificatory *poṣadha* rite, feeding him a meal worthy of a divine feast, offering him a clean turban and a bath, and anointing him with sandal and other fragrant ointments. The loom and other necessary implements are to be ritually washed with the five cow-products (urine, dung, milk, butter, and curd), and sanctified with perfumed water that has been strained to insure that no small creatures pollute it. Moving then to a location that is quiet and peaceful, the practitioner consecrates the place as a protective sphere and binds the weaver's head with the five-pointed crown of a bodhisattva. The "great protection" is complete. The fabric is now woven to the appropriate dimension. The text at this point inserts some verses in praise of the efficacious ritual means that have been taught in the way of mantras, insisting upon the necessity of correct practice in connection with those rituals involving *paṭa:*

> As for the accomplishment won through the three *paṭa*
> By men desiring supreme success,
> The violator of the rite will not succeed,
> Even if he's Indra, lord of [the goddess] Śaci. (*MMK,* p. 41, v. 17.)

Following this admonishment, we are told that the *paṭa* must be woven quickly, avoiding any delay, the acceptable numbers of days and nights for the work being given in detail in the text of the *MMK.* During the weaving of the *paṭa,* all of the weaver's activities, even defecation and urination, are hemmed in by ritual prescriptions, the practitioner attending all along to insure that nothing interferes with the flawless completion of the task. The finished cloth is rolled onto a bamboo rod and so readied for transport; the weaver is given his final payment and made happy with generous gifts.

The practitioner now takes the cloth to a pure location and, placing it there, begins a new round of protective rites, on behalf both of himself and of the *paṭa.* He should recall that the very mantras he now recites were uttered in the past by Mañjuśrī and the whole host of past buddhas, and, inspired by this thought, he should seek to realize all the ends of the mantra-practice. Remembering that failure will only perpetuate the round of saṃsāra, he should cultivate the enthusiastic faith that is the sole guarantee of success. We are now ready, in principle, to start painting.

The artist should be either a painter who has been well instructed by the practitioner or the latter himself. If he employs a painter, the practitioner should examine and consecrate him just as he had the weaver. The pigments are to be mixed with traces of camphor, sandal, and saffron, and an offering of incense is to be made. Following a round of mantra-recitation, many sorts of flowers are scattered on the *paṭa.* Taking one's seat on a *kuśa* mat facing east, one composes one's mind, visualizes the buddhas and bodhisattvas, picks up a very fine brush, and, not letting one's thoughts waver, begins to paint.

The *MMK* includes detailed descriptions of about a dozen iconographic arrangements, with remarks on their ritual employment. To the best of my knowledge, none of these correspond precisely to extant paintings, though the general features of composition are familiar enough from later Newari and Tibetan paintings. One example will suffice to provide some sense of the manner in which the *MMK* presents this material.

In the twenty-ninth chapter of the text, the Buddha reveals the potent six-syllable mantra of Mañjuśrī—*Oṃ vākyeda(ṃ) namaḥ!*—which is still recited to this day in Tibet, particularly by those wishing to gain the boon of Mañjuśrī's wisdom as an aid to study. In the *MMK,* however, it is not associated exclusively with this particular activity, but more generally with the alleviation of suffering and the attainment of supreme enlightenment. The practitioner, living on alms, observing the rite of thrice-daily ablution *(trikālasnāyī),* recites the mantra one hundred thousand times before commencing work on the *paṭa* associated with it. The artist (who after all may be the practitioner) must then assume the *poṣadha* vows, and make sure that the pigments to be utilized are uncontaminated. He paints Mañjuśrī at the center of the *paṭa,* seated upon a lotus, in the gesture of teaching the doctrine, adorned with all ornaments, in the form of a youth, and having one shoulder bared. To his left is Avalokiteśvara, holding lotus and fly-whisk, and to his right is Samantabhadra. Above Mañjuśrī, in the midst of clouds, are two *vidyādhara*s holding garlands. Below, the practitioner himself is to be depicted making offerings of incense. The figures are to be encircled by lofty peaks, and a lotus pond should be beneath them.

When the painting is completed it is to be affixed to the western side of a reliquary *caitya,* and worshipped with offerings of butter-lamps. One thousand eight jasmine flowers are to be thrown one-by-one by the practitioner, while consecrating them with the mantra, into Mañjuśrī's face. Then, he may hear the profound roar of the syllable *hum!* or else the *paṭa* will shake. The sound *hum!* will insure that he becomes king of all lands, while the shaking of the *paṭa* signifies his becoming a superior disputant, learned in all sciences, an attainment that recalls the primary use of the mantra in Tibet. Even if this be not achieved, later ritual success will nonetheless come easily. So concludes the rite of this *paṭa.* The well-ordered world of Mañjuśrī has been refined from the raw material of ordinary life in the form of a painted representation; but the process concludes not with the creation of the artifact alone; for the objective is the reordering of *our* world, a reordering whose successful conclusion is betokened by omens, or at the least by future ritual ease.

III

I now wish to propose a general analysis of the compositional principles undergirding the production and ritual of the *paṭa.* It is my contention that there are some very simple paradigms at work here, which can nevertheless generate considerable apparent complexity. In the present context it will not be necessary to elaborate a purely *syntactical* analysis, though I agree with Staal that such analysis offers a powerful means for the explanation of many aspects of ritual behavior. However, like Lawson and McCauley, among others, I do not join Staal in his rejection of the *semantic* analysis of religious ritual.[17] Indeed, though it will be clear that the compositional analysis proposed here would be consistent with a purely syntactical analysis, I believe that such analysis by itself would be incomplete if it did not also take account of the semantic features of rituals such as those with which we are here concerned. Nevertheless, because the compositional analysis offered here does not rigorously discriminate between the syntactical and semantic features of the rituals analyzed, its character remains informal.

To simplify matters, I shall be concerned initially only with ritual actions and their objects. A more complete analysis would explicitly have to include agency as well, though, significantly, the determination of the role of the artist *qua* tradesman (which, owing to its being the topic of much confusion in the secondary literature, is here a primary concern) does not require such analysis. This is, of course, a highly interesting feature of the proposed analysis, since it will help us to understand why the conception of "artist-as-meditator" is so problematic (but why, as we shall see, "meditator-as-artist" is not a similarly problematic category). In what immediately follows, then, one-term expressions of the form *"Fx"* must be read roughly as signifying that some *x* is the object of an action, *F,* performed by an unspecified agent (who in most instances is understood to be the *sādhaka,* the "adept" or "practitioner").

The primary compositional principle that clarifies the structure of the rituals of the *paṭa* surveyed above requires specification of three basic actions:

G Gather (the designated elements of, or requisites for...).
A Arrange (those same elements in some specified order).
C Consecrate (what has been so ordered).

Thus, where "painting" stands for the painted *paṭa* itself, "(G)painting" refers to the collecting of cloth, pigments, artist, and so forth, on an auspicious day in an appropriate place, all of which taken together are the prerequisites for the production of the painting. In that case, then, "(A)painting," putting the elements into a specified arrangement, is none other than the execution of the painted *paṭa*. "Consecration," as used here, is intended broadly; it refers to any ritual action that transforms its object into a vehicle for or locus of divine agency. Thus, in the case of the *paṭa*, either a *pratiṣṭhāvidhi* (that is, a ritual of the type that is ordinarily referred to as a "consecration" of an art object),[18] or a *paṭavidhi* (rite of the *paṭa*), like the rites concluding the execution of the painting of Mañjuśrī described briefly above, will satisfy the notation "(C)painting." The entire ritual of the painted *paṭa* therefore, may be summarized as being composed according to the formula:

(1) (GAC)painting.

Now recall some of the specific elements that must be gathered as requisites for the execution of the painted *paṭa*. First and foremost was the unpainted *paṭa*, which, as we have seen, required for its creation, among other elements, specially produced thread and an appropriately qualified weaver. The *paṭa*, once woven, was not, however, consecrated, but was only rolled onto a bamboo rod. It may seem, then, that the paradigm described above is in this case only imperfectly realized, thus:

(2) (GA)*paṭa*.

However, it is also clear that, before it can be painted, it must additionally be "protected" by means of mantras and rites of cleansing. "Protection" ("P") in fact may be consistently substituted for "consecration" in any of the ritual events governed by the ritual of the painted *paṭa* as a whole. So, for example, we may describe the painting of the *paṭa* more fully:

(3) (GAC)painting

(GAP)*paṭa* (GAP)*artist*

The "great protection," performed on the weaver and artist, actually crowned each craftsman as a bodhisattva. I believe this confirms that "protection" and "consecration" may usually be regarded as functionally similar.

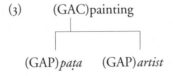

It will be clear enough that the compositional paradigm described here can then be extended to include the entire ritual sequence described above, beginning with the gathering of the cotton wool:

(4)

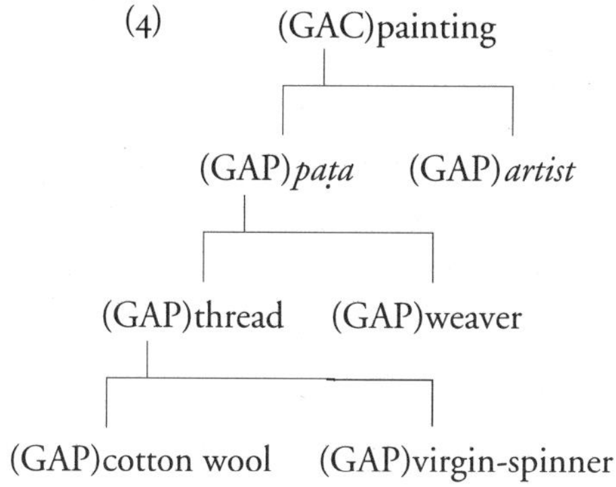

We commented earlier on the manner in which the ritual of the *paṭa* seems to involve a thoroughgoing ordering of the world. The foregoing analysis provides additional support for this suggestion, and clarifies, moreover, our conception of the purpose of such ordering: the appropriate ritual acts that rearrange the world create a tranformative opening of the world, through which divine agency—here specifically the activity of buddhas and bodhisattvas—may penetrate our own domains. In fact, the ritual of the *paṭa* may even be regarded as a small-scale enactment of the gathering, arranging, and consecrating of the entire world that is after all the aim of the Mahāyāna; and it is an enactment that contributes to the actualization of that aim. The proposed analysis further contributes in this connection to our understanding of an apparently paradoxical dimension of esoteric Buddhist doctrine, which always claims that, as the world-age steadily degenerates, ever more efficacious means are revealed in the tantras. Though this no doubt served as a rationale for the introduction and gradual acceptance of new tantras and tantric techniques, it may without much interpretive violence be taken to mean, too, that as the world becomes a messier place, so that the large-scale order of the Buddhist monastic community can no longer be well-maintained, the local, ephemeral, and often personal order engendered by high-powered techniques of ritual and yoga perforce become the primary points at which enlightened activity may enter the world.[19]

Before continuing further, one obvious objection must be addressed: the GAC-paradigm is in no way definitive of specifically Buddhist ritual; many other sorts of ritual, for example, the Jewish household rituals of the sabbath eve, may appear to exemplify the same paradigm: candles and wine, freshly baked bread, a clean table cloth, and other elements of a festive meal are gathered together, prepared and arranged, and then "consecrated" by the women of the house, when they perform the blessing over the sabbath candles shortly before sunset. Such general structural similarity among what may be broadly regarded as consecratory rituals belonging to greatly differing religious traditions, however, also suggests the correct resolution of the difficulty this raises; for *structural* similarity also underscores the pronounced *semantic* differences of our ritual actions. Thus, although

(GAC)sabbath table

and

(GAC)painted *paṭa*

are similar in that each represents an instance of "(GAC)*x*" in the context in which it occurs, those contexts also exclude the possibility of arbitrary substitution of specific elements, be they material requisites, specifications of time, place, or person, etc. Moreover, relevant fundamental understandings will differ greatly in differing contexts: the divine agency recalled through the sabbath blessings in Judaism, and the manner of its action in the human world, resemble the divine agency brought forth in the *paṭavidhi* at most in only an approximate fashion.[20] The precise contexts generated in specific traditions determine the values permitted as appropriate substitution instances of any "*x*," and these in turn contribute to the determination of the manner in which the functions "G," "A," and "C" are to be interpreted. The contextually determined interpretation of these functions further insures that restrictions governing permitted substitution values will not often be transgressed, and even then generally in characteristic ways that are tolerated by the context in question.

It is also true that, at some point, the process of ritual production must rely upon natural or manufactured goods that are not in fact produced as part of the ritual, though, in the case of manufactured goods, it may be required that they be produced in accordance with ritual stipulations (for instance, Passover matzoh, or the incense used by Tibetan Buddhists). Where natural produce is utilized, it is stipulated that it be "pure" or otherwise appropriate. It is possible to see here the basis for certain types of substitution that do in fact occur: for instance, the use of manufactured cloth for the religious paintings with which we are in the present instant concerned.

We should further note that in the rituals of the *paṭa* there is a great amount of redundancy: there's simply no way that the virgin, for instance, can have too much protection. It is this redundancy, when conjoined with the principle governing the employment of natural and imported goods that such goods be pure or well ordered relative to their class, that opens the way for the omission of entire stages of the ritual: the purchase of "pure," high quality thread, combined with its ritual cleansing and protection, may for instance be permitted as functionally equivalent to the longer process of harvesting cotton wool, consecrating a virgin-spinner, and so on. Thus these rituals lend themselves to varied expansion and abridgement, while preserving a relatively stable, underlying structure.

Finally, some remarks on agency are required; for if, in the examples given above, the spinner, weaver, and painter are in no wise to be regarded as agents, then it would appear that the analysis offered here has relegated them to the status of mere instruments, which was one of the positions I had proposed to refute, namely, that the creation of the ritual art of esoteric Buddhism serves the ritual in an exclusively instrumental fashion. Remark, however, that at every stage the craftspersons employed—even those who cleansed the cotton wool—were duly qualified, protected, or consecrated, so that in some measure the divine agency at work here might be thought of as working through them as well. It is precisely in and through their common participation in the agency of buddhas and bodhisattvas that those who assist the *sādhaka* are dignified above mere instruments, and become genuine collaborators in the ritual process that is in operation here.[21] With this it becomes possible to consider some aspects of artistic production in Tibet.

IV

We have, of course, no way of determining at the present time the extent to which the practice of adepts and artists in India during the Pāla period actually conformed with the ritual norms described and analyzed above. But comparative data gleaned from living traditions that were markedly influenced by Pāla religious and artistic practices may at least suggest plausible frames for our conception of the relationships holding among normative texts and practical conventions. Tibetan traditions of religious painting and sculpture, given their explicit and well-established debt to Pāla Buddhism, offer an appropriate point of departure for such research. We must take care, however, not to suppose that Tibetan practice is just a recapitulation of Indian: the tradition was transformed in the course of its transmission, so that, about some matters, we must assume that the texts really do reflect Indian practices, even where the Tibetans came to ignore or to alter certain of the prescriptions concerned. What I shall propose, therefore, is that a relatively consistent ethos governed the production of Indian and Tibetan Buddhist ritual art, but that, so long as that general ethos was maintained, many particular prescriptions could be regarded as options. It will be seen, moreover, that the very vague notion of "a relatively consistent ethos" can be given unambiguous expression by appealing to the principles of ritual composition discussed above—in sum, that the paradigms governing the production of Tibetan religious art appear to accord very well with those that may be derived from the *MMK*.

To begin, however, some ground-clearing is required; for the entire topic of the ritual dimension of Tibetan artistic production has been obscured by much misunderstanding regarding the supposed soteriological value of Tibetan painting and sculpture, or the lack thereof. As the late Chögyam Trungpa, Rinpoche felt obliged to point out, "It is widely thought that thangka painting is a form of meditation. This is not true."[22] The question this raises is examined in relation to our present subject matter by David Jackson and Janice Jackson:

> The misconception of the thangka painter as yogi no doubt mainly derives from textual sources. A number of texts, including both indigenous Tibetan treatises and translations from the Sanskrit, set forth the ritual steps and visualizations that should accompany the painting of certain images. Yet in their everyday practice few artists followed such methods. Though Tibetan painters on the whole were religiously minded, none of our teachers mentioned such practices as forming part of their standard method. Nevertheless, Tibetan Buddhism required that its painters be tantric initiates in a formal sense at least. According to Vajrayana Buddhism any artist who depicted the deities belonging to the four classes of Tantras had to be ritually initiated into each of these classes. Most Tibetan painters had in fact received such initiations *(dbang bskur)*.[23]

Though this seems to me to be correct in a very general manner, there are two emendations that I think must be made in order to comprehend the ritual role of the artist in a traditional setting: in the first instance, the "misconception of the thangka painter as yogi," which is after all a Western and not a Tibetan misconception, has probably had more to do with popular Western notions of Buddhist arts ("Zen and the art of thus-and-such") than with any sources, textual or otherwise, stemming from within the Tibetan tradition itself;[24] and, secondly, the requirement that "painters be tantric initiates in a formal sense at least" is without doubt a minimal fulfillment of a rule of ritual composition that may be derived from texts (like the passages from the *MMK* summarized above) that are here thought to be sources of the misconception. Appropriately initiated artists, so long as they are not thought to have irrevocably broken their vows, are "well-ordered" from the perspective we have been considering, and their craft therefore appropriately instantiates divine agency to some degree. In other words, as the texts insist, artistic practice remains part of a system of ritual, but because that part was seldom thought to be soteriologically efficacious by itself, the notion of artistic practice as *itself* exemplary soteriological discipline—that is, as yoga or meditation—simply fails to make sense from a traditional standpoint: those who speak of thangka painting in general as meditation are simply making a grammatical error. To suggest, however, by way of rectification, that there is no strong relationship between artistic and soteriological practices, is certainly a mistaken hyper-correction.

The *MMK* was not itself among the several important tantras that were regularly studied in the Tibetan monastic curriculum; besides some prayers known to every Tibetan schoolchild, the best-known work relating to the Mañjuśrī cult was, rather, the *Mañjuśrīnāmasaṃgīti (The Litany of Mañjuśrī's Names).*[25] Nonetheless, the *MMK* was known, among the cognoscenti at least, to have been the source of some of the more popular ritual and meditational practices *(sādhana)* focussing upon Mañjuśrī,[26] as well as of certain important legendary and historical traditions.[27] Of special interest here is a very late recasting of the *MMK's* rites of the *paṭa,* set down by the famous Rnying-ma-pa polymath 'Jam-mgon 'Ju Mi-pham-rgya-mtsho (1846–1912).[28] It will be sufficient for our purposes to consider just the first few lines:

> Here, in the extensive [ritual of the] *paṭa* of Mañjuśrī, one blesses the [cotton] wool and then causes a virgin to spin the thread. There are various large, medium, and small *paṭa* that one commissions a weaver to weave. At the outset, you perform the *sevā* [the ritual "service" of the deity, achieved through recitation of

> the mantra] by reciting the syllable *mu* one hundred thousand times on a mountain top.[29] Having taken the vows of refuge and of the enlightened attitude, the purification and dispelling [of obstacles] is performed with water [mixed with] sandal, camphor, and saffron on a pure piece of cotton cloth or silk. In a pure place, a pure painter, having partaken of the three white [foods, i.e., milk, yoghurt, and butter] and having donned white clothes, begins to paint at sunrise on an astrally auspicious full-moon day. He paints through half the day but no more. Painting in that way on each day, he will bring it to completion.

Mipham then continues his account with a survey of some of the important iconographic arrangements specified in the *MMK,* and of the rites that are to be performed in connection with the completed paintings.

What immediately strikes the reader of this account is the extreme condensation of Mipham's summaries of the *MMK's* elaborate discussions of the production of thread and cloth. The explanation, of course, is simply that, in Mipham's world—that of far eastern Tibet during the nineteenth century—cotton cloth and fabric were not locally manufactured, so that Indian rituals concerning their manufacture had long since passed into obsolescence, retaining only the incidental, antiquarian interest that scholars (and sometimes revivalists) like to find in the disused traditions of the past.

Moreover, while it was no doubt uncommon for Tibetan icons to be produced in precise accord with even those stipulations that it was possible to observe in Tibet—this probably occurred only when a lama or yogin undertook specific rituals requiring the commission of specific pieces of artwork (i.e., in cases closely resembling the situation described in the *MMK*)—it is nevertheless certain that Tibetan artists retained at least a general notion of the manner in which their *métier* was circumscribed by ritual norms. Thus, Gega Lama, a leading contemporary artist, writes:

> An artist...[w]hen portraying the passionless form (of the Buddha), or the divinities of the outer tantras,...should bathe regularly and be scrupulous in his conduct, keeping the precepts of lay ordination (assuming he is not an ordained monk): when portraying the divinities of the inner tantras, he must have received the appropriate empowerment and be maintaining the commitments thereof, ideally performing the meditation daily or at least reciting the mantra of the divinity continually. At the

start of the project, he should perform a ceremony to eliminate all potential obstacles; meditating on himself in the form of the appropriate protective divinity, the artist purifies the canvas; next, visualizing himself in the forms of the Buddhas of the five families, or of Vairocana..., he consecrates the pigments and brushes in a particular ceremony.... Until the project is completed, he must be able to devote unceasing energy to it, without procrastination; and when it is completed, he should know how to explain its qualities in order to gladden the patron, and to dedicate the virtue of the endeavor for the welfare of others in a spirit of celebration.[30]

figure 5. A Tibetan painter at work. Gtsang-gnas Monastery, near Barkham, Sichuan. 1990.

And the Sherpa painter, Kaba Par Gyaltsen, after demonstrating the manufacture of a brush to a Western student, comments:

> Brushes are like little gods. In fact, you should think of them all as the sword of Manjusri, the patron deity of our craft. You should never put a brush in your mouth as it's disrespectful. Always keep them in a high place and never allow them to fall to the floor.[31]

Hugh R. Downs, who recounts this, further describes the hermit and painter Au Leshi, who was well-known in the Sherpa and Tibetan Buddhist communities of eastern Nepal as one who did, in fact, integrate his painting with his meditational practice. Though Au Leshi's interpretation of his art as an extension of his contemplative practice was generally thought to be exceptional, yogins who were also artisans were not uncommon, and indeed, a special value was often attributed to the work of such yogin-artists, their paintings and sculptures being regarded as imbued with divine agency even prior to formal consecration.[32]

I believe, therefore, that Tibetan practice of the sacred arts traditionally remained continuous with the ritual ethos of Pāla Buddhism, wherein artistic creation was valued above all for its contribution to the ordering of our world and hence to the introduction of divine agency therein. Nevertheless, it is also probably safe to say that the explicit and self-conscious adherence to this ethos has diminished with the passage of time, and will no doubt continue to diminish given the social and political circumstances now obtaining in the Tibetan cultural world.

V

In concluding this chapter, I should like to return to some questions raised by the rich and fascinating exhibition that inspired its composition. In her introduction to the exhibition's catalogue, Susan L. Huntington writes:

> Artistic influence occurred in several ways. In some cases, foreign travellers returning from India brought away with them the memories of the temples, shrines, and images they had seen in the Pāla lands, and their descriptions must have enabled artists in their own countries to create works based on Pāla models. Some travellers physically transported objects of Pāla manufacture back to their homelands, including images, manuscripts, and other works of art that served to inspire artists in their native countries....
>
> "Influence" is all too often seen as a contagion or virus-like phenomenon that can hardly be rejected by its potential recipient. However, if a metaphor must be drawn to portray the nature of cultural influence, perhaps it should be likened to a signal that is not always heard, and if heard not always heeded....

> When we speak of Pāla internationalism, then, we are referring to a vigorously dynamic process, for at the same time that Pāla culture was disseminated, it was also nourished and perpetuated by its emulators.[33]

In most respects this is certainly correct, but I believe that Huntington's account does not sufficiently emphasize certain cardinal considerations in light of which the internationalization of Pāla religious culture, and the artistic styles that accompanied it, become at least minimally intelligible. So long as we focus upon the plastic arts as models that were imitated, ignored, or transformed, we perceive only hazily the motivations underlying the transmission of artistic models in the first place, and the motivations for producing works of the same type at home. However, when we take seriously the implications of the reconstitution of the world in ritual that was described earlier—and particularly its implications for attributions of relative purity, status, and worth—it becomes clear that a growing circle of participatory involvement in the systems of religious ritual in question would have entailed, among many other things, the diffusion of artistic style. The spread of a new type of popular music and dance, which may bring with it changes in styles of clothing, cosmetics, and hair, here provides a much more powerful metaphor than a radio signal. But regrettably so far—owing perhaps to the small degree of active collaboration among scholars in the various disciplines and area studies concerned—the ritual craze that swept through much of Asia from India, and especially from the Pāla domains towards the end of the first millennium and the beginning of the second, remains dimly perceived and even more poorly understood.

Notes

This chapter was first presented at the University of Chicago, at a symposium convened in connection with the installation at the Smart Gallery of Art of "The Art of Pāla India and Its International Legacy," curated by Susan L. Huntington and John C. Huntington. The exhibition catalogue is given in Huntington and Huntington 1990.

1 Bacon 1944: *Novum Organum,* first book of aphorisms, 39 *et seq.* Halbertal and Margalit 1992 offers a thorough and penetrating discussion of the problem throughout a broad range of Western philosophical and religious traditions.

2 Pierre Martin, quoted in Marshall 1970: 21.
3 Waddell 1971: 12.
4 *Bshes spring mchan 'grel,* fol. 2b, line 6.
5 Among twentieth-century Western writers on Hinduism and Buddhism, well-articulated misgivings about Western monotheisms and their dogmatic opposition to idolatry have, however, not been all that uncommon. In fact, the deliberate break with the Western religious mainstream on just these points is an important *leitmotif* running right through the discourse of the alternative religions inspired or influenced by Hinduism and Buddhism, from Theosophy onwards, not to mention such "New Age" phenomena as neo-Paganism and witchcraft. One of the clearest statements of opposition to traditional monotheism from a noted scholar of Hinduism is Daniélou 1964, who, for example, writes (p. 7): "[W]e may be nearer to a mental representation of divinity when we consider an immense number of different gods than when we try to stress their unity; for the number one is in a way the number farthest removed from infinity."
6 For a brief traditional statement about this point, see Dudjom 1991, vol. 1, pp. 98–99.
7 Griswold, Kim, and Pott 1968: 154–55. The view adopted by Huntington and Huntington (1990: 102) differs in points of detail: "The surviving art of the Pāla period is religious, meant to support meditation and visualization of the divine.... Every element, every gesture, and in many cases every nuance is imbued with philosophical and religious content. For lay practitioners, the complexities of the symbolism probably were not understood, but the images served for them as sources of instruction and inspiration." The understanding of the laity is perhaps underestimated here. I tend to think, rather, that iconographic symbolism was valuable for Hindus and Buddhists precisely because, at least in many of its essentials, it did form a common symbolic code, to which both those who had had elite training and those who did not were attuned. (The manner in which knowledge of iconographic symbolism may defy our preconceptions of cultural elites was underscored for me in November 1992, when, during a visit to Bhubanesvar, Orissa, a young brahman was attempting to explain to me the significance of the carvings adorning the temple with which he was associated. His little sister, a girl of about ten, began correcting him until, with some embarrassment, but also a measure of good humor, he ceded all iconographic authority to her.) Of course, regarding the full complexity of icons that were thought to be highly esoteric even within the tradition itself, understanding was probably possible only for initiates (who in the Buddhist esoteric traditions might nevertheless have been laymen).
8 One of the earlier contributors to the study of tantrism who seems to have appreciated the relationship between art and ritual in this context along lines similar to those I advance here was Heinrich Zimmer, on whose approach see the following chapter.
9 The edition used here is entered as *Āryamañjuśrīmūlakalpa* in the bibliography. My references to the MMK give page numbers according to Vaidya's edition,

with verse numbers where relevant. There are important differences among the available Sanskrit, Chinese, and Tibetan versions. The questions of dating and provenance are most recently and adequately surveyed in Matsunaga 1985.

10 Lalou 1930, Macdonald 1962. *Paṭa* are discussed briefly in Huntington and Huntington 1990: 99–100.

11 Lalou 1936.

12 The chapters of the *MMK* primarily devoted to *paṭa* are nos. 4–11 (pp. 39–85), 26 (pp. 226–33), and 29 (pp. 249–50), though there are many references to the ritual employment of *paṭa* elsewhere in the text as well. My reading of the text also takes account of Lalou's 1930 edition of the Tibetan.

13 The frequent mention of "purity" in what follows may strike the reader as being unnecessarily repetitive but paraphrases the text itself and is clearly one of its predominant concerns. Besides *śuci,* other terms relating to purity and cleanliness that one finds here include *śukla, śubha, saṃśodhana,* and *suśobhana.* In the present passage it is further specified that the place is to be "dustless" *(rajovigata).*

14 Gellner 1992 extensively demonstrates the correlation between elaborate ritual obligation and ethico-religious value in a spiritual environment that in some ways, at least, is continuous with that studied here. On p. 91 he writes, "High status and a large number of religious obligations are inseparably linked in Newar minds." As will become clear from the analysis proposed below, that which is hedged in by vows and regulations is relatively more ordered, thus "purer," than that which is not.

15 The precise meaning of this phrase is uncertain. Lalou, on the basis of the Tibetan, suggests reading *°gatimati-* where the available Sanskrit text has *°matigati-.*

16 This approximately means: "Homage to all Buddhas and Bodhisattvas, whose conduct accords with unobstructed intelligence. Homage to the king among emperors, who purifies and tranquilizes troubles, to the Tathāgata, the Arhat, the Genuinely Perfect Buddha. Thus: Oṃ! Purify it, purify it! O bearer of princely form, remover of all obstacles, most compassionate! Magically transform it, magically transform it! Recollect the vow! Be present, be present! Hum! Hum! Phaṭ! Phaṭ! Svāhā!"

17 Staal 1989 conveniently brings together, with additional new material, Staal's contributions to the theory of ritual. Lawson and McCauley 1990 elaborates a powerful theory of religious ritual systems, inclusive of their semantical features, with whose approach the present chapter is broadly in harmony.

18 On Indian and Tibetan Buddhist rituals that are technically designated as consecration rituals *(pratiṣṭhāvidhi),* see Bentor 1996.

19 For traditional notions of the progressive ordering of the Buddhist tantras, see Dudjom 1991: 268 ff. On the soteriological necessity of tantricism, cf. also Kapstein 1992, repr. as chap. 9 of Kapstein 2000a.

20 Of course, just as there are many Buddhisms, so too many Judaisms; I do not intend to suggest that either of these religions possesses a monolithic conceptual system. In the present example of the family service of the sabbath eve, I

have in mind the ritual and doctrinal world of contemporary Conservative Judaism in the United States.

21 Shaw 1994 argues at length that the role of women in Buddhist tantric practice, far from being that of objects of male practice, was one of active agency and creativity. While I am hesitant to attribute to artisans the degree of autonomy that Shaw maintains belonged to women tantrics in India, and though I also hesitate to accept her conclusions about this, it nevertheless seems certain to me that both cases do require a roughly similar reassessment of instrumentality and agency. We must wonder whether earlier generations of Western scholars tended to perceive generally oppressed social groups, such as women and artisans, as instruments solely owing to prejudgments fostered by Western modes of analysis, or whether we are now tending to emphasize agency owing to the inclinations encouraged by our contemporary academic milieu. Both alternatives may contain a measure of truth.

22 Trungpa 1975: 18.

23 Jackson and Jackson 1984: 12.

24 Suzuki 1959 is perhaps the most notorious example of a work by a respected scholar promoting the conflation of art and Buddhist enlightenment. Cf. the pointed review by Demiéville 1973: 496–97.

25 For an edition, translation, and much useful historical background, see R. M. Davidson 1981.

26 For example, the rites of the deity according to the tradition of Mati Paṇḍita, which are treated at length in *Sgrub thabs kun btus,* vol. 2.

27 E.g., Dudjom 1991, vol. 1, pp. 435, 507, 510. Cf. also Kapstein 1989: 240; repr. as chap. 7 of Kapstein 2000a: 133. On aspects of the early history of the transmission of the *MMK* in Tibet, see Imaeda 1981.

28 The passage cited here is found in his *'Jam dpal ras bris sogs kyi zin bris,* given in his *Sgrub skor,* in *Mi pham gsung 'bum,* vol. 25, pp. 249–55. Dan Martin has kindly informed me that he has recently located a similar summary of the same material in the writings of the early Bka'-brgyud-pa master Phag-mo-gru-pa Rdo-rje-rgyal-po (1110–70).

29 Mipham's discussion is here based on *MMK,* chaps. 25–27.

30 Gega Lama 1983, vol. 1, pp. 57–58.

31 Downs 1980: 105.

32 Besides the testimony of Downs 1980, I rely here on my own conversations with the late Au Leshi, and on discussions with the late Sebra Gomchen of Sikkim and other yogin-artists. The Ven. Tulshig Rinpoche specifically stated to me on one occasion that, because of the special circumstances of their manufacture, Au Leshi's paintings did not even require formal consecration. Tibetans very often attribute a sort of talismanic value to artwork executed by renowned yogins and lamas. For a particularly striking case of the convergence of artistry and yoga within traditional literature, see Dudjom Rinpoche 1991, vol. 1, pp. 626 ff., on the great Heruka image of Ukpalung.

33 Huntington and Huntington 1990: 69–71.

11. Schopenhauer's Śakti

Heinrich Zimmer's (1890–1943) name is not often invoked in connection with the contemporary study of Indian philosophy—and for good reason: Zimmer was no philosopher, and never identified himself as one. Nonetheless, his *Philosophies of India* has enjoyed long popularity and, in the public imagination at least, has caused Zimmer's name to be widely associated with Indian philosophy, much as Will Durant's *Story of Philosophy* created, for an earlier generation, a reputation for Durant as a philosophical publicist.[1] While there are aspects of Zimmer's work on Indian art and Tantricism that I think do command continuing philosophical interest, we should be clear at the outset about the decidedly non-philosophical orientation of Zimmer's scholarship and about the particular standpoint he adopted with respect to philosophy. For only when we have comprehended Zimmer's deliberate disaffinity with much of academic philosophy can we attempt to locate the genuine contributions to the philosophical study of classical India that may still be derived from his work.

In characterizing Zimmer's approach as "non-philosophical," I have in mind first and foremost his absolute disregard for what many contemporary philosophers would hold to be the indispensible features of philosophical method: rigorous definition and systematic argument, together with an insistence on well-crafted logical form as the appropriate vehicle for the elucidation of philosophical content. The immensity of Zimmer's disinterest here becomes apparent when we note that, with the exception of an appendix added to *Philosophies of India* by Joseph Campbell, the book makes not even perfunctory reference to the development of philosophical method in India, nor to the Nyāya and Vaiśeṣika schools and their Buddhist and Jaina counterparts, which represent (from a contemporary philosophical perspective, at least) the most characteristically *philosophical* aspects of classical Indian thought.[2] Nor do Zimmer's earlier writings in German make up for this striking omission from his American lectures.[3] A comment from perhaps the most influential of recent authorities on Indian philosophy, the late Bimal K. Matilal, underscores the significance of such an omission for current investigations of Indian philosophy:

> A considerable portion of Indian philosophy consists of a number of rigorous systems which are more concerned with logic and epistemology, than they are with transcendent states of euphoria. Verifications and rational procedures are as much an essential part of Indian philosophical thinking as they are in Western philosophical thinking. Thus, neglect of the study of Indian philosophy in modern philosophical circles is obviously self-perpetuating, for no one but the analytical philosophers will ever be able to recognize and make known in Western languages the counterpart to their own discipline.[4]

This is, perhaps, simply to affirm the regrettable but banal truth that Indologists have often been confused about the nature of philosophy, while philosophers generally can't read Sanskrit. Despite this, however, some Indologists of Zimmer's generation, and some even earlier, had already made sufficient contributions to the uncovering of India's past traditions in logic and philosophical argument so that, had Zimmer really been interested in this material, he might readily have found substantial resources at his disposal.[5]

Shall we conclude, then, that Zimmer merely used the term "philosophy" in the casual manner that non-philosophers are often wont to do, being either ignorant of or willfully ignoring the concerns of those who regard philosophy to be their proper domain? Perhaps Zimmer thought of philosophy in the way that I did when, as a nineteen-year-old student (who had read some Zimmer), I arrived in India for the first time and was delighted to discover that everyone I met—the *rickshaw-wālā,* the *pānwālā,* the *dhobī,* no less than the *sādhu* or the *paṇḍit*—was a *philosopher.* What I meant then was that almost everyone I spoke with seemed ready and able to express a complete worldview that could be regarded as providing a fully coherent explanation of everything: "This whole world is the gift of Maheśvara," "Brahman is everywhere, in every creature," "No one escapes the fruit of karma," or what have you. It is not my intention now to disparage these and similar adages, or those who pronounce them: such affirmations might well serve as the conclusions to or the points of departure for philosophical

figure 6. Śakti in action: Durgā slaying the buffalo-demon. Cave 21, Ellora, Maharashtra. Eighth century.

reflection. But they do not of themselves constitute philosophical reflection. Philosophy happens when we ask, for instance, just what is explained and how exactly the account that is offered serves to explain it, and whether or not the explanation is as coherent as its proponent affirms it to be.

Zimmer, to be sure, was not interested in one-line affirmations, either. He was primarily concerned with the delineation of worldviews, however, rather than with the rational arguments advanced in connection with them. And he was profoundly concerned with the possibilities for human transformation disclosed in connection with the great worldviews of ancient India. Between Zimmer the philosopher and the philosophical *pānwālā,* then, the difference lies at least partially in the degree to which they elaborate their accounts, and the erudition with which they do so. Still, some would certainly hold, and not without justification, that Zimmer's *Philosophies of India* comes close to exemplifying precisely what Bimal Matilal had in mind when he wrote:

> The mass of publications which purport to be about "Indian philosophy," generally written by people who are totally unqualified in the discipline and which earns the boredom and annoyance of the professional philosopher, requires a little further comment: "Indian philosophy" has unfortunately come to denote a group of occult religious cults, a system of dogmas, and an odd assortment of spirituality, mysticism, and imprecise thinking, concerned almost exclusively with "spiritual liberation." Books, pamphlets, and other materials dealing with this theme are quite considerable in number and unfortunately too easily available.[6]

That *Philosophies of India* was one of the books Matilal may have had in mind here is, perhaps, clear from Zimmer's own contention that, "Our academic secular philosophies are concerned rather with information than with that redemptive transformation which our souls require. And this is the reason why a glance at the face of India may assist us to discover and recover something of ourselves."[7]

To the view that Zimmer the philosopher was really a genial non-philosopher dabbling in a field about which he was largely ignorant, however, there is one important objection: Zimmer in fact knew quite a lot of philosophy. A philosophical layman, to be sure, he was nevertheless broadly conversant with Western philosophical traditions in general, and particularly knowledgeable about nineteenth-century German philosophy, so that his relationship with academic philosophy must be regarded as a considered one, rather than as the product of sheer ignorance and misinformation. He was well aware of the tension between normative academic notions of philosophy and what he referred to as "Indian philosophy," a problem he introduces in *Philosophies of India* with these words:

> Many remained reluctant, even in the first years of the present century, to confer on Hindu thought the dignifying title "philosophy." "Philosophy," they claimed, was a Greek term, denoting something unique and particularly noble, which had sprung into existence among the Greeks and had been carried on only by Western civilization. To support this contention, they could refer to the authority of the giant Hegel, who, a full century before them...had discussed India and China in his *Philosophy of Religion* and *Philosophy of History*... Hegel's argument—and it is still the argument of those who entertain the old reluctance to confer the title "philosopher" upon the immortal thinkers of India and China—is that something is missing from the Oriental systems. When they are compared with Western philosophy, as developed in antiquity and in modern times, what is obviously lacking is the ever renewed, fructifying close contact with the progressive sciences—their improving critical methods and their increasingly secular, non-theological, practically antireligious, outlook on man and the world. This is enough, we are asked to agree, to justify the Western restriction of its classical term.
>
> Here, it must be admitted, the Old Guard are quite correct.[8]

This is not entirely unobjectionable: one may point to the influence of increased mathematical and astronomical knowledge during the Hellenistic period on Indian cosmological speculation, or that of medicine on yogic physiological conceptions, or to the many relationships between the Vedic ritual and the sciences to whose rise it contributed, notably geometry and linguistics.[9] Nevertheless, despite such evidence as we do find in India of the mutual relationship between scientific thought and philosophical and religious speculation, it remains true that the sustained scientific orientation of much of Western philosophy, particularly after the Renaissance (when science and academic philosophy became increasingly allied in their antagonism to church dogmatics), sets it in apparently sharp contrast with much of the Indian tradition. It is only when we recall, however, that profoundly non-scientific and even anti-scientific movements have continued to emerge under the aegis of modern Western philosophy, that Zimmer's intention at last comes clear: in contrast to recent apologists for the technical dimensions of classical Indian thought, he is engaged in a polemical assault on scientism, the tendency of much of modern Western thought to eliminate from its purview all that cannot be reduced to modes of explanation derived from the natural sciences. Zimmer's approach to "Indian philosophy" is precisely conceived so as to underscore difference, and in so doing to affirm the romantic humanism that he regarded as the proper source of authentically human values, which he thought had been largely lost to the contemporary Western scientific outlook. His fundamental standpoint is confirmed by many other passages:

> Western philosophy has become the guardian angel of right (i.e., unprejudiced, critical) thinking. It has earned this position through its repeated contacts with, and unwavering loyalty to, the progressive methods of thought in the sciences. And it will support its champion even though the end may be the destruction of all traditional values whatsoever, in society, religion, and philosophy.[10]

That Zimmer's distaste for the elevation of scientific and technical virtuosity above all else was a determining feature of his intellectual orientation generally is firmly established by his own revealing autobiographical remarks. Recollecting his student days, he writes that:

> My teacher in Sanskrit, Heinrich Lueders, was an arch-craftsman in philology, in deciphering manuscripts, inscriptions, a skilled super-mechanic, one of the past masters of philological craft in the field of Indic studies. But he was not interested in Indian thought, a plain liberal citizen from the republic of Luebeck, anti-philosophic, indifferent to mysticism, and with a meager sense for artistic qualities and implications. I was brought up on a wholesome diet of stones instead of bread.[11]

And, a few pages later, again referring to Lueders, he adds: "When I awakened to my own capabilities, in 1924/5, in writing *Kunstform und Yoga im indischen Kunstbild,* I simply swept him overboard."[12]

Zimmer's pairing of "anti-philosophic" and "indifferent to mysticism" here is particularly illuminating: for Zimmer, "philosophy" in its true sense was not primarily academic philosophy at all; it was, rather, what is sometimes now referred to as "transformative philosophy"; that is, those movements in thought that have emphasized above all the capacity of humankind for liberative spiritual transformation. "Transformative philosophy" is concerned with the spiritual condition of the person as a whole, and in this respect overlaps with certain of the varied tendencies in nineteenth-century thought that have been called *Lebensphilosophie,* "philosophies of life." The philosophers whom Zimmer most admired—Schopenhauer, Nietzsche, Dilthey, Deussen—are among the foremost of the "life philosophers."

If we are to form now a clear conception of the most philosophically suggestive elements of Zimmer's thought, especially in relation to the philosophies of life, we would do better to turn from the college lecture series represented by *Philosophies of India* to the work in which, by Zimmer's own account, his personal approach to the study of ancient India first crystallized: *Artistic Form and Yoga in the Sacred Images of India.* This deeply personal monograph, though not a work of philosophy, is nonetheless remarkably evocative from a philosophical perspective: the reflections on interpretation, aesthetics, and tantric thought that are found within it remain, for the most part, vital even today. Indeed, it is perhaps only now, with the recent interest among students of India in interpretation theory and in tantricism, that an appropriate readership for Zimmer's masterwork has emerged.

Experience and Understanding in the Study of Indian Art

That Zimmer was familiar with Wilhelm Dilthey (1833–1911) is certain.[13] It is very difficult, however, to establish the direct impact of Dilthey's thought on Zimmer, and so it is perhaps better to speak here of some of those areas in which Zimmer's intellectual concerns seem at least to have resonated with Dilthey's, leaving the question of direct influence to one side. Seen in this manner, an affinity with Dilthey is apparent throughout Zimmer's *Artistic Form and Yoga,* a book that is paradigmatically an essay in interpretation. Though Zimmer does not attempt to set out a systematic theory of interpretation at any point, *Artistic Form and Yoga* provides us with ample evidence regarding some of the key assumptions that Zimmer made about hermeneutical practice.

Dilthey was one of the leading proponents of the life philosophies in nineteenth-century Germany. The characteristic orientation of these thinkers finds its clearest expression in the concept of *Erlebnis,* "lived experience," which they held to form the ground for all acts of expression, understanding, and interpretation. It is his emphasis on *Erlebnis* that constitutes one of Dilthey's greatest contributions to the phenomenology of Edmund Husserl (1859–1938) and his successors, and that gives to Dilthey's own thought an unmistakably phenomenological cast. In the same vein, it is the lived experience of the work of art that provides Zimmer with the point of departure for his interpretive investigations:

> The classical work of art directs its appeal to our eye, promising us a glimpse of the infinite if our gaze does but follow its mysterious, beckoning call; we still have to ask where the appeal of Indian sculpture is directed—it is certainly not directed to our inquisitive eye. For the Indian figures refuse to take notice of us or to make eye contact with us that, once established, might then guide our eye over their richness of forms. Classical art appeals to our eye and to our eye alone. Anyone brought under its spell is physically galvanized, transformed into pure sight. With Indian sculpture, we circle about in vague disquiet; it does not look at us, and in vain do we try to capture its gaze.[14]

The experience of the Western eye first encountering Indian sculpture is one of disquiet, disclosing that we do not yet know how to see what ostensibly stands within our gaze. Moved by this same disconcerting experience, Zimmer asks what the Indian tradition itself tells us of its sacred images. He finds an answer in the artistic prescriptions of the *purāṇas* and *tantras,* the devotional and esoteric texts that had been almost systematically avoided by nineteenth-century Indologists, who saw in these works merely endless perversions of fantasy and moral corruption. For Zimmer, however, these puzzling documents provide the keys permitting us to undertake a sympathetic and imaginative reconstruction of the Hindu ritual experience. We cannot emphasize too much that for Zimmer this reconstruction was inevitably an original act of intellectual interpretation; for he was disdainful of Western attempts to assimilate Eastern wisdom through any of the various forms of spiritualism or theosophy that emerged during the late nineteenth and early twentieth centuries and that sought an immediate intuition of, or communion with, the enlightenment of "the East." In Dilthey's terms, I think that Zimmer would have said that it is impossible for us simply to shed the preunderstanding that is the inheritance of our Western classical background; this preunderstanding *must* be the point of departure for our encounter with Indian art and religion.

The imaginative construction of the ritual practice, or *sādhana,* reveals the art object to express the unfolding of an inner vision in which the divine discloses itself. As such, the art object at once reflects the lived experience of the visionary and the purely transcendent nature of divinity, which may unfold in an inner vision but can never be considered to be an invention thereof. Dilthey, concerned as he was with the interpretation of Western art, emphasized that the art object was an expression of lived experience, but seems to have placed less stress on its transcendent character. For Zimmer, however, the lived experience that gave rise to the Indian work of art as its expression was paradigmatically *ritual experience,* while the deity whose radiant presence was disclosed therein belonged in its proper nature to a domain beyond any possible experience. Hence, the lived experience of Indian art was, for Zimmer, necessarily self-transcending.

The ritual function of the sacred image relates it immediately to functionally similar objects, and so, Zimmer insists, it should be studied together with the other sorts of schematic disclosures of the divine order, especially the Buddhist *maṇḍalas* and Hindu linear *yantras,* which had frequently been categorized in the West as quite apart from works of art.[15] By arguing that the sacred image, ritual manual, and *yantra* diagram stand in a clear relationship both to one another and to the transformative inner vision that is mediated through them, however, Zimmer is not just reshuffling a pack of Indological cards drawn at random. Rather, he wishes us to enter into an understanding of a *part* of the Indian experience of the sacred by endeavoring to comprehend the *whole.* In this his strategy reflects Dilthey's difficult conception of the role of the part-whole relationship in the interpretive act: only our understanding of the whole can disclose the significance of the part, while our grasp of the part must inform our understanding of the whole—understanding *(Verstehen)* irreducibly involves this circularity. And for evidence about what the whole might be like in the case of the complex formed by Indian sacred art, ritual, and literature, Zimmer rightly turned to the most comprehensive self-disclosures of the tradition itself, primarily the tantras.

Nevertheless, we must add that Zimmer's approach to interpretation, like Dilthey's, seems markedly positivistic when judged from a contemporary perspective: we may aspire, in Zimmer's world, to something approximating "correct" understanding, as he suggests by referring, for instance, to "the true essence of Indian art." Likewise, interpretation, for Dilthey, should arrive at something rather like objective truth. It has recently been fashionable to castigate such a view as being very obviously wrong. Against the fashionable assumption of the times, which in certain of its cruder expressions seems obviously to be self-refuting, the better corrective to the residual positivism of a Dilthey or a Zimmer is to maintain that although "correctness" of interpretation is seldom, if ever, uniquely determined, this still leaves room for determinations of incorrect interpretation: *mis*understanding is an ever-present possibility.[16] "Correctness" in this context is more like finding one's way into the right ballpark than it is like drawing the sole winning number in a game of chance. We may therefore reject Zimmer's tendency to adopt positivistic diction, while preserving much of his general orientation.

Zimmer's experiment in the interpretation of Indian sacred art was dependent throughout on his study of tantricism, an area that yielded some of his richest insights: in point of fact, this was the ballpark in which he chose to play out the game of interpretation. Accordingly, it is to this aspect of Zimmer's thought that we now turn.

Schopenhauer's Śakti

The Western philosopher in whose work Zimmer seems to have sustained the deepest genuine interest was Arthur Schopenhauer (1788–1860). Schopenhauer's peregrinations in Indian thought, and in the Upaniṣads above all, are well known, as are his famous comparisons of his own doctrines of the world-as-representation to the Vedāntic notion of the veil of *māyā* and of the extinction of the will to the Buddhist conception of nirvāṇa. Less well known, at least among English-speaking philosophers, is the remarkable impact of Schopenhauer's thought on the study of Indian thought and culture during the late nineteenth and early twentieth centuries, particularly in Germany. The Indologist and historian of philosophy Paul Deussen may be counted chief among the heirs to Schopenhauer's legacy here, and as we thumb through the pages of the *Jahrbuch der Schopenhauer-Gesellschaft,* we discover that Indological contributions are found there in remarkable numbers. Small wonder, then, that an early twentieth-century German Indologist, particularly one who was inclined to emphasize the primacy of lived experience, should have shown more than casual interest in Schopenhauer.

Zimmer's interest, however, was much more than casual, and he enjoyed a reputation as a Schopenhauer scholar in his own right, contributing, for example, the standard biographical summary of Schopenhauer to *Die*

Grossen Deutschen: Deutsche Biographie.[17] Nevertheless, his articles on Schopenhauer are really no more philosophical (at least in the "strict and technical" sense) than are his Indological writings, and may be best considered as contributions to the history of ideas.

Although Schopenhauer felt that he had identified several important affinities between his own philosophy and classical Indian thought, one issue that long perplexed him was the relationship between his concept of the will and its possible Indian antecedents. For some time, he entertained the idea that the notion of *brahman,* the cosmic principle in which subject-object distinctions vanish, was the closest analogue.[18] The will, for Schopenhauer, is the sole instance of what Kant had termed the "thing-in-itself" *(Ding-an-sich),* and in this respect it stands outside of all spatial and temporal determinations:

> The *will* as a thing in itself is quite different from its phenomenal appearance, and entirely free from all the forms of the phenomenal, into which it first passes when it manifests itself, and which therefore only concern its *objectivity,* and are foreign to the will itself. Even the most universal form of all ideas, that of being an object to a subject, does not concern it; still less the forms which are subordinate to this and which collectively have their common expression in the principle of sufficient reason, to which we know that time and space belong, and consequently multiplicity also, which exists and is possible only through these.[19]

The will as thing-in-itself, then, is free from all the characteristics of phenomenal existence, even one so apparently primary as the distinction of subject and object. Objectively, however, the will determines our experience in all of its phenomenal aspects. In this respect, it is eminently knowable:

> The word *will,* which, like a magic spell, discloses to us the inmost being of everything in nature, is by no means an unknown quantity, something arrived at only by inference, but is fully and immediately comprehended, and is so familiar to us that we know and understand that will is far better than anything else whatever.[20]

This is so because whenever we reflect upon ourselves, we find that the will proclaims its presence in our desires, motivations, inclinations, and so on, of whatever kind. Our introspective knowledge of the nature of the will and of the ultimacy of its dictates permits us to detect its handiwork elsewhere as well:

> [Whoever] will recognize this will of which we are speaking not only in those phenomenal existences which exactly resemble his own, in men and animals as their inmost nature, but the course of reflection will lead him to recognize the force which germinates and vegetates in the plant, and indeed the force through which the crystal is formed, that by which the magnet turns to the north pole.... all these, I say, he will recognize as different only in their phenomenal existence, but in their inner nature as identical, as that which is directly known to him so intimately and so much better than anything else, and which in its most distinct manifestation is called *will*.... It is the inmost nature, the kernel of every particular thing, and also of the whole. It appears in every blind force of nature and also in the preconsidered action of man; and the great difference between these two is merely in the degree of the manifestation, not in the nature of what manifests itself.[21]

Let us return now to Zimmer, whose vision of tantric religion had as its focal point the notion of *śakti,* which he defined in these terms:

> The central concept of tantric ideology is Śakti. Energy is held to be the essence of the world. Each personification of the Divine is seen as only one of the forms energy elects in order to make itself manifest. Eternal, divine Śakti divides itself into countless individual personifications of the Divine. But each divine personification, itself a manifestation of Śakti, develops Śakti further into a series of aspects that we may call its own *śaktis.* The idea of Śakti therefore frees the grand figures of the Hindu pantheon both from their autonomy as individuals and from their contentious rivalry with one another as a group, reducing them to the elemental concept they always had in common: to their very self, to divine energy. Śakti is the substance of the Divine; the diverse shapes it assumes are but apparitions—aspects of Śakti. The emergence of the idea of Śakti puts an end to a prolonged, ancient struggle for preeminence and sole authority among the separate ways we conceive of the Divine; no one of them emerges

figure 7. A dancing yoginī. Hirapur Temple, Orissa. Ninth century.

victorious from the conflict of sects and cults. Even though these ways vary in representing the richness of divine power and glory, they are of equal rank because each and every one, as a mere manifestation of the Divine, is subordinate to that idea ultimately constituting its divine nature: to Śakti, to divine energy.[22]

Further:

> Within the several, duller levels of our consciousness of the phenomenal world's many differentiations, *śakti* realizes itself above all in the consciousness of the individual human soul, in *jīva.* But since nothing can exist apart from this divine spiritual energy, the lower worlds of animals and plants—even mountains and rocks—are simply stages of the unfolding of the one single *Śakti* into which, in play, it divided to form the duality of consciousness. Their lack of spirituality, their insensate nature exist only as opposites to the dimly lit spirituality of human consciousness; bound to this consciousness by its own *māyā,* the spiritual, that energy, does not know itself as the Universal One.[23]

It is primarily in his emphasis on "the Divine" that Zimmer's formulation departs notably from Schopenhauer's.

Was Zimmer himself conscious that he had posited Schopenhauer's missing analogue? It is impossible to answer this with assurance on the basis of the passages cited above from *Artistic Form and Yoga,* but in a later article he himself underscored the connection:

> Was Schopenhauer den "Willen" nannte, heisst in Indien "shakti," d.i. "Kraft." ["What Schopenhauer termed 'Will,' is called 'shakti' in India, that is to say, 'power.'"][24]

We should note, however, that Zimmer's conception of *śakti* departed from Schopenhauer's doctrine of the will in at least one very striking respect. Whereas Schopenhauer regarded *eros* to be the unadulterated expression of will, from whose painful grasp freedom was to be realized only by the extinction of the will in what he took to be nirvāṇa, Zimmer saw the tantras as overcoming the explicit dualism of any such formulation:

> Everything in the world is Śiva and Śakti: in the sexual union of the spouses, the polar tension of the Divine's duality collapses into oneness; in this union, human consciousness crosses the borders of its isolation and enters a realm beyond polarities, to the point where it dissolves its polar nature—it becomes *nir-dvandva.* Eroticism in marriage is one means to the experiencing of one's own godlike nature, where the distinction between I and Thou

disappears, where the world falls away, where pain and desire and all the other polar opposites are transcended *(aufgehoben).*[25]

Zimmer was well aware of the persistent disparagement of the tantras in European academic circles, the tendency to see within them only the jumbled and incoherent fantasies said to be symptomatic of the corruption and degeneracy of later medieval Indian culture and religion. To his lasting credit as an interpreter of India, Zimmer recognized there to be much more to the story than that: the tantras in fact embody a system, a distinctive way of thought, that succeeds in resolving many of the tensions inherent in earlier Indian thought, and that informs Indian culture, especially its art and ritual, throughout. And in perceiving an affinity between the Hindu tantric concept of *śakti* and Schopenhauer's *Wille,* Zimmer became perhaps the first Western thinker to suggest the possibility of comparative philosophical reflection with respect to the tantras. One wonders, however, whether Zimmer's comparative insight could be profitably developed in an age to which Schopenhauer no longer speaks. Perhaps, then, it was for the best that in *Artistic Form and Yoga* the connection was left unspoken.

Philosophies of India will continue to be widely read, for it is an entertaining, though dated and now (about many matters) unfashionable, introduction to the world of ancient Indian religious thought.[26] To the study of Indian philosophy, however, Zimmer's enduring contribution is undoubtably *Artistic Form and Yoga.* The peculiar questions that Zimmer raises there, and the peculiar approach he adopts in seeking to resolve them, merit the continuing consideration of students of Indian art and esotericism, but equally the reflections of the philosophers.

Notes

1 Zimmer 1969 (originally published by the Bollingen Foundation in 1951). Like Zimmer, Durant also started out as a Schopenhauerian. I do not wish to suggest, however, that there were deep similarities between the two: Zimmer's vision of the transformative value of Indian spirituality is essentially at odds with Durant's insistence that "the story of civilization" is in most significant respects a Western tale.

2 Zimmer 1969: 605–14. A question that is raised throughout recent discussions of Zimmer is: how intrusive was Campbell as an editor? (See Case 1994). In connection with *Philosophies of India,* I believe that Campbell's "Editor's Foreword"

(pp. v–vii) can be regarded as a substantially reliable guide to his admirably restrained editorial contribution. This conclusion is supported by the comparison of *Philosophies* with those among Zimmer's German works that offer the clearest precedents for it, chiefly *Indische Sphären* (Zimmer 1963). Cf. also the descriptions of the lecture courses from which *Philosophies* was derived—Indo-Iranian u126 and Indian Philosophy u128—listed in the *Columbia University Bulletin of Information,* Forty-first Series, No. 35 (August 9, 1941), p. 129, and Forty-second Series, No. 31 (July 11, 1942): what we find here is a course outline essentially similar to the plan of *Philosophies,* and similarly omitting any reference to the traditions of Indian logic. I am grateful to John Hawley for having taken the trouble to locate these artifacts of semesters long past.

3 The best bibliographical survey is the "Selected Bibliography of Zimmer's Works," in Zimmer 1984: 261–67.

4 Matilal 1971: 11–12.

5 This is not the place to offer a bibliographical review of nineteenth- and early twentieth-century investigations of Indian logic and related matters. Among those whose works Zimmer should have encountered at one point or another, however, we might mention E. B. Cowell, Surendranath Dasgupta, B. Faddegon, Ganganatha Jha, Hermann Jacobi, A. B. Keith, H. N. Randle, Stanislaus Schayer, Theodore Stcherbatsky, and Giuseppe Tucci.

6 Matilal 1971: 10.

7 Zimmer 1969: 14.

8 Zimmer 1969: 29–30. Cf. Heidegger 1958: 35: "the name 'philosophy' summons us into the history of the Greek origin of philosophy." Heidegger, however, was not concerned simply to denote "something unique and particularly noble," as were the Hegelians to whom both he and Zimmer are alluding. Heidegger's concern, rather, was to point to the profoundly problematic nature of the historical phenomenon called 'philosophy,' and in this he and Zimmer would have found themselves, to some extent at least, in agreement. Refer to the introduction and chap. 8 of the present volume.

9 On relations between religion and science in ancient India, see, for instance, Staal 1982, and Zysk 1991.

10 Zimmer 1969: 31.

11 Zimmer 1984: 247.

12 Zimmer 1984: 249.

13 See Zimmer 1969: 28, 64.

14 Zimmer 1984: 11.

15 Zimmer's treatment of esoteric Buddhism generally leaves much to be desired: like other scholars of his generation, he simply assumed that later Indian Buddhism dissolved back into Hinduism, almost completely losing its own identity in the process. Despite this, Zimmer's remarks on esoteric Buddhism do show frequent flashes of insight that speak for his interpretive genius and independence of thought. One small but telling example: his recognition of the significance of Avalokiteśvara's mantra—*Oṃ Maṇipadme Hūṃ*—against the

long-held (and unfortunately still current) canard that this means "Hail to the Jewel in the Lotus!" The comparative analysis of Tantric mantras and the Tibetan Buddhist commentarial tradition both support Zimmer's contention (1984: 209) that *Maṇipadme* is in fact a feminine vocative meaning "O holder of the jewel and lotus!"—which are, indeed, the attributes held by Avalokiteśvara. The "jewel in the lotus" error appears to originate only in late nineteenth-century British scholarship. On this, see Lopez 1998, chap. 4.

16 The example of the "jewel in the lotus," mentioned in the preceding note, nicely illustrates the manner in which some misinterpretations do take on a life of their own, becoming virtually unchallenged in the process. Much of the study of Tantrism in fact seems to be characterized by established misunderstanding in just this way.

17 Zimmer 1936.

18 A judicious survey of Schopenhauer's relation with Indian thought, as understood in Europe during his lifetime, will be found in Halbfass 1988: 105–20.

19 Schopenhauer 1883, book 2, section 23. For an excellent recent assessment of Schopenhauer's doctrine of the will, and of his philosophy generally, see Hamlyn 1980.

20 Schopenhauer 1883, book 2, section 22.

21 Schopenhauer 1883, book 2, section 21.

22 Zimmer 1984: 153.

23 Zimmer 1984: 25.

24 Zimmer 1938: 270. Generally speaking, Zimmer's understanding of *śakti,* as of tantric thought generally, was profoundly indebted to the work of Sir John Woodroffe (Arthur Avalon), a debt that Zimmer gratefully acknowledged, e.g., in his autobiographical remarks in Zimmer 1984: 254. Woodroffe even came close to a Schopenhauerian formulation in the title of his collection of essays, *The World as Power* (1966), but, so far as I have been able to determine to date, never made this allusion explicit.

25 Zimmer 1984: 214.

26 One aspect of *Philosophies of India* strikes me as being profoundly problematic, in particular. This is Zimmer's much flaunted notion of an "Aryan-Dravidian synthesis." Zimmer seems to have harbored the view, popular during the nineteenth century (and made into a party dogma by the National Socialists, whom Zimmer detested), that different racial lines were rather strictly correlated with systems of belief. Thus, the history of ideas could be regarded as a story about the intermingling and dividing of human races. That Zimmer thought in these terms persistently, though perhaps without clearly thinking through the implications, may be seen in his autobiographical notes, Zimmer 1984: 253: "On her father's side [Zimmer's mother] was of German-Saxon extraction.... Her mother...was of Wendish stock.... This Saxon-Wendish stock is inclined to mysticism, as are kindred folk in Silesia.... This may account for my predilection for mysticism, myths, and symbols, while the Pre-German, Pre-Celtic, Pre-Aryan descent of my father from the ancient European matriarchal civilization

explains my penchant for the corresponding stratifications in ancient Pre-Aryan Hindu civilization (the Great Mother, the feminine principle in Tantrism)." (!) In fact, Zimmer probably inherited this nonsense directly from his father, also named Heinrich Zimmer (1851–1910), on whose own application of racialist theories to India, see Inden 1990: 178.

IV DOCTRINAL INTERPRETATION IN TIBET

12. From Kun-mkhyen Dol-po-pa to 'Ba'-mda' Dge-legs: Three Jo-nang-pa Masters on the Interpretation of the *Prajñāpāramitā*

I

IN AN OFT-CITED PASSAGE, the *Sandhinirmocanasūtra (The Sūtra That Sets Free [the Buddha's] Intention)* argues that the second turn of the wheel of the doctrine was provisional and surpassed, while the third and final turn alone was definitive and unsurpassed.[1] The paradigmatic sūtras of the second turn are generally thought to be those of the Prajñāpāramitā (Perfection of Wisdom) and the most authoritative commentaries on their intention to be the Madhyamaka writings of Nāgārjuna. However, along with those who would oppose his teaching, Dol-po-pa Shes-rab-rgyal-mtshan (1292–1361), the great proponent of the distinctively Jo-nang-pa doctrine of extrinsic emptiness *(gzhan-stong)*, clearly regarded the Prajñāpāramitā teachings to be in some sense definitive too. We may ask, then, how Dol-po-pa sought to resolve the apparent hermeneutical conflicts to which his position gave rise. This question, certainly, is of some importance: Tsong-kha-pa's decisive rejection of Dol-po-pa's approach to interpretation, and the formation of the Dge-lugs-pa commentarial tradition as one in many respects diametrically opposed to the Jo-nang-pa, are among the issues that must be related directly to it.[2]

Dol-po-pa, though perhaps in some respects an eccentric interpreter, was not so overwhelmed by his own vision that he lost sight of the foremost objections that might be raised against it. Scattered throughout his writings are hints about how he thought these were to be met; on the question of the interpretation of the second turn of the wheel, for example, a comment responding precisely to the line of criticism that Tsong-kha-pa would later refine and defend is found in his most famous work, the *Ri chos nges don rgya mtsho (Teachings for Mountain Retreat: The Ocean of Certainty):*

> Some hold the *[Sandhinirmocana]sūtra* to be of provisional meaning, but this is unreasonable, for such has been neither declared [in scripture], nor is it established by reason, and therefore [the sūtra in question] is of definitive meaning and unobjectionable.
>
> It is objected, however, that, because the middle turn is Madhyamaka, and the last Mind Only *(sems tsam, cittamātra),* then it is the middle that remains of definitive meaning, while the last remains provisional.
>
> But this is most exceedingly unreasonable, because there is neither scriptural authority nor reason [establishing] the final turn to be the proper canon *(rang-gzhung)* of Mind Only, for its teaching surpasses Mind Only, and it teaches the culminating significance of the Great Madhyamaka, and teaches [this] in accord with the culminating significance of the Vajrayāna. (*Dol-po-pa*, vol. 2, p. 228, l. 3f.; *Ri-chos*, p. 177, l. 3 f.)

It is clear why some such maneuver appealed to Dol-po-pa and other Tibetan proponents of similar positions; for sūtras typically considered paradigmatic of the third turn of the wheel, e.g., the *Laṅkāvatāra* and the *Gaṇḍavyūha*, do indeed teach much that surpasses Mind Only, at least given a relatively restricted doxographic perspective on that philosophical school. Indeed, these sūtras are not infrequently cited as authorities by such major teachers of the Madhyamaka as Candrakīrti and Śāntideva (and this of course was taken as providing some support for the conception of a "Great Madhyamaka" tradition surpassing the more widely known Madhyamaka philosophical schools, as understood doxographically).[3] Finally, there were many in Tibet who held that the Vajrayāna, the way of mantra, was in crucial respects a "higher" teaching than that of the sūtras, and that the apparent affinities of the Tantras with at least some of the sūtras of the third turn are more pronounced than are their affinities with the sūtras of the middle turn.[4] But where does this leave the Prajñāpāramitā itself? Dol-po-pa's discussion continues:

> The second turn...is not taught to be of provisional meaning and surpassed, etc., for the reason that it teaches Prajñāpāramitā,

> but rather because it teaches that which is not intrinsically empty to be intrinsically empty, and for other such reasons. The Prajñāpāramitā that is unborn, unceasing, primordially pacific, etc., is taught in the third turn and in the Vajrayāna. But it is taught [in these three respective divisions of the teaching] unclearly, clearly and exceedingly clearly...

In short, Dol-po-pa suggests that the Prajñāpāramitā sūtras, in their verbal form, do not always clearly articulate the teaching that is in fact their intention, which he variously characterizes as the teaching of buddha-nature *(tathāgatagarbha, de-bzhin-gshegs-pa'i snying-po),* nondual gnosis *(advaya-jñāna, gnyis-med ye-shes),* the Great Seal *(mahāmudrā, phyag-rgya chen-po),* the absolute thought of enlightenment *(pāramārthikabodhicitta, don-dam-pa'i byang-chub-sems),* etc., as well as that of emptiness *(śūnyatā, stong-pa-nyid),* reality *(dharmatā, chos-nyid),* perfection of wisdom *(prajñāpāramitā, shes-rab-kyi pha-rol-tu phyin-pa),* and so on. Dol-po-pa thus combines the formulation of a qualitative gradation of the teaching with a type of esotericism:[5] the *Kālacakra Tantra,* for instance, is in many respects held to be superior to the *Aṣṭasāhasrikā Prajñāpāramitā,* but their essence is suffused with the same radiant light, which just shines more brightly in the former. And this, he goes on to say,

> is the culminating emptiness-cum-compassion, means-cum-wisdom, which is the coalescent union of bliss and emptiness, the sole savor; and this is also the sole savor of the union of the expanse *(dbyings, dhātu)* and awareness, in which the culminating abiding nature of reality, as noesis and noetic object, is one. Such is the real *(mtshan-nyid-pa)* Prajñāpāramitā, the culmination of the Prajñāpāramitā of the ground and the Prajñāpāramitā of the result, the quiddity of [their] indivisible essence. The path whereby it is disclosed, and the canon which teaches these [topics under discussion], is only conventionally designated *(btags-pa-tsam).*

Dol-po-pa, however, does not only provide us with such general and idealized accounts of the Prajñāpāramitā teaching; his view of Prajñāpāramitā is developed in impressive detail in four major commentaries and several short commentarial notes devoted to the Prajñāpāramitā literature. The most important of these works are a detailed commentary on the *Abhisamayālaṃkāra* (The Ornament of Emergent Realization) and separate commentaries on the *Aṣṭadaśasāhasrikā*, the *Pañcaviṃśatisāhasrikā*, and the *Śatasāhasrikā* (respectively, the Perfection of Wisdom in Eight Thousand, Twenty-five Thousand, and One Hundred Thousand lines).[6] While a preliminary survey of this material suggests that Dol-po-pa generally restrained his inclination to read his philosophy of extrinsic emptiness into these texts, he nevertheless does not hesitate to articulate it when remarking on those passages in which the relative "unclarity" of the Prajñāpāramitā sūtras seems to intimate the "clarity" of the sūtras of the third turn, or the "exceeding clarity" of the Tantras. Thus, in a note on the sixth fascicle of the *Śatasāhasrikā*, he writes:

> The absolute ground of emptiness is extrinsic emptiness, self-emergent pristine cognition, the changeless absolute, *sugatagarbha*, the Great Madhyamaka, the real Prajñāpāramitā and the culminating Secret Mantra... *(Dol-po-pa,* vol. 3, p. 76.)

And elsewhere, in discussing the innate virtue of all dharmas—"which, being insubstantial, are empty, naturally luminous *(rang-bzhin-gyis 'od-gsal-ba, prakṛtiprakāśa)*, and therefore good *(dge-ba, kuśala)*"—Dol-po-pa briefly enumerates the deities of the Kālacakra, Hevajra, and other maṇḍalas, who, like Rūpavajrā ("she who is the adamantine nature of form") are taken to be apotheosized dharmas; for it is precisely the goodness of those dharmas, as disclosed in the Prajñāpāramitā, that is deified in the Tantras *(Dol-po-pa,* vol. 3, p. 277, l. 6f.).

II

We turn now to Rje-btsun Tāranātha (1575–1634), who is best known at present for his *History of Buddhism in India*, and for other historical and hagiographical writings. His work in its full scope, however, deserves to be more widely studied; above all, in my estimation, he should be regarded as one of the greatest contributors in any time, place, or methodological tradition to the study of tantrism and yoga, but this would take us beyond our present concerns.[7] Among the many topics that interested Tāranātha was the interpretation of his predecessor Dol-po-pa's teaching of "extrinsic emptiness" and its ramifications for our understanding of the Prajñāpāramitā. Particularly, given the long-standing interest that the *Heart Sūtra (Prajñāpāramitāhṛdaya Sūtra)* has enjoyed among Western students of Buddhism, his authorship of two commentaries on this short text resonates—whether sympathetically or not remains to be seen—with our own traditions of Buddhological knowledge.[8]

Those familiar with Donald Lopez's recent studies of the *Heart Sūtra* will already have some knowledge of the manner in which later Indian and Dge-lugs-pa commentators handled this text,[9] and will find that the material presented there may conveniently be compared with Tāranātha's glosses. To exemplify the latter in brief, let us consider Tāranātha's remarks on the familiar words near the sūtra's beginning:

> At that time, indeed, the Lord was absorbed in the samādhi called "Profound Illumination." And at that time, Āryāvalokiteśvara, a bodhisattva and mahāsattva, setting his course in the profound Prajñāpāramitā, thus caught a glimpse; he caught a glimpse of the five *skandhas* as empty of substance.[10]

Tāranātha's comment is as follows:

> "At that time, the Lord..." etc. It is "profound," because difficult to realize, namely, the abiding nature, Prajñāpāramitā. The pure cognition that realizes it as evident is "Illumination," which has the sense of an actual seeing. The absorption that is endowed with that pure cognition is samādhi, and the Lord is perpetually absorbed in that samādhi. Nevertheless, from the perspective of the disciples who are gathered there, it appears as if he became newly absorbed in that samādhi of Profound Illumination. Again, as soon as the Lord has become thus absorbed, Āryāvalokiteśvara, a bodhisattva and mahāsattva, catches a glimpse of an absorption that is connected with samādhi, the pure cognition whose course is the evident realization of the profound Prajñāpāramitā, and so abides in [that] noetic pure cognition. And through pure cognition he catches a glimpse of and meditatively cultivates the basis for an actual course in such Prajñāpāramitā, namely, [the realization] that the five *skandhas* are not established, and so empty, with respect to substantial essence. Because the five *skandhas'* substantial emptiness is taught [here] besides the profound Prajñāpāramitā, that establishes that the profound Prajñāpāramitā is not empty of its own essence; wherefore this is the first phrase [within the *Heart Sūtra*] expressly

> teaching the Madhyamaka of extrinsic emptiness. (*Tāranātha,* vol. 18, pp. 809–10.)

In other words, Prajñāpāramitā is the cognition that realizes the emptiness of the *skandhas,* but is not itself that emptiness. Thus, it is not intrinsically empty *(rang stong)* but only so in a relative, extrinsically empty *(gzhan stong)* sense, since it realizes the emptiness of the *skandhas.* The underlying message of the *Heart Sūtra* is thus taken to be an affirmation of the Jo-nang-pa teaching.

Now, we may ask, just what bearing does this have on the questions raised earlier regarding the interpretation of the second and final turns of the wheel? Tāranātha himself raises this as a brief afterword following the conclusion of the sūtra itself:

> Some may object, saying, "if this profound sūtra belongs among the sūtras of the middle turn, it's not right [to assert] that it teaches the Madhyamaka of extrinsic emptiness," or "if it does teach that, then there's no distinction of relative profundity between the middle and final turns." If such [objectors] do arrive, here's what you should tell them: the intention of all three turns is the Madhyamaka of extrinsic emptiness *(dbu ma gzhan stong).* Even in the first and middle turns there are occasionally phrases that teach [it] literally and clearly. In the [final] turn, which definitively ascertains the absolute, it is much more clear and extensive than in either the first or middle, and is disclosed there without concealment, and taught expansively. Thus, among the three turns there arise qualitative distinctions, while at the same time there is a single intention; so the two faults [mentioned above] do not apply. (*Tāranātha,* vol. 18, pp. 826 and 829.)

Thus, Tāranātha concludes by explicitly affirming precisely the hermeneutical strategies—namely, appeals to the hierarchical ordering of the teaching and to esotericism—that had been earlier employed by Dol-po-pa.

III

As is well known, the Jo-nang-pa school was effectively banned in Central and Western Tibet during the mid-seventeenth century, retaining there only one nuns' convent.[11] Sometime following the ban, the writings of both Dol-po-pa and Tāranātha were placed under seal, though it is not yet clear exactly when this occurred, and the "extrinsic emptiness" teaching was effectively anathematized. Much oral tradition, at least, maintains that the Sgo-mang College of 'Bras-spungs Monastery played a particularly active role in the move for what its hierarchy regarded as necessary doctrinal rectification. Sgo-mang itself adhered to the commentarial tradition of 'Jam-dbyangs-bzhad-pa (1648–1722), the founder of Bla-brang monastery in Amdo (now Gansu), in relatively close proximity to what are today the Jo-nang-pa strongholds of 'Dzam-thang and Rnga-khog.[12] 'Jam-dbyangs-bzhad-pa had vigorously criticized the extrinsic emptiness doctrine of the Jo-nang-pa,[13] and popular lore sometimes regards him to have been a major instigator of the sealing of the books. Indeed, the polemical attack on the Jo-nang-pa was continued by his successors at Bla-brang, notably Gung-thang Dkon-mchog-bstan-pa'i-sgron-me (1762–1823).[14] We have no evidence, however, that the Bla-brang hierarchy ever sought the actual suppression of the Jo-nang-pa in Amdo. It is important to bear this point in mind in connection with what follows.

While the teaching of extrinsic emptiness was thus effectively suppressed in Central Tibet, and philosophically attacked in Amdo, it was simultaneously revived in the eastern districts of Khams, in regions around the principality of Derge. Both a Karma Bka'-brgyud-pa master, the renowned grammarian Situ Paṇ-chen (1699–1774), and a noted luminary of the Rnying-ma-pa center of Kaḥ-thog, Dge-rtse Paṇḍita 'Gyur-med-tshe-dbang-mchog-sgrub (b. 1764), became philosophical converts and actively promoted the extrinsic emptiness line of interpretation, establishing the basis for much of later Bka'-brgyud-pa and Rnying-ma-pa doctrinal writing in the process. Dge-rtse Paṇḍita, in fact, even came to be regarded as an emanation of Dol-po-pa himself; and the account of the "Great Madhyamaka" found in Dudjom Rinpoche's *Fundamentals*, part 3, is in most respects derived from the work of this master.[15]

In sum, then, by the mid-nineteenth century the Jo-nang-pa found themselves in a relatively secure position in a few districts of Amdo, sandwiched between the vigorous Dge-lugs-pa opponents of their teaching, with their great center of power at Bla-brang to the northeast, and the congenial Bka'-brgyud-pa and Rnying-ma-pa revivers of Jo-nang-pa doctrinal interpretation, whose seats were located to the southwest in the virtually independent principalities of Khams. While I do not wish to advocate historical determinism with respect to commentarial practice here, it will nonetheless be clear, I think, that this peculiar configuration at least contributed to the next phase in the tale.

It was during my travels in Amdo in 1990 that I first heard of 'Ba'-mda' Thub-bstan-dge-legs-rgya-mtsho (1844–1904), a Jo-nang-pa master whose writings play an important role in contemporary Jo-nang-pa monastic education.[16] Indeed, he is one of three authors whose works form the primary basis for the curriculum, the other two, of course, being Dol-po-pa and Tāranātha. The complete biography of this master has not yet, to my knowledge, been published. However, two brief accounts have appeared in recent years that allow us at least to know his career in its general outlines.[17]

A native of 'Ba'-mda', adjacent to Dar-thang in southern Amdo, he was educated in his home district until about his nineteenth year. (The sectarian tradition in which he had his early training appears to have been Jo-nang-pa, though the details remain uncertain.) He then travelled to the Derge district, where he remained when he was in his early twenties. This was during precisely the period in which the activity of the so-called Ris-med ("eclectic" or, sometimes, "universalist") masters was at its height. Among those with whom he studied were two of the most influential of these luminaries, Rdza Dpal-sprul Rin-po-che (1808–87) and Kong-sprul Yon-tan-rgya-mtsho (1813–99). The latter, in particular, transmitted to him his teachings of the "six doctrines of Nāropā" *(Nāro chos-drug),* and this seems to have influenced him very deeply: one full volume (vol. 17) of his collected works is consecrated to these precepts of the Bka'-brgyud tradition, and in later life he established a retreat center in Amdo to perpetuate their practice.[18]

Though he was eager to continue his studies in Khams, an urgent summons from home, the reasons for which remain unclear, impelled him to return.[19] This proved, however, to be in some sense fortunate; for now he became directly affiliated with the nearby Jo-nang-pa center of 'Dzam-thang. Throughout his late twenties and thirties he appears to have been primarily involved in the study and practice of the teachings of the Jo-nang-pa tradition, eventually being called upon to teach in his own right.[20] Towards the end of his life he apparently became rather widely known; the praise Mi-pham is said to have showered upon him became famous among the religious of 'Go-log, where the saying, "the lama from Bamda was more learned than Mipham," assumed almost proverbial status,[21] and he was invited to return to Derge to become a tutor to the young Tā'i Si-tu, an invitation that he declined.[22] His prolific literary activity appears to have been largely the product of his last two decades.[23]

In 1992 I was very fortunate to be able to collect a set of his complete works, in twenty-two large *potis*, containing approximately eleven thousand two-sided folios. This material has proved to be full of surprises, the greatest of which, by far, is this: 'Ba'-mda' Dge-legs adheres, throughout almost all of his scholastic commentarial writing on non-tantric subjects, to the Dge-lugs-pa tradition of Bla-brang. This is rather like finding a French Hegelian who throughout his philosophical writing adheres to the analytic tradition of Princeton. Once I began to gain some sense of their contents, the eleven thousand folios piled high in my office steadily increased my perplexity. Slowly I have begun to piece together an account of 'Ba'-mda' Dge-legs's very unusual brand of eclecticism. This is still very tentative, but for what it is worth I offer a summary here.

'Ba'-mda' Dge-legs's debts to the Bla-brang curriculum are most extensive and obvious in his writings on subjects connected with the staples of a Tibetan monastic doctrinal education, Buddhist epistemology *(pramāṇa, tshad-ma),* Candrakīrti's *Madhyamakāvatāra (The Introduction to the Madhyamaka),* and the *Abhisamayālaṃkāra (The Ornament of Emergent Realization)* being foremost among the topics on which he wrote at length. So far as I have been able to determine—and because the writings of 'Ba'-mda' Dge-legs in the areas just mentioned are massive even by Tibetan standards (two tomes *(po-ti)* on the Tibetan debate logic *(bsdus-grwa)* approach to Pramāṇa (vols. 1–2), two on the *Madhyamakāvatāra* (vols. 9–10), and *seven* on the *Abhisamayālaṃkāra* (vols. 3–8, and 11)), I do not claim to have uncovered every relevant passage yet—his sole concern here was to elaborate a straightforward redaction of the Bla-brang curriculum, without attempting to relate it explicitly to distinctively Jo-nang-pa doctrines. In the opening invocation of his large commentary on the *Abhisamayālaṃkāra,* the *Phar-phyin snang-ba'i rgyan (The Ornament Illuminating the Perfections),* there is only the slenderest hint that he might have any other intention, when he praises Buddha Śākyamuni as "he who has arrived at the supreme transcendence of purity, bliss, and permanence" *('Ba'-mda',* vol. 3, no. 5, p. 2). This alludes to the four Perfections of purity, bliss, permanence and supreme self, taught, for instance, in the Mahāyāna version of the *Mahāparinirvāṇasūtra (Sūtra of the Great Parinirvāṇa).* Dge-lugs-pa interpreters generally regard these as being of provisional significance, while the Jo-nang-pa consider them definitive. Immediately following this one-liner, however, he addresses verses of praise to Tsong-kha-pa and 'Jam-dbyangs-bzhad-pa, so that it is not at all certain that the preceding allusion was intended to carry the weight one might otherwise attribute to it in a Jo-nang-pa context. And in reading the body of the commentary itself, one is impressed by the determination with which he steers clear of the troubled waters of extrinsic emptiness.

Are we, then, entitled to conclude that 'Ba'-mda' Dge-legs was a Jo-nang-pa who simply abandoned his school's most distinctive doctrine without comment? Well, not exactly. Many of his writings on tantric subjects, for instance, reveal a decisively Jo-nang-pa orientation. In his commentary on a rite of guru-devotion *(Guruyogasādhana)* by Dol-po-pa, 'Ba'-mda' adds a revealing annotation to the author's colophon. Dol-po-pa had signed this work tersely, using a favorite pen name: "...composed by Rton-pa-bzhi-ldan," meaning "the one endowed with the four orientations" (*pratisaraṇa,* on which see section 1.4 of the following chapter; *Dol-po-pa,* vol. 7, p. 393). 'Ba'-mda's commentary reads:

> This was declared by the one endowed with the four *pratisaraṇa,* namely, the all-knowing Dol-po-pa Shes-rab-rgyal-mtshan-dpal-bzang-po, who mastered the intention of all sūtras and tantras, and with captivating wisdom, roared with the great lion's battle-cry of the view of the great Madhyamaka, extrinsic emptiness, thus piercing with fear the hearts of wrong-viewing foxes. (*Bla ma'i rnal 'byor byin rlabs char 'bebs zhes bya ba rnam par bshad pa'i khrid yig yid kyi mun sel,* in *'Ba'-mda',* vol. 15, no. 33, p. 536.)

This hardly seems to be the remark of one who was prepared to abandon the *gzhan-stong* teaching in silence.

Now, we have seen earlier that Jo-nang-pa interpretation was committed to a type of esotericism, specifically to the view that the *gzhan-stong* doctrine represented not just the highest philosophical teaching of the Buddha, but also the teaching that was to be found concealed within *all* facets of the Buddha's doctrine, if only one knew how to glimpse it. In playing itself out among Dol-po-pa's Central Tibetan successors, this view had encouraged a tolerant and pluralistic orientation, so that the Jo-nang-pa early on became remarkably eclectic: the best examples of this tendency were no doubt Tāranātha's predecessor Rje-btsun Kun-dga'-grol-mchog (b. 1507)[24] and Tāranātha himself. As Gene Smith once argued, it was this that encouraged 'Jam-mgon Kong-sprul to adopt *gzhan-stong* as the foundation for his own eclectic enterprise during the nineteenth century.[25] What is significant here for our effort to make sense of 'Ba'-mda' Dge-legs (whose master in the Bka'-brgyud tradition was, let us recall, 'Jam-mgon

Kong-sprul) is this: these authors had already backed away from any inclination there may have been to treat the Prāsaṅgika-Mādhyamika line of interpretation that had been adopted by Tsong-kha-pa as "wrong view" *simpliciter*.[26] Rather, they held this to be an inferior, but nevertheless legitimate and propædeutically valuable, approach to Madhyamaka thought, which, once mastered, opened the way to an appropriate engagement in the "Great Madhyamaka," that is, the teaching of extrinsic emptiness. What I wish to propose, then, is this: the nineteenth-century eclectic movement in Khams encouraged some degree of bridge-building among sectarian traditions that, if not positively hostile, had usually been aloof from one another. 'Ba'-mda' Dge-legs, who had strong connections with this movement, appreciated the delicate situation of the Jo-nang-pa in Amdo, and certainly had great respect for the intellectual values refined in the course of a Dge-lugs-pa scholastic education, simply adopted the approach that was already in place for relating the Prāsaṅgika-Mādhyamika tradition to the "Great Madhyamaka" in order to achieve a wholesale appropriation of the Dge-lugs-pa scholastic system for his own lineage. This coup required not that he abandon the *gzhan-stong* teaching, but rather that he treat it as relatively esoteric. Again, turning to his commentarial glosses we find some evidence that this is precisely what was intended.

Among Tāranātha's writings there is a survey of the Bka'-gdams-pa approach to the bodhisattva's path (this was something of a Dge-lugs-pa specialty), and the work is one that well-illustrates Tāranātha's catholicity.[27] He adheres there strictly to the recognized authorities among the early Bka'-gdams-pa—for instance, Atiśa and the first generations of his followers—and avoids importing peculiarly Jo-nang-pa doctrines into that tradition. The closest he ever comes to this is in one brief allusion near the end of the book, where he discusses the achievement of buddhahood as the result of the path:

> On the level of the perfect Buddha, there is the culmination of the virtuous *dhyāna* of the Tathāgata. This fourth *dhyāna* is the pure cognition wherein the *garbha* is realized in direct perception, but that may be known in detail elsewhere. (*Tāranātha,* vol. Tsha (19), p. 440.)

'Ba'-mda' Dge-legs expands these lines as follows in his commentary:

> According to our own tradition, that of the proponents of extrinsic emptiness, in this, the fourth *dhyāna*, that is, the virtuous *dhyāna* of the Tathāgata, the pure cognition that is relative and heteronomous *(kun rdzob gzhan byung gi ye shes)* is destroyed. However, the culmination of the virtuous *dhyāna* of the Tathāgata is the pure cognition in which all aspects of the *sugatagarbha* are altogether perfectly realized in direct perception. This tradition may be known in detail elsewhere, namely, in [Dol-po-pa's] *Ri chos nges don rgya mtsho,* and other works. (*'Ba'-mda',* vol. 12, no. 19, pp. 793, l. 7–794, l. 2.)

Thus, the *gzhan-stong* teaching is taken to pertain in particular to the disclosure of buddhahood, and this warrants the treatment of it as a relatively esoteric doctrine, but certainly not its abandonment.

Mkhan-po Blo-grags's summary of 'Ba'-mda' Dge-legs's life maintains, as noted above, that most of his writings on the Dge-lugs-pa curriculum were mature works, dating from his later years. What is most unclear is just where he gained his exceptional Dge-lugs-pa background. His family seems to have had Jo-nang-pa connections, so that this was likely the tradition in which he received his early schooling.[28] There is some indication that his departure for Khams was motivated initially by a desire to study the five Indian treatises *(gzhung-chen lnga, bka'-pod lnga)* that formed the backbone of the traditional doctrinal curriculum, reflecting a youthful interest in the scholastic writings to whose exegesis he would later contribute abundantly. I have not yet ascertained, however, whether this reflects an early interest in particularly Dge-lugs-pa teaching, or whether instead the Jo-nang-pa in Amdo had traditionally followed the curriculum based upon the five treatises.[29] Most significant, certainly, were 'Ba'-mda' Dge-legs' own belief that he was an emanation of the 'Jam-dbyangs-bzhad-pa, and his repeated visions of this master and of the Thu'u-bkwan Rin-po-che, visions in which he honed his skills in debate.[30] We may propose that his later Dge-lugs–Jo-nang eclecticism was impelled in part by a desire to reconcile this conviction with his Jo-nang-pa training, as much as by an appreciation of the curricular value of Dge-lugs-pa schooling, for there are some suggestions that he sought to situate this material in the Jo-nang-pa curriculum as a propædeutic.[31]

The eventual recovery and publication of 'Ba'-mda' Dge-legs' biography will perhaps clear up some of these outstanding questions; and certainly the continuing study of his writings may be expected to illuminate still undiscerned facets of his thinking. As the sole known representative of the one brand of Tibetan eclecticism we once expected never to find, this unique master warrants the kind of sustained consideration that may help to shed light on the phenomena of Tibetan Buddhist intersectarian relations in general, and on the role of particular intellectual perspectives and practices within them.

Notes

Since 1990 I have acquired substantial new resources for the study of the Jo-nang-pa school of Tibetan Buddhism, and for this I am indebted above all to its living representatives in Sichuan. Many of the texts I have collected were published lithographically by a former Jo-nang-pa monk from 'Dzam-thang named A-khu Thogs-med, who was his monastery's business representative in Chengdu. A man in his middle years, A-khu Thogs-med was deeply committed to the preservation and dissemination of knowledge of the Jo-nang-pa tradition, and having published the three major collections required for contemporary Jo-nang-pa education, he wished to turn to the publication of the extant writings of Dol-po-pa's disciples. After I met him in Chengdu in 1992, he was very gracious in securing copies of Jo-nang-pa publications that I had not acquired earlier, and was eager to maintain some connection so that such materials could continue to be made available outside of China.

In 1994 A-khu Thogs-med was the victim of a fatal attack in Chengdu, the investigation of which, to the best of my knowledge, has never been resolved. The present chapter is based primarily on sources that would not have been available to me without A-khu Thogs-med's good efforts. If any small merit is to be found here, it is appropriate that it be dedicated to his memory.

For its support of my research in Sichuan in 1990 and 1992, I am grateful to the Committee for Scholarly Communication with the People's Republic of China (now the CSCC). For facilitating my acquisition of Jo-nang-pa writings from A-khu Thogs-med, I wish to thank the colleagues of the Ven. Thub-bstan-nyi-ma in Chengdu, above all A-khu Bu-phrugs.

1 Lamotte 1935: 85 (Tibetan text) and 206–7 (trans.). See also Kapstein 2000a: 112–14.

2 These issues and the previous researches relevant to their investigation are examined in Tauscher 1995; Hopkins 1999; Stearns 1995, 1999; and Kapstein 2000a, chap. 6.

3 Thus, for instance, 'Bri-gung Skyobs-pa 'Jig-rten-mgon-po (1143–1217) in his *Dam chos dgongs pa gcig pa'i rtsa tshig:* "There are those who hold the promulgations of Madhyamaka and the promulgations of Mind Only to be different,

but, according to the vajra-speech, the very same promulgations that teach Mind Only teach Madhyamaka" *(dbu ma'i bka' dang sems tsam pa'i bka' tha dad par 'dod de; rdo rje'i gsung sems tsam ston pa'i bka' nyid dbu ma ston par bzhed).* From *Dgoṅs gcig yig cha,* vol. 1, pp. 157–58. It is perhaps not without significance that Dol-po-pa was regarded as an emanation of 'Bri-gung Skyobs-pa.

4 See, for example, Dudjom 1991, vol. 1, pp. 191–216, 243–56, and 911–13.

5 I use "esotericism" here in the specific sense in which contemporary philosophers of religion understand it, that is, as referring to the assertion of a philosophical doctrine or intuition that, while not explicitly represented throughout the corpus being interpreted, is nevertheless held by its proponents to be present as the implicit or concealed message unifying the whole as its deepest or ultimate significance. In this sense efforts to identify, say, Advaita Vedānta as the teaching underlying all Hinduism are similarly esoteric.

6 *Dol-po-pa,* text nos. 7, 8, 9, 10, 12, 13. The commentaries on the three Prajñāpāramitā sūtras do not offer word-by-word explanations, of course, but detailed summaries, with glosses on selected topics, that attempt to illustrate the manner in which the *Abhisamayālaṃkāra* itself functions as a commentary on these sūtras.

7 Giuseppe Tucci's brief summary of Tāranātha's contributions (1949, vol. 1, pp. 128–31), of course, does emphasize his tantric writings. Recently, Arènes 1996: 289–381 examines aspects of Tāranātha's writings on Tārā.

8 Both are found in *Tāranātha,* vol. Tsa (18): *Shes rab kyi pha rol tu phyin pa'i snying po'i mdo rnam par bshad pa sngon med legs bshad,* pp. 601–806; and *Sher snying gi tshig 'grel,* pp. 807–29. In the latter the tenth and eleventh folios have been placed in incorrect order, and must be rearranged according to the following page sequence: 827, 828 (= fol. 10), 825, 826 (=fol. 11), 829 (=fol. 12). In the *dkar-chag* of the Phun-tshogs-gling edition of Tāranātha's works transcribed in Lokesh Chandra 1963: 18–33 (Tib.), the short commentary is listed as no. 533 in vol. Pa (p. 27), while the longer one, no. 602 in vol. Tsa (p. 30), is described as incomplete. There is, in addition, a recent xylographic edition of the short commentary from Bse-dgon-pa in Rnga-ba, Sichuan.

9 Lopez 1988b, 1996.

10 *Tena khalu samayena Bhagavān gambhīrāvasaṃbodhaṃ nāma samādhiṃ samāpannaḥ. Tena ca samayena Āryāvalokiteśvaro bodhisattvo mahāsattvo gambhīrāyāṃ prajñāpāramitāyāṃ caryāṃ caramāṇaḥ evaṃ vyavalokayati sma. Pañca skandhāṃs tāṃś ca svabhāvaśūnyaṃ vyavalokayati.* In translating *vyavalokayati (rnam par blta)* as "caught a glimpse," I am not seeking to propose this as a regular convention, but only to capture the nuance of Tāranātha's interpretation.

11 For bibliography on studies of the history and doctrine of the Jo-nang-pa, refer to my "Introduction and Catalogue" to *Dol-po-pa.* The exact circumstances of and reasons for the sanction against the Jo-nang-pa remain poorly understood, but no doubt had much more to do with contemporary political rivalries than with doctrine, which at most perhaps served as a pretext. See also Stearns 1999.

12 On the geographical setting of the former, see Ryavec 1994.

13 *Grub mtha' chen mo,* pp. 663–69. On the 'Jam-dbyangs-bzhad-pa, refer to Lokesh Chandra 1968.

14 Especially in his *Yid dang kun gzhi'i dka' gnas rnam par bshad pa mkhas pa'i 'jug ngogs,* which criticizes above all Dol-po-pa's disciple Sa-bzang Ma-ti Paṇ-chen (1294–1376).

15 Kong-sprul acknowledges Si-tu's influence upon his own *gzhan-stong* perspective; see, e.g., Hookham 1991: 277. Dudjom 1991: 169–216. For recent discussion of *gzhan-stong* thought in Eastern Tibet during the nineteenth-century, see Williams 1998a, Pettit 1999, and Kapstein 2000b.

16 *Dol-po-pa,* "Introduction and Catalogue," p. 4.

17 *Blo-grags I,* pp. 412–24; *'Ba'-mda'i Bsdus-grwa,* 568–71. A full-length *rnam-thar* is reported to have been in circulation prior to 1959, but has not yet reappeared.

18 *Blo-grags I,* pp. 413 & 417; *'Ba'-mda',* vol. 17. The retreat was established at Rdo-stod G.yu-thog-dgon.

19 *Blo-grags I,* p. 414.

20 *Blo-grags I,* pp. 414–16.

21 *'Ba'-mda' Bla-ma Mi-pham-las mkhas.* Tulku Thondup Rinpoche (currently of Cambridge, Mass.), a native of 'Go-log who was educated at Rdo-grub Chos-sde—a major Rnying-ma-pa monastery where 'Ba'-mda' Dge-legs's writings on *tshad-ma* (esp. *'Ba'-mda',* vol. 1, no. 1, also published in *'Ba'-mda'i Bsdus-grwa*) were part of the curriculum—first recounted this to me in 1990. This basis for this saying may be found in an anecdote given in *Blo-grags I,* p. 420, where a miraculous competition between Mi-pham and 'Ba'-mda' Dge-legs is reported: after Mi-pham had begun to make hail, his rival brought out the sun! Mi-pham is further said to have stated that, among the many learned persons he had encountered, only 'Ba'-mda' Dge-legs left him almost speechless in debate.

22 *Blo-grags I,* p. 418. The young incarnate was the eleventh Tā'i Si-tu, Padma-dbang-phyug-rgyal-po (1886–1952).

23 *Blo-grags I,* pp. 416 and 418–19.

24 This is best exemplified by his *Khrid-brgya,* concerning which see Kapstein 1995.

25 Smith 1970: 4.

26 *Blo-grags I,* p. 418, designates the view in question *snang-med rang-stong dbu-ma,* the "Madhyamaka of intrinsic emptiness without appearances." Mkhan-po Blo-grags (1920–75) himself, who is regarded by contemporary Jo-nang-pas to have been an emanation of Dol-po-pa, sought to complement 'Ba'-mda' Dge-legs' concessions to this line of interpretation with his own powerful reassertion of the properly Jo-nang-pa *gzhan-stong* view; see *Blo-grags II,* vol. 2.

27 *Rgyal ba'i bstan pa la 'jug pa'i rim pa skyes bu gsum gyi man ngag gi khrid yig bdud rtsi'i nying khu,* in *Tāranātha,* vol. Tsha (19). This is among the works that have already been noted by Tucci, 1949, vol. 1, p. 130. In the Phun-tshogs-gling *dkar-chag,* in Lokesh Chandra 1963, it is no. 529 in vol. Pa (p. 27).

28 His younger brother Zla-ba-grags-pa, for instance, was a recognized Jo-nang-pa *sprul-sku,* and abbot of 'Dzi-sribs-dgon-pa; *Blo-grags I,* pp. 424–27.

29 *Blo-grags I,* p. 413. Most of the lineages influenced by the old Bka'-gdams-pa scholasticism of Gsang-phu, however, emphasized precisely the same basic curriculum, even if otherwise opposed to the Dge-lugs-pa; so, for instance, the Karma Bka'-brgyud. As both the Ven. Ringu Tulku and Dr. George Dreyfus have reminded me, too, the de facto supremacy of the Dge-lugs-pa in Amdo was also an important condition here.

30 *Blo-grags I,* p. 419.

31 *Blo-grags I,* p. 416, in fact puts the point somewhat coarsely: "The great expositions and the like that he composed on Madhyamaka and Prajñāpāramitā are textbooks offering fine explanations, the clearest elucidations, on behalf of those of the degenerate age, who by nature are of dull acumen and stupid" *(khong gis brtsams pa'i dbu phar gyi rnam bshad chen mo sogs dus snyigs ma'i dbang po rtul po rmongs pa'i rang bzhin can dag la ches rab gsal byed pa'i zhib bshad kyi yig cha...).*

13. Mi-pham's Theory of Interpretation

Introduction

THIS CHAPTER takes for its subject matter the theory of interpretation advanced by the late Tibetan scholastic philosopher 'Jam-mgon 'Ju Mi-pham rgya-mtsho (1846–1912), referred to in the previous chapter as a friendly rival of 'Ba'-mda' Dge-legs. We will not be concerned with Mi-pham's actual application of this theory in his commentarial writing: his tremendous output (traditionally said to amount to thirty-two large Tibetan volumes) precludes our undertaking here a critical study, or even a perfunctory sketch, of his practice of interpretation.[1]

The scriptural corpus representing the transmitted doctrine (Skt. *āgama,* Tib. *lung*) of the Buddha, the enlightening teaching of the enlightened sage, is, by virtue of its extent and heterogenous composition, a source of bewilderment no less than of illumination for those who have not fully realized the founder's intention. In the face of apparent contradiction and obscurity, systematic interpretation is required, and, so that this does not become merely the arbitrary reformulation of the doctrine according to erroneous preconception or pure fancy, interpretive guidelines have been elaborated within the Buddhist tradition. We must thus distinguish carefully at the outset between Buddhist *interpretations* and Buddhist *rules for interpretation,* the latter being those directives whereby the former, representing the actual content of the teaching, may be established. Rules of thumb, however, if not grounded in reasonable extra-systemic foundations, may support the construction of fantastic theories (if unreasonable) or conduce to circularity (if purely intra-systemic).[2] A complete *theory of interpretation* should, therefore, be more than a miscellany of such rules; it must further ground its rules and indicate their proper application. Read with this in mind, the śāstric lists of rules for interpretation, familiar to many students of Buddhism, seem not to resolve satisfactorily the problem for whose solution they were drawn up.

We must distinguish, too, between *implicit* and *explicit* rules for or theories of interpretation. In our study of a given interpretation of the doctrine, for example, we may arrive at the conclusion that the interpreter is guided in his thinking by certain principles that, however, he never actually sets forth. For strictly formal reasons such a conclusion can never be more than probabilistic, though the particulars in any given case may strongly suggest our determination of the interpretive principles in question to be appropriate.[3] Nonetheless, it is only when an explicit statement of such principles is available to us that we can speak authoritatively of an actual *theory* of interpretation. This does not mean, of course, that explicit theoretical statements allow us to assume without further evidence that their author ever actually employed his theory in practice. Indeed, the examination of his actual interpretive work may lead us to discover that his explicit theory could not have supported his own avowed conclusions. We may in that case infer that our author misapplied his own theory, or that there are further implicit principles he assumed but did not set forth—that his theory was deficient even with respect to his own interpretive work. This problem need concern us no longer, for only the fundamental distinction made here between implicit and explicit rules is relevant to the present investigation.

These remarks may help to clarify the manner in which the central concerns of this chapter are to be related to the multifarious body of thought that we in the West call "hermeneutics." As a point of departure, at least, our problematic lies within the domain of scriptural interpretation. Specifically, it centers on the theory of the interpretation of Buddhist scriptures. As we proceed, however, it will become apparent that Mi-pham's theory addresses basic philosophical concerns, and that our understanding of just what, in Mi-pham's case, it is that can be termed "Buddhist hermeneutics" will have to be broadened accordingly.

The Scholastic Background

Mi-pham did not create his theory *ex nihilo.* Its antecedents, one and all, were found in traditions of scholastic exegesis that can be traced back to India—to sūtras such as the *Saṃdhinirmocana,* for example, and to such towering interpreters of the Buddha's doctrine as Asaṅga and Vasubandhu, Dharmakīrti and Candrakīrti. The historical evolution of all the many relevant themes cannot be surveyed here. What is most useful for our present purposes is some knowledge of the tradition on which Mi-pham immediately drew. We are fortunate that this is represented to some extent in the work of Mi-pham's senior contemporary, 'Jam-mgon Kong-sprul Blo-gros mtha'-yas (1813–99/1900).[4]

Kong-sprul's *Shes bya kun khyab mdzod (The All-Embracing Treasury of Knowledge)* was the last great Tibetan encyclopedia.[5] Its three volumes survey all branches of Tibetan scholastic learning with erudition and clarity, if not often with great originality. Of its ten books, the seventh is devoted to "the progressive disclosure of the lesson of superior discernment (Skt. *adhiprajñā*)" *(lhag pa shes rab kyi bslab pa rim par phye ba)*. The methods and objects of Buddhist scriptural interpretation are the subject matter of the first two chapters of that book: (i) "the ascertainment of the interpretive keys" *('jal byed kyi lde'u mig rnam par nges pa,* i.e., the keys that open up the treasure-house of the genuine doctrine, which is the object of interpretation, *gzhal bya'i dam chos rin chen mdzod khang);* and (ii) "the ascertainment of provisional and definitive meaning in connection with the three wheels, and of the two truths and dependent origination" *('khor lo gsum gyi drang nges dang bden gnyis rten 'brel rnam par nges pa)*. As the second of these treats the Buddha's teaching *qua* object of interpretation in particular, its contents would have to be surveyed in any thorough-going treatment of Tibetan hermeneutics.[6] It is the first, however, that encompasses the relevant background for Mi-pham's work, and so only its contents will be described here.

In his general introduction to "the ascertainment of the interpretive keys," Kong-sprul proposes that study (Tib. *thos pa;* Skt. *śrūti*) alone is productive only of rough understanding *(rags par go ba)* of its objects, and leaves us still subject to doubts. The demand for certainty (Tib. *nges shes;* Skt. *niścaya*) requires that we exercise discernment born of critical reasoning (Tib. *bsam byung gi shes rab;* Skt. *cintāmayī prajñā*), the medium of which is discursive thought (Tib. *yid kyi brjod pa;* Skt. *manojalpa*). The precise manner in which this is to be exercised with respect to the objects of study may be summarized with reference to the interpretive keys.

The keys themselves are considered throughout the remainder of the chapter. They fall into the two broad categories of those which are common (Tib. *thun mong;* Skt. *sādhāraṇa,* that is, to the interpretation of both sūtras and tantras), and those which are uncommon (Tib. *thun mong ma yin pa;* Skt. *asādhāraṇa,* that is, which uniquely pertain to the interpretation of tantras). To the first of these categories belong four sets of rules of thumb, which distinguish: (a) provisional meaning (Tib. *drang don;* Skt.

neyārtha) and definitive meaning (Tib. *nges don;* Skt. *nītārtha*); (b) four special intentions (Tib. *dgongs pa bzhi;* Skt. *catvāro 'bhiprāyāḥ*) and four hidden intentions (Tib. *ldem dgongs bzhi;* Skt. *catvāro 'bhisandhayaḥ*); (c) four orientations (Tib. *rton pa bzhi;* Skt. *catuḥpratisaraṇa*); and (d) four principles of reason (Tib. *rigs pa bzhi;* Skt. *yukti-catuṣṭayam*). The first three of these groups have been discussed at length elsewhere,[7] and will be considered briefly in connection with Mi-pham's work below (in section 1.4). The fourth has received little scholarly attention outside traditional Buddhist circles, and our efforts here will for the most part concern this set of rules.

Kong-sprul's discussion of the interpretive keys which apply uniquely to the tantras outlines the two sets of rules known as the six parameters (Tib. *mtha' drug;* Skt. *ṣaṭkoṭi*) and four modes (Tib. *tshul bzhi;* Skt. *caturvidha*). These have also been considered elsewhere and so need not detain us here.[8]

We should note that Kong-sprul nowhere seeks to explain the manner in which all these rules are to be applied, or the manner in which they complement, or relate to, one another. Presumably we are to master their use inductively, by discovering in the commentarial literature their actual utilization. This leaves Tibetan hermeneutics in roughly the condition of its pre-modern Western counterpart.[9] This state of affairs is Mi-pham's point of departure.

Kong-sprul's Definitions of the Four Principles of Reason

The four principles of reason are in Sanskrit called the *yukti-catuṣṭayam.*[10] The term *yukti,* which may mean "law, reason, proof, argument; what is correct, right, fit, appropriate,"[11] had been used in connection with the earliest efforts of Indian Buddhists to formulate canons of interpretation.[12] The precise enumeration of four *yukti* appears for the first time, it would seem, in the quintessentially hermeneutical scripture of the Mahāyāna, the *Saṃdhinirmocanasūtra (The Sūtra Which Sets Free the [Buddha's] Intention).* "The principles of reason," declares the Sage, "should be known to be four: the principle of dependence (Skt. *apekṣāyukti;* Tib. *ltos pa'i rigs pa*); the principle of efficacy (Skt. *kāryakāraṇayukti;* Tib. *bya ba byed pa'i rigs pa*); the principle of valid proof (Skt. *upapattisādhanayukti;* Tib. *'thad pa sgrub pa'i rigs pa*); and the principle of reality (Skt. *dharmatāyukti;* Tib. *chos nyid kyi rigs pa*)."[13] Henceforth, this enumeration of the four principles of reason would remain a stable feature of the Indian, and later Tibetan, Buddhist scholastic traditions. The precise manner in which the four were individually defined and the manner of their interrelation were, however, subject to considerable variation. Kong-sprul's definitions relate rather closely to those given in the *Abhidharmasamuccaya (Compendium of the Abhidharma)* by Asaṅga and its commentaries.[14] They are as follows:

> (i) The first is dependent production. It is a principle of reason that in dependence upon the seed the shoot emerges. It is a principle of reason that in dependence upon unknowing (Tib. *ma rig pa;* Skt. *avidyā*), existence-factors (Tib. *'du byed;* Skt. *saṃskāra*) and the other [links in the chain of] dependent origination (Tib. *rten 'brel;* Skt. *pratītyasamutpāda*) emerge. It is a principle of reason that visual consciousness does not emerge by itself *(rang bzhin mi 'byung gi),* but that in dependence upon both the ocular faculty and form as an object it emerges. Such are [examples of] the principle of dependence. (ii) The sense faculty, object and consciousness, and so forth, act to effect the apprehension of the proper object [of the sense consciousness in question], but do not so effect [apprehension of] other meaningful forms (Tib. *don;* Skt. *artha*). It is a principle of reason that when visual consciousness occurs it effects vision directed upon form, but it is not fit *(mi 'os pa)* to hear sound. And the ocular faculty can effect the production of visual consciousness, but cannot produce auditory or other consciousnesses. Further, it is a principle of reason that a barleycorn produces barley, but it is not a principle of reason for buckwheat, peas, and so forth to be born [from it]. Such is the principle of efficacy. (iii) The logic of inference is exemplified by knowing from smoke that there is fire and by recognizing the presence of water from moisture. The logic of direct perception is [exemplified by] the six consciousnesses and the yogin's spiritual vision *(rnal 'byor pa'i sems kyis mthong ba).* The infallible utterances enunciated by the Buddha constitute scriptural authority (Tib. *lung;* Skt. *āgama*). These form the principle of logic *(tshad ma'i rigs pa),* or the principle of valid proof. (iv) It is a principle of reason that water falls downwards and not a principle of reason that it falls upwards. [The principle here considered] also includes generic properties (Tib. *chos spyi;* Skt. *sāmānyadharma*) and individuating characteristics (Tib. *rang gi mtshan nyid;* Skt. *svalakṣaṇa*), such as the sun's rising in the east, the solidity of earth, the wetness of water, the heat of fire,

> and the motility of air, as well as emptiness and absence of self. These, which are well known as thus abiding by their own natures from all eternity *(thog ma med pa'i dus nas),* are the principle of reality.[15]

The Tibetan *rigs pa,* like its Sanskrit counterpart *yukti,* is a term whose reference may be either extramental or psychological—note the analogy to the English *reason,* when taken to include, for example, *the reason it happened* as well as *his reason for doing it.* In passages such as the one given here, it appears possible to propose two main approaches to the interpretation of the doctrine: either it may be taken to be a doctrine of natural fitness, that is, one which holds that the world is such that it is in some sense fitting and correct that, for instance, shoots come from seeds and inferences allow us to know certain things; or, to adopt a Kantian tack, it may be a way of describing the *a priori* conditions for knowledge, such that it is reasonable to maintain that *x* causes *y* just because we can know the event at hand under no other description than a causal one. I do not believe that Kong-sprul's discussion of the four principles is formulated with sufficient precision to permit of an exact determination here. Some clarification will be forthcoming below, especially when we consider Mi-pham's treatment of the principle of reality. This, however, is one of several problems relating to the four principles of reason, which remain unresolved.

It should be noted, too, that the four principles of reason differ from the other three groups of rules of thumb listed above, in that they are not ostensibly rules for the interpretation of scripture. Kong-sprul tells us nothing regarding their actual role in scriptural interpretation. We must wonder: can their occurrence here be merely a classificatory accident?[16]

Mi-pham's Theory: Sources

Mi-pham sketched out his theory of interpretation in two works: (a) a short verse tract entitled *Don rnam par nges pa shes rab ral gri (The Sword of Discernment: An Ascertainment of Meaning),* written in 1885, his fortieth year;[17] and (b) in the final section of his *Mkhas pa'i tshul la 'jug pa'i sgo (Introduction to Scholarship),* a lengthy scholastic manual intended for more or less elementary instruction, composed in 1900.[18] He also treated the four principles of reason, the foundation of his approach, at some length in his mammoth commentary on the *Mahāyānasūtrālaṃkāra (The Ornament of the*

Mahāyāna Sūtras), his last great exegetical work, written in 1911, the year preceding his decease.[19] This last mentioned, having been composed primarily to facilitate our understanding of the root-text and depending to a great extent on the commentary of Sthiramati,[20] does not contribute much to our knowledge of Mi-pham's own theory. It is clear that his conception of this attained much of its final form with his composition of *The Sword of Discernment,* for the exposition in the *Introduction to Scholarship* is little more than a prose restatement of the contents of the former work. Hence, in what follows, my primary aim will be to offer an account of the theory developed in *The Sword of Discernment,* drawing on the *Introduction to Scholarship* and, where relevant, others among Mi-pham's writings, only in order to clarify and fill out the argument. I have also made free use of Mi-pham's own annotations on *The Sword of Discernment,*[21] and of Mkhan-po Nus-ldan's on the *Introduction to Scholarship.*[22] The outline to be followed here is based on the one formulated by Mi-pham himself for the *Introduction to Scholarship,*[23] which is followed, too, by Mkhan-po Nus-ldan. While adhering as closely as possible to the actual words of these texts, I do not offer here a translation, but rather a paraphrase, with occasional digressions and insertions for which I alone am responsible (but which, I believe, are in no case inappropriate or misleading). Of course, it will not be possible in this summary to present and analyze each and every important concept and argument presupposed. My presentation must thus be somewhat elliptical, as is Mi-pham's own.

Mi-pham's Theory: Exposition

1.0. The teaching of the Buddha is profound and vast *(zab cing rgya che),* and therefore hard to understand *(rtogs dka' ba).* Those who wish to savor its meaning require intellectual illumination, which *The Sword of Discernment* is intended to provide.

The Buddha's entire teaching, in all its many dimensions, can be subsumed under two fundamental categories: that teaching which is consistent with the mundane truth that conceals reality (Tib. *'jig rten kun rdzob kyi bden pa;* Skt. *lokasaṃvṛtisatya*); and that which reveals the absolutely valuable truth that is reality (Tib. *dam pa'i don gyi bden pa;* Skt. *paramārthasatya*). These two categories are the domains of two fundamental "logics of investigation" *(dpyod pa'i tshad ma),* which are directed upon the two truths respectively. These in turn are wholly subsumed by the four principles of reason.

1.1. The Principles of Efficacy and Dependence

Whatever appears in the world comes into being through some cause, this being expressed in the fundamental Buddhist doctrine of dependent origination. Nothing appears independent of its proper causal nexus (Tib. *rgyu yi tshogs pa;* Skt. *hetusāmagrī*): lotuses do not just blossom in space. When a causal nexus is complete it effects the production of its proper result—this is the principle of efficacy. Conversely, whatever is by nature an effect depends upon its proper causal nexus—this is the principle of dependence. The two, of course, are not equivalent: they do not entail that all causes are themselves effects, nor that all effects are causes. We can restate these two principles in the simplest of terms:

(i) Principle of efficacy: Every cause has an effect.
$(x)(x \text{ is a cause} \supset (\exists y)(x \text{ causes } y))$.

(ii) Principle of dependence: Every effect has a cause.
$(x)(x \text{ is an effect} \supset (\exists y)(y \text{ causes } x))$.

We will simply assume for the moment that we understand what it means to be a *cause,* to be an *effect,* and *to cause.* Indeed, we function quite adequately in our daily lives without questioning these assumptions. It is the functional utility of these concepts, in fact, that characterizes them as belonging to the logic of the truth which conceals reality.[24] It is on this basis that we undertake or desist from actions in the world, and here we find the root of our technologies, arts, and other branches of learning. That is to say, all practical endeavor is grounded only in our knowledge of the positive and negative contingencies of things (Tib. *gnas dang gnas ma yin pa;* Skt. *sthānāsthāna*).[25]

1.2. The Principle of Reality

1.2.0. Mi-pham, it will be remarked, has altered the canonical sequence of the four principles of reason. The principle of valid proof, originally and throughout much of the later scholastic tradition third in the list, has traded places with the the principle of reality. In this Mi-pham is following the eleventh-century Rnying-ma-pa master Rong-zom Chos-kyi bzang-po,[26] though the arrangements found in both the *Mahāyānasūtrālaṃkāra* and Candragomin's *Nyāyālokasiddhi* offer precedents as well.[27] The motive underlying the change of order will become clear below. Mi-pham's discussion divides the principle of reality into two subsections, corresponding to the two truths, namely, conventional reality (Tib. *tha snyad kyi chos nyid;* Skt. *vyāvahārikadharmatā*) and absolutely valuable reality (Tib. *don dam pa'i chos nyid;* Skt. *pāramārthikadharmatā*).

1.2.1. Conventionally all things, according to their particular essences *(rang rang gi ngo bo nyid kyis),* possess specific individuating characteristics (Tib. *rang mtshan;* Skt. *svalakṣaṇa*), and possess, too, the generic characteristics (Tib. *spyi mtshan;* Skt. *sāmanyalakṣaṇa*) of the classes to which they belong. Inclusion *(sgrub)* and exclusion *(sel)* determine for any given entity limitlessly many attributes. One way of categorizing these with respect to meaningful forms that are directly apprehended *(mngon sum gyis yongs gzung don)* is to speak of the opposition of substance (Tib. *rdzas;* Skt. *dravya*) and attribute *(ldog).* The former, as the unique locus of its specific individuating characteristics, is a concretum (Tib. *rdzas yod;* Skt. *dravyasat*), whose apprehension is non-conceptual (Tib. *rtog med;* Skt. *nirvikalpaka*). The latter, attributed to the object in question by a conceptualizing agent (Tib. *rtog bcas yid;* Skt. *savikalpakamanas*) which "divides and combines" *(phye zhing sbyor),*[28] is both a generic characteristic and abstractum (Tib. *btags yod;* Skt. *prajñaptisat*). The categories thus elaborated may be multiplied manyfold. Inasmuch as they are conventionally adequate *(tha snyad don mthun)* they unquestionably correspond to reality.

In addition to the categories of substance and attribute, individuating and generic characteristic, concretum and abstractum, which Mi-pham explicitly assigns to conventional reality, his tradition maintains that what we would term necessary truths are to be classed here as well.[29] The conventional aspect of the principle of reality further plays a foundational role with respect to the concept of causality, as will be indicated below (in par. 1.2.3).

1.2.2. The principles of efficacy, dependence, and reality, as introduced thus far, are all principles belonging to the conventional logic of investigation. The *absolute* logic of investigation is presented as a second aspect of the principle of reality, but all three of the principles introduced up until now are brought into play again at this juncture.

So far we have taken the concepts of cause, effect, and individual essence as primitives upon which we actually rely in our daily lives, even if we are at a loss to explain them. The "great arguments" *(gtan tshigs chen mo)* of the Madhyamaka[30] are now called upon to demonstrate that there is no causal agent which acts to generate the result,[31] that results do not come to be through depending upon such causal agents,[32] and that individual essences are merely convenient fictions.[33] The three gates to liberation (Tib. *rnam thar sgo gsum;* Skt. *trīṇi vimokṣamukhāni*) are thus thrown open: causes stripped of efficacy are unmarked (Tib. *mtshan ma med pa;* Skt. *animitta*); results that are not dependent entities can no longer be objects of expectation (Tib. *smon pa med pa;* Skt. *apraṇihita*); and reality itself cannot be hypostatized through such fancies as individual essence (Tib. *ngo bo nyid med pa;* Skt. *niḥsvabhāvatā*).[34]

1.2.3. Returning now to the domain of convention, efficacy and dependence are actual features of the conventional reality of beings *(tha snyad kyi dngos po'i chos nyid)*. So, for instance, fire is essentially warm—it is the very nature of the thing to be so. But it is equally the nature of fire to effect the state of being burnt and to depend upon fuel for its own being. Hence, the principles of reason find their limit *(mtha')* in the principle of reality. We cannot ask *why* fire is hot, burns, or depends upon fuel. Such is the way of reality. To seek for further reasons is futile.[35]

It should now be clear that the principle of reality will not permit the sort of very simple formulation advanced above for the principles of efficacy and dependence. It does seem possible, though, to suggest a tentative statement outlining an approach to its precise formulation. Let us assume that for all *x*, where *x* is an individual, fact, or state of affairs, there is some (possibly infinite) set of individuating and generic properties $\{P_1, P_2, \ldots P_n \ldots\}$, such that being *x* entails instantiating all and only $\{P_1, P_2, \ldots P_n \ldots\}$. Let us call $\{P_1, P_2, \ldots P_n \ldots\}$ the "complete concept of *x*," and further assume that the complete concept of *x* will include as a subset the causal properties of *x*, namely, those that are subsumed in the principles of efficacy and dependence. We may assert, then, that a *complete definition* (or *analysis* or *explanation*) of *x* is one in which the properties entailed by those mentioned in the *definiens* (or *analysans* or *explanans*) are all and only those that are constitutive of the complete concept of *x*. The conventional aspect of the principle of reality, taken metaphysically, would then amount to the principle that the reality of a thing is exhausted in its complete concept; and, taken epistemologically, it would amount to the assertion that a thing is known when one attributes to it some set of properties that constitute a complete definition of that very thing. The absolute aspect of the principle of reality would then be a negative thesis to the effect that the complete concept of a thing neither involves, nor entails, the intrinsic being of that thing. (This formulation can apply only to the absolute *qua* denotation, on which see par. 1.3.3 below.)

1.2.4. Thus, we see that, for Mi-pham, the two logics of investigation are subsumed within the three principles of reason considered so far; and these are in turn subsumed within the single principle of reality. The metaphysical character of these principles and also their role in the guidance of thought he affirms in these words:

> Because it is appropriate *('os)* and reasonable *(rigs pa nyid)* that the nature of things that are objects of knowledge should so abide, one speaks of "principles of reason." Or, one speaks of "principles of reason" with reference to judgment that accords with that *(de dang mthun par gzhal ba)*.[36]

1.3. The Principle of Valid Proof

1.3.0. Having grouped together the principles of efficacy, dependence, and reality as fundamentally metaphysical principles, which pertain by extension to the adequate judgment, Mi-pham turns to treat the remaining principle of reason. From the *Saṃdhinirmocana* onwards, this principle had invariably been taken to subsume the topics dealt with in Buddhist logic and epistemology (Tib. *tshad ma;* Skt. *pramāṇa*),[37] and Mi-pham accordingly elaborates here a terse, but remarkably complete, treatise on precisely this subject. As we shall see below, there is a clear sense in which Buddhist logic is essentially hermeneutical. As a result it is impossible to cut material from Mi-pham's presentation without losing much that is important for his theory as a whole. At the same time, limitations of space require that rather severe abridgements be made at this point. So I will have to assume that readers presuppose here the inclusion of the Dignāga-Dharmakīrti theory of direct perception (Tib. *mngon sum;* Skt. *pratyakṣa*), inference (Tib. *rang don rjes dpag;* Skt. *svārthānumāna*), and argument (Tib. *gzhan don rjes dpag;* Skt. *parārthānumāna*).[38] The remarks that follow (in paragraphs 1.3.1–4) are intended only to indicate some interesting points of emphasis in Mi-pham's discussion.

1.3.1. If the determinations *(sgro 'dogs gcod pa)* made with respect to one's own mental states *(rang sems)* were similar to those made with respect to the physical forms experienced through direct perception, there would have to be another awareness of that, *ad indefinitum.* Therefore, self-reference must be distinguished from awareness cognizing an object. This self-clarification (Tib. *rang gsal;* Skt. *svaprakāśa*) is self-presenting awareness

(Tib. *rang rig;* Skt. *svasaṃvedana*). All that is experienced through other modes of direct perception is ascertained *as* direct perception through self-presentation. If that were not the case, direct perception would in effect be epistemically unfounded *('grub mi 'gyur te).* Inference is rooted in direct perception. Direct perception is, in turn, made certain by self-presentation. After arriving at this, the experience of one's own mind, with respect to which there can be no error *(ma 'khrul blo yi nyams myong),* there can be no further proof (Tib. *sgrub byed;* Skt. *sādhana*).[39]

1.3.2. Having grasped objects as general objectives (Tib. *don spyi;* Skt. *arthasāmānya*), one associates them with words and they become conceptualized *(ming dang bsres te rtog byed);* conceptual thought then multiplies various conventions. Even among persons who do not know the relevant signs (for instance, pre-verbal infants), the general objective appears to the mind; then, it is through concepts that are capable of being associated with words *(ming dang 'dres rung rtog pa)* that they enter into or desist from actions with respect to objects. Without the conceptualizing intellect, there could be no conventions of refutation and proof, and so none of the topics of inference and learning could be communicated. Concepts permit us to ponder and to undertake future objectives, and so forth, even though these are not directly evident.[40] If there were no inferences, which involve concepts, everything would be as if one had just been born. (That Mi-pham, as a representative of a spiritual tradition that places much emphasis on transcending conceptual states of mind, insists here on the value of conceptual processes is illuminating. His exposition makes it clear that the nonconceptual intuition to which the Buddhist practitioner aspires cannot be regarded as simply a regression into preconceptual chaos.)

1.3.3. In *The Sword of Discernment,* but not in the *Introduction to Scholarship,* Mi-pham introduces a way of subdividing the two logics of investigation, conventional and absolute, that is worth noting owing both to the emphasis he placed upon it in other works,[41] and the emphasis placed upon it by his successors.[42] The conventional is divided into an impure realm of what is perceived as being on hand in the ordinary world *(ma dag tshu rol mthong ba),* and a pure realm of supramundane visionary experience *(dag pa'i gzigs snang).* The absolute is divided into the absolute *qua* denotable (Tib. *rnam grangs kyi don dam;* Skt. *paryāyaparamārtha*) and the absolute *qua* undenotable (Tib. *rnam grangs ma yin pa'i don dam;* Skt. *aparyāya-paramārtha*).[43] The former division is required in order that our logic and epistemology be rich enough to embrace both mundane *and* visionary experience, and their objects, without reducing one to the other (as behaviorists do when they attempt to describe, e.g., the believer's sense of divine presence). The latter division prevents us from confusing *discourse* about the absolute with its ineffable *realization,* in which the dichotomy of the two truths is transcended in their coalescence. This realization may be spoken of as the sole truth of nirvāṇa. The pristine cognition (Tib. *ye shes;* Skt. *jñāna*) of enlightenment and its embodiment (Tib. *sku;* Skt. *kāya*) here converge: the noetic agent (Tib. *shes byed;* Skt. *jñātṛ*) and its object (Tib. *shes bya;* Skt. *jñeya*) are undivided.

1.3.4. It may be objected that, because the first three principles of reason already subsume the categories that apply to our understanding of the world and the arguments that conduce to receptivity to absolute value, the elaboration of this last principle of reason is quite unnecessary, being largely redundant. In replying to this, Mi-pham asks that we consider two ways in which the objection might be construed. First, it may be taken as asserting that we need not be epistemologists in order to *know*—that we need not, in other words, have studied formal logic in order to reason correctly. This is, of course, perfectly true, but it does not establish any redundancy here. Taken this way, the objection thus involves a confusion between the act of knowing and that of the inquiry into what it is to know, the act of inferring and the study of the principles of sound argument.[44] Alternatively, the objector may be suggesting that our foregoing consideration of the absolute should already have led us to conclude that the distinctions made here are not ultimately valid, and so should be dispensed with even conventionally. But this leads to great absurdity: we would then be incapable, even in our daily affairs, of distinguishing between a thing and its opposite. For one who has been in this manner misled by the notion of absolute realization—a realization in which all affirmation and denial have been utterly transcended—so that he now *affirms* utter nonsense, the principle of valid reason should hardly be considered unnecessary.

1.4. The Four Orientations

1.4.0. When one has achieved certainty with respect to the two truths by means of the four modes of reasoning—that is, has freed one's intellect from ignorance (Tib. *ma rtogs;* Skt. *apratipatti*), misunderstanding (Tib. *log rtogs;* Skt. *vipratipatti*), and doubt (Tib. *the tshom;* Skt. *saṃśaya*)—four changes of orientation are automatically realized *(shugs kyis 'byung)* with respect to the intention of the Buddha's doctrine. As we might say, the philosophical insight previously cultivated has now contributed to the formation of a preunderstanding that is appropriate to the task of correctly interpreting the Tathāgata's liberating message.

1.4.1. One orients oneself to the the *dharma,* and not to persons *(gang zag la mi rton, chos la rton).* For it is the path that liberates, not its propounder. The latter may appear in any guise: it is taught that the Sugata himself, for example, according to the requirements of those to be trained, once emanated as a butcher. And even if he who propounds the doctrine appears to be otherwise excellent, it is of no benefit if the content of his teaching contradicts the Mahāyāna: Māra, for instance, emanated in the guise of the Buddha.

1.4.2. Having oriented oneself to the dharma, one orients oneself to its *content,* and not to its verbal conventions *(tshig la mi rton, don la rton).* Because the motivation for utterance (Tib. *brjod 'dod;* Skt. *vivakṣā*) is to convey some content, then, so long as a given concatenation of signs has given rise to such understanding, further verbal elaboration is unnecessary: it is like seeking an ox that has already been found. There is no limit to the possible analysis of objects, and so forth, associated with even a single expression like "Fetch the wood!" But if the utterance of that phrase alone permits of understanding, then the purpose of the verbalization is exhausted.

1.4.3. In penetrating the content, having come to know provisional meaning and definitive meaning, one orients oneself to *definitive meaning,* and not to provisional meaning *(drang don la mi rton, nges don la rton).* The Omniscient One taught the sequence of vehicles as the rungs of a ladder in accord with the predispositions, faculties, and attitudes of his disciples. There are statements which he purposefully made with an intention (Tib. *dgongs pa;* Skt. *abhiprāya/sandhyā*) directed to a given intended stratum of meaning *(dgongs gzhi),* but which a critical analysis calls into question if taken literally (Tib. *sgra ji bzhin pa;* Skt. *yathārutam*). These are exemplified by the four special intentions and four hidden intentions. Thus, regarding the four philosophical systems and the culminating Vajrayāna, that part of the teaching not clearly disclosed in a lower system is elucidated by a higher one. It is by seeing both what accords with scripture and what is proven by reason that one grasps definitive meaning. In the case of the

Vajrayāna, whose teachings are "sealed" by the six parameters and four modes, reason can establish the intended content only in association with the precepts transmitted by the appropriate lineage.[45]

1.4.4. If one is to assimilate the definitive meaning of the doctrine, then one must orient oneself to non-dual *pristine cognition*, and not to (mundane) consciousness *(rnam shes la mi rton, ye shes la rton)*. For consciousness is that mind that apprehends objects *(gzung 'dzin sems)*, and is entangled in word and concept *(sgra rtog rjes 'brangs)*. That mind's very nature is objectification (Tib. *dmigs pa can gyi bdag nyid;* Skt. *sālambanātmaka*), which is embodied in the dichotomy of apprehended objects and the apprehensions of them; and such acts of apprehension are all non-veridical *(rdzun)*[46] and so cannot touch reality. Attitudes which objectify may grasp their objects as beings *(dngos por dmigs)*, non-beings *(dngos med dmigs)*, the conjunction of being and non-being *(dngos dngos med gnyis su dmigs)*, or the negation of both being and non-being *(gnyis med dmigs)*.[47] But these objectifications are all equally said to be "Māra's range of activity" *(bdud gyi spyod yul)*.[48] The process of objectification is not terminated by refutation or proof; for only when one sees what is *as it is*, without refutation or proof, is one freed.[49] Released from all apprehended objects and apprehensions, self-emergent and self-luminous, pristine cognition unfolds.

1.5. The Eight Treasures of Brilliance

The realization of immediate insight into the nature of reality brings with it the emergence of spiritual faculties that contribute to a profound ability to convey to others the significance of the Buddha's message. These faculties are spoken of in the *Lalitavistarasūtra* as "treasures of brilliance" *(spobs pa'i gter)*,[50] and are said to be eight in number: (i) the treasure of mindfulness, so that forgetfulness is overcome; (ii) the treasure of intellect, whereby one remains critical; (iii) the treasure of realization, which is here specifically the comprehension of the entire corpus of Buddhist scripture; (iv) the treasure of retention, which is distinguished from mindfulness in that retention has as its specific objects the topics of formal study; (v) the treasure of brilliance, which is the ability to satisfy the spiritual needs of others by means of eloquent speech; (vi) the treasure of dharma, whereby one acts to preserve the doctrine; (vii) the treasure of an enlightened spirit, so that one maintains a constant affinity with the Three Jewels of the Buddhist religion; and (viii) the treasure of actual attainment, for one is now fully receptive to unborn reality. Endowed with these treasures, one upholds the doctrine, reveals to others what is to be undertaken and what is to be abandoned, and in the end comes to realize for oneself the full enlightenment of a Buddha.

Some Contemporary Reflections

We began this inquiry by considering Buddhist hermeneutics to be the explicit theory guiding Buddhist scriptural interpretation, and we have followed its course as it has merged with Buddhist philosophy as a general framework for Buddhist exegesis and practice. Turning now to our Western traditions of hermeneutical thought, what might be derived from their juxtaposition with Mi-pham's contribution? A comprehensive answer to this question cannot be formulated hastily. I will content myself to consider briefly two related problems that have come to my attention in the course of this research. These concern the dichotomy of *explanation* and *understanding,* and the conflict of fundamentally *ontological* with fundamentally *epistemological* orientations. Mi-pham, of course, knew nothing of Western philosophy. I therefore make no claim to represent here the manner in which he might have treated these issues in their contemporary context.

Hermeneutical philosophy since Dilthey has generally affirmed there to be two distinct scientific methodologies: a methodology of *explanation* that is appropriate to the natural sciences; and a methodology of *understanding (Verstehen)* that is appropriate to the human sciences. This was advocated against the view of the positivist tradition, which maintained that the methods of the human sciences could in fact be reduced to those of the natural sciences. In mid-twentieth century philosophy this monomethodological view was powerfully asserted in Hempel's covering law theory,[51] which occasioned a sustained debate within the analytic tradition through the challenges framed by such disciples of Wittgenstein as Anscombe and von Wright.[52] The last mentioned, in particular, has explicitly related his own insistence upon an irreducible distinction of "two great process categories"—causation and intentional agency, which are respectively the domains of the operations known as explanation and understanding—to the work of thinkers associated with the continental hermeneutical tradition. At the same time, philosophers within the hermeneutical tradition, especially Ricoeur, and within the analytic tradition, for instance, Davidson and Searle, have in various ways questioned the validity of the distinction, though without wishing to resurrect Hempel's program in its particulars.[53] The controversy thus bridges the gulf between two major philosophical traditions which have often seemed incapable of constructive interaction. Let us now inquire into the manner in which the dispute reflects upon certain features of Mi-pham's thought.

We are concerned here, of course, with the principles of efficacy and dependence, especially in the light of Mi-pham's assertion that these are the basis for our undertaking or desisting from actions in the world. This suggests that Mi-pham would have denied there being any absolute gulf separating the realm of intentional undertaking from that of causation. It thus appears, *prima facie,* that his thought is in conflict with the views of those who insist on a thorough-going dualism here. Does this point to a fundamental defect in Mi-pham's system at this point?

Before we can answer this question, we should note that many of the contemporary causalists have conceded a major point to philosophers such as von Wright: they have largely abandoned the logical positivists' program of relying on causality to explain away the intentional features of human action. But they insist nevertheless that intentional attitudes may themselves function causally. This von Wright, for instance, would deny. I believe that Buddhist thought in general, and Mi-pham in particular, would support some version of the causalist approach to the problem. In his treatment elsewhere of the fundamental doctrine of dependent origination (Skt. *pratītyasamutpāda;* Tib. *rten cing 'brel bar 'byung ba*), Mi-pham recalls the distinction between an inner causality *(nang gi rten 'brel)* and an outer causality *(phyi yi rten 'brel)*.[54] The former is embodied in the traditional Buddhist scheme of the twelve links of dependent origination, beginning with ignorance and ending in old age and death; and the latter describes natural processes, such as the growth of a plant from the seed. I take this distinction to be at least analogous to von Wright's distinction between two great process categories. But Mi-pham, like Davidson, parts company from von Wright by maintaining both processes to be *causal,* though it is important to note that this is asserted without seeking to reduce one category to the other. A detailed analysis of the relevant Buddhist doctrines in Mi-pham's formulation of them cannot be undertaken here. Suffice it to say, however, that in the absence of such an undertaking it is by no means obvious that Buddhist thought is lacking in the conceptual richness required to deal adequately with the conflicting claims of causation and agency. If Mi-pham's theory is defective at this point (as it may yet prove to be), more than a general objection to causalism would be necessary to show wherein a supposed fault may lie.

With regard to the problem of the conflict between ontological and epistemological orientations, it may be said that Western philosophy since Kant has generally moved between two poles, which assert respectively the primacy of *being* and, in line with Kant's "Copernican Revolution," the primacy of *knowing.* The distinction complements, in some respects, that which obtains with respect to the two process categories. When we emphasize an epistemological and agent-centered orientation to the exclusion of the ontological and causalist, we tend towards idealism; and when we adopt an opposite orientation, we swing in the direction of positivism. And other orientations also have been realized with respect to these fundamental divisions. This problem of conflicting orientations, however, does not seem to exist for Mi-pham. In the following brief remarks I will offer one explanation for this, without committing myself to any opinion on the implications for contemporary Western philosophical investigations.

Mi-pham's most novel contribution to the discussion of the four principles of reason was perhaps his reduction of the principles of efficacy and dependence to that of reality. As we have seen, this is where why-questions must reach their end. At the same time, in elaborating the principle of valid proof, he sought the ultimate foundations for his epistemology in the phenomenon of self-presentation. We thus have two fundamental grounds, the first of which is ontological and the second epistemological. What I wish to suggest here is that no tension arises between them because Mi-pham never seeks to reduce one to the other, holding instead that without such reduction the two foundations nonetheless converge. That they do so is ultimately entailed, of course, by Mi-pham's conception of the absolute as involving the coalescence of noetic agent and object. But it is significant, too, that even within the domain of convention they are not to be thought of as being wholly disparate.[55] For self-presentation confronts us in all our conscious moments with the unity of being and knowing. How does my being in pain allow me to know that I am in pain? It just does. No further answer is required. Being and knowing are here no different. And it is characteristic of Rnying-ma-pa thought to find in our ordinary states of awareness *(rig pa)* a subtle but abiding link with the ineffable truth of enlightenment.[56]

Buddhism As a Hermeneutical Endeavor

Mi-pham's theory of interpretation clearly ramifies beyond the apparent limits of scriptural interpretation plain and simple. In concluding this presentation of it, I wish to consider a few of the implications of Mi-pham's work for our general conception of Buddhist hermeneutics.

Mi-pham's discussion is divided into three main phases. First, the four principles of reason are taught so that we might comprehend the fundamental doctrine of Mahāyāna metaphysics, that of the two truths. Armed with this insight, we set out to transform certain basic orientations that pertain to our understanding of Buddhist scripture and doctrine in the second phase. And finally, realizing the fruit of this transformation, we gain the endowment of the eight treasures of brilliance. This seems to bear more than accidental resemblance to the systematic teaching of the doctrine according to the categories of ground *(gzhi)*, path *(lam)*, and result *('bras-bu)*. Let us note, however, that with the sole exception of the eight treasures, all the major categories employed by Mi-pham are those expounded in the earlier scholastic tradition in particular association with the problems of textual interpretation. It would thus seem to be the case that for Mi-pham the principles of interpretation are really no different from the principles of Buddhist philosophy overall. I believe that this is as it should be.[57]

Vasubandhu, in a frequently cited verse (*Abhidharmakośa,* 8.39), divided the teaching into the two great domains of transmitted doctrine (Skt. *āgama,* Tib. *lung*) and realization (Skt. *adhigama;* Tib. *rtogs-pa*). No English translation can convey the resonance of these technical terms, which are both derived from the same Sanskrit root. (In Tibetan, too, this is lost.) Perhaps we can suggest it by saying that the transmitted doctrine is that which *comes down* to us, while realization is that which *comes through* when the transmission is rightly understood. Vasubandhu associated these two domains with two sorts of spiritually meaningful activity: exegesis and practice. Jointly, they guarantee the continuing integrity of the Buddha's teaching in the world. Now, what I wish to propose here is that we regard both of these activities to be fundamentally interpretive. In the first, receptivity and acumen must open us to the descent of the teaching, for that only occurs when we are capable of understanding the Buddha's intention. In the second, we similarly open ourselves to the realization of reality *qua* absolute value, for that cannot come through to us until we are ready to comprehend the real order of things. Clea ly a Buddhist theory of interpretation must in the final analysis embrace both domains; for it is through the interpretive act that scripture on the one hand and reality on the other are in fact comprehended.

In developing a Buddhist theory of interpretation in this manner Mi-pham was not, of course, undertaking a radical program; he was no revolutionary breaking with tradition in order to forge previously undiscovered pathways in Buddhist thought. Like most Buddhist philosophers, he was engaged in the on-going process of unpacking the contents of the received tradition. The very inclusion of the four principles of reason among the rules of thumb for interpretation was already indicative of the inseparability of Buddhist hermeneutics from Buddhist logic and metaphysics.[58] The hermeneutical character of the Dignāga-Dharmakīrti system, too, had been clearly enunciated long before Mi-pham's time—for instance, by the seventh Karma-pa Chos-grags rgya-mtsho (1454–1506), who introduced his monumental exposition of that system with these words:

> The Buddha, that Transcendent Lord, who embodies logic...set in motion the wheel of the doctrine which is infallible with respect to both provisional and ultimate meaning, so that the genuinely significant, which had been previously unknown, might be clearly known without error. And that [doctrine], according to the faculties of individual disciples, abides in various forms, to wit, provisional meaning, definitive meaning, literal, metaphorical, having a special intention, and having a hidden intention. Seeing that its meaning is thus hard for disciples to understand, that great soul Dignāga well established all the scriptures of the Sugata by means of three logics, so that they could be easily understood through the science of logical argument, and so that ignorance, misunderstanding, doubt, and so forth might be removed.[59]

It will not be possible to explore this theme in greater detail here. It will be enough to affirm that there is a fundamental sense in which Buddhadharma is a *hermeneutical* endeavor and that this is revealed certainly in our consideration of Mi-pham. Buddhism is hermeneutical in that it demands that we confront and come to understand the message of the Sugata; it is hermeneutical in that it requires a reinterpretation of the world within which we find ourselves and equally a redefinition of ourselves within that world; and it is hermeneutical in that it will not allow us to remain silent, but demands that we enunciate, i.e. interpret for others, the message and the reality with which we have struggled.

Notes

The topic for this chapter was suggested, and the relevant writings of Mi-pham brought to my attention, by the late Mkhan-po Sangs-rgyas bstan-'dzin Rin-po-che of Ser-lo dgon-pa, Nepal. Mkhan-po Dpal-ldan shes-rab, currently residing in New York, indicated to me the important contributions of Candragomin and Rong-zom-pa, and their influence on Mi-pham and the later adherents of his school. I am grateful to them both for advice and critical conversation in connection with this research.

1 On the life and contributions of this master, see Goodman 1981; Dudjom 1991, vol. 1, pp. 869–80; Williams 1998a, 1998b; Pettit 1999; and Kapstein 2000b.

2 The circularity that seems to me to be problematic here is not a feature of the so-called "hermeneutic circle" in general. According to Dilthey's conception of the latter, the interpreter is not expected to (and indeed cannot) exclude as irrelevant all elements of his pre-understanding which have their origins outside the particular text under consideration. The concept of the hermeneutic circle thus tells us that we cannot understand the text without already understanding the text *in part*. But the circularity to which I here object arises instead when we insist that to understand the text we must refer *only* to the text, and nothing more.

3 My reservations with respect to implicit hermeneutics stem from the following considerations: Let us suppose that an individual *a* has interpreted a text *b* and that his interpretation is represented by some body of conclusions *C*. Let us further suppose that there is some theory *T* such that if *b* is read in the light of *T* one would tend to conclude *C*. These suppositions *do not* jointly entail *a*'s having interpreted *b* in the light of *T*. Given these bare bones there is in fact nothing whatsoever that can be said of *a*'s implicit hermeneutic. These considerations notwithstanding, I do not disagree with Robert Gimello and David Tracy in their insistence (expressed in the discussions held during the 1984 Kuroda Institute conference at which this chapter was first presented) that Buddhist hermeneutics will often require extending our inquiry to implicit principles of interpretation if we are to investigate Buddhist hermeneutics at all. In such instances we will, of course, have more than bare bones upon which to base our hypotheses. Lest there be some misunderstanding about this, my point here is simply to indicate something of the theoretical limits of this process, and to define my own investigations in terms of those limits.

4 Kong-sprul and Mi-pham were among the closest disciple-colleagues of nineteenth-century Tibet's greatest visionary, 'Jam-dbyangs Mkhyen-brtse'i dbang-po (1820–92). The best survey to date of these masters and their intellectual and spiritual milieu remains Smith 1970. Kong-sprul was, in fact, one of Mi-pham's teachers, but available information on his instruction to him leaves unclear whether he influenced Mi-pham with respect to the present subject matter. On their relationship see Dudjom 1991, vol. 1, pp. 871 and 875.

5 The original Dpal-spungs edition of this work is reproduced in Lokesh Chandra 1970. Citations in the present chapter, however, refer to *Shes bya kun khyab.*

6 It is this aspect of Tibetan hermeneutics that has perhaps received the most attention from Tibetan thinkers themselves, e.g., in Tsong-kha-pa's tour de force, the *Drang nges legs bshad snying po,* a complete translation of which is available in Thurman 1984. See now also Hopkins 1999. On the two truths, in particular, refer to chap. 8 of the present volume.

7 Among recent contributions see, for example, Thurman 1978; Lipman 1980; Broido 1984; and Arènes 1996, append. 3.

8 See especially the contributions of Broido and Thurman to Lopez 1988a and the references therein.

9 Cf. Bleicher 1980: 14: "The limitation of the pre-Schleiermacher effort consisted…in the lack of reflection that transcended merely methodological considerations—which themselves did not reach any systematic formulation and remained on the level of ad hoc insights that were forthcoming from interpretative practice."

10 *Mahāyānasūtrālaṃkāra,* chap. 19, v. 45d. Elsewhere the Sanskrit phrase is *catasro yuktayaḥ,* e.g., *Abhidharmasamuccayabhāṣya,* p. 99, no. 125. Cf., too, *Śrāvakabhūmi,* pp. 141–43, 369.

11 Cf. Monier-Williams 1899: 853.

12 The Pali equivalent *yutti* represents a basic category of scriptural analysis in both the *Nettippakaraṇaṃ* and the *Peṭakopadesa.* See Ñāṇamoli 1962: 36ff., and 1965: 116ff. *Yutti* is here translated as "a construing." Cf., also, the concept of *yukti* as it occurs in the *Tattvārtha* chapter of the *Bodhisattvabhūmiḥ,* pp. 25ff.; and the translation by Willis 1979: 150. See further Scherrer-Schaub 1981.

13 Lamotte 1935, chap. 10, para. 7.4.7° (text and translation). Lamotte mistook *rigs pa* in this context to be a translation of the Sanskrit term *nyāya* rather than *yukti.* His attempt to translate the lengthy and difficult passage which adumbrates the four principles of reason he qualifies with these words: "Cet exposé de logique bouddhique étant très special, nous avons cru bien faire de conserver les termes techniques sanscrits dans notre traductions."

14 *Abhidharmasamuccaya,* p. 81; *Abhidharmasamuccayabhāṣya,* para. 125. For a translation of the former see Rahula 1971: 136. This, however, is somewhat flawed in the passage here cited: Rahula has without explanation read *sākṣātkrīyāsādhanayukti* for Pradhan's entirely correct reading of *upapattisādhanayukti.*

15 *Shes bya kun khyab,* 3.11–12.

16 Neither do the doxographers of the other Tibetan traditions offer us much assistance at this point. E.g., the Dge-lugs-pa scholar Lcang-skya Rol-pa'i rdo-rje (1717–86), in *Grub mtha' lhun po'i mdzes rgyan,* p. 151, says that "relying on these four principles of reason, too, one penetrates the significance of the Jina's scriptures." But this is rather uninformative.

17 *Don rnam nges shes rab ral gri.*

18 *Mkhas 'jug,* fols. 148b–161b. For a general introduction to this work see Goodman 1981 and Kawamura 1981.

19 *Mi pham gsung 'bum,* vol. A, pp. 667–68.
20 *Sūtrālaṃkāravṛttibhāṣya,* vol. 2, pp. 403–10.
21 *Don rnam par nges pa shes rab ral gri mchan bcas,* in *Mi pham gsung 'bum,* vol. PA, pp. 787–820.
22 *Mkhas 'jug mchan 'grel,* pp. 653–94. At least three commentaries on the *Don rnam nges shes rab ral gri* itself are also known: *Don rnam nges 'grel thub bstan snang byed, Don rnam nges 'grel lung rigs do shal,* and a recent commentary by Mkhan-po Dpal-ldan-shes-rab.
23 *Mkhas 'jug sa bcad,* pp. 20b–22b.
24 Dharmakīrti's definition of absolute reality, i.e. efficacy (Skt. *arthakriyā*), is here taken as the mark of veridical being in the domain of the concealment of the absolute. See *Pramāṇavārttika,* p. 100: "What is capable of effecting a result is here [defined as] absolute being." Cf., also, Mikogami 1979, Dreyfus 1997.
25 Goodman 1981: 71, translates this term as "what is possible and what is impossible"; and Kawamura 1981: 114, gives "what is inevitable and what is impossible." The latter is certainly incorrect and the former inaccurately suggests that both logical and empirical possibility are to be included here. But Mi-pham himself, *Mkhas 'jug,* 231ff., makes it quite clear that this topic concerns only empirical possibility. Accordingly, "positive contingencies" *(gnas)* refers here to natural and other processes—e.g., a rice stalk growing from a riceseed—and "negative contingencies" *(gnas ma yin pa)* to empirically impossible processes—e.g., a cat growing from a rice seed.
26 See his *Snang ba lhar bsgrub.*
27 The Sanskrit title of the text last mentioned is also given as *Nyāyasiddhyāloka, P.* 5740, translated by Śrīsiṃhaprabha and Vairocana, although it is not listed in the early ninth-century *Ldan dkar dkar chag* as given by Lalou 1953. The text is noted, but not analyzed, by Vidyabhusana 1971: 336. Vidyabhusana assigns the author to "about 925 A.D.," but if the attribution of the translators is correct he would have been active over a century earlier. See further Steinkellner 1984.
28 Cf. the distinctions made by Aquinas 1962: 17: "There is a twofold operation of the intellect.... One is the understanding of simple objects, that is, the operation by which the intellect apprehends just the essence of the thing alone; the other is the operation of composing and dividing. There is also a third operation, that of reasoning, by which reason proceeds from what is known to the investigation of things that are unknown. The first of these operations is ordered to the second, for there cannot be composition and division unless things have already been apprehended simply. The second, in turn, is ordered to the third, for clearly we must proceed from some known truth to which the intellect assents in order to have certitude about something not yet known." Cf., also, Aristotle, *De Anima,* book 3, chap. 6. For Mi-pham's indications concerning the passage from the operation of division and combination to that of reasoning, see below, paras. 1.3.1–2.
29 I am indebted to Mkhan-po Dpal-ldan shes-rab for having clarified this point.

By now it will be obvious to readers familiar with recent Western philosophy that "conventional" is not used here with the same meaning it has had in the philosophy of science since Poincaré. For even the necessary truths of logic and mathematics, which may be known *a priori,* are here termed "conventional" (Skt. *sāṅketika;* Tib. *tha snyad pa*). But "conventional" in its Buddhist uses should not be taken to imply "freely chosen from a given set of alternatives," and much less "arbitrary." It refers, rather, to all language and propositional knowledge, and to the principles to which they conform and to their objects; for none of these is or directly points to that absolute reality whose realization is spiritual liberation. That absolute, of which not even the categories of the one and the many or of being and non-being can be affirmed, wholly transcends the familiar conventions of logic, experience, language, and thought.

30 For the four major arguments traditionally enumerated in the scholastic treatises of the Madhyamaka school see Ruegg 1981: 112. A detailed account of their exposition according to the Dge-lugs-pa tradition is found in Hopkins 1983, part 2, "Reasoning into Reality." Here I follow Mi-pham's own discussion, as given in *Mkhas 'jug,* 133b–140a. The enumeration of three arguments in the passage which follows, rather than the traditional four, is explained by the fact that the fourth, the "Great Interdependence Argument" *(rten 'brel chen po),* is held to apply equally to the analyses of cause, result, and essence. Mi-pham's approach to Madhyamaka interpretation has recently received detailed treatment in Pettit 1999 and, inter alia, in Williams 1998a, 1998b.

31 The argument applied to causes, called "Diamond Fragments" *(rgyu la dpyod pa rdo rje gzegs ma),* proceeds from the assumption that if an individual thing comes into being as the result of some cause, then that cause must either be the thing itself or something other. The supposition that it is the thing itself leads to an infinite regress, whereas the assumption that the cause is other cannot be sustained owing to the absence of any intrinsic relationship between the supposed cause and its result. Having denied these two alternatives, nothing is gained by supposing that their conjunction might explain causation; and their joint negation leads to the absurdity of things coming into being causelessly. The argument is intended to demonstrate that the concept of cause is radically defective, i.e., empty.

32 The reality of the result is challenged by the "negation of the coming into being of an existent or of a non-existent" *('bras bu la dpyod pa yod med skye 'gog).* Whatever comes into being, it is supposed, must be something that exists, does not exist, conjoins existence and non-existence, or neither exists nor does not exist. Following an argumentative strategy similar to that of the critique of cause, one is led to conclude that the concept of result (i.e., of something that is brought into being) is also defective.

33 The argument employed here intends to reduce to absurdity the notions of the one and the many *(ngo bo la dpyod pa gcig du bral),* with the result that the concept of individual essence is overthrown. As applied to material bodies the argument is similar to Kant's second antinomy. But in the case of spiritual substance

it depends on the denial of the unity of consciousness, both through appeal to an assumption of temporal parts and in the light of Humean considerations with respect to the variegation of consciousness. Mi-pham analyzed this argument in extenso in his commentary on Śāntarakṣita's *Madhyamakālaṃkāra,* the *Dbu ma rgyan gyi rnam bshad 'jam dbyangs bla ma dgyes pa'i zhal lung,* in *Mi pham gsung 'bum,* vol. 12, pp. 1–359. On the "neither one nor many" argument, see Tillemans 1983, 1984.

34 Cf. Lamotte 1962: 148, n. 16.

35 Despite the peculiarities of diction, Mi-pham's point here seems to be similar to that made by Aristotle, *Metaphysics,* book 7, chap. 17, 1041a. (trans. W.D. Ross): "Now 'why a thing is itself' is a meaningless inquiry (for [to give meaning to the question 'why'] the fact or the existence of the thing must already be evident—e.g., that the moon is eclipsed—but the fact that a thing is itself is the single reason and the single cause to be given in answer to all such questions as 'why the man is man, or the musician musical', unless one were to answer 'because each thing is inseparable from itself, and its being one just meant this'...)." Cf., also, *Posterior Analytics,* book 2, chaps. 4–7.

36 *Mkhas 'jug,* 150a6–b2.

37 The presentation found in the *Saṃdhinirmocana* thus has the distinction of being one of the earliest Buddhist presentations of these topics. The *pramāṇas* are listed there as falling under three categories: direct perception, inference, and scriptural authority. Later Buddhist logicians tended to refrain from enumerating the last of these as a separate epistemic authority, but recall Kong-sprul's remarks cited above.

38 A valuable account of this system remains Stcherbatsky's dated opus, *Buddhist Logic* (1962), originally published in 1930. Useful lists of relevant sources are found in Tharchin 1979: 237–70; and Steinkellner 1979: 10–19. See now, also, Dreyfus 1997 and Tillemans 1999.

39 The issues raised in this passage are of central importance to contemporary epistemology, and require much further study in their Buddhist formulations. The epistemic primacy of self-presentation *(svasaṃvittiḥ)* was sharply contested by those within the Buddhist tradition who maintained this concept to be fundamentally incoherent, like the notion of a sword being used to cut itself. Cf. *Bodhicāryāvatāra,* chap. 9, v. 18. Also problematic was the precise nature of the chain leading from discrete self-presentations through sensory perceptions to inferential knowledge of the world. For contemporary philosophical discussions of these and related questions see Chisholm 1966. The connection between the Buddhist notion of *svasaṃvittiḥ* and recent investigations of self-presentation appears to have been first explicitly noted by Williams 1983a. (Williams, it should be noted, uses "self-consciousness" where I prefer "self-presentation.") Williams 1998a provides a detailed investigation of this topic, focusing upon Mi-pham's contributions. See further Kapstein 2000b.

40 One interesting question that can be raised here is whether Buddhist philosophers regarded future states of affairs as having determinate truth-value. On the

question of *don-spyi* (objective generalities), see now Dreyfus 1997, chap. 14, and Kapstein 2000a: 89–97.

41 See especially his *Nges shes rin po che'i sgron me,* translated now in Pettit 1999.

42 Particularly noteworthy here is Bod-pa sprul-sku Mdo-sngags-bstan-pa'i nyi-ma's *Lta grub shan 'byed* and its autocommentary, on which see Lipman 1992.

43 On this distinction see Ruegg 1981: 64 and 88.

44 In point of fact this very confusion has been an obstacle to the study of the development of Indian logic. See, e.g., Vidyabhusana 1971: 500, n. 1.

45 Note that it is here that Mi-pham situates most of the interpretive rules of thumb enumerated in the standard scholastic manuals. Refer to the section on "the scholastic background" above, and the articles referred to in nn. 7 and 8.

46 Non-veridical, that is, in the absolute sense, which does not preclude their being *conventionally* veridical.

47 From a philosophical perspective it is of supreme interest that while Mi-pham considers, e.g., the conjunction of being and non-being to be a metaphysical absurdity, he nonetheless maintains that it can be in some sense *objectified.* This merits comparison with certain of the proposals of Alexius Meinong as detailed in his "Theory of Objects," translated in Chisholm 1960. A lucid introduction to Meinong's theory may be found in Linsky 1967, chap. 2.

48 This is so because the conventional dichotomy of subject and object is a fundamental aspect of the unknowing which is the root of saṃsāric entanglement. For the precise formulation of this in accord with the cosmogony of the Rnying-ma-pa school, see Dudjom 1991, vol. 1, pp. 54–57.

49 Cf. *Ratnagotravibhāga,* p. 76, 1.154; and *Abhisamayālaṃkāra,* 5.21.

50 *Lalitavistara,* p. 317. The *sūtra* refers to them merely as the "eight great treasures" (Skt. *aṣṭau mahānidhānāni).*

51 Hempel 1949.

52 Anscombe 1957 and von Wright 1971. An introduction to the domain in which analytic philosophy and hermeneutics intersect is provided by Howard 1982. See, also, Thompson 1981.

53 For a concise presentation of Paul Ricoeur's view here see Ricoeur 1981, chap. 5, "What Is a Text? Explanation and Understanding." Ricoeur does not seek to deny that explanation and understanding are distinct operations, but refuses to accept Dilthey's absolute bifurcation of their respective domains. In sum (p. 157) "...it will be upon the same terrain, within the same sphere of language *(langage),* that explanation and interpretation will enter into debate." By contrast, analytic critics have tended to focus upon the supposed dichotomy between the two process categories of natural causation and intentional agency. See Davidson 1980 and Searle 1983, chap. 4, "Intentional Causation." One philosopher who has systematically examined both the causation-agency and the explanation-understanding dichotomies is Chisholm. In *Person and Object* (1979), pp. 69–72 ("The Agent as Cause"), he denies that there is any "unbridgeable gap" between the members of the former pair, whereas in *The Foundations of Knowing* (1982), chap. 7 (*"Verstehen:* The Epistemological Question"), he concludes

that the latter distinction is indeed a significant one. Implicit in Chisholm's work, therefore, is the important observation that strict parallelism between these two distinctions need not be presupposed. At the time of this writing I have no clear sense of how Buddhist epistemologists would have treated the notion of *Verstehen,* though I suspect that, in many contexts, their conception of "comprehension," or "realization" *(rtogs-pa, pratipatti),* would have accorded more closely with understanding than with explanation, as contemporary philosophers understand these terms.

54 *Mkhas 'jug,* section 4.

55 Cf. Husserl, 1962, vol. 2, part 2, section 5, p. 174: "There are not two things... which are present in the experience; we do not experience the object and, beside it, the intentional experience which relates to it..."

56 On this see now Williams 1998a, and Kapstein 2000b.

57 When we survey the history of Western hermeneutics since Schleiermacher, we similarly find theory of interpretation becoming fused with more general aspects of epistemology, metaphysics, and the philosophy of language. What I wish to suggest at this juncture is that any theory of interpretation which generalizes its concerns beyond the elaboration of the rules of thumb required in connection with the study of a given corpus must inevitably undergo some such transformation, for the reason that interpretive acts and their objects, when considered in general and not specified, are none other than rational and linguistic acts and their objects. If this is so, then hermeneutics as scriptural interpretation will be in essence the conjunction of the appropriate domains of general philosophical inquiry with those rules that are elaborated specifically to link such inquiry with the scriptural corpus under consideration. And this seems to be just what is accomplished by the Buddhist enumerations of interpretive keys. If, in the light of these observations, we turn to Western scholastic traditions, I think we will find that logic, theology, rational psychology, etc., are within those traditions hermeneutical in just the same sense that Buddhist philosophy is here claimed to be hermeneutical.

58 It is of interest in this connection that the first Western work explicitly consecrated to interpretation theory was a treatise on logic, Aristotle's *De Interpretatione.* Consider in this regard the remarks of Gadamer 1982: 278–89, where the focus is, however, on the relevance of Aristotle's *Ethics.*

59 Karma-pa VII Chos-grags rgya-mtsho, *Tshad ma rigs gzhung rgya mtsho,* vol. 1, p. 5, lines 1–5: *tshad mar gyur pa'i sangs rgyas bcom ldan 'das de nyid kyis...chos kyi 'khor lo gnas skabs dang mthar thug gi don la bslu ba med cing sngar ma shes pa'i yang dag pa'i don phyin ci ma log pa gsal bar shes pa'i slad du bskor bar mdzad la/ de'ang gdul bya so so'i dbang gis drang ba'i don dang/ nges pa'i don dang/ sgra ji bzhin pa dang/ ji bzhin ma yin pa dang dgongs pa can dang/ ldem por dgongs pa ci rigs pa'i tshul gyis gnas pa las/ de'i don gdul bya rnams kyis rtogs dka' bar gzigs nas gtan tshigs rigs pa'i sgo nas bde blags tu rtogs par bya ba dang/ ma rtogs pa dang/ log par rtogs pa dang/ the tshom la sogs pa bsal ba'i slad du bdag nyid chen po phyogs kyi glang pos bde bar gshegs pa'i gsung rab ma lus pa tshad ma gsum gyis legs par gtan la phab ste/*

V PHILOSOPHICAL TEXTS IN TRANSLATION

14. Vasubandhu and the Nyāya Philosophers on Personal Identity

A Note on the Translated Texts

THE TEXTS IN THIS CHAPTER represent major contributions by three classical Indian philosophers to the development of arguments concerning the self and personal identity. (In addition, as an appendix to chapter 3 I have translated a brief discussion of related subject matter, from the philosophical notes of a renowned Tibetan Buddhist scholar of the late eighteenth–early nineteenth century.) In the remarks introducing each text selection, I will say a few words about the works here translated, and provide bibliographic details on the editions and earlier translations used in preparing the translations offered here.

I Vasubandhu's Treatise on the Negation of the Person

The *Treatise on the Negation of the Person (Pudgala-pratiṣedha-prakaraṇa),* also known as the *Ascertainment of the Person (Pudgala-viniścayaḥ),* forms the ninth chapter of Vasubandhu's autocommentary on his *Treasury of the Abhidharma (Abhidharmakośa),* a monumental compilation of the doctrines and arguments codified primarily in the Kashmir branch of the Vaibhāṣika school of early Buddhist scholasticism. The *Treatise on the Negation of the Person* itself has something of the character of an appendix, for it does not comment on any part of the root-text that actually forms the basis for the preceding chapters. Rather, as Stcherbatsky pointed out, it forms a supplement whose purpose is to explicate the most notable omission from the main text, namely, the omission of an explicit theory of the self.

The complete *Treasury of the Abhidharma,* including the autocommentary, was translated twice into Chinese (during the sixth and seventh centuries) and once into Tibetan (during the eighth century). Until the original Sanskrit text was edited and published in the 1960s and 70s (in independent editions by Pradhan and Śāstrī, respectively), these early translations were the sources upon which scholars had to rely. Theodore Stcherbatsky published his pioneering translation of the *Treatise on the Negation of the Person* from Tibetan into English in 1920, and this was followed in 1923–31 by L. de La Vallée Poussin's monumental translation of the entire *Treasury of the Abhidharma* and its commentary from Chinese into French. (La Vallée Poussin's work has been more recently translated into English by Pruden.) Stcherbatsky's translation suffers from the inevitable difficulties of an unprecedented work of scholarship, but also from some problems which I think run throughout Stcherbatsky's work in English: he was not a native speaker of English, and his style remained forever unidiomatic; and in his eager search for Western philosophical terms to serve as equivalents for Buddhist technical terms, his decisions were sometimes unfortunate. Thus, for instance, his insistence on rendering *prajñapti* (*btags-pa/'dogs-pa,* translated here as "conceptual construct") as "nominal," has had the unfortunate result—which he also reinforced in his *Buddhist Logic* (1930)—of creating the impression that the Buddhist-Brahmanist controversies were a neat equivalent of Western Nominalist-Realist disputes. That there is some resemblance here few will contest, and certainly Stcherbatsky deserves credit for having first noticed that resemblance; but it is very misleading to press this point too far. (See, further, the remarks on nominalism in the following chapter, section 4.) Stcherbatsky's approach provided a remarkable beginning for a new field of research, but now, more than three-quarters of a century later, we have advanced considerably, both philologically and philosophically. I should note, too, that I think Stcherbatsky sometimes simply mistranslates, and that at points he misses the drift of the argument altogether.

La Vallée Poussin's translation of the *Treasury of the Abhidharma* remains, I believe, among the most splendid achievements of Western Buddhist scholarship to date. No Western scholar (except perhaps his own pupil, the late Msgr. Étienne Lamotte) has ever mastered the literature of the Buddhist tradition on such a grand scale, or with such depth of insight. I have found La Vallée Poussin's work to be an indispensible companion in the course of preparing my own translation, which depends primarily on the Sanskrit edition brought out by Swāmī Dwārikādās Śāstrī. In addition, I have consulted the Tibetan text throughout. Following is complete information on the texts and translations consulted:

Vasubandhu, *Pudgalaviniścayaḥ*. Swāmī Dwārikādās Śāstrī, ed., *Abhidharmakośam*, vol. 4. Varanasi: Bauddha Bharati, 1973. [*Abhidharmakośa*, 1189–1232.]

Chos mngon pa mdzod kyi bshad pa. Sde-dge canonical ed. *T.* 4090; *D. Bstan-'gyur, Mngon-pa*, vols. *ku-khu*. Eighth-century Tibetan translation of the *Abhidharmakośabhāṣya*, the autocommentary on the *Treasury of the Abhidharma*. The *Treatise on the Negation of the Person* is contained in vol. *khu*, folios 82a.1–95a.7.

Louis de La Vallée Poussin, *L'Abhidharmakośa de Vasubandhu*. Brussels: Institut Belge des Hautes Études Chinoises, 1971. 6 vols. (Reprinted from the 1923–31 Paris ed. The *Treatise on the Negation of the Person* is found in vol. 5, pp. 227–302.)

Theodore Stcherbatsky, *The Soul Theory of the Buddhists*. Delhi: Bharatiya Vidya Prakashan, 1976. (Reprinted from the 1920 Soviet Academy of Sciences' ed.)

To help guide the reader who knows Sanskrit or Tibetan, I give the pagination of the original texts (as well as of the two translations just mentioned) in notes following each of the section headings.

The section headings themselves, as well as italicized introductory expressions—for instance, *Question, Objection, We respond,* etc.—are not found in the original texts and are intended to orient the reader to Vasubandhu's argument. Earlier translators have attempted to do this by assigning each passage to a specific interlocutor, and so construing the text as a dialogue throughout. Though Vasubandhu's work clearly does betray its origins in earlier dialogic works, it seems to me that the dialogue here is by and large left implicit, and that many passages can best be interpreted as the internal dialogue of a single thinker. The present translation reflects this view of the text.

The translation was completed in 1986 as part of my Ph.D. dissertation. A translation of the same text by James Duerlinger was published in 1989, leading me to abandon thoughts of publishing this version at that time. Nevertheless, over the years since, my students have sometimes remarked that it would be useful to have this version readily available in print, and I have included it here in response to their encouragements.

Translation

1. The self and worldly bondage[1]

Question. Now, then, is no liberation [from the round of saṃsāra] to be found outside of this [teaching of the Buddha]?

No, it is not.

Why so?

Owing to preoccupation with false views of self. For [our opponents] have not determined that the conceptual construction "self" refers to the bundle-continuum alone.

What then?

They imagine that the self is a discrete substance. Moreover, the negative affections are born from grasping-as-self.

2. The epistemological argument for the non-self principle[2]

Question. How is it known that this designation "self" applies to the bundle-continuum alone, and not to some other designatum?

Because there is neither acquaintance with nor inference to [the posited self]: Thus, whatever things there are are apprehended by acquaintance whenever there is no obstruction. So, for example, the six objects and the intellect. On the other hand, [they may be apprehended] inferentially, as are the five sense faculties. In that case this is the inference: There being [some] cause, the absence of an effect is noted in the absence of some other cause, and in the presence [of that additional cause] the presence [of the effect in question is noted]. So it is, for instance, in the case of a shoot. Now, [in the case of the inference which establishes the sense faculties], there is a manifest object and a cause [which contributes to the perception of that object, namely] the attention [of the subject directed upon it]. But the apprehension of the object may be absent or, again, present. E.g., [it is absent] among the blind, deaf, etc., and [it is present] among those who are not blind, not deaf, etc. Hence, in that case, the absence or presence of another cause is ascertained. And that which is that other cause is the sense faculty. That is the inference [in the case of the sense faculties]. But because there are no such [perceptions or inferences] of the self, [it follows that] there is no self.

3.–6. The dispute with the "personalists"

3. The "personalist" controversy introduced[3]

Objection. Nonetheless, the Vātsīputrīyas hold that there is a person.

Now, this must be examined: do they hold it to be substantial, or conceptually constructed?

What is [meant by] "substantial," and what [by] "conceptually constructed?"

If, like physical form, etc., it is a discrete entity, then it is substantial. But if like milk, etc., it is a *collectivum,* then it is conceptually constructed.

What follows from this?

If it is substantial, then because it is essentially separate, it must be said to be discrete from the bundles, just as the bundles are one from the other. And its cause must be stated. If, on the other hand, it is unconditioned, this would imply [that the Vātsīputrīyas hold] a non-Buddhist view, and [that the person they posit] is inefficacious.

But if it be conceptually constructed?

We too affirm just that.

But it is neither substantial nor conceptually constructed.

What then?

Depending upon the bundles which are inwardly held now, the person is conceptually constructed.

We do not understand this blind prattle, whose meaning is indistinct! What is [meant here by] "depending upon?" If the meaning is *objectively directed upon* the bundles, then the conceptual construction "person" applies to them. For example, objectively directed upon physical form, etc., the conceptual construction "milk" [applies] to them [i.e., to the color, odor, etc., which collectively are designated "milk"]. But if the meaning is *causally founded upon* the bundles, then that very fault applies, because the bundles are then the cause of the conceptual construction "person."

4. Fire and fuel[4]

Objection. It is not conceptually constructed in that manner.

Then how so?

As is fire, depending upon fuel.

How is it that fire is conceptually constructed depending upon fuel?

Though the fire is not conceptually constructed without fuel, one can neither assert that fire is discrete from fuel, nor that it is non-discrete. For if it were discrete, the fuel would be not hot; and if it were not discrete, then the combustible would itself be the combustion. Just so, though the person is not conceptually constructed in the absence of the bundles, one cannot assert that it is discrete from the bundles, because that implies permanence; nor that it is not discrete, for that implies annihilation.

But now tell us: what is fuel, and what fire? Then we'll know how it is that, depending upon fuel, fire is conceptually constructed!

What can be said in response? Fuel is the combustible and fire is the combustion.

But here one must state what is the combustible, and what the combustion. Now, in the world it is said that wood and so forth that have not been ignited are fuel, or the combustible. And that which is ignited is fire, or the combustion. It is that which is ablaze and intensely hot, that by which that [fuel] is scorched and burned; for it effects an alteration of continuum. Both of these, too, are eightfold substances. Moreover, the fire arises founded upon that fuel, just as, for example, yogurt is founded upon milk, or mead upon honey. Hence, it is said, "depending upon the fuel." But because [the fire] is [in that case] temporally discrete from that [fuel], it is other. If, in the same way, the person came into being causally founded upon the bundles, then it would be discrete from them and impermanent. On the other hand, [if you hold that] when wood, etc., are ignited, then the heat which is present is fire, and the three elements [earth, water, and air] coexisting with that are fuel, then their discreteness is proven; for their defining characteristics are different. Moreover, the meaning of "depending upon" must be stated [in accordance with this last explanation]. How is it that depending upon that fuel the fire is conceptually constructed? For neither [in this case] is that [fuel] the cause of the [fire], nor [is it the cause] of its conceptual construction, because the fire itself is the cause of its conceptual construction. Whether [it be asserted that] "depending upon" has the meaning of "foundation" or that of "co-existing," *ex hypothesi* the person is distinctly discrete from the bundles; for the bundles are thus the foundation of, or that which has come into being along with, the person. And their absence implies the absence of the person, as the absence of fuel does that of fire. Moreover, when you say, "if the fire were discrete from the fuel, the fuel would be not hot," then what is this "hot?" If it be heat, then, indeed, the fuel is not hot, for they are essentially different elements.

But if it means "heat-possessing," then it is established to be hot, even though it be other than essentially hot fire; for it is conjoined with heat. Thus, discreteness is no fault. And moreover, it may be held that all that is ablaze—wood, etc.—is both fuel and fire.

Then, too, the meaning of "depending upon" must be stated. And persons would then be just bundles—their being-no-different is incontrovertibly implied. Hence, it is not established that the person is conceptually constructed depending upon the bundles, just as fire is, depending upon fuel. And if this [person] cannot be affirmed to be discrete from the bundles, then it is implied that it cannot be affirmed that there are five sorts of knowable: past, future, occurrent, unconditioned, and ineffable. For it must be affirmed that it is neither the fifth nor not the fifth among "past" [i.e., the bundles being by no means ineffable, the person cannot be both ineffable and not affirmed to be discrete from the bundles].

5. *Is the person an object?*[5]

5.1. *Question.* When the person is conceptually constructed, is it that, objectively directed upon the bundles, it is conceptually constructed? Or upon the person?

If directed upon the bundles, then the conceptual construction "person" applies to them alone; for there is no apprehension of the person. And if the person? Then how is it that depending upon the bundles there is the conceptual construction [of the person]? For the person itself must be the cause of that [conceptual construction].

Objection. Now, it is thought that, there being the bundles, the person is apprehended; therefore it is said that its conceptual construction depends on the bundles.

If that were the case, then, because the apprehension of visible form occurs whenever there are eye, attention, and light, [its] conceptual construction should be said to be depending on them. And, as with visible form [which is discrete from eye, etc.], the discreteness of the person [from the bundles] is clear.

5.2. Then it should be said [in order to interrogate further our opponents]: the person is the object of how many of the six consciousnesses?

Of [all] six—so they [the Personalists] say.

How so?

If the person is apprehended, causally founded upon the visible forms which are the objects of eye consciousness, then the person must be said to be the object of eye consciousness. But one must not say that it is or is not the visible forms. Just so, if the person is apprehended founded upon the regular principles which are objects of mental consciousness, [then] the person must be said to be the object of mental consciousness. But one must not say that it is or is not those regular principles. Thus, it is similar to milk and so forth. If milk and water are apprehended, causally founded upon the visible forms which are objects of eye consciousness, then milk and water must be said to be objects of eye consciousness. But one must not say that they are or are not the visible forms. Similarly, they must be said to be the objects of olfactory, gustatory, and bodily consciousness. But one must not say that they are or are not tactile [or visual, olfactory, or gustatory] things. Do not let there be the implication that both milk and water are four! Hence, just as visible forms, etc., collectively, are conceptually constructed as being milk or water, so too the bundles [are conceptually constructed as being] the person—this is established.

Concerning what has been said, what is the meaning of this sentence: "the person is apprehended, causally founded upon visible forms that are the objects of eye consciousness"? Are the visible forms the cause of the apprehension of the person? or is it that in apprehending visible forms, the person is apprehended? If [you say that] the visible forms are the cause of the apprehension of the person, and that, therefore, it should not be said to be discrete from them, [then we respond that] if that is the case, then visible form, too, must not be said to be discrete from light, the eye, and attention; for they are the cause of the apprehension of it. But if in apprehending visible forms, the person is apprehended, then is it apprehended by that very [act of] apprehension, or by another? If by that very one, then the person is not essentially separate from visible form; its conceptual construction [applies] to visible form alone. How then does one differentiate them, saying, "this is visible form, that is person." And if one does not thus differentiate them, how is this asserted, that there *is* visible form and there *is* a person. For it is per force of the apprehension that its being is asserted. So should it be repeated [going through the entire list of objects] down to the regular principles. And if [it is apprehended] by another [act of apprehension]? It must then be discrete from visible form, for the apprehension [of it] is at a different time, just as is [the perception of] yellow from [an earlier perception of] blue, and just as one moment from another moment. So should it be repeated [going through the entire list of objects] down to the regular principles.

But just as with visible form and the person, so the apprehension of them must not be said to be discrete or not discrete.

In that case, even that which is conditioned becomes ineffable, which breaks from [our own Buddhist] philosophy. For, if it is the case that "one must not say that it is or is not visible form," then why has the Fortunate Lord said, "visible form is not self..." [and continued] up to "consciousness is not self?"

5.3. *Question.* [According to the Personalists] does that eye consciousness whereby the person is apprehended arise causally founded upon visible forms, or upon the person, or upon both?

If it arises causally founded upon visible forms, then there cannot be consciousness of the person in the manner of sound, etc. For when there is eye consciousness, that very object causally founded on which the consciousness arises is indeed its objective condition. Or does it arise depending upon the person, or on both? This would transgress sūtra. For it is certainly held in a sūtra that "causally founded on two is the arising of consciousness":

> Thus, O monk, the eye is the cause and the visible forms are the conditions for the arising of eye consciousness. Why is that? Whatever there is, O monk, that is eye consciousness, all that is causally founded upon eye and visible forms.

Moreover, the person must thus be impermanent; for it says in a sūtra:

> Which are the causes and which are the conditions for the arising of consciousness, those too are impermanent.

5.4. *We affirm.* If the person is not its [i.e., consciousness's] object, then it is not to be cognized by it. If, moreover, the person is asserted to be the object of consciousness of the six consciousnesses, then because it is the object of consciousness of auditory consciousness, it must be discrete from visible form, like sound. And it must be discrete from sound, like visible form, because of being an object of consciousness for eye consciousness. This is to be applied in the cases of other [consciousnesses] as well. And this [assumption of the Personalists] is in contradiction with the words of a sūtra:

> O brahman, as for these five sense faculties, which have various domains, various objects, each experiences its own domain and object; they do not experience the domain and object of any other. Such are the visual faculty, the aural faculty, the nasal faculty, the gustatory faculty and the corporeal faculty. The mind

> experiences the domain and object of these five faculties; and mind is their support.

Again, the person is not an object. If not an object, it is then not an object of consciousness.

Objection. If this is so, then even the mind faculty must be invariable [with respect to its specific object]. As it says in the *Ṣaṭprāṇakôpama* ["Example of the Six Species"]:

> These six faculties, which have various domains, various objects, desire their respective domains and objects.

We respond. There, it is not the sense faculties that are spoken of as "sense faculties." For those five and their [respective] consciousnesses cannot possibly desire to see and so forth. Hence, it is the mental consciousness that is brought forth by their power that is spoken of as "sense faculty." And that mental consciousness which solely is brought forth by the power of the mind desires in no wise the object of the others. Hence, there is not this [supposed] fault. So, too, the Fortunate Lord, having said, "O monks, I will reveal all enumerations of regular principles that are objects of higher knowledge..." [then goes on to say]:

> The eye is an object of higher knowledge, [so too] visible forms, eye consciousness, eye contact, and that pleasure, pain, or absence of pleasure and pain that arises as an inner sensation conditioned by eye contact...

and so on up to:

> ...conditioned by mind contact. This is the enumeration of regular principles, all the objects of higher knowledge and of thorough knowledge.

Hence, just this much is determined to be the object of higher knowledge and of thorough knowledge; not the person. Therefore, neither is it an object of consciousness; for discernment and consciousness have just the same objects. The Personalists, envisioning that "we see the person with the eye," have acquired the [false] viewpoint that "we see self with what is not self." In a sūtra, moreover, the Transcendent Lord has determined that "the denomination 'person' [applies] to the bundles alone." Thus the *Mānuṣyakasūtra:*

> Founded upon eye and visible forms, eye consciousness arises. From the conjunction of three, contact. Born together with contact are sensation, conceptualization, and attention. Thus, the four bundles which are not physical form [i.e., sensation, conceptualization, motivation, and consciousness], and the eye which is physical form. This much is said to be the human being. Here these are synonyms: "being," "man," "human progeny," "vital person," "nourished soul," "inner person," "person," "life," "creature." Here this is the assertion: "I see visible forms with the eye." Here this is the convention: "That long-living one named such-and-such, of such-and-such family, of such-and-such clan, having such-and-such nourishment, experiencing such-and-such pleasure and pain, having such-and-such a life span, enjoying such-and-such longevity, having such-and-such an end to life." Just so, O monks, all this is mere name. All this is mere convention. All these principles are impermanent, conditioned, and projected volitionally; they are dependently originated.

And the Fortunate Lord has said that a sūtra of definitive meaning is to be relied upon. Therefore, this is not investigated further.

6. Questions of scriptural interpretation[6]

6.1. *We affirm.* It is, moreover, said: "Everything exists, O brahman, inasmuch as there are twelve activity fields." Thus it is established that if this person is not [to be classed as a member of] an activity field, it does not exist. If it is [so classed within] an activity field, then it is not ineffable. Among them [the Personalists], too, one sees [this scripture]:

> As far, O monk, as [there is] an eye, as far as [there are] visible forms...etc., so far, O monk, the Tathāgata denominates everything.

In the *Bimbisārasūtra,* too, it is said:

> "Self," "self," O monks, so has the infantile, uneducated, common person fallen into imaginings. Here there is neither self nor that which is of the self. This suffering, in arising, arises...etc.

And the *arhantī* Śailā[7] has said, addressing Māra:

> Do you think, O Māra, that there is a "being?"
> You're under the spell of views!
> This mass of conditions is empty;
> No being is found here.
>
> Just because there's an assemblage of parts,
> The denomination "chariot" comes to mind.
> In the same way, depending on the bundles,
> One speaks of a "being" conventionally.

And in the *Kṣudraka Āgama,* addressing a poor brahman it is said:

> Listen now respectfully to the doctrine that undoes all knots,
> Of how the mind is sullied, of how the mind is cleansed.
> There is neither self nor [possession] of self; [these are] erroneously conceived.
> Here there is neither being nor self, but regular principles that have causes.
> Thinking on all of these—the twelve limbs of becoming,
> The bundles, activity-fields and bases—one apprehends not the person.
> See the inner emptiness! See emptiness without!
> Neither is he found at all, who cultivates emptiness!

Just so it is said:

> There are five evil consequences of the apprehension of self: (1) one has views of self, views of beings, views of life; (2) one becomes no different from the non-Buddhists; (3) one turns off on a detour; (4) one's mind does not penetrate emptiness, does not have confidence in it, does not abide in it, nor become liberated in it; and (5) one does not refine the sublime principles [of enlightenment].

Objection. But they [the Personalists] do not make of this text an authority.

For what reason?

They say, "This is not recited in our tradition."

What then? Is the tradition their authority, or the Buddha's utterance? If the tradition is their authority, then the Buddha is not their teacher, and they are not "sons of Śākya." But if the Buddha's utterance is [their] authority, then why is this text not an authority?

Because this is not the Buddha's utterance.

Why so?

It is not read in our tradition.

This is unreasonable.

What here is unreasonable?

To say that a book which is transmitted in all the other traditions, and which contradicts neither sūtra nor reality, is not the Buddha's utterance because "we do not recite it" is mere recklessness. Moreover, do they not have this sūtra: "All principles are non-selves?"

Objection. One might maintain that the person is neither a regular principle nor other than a regular principle.

If so, it cannot be established to be an object of mental consciousness, for it is determined that "founded upon two is the arising of consciousness."

Here, however, it is thought that "self" is erroneously applied to non-self, but not so to self.

What follows? The bundles, activity-fields and bases are not self and, what was said before—"it must not be said to be visible forms, nor not"—has been excluded. It is said in another sūtra:

> O monks, whichever mendicants or brahmans perceive what they consider to be "a self," all of them [perceive] only these five acquisitive bundles.

Therefore, all grasping of self [applies] only to non-self. So it is said:

> Whoever remembering past abodes, has remembered, remembers, or will remember them, all of those [remember] only the five acquisitive bundles.

Objection. If that is so, then why did [the Buddha] say: "In past time, I was one with [such-and-such] form?"

Thus variously he demonstrates [the meaning of the passage beginning] "whoever remembering..." If one were to see the person as having form, that would imply a view which hypostatizes the ephemeral, which here would be [to seek] a refuge in what is not taught. Therefore, the person is a conceptual construct, like a heap or a stream.

6.2. *Objection.* If this were so, then the Buddha would not be omniscient, for there would be no thought or mental event which knows everything, owing to momentariness. But the person might know.

In this case it is affirmed that when the thought is destroyed the person is not destroyed, wherefore its permanence is affirmed. Moreover, we do not declare the Buddha to be omniscient owing to manifest knowledge of everything.

What then?

Owing to potentiality: the continuum called "Buddha" has this potentiality, namely, that by merely intending it, unerring knowledge arises about what is desired. On this it is said:

> By the continuum, owing to potentiality,
> As a fire desiring to consume all;
> So the all-knowing one [cognizes] the desired object,
> For the knowing of all is not simultaneous.

Question. How is this known?

We respond. From the statement beginning "Past...":

> Those who were perfect Buddhas in the past,
> And those who will be future perfect Buddhas,
> And he who is the perfect Buddha here,
> Remove the grief of the many.

6.3. *Objection.* You hold the bundles alone to be three-timed [belonging to past, present, and future], not the person; but if the bundles were the person, then why did [the Buddha] say this:

> O monks, I will teach the burden, the taking up of the burden, the casting off of the burden, and the bearer of the burden?

Why shouldn't this have been said?

Because the burden itself is not rightly the burden bearer.

Why so?

Because this is not seen.

Neither is it rightly ineffable.

Why so?

Because this is not seen. And because it is then implied that the one who takes up the burden is not subsumed by the bundles. The Fortunate Lord has taught the meaning of the burden-bearer:

> The one who is that long-living one, with such-and-such a name...up to...with such-and-such longevity, with such-and-such an end to life.

What he has made known thus, should not be known otherwise, i.e., as "permanent" or "ineffable." The bundles indeed come to harm the bundles, that is the later by the earlier. Thus they are spoken of as burden and burden bearer. For burden has the meaning of "harm."

6.4. *Objection.* There is indeed a person, for it is said: "'There is no being that comes into being' is a false view."

Who is it that says, "There is no being that comes into being?" We say in the *Mānuṣyakasūtra* that "just as beings are, so the Fortunate Lord has classified them." Hence, who deprecates the bundle-continuum called "the being which comes into being hereafter" has this false view: "There is no being that comes into being." For the coming-into-being is of the bundles. If this deprecation of the person were a false view, how then would it be renounced? It cannot be an object of renunciation [on the paths] of insight or of cultivation, because the person is not included among the truths.

And if [one objects that] because of the statement "one person, coming into being, comes into being in the world," there are no bundles?

Not so! For "one" is conventionally applied to *collectiva*—as [in the phrases] "one sesamum seed" or "one rice grain," so also in "one heap" and "one saying." Moreover, you must state whether the person is conditioned; for you affirm it to come into being.

It does not come into being in the manner of the bundles, from being not previously manifest.

How then?

Due to acquiring other bundles. Just as it is said that "he became a ritualist" or "he became a grammarian" due to the acquisition of knowledge; "he became a monk" or "he became an ascetic" due to the acquisition of tokens; or "he became old" or "he became ill" due to the acquisition of a condition.

Not so! For that is denied. It has been denied in a sūtra by the Fortunate Lord, [namely] in the *Paramārthaśūnyatā:*

> So it is, O monks, that there is action, there is ripening [of the effects of action], but no actor is apprehended, who casts off these bundles and links up with other bundles, except for what are called regular principles.

And it is said in the *Phalgusūtra:*

> I do not say "acquired by Phalgu."

Therefore, there is no acquirer of the bundles, neither one who casts them off.

What is it then, sir, that is made an example, referring to the "ritualist" and so on through "invalid?" Perhaps the person?

That is not established.

Then thought and mental events?

No! They originate unprecedented at every moment.

Then the body?

The same of that [for the body also comes into being in a momentary series]. Moreover, just as body, knowledge, and token [must be other than the supposed person], so the otherness of bundles and person is entailed. Old age and illness are indeed otherness of body, for the transformationalism of the Sāṃkhyas has been refuted. Therefore, these are poor examples. If unprecedented coming-into-being is attributed to the bundles, but not to the person, then it is other than them and permanent—this is clearly indicated. By saying, "five bundles and one person," how can one not speak of [their] otherness?

How then [can one speak of] "four elements, but one form"; for form is not other than the elements?

The fault is partisan.

Belonging to which party?

To the "element-only" party. But even so, as form is element-only, so it is affirmed that person is bundle-only.

6.5. *Objection.* If the person is bundle-only, then why has the Fortunate Lord not declared "whether the life and the body are [same] or other?"

Because [the Buddha was responding] with reference to the questioner's intention. For he [the questioner] asked with reference to a single life-substance that is the inner active person. And that does not exist in any respect, so how is its difference or non-difference to be declared? It is like [speaking of] the hardness or softness of the tips of the tortoise's hairs. This knot was already untied by our predecessors. The elder Nāgasena, being approached by the king of Kaliṅga, was thus addressed:

> "I ask you, sir: mendicants are talkative, so if I ask you something, please declare an answer to it!"
> "Ask away," he said and was asked,
> "Is the life the body, or is life one thing and body another?"
> "This is undeclared," said the elder.
> He said, "But, sir, I had you previously make a promise not to declare otherwise! Why have you said, on the contrary, 'This is undeclared?'"
> The elder spoke: "I too might ask you, Great King: kings are talkative, so if I ask you something, please declare an answer to it."
> "Ask away," he said and was asked,
> "About that mango tree that is in your residential quarters, are its fruits sour, or are they sweet?"
> "There is no mango tree in my residential quarters," he said.
> "But, Great King, I had you previously make a promise not to declare otherwise. Why then have you said, on the contrary, 'There is no mango?'"
> He said, "How am I to declare the sourness or sweetness of the fruits of a nonexistent tree?"
> "Just so, Great King, that life does not exist. How am I to declare its difference or non-difference from the body?"

Objection. Then, why did not even the Fortunate Lord say, "It is not."

Because [he responded] with reference to the questioner's intention, for he [the questioner] might have come to believe that the bundle-continuum of which there is the so-called life also is non-existent, and so fall into a false view, through ignorance of dependent origination. And he could not bear that teaching. Hence, this indeed is ascertained, for the Fortunate Lord has said *in extenso:*

> Ānanda! "There is a self"—so, being questioned, might I declare to the mendicant of the Vatsa clan; but surely that would not suit the statement, "All principles are non-selves."
>
> Ānanda! "There is no self"—so, being questioned, might I declare to the mendicant of the Vatsa clan; but the mendicant of the Vatsa clan has been bewildered even previously to such an extent that he would [again] become bewildered, [thinking], "Formerly I had a self, and now I have none!"
>
> "There is a self," Ānanda, suggests eternalism. And "there is no self," Ānanda, suggests nihilism.

Here, too it is said:

> The Conqueror teaches the doctrine as a tigress carries her cubs:
> Beware of the sharp teeth of views, and of being dropped in the karmic abyss!
> Affirming existence of self, one is pierced by the teeth of views;
> Not to realize conventional truth would be to drop the virtuous cub.

Further, it is said:

> Due to [its] nonexistence the Fortunate Lord did not speak
> Of life as a discrete entity.
> But neither did he say "it is not," so as not to suggest
> Its nonexistence as a conceptual construction.
> For where there's a bundle-continuum,
> Good and evil results may be found.
> But there is no so-called "life,"
> For the nonexistence of life has been taught.
> He has not said that "life" exists among
> The bundles even as a conceptual construct;
> [For] then such people as lack good fortune
> Would not realize emptiness.
> So he has not said that it is,
> When asked whether self is or is not.
> Thus, referring to the questioner's intention,
> Why has he never said that it is?

The non-declaration, too, of the world's eternity, etc., has reference to the questioner's intention. For, if self were held to be the world, then, owing to its nonexistence, the fourfold declaration would be invalid. Then, [the declaration] that "the whole of cyclic existence is the world" is also invalid. If the world is eternal then no one would attain complete nirvāṇa. But if it is impermanent, then all would be annihilated. If both are determined, then some might attain complete nirvāṇa and some not. If both are not the case, then it can only be that there is neither complete nirvāṇa, nor not complete nirvāṇa. Hence, the fourfold determination of complete nirvāṇa is not declared owing to [nirvāṇa's] dependence upon the path, as in the example of the Nirgrantha ascetic's bird.[8] Similarly, there can be no fourfold declaration as to whether "the world has an end." For this quartet has the same significance. Just so, the mendicant Muktika, having thus questioned the four [alternatives], questioned further:

> "Does the whole world pass beyond owing to this path, or does only part of the world?" The Elder Ānanda answered, "Just what you, Muktika, have at first asked the Fortunate Lord, you ask this very same thing now phrasing it thus."

Similarly all [four alternatives are excluded in this case]. "That there exists the tathāgata after death"—this, too, was not declared owing to reference to the intention of the questioner. For he asked making of the tathāgata a "liberated self." Hence, the Personalists must be interrogated thus: Why [given your view] does the Fortunate Lord declare that there is a living person, but does not declare [that the person exists] thus after death?

That would imply the fault of eternalism.

But why has he declared thus: "Maitreya! in a future time you will become a tathāgata, an arhat, a fully enlightened one?" And why has he declared the birth of a disciple in past time, saying, "so-and-so was born in such-and-such"; for this too implies eternality. If, moreover, the Fortunate Lord, having at first seen the person, no longer saw it after final nirvāṇa, and hence did not declare it owing to ignorance, then that repudiates the teacher's omniscience; otherwise it should have been affirmed that "it is not." Alternatively, "he sees [that there is a person], but without speaking [of it]" entails both its existence and eternality. Alternatively, "it can't be said whether or not he sees"—this then gradually makes it impossible to say whether or not the Fortunate Lord is omniscient.

Objection. There is indeed a person, for it is said to be a false view that my self does not exist in truth and abidingly.

But it is also said to be a false view that it does; wherefore this is not reliable. The masters of the abhidharma say, moreover, that both of these are views which grasp extremes, that is, views subsumed by eternalism and nihilism. And that is correct. As it says in the *Vātsyasūtra:*

> "There is a self," Ānanda, entails eternalism. "There is no self," Ānanda, entails nihilism.

6.6. *Objection.* If, then, there is no person, who transmigrates? For it is not correct to say that this transmigration transmigrates. As the Fortunate Lord has said:

> Migrant beings tainted by ignorance transmigrate.

Now, how is it that the person transmigrates?

By abandoning and assuming differing bundles.

This position has already been answered. Just as fire, which is instantaneous, migrates continuously, so the so-called being, a bundle-aggregate, acquisitive owing to thirst, transmigrates. So it is said.

But if this is merely the bundles, then why did the Fortunate Lord say: "I, indeed, at that time, on that occasion, became the teacher named Sunetra?"

Why shouldn't that have been said?

Owing to difference of bundles.

But, if this were the person, then it would be eternal! Hence, "I, indeed, was he" denotes being one continuum. E.g., "that very fire, burning, has approached." If there were a self, the tathāgata would see it clearly. And the grasping-of-self and the self-love of the seer would become firmer. Also, his grasping-of-self towards the bundles would increase, for as the sūtra says, "There being self, 'mine' comes into being." He would have the view which reifies the ephemeral. And there being a view of mine, so too love of mine. Thus, this one who is enravelled in the bonds of firm love of self and mine would become far distant from liberation.

It may be held that indeed love is not directed upon the self.

But how can it be correct that love arises with respect to non-self, having mistaken it for self, but that it does not arise with respect to self? Therefore, two cankerous views have developed in this teaching—that of those who grasp the person, and that of those who grasp the non-being of all. And those tīrthakaras [non-Buddhists], who think of the self as a separate substance, invariably possess the fault of being without liberation.

7. Memory and Personal Identity[9]

7.1. *Objection.* If, then, there is no self whatsoever, then how is it that among instantaneous mental events there occurs memory or recognition of objects experienced long before?

Owing to a distinctive mental event, following from an act of concept formation directed upon the object of memory.

What sort of distinctive mental event is it, from which memory immediately follows?

From one endowed with an act of concept formation, etc., which has a resemblance to and connection with the enjoyment of that [object], and whose force is not destroyed by peculiarities of the support [i.e. the body], grief, distraction, etc. For even though it may resemble that [object], a distinctive mental event not caused by it has not the capacity to produce memory, and even if it follows from it, that [mental event] which resembles another [object] has not the capacity to produce memory; for the capacity is not found elsewhere.

Now, how is it that what has been seen by one mind is remembered by another? For thus [according to your account] what was seen by Devadatta's mind might be remembered by Yajñadatta.

Not so, owing to lack of connection. For those two [Devadatta's act of seeing and Yajñadatta's apparent memory] have no connection as do two [mental events] belonging to the same continuum, because they are not related as cause and effect. Moreover, we do not say, "what was seen by one mind is remembered by another." But rather that the other mind which remembers comes into being from the mind which sees, as has been said, through the transformation of the continuum. What fault is there here? Moreover, recognition occurs only owing to memory.

If there is no self, who remembers?

What is the meaning of "remembers"?

Memory grasps the object.

Is that grasping other than memory?

What then does the remembering?

It has been stated what does it, namely, the specific mental event that is the cause of the memory. What, then, is spoken of as "Caitra remembers," is spoken of owing to a perceived state of being caused by that continuum called "Caitra," namely, that "Caitra remembers."

There being no self, whose is the memory?

What's the meaning of the genetive case [of the pronoun "whose"]?

Possessive. E.g., who is the possessor of what? E.g., Caitra of a cow.

In what sense is he the possessor?

Because its utilization depends on him, as a draught animal, milch cow, etc.

But memory is to be utilized for what? For this is the manner in which [its] possessor must be sought.

For the object to be remembered.

For what reason is it to be utilized?

For memory.

What gems from the mouths of those who have been well-raised! So it's to be utilized for that reason. Well, how is it to be utilized? By production, or by dispatch?

Because memory is without movement, by production?

But then the cause must be the possessor, and it the result. Wherefore, the cause has the power [to determine] the effect; and through the effect, what has it is the cause. Thus, what is the cause of the memory is its [possessor]. Thus, having taken as one the continuum of the assemblage of conditions called "Caitra," it is spoken of as the possessor of the so-called "cow." Thinking of him as being thus a cause of the production of its movement and change, there is nonetheless no one called "Caitra," nor is there a cow. Hence, even in that case, there is no being-a-possessor above and beyond being-a-cause.

7.2. *Question.* In that case, who cognizes? Of whom is there consciousness? This and more must be stated!

What's special here is the appropriate cause, i.e., sense-faculty, object and attention.

But it may be said, because states of being have reference to beings, all states of being depend upon beings. E.g., "Devadatta goes"—here the state of going refers to the one who goes, Devadatta. In the same way, consciousness is a state of being. Therefore, he who cognizes must be.

It should be said: what is this "Devadatta?" If the self, then that indeed remains to be proven. Or the conventional person? That too is not one, for the conditions are so-named. In that case, Devadatta goes just as he cognizes.

And how does Devadatta go?

The instantaneous conditions in an unbroken continuum—which is regarded by childish persons, who grasp it as a unified lump of existence, as the so-called "Devadatta"—are the cause of its own coming-into-being elsewhere, which is spoken of as "Devadatta goes." For "going" is that very coming-into-being-elsewhere. E.g., "going" designates the passage of the continua of flames and words. Similarly, too, there being causes of consciousness, they are spoken of as "Devadatta cognizes." The Sublime also speak using such denominations, for the sake of convention.

As for what it says in the sūtra, namely, that "consciousness cognizes," what in that case does consciousness do?

It does nothing whatever. Just as it is said that the effect conforms to the cause, by being similar in nature without having done anything, so too it is said that "consciousness cognizes," by being similar in nature without having done anything.

But how is it similar?

By having the feature of that [i.e., its object]. Hence, it is said that one cognizes the object, and not the sense faculty, because [the object] arises from its sense faculty. As otherwise, just so, here too there is no fault in saying, "consciousness cognizes," because the continuum of consciousness is consciousness's cause. For an agentive term [is used to express] the cause. E.g., [in the phrase] "the bell cries." Moreover, as a lamp-light moves, so consciousness cognizes.

Now, how does a lamp-light move?

"Lamp-light" designates the continuum of a flame; it is said to move to a place whenever it comes into being elsewhere. Thus, consciousness, too, designates the mental continuum; and it is said to cognize some object whenever it is coming into being with respect to that object. Again, just as when form arises and persists, that which is is no object other than [its] state of being, so too with respect to consciousness.

7.3. *Objection.* If consciousness arises from consciousness and not from self, then why does it neither always arise similarly, nor according to a fixed order, e.g., sprout, shoot, leaf, etc.?

Because the mark of the conditioned is that, what persists becomes otherwise. For this is the essence of the conditioned, namely that necessarily there comes about the otherness of what continues. For otherwise, those perfectly absorbed in concentration, if their bodies and minds coming into being [in each successive instant] are similar, then, because there is no difference from the first instant, later too they would not re-emerge [from states of meditative equipoise] by themselves, [but would remain eternally absorbed]. Also, there is fixed order among mental states, because what is to arise from such-and-such only arises from that. For when some similarity of features occurs, then there is a potency, owing to the specifics of class. E.g., if, following the thought of a woman, the thought of rejecting her body or the thought of her father, son, etc., should arise, then again when later on, owing to the transformation of the continuum, the thought of a woman arises, then, because of being of that class, it is capable of giving rise to the thought of rejecting her body, or the thought of her father, son, etc., but is not otherwise capable. Moreover, if from the thought of a woman a great many thoughts have gradually arisen, then those which are most frequent [or clearest], or most proximate arise, because they have been most forcefully cultivated, except when there are simultaneous special conditions external to the body.

Why does that which has been most forcefully cultivated not perpetually bear fruit?

Because the mark of the conditioned is that, what persists becomes otherwise. And that becoming otherwise conforms to the fruition of other cultivations. But this only generally pertains to all types of mind, while the buddhas have mastery over the knowledge of immediate causes, as is said:

> The totality of the causal features of a single peacock feather's eye
> Is not knowable except by an omniscient one,
> For the knowledge of that is the power of omniscience.

How much more is this true of the distinctions of immaterial minds!

7.4. *We maintain.* As for those tīrthikas [non-Buddhists] who believe that the arising of mental events originates in the self, this clear objection is urged against them: why is it that [it] comes into being neither in just the same manner, nor according to a fixed order, like that of shoot, stem and leaf? If the response is "owing to dependence upon a particular connection with the mind"—that is not so, because another connection is not established. This is because of the complete difference of the two things [supposedly] connected, because the defining characteristic of the so-called "connection" is acquisition where previously there was no acquisition; and this implies the complete difference of the self [from what it acquires]. Hence, it is implied that transformation of self follows from transformation of mind, and analogously for annihilation.

But if they are partially connected?

No, because it is not the case that the part of one is of the other. Or, let there be a connection. That being so, how is there a particular connection if the mind is permanently without particularity?

Owing to dependence upon a particularity of intellect?

To that the objection is raised: what sort of particularity of intellect?

From that connection of self and mind, which depends upon particular conditions.

So let it be from that very mind which depends upon particular conditions. In that case, no power of the self is found at all, just as when a medical charlatan pronounces his "abracadabra" during the manufacture of medicine.

There being a self, that pair [mind and conditions] also exists?

Mere words!

Perhaps it is a support?

As what is the support of what? For they are not supported in the manner of a mural painting or jujube fruits, and so forth, and it is not a support in the manner of a wall, or a bowl, etc. Thus, it is not a support in this way, because of the faults of resistance and spatial separation [which are attributes of physical things but not of minds or of the posited self].

How then [might it be a support]? As earth, which possesses fragrance, etc.?

We're simply delighted! For this affirms our tenet—"there is no self." E.g., the earth is no different from fragrance, etc. [i.e., from the collection of atoms and real properties of which it is aggregated]. For what honest person maintains with certainty that earth is discrete from fragrance, etc.? As for the convention "odor, etc., of earth," its purpose is to distinguish. E.g., those very odors, etc., called in this fashion may be known as such [i.e., as odors of earth, or flowers, etc.], and not as any other. This is just as when one speaks of a body made of wood.

Given that there is dependence upon particular conditions, why is it that all cognitions do not arise at once?

Because whichever one is most powerful obstructs the others.

Then why does not that powerful one perpetually bear fruit?

Whatever is the principle in this case [i.e., that what is conditioned is in the end annihilated], let that be so when it has been cultivated [i.e., when its potency is exhausted]. But nonetheless the self is thought to be without purpose.

But the self must be affirmed. Because memory, etc., belong to the category of quality, and because what belongs to the category of quality must be supported by substance, because their having some other support is incorrect.

Not so; for their belonging to the category of quality is not established. For, according to us, everything that exists is substance. For it is said, "The fruits of mendicancy are six substances." Moreover, their being supported by substance is not established. For the meaning of "support" has been examined above. Therefore, this is a slight matter.

7.5. *Question.* If there is no self, then why undertake deeds, i.e., that "I may be happy," or "I may not be miserable"? What is this "I," which is the object of this I-assertion?

The object is the bundles.

How is that known?

Because there is attachment to them. For there is co-referentiality with the thought of paleness, etc.: "I am pale"; "I am dark"; "I am stout"; "I am lean"; "I am old"; "I am young." Thus, this I-assertion is found to be co-referential with the thought of paleness, etc. But the self is not held to have such features. Therefore, this is understood to apply to the bundles. The body which serves the self also has the designation of "self." E.g., what this is, that [very same thing also] is I.

Objection. What this one is is my servant, who [given your opinion] should then have the designation "self" in that he serves my self, but he is not [the object of] the I-assertion. There being [in this case] the apprehension of a body, even though it be another's body, why then is there no [I-assertion]?

Owing to lack of connection. For that mind or body with which there is a connection is that with reference to which the I-assertion arises, not elsewhere; for that has been cultivated in beginningless saṃsāra.

What kind of connection?

One of causal nature.

If there is no self, whose is this I-assertion?

This has already come up: "What is the meaning of this genitive…that which is its cause is [its possessor]."

And what [in the present instance] is its cause?

That mind, endowed with ignorance, completely cultivated through former [acts of] I-assertion, which has as its object its own continuum. [That is to say, the referent of an act of I-assertion is simply the continuum in which that act occurs.]

7.6. *Question.* There not being a self, who is this who is happy or miserable?

That basis on which happiness or misery has arisen. E.g., the tree has flowered, the grove has ripened. [These are held to exemplify processes undergone by paradigmatic continuants.]

What, moreover, is their [i.e., happiness's or misery's] basis?

The six activity fields [of the sense faculties and intellect], in which sense has already been explained.

There being no self, who is the doer of these deeds? And who is the enjoyer of their fruit?

What is the meaning of "doer?"

The doer is the one who does; the enjoyer is the one who enjoys.

Synonyms have been offered, not meaning.

The Definers [i.e., lexicographers in the grammatical tradition] say that this is the mark of the "doer": "the doer is autonomous."

Now, whose autonomy is there with respect to what effects?

In the world Devadatta's is seen with respect to bathing, sitting, locomotion, etc.

But what is it that you term "Devadatta"? If the self, then that remains to be proven. Then the five bundles? In that case, those are the doer. Moreover, this action is threefold: action of body, speech, mind. There, with respect to actions of body [and speech], they are undertaken depending upon the mind. And those of mind are undertaken depending upon a proper cause with respect to body [and speech]. That being so in that case, nothing at all has autonomy. For all things come about depending on conditions. And a self, too, which is not dependent because it is affirmed to be not a cause, is neither established to be autonomous. Therefore, no doer characterized in that manner is apprehended. That which is the dominant cause of something is called its doer. But the self is not found to be a cause with respect to anything. Therefore, there cannot thus be a self. For, from recollection there is interest; from interest consideration; from consideration willful effort; from willful effort vital energy; and from that, action. So what does the self do here? And what is the enjoyment of the fruit [of the action], wherefore this self is thought to be enjoyer of what [it] does? If [you say that it is] the apprehension, [we respond that] the self has no capacity to apprehend, because that has been refuted with respect to consciousness [in section 7.2. above].

7.7. *Question.* If there is no self, how is it that sin and merit do not accrue to insentient loci?

Because they do not support sensations, etc., of which the support consists of the six activity fields, not self, as has been said.

How is it that, there being no self, fruit arises in the future life from exhausted deeds?

Even if there were a self, how would fruit arise in the future life from exhausted deeds?

From the right and wrong supported by it.

"As what is supported by what...?"—the answer [to that supposition] has already been expressed thus [in section 7.4. above].

So, let it be from unsupported right and wrong.

We, in any case, do not say that the fruit arises in the future life from exhausted deeds.

What then?

From the distinctive feature of the transformation of that continuum, like seed and fruit. "As the fruit arises from the seed"—so it is said. It does not arise from an exhausted seed, but neither [does it arise] immediately.

What then?

From the distinctive feature of the transformation of that continuum; from the completion of the sequence of sprout, stem, leaf, etc., culminating in the flower [which transforms into the fruit].

If that [fruit] is completed from the flower, then why is it called the fruit of that seed? Because that potency belonging to it [i.e., the seed] [is generated] in the flower only mediately. For if that [seed] did not precede, then there would not be the capacity to arise as a fruit of that sort. Thus, the fruit of the action has arisen—so it is said. And that has not arisen from exhausted action, and also not immediately.

What then?

From the distinctive feature of the transformation of that continuum.

What, then, is the continuum? What the transformation? What the distinctive feature?

That which, preceded by deeds, is an on-going coming-to-be of mental events, is a continuum. Its arising otherwise is transformation. And, moreover, that potency, which immediately produces the fruit, being distinct from [that involved in] other transformations, is the distinctive feature of the transformation. E.g., a mind at the point of death which grasps for rebirth. And though various sorts of deeds precede, that deed which is weightier, or proximate, or reinforced by practice, is one which has generated a potency that shines forth, but not so another. As it is said:

> Which is weighty, which is close,
> Which is practiced, and which was done before,

Is ripened ever earlier in the round of deeds.

There, the power to produce the fruit of maturation, which belongs to the maturational cause, having produced the maturation, subsides. But the power to produce the fruit of accordance, which belongs to the cause of the overall fortune, subsides among those who are defiled only when an antidote arises, and it subsides altogether among the undefiled when the mind continuum reverts altogether.

Now, why from a maturation does a following maturation not arise, just as from the fruit of a seed another fruit?

The example is not equivalent in all respects. Moreover, in that case it is not from the fruit that the following fruit arises.

What then?

From a distinctive alteration born from a distinctive incubation. For what brings into being there the sprout, which is a kind of [aggregation of] elements, that is the seed, not anything else. Moreover, whether due to verbal convention or to resemblance, the preceding continuum is called the seed. Thus, here too, from that maturation, if alterations of mind arise, whether virtuous but corrupt [i.e., worldly], or unvirtuous, which are born from the distinctive condition of, e.g., studying true or false doctrines, from that too further alteration arises, and not otherwise—this much is similar. Otherwise, moreover, this should be known: as a citron flower stained with lac gives rise, in the "fruit," to a red stamen, this being born from the distinctive transformation of the continuum, but from that no other [subsequent flower with a red stamen is born], so too from the maturation born of deeds there is no further maturation. This has been taught coarsely in accord with our understanding. But through deeds divided according to their various powers, the passage of a continuum so effected to such a condition as is its manifest fruit—this is within the range of the buddhas!

II Vātsyāyana and Uddyotakara on the Aphorisms of Reason: Selections from the Nyāyasūtra Commentaries

The texts translated in this section are some of the main expressions of opposition to the Buddhist view of the self, as formulated by thinkers of the old Nyāya tradition. In the *Nyāyasūtra* itself (compiled c. mid-second century C.E.), the "proof of the self" is the topic of just one terse aphorism (1.1.10), while the aphorisms making up book 3 of the same work are concerned not to demonstrate the reality of the self, but rather set forth its properties, among other topics. A fuller treatment of the self begins to emerge in the commentarial literature, and it is in the earliest extant commentary, the *Nyāyabhāṣya* of Vātsyāyana (c. 400) that we find the "proof of the self" elaborated into a relatively thorough argument directed against an unnamed Buddhist opponent.

The Nyāya challenge to the Buddhists, however, finds particularly rich expression in the work of Uddyotakara (c. 600), whose compendious *Nyāyavārttika* forms a subcommentary on Vātsyāyana's *Nyāyabhāṣya.* Uddyotakara not only considerably expands Vātsyāyana's comments on *Nyāyasūtra,* 1.1.10, but he also adds a detailed introduction to book 3, in which he works out some of his objections to the Buddhist position at length. I think that it is fair to say that many of the later Nyāya works on the subject matter with which we are concerned here, especially the important writings of Vācaspatimiśra (ninth century?) and Udayana (late tenth century), represent in large measure the continuation of Uddyotakara's line of thought.

Despite Uddyotakara's philosophical and historical importance, however, his work suffers from a virulent polemical style—sometimes he seems to lose the thread of his own argument in favor of striking satirical blows, no matter how low they might be—and thus too often his arguments are purely sophistical. These faults have undoubtably discouraged scholars from giving Uddyotakara's writing the philosophical consideration it certainly deserves, though recent work by Potter, Matilal, and Chakrabarti is indicative of renewed philosophical interest.

The *Nyāyasūtra* and its commentary by Vātsyāyana have been translated into English on several occasions, while a complete translation of Uddyotakara has been done only once. Among these translations, the work of Gaṅganātha Jhā stands out, and merits some attention in its own right. Jhā was an incredibly prolific scholar. At the beginning of his career, in the latter part of the nineteenth century, the writings of the great Indian philosophers of the first millennium C.E. (with perhaps the exception of Śaṅkara) had been seldom studied and were only poorly understood. Jhā undertook to edit and translate a substantial body of the most important texts of that period, and in so doing paved the way for the systematic philosophical and historical investigation of them. One of Jhā's greatest virtues, from the philosopher's perspective, was that, unlike many pure philologists, he had deep insight into the philosophical arguments presented in his sources, so that his translations remain often useful to the specialist in classical Indian philosophy, especially when the original Sanskrit is so laconic that, but for Jhā, the line of argument would be almost impenetrable. Despite my great admiration for (and almost constant reliance upon) Jhā's work, however, it seems to me that its value for non-specialists is much reduced for the following reasons: his own English style is rather archaic, and his choice of philosophical terminology does not accord so well with contemporary usage among English-speaking philosophers; his own early background in the "new school" of Indian logic (Navya-Nyāya) colored his entire perspective in such a way that he not infrequently adopts anachronistic renditions for certain key terms and concepts; and, as he himself admitted, he had no specialized background in Buddhism, so that his treatment of Buddhist materials is sometimes not very satisfactory. In addition to Jhā's translations, I have also consulted Gangopadhyay and Chattopadhyay's translation of Vātsyāyana, Śāstrī's Hindi translation of the same, and Chakrabarti's partial translation of the introduction to *Nyāyavārttika,* book 3.

Following are the works consulted in preparing the present translations:

Taranatha Nyaya-Tarkatirtha, Amarendramohan Tarkatirtha, and Hemantakumar Tarkatirtha, eds. *Nyāyadarśanam.* Kyoto: Rinsen Book Company, 1984. (Reprinted from the 1936–44 Calcutta Sanskrit Series ed.) Includes the complete Sanskrit texts of Gautama's *Nyāyasūtra,* Vāstyāyana's *Bhāṣya,* Uddyotakara's *Vārttika,* and Vācaspatimiśra's *Tātparyaṭīkā.*

Gaṅganātha Jhā, *The Nyāya Sūtras of Gautama.* Reprinted, Delhi: Motilal Banarsidass, 1984. 4 vols. Includes complete translations of the commentaries of Vātsyāyana and Uddyotakara.

Mrinalkanti Gangopadhyay and Debiprasad Chattopadhyay, trans., *Nyāyasūtras.* Calcutta: Indian Studies Past and Present, 1967. 5 vols.

Arindam Chakrabarti, "The Nyāya Proofs for the Existence of the Soul." *Journal of Indian Philosophy* 10 (1982):. 211–38. Includes a partial translation of the introduction to book 3 of Uddyotakara's *Nyāyavārttika.*

Swāmī Dwārikādāsa Śāstrī, *Nyāyadarśanam.* Varanasi: Bauddha Bharati, 1976. Sanskrit text of Vātsyāyana's *Nyāyabhāṣya,* accompanied by a Hindi translation and commentary.

Translations

A. Vātsyāyana's Bhāṣya on Nyāyasūtra, 1.1.10.[10]

[Among the substances] the self is not grasped through direct acquaintance. But then is it established only through received scripture? No; for it is to be established through inference.

How then?

> Desire and hatred, willful effort, pleasure and pain, and knowledge are the marks of the self. *[icchā-dveṣa-prayatna-sukha-duḥkha-jñānāny ātmano liṅgam.]*

The self, having [previously] acquired pleasure through contact with an object of a certain type, desires to possess an object of that very type when it perceives it. It is the mark of the self that this desire-to-possess occurs, because a single seer unites *(pratisaṃdhā)* the [individual acts of] seeing. For even with respect to a fixed object, that [unification] cannot be based solely upon discrete mental events *(buddhibheda),* e.g., [the discrete mental events associated with] different bodies. Just so, because [individual acts of] seeing are united by one seer of many objects, there is aversion toward a [previously experienced] cause of suffering; and when, for example, its object is an established cause of pleasure, then, perceiving an object of that type, it strives to possess it, and this would not be the case if there were not one seer of many that unites [the individual acts of] seeing. And it would not be possible if there were only [discrete] mental events [directed upon] fixed objects, just as [is the case when those mental events are associated with] different bodies. In the same way, willful effort with respect to the cause of suffering is explained. Recalling pleasure or pain, this one, undertaking the means to achieve that [pleasure or to avoid that pain], realizes pleasure, or realizes pain, and thus experiences pleasure or pain. The reason is as stated before. [I.e., "this would not be the case if there were not one seer…"] Desiring to know *(bubhutsamāna),* moreover, this one reflects, "What is…?" And, having reflected, it knows, "This is…" It is the mark of the self that this knowledge is grasped as being the indivisible agent *(abhinna-kartṛka)* both of the desire to know and of the act of reflection. The reason is just as was stated before.

There [in the foregoing argument], "for example, different bodies" is to be analyzed thus: [Given the view] of the non-self advocate [*anātmavādin,* i.e., the Buddhist], just as discrete mental events having fixed objects [but occurring] in different bodies are not united, so too a single body's objects ought not to be united; for a special feature *(viśeṣa)* is absent [namely, a unifier]. It is a commonplace [when speaking] of a single being, that memory is of what he himself has perceived, not of what another has perceived. Similarly, it is a commonplace [when speaking] of diverse beings, that what one has perceived is not remembered by another. Neither of these two [commonplaces] can be established by the non-self advocate. Therefore, it is proven: The self is.

B. Uddyotakara's Vārttika: comments on passage A.[11]

"Desire..." is the sūtra whose purpose is to distinguish the self from those which belong to its class [that is to say, from the other objects of perception and knowledge] and those which do not [i.e., the means of perception and knowledge]. Alternatively, its purpose is to link scripture with inference, that is, its purpose is to link the self, which is established by scripture, with inference. Alternatively, its purpose is to illustrate the convergence of means of knowledge [which in this case are scriptural authority and inference], for when I said previously that "the means of knowledge converge" it was with this object in mind.

It says in the *Bhāṣya,* "through contact with an object of a certain type." There [in the passage which begins with those words], it is the unification of desire, etc., that establishes the existence of the self. The question to be examined is this: how is it that desire, etc., cause there to be knowledge of the unapprehended self? It is because of the sharing of a single object with memory; for singularity of agency is established because desire, etc., have the very same objects as memory. For [otherwise] there is no unification of diverse agents, diverse objects and diverse stimuli. For the cognitions of form, taste, odor, and texture are not united; for it is not the case that "what form I have seen, that is this texture, and what texture I have felt, that is the form I see." Neither is there found any unification with Yajñadatta, when it is Devadatta who has seen something. For it is not the case that what Devadatta saw, I, Yajñadatta, saw. Why so? Because of the determination of the objects of different minds. According to those who propound the non-self view, there can be no determinate objects whose forms are here and there differentiated, and thus there is no reason for unification. Therefore, that which unites is the self.

And if one objects that there is unification owing to there being cause and effect?

In other words, you think that the unification is not due to singularity of agency. But what then?

It is due to there being cause and effect. From the distinctions of ever earlier mental events, other, successively later, mental events come into being endowed with the whole mass of potencies in conformity with the potencies of the earlier mental events. Hence, even though there is diversity, there is unification owing to there being cause and effect, as in the case of a seed, etc. Thus, the shoot becomes manifest immediately after the rice grain. Its conformity with the potency of rice is established by its precedent [i.e., the rice grain]. Thereafter, being involved with the elements, a further rice grain is generated, not a barley grain; for that was not its precedent. Just so, in the present case, the unification of mental events belonging to a single continuum is due to the establishment of cause and effect, and it excludes the mental events belonging to another continuum, because they are not the precedent [of the present mental events of the continuum in question]. But the unification is not due to there being a unique agent, because that is not perceived. This unification being otherwise [i.e., explicable by other than the posit of an irreducible self], it cannot establish the being of the self.

But that is not so; because diversity has not been precluded [by the assumption of the continuum]; that is to say, affirming the unification to be due to there being cause and effect does not preclude diversity.

Why so?

There being cause and effect indeed supports [the assumption of] diversity; and where both sides in this argument agree that there is diversity, no unification is to be found.

Why is that?

Because what one has experienced is not remembered by another; and the unremembered cannot be united [with such a continuum], because, there being no cause and effect, it is not established.

But we do not say that wherever there is cause and effect unification is found; what we assert is that it is not found in the absence of cause and effect, because then there is no precedent. Therefore, this objection [that our causalism implies diversity] does not accord with our meaning.

But that is incorrect, because it does not get to the heart of the dispute. Saying this, sir, you have not gotten to the heart of it. What I have said is that [unification] is not seen where there is diversity. You have said that it is not seen where there is diversity, owing to the absence of cause and effect. Thus, owing to uncertainty, the heart of the dispute has not been reached.

The same also applies to yourself; by saying "because [unification] is not seen where there is diversity," neither have you gotten to the heart of the dispute.

Because of your affirmation [of our own premise of diversity] you are without a response; and it was by saying "the same [also applies to yourself]" that you so affirmed.

Not so, it was owing to want of proof; that is, I have not proven unification owing to there being cause and effect. Rather, because [the unification] possibly occurs otherwise [i.e., in the absence of a persisting self], it is stated that [your] reason has the fault of not proving that which is its purpose.

Not so, because you have not comprehended the significance of that reason. You have not understood the reason in particular, but have declared the reason to be flawed, saying "it may be otherwise," only with respect to the reason in general. But this unification has been particularly qualified: there is unification with memory owing to there being one object of both earlier and later cognition; but such memory cannot occur according to [the hypothesis advanced by] your side.

Why so?

Because one does not remember what another has experienced. That is to say, there is no memory by one of what another has experienced; it is not the case that another remembers what another experienced, and yet *there is* memory; therefore, it is reasonable for unification to be affirmed by that side for which memory is possible.

You attribute to us [the view that] memory does not occur; but, on the contrary, on our side it is not the case that memory is not possible.

How so?

It is due to there being cause and effect that the body-mind continuum *(kāya-citta-santāna)* in which memory and experience occur is the body-mind continuum which is both rememberer and experiencer.

Not so; because of the instability of mental events. For that which is impressed with what leaves a trace is seen to be stable, and there is no stability among mental events. And because of the absence of relationship; for that which is impressed with what leaves a trace is seen to be related [to it], but among mental events there can be no relationship with what leaves a trace.

It may be objected that "the trace is an occurrence among mental events characterized by some power." That is to say, it is thought that owing to a particular characteristic of consciousness, which co-existed with an earlier mental event, a mental event occurs characterized by the power of what preceded, and that is spoken of as its "trace, which is an occurrence among mental events characterized by some power."

It is in reference to this [very notion] that I have said, "because of instability, and because there is no relationship with what leaves the trace." That characteristic of consciousness that co-existed with the earlier mental event performs no useful function in connection with consciousness in the present or in the future.

Why so?

Just because, as it comes into being in the present, without deformation, exactly so, it is annihilated; and so it is not related to [anything that will occur in] the future, and what is unrelated does not leave traces. Therefore, to say that there is memory because of there being cause and effect is the trace of deficient education! And for this reason, too, there is no memory on your side: because states of being are dependent on beings. For every state of being depends on a being, just as origination on causal efficacy. Now, the being associated with memory should be either an object of action or an agent. [E.g., when one speaks of] "the cooking of rice," [the being referred to is] an object of action [i.e., the rice]; and [when speaking of] "Devadatta's gait," it is an agent [i.e., Devadatta]. Then, [in the case of memory] that [being] is not the object of the action, for there may be [memory] even when that [object of memory] does not exist. That is to say, when one remembers something not existing, then memory would be without foundation. But the agent is its foundation, and therefore [memory] may be realized on our side, but not on yours.

Why so?

Because you do not affirm there to be an agent. For you do not establish the existence of the agent in order that there be memory. Memory is foundationless on your account, and that is without [the support of] inference; for foundationless effects are not perceived. All effects are seen to have foundations, for instance, visible form, etc. Memory is one such [effect]; therefore, it has a foundation.

But the conventions "state of being," etc., refer to effect and cause. The instant of [the occurrence of] the effect is a "state of being," and the causal instant is a "being." What purpose, then, in supposing there to be some other being?

But that is not so, owing to temporal distinction; for cause and effect, being temporally distinct, cannot be of the nature of support and what is supported, e.g., a bowl and jujube fruits.

But then, this may be the case: origination is the "state of being" and what originates is the "being." Memory also originates, wherefore its origination will also be a "state of being," and memory, as what originates, will be a "being."

That, too, is wrong; both because of contradiction and absence of assertion. If origination is distinct from memory, there is a contradiction [in your position], and its [origination's] essential nature must be stated, for according to you, origination is no different from what originates. And if your thought is that origination is something different, then its essential nature must be stated. And to describe its essential nature would contradict [your] treatise.

Why so?

Origination has a connection with the existence of its proper cause, and existence is qualified by connection with a proper cause, both of which contradict what [your] treatise affirms.

Then, is it preceded by an origination that is no different from the memory?

In that case, it is vacuous to state what occurs on what [basis].

The origination is the state of being, and what originates is the memory?

To say so would be reasonable only if one were to say that the origination of memory is a state of being. Or, if memory is the state of being, then it [the origination] must be the being. Why? Because, as was said earlier, a state of being has reference to a being. Therefore, on your side memory is not at all possible, and without memory there is no unification. But [in fact] there is unification. Therefore, that which is the agent of this is a discrete and unique object, the self. The sūtra may also be interpreted as a direct inference. Thus, for instance, Devadatta's cognitions of visible form, flavor, odor, and texture bear the mark of one and many; for they are unified together by the cognition "I." Similarly, the cognitions of many persons, who have previously entered into an agreement, [are linked together] during the single instant when the dancing-girl raises her brow. Or else "Desire and hatred, willful effort, pleasure and pain, and knowledge are the marks of the self" may be explained differently: desire, etc., are qualities. That qualities are dependent entities is axiomatic. There being qualities is proven by differentiation: they are not genus, species or inherence, because they are impermanent. And they are not substance or action, because, like sound, they inhere in a substantial medium, etc.—with such a view to what they [desire, etc.] have in common, the inference [that they are qualities and so must inhere in some substance] is established because of impermanence, the dependency of desire, etc.; and also because of efficacy, as in the case of shape, etc. Because they are not extended in the manner of material substance, their being qualities of the body is negated. That being negated, they can only be qualities of the self. Thus, by differentiation it is proven that there is a self.

C. Extracts from Uddyotakara's Introduction to Nyāyasūtra, Book 3.[12]

Now, there follows the investigation of the objects of authoritative knowledge. To be investigated immediately is that about which, as its object, ego-construction continuously weaves saṃsāra, but which, when its nature is known, becomes the cause of an end to saṃsāra. That, of course, is the self, and so the self is to be examined. But, concerning it, what is to be examined? Is it different or not from body, sense faculty, intellect, and mental events?

Objection! [We can't begin to examine that question], because the subject [i.e., the self] is not proven to be! Difference and non-difference are [supposed to be] properties of the self, and so long as there is a subject as property-possessor, there are its properties; but the subject here is not proven to be. And it is not proper to examine the properties of a subject that is not proven to be. Therefore, let the existence of the subject itself be established.

Not so! The sūtra beginning "Desire…" [Given in passage **A.** above] has already proven the self to be. The sūtra beginning "Desire…" has established the real existence of the self; and that being established, it is proper for the examination [of its properties] to follow immediately. Moreover, there is no disputation; for no philosopher disputes the real existence of the self, but its particular characteristics are disputed thus: is the self merely the body? is the self intellect and so forth? is the self an aggregation? is the self something separate? So, the objection that it is improper to dispute about particular properties when the very being of the self is not established is itself not correct; wherefore the examination of properties is quite proper. Moreover, there is no proof that establishes its non-being. That is to say that there is no proof that establishes the non-being of the self implies that there is no dispute concerning its real existence.

But some object, saying, "It does not exist; for it has not come into being." That is, there is no self, because it has not come into being; and so is like a rabbit-horn [a nonexistent fancy].

There, the phrase "there is no self" is self-contradictory. This word "self," which is co-referential with the phrase "there is no" does not establish the non-being of the self.

For what reason?

"Self" designates being, while "there is no" is its negation. Whatever is negated in terms of somewhere is therefore elsewhere. E.g., the co-referentiality of the word "pot" with "there is no" cannot establish the non-existence of the pot, but is a negation with respect to specifications of place or time. "There is no pot" may negate a specification of place, e.g., "there is no pot in the house," or it may negate a specification of time, e.g., "there is none now," or [of position, e.g.] "it is not in front of...," or "it is not above..." No such negation amounts to a non-affirmation of the pot's being. Therefore, we ask whether "there is no self" is a negation of a specification of place or a specification of time. If one responds that it is a negation of a specification of place, that cannot be correct with respect to the self, because it is non-spatial. Moreover, by negating a specification of place the self is not thereby negated. Or is your intention as follows: "The body is not the self?" Then whose body is it with respect to which the self is negated? Or is your negation to the effect that "the self is not within the body?" Then whose body is it with respect to which the self is said to be not within?

Well then, where is the self?

Nowhere at all!

But now haven't you said "there is no...?"

It's not "there is no...," because only a specification was negated.

What's this verbal trick! So, it's not in the body, not elsewhere, and not not?

This "verbal trick" is simply to tell it like it is! For this self is nowhere at all, and therefore I've said so. Neither is a negation of temporal specification appropriate with respect to the self, because it is free from temporal distinctions, that is, there is no distinguishing the three times in reference to the self, because it is permanent. That the self is permanent we will establish below, in the sūtra beginning, "Cultivated before..." Therefore, there is no negation of temporal specification [with reference to the self]. Moreover, in undertaking to negate the self, the object of the word "self" must be stated. For we do not perceive any singular term as being meaningless. Thus, it might be established that the object of the word "self" is the body, etc., but in this manner our objection would not be overturned.

Why so?

Because then "there is no self" would mean "there is no body, etc."

Then, [we hold that it is] just what you imagine the self to be [i.e., an eternal, immaterial substance] that it is not.

But we do not *imagine* there to be a self. For "imagination" is the having of an object of cognition in which there is the projection of a property common both to what is not such-and-such and to those things which really are.[13]

And we do not establish the self in such a manner. By saying "just what you imagine to be the self" you raise the question, just how do we imagine the self? Is it as being or as non-being? If it is as being, then what is the common property shared by what is and what is not, whereby the self is an object of imagination? And by saying that self has something in common with non-self, self is affirmed, for what is not and what is have no common property. Now, imagining body and the other objects of ego-construction to be the self is erroneous, but this would not overturn our objection, because this is to affirm the being of an object of ego-construction that is distinct from body, etc. Perhaps you think that a singular term is not necessarily meaningful, e.g., "empty" or "darkness," and thus the objection is not overturned. But the word "empty" has this meaning: an unprotected [that is, ownerless] object, which is thus an object of use only to dogs, is "empty."[14] The word "darkness" has as its object whatever substance, attribute, or action has the mark of not being perceived. Wherever there is no proximity of light, the substances, etc., that are there are spoken of using the word "darkness." And by saying that the word "darkness" is meaningless, you contradict the position of your own school, which says, "darkness [is established] because of being a form to be acquired in connection with the four [elements]." Therefore, there is no meaningless word. And, moreover, just by saying, "there is no self," you contradict your own school.

Why so?

"'Form, O master, is not I. Neither are sensation, motivation, or consciousness I.' In this way, O monk, you are not form. Neither are you sensation, motivation, or consciousness."—This negates the bundles—form, etc.—as objects of "I." This is a negation of specification, not a negation in general. In not affirming the self, you ought also to it negate in general: e.g., "I am not, nor are you." Or else the partial negation is to the effect that the ego-construction has as its object a *collectivum.* In that case, one should say that the object of the ego-construction is a *collectivum* above and beyond physical form and the other five bundles. And by affirming the *collectivum* which is distinct from them to be the object of ego-construction the concept is delineated: self is a *collectivum.*

But [the *collectivum*] is not distinct; no single cognition captures the "I."

But we do not find a singular term applied to the many. Moreover, physical form and the other bundles, whether singly or collectively, are not the self—ego-construction [which grasps them as such] is the determination of something as what it is not.

So, let it be a mistaken cognition. How would that refute us?

How can it fail to refute you, that mistaken cognitions [according to your account] thus mimic true ones? Moreover, by not affirming the self, it is impossible to establish the teaching of the Tathāgata as a meaningful one. And it is not the case that this is not explicit, because of what is expressed in the *Sarvābhisamayasūtra.* In that it is said that saying "there is no self" contradicts your own school, thus: "I will teach the burden, O monks, and the bearer of the burden: the five bundles are the burden, and the burden-bearer is the person." And the sūtra says, "It is an erroneous view to hold that the self is not." Moreover, the reason [adduced in support of the view that there is no self], namely, "because it has not been produced," is contradicted by reason of being [simply] an exclusion of the other alternative. To have been produced and not to have been produced are properties of entities.

Now what is "to have been produced" and what is "not to have been produced"?

Whose being involves causes has been produced; whereas whose being does not involve causes is unproduced.

Why so?

Because the negative particle [in "not to have been produced"] has as its object to negate production; this application of the negative particle is a negation of production. That is to say, "its production is not found." Thus, to say that it is unproduced does not amount to a negation of the self. It is like [the expression], "the pot is water-less" [where the pot itself is not negated].

But in the case under discussion, "unproduced" is a negation of being.

Then your assertion and the logical reason [you adduce in favor of it] are one! "Unproduced," indeed, is a property; and it is not reasonable for a property to be autonomous, for it inheres in something other. And that to which this property belongs is the self. Hence, there is a contradiction [in your argument]. But if you are saying that there is a property, but no property-possessor, then you are involved in an incontrovertible self-contradiction; for there are no autonomous properties. What, moreover, is the meaning of "because of being unproduced?" If the meaning is that it has no birth, then that is not established; for the self possesses birth.

What, then, is the birth of the self?

A connection with an unprecedented embodied condition, that is, with body, sense faculty, intellect, and sensation.

Well, then, "unproduced" means "causeless."

In that way nothing is refuted! And the logical reason involves a contradiction [with your original assertion, namely, that there is no self, not that it is a causeless thing.] Because of the permanence of that which is causeless, in proving non-being you have proved permanence instead! Thus, your reason involves a contradiction. So the assertion and reason contradict one another: the object of the assertion is "there is no self," whereas that of the reason is that it [the self] has a relationship with perpetual being. Because these two, assertion and reason, have non-being and being as their respective objects, they are contradictory. In the same way, similar faults beset such other [logical reasons] as "because of absence of a material cause," "because no material cause for birth is acquired," "because of inefficacy," "because of causelessness," etc. So, too, when it is said that "it is like a rabbit-horn," this too is an unproven example.

Why is that?

Because the word "rabbit-horn" has a relationship as its object, a negation of the relationship is not a negation of a horn.

But the example should be the relationship between rabbit and horn.

That too is incorrect, for there might occur a relationship between a rabbit and a horn.

That contradicts ordinary usage.

So you think that if there were a horn on a rabbit, ordinary usage would be contradicted!

But it is not contradicted in that way. For worldly usage is due to the negation of there being a cause-and-effect relationship here. That is to say, the world denies [there being rabbit-horns] just in so far as horn is neither cause nor effect of rabbit. But just as there is a cause-and-effect relationship between cow and horn, just so there is no cause-and-effect relationship between rabbit and horn.

But the negation of the cause-and-effect relationship does not imply non-being. For it is not the case that where thus-and-such is neither cause nor effect of such-and-such, then it is not; for instance, Devadatta's pot [which, though it exists, has no causal relationship with Devadatta]. So, when one says, "there is no rabbit-horn," he should be interrogated as follows: is this a general negation or a particular negation? If you say "general negation," then that cannot be correct, for no such general negation is possible. For then "there is no rabbit-horn" implies "there is no cow-, or any other sort of horn that has any relationship with the rabbit," and that cannot be; for it is not the case that those [cow- and other horns] are not. Then is it a partial negation? That is, is some particular horn negated with respect to rabbit, so that the rabbit is neither its cause nor its effect? That [partial negation] negates this [particular] cause-and-effect relationship; that is to say, cause-and-effect relationships are found elsewhere, but are negated in this case. Hence, the example cannot establish absolute non-being. Similar considerations apply to the non-being of sky-flowers, etc.

And if one objects that there is no self, because it is not apprehended?

Here, too, the assertion, and so forth, are flawed, and the example is flawed, just as before. "By reason of no apprehension" is thus not correct. The absence of apprehension is not proven, because the self is the object of direct acquaintance and the other means of knowledge. Thus, the self is apprehended through direct acquaintance. How so? The consciousness of "I," which conforms to the distinctions of the nature of the object, and which does not depend upon memory of marks, the possessor of the marks, and their relationship, is direct acquaintance just as is the cognition of physical form. Concerning what you yourself, with perfect confidence, establish to be direct acquaintance, in virtue of what is it [said to be] direct acquaintance? You must establish it as being consciousness alone, which does not depend upon the relationships among marks, etc., and which is self-presented. So then you think there to be an I-cognition, but that its object is not the self? Well, then show us its object! If you say that it is physical form, etc., then you think physical form, etc., to be the objects of ego-construction. Just so it is said that, "Self is so-called owing to its being a stimulus for the origination of the object of ego-construction."

But that is not so, for that is not the case and it has been thus negated. Thus, [the Buddha] has negated [the assumption that] the ego-construction applies to physical form, etc.: "I am not form. Just so, O monk, you are not form." Therefore, physical form, etc., are not the objects of ego-construction. And this ego-construction is never found [to apply] to form, etc. For it is never the case that "I am physical form," or "I am sensation," etc.

But it is the case that "I am pale," or "I am dark."

We say that it is not.

How so?

For it is not the perceiver's cognition that, "This pale form which is mine—that is I." But merely through elision of a grammatical possessive [does one say], "I am pale," which thus has a possessive meaning [i.e., "my body is pale"]. This being so, it is not really the case [that the "I" in such expressions as "I am pale" refers to the body].

Why is that? Why do you think that [this is an instance of] "the elision of the possessive, etc., which is indicative of possessive meaning, but not really the case?"

It is because it reveals co-referentiality with the cognition "mine." That is to say, this I-cognition also applies to that which is the object of the cognition "mine." It is owing to this co-referentiality with the cognition "mine" that there is an elision of the possessive.

But this co-referentiality of the I-cognition with the cognition "mine" is found whenever there is difference, owing to usefulness. That is to say, the ego-construction is found to be co-referential with the cognition "mine" with respect to useful things—"what that is, such am I." It is said here that the I-cognition with respect to physical form and the other bundles is a cognition [which attributes] thus-and-such to what is not thus-and-such. But because [in that case] the self is the object of the I-cognition, just in that respect there is direct acquaintance [with that self]. Moreover, the self is apprehended by inference, as was stated in the sūtra "Desire...etc." Besides this, there is scriptural authority. Because those three epistemic authorities [direct acquaintance, inference, and scripture] have a single object, they converge in establishing the self. And there is no other epistemic authority that would overturn them. Therefore, "because there is no apprehension" is not established as a logical reason. "By reason of lack of apprehension" is further doubtful, there being three bases. That is, there may be three bases for lack of apprehension: apprehender, apprehension, and apprehended object. The doubt arises when one asks, in this instance of lack of apprehension, "it is due to the absence of which one [of the three]?" If you say that it is the apprehended object, then you are only repeating your original assertion. The original assertion cannot be its own proof, so such lack of apprehension cannot serve as the logical reason. Moreover, what is the ground upon which the non-apprehension depends in order to establish the non-being of the self? If you establish it to be the self, then you contradict your statement that there is no self. Then, let there be no ground—in that case, what is the purpose of the proof? For one cannot establish a groundless property [here = non-being] to be the *probandum*. Then the non-apprehension itself is not? In that case, just what are you trying to prove by saying, "by reason of non-apprehension?"

Notes

1 *Abhidharmakośa,* 1189.1–4; *D.* 82a1–2; Stcherbatsky 1976: 10–11; La Vallée Poussin 1971: vol. 5, 230.

2 *Abhidharmakośa,* 1189.5–1191.2; *D.* 82a2–6; Stcherbatsky 1976: 11–12; La Vallée Poussin 1971: vol. 5, 231–32.

3 *Abhidharmakośa,* 1191.3–1193.3; *D.* 82a6–b4; Stcherbatsky 1976: 12–13; La Vallée Poussin 1971: vol. 5, 232–34.

4 *Abhidharmakośa,* 1193.4–1195.10; *D.* 82b4–83b3; Stcherbatsky 1976: 14–18; La Vallée Poussin 1971: vol. 5, 234–37.

5 *Abhidharmakośa,* 1195.11–1201.10; *D.* 83b3–86a3; Stcherbatsky 1976: 18–27; La Vallée Poussin 1971: vol. 5, 237–46.

6 *Abhidharmakośa,* 1202.10–1215.10; *D.* 86a3–90b6; Stcherbatsky 1976: 27–50; La Vallée Poussin 1971: vol. 5, 247–73.

7 She is here equivalent to the Vajirā of the Theravāda tradition (chap. 3 above).

8 Yaśomitra explains (*Abhidharmakośa,* 1212) that a Nirgrantha ascetic once approached the Buddha holding a bird, and demanded to known whether it was living or not. If the Buddha had answered affirmatively, the ascetic would have squeezed out its life to demonstrate that the Buddha answered falsely, but would have preserved it had the Buddha declared it to be dead. The Buddha, therefore, did not offer a declarative response.

9 *Abhidharmakośa,* 1215.11–1231.10; *D.* 90b.6–95a.4; Stcherbatsky 1976: 50–76; La Vallée Poussin 1971: vol. 5, 273–300.

10 *Nyāyabhāṣya,* 1.184–88; Jhā 1985 1.216–19; Gangopadhyay and Chattopadhyay 1967 1.72–74; Śāstrī 1976 26–28.

11 *Nyāyavārttika,* 1.184–93; Jhā 1985: 1.219–33.

12 *Nyāyavārttika,* 2. 697–706; Jhā 1985, 3. 1067–1083; Chakrabarti 1982: 227–36.

13 Thus, for instance, in imagining a rabbit with a horn, one projects the property of horn-possession, which cows, for instance, really have, to rabbits, which do not have that property.

14 This is not a mistranslation, but is a derisive pun on the Buddhist technical term "empty" *(śūnya),* which plays on its near-homonymity with the Sanskrit word for dog, *śvan.*

15. Abhayākaragupta on the Two Truths

Introduction

ABHAYĀKARAGUPTA was among the last great masters of Buddhism in India. Active at the famous monastery of Vikramaśīla during the reign of Rāma Pāla (c. 1100), he wrote prolifically on most major areas of Buddhist practice and thought: Mahāyāna doctrine and the path, and Tantric ritual and meditation are all encyclopedically represented in the writings that survive.[1] Through both his impact on Tibetan visitors to Vikramaśīla, and the continuing activity of his successors in connection with the transmission of Indian traditions to Tibet, he came also to exert a remarkable influence upon the formation of Tibetan Buddhism, particularly during the twelfth through fourteenth centuries. Nevertheless, because his works have received little attention in contemporary scholarship, his importance as an exemplar of Buddhism under the Pāla dynasty as well as his legacy in Tibet have remained largely unknown.

Abhayākaragupta's masterwork on the path of the Mahāyāna is the *Munimatālaṃkāra (The Ornament of the Sage's Intention),* from which the selection translated below is drawn. The text, which unfortunately does not appear to survive in the original Sanskrit, was translated by the author's Tibetan disciple Dpang-zho Gsal-ba-grags at Nālandā, and later revised by Dpang Lo-tsā-ba Blo-gros-brtan-pa (1276–1342). It was widely studied in Tibet through at least the fourteenth century, after which time it seems to have been supplanted by indigenous Tibetan treatises treating similar subject matter, and often adhering to the model of Atiśa's famous "Lamp on the Path of Enlightenment" *(Bodhipathapradīpa).* Given the considerable difficulty in this case of Abhayākaragupta's text, and the remarkable literary clarity achieved by Tibetan authors of works on the path—notably Sgam-po-pa, Sa-skya Paṇḍita, Klong-chen-pa, and Tsong-kha-pa—it is easy enough to see why this displacement might have taken place. Nevertheless, the reader of the *Munimatālaṃkāra* cannot but be impressed by the strong correspondences one sometimes finds between aspects of Abhayākaragupta's work and formulations found in later Tibetan writings. Indeed, the title of Sa-skya Paṇḍita's major path-text, the "Clarification of the Sage's Intention" *(Thub pa'i dgongs pa rab tu gsal ba),* no doubt alludes to Abhayākaragupta's treatise.

The only commentary available on the *Munimatālaṃkāra* is an interlinear series of annotations *(mchan 'grel)* found in just two of the Tibetan canonical editions of the text (Peking and Narthang). Wayman 1984 argues that this is Abhayākaragupta's own work and that it demonstrates the Indian origins of the Tibetan genre of interlinear commentary. This, however, is certainly incorrect. The fact, for instance, that the Tibetan translation of the name of the Vikramaśīla monastery *(Rnam-gnon-tshul)* in the author's colophon is glossed with its Sanskrit equivalent in the commentary clearly points to Tibetan, not Indian, authorship. The interlinear commentary on the *Munimatālaṃkāra* is thus a Tibetan supplement intended to clarify aspects of this difficult text, and, given the evidence of the translators' colophons, it was most likely composed by the last of the translators to have worked on the *Munimatālaṃkāra,* the noted Sanskritist Dpang Lo-tsa-ba Blo-gros-brtan-pa.[2] The commentary, if truth be told, often does not address the problems a contemporary Western reader is likely to encounter, though it does usefully identify the sources of many quotations left unidentified in Abhayākaragupta's own text.

The passage translated here is drawn from the final section of the lengthy first chapter of the *Munimatālaṃkāra,* entitled the "appearance of the enlightened mind *(bodhicitta)*" *(byang chub kyi sems kyi snang ba'i le'u, *bodhicittālokaparicchedа).*[3] The chapter as a whole traces the course of the path from the initial cultivation of the aspiration to enlightenment *(bodhipraṇidhicitta)* through to the development of discernment, or wisdom *(prajñā),* and it is in this context that the analysis of the two truths is introduced. In its general orientations, Abhayākaragupta's discussion is clearly reminiscent of that of his predecessor at Vikramaśīla, Prajñākaramati, whose remarks we considered in chapter 8 above. One important difference, however, is that Abhayākaragupta, perhaps influenced by the approach of Śāntarakṣita and certainly anticipating later Tibetan developments, more fully engages the *pramāṇa* tradition of Dharmakīrti, even in this Madhyamaka context.

The translation presented below is intended only as a preliminary effort, introducing an aspect of Abhayākaragupta's work that complements earlier essays in this volume, particularly chapters 7 and 8. It will be evident, too, that there are also affinities with the Tibetan materials discussed in chapters 12 and 13. It is possible that Dol-po-pa, especially, was directly influenced by the text here considered; for we know that he much admired Abhayākaragupta, and was a close student of his tantric œuvre. I offer this translation not as a definitive interpretation of this challenging text—for it is certainly not that—but rather as a stimulus to further investigation of an author who merits far greater investigation than he has received to date. The encyclopedic character of Abhayākaragupta's writings particularly recommends them as a source for the study of monastic Buddhist learning during the later Pāla dynasty.

The interpretation provided here is given without annotation and other apparatus. I have added section headings, bracketed comments when this appeared useful, and Sanskrit equivalents for technical expressions, as aids to understanding. I have also identified citations, where possible, in edited Sanskrit texts. (However, translation of citations always accords with the form in which they are given in the present Tibetan text.) My aim throughout has been philosophical intelligibility, while accepting the limitations of philological minimalism. (As Theodore Stcherbatsky and Sylvain Lévi suggested long ago, texts such as these really merit a *double* translation.) One particular point requires special comment: the term *saṃvṛtisatya*—which is variously rendered as relative, conventional, transactional, or superficial truth or reality; and in chapter 8 above as "occluded" truth—is of central importance in the present discussion, and is treated here from a variety of differing viewpoints. At one point or another, any of the translations just suggested might be appropriate, though none of them seems adequate in all contexts of use. I have therefore adopted the expedient here of translating *saṃvṛtisatya* as "ostensible truth," which has the merit of being intelligible throughout this selection, without straining English style beyond the limits to which it is already pushed in translations of Buddhist philosophical texts.

In translating this selection, I have utilized both the Derge (*T.* 3903, in *D. Bstan-'gyur, Dbu-ma,* vol. A: 73b–293a) and Peking (*P.* 5299, in vol. 101: 146.5–277.4) editions of the *Munimatālaṃkāra.* (The passage given here spans folios 137b–145b in the former and plates 184.3–189.5 in the latter.) In general, I have preferred the readings supplied by the Peking text where there have been significant variants between the two, though in a small number of cases, too, I have adopted the readings of the Derge edition.

Translation

1. Four Truths, Two Truths, and One Truth[4]

These eighteen bases *(dhātu)* alone, when condensed in one way are established to be the twelve activity fields *(āyatana),* and when extremely condensed in another the five bundles *(skandha).* They, indeed, *are* the four truths: suffering *(duḥkha),* origination *(samudaya),* cessation *(nirodha),* and the path *(mārga).* They are also the three natures *(svabhāva):* imaginary *(parikalpita),* dependent *(paratantra),* and absolute *(pariniṣpanna).* They are also two: the ostensible truth *(saṃvṛtisatya)* and the truth of the ultimate objective *(paramārthasatya).* They are, moreover, one alone: the undivided *(advaya)* truth of the ultimate objective. That, indeed, is beyond conceptual elaboration *(niṣprapañcita).* That alone is the great vehicle *(mahāyāna),* the transcendent perfection of wisdom *(prajñāpāramitā),* the spirit of enlightenment that is the ultimate objective *(pāramārthikabodhicitta).*

Among those [four truths], what is to be renounced *(heya)* is the aspect that is altogether afflicted *(saṃkliṣṭa),* whose result *(phala)* is the truth of suffering, which is appropriated by means of the truth of origination. What is to be undertaken *(upādeya)* is the aspect of purification *(vyavadāna),* whose result is the truth of cessation, which is appropriated by means of the truth of the path. The proper essence of the truth of the ultimate objective is the truth of cessation. Therefore, [because the three truths of suffering, origination, and the path comprise the ostensible truth,] there are only two truths. As it says in *The Sūtra of the Meeting between Father and Son* (*Pitaputrasamāgamanasūtra, T.* 60; *Bodhicaryāvatārapañjikā,* p. 175):

> The world-knower by himself has seen these two truths,
> Not having heard them from others.
> They are the ostensible and the ultimate objective.
> There is no third truth at all.

Similarly, it says in *The Sublime Dialogue with Brahmā* (*Āryabrahmaviśeṣacintiparipṛcchā, T.* 160):

> There is no suffering, there is no origination of suffering, there is no cessation, neither is there a path which is a noble truth *(āryasatya).* Nonetheless, Brahmā! this suffering without coming-into-being is a noble truth. This origination without movement

> is a noble truth. This total cessation without coming-into-being or ceasing-to-be is a noble truth. This loving cultivation of the path with respect to all principles, which are equivalent, is a noble truth.

Therefore, with respect to the ultimate objective, suffering and the other truths do not exist. In order to turn the mind from saṃsāra and on behalf of the pious attendants *(śrāvaka),* they were merely taught through such topics as impermanence in order to introduce only the reality of personal selflessness *(pudgalanairātmyatattva);* but they were not [taught] with reference to the teaching of both selflessnesses [of persons and of principles]—that must be understood.

2. *Two Truths and Three Natures*[5]

Those who disparage ostensible reality, those whose intelligence is perverted through obsessive study of mistaken treatises, etc., and those who, with respect to what is conventional, non-existent, and mere falsehood, exaggeratedly attribute entities that are permanent, etc., [to ostensible reality,] and who grasp form, etc., as being as *they appear*—because their intellects have fallen into the extremes of disparagement and exaggerated attribution, they do not enter into the extremely profound ocean that is the way of the ultimate objective as is proper, namely, "without two extremes." Therefore, in the *Sūtra Which Sets Free the Intention (Saṃdhinirmocanasūtra),* the Transcendent Lord has for that very reason taught the intentions of the three absences of essence, elucidating the teachings of not-coming-into-being, etc., which have reference only to the ultimate objective. Thus, he has scripturally established the middle path *(madhyamā pratipat),* without two extremes, as being solely of definitive significance *(nītārtha).*

In that context, whatever, when left unexamined, is nevertheless believed and seen in the manner of apparition, that thing, which has arisen in interdependence, exemplifies the dependent nature. That, moreover, comes into being ostensibly by the force of conditions that are external to it, but not by its own nature; wherefore, coming-into-being is determined to be devoid of an essential nature. Whatever arises in interdependence is just empty by nature.

With reference to just that dependent nature, permanence and impermanence and other such natures that, in reality, are projected upon it, are the imputed nature. Because the imputed nature is not established as such, it is determined to be devoid of a definite nature. This absence of essential nature is in fact determined just with reference to the dependent nature, because its defining characteristic is imputed just to that [dependent nature].

That which abides always, in reality, as the natural essencelessness of all principles *(dharma)* is the absolute nature, because that is established to be always free from projections. As it says in the *Sandhinirmocanasūtra* (*T.* 106):

> With reference to the dependent characteristic and the absolute characteristic, the perpetual absence, in all aspects, of either affliction or purification, and nonobjectification with respect to it—these are all said to be the characteristic of emptiness.

Moreover, referring to passion, etc.: exaggeratedly attributing substantial nature to ostensible things, which exemplify the dependent characteristic—as causes of affliction, as effectuators of saṃsāra, or as obstructors of the antidotal aspects [of the path], etc.—is the imputed characteristic with reference to them. In the ostensible reality of the yogins *(yogisaṃvṛti)*, because there is [a realization of] the absolute inasmuch as the absolute is inerrantly established, there is an exaggerated attribution of substantial reality [which imputes] the characteristic of the absolute to the factors of enlightenment and other aspects of purification, [which are thus grasped] as the decisive defeaters of whatever opposes [enlightenment] and as the true effectuators of nirvāṇa, and so forth—that is the imputed characteristic with reference to them. Concerning these principles whose nature is the imputed characteristic, neither of those two [ostensible causes of affliction or of purification] exists in the naturally radiant expanse of reality, because ultimately there are no afflictions, etc. This is because these afflicted and purificatory principles, being all ultimately unoriginated, are of a single taste *(ekarasa)*, so that it is not reasonable to divide them. Therefore, because both alike abide as empty but valid in terms of their ostensible truth *(tathyasaṃvṛtisatya)*, there is no fault of negating [the ostensible distinction between] the afflicted and purificatory dimensions. That is what is said, too, in the two-thousand-five-hundred-verse *Prajñāpāramitā* (*Suvikrāntavikrāmiparipṛcchā, T.* 14):

> Suvikrāntavikrāmin! Form is neither a locus of passion nor a locus of dispassion. So, too, for sensation, perception, motivations, and consciousness. The perfection of wisdom *(prajñāpāramitā)* is their reality as not-being-passion and their reality as not-being-dispassion. Similarly, form is neither a locus of aversion nor a

> locus of inaversion, neither a locus of stupidity nor a locus of non-stupidity. Similarly, the perfection of wisdom, with respect to consciousness as it is, is this reality of non-stupidity and this reality of not non-stupidity. Form is neither afflicted nor pure. The perfection of wisdom is this non-affliction and this non-purity among them [i.e., form and the remaining skandhas].

3. The Meaning of "Ostensible" [6]

Nevertheless, is it not said, "ostensibly [things] come to be"? In this case, what is [the meaning of] "ostensible"?

What is said to be "ostensible" is the bewildered intellect that has projected erroneous features of things upon things that are devoid of substantial nature. This is because here [things] are obscured, or because it causes, as it were, the occlusion of reality. As it says in a sūtra (*Laṅkāvatāra,* 10.429):

> Ostensibly things come into being.
> Ultimately there is no substantial nature.
> That absence of substantial nature, bewilderment,
> Is held to be valid ostensibly.

Because they have thus emerged, all false things which are thus indicated are spoken of as ostensible. Regarding that, moreover, the force of the maturation of beginningless, bewildered dispositions *(vāsanā)* reveals things from nothing as if they genuinely existed, and which thus come into being among all creatures. Owing to this, by the force of the mental activity directed upon them, all such essentially false things are spoken of as ostensible. These are not genuinely of the essential nature of real substances, because their way of appearing is not what really is *(tattva).* Neither are they, like the rabbit's horn, perpetually nonexistent essences, because they distinctly appear with features that are well enough when left unanalyzed. In that way, the verbal convention "ostensible truth" is adopted [to speak of] what is projected by false-featured cognition with respect to all things, in the manner of essences determined by persons subject to bewildered cognition with respect to illusory persons [magically created by an illusionist] and so forth. And the truth of the ultimate objective is that essence which is ascertained by valid epistemic operations with respect to all things, in the manner of the essences determined by unadulterated consciousness, [which recognizes as illusion] those illusory persons and so forth.

Thus, depending upon the two truths, ostensible and ultimate, whose essences are [respectively] determined by bewildered and unbewildered cognition, it is established that ostensibly, for those with eye disease, etc., there exist hairlines and other such apparent objects, while for the proponents of percepts [*vijñaptivādin,* the adherents of Mind Only,] there exist both the features of apprehended object and apprehending subject, though they do not exist ultimately. Owing to the distinctions made with reference to this, there is no contradiction [in the establishment of the two truths,] and so it is for all things.

Therefore, the ostensible, bewildered essence, as thus explained, in reality is without coming-into-being, but nevertheless it seems manifest that things come into being from something. Hence, depending on that, one says that "ostensibly things come to be," though ultimately there is no coming-to-be.

Because they have inerrant objectives as their objects, all cognitions born of authentic study, thought, and contemplation alone are spoken of as "ultimate objectives," for they are said to have the ultimate as their objective.

There is a distinction to be made in terms of direct and indirect [cognition of the ultimate]. Owing to that, all things are realized just to be without coming-to-be. Correct cognition tells us that these are not established as coming-to-be. Furthermore, what is not examined is ostensible reality. Thus, discernment born of thought arises by force of sound epistemic operations that have engaged in the inerrant ascertainment of reality [and, in this sense, it is "indirect"]. Similarly, there is [discernment] born of contemplation, which is said to analyze the significance of reality by means of either direct investigation or of that which accords with its basis.

That which turns its back on the significance of reality is said to be a false investigation. All cognitions which apprehend false features, whose back is turned to the significance of reality, due to their being opposed to that [reality], are unexamined. They are neither non-discursive gnosis *(nirvikalpakajñāna),* nor mere absence of analysis. Therefore, all things of false nature, whose natures are well-known, are thus merely ostensible. Moreover, the ostensible is that which is accepted in the world *(lokaprasiddha);* for those objects which are well-known to the whole world are held to be just ostensible.

Not every object is within the scope of all faculties, because some [faculties] perceive only some [objects]. Therefore, all the ascertainments determining deeds and their results, etc., which remain extremely inevident *(atiparokṣa)* are solely [within the scope of] omniscient gnosis. But other [matters, which are not "extremely inevident"] are [known] through the remaining cognitions [i.e., mundane consciousness in contradistinction to omniscient gnosis].

Some authors of śāstra say that, opposing what is well-known, things that are analyzed as being of the nature of imputations and so forth are said to exist as errant ostensibles *(mithyāsaṃvṛti),* for they are not well-known [to valid ostensible truth]. As for that which is investigated following on the basis of what is well-known—for instance,

> This is not a self or a being.
> These principles have a causal basis—

this is said to exist as valid ostensible truth.

Therefore, although the authors of śāstra have elaborated many [sorts] of natures, this does not imply that things have many natures that are mutually contradictory.

Again, illusion is a synonym of the ostensible, and untruth is a synonym of illusion. Though illusory objectives are of the nature of bewildered cognition, there is no implication that it is cognition that *is* the [illusory] thing [perceived]. This is because [when there is bewildered cognition] there is an appearance in which a false feature *(mithyākara)* is apprehended, and because the true and the false are mutually contradictory in essence. Therefore, because that whose nature is false would become true [insomuch as cognition itself *is* the illusion], the cognition would neither be bewildered, nor of variegated nature; for there would be no essential contradiction in the one [appearance].

As for false natures, too, because they are false, [and assuming the strict identity of consciousness and its object,] cognition would not be true even in respect to its being bewildered; because the natures [of consciousness and its object] must be without mutual variation, and because, being one, they can be neither parts *(avayava)* nor part-possessors *(avayavin)* [with respect to one another]. Therefore, because cognition, too, is false [under this description], this is quite different from the inner constitution of the knowable.

4. Against "Nominalism"[7]

There is a misunderstanding that the ostensible is merely nominal *(śabdamātra),* but no follower of the Sugata holds the ostensible to be merely nominal. As for what it says in a sūtra,

All of these are only names,
Abiding just in perception.
There is no expressed referent,
Apart from the act of expression—

this indicates that the expression and its referent just abide in conceptual activity; [and this is] in order to refute the tenet of those who imagine the expression to be just a substantial thing and its referent to be something else again. For here, "perception" *(saṃjñā)* is conceptual activity *(kalpanā);* and it is just the essence of conceptual activity that is evidently intended by the word "name" [used in this verse to mean] "act of expression." It [the "name"] is not the object that appears to auditory cognition; for that is not in itself an act of expression. Moreover, if [everything] were exhausted only in that [i.e., in names alone,] then all things would not appear variously—as visible form, etc.—and there could be no determination of the *skandhas,* and so forth. Just as, with reference to many illusory persons, there is the imputed application of an essence whose feature is the objective generality *(arthasāmānya)* [corresponding to] the repeated term "person," so too with reference to things inasmuch as they are essenceless with regard to the ultimate objective. That which is expressible as an essence exaggeratedly attributed to the ultimate objective is solely ostensible; for that [ultimate objective] transcends all elaborations *(prapañca).* So it is said in a sūtra (*Āryasaṃvṛtiparamārthanirdeśasūtra,* T. 179):

> O son of the gods! If, in terms of the ultimate objective, the truth of the ultimate objective were to be an essence within the reach and range of body, speech, and mind, then it would not be counted as truth, but would be merely ostensible truth. But on the contrary, in terms of the ultimate objective, the truth of the ultimate objective transcends all conventional signs.

Moreover, the momentariness of things is ostensible. The ultimate objective is the emptiness *(śūnyatā)* that is definitive of all those things of changeable nature, their natural essencelessness. And that is permanent, because it abides throughout all time, whether or not tathāgatas arise.

5. The Ostensible and Epistemic Authority[8]

If the ostensible is an epistemic authority *(pramāṇa),* then in what sense is it ostensible? But if it is not an epistemic authority, then how is selflessness proven on this basis?

This [objection] is incorrect; for, just as an inferential cognition proceeds from the apprehension of a universal that is false [in that all universals are conceptual constructions], and hence is ostensible in essence, nevertheless it is held to be an epistemic authority just insomuch as it brings about the acquisition of the intended objective efficacy *(arthakriyā)*. In the same way, certain ostensible things, despite being false in their own essence, are said to be "epistemic authorities" just in that they are not deceptive with respect to worldly or transcendent objectives, owing precisely to what transpires in the progressive course of appropriate study, critical reflection, and so forth [whose subject matter consists in "certain ostensible things" such as selflessness, etc.]. And their opposites are *not* epistemic authorities. All such determinations of epistemic authority, etc., are only due to convention *(vyavahāra)*—because this is established in the *Pramāṇavārttika,* etc., it is beside the point to elaborate upon it here.

All that is ostensible, moreover, has already been established to be in no way the essence of things. Therefore, the appropriation of these ostensible things, such as trees and so forth, is reasonably established to be only a beginningless, insubstantial self-adequation. Neither are consciousness, etc., substantial; because they are the contradictories of that. Therefore, with reference to what is well-known when left unexamined—the exaggerated attributions of coming-into-being, abiding, destruction, etc.—these are determined to be ostensible truth, and similar to apparitions, dreams, the city of angels *(gandhārvanagara),* conjurations, and so forth.

As for these exaggerated attributions such as coming-into-being, etc., the ascertainment of their absence by means of genuine epistemic authority is that truth which is the truth of the ultimate objective. As it says in the *Dharmasaṃgīti* (*T.* 238):

> The absence of coming-into-being is truth. Principles like coming-into-being are loci of untruth, falseness, and deception.

Because this absence of coming-into-being accords with the ultimate objective, it is spoken of as the ultimate objective, but it is not so in fact; because in reality *(vastutas)* the ultimate objective transcends all elaborations. Though the absence of coming-into-being just alone is not to be taught [to be the ultimate] in all aspects, nevertheless, owing to conventional usage *(vyavahāravaśāt),* it is taught that the unconditioned is the reality of conditioned things without exception. Because both coming-into-being and its absence abide throughout all time, they are also taught to be unconditioned, but that is not to say that [the ultimate] is of the essence of those two; for it is characterized as transcending all essences. As it says in the **Mahāprasādotpādanasūtra* (cf. *Mūlamadhyamakakārikā,* chap. 18, v. 9):

> Not realized elsewhere, pacific,
> Unelaborated by elaborations,
> Non-conceptual, not various—
> This is characteristic of suchness *(tathatā).*

Just so, the twenty-two [modes of the] cultivation of [the enlightened] mind *(cittotpādana)* [as are taught in the *Abhisamayālaṃkāraśāstra*] are merely ostensible, together with [their] particular [subdivisions]. And so it is, moreover, [in this context] that "particular," "qualification," "attribute," and "principle" are no different in meaning; and "particularized," "qualified," "locus of attributes," and "locus of principles" are no different in meaning.

Whenever, owing to the apprehension of a self-marking particular *(svalakṣaṇa),* a term for a principle is used to express the locus of the principle [e.g., "there's a *blue* thing here"], at that time the principle is ostensibly designated a "reality" *(dharmatā)*—this determination of utterance meaning *(śabdārtha)* emerges from the [system of] signs *(saṅketa).* Utterance meaning may be affirmative or negative. Those, moreover, may be understood at once from the utterance which expresses an affirmation, as in the case of [the understanding of] "a taintless, white, hundred-petalled [flower]," [which arises] from [hearing] the utterance "white lotus." The cognition that is engendered by the utterance has as its object a particular essence that is devoid of exaggerated attribution. For that very reason, it is an exclusion of the extraneous *(anyāpoha),* whose intention is without such contents as genus [*jāti,* and other imputed categories], and precisely without an entity corresponding to the intended object. If, moreover, one objects that, because there is then no entity corresponding to the object, the object of the exclusion must be an object that is a non-entity, then [we may respond that] with respect to that, too, the subject, due to self-assertion, [apprehends] its intended objective as an object, even though there is in fact no object. And even insomuch as the subject is oriented to an objective, it is not so in all respects, but rather [when there is an intentional act] whose essence is delimited by a single differential. [The content of the act, in other words, is determined by what it excludes.]

That aspect of an entity whose nature is without any heterogeneity is its conceptual range, [corresponding to] the meaning of the utterance. As it is said (cf. *Pramāṇavārttika, Svārthānumānapariccheda,* v. 48cd):

> How can an essence that is unascertained
> Be the object of that ascertainment?

Therefore, because [in that case] other utterances may apply, [only] that nature which eliminates each heterogenous category is an aspect of the entity, [corresponding to] the meaning of the utterance. All conventional usages—negations and affirmations—have that alone as their basis, owing to the presence of that [aspect of the entity], and the absence of what is heterogenous and devoid of that [same aspect].

Because the negation of a predicate *(paryudāsapratiṣedha)* has the nature of an elimination [of some predicate or qualification], so that it is not a mere absence, when the negation is comprehended and expressed through an utterance, there is just the expression of a difference. Just as that negative utterance eliminates an exaggeratedly attributed feature, expressing it in terms that entail an affirmation, [e.g., "there *is* something *not blue* here"], and while the existential negation *(prasajyapratiṣedha),* whose nature is no essence whatever, entails no-thing-ness [e.g., "there *is no* blue thing" *simpliciter*], in the same way an affirmation expresses an affirmative essence, but without overlooking the differential essence that opposes [what is affirmed] to what is other [e.g., "there *is* something blue (and *not* otherwise) here"]. For these reasons, the intended meaning for the auditor may be an unrestrictively qualified convention, in that it does not preclude other qualifications, as [when one speaks of] "the mind being without substance *and* empty"; or, it may be a restrictively qualified convention, in that it does preclude other qualifications, as [when one speaks of] the "insubstantiality," or "emptiness" of consciousness. But in terms of the ultimate objective, because principles such as consciousness and the reality that is emptiness are without substantial nature, there is neither qualification nor the absence of qualification. So it is said (in the *Pramāṇavārttika, Parārthānumānapariccheda,* v. 182):

> In investigating the ultimate objective,
> Such [qualifications] are not established.

It is in ostensible word and meaning
That reality and alterity are negated.

Moreover, (the *Pramāṇavārttika, Svārthānumānapariccheda,* v. 169cd) says:

Because the differential is without essence,
There can be no analysis of sameness or difference.

Therefore, conditioned characteristics, such as the whiteness of the moon and so forth, are the ultimate characteristic in a unity coextensive with what is ostensible, which is entirely inexpressible in terms of self-identity or alterity. This is because it is only with reference to an entity that there can be a conception of self-identity or alterity, and the general characteristic of the ultimate objective is that, because it is without the essence of an entity, it is entirely inexpressible in terms of self-identity or alterity. For where there is an existing entity, there emerge the conceptions of self-identity or alterity, but given that entities are without substantial nature, that is not the case—this involves no contradiction at all.

That ultimate objective whose nature is gnosis *(jñānātmakaparamārtha),* moreover, whose characteristic is suchness that is coextensive with the ostensible, is held to be uniquely the feature of the ultimate objective; for as it says in the Perfection of Wisdom:

> Subhūti! What is ostensible in the world *(lokasaṃvṛti)* is not one thing and the ultimate objective another; for it is just the suchness of what is ostensible in the world that is the suchness of the ultimate objective.

Thus, because that ultimate objective whose nature is gnosis is no different from apparition and so forth, it is also the very essence of valid ostensible reality. Because it is in accord with the realization of just what is, it is also the very essence of the ultimate objective. Though these involve a difference of emphasis, with respect to each, there is no essential contradiction between the two. Therefore, the determinations of the various principles and loci of principles, etc., are merely conventional—by affirming this [it is entailed that] ultimately the cultivation of [enlightened] aspiration, etc., is neither qualified nor without qualification.

6. Madhyamaka and Mind Only[9]

Concerning what is said in the *Āryadaśabhūmikasūtra*—"O sons of the gods! these three realms are mind alone"—it is not taken to be ultimately so, because in other sūtras it is the absence of substantial nature *(niḥsvabhāvatā)* that is taught at length. Rather, Mind Only *(cittamātra)* is exclusively taught in order to provide an ingress into the oceanic ways of the ultimate objective—so it is that you should grasp it.

In that way, those who cannot realize at once that all principles, without exception, are without substantial nature gradually penetrate the absence of substantial nature of external objects by relying on Mind Only. Hence it is said (in the *Laṅkāvatāra):*

> In this way, those who look analytically
> Come to negate apprehended object and apprehending subject.

Thereafter, by stages, when one investigates the nature of Mind Only, having fully comprehended it as selflessness, one penetrates the profound way *(gambhīranaya).*

Ostensibly, in accordance with consciousness, external objects also abide. Otherwise, there would be a contradiction with what is stated in the *Āryadaśabhūmikasūtra,* namely, that on the eighth stage *(bhūmi)* the bodhisattva comes to know the number of atoms in the universe *(lokadhātu)* and so forth. As it says at great length (*Daśabhūmika,* p. 44, lines 18–22):

> He well knows even those that are subtle, and knows well, too, those that are great, and unlimited, and their divisions. He knows well also how many subtle atoms of the elemental base of earth there are in the universe. Similarly, he knows well the elemental bases of water, of fire, and of wind.

There would also be a contradiction with common knowledge; for external objects are well known, just as is consciousness. Both, however, when examined by reason, do not stand up to scrutiny, and so are non-entities. In conventional truth, however, both things are very well known to [everyone] even simple milkmaids.

The fruit which is spoken of in Mind Only is the negation of the agent *(kartṛ)* and the enjoyer *(bhoktṛ)* imputed by others [i.e., non-Buddhists]; for, even conventionally, no other agent, etc., is established besides mind alone.

Again, [Mind Only is taught] in order to demonstrate the mind's preeminence with reference to all principles, because the mind precedes all principles.

Regarding the saying, "mind itself which has no object," and similarly (*Laṅkāvatāra,* 10.155ab):

> The mind that is agitated by latent dispositions *(vāsanā)*
> Emerges appearing as an object—

these and other such citations should be taken to affirm just that [mental acts] are certainly accompanied by features [*ākāra,* of their apparent objects], because it is impossible for a featureless mind to apprehend any object whatsoever. Therefore, because no objective feature appears besides the mental feature, by refuting that [objective feature], it is precisely proven that the mind is accompanied by features; but on that basis it is not realized that there are no external objects.

What's more, the Transcendent Lord has taught [Mind Only] on behalf of persons who might be trained by it, in view of [their adherence to] teachings such as the existence of the self. As it says in the *Laṅkāvatāra* (2.121):

> As a doctor bestows medicines
> On patients who are ill,
> So too the Buddha teaches
> Mind Only to sentient beings.

He has not taught this in order to deceive others; for it is a fruitful teaching, which brings happiness to persons who may be trained by it. The Transcendent Lord has spoken no falsehood, because truthfulness is just what is beneficial to others. As the exalted Nāgārjuna says (in the *Ratnāvali,* chap. 2.35cd):

> That which solely benefits others is truth.
> Its opposite, because it brings no benefit, is falsehood.

Others, however, hold that because just Mind Only is in essence self-evidently proven, ostensibly it so abides, while external objects do not abide even ostensibly; for they are not established except as features of mind. Therefore, [they say,] in order to properly indicate that, the Transcendent Lord has taught that entities are just mind alone.

In that way, it may be that ostensibly there are external objects or merely percepts *(vijñaptimātra),* but [those two alternative views] are not, in all aspects, the transmitted teachings [of the Buddha] that indubitably carry conviction regarding the genuine establishment of the essence of things. Thus, those who in arrogance conceptualize the nature of things—while failing to grasp rightly the way of the scriptures of the Transcendent Lord—disparage the Transcendent Lord, and bring themselves and others to ruin. All those substantialists [i.e., both the realists and the idealists], insomuch as they errantly teach the real nature of principles *(dharmatattva),* are just teaching a counterfeit perfection of wisdom. Only those who propound the absence of the substantial essence of all principles are inerrant.

For that reason, those who are intelligent will faithfully reject views that abandon the profound doctrines, and, taking as an epistemic authority the Transcendent Lord alone, will consider that they have failed to grasp [the profound doctrine] owing only to their own ignorance. Thus, engendering exceptional devotion to the profound sūtras, they will make manifest efforts to study, retain, and meditate upon them. They will encourage others rightly to take them up, and they will pray to cultivate their own devotion. For so it is that the tathāgatas alone are the unique epistemic authority of direct perception *(pratyakṣapramāṇa).* They do not objectify any entity as genuine; for as it says in the *Bodhisattvapiṭaka* (*T.* 56):

> Again, if you ask, "What is it to see all principles as they are?"
> it is no seeing at all.

And in the *Dharmasaṅgīti:*

> The unseeing of all principles is genuine seeing.

7. *The Perception of Yogins and the Inference of Essencelessness*[10]

Nevertheless, one may ask, given that in the perception of yogins all principles are selfless, how then is it that, with respect to a non-entity, consciousness *(vijñāna)* of a non-entity is not produced?

This, too, is not correct; for we do not affirm that, with respect to such non-entities as rabbit-horns, there are particular cognitions produced by perception. On the contrary, because great yogins have practiced the contemplation of all principles as resembling mirages and optical illusions, attained the absorption *(samādhi)* that emerges from the highest limit of the contemplation of the genuine objective, and so have come to be endowed with exceptional, inconceivable power, an exceedingly lucid gnosis arises for those yogins, in which the reality of the selflessness of each and every principle is disclosed. It is that that is spoken of as the "unseeing of reality," and in essence it is not an existential negation. Thus, the Transcendent Lord has stated (in the *Laṅkāvatāra*):

> Mahāmati! the bodhisattva should be taught that all principles are like apparitions and dreams; for they are characterized as seen and unseen.

In that way, they are characterized as visible in conventional terms, but the characteristic of invisibility is the ultimate objective alone—such is the meaning of the sūtra. It was with respect to just this that the venerable Ārya Nāgārjuna said (in the *Yuktiṣaṣṭika*):

> Mundane being and nirvāṇa—
> Neither one exists.
> It is just the thorough knowledge of mundane being
> That is spoken of as "nirvāṇa."

Although all principles, in terms of the ultimate objective, are of one taste in that they are without coming-into-being, so that perception also is ultimately without substantial nature, nevertheless, relying upon the ostensible truth, the determinations of perceptions and so forth all remain undisturbed. In conventional terms, neither the yogin's cognition, nor even the cognition of the ordinary person *(pṛthagjana),* is rejected as a basis for the determination of exalted individuals *(āryapuruṣa),* etc. But, on the other hand, whatever is forever without even ostensible basis does not come into being even in conventional terms, for instance, the rabbit's horn. What does exist comes into being, as do apparitions and reflections. Thus, in the same way that, owing to the provision of charms, drugs, etc., various apparitions, like elephants and so on, come forth, so too, owing to the afflictions *(kleśa)* and deeds *(karma)* of sentient beings, the apparitions of coming-into-being, etc. And for yogins, too, owing just to their provision of merit *(puṇya)* and wisdom *(jñāna),* the apparitions of the yogin's gnosis, etc., come forth. But because they, like the illusionist, entirely know the apparition for what it genuinely is, they are in reality without manifest craving, and armor themselves to benefit others. As it says in the *Dharmasaṃgīti:*

Those skilled in perfect enlightenment,
Have thus known beings from before;
Knowing the three worlds to be like an emanation,
They armor themselves for beings.

Those who, with respect to coming-into-being and other such apparitions, manifestly hanker after them as veridical, as being just as they are seen to be, are like childish persons wrapped up in fancy; because they engage in errant craving, they are spoken of as children.

In saying that, "this is to be genuinely realized through the yogin's perception," there is nothing unreasonable; for the learned have explained the defining characteristic of perception thus: "perception is free from conceptualization and unbewildered" (*pratyakṣam kalpanāpoḍham abhrāntam, Nyāyabindu,* 1.4). And owing to the force of practice, an exceedingly clear cognition may arise even with respect to impure objects; for example, for those tainted by desire, suffering, fear, madness, etc., due to very much cultivation [of those states], very clear cognitions arise in which, [for instance,] a woman appears [to a man obsessed with desire], and analogously [for the other states mentioned]. It may ever be the case that they see these things as if present before them, and so behave bodily in various unpredictable ways.

For those reasons, some who practice contemplation upon reality, as it is expounded, are plausibly said to produce an exceedingly lucid cognition. And that cognition which thus appears lucidly is solely non-conceptual; for, in that which is conceptually agitated the feature of lucidity does not arise. This has been treated in detail in the *Pramāṇavārttika* and elsewhere.

Our teachers [Dignāga and Dharmakīrti], moreover, have divided perception into two: that of the yogins, and that of the rest. The perception of the rest is not said to be unbewildered with respect to the ultimate objective. Otherwise, we would all be exclusively yogins, and there would be none who see what is present here below *(arvāgdṛk).*

Conventionally, one only speaks of being "unbewildered" with reference to just what objects are well-known and undeceptive *(avisaṃvādin),* in the same manner as dreams, etc. The perception of such yogins as the *śrāvakas*, etc., who have penetrated only the selflessness of persons, is thus an epistemically authoritative perception *(pratyakṣapramāṇa),* because it is undeceptive with respect to that. But it is not [that perception] whose scope includes reality in all its aspects. Because the perception of the Transcendent Lord alone is that whose scope includes reality in all its aspects, in point of fact just that is undeceptive and so unbewildered with respect to reality in all its aspects in particular. Therefore, the buddhas, who are transcendent lords, have eminently known all principles to be without characteristic. It is not implied, moreover, that omniscient gnosis is itself an entity; for that is also included among all principles, with respect to whose absence of characteristic [the Buddha] is manifestly and perfectly awakened *(abhisaṃbuddha)*. So it says in the *Āryaśatasāhasrikā Prajñāpāramitā:*

> Omniscient gnosis has the characteristic of perception; and that, too, is what the Tathāgata has manifestly and perfectly awakened to as "without characteristic."

The exaggerated attributions, on the part of childish persons, of a substantial and ultimate essence to false appearances that are objects in the scope of conventional perception, like dreams and so forth, are annulled *(bādhyate)* by inference; and, as they are annulled, it is established that ultimately all principles are without substantial nature. The Transcendent Lord has himself precisely stated that what is established by that annulment has the epistemic authority of inference. Thus, in the *Anavataptanāgarājaparipṛcchā* (*T.* 156; *Prasannadapā,* p. 105):

> That which is born from conditions is unborn;
> Its birth is from no substantial nature.
> What is in the power of conditions is said to be empty;
> And whoever knows emptiness is meticulous.

In the *Sāgaramatinirdeśa* (*T.* 152), as well:

> What arises in interdependence
> Has no substantial nature.
> What is without substantial nature
> Emerges nowhere at all.

Similarly, (in the *Laṅkāvatāra,* 10.709):

> Just as in a mirror
> A form is neither one nor other,
> But appears though not existing,
> So, too, in reality, substantial nature.

Ārya [Nāgārjuna] also says, in the *Madhyamakaśāstra* (24.18):

What arises in interdependence
Is said to be emptiness.
It is dependently designated.
That is the middle path.

The teacher [Dharmakīrti] similarly says (*Pramāṇavārttika, Pratyakṣa-pariccheda,* v. 360):

When entities are analyzed,
No entity is found there.
This is because among them
There is no nature of one or of many.

The demonstrations that interdependent arising is without an essence that is one or many are these:

[A1] What arises interdependently is empty in ultimate nature, like an apparition.
[A2] All principles arise interdependently.
[[A3] Therefore, all principles are empty in ultimate nature, like apparitions.]

[B1] What is ultimately without a nature that is one or many is without substantial nature, like a reflection.
[B2] All principles are ultimately without a nature that is one or many.
[[B3] Therefore, all principles are without substantial nature, like reflections.]

Because the textual traditions of these two proofs *(prayoga)* will not be understood by those unfamiliar with dialectics, I fear they will not attend to them, and so have not set them forth here at length. In brief, I have thoroughly explained them in my *Madhyamakamañjarī.*[11]

Those who are learned should study them there.

Notes

1 In *T.* twenty-two works are attributed to his authorship: 1198, 1380, 1383, 1498, 1499, 1500, 1618, 1654, 1831, 2036, 2484, 2491, 3140, 3141, 3142, 3266, 3613, 3743, 3766, 3805, 3903, 3970. A number of his other writings are referred to, but appear not to be available at present (see, for instance, n. 11 below). In addition, he collaborated with Pa-tshab Tshul-khrims-rgyal-mtshan on the translation of the entire series of 161 sādhanas given in *T.* 3144–3304. This series is very closely related to *Sādhanamālā,* and strongly influenced later Tibetan sādhana collections. Sanskrit manuscripts of a number of Abhayākaragupta's writings are known, but only the *Niṣpannayogāvali* (*T.* 3141 in Tibetan) has so far been edited in full. The *Vajrāvali* (*T.* 3140), in particular, was one of the most important later Indian Buddhist tantric works, and survives in the original in a large number of manuscripts in Nepal and elsewhere. Selected passages are edited in Bhattacharyya 1981

2 *D.* 293a: "The great redacting translator, venerable Blo-gros-brtan-pa, the *bhikṣu* of Dpang, well corrected [the text], purely translated it, and established its final redaction, on the basis of the provisions achieved by the spiritual benefactors Dog-shing-dbon-po, Bde-ba-chos-kyi-bzang-po, and others. Later, that same venerable Blo-gros-brtan-pa compared as much as possible the correlations between sections of this texts and [the corresponding] sections of other texts, and well examined them in accord with Indian manuscripts. On this basis, he redacted it, and corrected it, having thoroughly examined the meaning." *(zhu chen gyi lo tsā ba dpang dge slong dpal ldan blo gros brtan pas/ dge ba'i bshes gnyen dog shing dbon po dang/ bde ba chos kyi bzang po la sogs pas/ mthun rkyen bsgrubs pa la brten nas/ legs par bcos nas dag par bsgyur cing zhus te gtan la phab pa'o// // slar yang dpal ldan blo gros brtan pa de nyid kyis gzhung 'di'i skabs dang gzhung lugs gzhan gyi skabs mthun pa ji snyed rnyed pa rnams sbyar zhing rgya dpe dang gtugs te legs par brtags shing dpyad nas zhus chen bgyis la/ don la yang legs par dpyad pas shin tu dag par bgyis pa'o/ /).* Because the interlinear commentary is in large measure concerned to identify the sources of quotations left unspecified in the main text, it is at least plausible that it is the product of Blo-gros-brtan-pa's effort to "compare as much as possible the correlations."

3 The *Munimatālaṃkāra* is divided into four chapters, of which the first, third, and fourth are each, in terms of both conception and length, substantial treatises: 1. "appearance of the enlightened mind" *(byang chub kyi sems kyi snang ba'i le'u, *bodhicittālokapariccheda,* folios 73b–151b in *D.);* 2. "appearance of the cultivation of the enlightened mind" (*byang chub kyi sems sgom pa'i snang ba'i le'u, *bodhicittabhāvanālokapariccheda,* 151b–168b); 3. "appearance of the eight emergent realizations *(abhisamaya,* as taught in the *Abhisamayālaṃkāra)"* (*mngon par rtogs pa brgyad kyi snang ba'i le'u, *aṣṭābhisamayālokapariccheda,* 168b–225a); 4. "appearance of [enlightened] attributes" (*yon tan gyi snang pa'i le 'u, *guṇālokapariccheda,* 225a–292a).

4 *D.* 137b–138b; *P.* 184.3.8–184.5.5.

5 *D.* 138b–139b; *P.* 184.5.5–185.4.1.
6 *D.* 139b–140b; *P.* 185.4.1–186.3.4.
7 *D.* 140b–141a; *P.* 186.3.4–186.5.1.
8 *D.* 141a–142b; *P.* 186.5.1–187.5.5.
9 *D.* 142b–144a; *P.* 187.5.5–188.5.2.
10 *D.* 144a–145b; *P.* 188.5.2–189.5.8.
11 This is among Abhayākaragupta's missing works. It seems never to have been translated into Tibetan, and no Sanskrit text of it is available. Nonetheless, a Sanskrit manuscript bearing this title has been rumored recently to exist. The present author would be grateful to any reader who can help to locate it.

Bibliography

Canonical Collections and Catalogues

The editions of specific canonical texts in Pali and Sanskrit used here will be found listed in the following section.

D Sde-dge edition of the Tibetan Buddhist Canon.

P Daisetz T. Suzuki, ed., *The Tibetan Tripitika: Peking Edition* (Kept in the Library of the Otani University, Kyoto). Tokyo/Kyoto: Tibetan Tripitika Research Institute, 1961.

T Hakuju Ui, Munetada Suzuki, Yenshō Kanakura, and Tōkan Tada, eds., *A Complete Catalogue of the Tibetan Buddhist Canons (Bkaḥ-ḥgyur and Bstan-ḥgyur).* Sendai: Tōhoku Imperial University, 1934.

Taishō Refer to Demiéville, Durt, and Seidel 1978.

Sanskrit and Pali References

Abhidharmakośa
Vasubandhu, *Abhidharmakośam,* Swāmī Dwārikādās Śāstrī, ed. 4 vols. Varanasi: Bauddha Bharati, 1970–72.

Abhidharmasamuccaya
Abhidharma Samuccaya of Asaṅga, Prahlad Pradhan, ed. Santiniketan: Visva-Bharati, 1950.

Abhidharmasamuccayabhāṣya
Abhidharmasamuccayabhāṣyam, Nathmal Tatia, ed. Patna: K.P. Jayaswal Research Institute, 1976.

Abhisamayālaṃkāra
Abhisamayālaṃkārakārika, in P.L. Vaidya, ed., *Aṣṭasāhasrikā,* Buddhist Sanskrit Texts 4. Darbhanga: Mithila Institute, 1960.

Abhisamayālaṃkārāloka
Haribhadra, *Abhisamayālaṃkārāloka,* in P. L. Vaidya, ed., *Aṣṭasāhasrikā.* Buddhist Sanskrit Texts 4. Darbhanga: Mithila Institute, 1960.

Ātmatattvaviveka
Udayana, *Ātmatattvaviveka.* Varanasi: Chaukhamba Sanskrit Series, 1936–40.

Āryabhadracaripraṇidhānarāja
Āryabhadracaripraṇidhānarāja, Skt. and Tib. ed. Suniti Kumar Pathak. Gangtok: Namgyal Institute of Tibetology, 1961.

Āryamañjuśrīmūlakalpa
Āryamañjuśrīmūlakalpa, in P.L. Vaidya, ed., *Mahāyānasūtrasaṅgraha, Part II,* Buddhist Sanskrit Texts 18. Darbhanga: Mithila Institute, 1964. [Essentially a reprint of the edition published by T. Ganapati Sastri in the Trivandrum Sanskrit Series, Nos. 70 (1920), 76 (1922), and 84 (1925).]

Udāna
Udānam, Paul Steinthal, ed. London: Pali Text Society, 1885.

Kathāvatthu
Kathāvatthu, Arnold C. Taylor, ed. 2 vols. London: Pali Text Society, 1894.

Kathāvatthu Aṭṭhakathā
Buddhaghosa, "Kathāvatthu-ppakaraṇa-Aṭṭhakathā," I. P. Minayeff, ed. *Journal of the Pali Text Society.* London: Pali Text Society, 1889.

Karaṇḍavyūha
Avalokiteśvara-guṇa-karaṇḍavyūha, in P.L. Vaidya, ed., *Mahāyānasūtrasaṅgraha, Part I.* Buddhist Sanskrit Texts 17. Darbhanga: Mithila Institute, 1961.

Kāvyādarśa
Daṇḍin, *Kāvyādarśa,* Skt. and Tib. ed. Anukul Chandra Banerjee. Calcutta: University of Calcutta, 1939.

Guhyādi-aṣṭasiddhisaṅgraha
Guhyādi-aṣṭasiddhisaṅgraha, Samdhong Rinpoche and Vrajvallabh Dwivedi, eds. Rare Buddhist Text Series 1. Sarnath: Central Institute of Higher Tibetan Studies, 1987.

Tattvasaṅgraha
Śāntarakṣita, *Tattvasaṅgrahaḥ,* Swāmī Dwārikādāsaśāstrī, ed. Vārāṇasī: Bauddha Bhāratī, 1968.

Tattvasaṅgrahapañjikā
Kamalaśīla, *Tattvasaṅgrahapañjikā,* in *Tattvasaṅgraha.*

Tarkajvāla
Bhāvaviveka. *Tarkajvāla* on *Madhyamakahṛdaya, P.* 5256, *T.* 3856.

Tarkabhāṣā
Tarkabhāṣā: A Manual of Buddhist Logic, B. N. Singh, ed. Varanasi: Asha Prakashan, 1988.

Daśabhūmika
Daśabhūmikasūtram, P.L. Vaidya, ed. Buddhist Sanskrit Texts 7. Darbhanga: Mithila Institute, 1967.

Daśopaniṣad
Daśopanishads with the Commentary of Sri Upanishad-Brahma-Yogin, C. Kunhan Raja, ed. 2 vols. Madras: Adyar Library, 1936.

Niṣpannayogāvali
Abhayākaragupta, *Niṣpannayogāvalī,* Benoytosh Bhattacharya, ed. Gaekwad's Oriental Series 109. Baroda: Oriental Institute, 1972.

Nyāyakandalīvyākhyā
Śrīdhara, *Nyāyakandalīvyākhyā,* in Durgādhara Jhā, ed., *Praśastapādabhāṣya.* Varanasi: Sampurnanand Sanskrit Vishvavidyalaya, 1977.

Nyāyakośa
Bhīmācārya Jhalakīkar, *Nyāyakośa,* Bombay Sanskrit and Prakrit Series, No. 49, 1893. [Reprinted on the basis of the 1928 revised edition. Poona: Bhandarkar Oriental Research Institute, 1978.]

Nyāyatātparyaṭīkā
Vācaspati Miśra, *Nyāyatātparyaṭīkā,* in *Nyāyadarśana.*

Nyāyadarśana
Nyāyadarśanam, Taranatha Nyaya-Tarkatirtha, Amarendramohan Tarkatirtha, and Hemantakumar Tarkatirtha, eds. Kyoto: Rinsen Book Company, 1984. Reprinted from the 1936–44 Calcutta Sanskrit Series edition.

Nyāyabhāṣya
Vātsyāyana, *Nyāyabhāṣya,* in *Nyāyadarśana.*

Nyāyavārttika
Uddyotakara, *Nyāyavārttika,* in *Nyāyadarśana.*

Nyāyasūtra
Akṣapāda Gautama, *Nyāyasūtra,* in *Nyāyadarśana.*

Pramāṇavārttika
Dharmakīrti, *Pramāṇavārttika,* Swāmī Dwārikādāsa Śāstrī, ed. Vārāṇasī: Bauddha Bhāratī, 1968.

Pramāṇavārttika-svavṛtti
Raniero Gnoli, *The Pramāṇavārttikam of Dharmakīrti: The First Chapter with the Autocommentary.* Serie Orientale Roma 23. Rome: Is.M.E.O., 1960.

Praśastapādabhāṣya
Praśastapādabhāṣya, Durgādhara Jhā, ed. Varanasi: Sampurnanand Sanskrit Vishvavidyalaya, 1977.

Prasannapadā
Candrakīrti, *Prasannapadā,* in P. L. Vaidya, ed., *Madhyamakaśāstram,* Buddhist Sanskrit Texts Series 10. Darbhanga: Mithila Institute, 1960.

Buddhacarita
The Buddhacarita, or Acts of the Buddha, E. H. Johnston, ed. Repr. Delhi: Motilal Banarsidass, 1972.

Bodhicaryāvatāra
Śāntideva, *Bodhicaryāvatāra,* P. L. Vaidya, ed. Buddhist Sanskrit Texts Series 12. Darbhanga: Mithila Institute, 1960.

Bodhicaryāvatārapañjikā
Prajñākaramati, *Bodhicaryāvatārapañjikā,* in *Bodhicaryāvatāra.*

Bodhisattvabhūmi
Bodhisattvabhūmiḥ, Nalinaksha Dutt, ed. Tibetan Sanskrit Works Series 7. Patna: K.P. Jayaswal Research Institute, 1978.

Madhyamakālaṃkāra
Śāntarakṣita, *Madhyamakālaṃkāra.* Refer to Ichigō 1989.

Madhyamakāvatāra
Louis de la Vallée Poussin, *Madhyamakāvatāra par Candrakīrti.* Bibliotheca Buddhica 9. Repr. Delhi: Motilal Banarsidass, 1992.

Mahāyānasūtrālaṃkara
Mahāyānasūtrālaṃkāra, S. Bagchi, ed. Buddhist Sanskrit Texts 13. Darbhanga: Mithila Institute, 1970.

Milindapañha
Milindapañho, Swāmī Dwārikādāsa Śāstrī, ed. Bauddha Bharati Series 13. Varanasi, 1979.

Mūlamadhyamakakārikā
Mūlamadhyamakakārikā, in P. L. Vaidya, ed., *Madhyamakaśāstram,* Buddhist Sanskrit Texts 10. Darbhanga: Mithila Institute, 1960.

Raghuvaṃśa
Kālidāsa, *Raghuvaṃśam,* Narayan Ram Acharya, ed. Bombay: Nirnaya Sagar Press, 1948.

Ratnagotravibhāga
Ratnagotravibhāga Mahāyānottaratantraśāstra, E. H. Johnston, ed. Patna: Bihar Research Society, 1950.

Ratnāvalī
Michael Hahn, *Nāgārjuna's Ratnāvalī,* vol. 1, *The Basic Texts.* Bonn: Indica et Tibetica, 1982.

Laṅkāvatāra
Laṅkāvatārasūtram, P. L. Vaidya, ed. Buddhist Texts Series 3. Darbhanga: Mithila Institute, 1963.

Lalitavistara
Lalitavistara, P. L. Vaidya, ed. Buddhist Texts Series 1. Darbhanga: Mithila Institute, 1958.

Viṃśatikā
Vasubandhu, *Viṃśatikā,* in Lévi 1925, with emendations in Lévi 1932. [The many recent republications of the Sanskrit text, e.g., K.N. Chatterjee, *Vijñaptimātratāsiddhi* (Varanasi: Kishor Vidya Niketan, 1980), often fail to take account of Lévi's emended readings.] The Tibetan text was first edited in La Vallée Poussin 1912, and a bilingual Sanskrit-Tibetan text was given in N. Aiyaswami Sastrin, *Viṃśatikā* (Gangtok: Namgyal Institute, 1964). For Xuanzang's Chinese version, see Hamilton 1938.

Vimalaprabhāṭīkā
Vimalaprabhā, vol. 1, Jagannatha Upadhyaya, ed. Bibliotheca Indo-Tibetica Series 11. Sarnath: Central Institute of Higher Tibetan Studies, 1986. Vol. 2, Samdhong Rinpoche and Vrajvallabh Dwivedi, eds. Rare Buddhist Texts Series 12. Sarnath: Central Institute of Higher Tibetan Studies, 1994. Vol. 3, Samdhong Rinpoche and Vrajvallabh Dwivedi, eds. Rare Buddhist Texts Series 13. Sarnath: Central Institute of Higher Tibetan Studies, 1994.

Visuddhimagga
Buddhaghosa, *Visuddhimagga,* Henry Clark Warren, ed. Harvard Oriental Series 41. Cambridge: Harvard University Press, 1950.

Vaiśeṣikasūtra
Vaiśeṣikasūtra, Jambuvijaya Muni, ed. Gaekwad's Oriental Series 136. Baroda: Oriental Institute, 1961.

Śatapatha Brāhmaṇa
Śatapatha Brāhmaṇa, Julius Eggeling, trans. Sacred Books of the East 12, 26, 41, 43, 44. Oxford: Clarendon Press, 1882–1900.

Śabdakalpadruma
Rādhākāntadeva, *Śabdakalpadrumaḥ.* Caukhamba-Saṃskṛta-granthamālā 93. Varanasi: Caukhamba Sanskrit Series, 1961. Repr. of Calcutta edition, 1886.

Śikṣāsamuccaya
Śāntideva, *Śikṣāsamuccayaḥ,* P. L. Vaidya, ed. Buddhist Sanskrit Texts Series 11. Darbhanga: Mithila Institute, 1961.

Śravakabhūmi
The Śravakabhūmi of Ācārya Asaṅga, Karunesha Shukla, ed. Tibetan Sanskrit Works Series 14. Patna: K.P. Jayaswal Research Institute, 1973.

Śrīśaṅkaragranthāvalī
Śrīśaṅkaragranthāvalī, vol. 1. Delhi: Motilal Banarsidass, 1964.

Ṣaḍdarśanasamuccaya
Mahendra Kumar Jain, ed., *Ṣaḍdarśanasamuccaya.* 3rd edition. New Delhi: Bharatiya Jnanpith, 1989.

Saṃyuttanikāya
Saṃyutta Nikāya, Léon Feer, ed. 5 vols. London: Pali Text Society, 1884–98.

Satyasiddhiśāstra
The Satyasiddhiśāstra of Harivarman, reconstructed and translated by N. Aiyaswami Sastri. Gaekwad's Oriental Series 159 and 165. Baroda: Oriental Institute, 1975. [Note that recent authorities prefer *Tattvasiddhi* as the likely reconstruction of Harivarman's title.]

Saṃdhinirmocanasūtra
Étienne Lamotte, *Saṃdhinirmocanasūtra: L'explication des mystères.* Paris: Adrien Maisonneuve, 1935.

Sambandhaparīkṣā
Dharmakīrti, *Sambandhaparīkṣā,* in Swāmī Dwārikādāsa Śāstrī, ed., *Vādanyāyaḥ Sambandhaparīkṣā ca,* pp. 139–49. Varanasi: Bauddha Bharati, 1972.

Sarvadarśanasaṅgraha
Sāyaṇa Mādhava, *Sarvadarśanasaṅgraha.* Vasudev Abhayankar, ed. Poona: Bhandarkar Oriental Research Institute, 1978.

Sarvasiddhāntasaṅgraha
The Sarva-siddhānta-saṅgraha of Śaṅkarācārya, M. Raṅgācārya, ed. Madras: Government Press, 1909.

Sādhanamālā
Sādhanamālā, Benoytosh Bhattacharya, ed. Gaekwad's Oriental Series 26 and 41. Repr. Baroda: Oriental Institute, 1968.

Suhṛllekha
Nāgārjuna, *Suhṛllekha.* Tibetan text edited in Dietz 1984.

Sūtrālaṃkāravṛttibhāṣya
Sthiramati, *Sūtrālaṃkāravṛttibhāṣya,* 2 vols. Repr. of the Derge Tanjur edition. Rumtek, Sikkim, 1976.

Saundarananda
E. H. Johnston, *The Saundarananda of Aśvaghoṣa.* Repr. of 1928 Lahore edition. Delhi/Patna/Varanasi: Motilal Banarsidass, 1975.

Hitopadeśaḥ
Nārāyaṇa Paṇḍita, *Hitopadeśaḥ,* Kāśināth Pāṇḍuraṅg Parab, ed. Mumbai: Nirṇayasāgara Buk Prakāśan, 1968.

Tibetan References

Mkhas 'jug
'Jam-mgon 'Ju Mi-pham-rnam-rgyal-rgya-mtsho, *Mkhas pa'i tshul la 'jug pa'i sgo.* Tashijong: Sungrab Nyamso Gyunphel Parkhang, 1964.

Mkhas 'jug mchan 'grel
Mkhan-po Nus-ldan, *Mkhas pa'i tshul la 'jug pa'i sgo'i mchan 'grel legs bshad snang ba'i 'od zer.* Delhi: Lama Jurme Drakpa, 1974.

Mkhas 'jug sa bcad
'Jam-mgon 'Ju Mi-pham-rnam-rgyal-rgya-mtsho, *Mkhas 'jug gi sa bcad mdor bsdus pa pad dkar phreng ba.* Tashijong: Sungrab Nyamso Gyunphel Parkhang, 1965.

Grub mtha' chen mo
'Jam-dbyangs-bzhad-pa, *Grub mtha' chen mo,* in *Collected Works of 'Jam-dbyaṅs-bźad-pa,* vol. 14. New Delhi: Ngawang Gelek Demo, 1972.

Grub mtha' lhun po'i mdzes rgyan
Lcang-skya Rol-pa'i rdo-rje, *Grub pa'i mtha'i rnam par bzhag pa gsal bar bshad pa thub bstan lhun po'i mdzes rgyan.* Sarnath: The Pleasure of Elegant Sayings Printing Press, 1970.

Dgongs gcig yig cha
Dgoṅs gcig yig cha. 2 vols. Bir: D. Tsondu Senghe, 1975.

Sgra sbyor bam gnyis
Mie Ishikawa, *A Critical Edition of the Sgra sbyor bam po gnyis pa, An Old and Basic Commentary on the Mahāvyutpatti.* Studia Tibetica 18. Tokyo: The Toyo Bunko, 1990.

Sgrub thabs kun btus
Sgrub thabs kun btus. 14 vols. Dehra Dun: G. T. K. Lodoy, N. Lungtok, and N. Gyaltsan, 1970.

Nges shes rin po che'i sgron me
See Pettit 1999.

Tāranātha
Rje btsun Tāranātha'i bka' 'bum yongs rdzogs. 23 vols. 'Dzam-thang/Chengdu: A-khu Thogs-med, 1990.

Lta grub shan 'byed
Bod-pa sprul-sku Mdo-sngags-bstan-pa'i nyi-ma, *Lta grub shan 'byed gnad kyi sgron me.* Chengdu: Si khron mi rigs dpe skrun khang, 1996.

Don rnam nges shes rab ral gri
'Jam-mgon 'Ju Mi-pham-rgya-mtsho, *Don rnam par nges pa shes rab ral gri,* xylograph from Ser-lo mgon-pa, Nepal, based on the Rdzong-sar edition, 10 folios. [A

typeset edition, with Mi-pham's annotations, is also given in *Mkhas pa'i tshul la 'jug pa'i sgo zhes bya ba'i bstan bcos*, pp. 31–64. Chengdu: Si khron mi rigs dpe skrun khang, c. 1990.]

Don rnam nges 'grel thub bstan snang byed
Lhag-bsam-bstan-pa'i-rgyal-mtshan, *Don rnam par nges pa shes rab ral gri'i 'grel pa thub bstan yongs su rdzogs pa'i snang byed: a commentary on 'Jam-mgon 'Ju Mi-pham-rgya-mtsho's Don rnam par nges pa shes rab ral gri*. Bylakuppe: Pema Norbu Rinpoche, 1984.

Don rnam nges 'grel lung rigs do shal
Mkhan-po Zla-ba'i-'od-zer, *Don rnam nges kyi 'grel pa lung rigs do shal: a commentary on Mi-pham-rgya-mtsho's Don rnam par nges pa shes rab ral gri*. Gangtok: Pema Thinley for Ven. Dodrupchen Rinpoche, 1985.

Dol po pa
The 'Dzam-thang Edition of the Collected Works of Kun-mkhyen Dol-po-pa Shes-rab-rgyal-mtshan. Collected and presented by Matthew Kapstein. 7 vols. [in 10 physical vols.] in Tibetan and 1 vol. introduction and descriptive catalogue in English. New Delhi: Shedrup Books and Sherab Drimey, 1992/3.

Drang nges legs bshad snying po
Tsong-kha-pa Blo-bzang-grags-pa, *Drang nges legs bshad snying po*. In *Rje Tsong kha pa chen po'i gsung 'bum*, vol. Pha. Xining: Mtsho sngon mi rigs dpe skrun khang, 1987.

Snang ba lhar bsgrub
Gsang sngags rdo rje theg pa'i tshul las snang ba lhar bsgrub pa Rong zom chos bzang gis mdzad pa, in *Selected Writings of Roṅ-zom Chos-kyi-bzaṅ-po*, Smanrtsis Shesrig Spendzod, vol. 73, pp. 125–51. Leh: S.W. Tashigangpa, 1973.

'Ba' mda'
'Ba' mda' bla ma Thub bstan dge legs rgya mtsho'i bka' 'bum, 22 vols. 'Dzam-thang/Chengdu: A-khu Thogs-med, c. 1990. [A catalogue of contents is given in Kapstein 1997.]

'Ba' mda'i Bsdus grwa
['Ba'-mda'] Thub-bstan-dge-legs-rgya-mtsho, *Bsdus grwa'i spyi don rin chen sgron me*. Beijing: Krung go'i bod kyi shes rig dpe skrun khang, 1990.

Mi pham gsung 'bum
Mi pham gsung 'bum, Sde dge par ma sogs. Paro: Dilgo Khyentsey Rinpoche, 1982; and *Collected Writings of 'Jam-mgon 'Ju Mi-pham rgya-mtsho*. Gangtok: Sonam Topgay Kazi, 1976.

Blo grags I
Mkhan-po Blo-gros-grags-pa, *Jo nang chos 'byung zla ba'i sgron me*. Beijing: Krung go'i bod kyi shes rig dpe skrun khang, 1992.

Blo grags II
Selected Historical and Doctrinal Writings of 'Dzam-thang Mkhan-po Blo-gros-grags-pa. Collected and presented by Matthew Kapstein, 2 vols. in Tibetan with English introductions. Dharamsala: Library of Tibetan Works and Archives, 1993.

Tshad ma rigs gzhung rgya mtsho
Karma-pa VII Chos-grags rgya-mtsho, *Tshad ma rigs gzhung rgya mtsho.* 2 vols. Thimphu: Topga Tulku, 1973

Tshad ma lam rim
Gnyid-mo-che'i rmi-lam-gyi rol-mtshor shar-ba'i bstan-bcos ngo-mtshar zla-ba'i snang-brnyan, in Thu'u-bkwan Chos-kyi nyi-ma, *Lcang-skya Rol-pa'i rdo-rje'i rnam-thar,* pp. 634–50. Lanzhou: Gansu Nationalities Press, 1989.

Ri chos
Dol-po-pa Shes-rab-rgyal-mtshan, *Ri chos ṅes don rgya mtsho: a treatise on the philosophical basis and practice of Buddhist contemplation.* Gangtok: Dodrup Sangyey Lama, 1976.

Shes bya kun khyab
Kong-sprul Yon-tan rgya-mtsho (= Blo-gros mtha'-yas), *Shes bya kun khyab,* 3 vols. Beijing: Minorities Press, 1982.

Bshes spring mchan 'grel
'Jam-dbyangs-blo-gros-rgya-mtsho (= Zhe-chen Rgyal-tshab Padma-rnam-rgyal), *Bshes spring gi mchan 'grel padma dkar po'i phreng ba.* Rewalsar, n.d.

Sa skya mkhas 'jug
Sa-skya Paṇḍita Kun-dga'-rgyal-mtshan, *Mkhas pa rnams 'jug pa'i sgo zhes bya ba'i btsan bcos.* Beijing: Mi rigs dpe skrun khang, 1981.

Sems nyid rang grol
Klong-chen Rab-'byams-pa, *Sems nyid rang grol,* in *Rang grol skor gsum: structured presentations of Nyingmapa Dzochen* [sic] *theory and practice.* Gangtok: Dodrup Chen Rinpoche, 1973.

Western Language References

Abe, Masao. 1989. *Zen and Western Thought.* Honolulu: University of Hawai'i Press.

Abe, Ryūichi. 1999. *The Weaving of Mantra: Kūkai and the Construction of Esoteric Buddhist Discourse.* New York: Columbia University Press.

Abegg, Emil. 1956. "Geist und Natur in der Indischen Philosophie." *Asiatische Studien* 10: 60–78.

Abhyankar, Kashinath Vasudev. 1961. *A Dictionary of Sanskrit Grammar.* Gaekwad's Oriental Series, No. 134. Baroda: Oriental Institute.

Anacker, Stefan, trans. 1984. *Seven Works of Vasubandhu, the Buddhist Psychological Doctor.* Delhi: Motilal Banarsidass.

Anderson, Dines. 1968. *A Pāli Reader.* Copenhagen, 1917. Repr. Kyoto: Rinsen-Shoten.

Anscombe, G.E.M. 1957. *Intention.* Ithaca: Cornell University Press.

Apte, Vanam Sivaram. 1958. *Sanskrit-English Dictionary,* edited by P. K. Gode and C. G. Karve. Poona: Prasad Prakashan.

Aquinas, St. Thomas. 1962. *Aristotle: On Interpretation,* translated by Jean T. Oesterle. Milwaukee: Marquette University Press.

Arènes, Pierres. 1996. *La Déesse Sgrol-ma (Tārā): Recherches sur la Nature et le Statut d'une Divinité du Bouddhisme Tibétain.* Orientalie Lovaniensia Analecta 74. Leuven: Peeters.

Aristotle, see McKeon 1941.

Aung, Shwe Zan, and Caroline Rhys Davids. 1915. *Points of Controversy.* London: Pali Text Society.

Bacon, Francis. 1944. *Novum Organum,* in *Advancement of Learning and Novum Organum.* New York: Wiley.

Barnes, Jonathan. 1979. *The Presocratic Philosophers.* London: Routledge.

Basham, Arthur L. 1959. *The Wonder That Was India.* New York: Grove Press.

Bechert, Heinz, ed. 1991–92. *The Dating of the Historical Buddha,* 2 vols. Abhandlungen der Akademie der Wissenschaften in Göttingen 189, 194. Göttingen: Vandenhoeck & Ruprecht.

Beck, Lewis White. 1960. *A Commentary on Kant's Critique of Practical Reason.* Chicago: University of Chicago Press.

Beckner, Morton O. 1967. "Vitalism," in Paul Edwards, ed., *The Encyclopedia of Philosophy.* vol. 8, pp. 253–56. New York: Macmillan.

Bentor, Yael. 1996. *Consecration of Images and Stupas in Indo-Tibetan Tantric Buddhism.* Leiden/New York: E. J. Brill.

Bernard, Paul. 1973. *Fouilles d'Aï Khanoum,* vol. 1. Paris: Éditions Klincksieck.

Bernhard, Franz. 1967. "Zur Entstehung einer Dhāraṇī." *Zeitschrift der Deutschen Morgenländischen Gesellschaft* 117: 148–68.

Bhattacharya, Kamaleshwar. 1973. *L'Ātman-Brahman dans le Bouddhisme Ancien.* Paris: École Française d'Extrême-Orient.

Bhattacharya, D.C. 1981. "The Vajrāvalī-nāma-maṇḍalopāyikā of Abhayākaragupta," in Michel Strickmann, ed., *Tantric and Taoist Studies in Honour of R.A. Stein,* vol. 1, pp. 70–95, in *Mélanges Chinois et Bouddhiques,* vol. 20. Brussels: Institute Belge des Hautes Études Chinoises.

Biardeau, Madeleine. 1968. "L'*ātman* dans le commentaire de Śabarasvāmin." *Mélanges d'Indianisme,* pp. 109–25. Paris: E. de Boccard.

Biderman, Schlomo, and Ben-Ami Scharfstein, eds. 1989. *Rationality in Question: On Eastern and Western Views of Rationality.* Leiden/New York/Copenhagen/Cologne: E. J. Brill.

Bleicher, Josef. 1980. *Contemporary Hermeneutics.* London: Routledge and Kegan Paul.

Bocheński, I. M. 1970. *A History of Formal Logic,* Ivo Thomas, trans. New York: Chelsea.

Braarvig, Jens. 1985. *"Dhāraṇī* and *Pratibhāna:* Memory and Eloquence of the Bodhisattvas." *Journal of the International Association of Buddhist Studies* 8/1: 17–29.

Braarvig, Jens. 1997. "Bhavya on Mantras: Apologetic Endeavours on Behalf of the Mahāyāna," in Agata Bareja-Starzyńska and Marek Mejor, eds. *Aspects of Buddhism: Proceedings of the International Seminar on Buddhist Studies.* Studia Indologiczne 4, pp. 31–40. Warsaw: Oriental Institute.

Brehier, Émile. 1963. *The History of Philosophy,* Joseph Thomas, trans., 7 vols. Chicago/London: The University of Chicago Press.

Brentano, Franz. 1966. *The True and the Evident,* Roderick M. Chisholm, Ilse Politzer, and Kurt R. Fischer, trans. New York: Humanities Press.

Brentano, Franz. 1973. *Psychology from an Empirical Standpoint,* Antos C. Rancurello, D. B. Terrell, and Linda L. McAlister, trans. New York: Humanities Press.

Brentano, Franz. 1975. *On the Several Senses of Being in Aristotle,* Rolf George, trans. Berkeley/Los Angeles/London: University of California Press.

Brentano, Franz. 1977. *The Psychology of Aristotle.* Berkeley/Los Angeles/London: University of California Press.

Broad, C.D. 1925. *The Mind and Its Place in Nature.* London: Routledge and Kegan Paul.

Broad, C.D. 1978. *Kant—An Introduction.* Cambridge: Cambridge University Press.

Brody, Baruch A. 1980. *Identity and Essence.* Princeton: Princeton University Press.

Broido, Michael M. 1984. *"Abhiprāya* and Implication in Tibetan Linguistics." *Journal of Indian Philosophy* 12: 1–33.

Bugault, Guy. 1994. *L'Inde pense-t-elle?* Paris: Presses Universitaires de France.

Cabezón, José Ignacio. 1992. *A Dose of Emptiness.* Albany: State University of New York Press.

Carrithers. Michael, Steven Collins, and Steven Lukes, eds. 1985. *The Category of the Person.* Cambridge: Cambridge University Press.

Case, Margaret, ed., 1994. *Heinrich Zimmer: Coming into His Own.* Princeton: Princeton University Press.

Chaignet, A. Ed. 1873. *Pythagore et la Philosophie Pythagoricienne,* vol. 2. Paris: Didier.

Chaignet, A. Ed. 1887. *Histoire de la Psychologie des Grecs,* vol. 1. Paris: Hachette.

Chakrabarti, Arindam. 1982. "The Nyāya Proofs for the Existence of the Soul." *Journal of Indian Philosophy* 10: 211–38.

Chakrabarti, Arindam. 1985. "Plato's Indian Barbers," in Matilal and Shaw, eds., *Analytical Philosophy in Comparative Perspective,* Synthèse Library. Dordrecht: D. Reidel.

Chattopadhyay, Debiprasad, and Mrinalkanti Gangopadhyay, eds. 1990. *Cārvāka/Lokāyata: An Anthology of Source Materials and Some Recent Studies.* New Delhi: Indian Council of Philosophical Research.

Chemparathy, George. 1972. *An Indian Rational Theology.* Vienna: De Nobili Research Library.

Chimpa, Lama, and Alaka Chattopadhyaya. 1980. *Tāranātha's History of Buddhism in India.* Atlantic Highlands, NJ: Humanities Press.

Chisholm, Roderick M., ed. 1960. *Realism and the Background of Phenomenology.* Glencoe, IL.: Free Press.

Chisholm, Roderick M. 1966. *Theory of Knowledge.* Englewood Cliffs, NJ: Prentice-Hall.

Chisholm, Roderick M. 1979. *Person and Object.* La Salle, IL: Open Court.

Chisholm, Roderick M. 1981. *The First Person.* Minneapolis: University of Minnesota Press.

Chisholm, Roderick M. 1982. *The Foundations of Knowing.* Minneapolis: University of Minnesota Press.

Collins, Steven. 1982a. *Selfless Persons.* Cambridge: Cambridge University Press.

Collins, Steven. 1982b. Review of Pérez-Remón 1980, in *Numen.* 29/2: 250–71.

Collins, Steven. 1994. "What Are Buddhists *Doing* When They Deny the Self?" in Frank E. Reynolds and David Tracy, eds., *Religion and Practical Reason,* pp. 59–86. Albany: State University of New York Press.

Collins, Steven. 1997. "A Buddhist Debate about the Self; and Remarks on Buddhism in the Work of Derek Parfit and Galen Strawson." *Journal of Indian Philosophy* 25: 467–93.

Conze, Edward. 1963. "Spurious Parallels to Buddhist Philosophy." *Philosophy East and West,* 13/2.

Conze, Edward. 1967. *Buddhist Thought in India: Three Phases of Buddhist Philosophy.* Ann Arbor: University of Michigan Press.

Conze, Edward. 1969. *Buddhist Meditation.* New York/Evanston: Harper and Row.

Copleston, Frederick C. 1955. *Aquinas.* Harmondsworth: Penguin.

Copleston, Frederick C. 1980. *Philosophies and Cultures.* Oxford: Oxford University Press.

Copleston, Frederick C. 1982. *Religion and the One.* New York: Crossroad.

Coward, Howard G., Julius J. Lipner, and Katherine K. Young. 1989. *Hindu Ethics: Purity, Abortion, and Euthanasia.* Albany: State University of New York Press.

Cowell, E.B. and A.E. Gough, trans. 1904. *The Sarva-Darsana-Samgraha, or Review of the Different Systems of Hindu Philosophy.* London: Kegan Paul, Trench, Trübner and Co.

Cox, Collett. 1995. *Disputed Dharmas: Early Buddhist Theories of Existence.* Studia Philologica Buddhica Monograph Series 11. Tokyo: The International Institute for Buddhist Studies.

Dampier, Sir William Cecil. 1971. *A History of Science and Its Relations with Philosophy and Religion.* Cambridge: Cambridge University Press.

Daniélou, Alain. 1964. *Hindu Polytheism,* Bollingen Series 73. New York: Pantheon.

Daor, Dan, and Ben-Ami Scharfstein. 1979. "In Answer to Antony Flew: The Whiteness of Feathers and the Whiteness of Snow." *Journal of Chinese Philosophy* 6: 37–53.

Dasgupta, Surama. 1961. *Development of Moral Philosophy in India.* New York: Frederick Ungar.

Davidson, Donald. 1980. *Essays on Actions and Events.* Oxford: Clarendon Press.

Davidson, Ronald M. 1981. "The Litany of the Names of Mañjuśrī." *Mélanges Chinois et Bouddhiques,* 20: 1–69.

Daye, Douglas D. 1978. "Buddhist Logic," in Charles S. Prebish, *Buddhism: A Modern Perspective.* University Park, PA: Pennsylvania State University Press.

Daye, Douglas D. 1985. "Some Epistemologically Misleading Expressions: 'Inference' and 'Anumāna', 'Perception' and 'Pratyakṣa'," in Bimal Krishna Matilal and Jaysankar Lal Shaw, eds., *Analytical Philosophy in Comparative Perspective,* pp. 231–52. Dordrecht: D. Reidel.

Dehejia, Vidya. 1986. *Yoginī Cult and Temples: A Tantric Tradition.* New Delhi: National Museum.

de Mallmann, Marie-Thérèse. 1986. *Introduction à l'iconographie du Tāntrisme bouddhique.* Paris: Adrien Maisonneuve.

Demiéville, Paul. 1973. *Choix d'études bouddhiques (1929–1970).* Leiden: E. J. Brill.

Demiéville, Paul, Hubert Durt, and Anna Seidel. 1978. *Répertoire du canon bouddhique sino-japonais, édition de Taishō.* Fascicule annexe du Hōbōgirin. Paris: Adrien-Maissoneuve.

de Silva, Lily. 1981. *Paritta: A Historical and Religious Study of the Buddhist Ceremony of Peace and Prosperity in Sri Lanka.* Spolia Zeylanica 36/1. Colombo: Department of Government Printing.

Deussen, Paul. 1965. *The Philosophy of the Upanishads,* A.S. Geden, trans. New York: Dover.

Deutsch, Eliot, and Ron Bontekoe, eds. 1997. *A Companion to World Philosophies.* Oxford: Basil Blackwell.

Dietz, Siglinde. 1984. *Die Buddhistische Briefliteratur Indiens.* Asiatische Forschungen 84. Wiesbaden: Otto Harrossowitz.

Donner, Neal. 1987. "Sudden and Gradual Intimately Conjoined: Chih-i's Tien-t'ai View," in Peter N. Gregory, ed., *Sudden and Gradual: Approaches to Enlightenment in Chinese Thought,* Studies in East Asian Buddhism 5. Honolulu: University of Hawai'i Press.

Downs, Hugh R. 1980. *Rhythms of a Himalayan Village.* New York: Harper and Row.

Dravid, Raja Ram. 1972. *The Problem of Universals in Indian Philosophy.* Delhi: Motilal Banarsidass.

Dreyfus, Georges. 1997. *Recognizing Reality.* Albany: State University of New York Press.

D'Sa, Francis X. 1980. *Śabdaprāmaṇyam in Śabara and Kumārila: Towards a Study of the Mīmāṃsā Experience of Language.* Indologisches Institut der Universität Wien. Leiden: E. J. Brill.

Dudjom Rinpoche, Jikdrel Yeshe Dorje. 1991. *The Nyingma School of Tibetan Buddhism: Its Fundamentals and History,* Gyurme Dorje and Matthew Kapstein, trans. 2 vols. Boston: Wisdom Publications.

Duerlinger, James. 1989. "Vasubandhu's 'Refutation of the Theory of Selfhood.'" *Journal of Indian Philosophy* 17: 129–87.

Duerlinger, James. 1993. "Reductionist and Nonreductionist Theories of Persons in Indian Buddhist Philosophy." *Journal of Indian Philosophy* 21: 79–101.

Duerlinger, James. 1997–2000. "Vasubandhu's Philosophical Critique of the Vāstīputrīya's Theory of Persons." Parts I, II, and III. *Journal of Indian Philosophy* 25: 307–35, 26: 573–605, and 28: 125–70.

Dumont, Louis. 1970. *Religion, Politics and History in India: Collected Papers in Indian Sociology*. The Hague: Mouton.

Dumont, Louis. 1980. *Homo Hierarchicus: The Caste System and Its Implications*. Rev. English ed. Chicago: University of Chicago Press.

Dutt, Nalinaksha. 1942. *Gilgit Manuscripts*. 4 vols. in 9 fascicles. Repr. Delhi: Sri Satguru Publications, 1984.

Eckel, Malcolm David. 1987. *Jñānagarbha's Commentary on the Distinction between the Two Truths*. Albany: State University of New York Press.

Eckel, Malcolm David. 1992. *To See the Buddha: A Philosopher's Quest for the Meaning of Emptiness*. Princeton: Princeton University Press.

Edgerton, Franklin. 1953a. *Buddhist Hybrid Sanskrit Grammar and Dictionary*. New Haven: Yale University Press.

Edgerton, Franklin. 1953b. *Buddhist Hybrid Sanskrit Reader*. New Haven: Yale University Press.

Edgerton, Franklin. 1965. *The Beginnings of Indian Philosophy*. Cambridge, MA: Harvard University Press.

Engle, Artemus Bertine. 1983. "The Buddhist Theory of Self According to Ācārya Candrakīrti." Ph.D. dissertation. University of Wisconsin, Madison.

Flew, Antony G. N. 1964. *Body, Mind, and Death*. New York: Macmillan.

Flew, Antony G. N. 1971. *An Introduction to Western Philosophy*. Indianapolis/New York: Bobbs-Merrill.

Flew, Antony G. N. 1979. "The Cultural Roots of Analytical Philosophy." *Journal of Chinese Philosophy*, 6: 1–14.

Francke, Frederick, ed. 1982. *The Buddha Eye*. New York: Crossroad.

Franco, Eli. 1987. *Perception, Knowledge, and Disbelief: A Study of Jayarāśi's Scepticism*. Stuttgart: Franz Steiner Verlag.

Franco, Eli. 1997. *Dharmakīrti on Compassion and Rebirth*. Wiener Studien zur Tibetologie und Buddhismuskunde 38. Vienna: Arbeitskreis für Tibetische und Buddhistische Studien, Universität Wien.

Frazer, James G. 1922. *The Golden Bough*. London: Macmillan.

Gadamer, Hans-Georg. 1982. *Truth and Method.* New York: Crossroad.

Gallop, David, trans. 1975. *Plato's Phaedo.* Oxford: Clarendon Press.

Ganeri, Jonardon. 2001. *Philosophy in Classical India.* London/New York: Routledge.

Gangopadhyaya, Mrinalakanti. 1981. *Indian Atomism.* Atlantic Highlands, NJ: Humanities Press.

Garfield, Jay L. 1990. "Epoché and Śūnyatā: Scepticism East and West." *Philosophy East and West* 40/3: 285–308.

Garfield, Jay L. 1995. *The Fundamental Wisdom of the Middle Way.* New York: Oxford University Press.

Gega Lama. 1983. *Principles of Tibetan Art.* Darjeeling: Jamyang Singe.

Gellner, David N. 1992. *Monk, Householder, and Tantric Priest: Newar Buddhism and Its Hierarchy of Ritual.* Cambridge: Cambridge University Press.

Giles, James. 1993. "The No-Self Theory: Hume, Buddhism, and Personal Identity." *Philosophy East and West* 43: 175–200.

Gokhale, V. V. 1958. "The Vedānta Philosophy Described by Bhavya in his Madhyamakahṛdaya," *Indo-Iranian Journal* 2/3: 165–80.

Gokhale, V. V. 1963. "Masters of Buddhism Adore the Brahman through Non-Adoration," *Indo-Iranian Journal* 5/4: 271–75.

Gombrich, Richard. 1988. *Theravāda Buddhism: A Social History from Ancient Benares to Modern Colombo.* London/New York: Routledge and Kegan Paul.

Gonda, Jan. 1979. *Les religions de l'Inde: 1—védisme et hindouisme ancien.* Paris: Payot.

Goodman, Steven D. 1981. "Mi-pham rgya-mtsho: an account of his life, the printing of his works, and the structure of his treatise entitled *Mkhas-pa'i tshul la 'jug pa'i sgo,"* in Ronald M. Davidson, ed. *Wind Horse,* vol. 1: 58–78. Berkeley: Asian Humanities Press.

Graham, A.C. 1964. "The Place of Reason in the Chinese Philosophical Tradition," in Raymond Dawson, ed., *The Legacy of China.* Oxford: Clarendon Press.

Graham, A.C. 1989. *Disputers of the Tao: Philosophical Argument in Ancient China.* La Salle, IL: Open Court.

Granoff, Phyllis. 2000. "Other People's Rituals: Ritual Eclecticism in Early Medieval Indian Religions." *Journal of Indian Philosophy* 28/4: 399–424.

Griffiths, Paul. 1986. *On Being Mindless: Buddhist Meditation and the Mind-Body Problem.* La Salle, IL: Open Court.

Griffiths, Paul. 1990. "Denaturalizing Discourse," in Frank E. Reynolds, and David Tracy, eds. *Myth and Philosophy*, pp. 57–91. Albany: State University of New York Press.

Griffiths, Paul. 1994. *On Being Buddha: The Classical Doctrine of Buddhahood.* Albany: State University of New York Press.

Griffiths, Paul. 1999. *Religious Reading: The Place of Reading in the Practice of Religion.* New York: Oxford University Press.

Griswold, Alexander B., Chewon Kim, and Peter H. Pott. 1968. *The Art of Burma, Korea, Tibet.* New York/Toronto/London: Greystone Press.

Gudmunsen, Chris. 1977. *Wittgenstein and Buddhism.* London: MacMillan.

Guenther, Herbert V. 1963. *The Life and Teaching of Nāropa.* London: Oxford University Press.

Gyatso, Janet, ed. 1992. *In the Mirror of Memory: Reflections on Mindfulness and Remembrance in Indian and Tibetan Buddhism.* Albany: State University of New York Press.

Hackforth, R. 1952. *Plato's Phaedrus.* Cambridge: Cambridge University Press.

Hackforth, R. 1955. *Plato's Phaedo.* Cambridge: Cambridge University Press.

Hadas, Moses, ed. 1967. *Solomon Maimon: An Autobiography.* New York: Schocken.

Hadot, Pierre. 1992. *La Citadelle intérieure. Introduction aux Pensées de Marc Aurèle.* Paris: Fayard.

Hadot, Pierre. 1995a. *Qu'est-ce que la philosophie antique?* Paris: Gallimard.

Hadot, Pierre. 1995b. *Philosophy as a Way of Life,* Arnold I. Davidson, ed. Michael Chase, trans. Oxford: Blackwell.

Hadot, Pierre. 1998. *Plotinus, or The Simplicity of Vision,* Michael Chase, trans. Chicago/London: University of Chicago Press.

Hahn, Michael. 1971. *Jñānaśrīmitras Vṛttamālāstuti: Eine Beispielsammlung zur altindischen Metrik nach dem tibetischen Tanjur zusammen mit der mongolischen Version.* Asiatische Forschungen 33. Wiesbaden: O. Harrassowitz.

Hakeda, Yoshito S. 1972. *Kūkai: Major Works.* New York/London: Columbia University Press.

Halbertal, Moshe, and Avishai Margalit. 1992. *Idolatry,* Naomi Goldblum, trans. Cambridge, MA: Harvard University Press.

Halbfass, Wilhelm. 1988. *India and Europe: An Essay in Understanding.* Albany: State University of New York Press. [Revised translation of *Indien und Europa.* Basel/Stuttgart: Schwabe & Co, 1981.]

Halbfass, Wilhelm. 1991. *Tradition and Reflection: Explorations in Indian Thought.* Albany: State University of New York Press.

Halbfass, Wilhelm. 1992. *On Being and What There Is: Classical Vaiśeṣika and the History of Indian Ontology.* Albany: State University of New York Press.

Hamilton, Clarence H. 1938. *Wei Shih Er Shih Lun.* American Oriental Series, vol. 13. New Haven: American Oriental Society.

Hamlyn, D. W. 1980. *Schopenhauer.* London: Routledge and Kegan Paul.

Harvey, Peter. 2000. *An Introduction to Buddhist Ethics.* Cambridge: Cambridge University Press.

Hattori, Masaaki. 1968. *Dignāga, On Perception.* Harvard Oriental Series, vol. 47. Cambridge, MA: Harvard University Press.

Hayes, Richard. 1988. "Principled Atheism in the Buddhist Scholastic Tradition." *Journal of Indian Philosophy* 16: 1–28.

Hedinger, Jürg. 1984. *Aspekte der Schulung in der Laufbahn eines Bodhisattva.* Wiesbaden: Otto Harrassowitz.

Hegel, Georg Wilhelm Friedrich. 1928. *Vorlesungen über die Geschichte der Philosophie,* vol. 1, in *Sämtliche Werke,* Hermann Glocker, ed. Stuttgart: Frommanns Verlag.

Heidegger, Martin. 1958. *What Is Philosophy?* William Kluback and Jean T. Wilde, trans. N.p.: Twayne Publishers.

Heidegger, Martin. 1962. *Being and Time.* John Macquarrie and Edward Robinson, trans. New York: Harper and Row.

Heidegger, Martin. 1971a. "Plato's Doctrine of Truth." John Barlow, trans. in William Barrett and Henry D. Aiken, eds. *Philosophy in the Twentieth Century,* vol. 3, *Contemporary European Thought,* pp. 173–92. New York: Harper and Row.

Heidegger, Martin. 1971b. "Letter on Humanism." Edgar Lohner, trans. in William Barrett and Henry D. Aiken, eds. *Philosophy in the Twentieth Century,* vol. 3, *Contemporary European Thought,* pp. 192–224. New York: Harper and Row.

Heidegger, Martin. 1971c. *On the Way to Language,* Peter D. Hertz, trans. New York: Harper and Row.

Heidegger, Martin. 1975. *Early Greek Thinking: The Dawn of Western Philosophy,* David Farrell Krell and Frank A. Capuzzi, trans. New York: Harper and Row.

Heidegger, Martin. 1998. *Pathmarks,* William McNeill, ed. Cambridge: Cambridge University Press.

Heimann, Betty. 1964. *Facets of Indian Thought.* New York: Schocken.

Hempel, Carl G. 1949. "The Function of General Laws in History," in Herbert Feigl and Wilfred Sellars, eds. *Readings in Philosophical Analysis*, pp. 459–71. New York: Appleton-Century-Crofts.

Herman, A.L. 1983. *An Introduction to Buddhist Thought.* Lanham, MD: University Press of America.

Hesse, Hermann. 1950. *Siddhartha: Eine indische Dichtung.* Suhrkamp Verlag.

Hoffman, Yoel. 1982. *The Problem of the Self, East and West.* Calcutta: Mukhopadhyay.

Hollis, Martin, and Steven Lukes, eds. 1982. *Rationality and Relativism.* Cambridge, MA: MIT Press.

Hookham, S. K. 1991. *The Buddha Within.* Albany: State University of New York Press.

Hopkins, Jeffrey. 1983. *Meditation on Emptiness.* London: Wisdom Publications.

Hopkins, Jeffrey. 1999. *Emptiness in the Mind-Only School of Buddhism.* Berkeley/Los Angeles/London: University of California Press.

Horner, I.B., trans. 1963. *Milinda's Questions.* London: Luzac & Company.

Horsch, Paul. 1956–58. "Le principe d'individuation dans la philosophie Indienne." *Asiatische Studien* 10 (1956): 60–78, continued in *Asiatische Studien* 11 (1957–58): 29–41, 121–42.

Howard, Roy J. 1982. *Three Faces of Hermeneutics.* Berkeley: University of California Press.

Hulin, Michel. 1978. *Le Principe de l'Ego dans la Pensée Indienne Classique.* Paris: Institut de Civilisation Indienne.

Hume, David. 1888. *A Treatise of Human Nature,* L. A. Selby-Bigge, ed. Oxford: Clarendon Press.

Huntington, C. W., Jr., with Geshé Namgyal Wangchen. 1989. *The Emptiness of Emptiness: An Introduction to Early Indian Mādhyamika.* Honolulu: University of Hawai'i Press.

Huntington, Susan L., and John C. Huntington. 1990. *Leaves from the Bodhi Tree: The Art of Pāla India (8th–12th Centuries) and Its International Legacy.* Seattle/London: The Dayton Art Institute in association with the University of Washington Press.

Husserl, Edmund. 1962. *Recherches Logiques,* Hubert Élie et al., trans. 4 vols. Paris: P.U.F.

Ichigō Masamichi. 1989. "Śāntarakṣita's *Madhyamakālaṃkāra,*" in Luis O. Gómez and Jonathan A. Silk, eds. *Studies in the Literature of the Great Vehicle: Three*

Mahāyāna Buddhist Texts. Ann Arbor: Center for South and Southeast Asian Studies.

Ichimura Shohei. 1980. "A Study of the Mādhyamika Method of Refutation, Especially of Its Affinity to that of Kathāvatthu." *Journal of the International Association for Buddhist Studies* 3: 7–15.

Iida Shotaro. 1980. *Reason and Emptiness: A Study in Logic and Mysticism.* Tokyo: Hokuseido Press.

Imaeda, Yoshiro. 1981. "Un extrait tibétain du *Mañjuśrīmūlakalpa* dans les manuscrits de Touen-houang," in *Nouvelles contributions aux études de Touen-houang,* pp. 303–20. Geneva/Paris: Librairie Droz.

Inagaki Hisao. 1999. *Amida Dhāraṇī Sūtra and Jñānagarbha's Commentary.* Ryukoku Literature Series 7. Ryukoku Gakkai.

Inden, Ronald. 1990. *Imagining India.* Oxford: Basil Blackwell.

Jackson, David P., and Janice A. Jackson. 1984. *Tibetan Thangka Painting: Methods & Materials.* Boulder: Shambhala.

Jackson, Roger R. 1993. *Is Enlightenment Possible? Dharmakīrti and rGyal tshab rje on Knowledge, Rebirth, No-Self and Liberation.* Ithaca: Snow Lion.

Jackson, Roger R. 1994. "A Tantric Echo in Sinhalese Theravāda?" *Dhīḥ—Journal of Rare Buddhist Texts Research Project* 18: 121–40.

Jackson, Roger R., and John J. Makransky, eds. 2000. *Buddhist Theology: Critical Reflections by Contemporary Buddhist Scholars.* Richmond, Surrey: Curzon Press.

Jacobson, Nolan Pliny. 1974. *Buddhism: The Religion of Analysis.* Carbondale, IL: Southern Illinois University Press.

James, William. 1925. *The Varieties of Religious Experience.* New York/London: Longmans, Green, and Co.

Jaspers, Karl. 1962. *The Great Philosophers.* Hannah Arendt, ed. Ralph Manheim, trans. New York: Hartcourt, Brace, and World.

Jayatilleke, K.N. 1963. *Early Buddhist Theory of Knowledge.* London: George Allen and Unwin.

Jhā, Gaṅgānātha. 1984. *The Nyāya Sūtras of Gautama.* 2 vols. Delhi: Motilal Banarsidass. [Repr. of 1912–19 edition.]

Jones, J. J., trans. 1949. *The Mahāvastu.* Vol. 1. Sacred Books of the Buddhists 16. London: Luzac.

Kahn, Charles H. 1973. *The Verb 'Be' in Ancient Greek.* Dordrecht: Reidel.

Kahn, Charles H. 1978. "Linguistic Relativism and the Greek Project of Ontology," in Mervyn Sprung, ed., *The Question of Being: East-West Perspectives*, pp. 31–44. University Park/London: Pennsylvania State University Press.

Kajiyama, Y. 1973. "Three Types of Affirmation and Two Types of Negation in Buddhist Philosophy." *Wiener Zeitschrift für die Kunde Südasiens* 17: 161–75.

Kant, Immanuel. 1927. *Kant's Critique of Practical Reason and Other Works on the Theory of Ethics*, Thomas Kingsmill Abbott, trans. 6th ed. London: Longmans, Green, and Co.

Kant, Immanuel. 1965. *Critique of Pure Reason*. Norman Kemp Smith, trans. New York: St. Martin's.

Kapstein, Matthew T. 1986a. "Self and Personal Identity in Indian Buddhist Scholasticism: A Philosophical Investigation." Ph.D. dissertation. Brown University.

Kapstein, Matthew T. 1986b. "Collins, Parfit and the Problem of Personal Identity in Two Traditions." *Philosophy East and West* 36/3: 289–98.

Kapstein, Matthew T. 1989. "The Purificatory Gem and Its Cleansing: A Late Tibetan Polemical Discussion of Apocryphal Texts." *History of Religions* 28/3: 217–44. Repr. as chap. 7 of Kapstein 2000.

Kapstein, Matthew T. 1992. "Samantabhadra and Rudra: Innate Enlightenment and Radical Evil in Tibetan Rnying-ma-pa Buddhism," in Frank E. Reynolds and David Tracy, eds., *Discourse and Practice*, pp. 51–82. Albany: State University of New York Press. Repr. as chap. 9 of Kapstein 2000.

Kapstein 1992/3. Catalogue to *The 'Dzam-thang Edition of the Collected Works of Kun-mkhyen Dol-po-pa Shes-rab-rgyal-mtshan*. New Delhi: Shedrup Books and Konchhog Lhadrepa.

Kapstein, Matthew T. 1995. "gDams-ngag: Tibetan Technologies of the Self," in Roger Jackson and José Cabezón, eds., *Tibetan Literature: Studies in Genre*. Ithaca: Snow Lion Publications.

Kapstein, Matthew T. 1997. "From Dol-po-pa to 'Ba'-mda' Dge-legs: Three Jonang-pa Masters on the Interpretation of *Prajñāpāramitā*." In Helmut Krasser, Michael Torsten Much, Ernst Steinkellner, and Helmut Tauscher, eds., *Tibetan Studies: Proceedings of the Seventh Seminar of the International Association for Tibetan Studies*, vol. 1, 457–75. Vienna: Austrian Academy of Science.

Kapstein, Matthew T. 2000a. *The Tibetan Assimilation of Buddhism: Conversion, Contestation and Memory*. New York: Oxford University Press.

Kapstein, Matthew T. 2000b. "We Are All Gzhan stong pas." *Journal of Buddhist Ethics* 7: 105–25.

Kapstein, Matthew T. 2002. "The Indian Literary Identity in Tibet," in Sheldon Pollock, ed., *Literary Cultures in History*. Berkeley: University of California Press.

Karunadasa, Y. 1967. *Buddhist Analysis of Matter.* Colombo: Department of Cultural Affairs.

Kawamura, Leslie S. 1981. "An Analysis of Mi-pham's *mKhas-'jug,"* in Ronald M. Davidson, ed. *Wind Horse,* vol. 1, pp. 112–26. Berkeley: Asian Humanities Press.

Keith, Arthur Berriedale. 1925. *The Religion and Philosophy of the Veda and Upanishads.* Cambridge, MA: Harvard University Press.

Kirk, G.S., and J.E. Raven. 1971. *The Presocratic Philosophers.* Cambridge: Cambridge University Press.

Kochumuttom, Thomas A. 1982. *A Buddhist Philosophy of Experience.* Delhi: Motilal Banarsidass.

Kretzmann, Norman. 1966. "Omniscience and Immutability." *Journal of Philosophy* 63.

Kripke, Saul A. 1981. *Naming and Necessity.* Cambridge, MA: Harvard University Press.

Krishna, Daya 1991. *Indian Philosophy: A Counter Perspective.* New Delhi: Oxford University Press.

Lalou, Marcelle. 1930. *Iconographie des Étoffes Peintes (paṭa) dans le Mañjuśrīmūlakalpa,* Buddhica, Series 1, vol. 6. Paris: P. Geuthner.

Lalou, Marcelle. 1936. *"Mañjuśrīmūlakalpa* et *Tārāmūlakalpa." Harvard Journal of Asiatic Studies* 1: 327–49.

Lalou, Marcelle. 1953. "Les Textes Bouddhiques au Temps du Roi Khri-sroṅ-lde-bcan." *Journal Asiatique* 241/3: 313–53.

Lamotte, Étienne. 1935. *Saṃdhinirmocanasūtra: L'explication des mystères.* Paris: Adrien Maisonneuve.

Lamotte, Étienne. 1944. *Le Traité de la Grande Vertu de Sagesse,* vol. 1. Louvain: Institut Orientaliste.

Lamotte, Étienne. 1962. *L'Enseignement de Vimalakīrti.* Louvain: Publications Universitaires.

Lamotte, Étienne. 1970. *Le Traité de la Grande Vertu de Sagesse,* vol. 3. Louvain: Institut Orientaliste.

Lamotte, Étienne. 1976. *Histoire du Bouddhisme Indien.* Louvain: Institut Orientaliste.

Larson, Gerald James. 1979. *Classical Sāṃkhya,* 2nd ed. Delhi: Motilal Banarsidass.

Larson, Gerald James, and Eliot Deutsch, eds. 1988. *Interpreting Across Boundaries: New Essays in Comparative Philosophy.* Princeton: Princeton University Press.

La Vallée Poussin, Louis de. 1912. "Viṃśakakārikāprakaraṇa." *Le Muséon* 31: 53–90.

La Vallée Poussin, Louis de. 1925. "La Controverse du Temps et du Pudgala dans le Vijñānakāya." *Études Asiatiques,* Publications de l'École Française d'Extrême-Orient 1: 343–76.

La Vallée Poussin, Louis de. 1971. *L'Abhidharmakośa de Vasubandhu.* 6 vols. Brussels: Institut Belge des Hautes Études Chinoises.

Law, Bimala Churn. 1969. *The Debates Commentary.* London: Pali Text Society.

Lawson, E. Thomas, and Robert N. McCauley. 1990. *Rethinking Religion: Connecting Cognition and Culture.* Cambridge: Cambridge University Press.

Lévi, Sylvain. 1925. *Vijñaptimātratāsiddhī.* Paris: H. Champion.

Lévi, Sylvain. 1932. *Materiaux pour l'étude du système Vijñaptimātra.* Paris: H. Champion.

Lindtner, Christian. 1981. "Atiśa's 'Introduction to the Two Truths,' and Its Sources," *Journal of Indian Philosophy* 9: 161–214.

Linrothe, Rob. 1999. *Ruthless Compassion: Wrathful Deities in Early Indo-Tibetan Esoteric Buddhist Art.* London: Serindia.

Linsky, Leonard. 1967. *Referring.* London: Routledge and Kegan Paul.

Lipman, Kennard. 1980. "*Nītārtha, Neyārtha,* and *Tathāgatagarbha* in Tibet." *Journal of Indian Philosophy* 8: 87–95

Lipman, Kennard. 1992. "What Is Buddhist Logic?" in S.D. Goodman and R. M. Davidson, eds., *Tibetan Buddhism: Reason and Revelation.* Albany: State University of New York Press.

Locke, John. 1974. *An Essay Concerning Human Understanding,* Peter H. Nidditch, ed. Oxford: Clarendon Press.

Lokesh Chandra, ed. 1963. *Materials for a History of Tibetan Literature,* part 1. New Delhi: International Academy of Indian Culture.

Lokesh Chandra. 1968. "The life and works of 'Jam-dbyaṅs-bźad-pa," *Central Asiatic Journal* 7: 45–49.

Lokesh Chandra. 1970. *Kongtrul's Encyclopedia of Indo-Tibetan Culture,* Śatapiṭaka Series 80. New Delhi: International Academy of Indian Culture.

Lopez, Donald S., Jr., ed. 1988a. *Buddhist Hermeneutics.* Honolulu: University of Hawai'i Press.

Lopez, Donald S., Jr. 1988b. *The Heart Sūtra Explained: Indian and Tibetan Commentaries.* Albany: State University of New York Press.

Lopez, Donald S., Jr., ed. 1995. *Curators of the Buddha: The Study of Buddhism under Colonialism.* Chicago: University of Chicago Press.

Lopez, Donald S., Jr. 1996. *Elaborations on Emptiness: Uses of the Heart Sūtra.* Princeton: Princeton University Press.

Lopez, Donald S., Jr. 1998. *Prisoners of Shangri-la: Tibetan Buddhism and the West.* Chicago/London: University of Chicago Press.

Löwith, Karl. 1967. *From Hegel to Nietzsche: The Revolution in Nineteenth Century Thought,* David E. Green, trans. Garden City, N.J.: Doubleday Anchor.

Macdonald, Ariane. 1962. *Le Maṇḍala du Mañjuśrīmūlakalpa.* Paris: Adrien-Maisonneuve.

Mackie, J. L. 1967. "Mill's Methods of Induction," in Paul Edwards, ed., *The Encyclopedia of Philosophy* 5: 324–32. New York: Macmillan.

Makransky, John J. 1997. *Buddhahood Embodied: Sources of Controversy in India and Tibet.* Albany: State University of New York Press.

Makreel, Rudolf A. 1992. *Dilthey: Philosopher of the Human Sciences,* 3rd ed. Princeton: Princeton University Press.

Malandra, Geri. 1993. *Unfolding a Maṇḍala: The Buddhist Cave Temples at Ellora.* Albany: State University of New York Press.

Marshall, P. J., ed. 1970. *The British Discovery of Hinduism in the Eighteenth Century.* Cambridge: Cambridge University Press.

Martin, C.B., and M. Deutscher. 1966. "Remembering." *The Philosophical Review* 75: 161–96.

Masson-Oursel, Paul. 1938. *La Philosophie en Orient.* Paris: Librairie Félix Alcan.

Matilal, Bimal Krishna. 1968. *The Navya-Nyāya Doctrine of Negation.* Harvard Oriental Series, vol. 46. Cambridge, MA: Harvard University Press.

Matilal, Bimal Krishna. 1971. *Epistemology, Logic and Grammar in Indian Philosophical Analysis.* The Hague: Mouton and Co.

Matilal, Bimal Krishna. 1973. "A Critique of the Mādhyamika Position," in M. Sprung, ed., *The Problem of Two Truths in Buddhism and Vedānta,* pp. 54–63. Dordrecht/Boston: D. Reidel.

Matilal, Bimal Krishna. 1977. *Nyāya-vaiśeṣika,* in Jan Gonda, ed., *A History of Indian Literature,* vol. 6, fasc. 2. Wiesbaden: Otto Harrassowitz.

Matilal, Bimal Krishna. 1982. *Logical and Ethical Issues of Religious Belief.* Calcutta: University of Calcutta.

Matilal, Bimal Krishna. 1986. *Perception.* Oxford: Clarendon Press.

Matilal, Bimal Krishna. 1990. *The Word and the World.* New Delhi: Oxford University Press.

Matilal, Bimal Krishna. 1998. *The Character of Logic in India*, ed. Jonardon Ganeri and Heeraman Tiwari. Albany: State University of New York Press.

Matilal, Bimal Krishna, and Arindam Chakrabarti, eds. 1994. *Knowing From Words: Western and Indian Philosophical Analysis of Understanding and Testimony.* Dordrecht: Kluwer.

Matsunaga Yūkei. 1985. "On the Date of the *Mañjuśrīmūlakalpa*," in Michel Strickmann, ed., *Tantric and Taoist Studies in Honour of R. A. Stein*, vol. 3, pp. 882–94, in *Mélanges Chinois et Bouddhiques*, vol. 22. Brussels: Institut Belge des Hautes Études Chinoises.

May, Reinhard. 1996. *Heidegger's Hidden Sources: East Asian Influences on His Work*, Graham Parkes, trans. London/New York: Routledge.

McDermott, A.C. Senape. 1970. *An Eleventh Century Logic of 'Exists.'* Foundations of Language, Supplementary Series, vol. 11. Dordrecht: D. Reidel.

McEvilley, Thomas. 1982. "Pyrrhonism and Mādhyamika," *Philosophy East and West* 32: 3–35.

McKeon, Richard, ed. 1941. *The Basic Works of Aristotle.* New York: Random House.

Mehta, J.L. 1978. "Heidegger and Vedanta: Reflections on a Questionable Theme." *International Philosophical Quarterly* 18: 121–49. Repr. in J. L. Mehta 1985, *India and the West: The Problem of Understanding.* Chico, CA: Scholars Press; and in Parkes 1987: 15–45.

Mehta, Mohan Lal. 1954. *Outlines of Jaina Philosophy.* Bangalore: Jaina Mission Society.

Miller, Fred D., Jr. 1982. "Aristotle against the Atomists," in Norman Kretzmann, ed., *Infinity and Continuity in Ancient and Medieval Thought*, pp. 87–111. Ithaca: Cornell University Press.

Mikogami Esho. 1979. "Some Remarks on the Concept of Arthakriyā." *Journal of Indian Philosophy* 7: 79–94.

Mohanty, Jitendra Nath. 1992. *Reason and Tradition in Indian Thought.* Oxford: Clarendon Press.

Monier-Williams, Monier. 1899. *A Sanskrit-English Dictionary.* Oxford: The Clarendon Press.

Murti, T. R. V. 1960. *The Central Philosophy of Buddhism.* London: George Allen and Unwin.

Nagao, Gadjin M. 1991. *Mādhyamika and Yogācāra*, Leslie S. Kawamura, trans. Albany: State University of New York Press.

Ñāṇamoli, Bhikkhu, trans. 1962. *The Guide.* London: Luzac and Company.

Ñāṇamoli, Bhikkhu, trans. 1965. *The Pitaka-Disclosure.* London: Luzac and Company.

Narain, A. K. 1957. *The Indo-Greeks.* Oxford: Clarendon Press.

Newland, Guy. 1992. *The Two Truths.* Ithaca: Snow Lion Publications.

Nozick, Robert. 1981. *Philosophical Explanations.* Cambridge, MA: Harvard University Press.

Nussbaum, Martha. 1986. *The Fragility of Goodness: Luck and Ethics in Greek Tragedy and Philosophy.* Cambridge: Cambridge University Press.

Nussbaum, Martha. 1994. *The Therapy of Desire: Theory and Practice in Hellenistic Ethics.* Princeton: Princeton University Press.

Oetke, Claus. 1988. *"Ich" und das Ich: analytische Untersuchungen zur buddhistisch-brahmanischen Ātmankontroverse.* Stuttgart: F. Steiner Verlag Wiesbaden.

O'Flaherty, Wendy Doniger, ed. 1983. *Karma and Rebirth in Classical Indian Traditions.* Delhi: Motilal Banarsidass.

Olivelle, Patrick. 1996. *Upaniṣads.* Oxford University Press.

Organ, Troy Wilson. 1964. *The Self in Indian Philosophy.* The Hague: Mouton and Co.

Pachow, W. 1980. *Chinese Buddhism: Aspects of Interaction and Reinterpretation.* Washington, D.C.: University Press of America.

Parfit, Derek. 1984. *Reasons and Persons.* Oxford: Clarendon Press.

Parkes, Graham, ed. 1987. *Heidegger and Asian Thought.* Honolulu: University of Hawai'i Press.

Passmore, John. 1969. *Philosophical Reasoning.* New York: Basic Books.

Pegis, Anton C., ed. 1945. *Basic Writings of Saint Thomas Aquinas.* New York: Random House.

Penelhum, Terence. 1967. "Personal Identity," in Paul Edwards, ed., *The Encyclopedia of Philosophy,* vol. 6, pp. 95–107. New York: Macmillan.

Pérez-Remón, Joaquín. 1980. *Self and Non-Self in Early Buddhism.* The Hague/Paris/New York: Mouton Publishers.

Perrett, Roy W. 1998. *Hindu Ethics: A Philosophical Study.* Monograph of the Society for Asian and Comparative Philosophy 17. Honolulu: University of Hawai'i Press.

Perry, John ed. 1975. *Personal Identity.* Berkeley/Los Angeles/London: University of California Press.

Pettit, John. 1999. *Mipham's Beacon of Certainty.* Boston: Wisdom Publications.

Piatigorsky, Alexander. 1984. *The Buddhist Philosophy of Thought.* New York: Barnes and Noble.

Pollock, Sheldon. 1985. "The Theory of Practice and the Practice of Theory in Indian Intellectual History." *Journal of the American Oriental Society* 105/3: 499–519.

Popkin, Richard H. 1979. *The History of Scepticism from Erasmus to Spinoza.* Berkeley: University of California Press.

Potter, Karl H. 1963. *Presuppositions of India's Philosophies.* Englewood Cliffs, NJ: Prentice-Hall.

Potter, Karl H. 1977. *Encyclopedia of Indian Philosophies: Indian Metaphysics and Epistemology: The Tradition of Nyāya-Vaiśeṣika up to Gaṅgeśa.* Princeton: Princeton University Press.

Putnam, Hilary. 1981. *Reason, Truth and History.* Cambridge: Cambridge University Press.

Quinn, Philip L. 1978. "Some Problems about Resurrection." *Religious Studies* 14: 343–59.

Qvarnström, Olle. 1989. *Hindu Philosophy in Buddhist Perspective.* Lund Studies in African and Asian Religions 4. Lund: Plus Ultra.

Radhakrishnan, Sarvepalli. 1953. *The Upanishads.* London: George Allen and Unwin.

Rahula, Walpola. 1971. *Le Compendium de la Super-Doctrine d'Asaṅga.* Paris: École Française d'Extrême-Orient.

Raju, P.T. 1985. *Structural Depths of Indian Thought.* Albany: State University of New York Press.

Rawski, Evelyn S. 1998. *The Last Emperors: A Social History of Qing Imperial Institutions.* Berkeley/Los Angeles/London: University of California Press.

Rawson, Joseph N. 1934. *The Kaṭha Upaniṣad.* London: Oxford University Press.

Renou, Louis, and Jean Filliozat. 1985. *L'Inde Classique: Manuel des études indiennes.* Vol. 1. Paris: Maisonneuve. [Repr. of 1947–49 ed.]

Rhys Davids, T. W., trans. 1890. *The Questions of King Milinda,* in F. Max Müller, ed., *The Sacred Books of the East,* vol. 35. Oxford: Oxford University Press.

Ricoeur, Paul. 1981. *Hermeneutics and the Human Sciences,* John B. Thompson, ed. and trans. Cambridge: Cambridge University Press.

Robinson, Richard H. 1976. *Early Mādhyamika in India and China.* 2nd ed. Delhi: Motilal Banarsidass.

Rorty, Amélie Oksenberg, ed. 1976. *The Identities of Persons.* Berkeley/Los Angeles/London: University of California Press.

Rorty, Richard. 1980. *Philosophy and the Mirror of Nature.* Princeton: Princeton University Press.

Rorty, Richard, J.B. Schneewind, and Quentin Skinner, eds. 1985. *Philosophy in History.* Cambridge: Cambridge University Press.

Ruegg, David Seyfort. 1963. "The Jo naṅ pas: A School of Buddhist Ontologists according to the Grub mtha' śel gyi me loṅ." *Journal of the Americal Oriental Society* 83: 73–91.

Ruegg, David Seyfort. 1981. *The Literature of the Madhyamaka School of Philosophy in India.* Wiesbaden: Otto Harrassowitz.

Ryavec, Karl E. 1994. "Important New Sources for the Study of Tibetan Geography: An Analysis of a Recent Chinese County Place Name Index of Dzamthang in Eastern Tibet." *Central Asiatic Journal* 38/2: 214–34.

Sahu, Nabin Kumar. 1984. *Khārevala.* Bhubaneswar: Orissa State Museum.

Said, Edward W. 1979. *Orientalism.* New York: Vintage Books.

Saksena, S.K. 1951. "Authority in Indian Philosophy." *Philosophy East and West* 1/3: 38–49. [Repr. in R.T. Blackwood and A.L. Herman, eds. 1975. *Problems in Philosophy: West and East,* pp. 247–56. Englewood Cliffs, NJ: Prentice-Hall.]

Schäfer, Peter and Hans G. Kippenberg. 1997. *Envisioning Magic: A Princeton Seminar and Symposium.* Leiden/New York/Cologne: E. J. Brill.

Scharfe, Hartmut. 1977. *Grammatical Literature,* in Jan Gonda, ed., *History of Indian Literature,* vol. 5, fasc. 2. Wiesbaden: O. Harrassowitz.

Scharfstein, Ben-Ami. 1989. *The Dilemma of Context.* New York: New York University Press.

Scharfstein, Ben-Ami. 1998. *A Comparative History of World Philosophy from the Upanishads to Kant.* Albany: State University of New York Press.

Schayer, Stanislaw. 1929–30. "Feuer und Brennstoff." *Rocznik Orjentalistyczny* 7: 26–52.

Schayer, Stanislaw. 1931–32. "Kamalaśīlas Kritik des Pudgalavāda." *Rocznik Orjentalistyczny* 8: 68–93.

Schayer, Stanislaw. 1932–33. "Studien zur indischen Logik." *Wydzial Filologiczny, Bulletin International,* 1932: pp. 98–102 and 1933: pp. 90–96. Krakow: Polska Akademia Umiejetnosci.

Scherrer-Schaub, Cristina. 1981. "Le terme *yukti:* Première étude." *Asiatische Studien* 35/2: 185–99.

Schopen, Gregory. 1997. *Bones, Stones, and Buddhist Monks: Collected Papers on the Archaeology, Epigraphy, and Texts of Monastic Buddhist in India.* Honolulu: University of Hawai'i Press.

Schopenhauer, Arthur. 1883. *The World as Will and Idea,* R. B. Haldane and J. Kemp, trans. London: Kegan Paul, Trench, Trubner and Co.

Searle, John R. 1983. *Intentionality.* Cambridge: Cambridge University Press.

Sharma, Dhirendra. 1969. *The Differentiation Theory of Meaning in Indian Logic.* The Hague: Mouton and Co.

Shaw, Miranda. 1994. *Passionate Enlightenment: Women in Tantric Buddhism.* Princeton: Princeton University Press.

Shoemaker, Sydney. 1984. *Identity, Cause, and Mind.* Cambridge: Cambridge University Press.

Shoemaker, Sydney and R. Swinburne. 1984. *Personal Identity.* Oxford: Basil Blackwell.

Shulman, David. 1994. "On Being Human in the Sanskrit Epic: The Riddle of Nala." *Journal of Indian Philosophy* 22: 1–29.

Siderits, Mark. 1982. "More Things in Heaven and Earth." *Journal of Indian Philosophy* 10: 187–208.

Siderits, Mark. 1985. "The Prabhākara Mīmāṃsā Theory of Related Designation," in Bimal Krishna Matilal and Jaysankar Lal Shaw, eds., *Analytical Philosophy in Comparative Perspective,* pp. 253–97. Dordrecht: D. Reidel Publishing Co.

Siderits, Mark. 1986. "The Sense-Reference Distinction in Indian Philosophy of Language." *Synthèse* 69: 81–106.

Siderits, Mark. 1989. "Thinking on Empty: Madhyamaka Anti-Realism and Canons of Rationality," in Biderman and Scharfstein 1989: 231–49.

Siderits, Mark. 1997. "Buddhist Reductionism." *Philosophy East and West* 47: 455–78.

Silburn, Liliane. 1955. *Instant et Cause.* Paris: Vrin.

Sinari, Ramakant A. 1984. *The Structure of Indian Thought.* New Delhi: Oxford University Press.

Skilling, Peter. 1992. "The *Rakṣā* Literature of the *Śrāvakayāna.*" *Journal of the Pali Text Society* 16: 109–82.

Skilling, Peter. 2000. "Vasubandhu and the *Vyākhyāyukti* Literature." *Journal of the International Association of Buddhist Studies* 23/2: 297–350.

Slusser, Mary Shepard. 1982. *Nepal Mandala: A Cultural Study of the Kathmandu Valley.* Princeton: Princeton University Press.

Smith, E. Gene. 1969. "The Biography of Lcang-skya Rol-pa'i-rdo-rje." *Collected Works of Thu'u-bkwan Blo-bzang-chos-kyi-nyi-ma,* vol. 1. New Delhi: Ngawang Gelek Demo.

Smith, E. Gene. 1970. "Introduction" to *Kongtrul's Encyclopedia of Indo-Tibetan Culture,* Śatapiṭaka Series 80. New Delhi: International Academy of Indian Culture.

Snellgrove, David L. 1987. *Indo-Tibetan Buddhism: Indian Buddhists and Their Tibetan Successors.* Boston: Shambhala.

Sprung, Mervyn, ed. 1973. *The Problem of Two Truths in Buddhism and Vedānta.* Dordrecht/Boston: D. Reidel.

Sprung, Mervyn. 1979. *Lucid Exposition of the Middle Way.* Boulder, CO: Prajñā Press.

Staal, J. Frits. 1962. "Contraposition in Indian Logic," in Ernest Nagel, Patrick Suppes, and Alfred Tarski, eds., *Logic, Methodology, and Philosophy of Science: Proceedings of the 1960 International Congress,* pp. 634–49. Palo Alto, CA.

Staal, J. Frits. 1965. "Euclid and Pāṇini." *Philosophy East and West* 15: 99–116.

Staal, J. Frits. 1982. "Ritual, Grammar, and the Origins of Science in India." *Journal of Indian Philosophy* 10: 3–35.

Staal, J. Frits. 1989. *Rules Without Meaning: Ritual, Mantras and the Human Sciences.* New York: Peter Lang Publishing.

Stcherbatsky, Theodore. 1962. *Buddhist Logic.* Repr. ed., 2 vols. New York: Dover.

Stcherbatsky, Theodore. 1976. *The Soul Theory of the Buddhists.* Delhi: Bharatiya Vidya Prakashan.

Stearns, Cyrus. 1995. "Dol-po-pa Shes-rab rgyal-mtshan and the Genesis of the *Gzhan-stong* Position in Tibet." *Asiatische Studien/Études Asiatiques* 44/4: 829–52.

Stearns, Cyrus. 1999. *The Buddha from Dolpo.* Albany: State University of New York Press.

Steiner, George. 1978. *Martin Heidegger.* London: Fontana.

Steinkellner, Ernst. 1979. *Dharmakīrti's Pramāṇaviniścayaḥ,* Teil II—Übersetzung und Anmerkungen. Vienna: Verlag der Österreichischen Akademie der Wissenschaften.

Steinkellner, Ernst. 1984. "Miszellen zur erkenntnistheoretisch-logischen Schule des Buddhismus IV. Candragomin, der Autor des Nyāyasiddhyāloka." *Wiener Zeitschrift für die Kunde Südasiens* 28: 177–78.

Störig, Hans Joachim. 1962. *Kleine Weltgeschichte der Philosophie.* Stuttgart: Im Bertelsmann Lesering.

Strawson, P. F. 1966. *The Bounds of Sense.* London: Methuen & Co.

Strickmann, Michel. 1996. *Mantras et mandarins: Le bouddhisme tantrique en Chine.* Paris: Gallimard.

Suzuki, Daisetz T. 1930. *Studies in the Lankavatara Sutra.* London: Routledge and Kegan Paul.

Suzuki, Daisetz T. 1959. *Zen and Japanese Culture,* Bollingen Series 46. New York: Pantheon Books.

Taber, John. 1990. "The Mīmāṃsā Doctrine of Self-Recognition." *Philosophy East and West* 40: 35–57.

Takeuchi Yoshinori. 1982. "The Philosophy of Nishida," in Frederick Francke, ed. *The Buddha Eye,* pp. 179–202. New York: Crossroad.

Tauscher, Helmut. 1995. *Die Lehre von den Zwei Wirklichkeiten in Tsoṅ kha pas Madhyamaka-Werken,* Wiener Studien zur Tibetologie und Buddhismiskunde 36. Vienna: Arbeitskreis für Tibetische und Buddhistische Studien Universität Wien.

Taylor, Charles. 1985. "Philosophy and Its History," in Rorty, Schneewind, and Skinner 1985: 17–30.

Taylor, Charles. 1989. *Sources of the Self: The Making of the Modern Identity.* Cambridge, MA: Harvard University Press.

Tharchin, Geshe Lobsang. 1979. *The Logic and Debate Tradition of India, Tibet, and Mongolia.* Freewood Acres, NJ: Mahayana Sutra and Tantra Press.

Thompson, Evan. 1986. "Planetary Thinking/Planetary Building: An Essay on Martin Heidegger and Nishitani Keiji." *Philosophy East and West* 36/3.

Thompson, John B. 1981. *Critical Hermeneutics: A Study in the Thought of Paul Ricoeur and Jürgen Habermas.* Cambridge: Cambridge University Press.

Thurman, Robert A.F. 1978. "Buddhist Hermeneutics." *Journal of the American Academy of Religion,* 46/1: 19–39

Thurman, Robert A.F. 1984. *Tsong Khapa's Speech of Gold in the Essence of True Eloquence.* Princeton: Princeton University Press.

Tice, Terrence N. and Thomas P. Slavens. 1983. *Research Guide to Philosophy.* Sources of Information in the Humanities No. 3. Chicago: American Library Association.

Tillemans, Tom J. F. 1983. "The 'Neither One nor Many' Argument for *Śūnyatā* and its Tibetan Interpretations," in *Contributions on Tibetan and Buddhist Religion and Philosophy,* Ernst Steinkellner and Helmut Tauscher, eds., pp. 305–20. Vienna: Arbeitskreis fur Tibetische und Buddhistische Studien Universität Wien.

Tillemans, Tom J. F. 1984. "Two Tibetan Texts on the 'Neither One nor Many' Argument for *Śūnyatā*." *Journal of Indian Philosophy* 12: 357–88.

Tillemans, Tom J. F. 1999. *Scripture, Logic, Language: Essays on Dharmakīrti and His Tibetan Successors.* Boston: Wisdom Publications.

Tobey, Jeremy L. 1975–77. *The History of Ideas: A Bibliographical Introduction,* 2 vols. Santa Barbara/Oxford: Clio Press.

Trungpa Rinpoche, Chögyam. 1975. *Visual Dharma: The Buddhist Art of Tibet.* Berkeley/London: Shambhala.

Tucci, Giuseppe. 1949. *Tibetan Painted Scrolls.* 3 vols. Rome: Libreria dello Stàto.

Tuck, Andrew P. 1990. *Comparative Philosophy and the Philosophy of Scholarship.* New York: Oxford University Press.

Tylor, Edward. 1871. *Primitive Culture.* London: Murray.

Van Bijlert, Victor. 1989. *Epistemology and Spiritual Authority.* Wiener Studien zur Tibetologie und Buddhismuskunde 20. Vienna: Arbeitskreis für Tibetische und Buddhistische Studien Universität Wien.

Van Cleve, James. 1981. "Reflections on Kant's Second Antinomy." *Synthèse* 47.

Vartanian, Aram. 1967. "Stahl, Georg Ernst," in Paul Edwards, ed., *The Encyclopedia of Philosophy,* vol. 8, p. 4. New York: Macmillan.

Venkataramanan, K. 1953. "Saṃmitīya-nikāya-śāstra." *Visvabharati Annals* 5: 153–243.

Versnel, H. S. 1991. "Some Reflections on the Relationship Magic–Religion." *Numen* 37: 177–97.

Vetter, Tilman. 1984. *Der Buddha und seine Lehre in Dharmakīrtis Pramāṇavārttika.* Wiener Studien zur Tibetologie und Buddhismuskunde 12. Vienna: Arbeitskreis für Tibetische und Buddhistische Studien Universität Wien.

Vidyabhusana, Satis Chandra. 1971. *A History of Indian Logic.* Delhi: Motilal Banarsidass.

von Wright, Georg Henrik. 1971. *Explanation and Understanding.* Ithaca: Cornell University Press.

Waddell, L. Austine. 1971 [1894, 1939]. *The Buddhism of Tibet or Lamaism.* Cambridge: W. Heffer and Sons.

Walshe, Maurice, trans. 1995. *The Long Discourses of the Buddha: A Translation of the Dīgha Nikāya.* Boston: Wisdom Publications.

Warder, A.K. 1963. "The Earliest Indian Logic." *Proceedings of the 25th International Congress of Orientalists,* vol. 4 (Moscow): 56–68.

Warder, A.K. 1970. *Indian Buddhism.* Delhi: Motilal Banarsidass.

Warder, A.K. 1973. "Is Nāgārjuna a Mahāyānist?" in Sprung 1973: 78–88.

Watanabe, Fumimaro. 1983. *Philosophy and Its Development in the Nikayas and Abhidhamma.* Delhi: Motilal Banarsidass.

Wayman, Alex. 1984. "The Interlineary-type Commentary in Tibetan," in Louis Ligeti, ed., *Tibetan and Buddhist Studies Commemorating the 200th Anniversary of the Birth of Alexander Csoma de Körös,* vol. 2, pp. 367–79. Budapest: Akadémiai Kiadó.

Wedberg, Anders. 1982. *A History of Philosophy,* vol. 1. Oxford: Clarendon Press.

Wedemeyer, Christian K. 2001. "Tropes, Typologies, and Turnarounds: A Brief Geneology of the Historiography of Tantric Buddhism." *History of Religions* 40: 223–59.

Whitehead, Alfred North and Bertrand Russell. 1962. *Principia Mathematica to *56.* Cambridge: Cambridge University Press.

Whorf, Benjamin L. 1956. *Language, Thought and Reality.* Cambridge, MA: MIT Press.

Williams, Paul. 1983a. "On *rang rig,*" in *Contributions on Tibetan and Buddhist Religion and Philosophy,* Ernst Steinkellner and Helmut Tauscher, eds., pp. 321–32. Vienna: Arbeitskreis fur Tibetische und Buddhistische Studien Universität Wien.

Williams, Paul. 1983b. "A Note on Some Aspects of Mi Bskyod Rdo Rje's Critique of Dge Lugs Pa Madhyamaka." *Journal of Indian Philosophy* 11: 125–45.

Williams, Paul. 1989. *Mahāyāna Buddhism: The Doctrinal Foundations.* London/New York: Routledge.

Williams, Paul. 1998a. *The Reflexive Nature of Awareness: A Tibetan Madhyamaka Defence.* Surrey: Curzon.

Williams, Paul. 1998b. *Altruism and Reality: Studies in the Philosophy of the Bodhicaryāvatāra.* Surrey: Curzon.

Willis, Janice Dean. 1979. *On Knowing Reality.* New York: Columbia University Press.

Willman-Grabowska, Helena. 1929–30. "L'idée de l'ātmán du Rig-Veda aux Brāhmaṇa." *Rocznik Orjentalistyczny* 7: 10–25.

Wilson, Margaret Dauler. 1982. *Descartes.* London: Routledge and Kegan Paul.

Winternitz, Maurice. 1972. *A History of Indian Literature,* S. Ketkar, trans. New Delhi: Oriental Books Reprint Corp.

Wittgenstein, Ludwig. 1953. *Philosophical Investigations.* London/New York: Macmillan.

Woodroffe, John. 1966. *The World As Power.* 3rd ed. Madras: Ganesh and Co.

Zaehner, R. C. 1966. *Hindu Scriptures.* London/Melbourne/Toronto: Dent.

Zimmer, Heinrich. 1936. "Arthur Schopenhauer. 1788–1869," in Willy Andreas and Wilhelm von Scholz, eds., *Die Grossen Deutschen: Deutsche Biographie,* vol. 3, pp. 236–51. Berlin: Ullstein. [2nd ed., rev. by Kurt Rossmann, vol. 3, pp. 134–51. Berlin: Ullstein.]

Zimmer, Heinrich. 1938. "Schopenhauer und Indien." *Jahrbuch der Schopenhauer-Gesellschaft* 25: 266–73.

Zimmer, Heinrich. 1963. *Indische Sphären,* 2nd ed. in *Gesammelte Werke,* vol. 5. Zurich: Rascher.

Zimmer, Heinrich. 1969. *Philosophies of India,* Joseph Campbell, ed. Bollingen Series 26. Princeton: Princeton University Press.

Zimmer, Heinrich. 1984. *Artistic Form and Yoga in the Sacred Images of India,* Gerald Chapple and James B. Lawson, trans. Princeton: Princeton University Press.

Zysk, Kenneth G. 1991. *Asceticism and Healing in Ancient India: Medicine in the Buddhist Monastery.* New York: Oxford University Press.

Index of Personal Names

Index of Subjects and Technical Terms

Index of Texts

About Wisdom

Wisdom Publications
199 Elm Street
Somerville, Massachusetts 02144 USA
Telephone: (617) 776-7416 • Fax: (617) 776-7841
Email: info@wisdompubs.org • www.wisdompubs.org

Studies in Indian and Tibetan Buddhism

This series was conceived to provide a forum for publishing outstanding new contributions to scholarship on Indian and Tibetan Buddhism and also to make accessible seminal research not widely known outside a narrow specialist audience, including translations of appropriate monographs and collections of articles from other languages. The series strives to shed light on the Indic Buddhist traditions by exposing them to historical-critical inquiry, illuminating through contextualization and analysis these traditions' unique heritage and the significance of their contribution to the world's religious and philosophical achievements. We are pleased to make available to scholars and the intellectually curious some of the best contemporary research in the Indian and Tibetan traditions.